Structure and Change in Indian Society

Structure and Change in Indian Society

edited
by
Milton Singer
and
Bernard S. Cohn

AldineTransaction
A Division of Transaction Publishers
New Brunswick (U.S.A.) and London (U.K.)

First paperback printing 2007

Copyright © 1968 Wenner-Gren Foundation for Anthropological Research, Inc.

This book is printed on acid-free paper that meets the American National Standard for Permanence of Paper for Printed Library Materials.

Library of Congress Catalog Number: 2007026441
ISBN: 978-0-202-36138-3
Printed in the United States of America

Library of Congress Cataloging-in-Publication Data

Structure and change in Indian society / [edited by] Milton Singer and
    Bernard S. Cohn.
       p. cm.
    Originally published: Chicago : Aldine Pub. Co., 1968.
    Includes bibliographical references and index.
    ISBN 978-0-202-36138-3 (alk. paper)
         1. Caste—India. 2. India—Social conditions. I. Singer, Milton B.
    II. Cohn, Bernard S., 1928-2003.

HT720.S8 2007
306.0954—dc22

                                                   2007026441

ACKNOWLEDGMENTS

W E ARE INDEBTED to many people for help with the conference and the preparation of this volume. We want especially to record our gratitude to Mrs. Lita Osmundsen, Director of Research of the Wenner-Gren Foundation, for the Foundation's support of the conference and publication; to Sol Tax for making available the facilities of the Center for Continuing Education and for his indispensable advice and help with all the arrangements; and to Stephen Barnett, David Lelyveld, Peter McGregor, Raymond Owens, and Richard Tubesing for reporting the conference discussions. We also wish to thank Sara Lindholm, for help with the transcription of Indian words and proofreading, and for preparing the index, and Helen Singer, for help with copy-editing.

M. S.
B. C.

PREFACE

ALL THE PAPERS in this volume except one were presented in their original form to a conference on Social Structure and Social Change in India held at the University of Chicago, June 3–5, 1965. The conference was co-sponsored by the Wenner-Gren Foundation for Anthropological Research and the Committee on Southern Asian Studies of the University of Chicago. In addition to the authors of the papers, more than fifty invited participants and observers were present at this conference (see Appendix for complete list).

The proposal for the conference originated with William Rowe and Bernard Cohn, who saw it as an opportunity to present and review research in the social anthropology of South Asia which had been carried on over the last fifteen years, but had not yet been reported in monographic form. They and many of the younger anthropologists who had been engaged in this research hoped that the conference and the publication of its papers would bring to the attention of their colleagues in anthropology and in other fields some significant recent developments in South Asian social anthropology, as the Chicago conference and volume on *Village India* edited by McKim Marriott had done over a decade before. In this brief preface, I should like to introduce these developments to the reader who is not a South Asianist, and to relate them to the mainstream of contemporary social anthropology.

It is a regrettable but undeniable fact that the social anthropology of South Asia, and of Southeast Asia as well, is thought of by many social anthropologists as peripheral to the mainstream of social anthropology. This is of course a quite unhistorical view, since at any given time the mainstream draws its strength from the particular tributaries which happen to be feeding it. In the 1930's and 1940's, for example, field work in Africa, which was of very high quality, was practically identified with the mainstream. So in the 1950's and 1960's, beginning with M. N. Srinivas' *Religion and Society among the Coorgs of South India*, a vigorous flow comes into the mainstream from Southern Asia. The date of publication of Srinivas' study, 1952, does not mark the first entry of South Asian social anthropology into the main course. Radcliffe-Brown, Srinivas' teacher at Oxford, had already published *The Andaman Islanders* in 1922, and W. H. R. Rivers, Radcliffe-Brown's teacher, inaugurated the modern-style social anthropological monograph in 1906 with his work *The Todas*. These are, to be sure, rare freshets in the anthropological stream. Between 1906 and 1952, the bulk of South Asian anthropology consists of descriptive ethnography and speculative ethnology, except for some of the work of Hocart, Bouglé, Ghurye, and Hutton, and some papers by Emeneau, Mandelbaum, and Opler and Singh. I do not mean to depreciate the value of the works of such men as Risley, Crooke, Blunt, and Thurston, or of the Indian Gazetteer reports. We read these works, however, not for powerful concepts or fruitful methods in social anthropology but for useful compilations of information.

After 1952, South Asian social anthropology shows a sustained pattern of growth which has not yet reached its peak. Conceptually and methodologically, this growth owes much to the earlier models of Rivers and Radcliffe-Brown, but it has also gone beyond these models and shows the influence of other conceptual models, Redfield's and Lévi-Strauss's, for example, as well as of the distinctive features of South Asian society and culture. The contribution of the papers in this volume to the growth pattern of South Asian social anthropology is perhaps best summarized in terms of the distinctive modifications they introduce to the study of social structure and social change.

The basic social units of joint family, caste, and village are not taken in any of these papers as structural or cultural isolates. They are seen rather as intimately connected with one another and with other social units, through social networks of various kinds. This non-isolationist point of view was already adopted by social anthropologists with respect to village studies in the Village India seminar of 1954 (see Marriott [Ed.], *Village India*, 1955) and became the point of departure for the Redfieldian concept of a civilization as a structure of such networks and cultural centers (see Redfield and Singer, "The Cultural Role of Cities," 1954; Redfield, *Peasant Society and Culture*, 1956; Cohn and Marriott, "Centers and Networks in the Integration of Indian Civilization," 1958; Singer [Ed.], *Traditional India, Structure and Change*, 1958; Singer, "The Social Organization of Indian Civilization." *Diogenes,* 1964; Singer [Ed.], *Krishna Myths, Rites and Attitudes,* 1966). The interest of the present papers, however, is directed to the specific patterns of interconnection which can be traced through empirical studies of particular groups in particular localities, and to the changes in such patterns. Generalizations about all-India patterns, or all-South Asia patterns, are not eschewed; they are attempted rather as tentative hypotheses based on a number of specified localized studies, as in Mandelbaum's generic description of the interrelations of family, *jāti,* and village, or Kolenda's correlations of joint family, caste, region, and other variables. Even cross-cultural generalizations about "the caste system" in India and the U.S., as in Harper's paper, must prove themselves against the specific social and cultural contexts in which "the system" operates in each country. This requirement was repeatedly affirmed in the discussions at the conference, and the failure to agree on whether it is American Negro-white relations, or the relations of religious denominations and ethnic groups, or the battle of the sexes, that constitutes the best analogy with the Indian caste system, shows that such comparisons are easier to suggest than to demonstrate.

Nowhere was this empirical mindedness of the conference more in evidence than in the papers and discussion on the structure of intercaste relations. The traditional view of the caste system as a single hierarchy of the four varnas—Brahmans, Kshatriyas, Vaishyas, Shudras, with a fifth Untouchable order beneath the others—seems in these papers and discussion to have been pluralized into as many hierarchies and structures as there are operational methods for determining them. Schwartzberg, a geographer, uses criteria of spatial location and dominance to map "caste regions." Elder, a sociologist, employs an attitude questionnaire to test for regional differences in attitudes toward intercaste relations. Marriott, a social anthropologist, seeks to determine the order of caste-ranking in a village with the help of a matrix analysis of verbal opinions and behavioral interactions. Three linguists, Bright, Ramanujan, and McCormack, apply recent techniques of anthropological linguistics and sociolinguistics to study how Brahmans talk with non-Brahmans as well as with each other.

The results of these different operational methods are not quite the pluralistic disarray of structures of intercaste relations one might have expected. Local and regional differences make themselves felt, to be sure, but it is surprising, too, to find that the traditional varna system still has relevance for these empirical studies. Marriott's caste-ranking studies found so much consensus about local caste hierarchies between collective verbal opinions and interactional behavior that several members of the conference protested the possible oversight of individual variability of both opinion and behavior.

Clearly there is nothing in empirical local studies as such that forecloses the possibility of agreement between the results of different operational methods for determining the structures of intercaste relations, or of significant relationships between the local structures and the supra-local norms of the scriptural texts and ideological movements. Marriott's functional explanation of such agreements and relations—the ranking of castes is what the people of a local community collectively believe it to be, and people know what the ranks of castes are by looking at actual, formal interactions of certain significant kinds (especially transfers of food and services, among persons belonging to different castes)—not only reconciles subjective and objective methods of caste-ranking but opens a new field for research into the relations between local cognitive and behavioral structures, and the relation of both to the great traditional structures of the Dharmashastras and other texts. The failures of consensus among these different kinds of structures may, as I have argued elsewhere, be as revelatory of significant functional and dynamic processes as close agreement among them would be (see "The Social Organization of Indian Civilization," pp. 99ff.). In any case, Orenstein's attempt to codify the traditional varna structure by applying the linguistic analogy of a grammar and code to the scriptural texts, brings the social anthropologist into direct contact with the materials and methods of the Indologist.

The functional relation of religion to social structure was the central focus of River's monograph on the Todas, Radcliffe-Brown's on the Andamanese, and Srinivas' on the Coorgs. The characteristic problem of these classic studies was to identify the religious cults associated with the different basic units of social structure—family, village, caste, etc.—and to trace the network of functional relations which bound them together. While this kind of study has been done after 1952, notably by Louis Dumont's *Une sous-caste de l'Inde du Sud*, many recent studies, including those represented by the papers in this volume, have extended the approach in two different directions. There is now an interest, on the one hand, in tracing the functional relations of other aspects of culture to social structure: of politics to social structure, of economics to social structure,

of law to social structure, of language to social structure, etc. The work of
F. G. Bailey, Barth, Béteille, T. S. Epstein, and Gough, among others, illustrates
this trend. At the same time, there is a new interest in the conditions and course
of change in these functional relationships. Nicholas, for example, seeks to determine the generic interrelations at the village level of political conflict, land
tenure, and social structure, and how these are being changed by the coming
of universal suffrage and land reform. Hazlehurst analyzes the political alliances
made during a municipal election in a North Indian town to trace the influence
of growing urbanization, and the economic and political opportunities that go
with it, on the caste system. His statement that caste is "a composite of tenuously
articulated parts" in the dynamics of social change might, with appropriate
changes, be converted into a general formula for the other case studies as well.
Galanter's finding of a transformation in the judicial recognition of castes from
a conception of them as parts of a sacred order to a view of them as voluntary,
autonomous associations, political pressure groups, or religious denominations,
seems to go beyond Hazlehurst's formula. Yet, during the conference discussions,
when one member proposed to apply Galanter's typology as a sequence of phases
to the last hundred years of Indian social history, the proposal was strongly
resisted on the grounds that the available evidence did not demonstrate such
fixed sequences.

Whether this resistance is an expression of a negative attitude toward evolutionary theories of social and cultural change I am not sure, but it is a striking fact
that none of the papers in the volume tries to make a case for social change as
a transformation of structural and cultural types. The only generic processes of
social change that received wide recognition at the conference were Srinivas'
complementary processes of "Sanskritization" and "Westernization." His paper
and Rowe's offer some new historical materials on the operation of these processes
during the pre-British and the British periods. Lynch's paper, which deals with a
contemporary upward mobile group that has rejected Sanskritization for political
participation, recalls Bailey's Orissa studies and suggests that post-independence
parliamentary democracy and the organization of political parties bring new
paths for upward mobility. Whether this also introduces a new generic process
of change, which Lynch calls "elite emulation," or whether it is but a changing
phase in the same historical process, as Srinivas suggests in his recent book *Social
Change in Modern India*, is a debatable issue. The question is not Maitland's:
whether anthropology will become history or nothing; Cohn's work demonstrates
that it can become a history of the relations of politics to social structure.

This issue is also raised by the conversion of Hindus to Buddhism, to Christianity, and to Islam, as well as to socialism, communism, and other ideological movements. These are not cases of "Sanskritization," if this process is defined, as Srinivas
defined it in 1952, as the process whereby a low caste moves up in the caste hierarchy by taking over the Sanskritic customs, rites, and beliefs of the Brahmans.
If, however, we use Srinivas' later and broader definition of Sanskritization as the
process "by which a 'low' Hindu caste, or tribal or other group, changes its
customs, ritual, ideology and way of life in the direction of a high, and frequently,

'twice-born' caste" (1966), then we can see the close family relation between these different paths to upward social mobility. I doubt, however, that the suggestion made by some writers that we subsume all these processes under a concept of "social mobility" does justice to the peculiarities of Indian society and culture. This concept minimizes the important fact that the social hierarchy is also a hierarchy of ritual purity and pollution, and that social mobility, upward or downward, also involves a *cultural* mobility in ritual status. The constitutional abolition of untouchability and general secularizing trends may be contracting the scope of ritual pollution in social relations, but ritual pollution continues an important and pervasive element in them, and Sanskritization continues to operate as the dynamic aspect of the ritual and cultural structure.

Srinivas has often remarked that Sanskritization involves a change in position in the caste system but not a change in the system itself. Yet the system is changing, with the formation of voluntary caste associations and their entry into political alignments and into industrial employments. A core of caste endogamy and commensality may persist, but new patterns of social relations are also emerging in these new contexts. These processes of change are not adequately defined in terms of the social anthropological concepts of "equilibrium adjustments" or "structural change." There are no linear transformations of "structural types," and yet there is significant social movement and change. One might interpret this situation by arguing that the gradualness of change in Indian society is simply a reflection of the limited amount of industrialization, urbanization, and modernization; another, and to my mind equally plausible explanation is that Indian civilization has built into it adaptive mechanisms for incorporating new techniques, new ideas, and newcomers with only a gradual displacement of the old. These two explanations are not necessarily in conflict, although a test between them will come with an acceleration of the forces of modernization.

These general observations are also applicable to the papers on the joint family. Here, too, the evidence of specific empirical studies does not support the widespread belief that the joint family is "breaking down," or that it is being transformed under industrialization and urbanization into a Western-style nuclear family. Kolenda's paper, on the contrary, challenges the common use of statistics on the relative frequency of nuclear to joint families in support of the "breakdown" thesis, by demonstrating the significant variations in definitions of family types and in the distributions of these types with region, caste, and other variables. Gould's paper casts further doubt on the thesis of linear transformation of "structural types" by applying Fortes' concept of the "domestic cycle" to data on the Indian joint family in a small town. His results suggest that a preponderance of the percentage of joint or nuclear families in one time period over another does not necessarily mean structural change. It may only indicate a cyclical rearrangement.

Such results are leading students of the Indian joint family to greater skepticism about the "breakdown" thesis, especially when the thesis is based on census data and massive statistical surveys. Scholars are turning instead to intensive, functional studies of the adaptive changes which particular families in particular villages, towns, cities, and regions are undergoing. My own paper and Patterson's illustrate the use of family histories for study of these problems. Perhaps social anthropologists will be encouraged by these trends in South Asian social anthropology to extend "the genealogical method" to the study of change in other areas. Perhaps, too, they will be persuaded by these papers to recognize that the study of Indian society reveals novel social forms and processes that call for novel concepts, methods, and theories in social anthropology. To this renewal, we hope that the papers in this volume, and the forthcoming monographs from which many are selections, will make a contribution worthy of India's reputation in the past as a rich source of modern anthropological and comparative studies.

MILTON SINGER

TRANSCRIPTION OF INDIAN WORDS

T HE PRESENT VOLUME includes words from over a half dozen major Indian languages. With the exception of the phonemic transcriptions of spoken Kannada, Tamil, and Tulu in Part VI, the standard for transcription has been literary; that is, an attempt has been made to transliterate the words from their written forms in the regional languages. The standard conventions have been followed for representing long vowels (*ā, ī, ū*) and retroflex consonants (*ṛ, ṭ, ḍ*, etc.). An interconsonantal *ṛ* represents vocalic *r*, which is pronounced *ri* as in *rich*. Aspiration is indicated by an *h* following the consonant, whereas *c* represents *ch* as in "charity" and *ś* and *ṣ* represent palatal and retroflex variations of *sh* respectively, An *ṃ* indicates the nasalization of the preceding vowel, as in *vaṃś*.

In Part VI the contemporary linguistic usages of the authors have been followed. Long vowels are represented by double or geminate letters, and a tilde indicates nasalization.

Diacritics have been used on italicized words only. Proper names of persons, castes and tribes, and geographic features have been reproduced in Roman script without diacritics, as have all words defined in Webster's New International Dictionary (1961).

CONTENTS

I. CASTE AND SOCIAL STRUCTURE

II. THE STRUCTURE OF INTERCASTE RELATIONS

III. IS THE CASTE SYSTEM CHANGING?

IV. CASTE IN POLITICS, ECONOMICS, AND LAW

PART I:
Caste and Social Structure

1. NOTES ON THE HISTORY OF THE STUDY OF INDIAN SOCIETY AND CULTURE

BERNARD S. COHN

THE STUDY of social change and acculturation has become over the last 35 years one of the anthropologist's major activities. Until quite recently the American Indians and African and Latin American societies and cultures have been the locus of most social change and acculturation studies.

The American Indian studies have tended to focus on the overwhelming effects that white American society has had on tribal groups. The African studies have tended to focus on the direct and indirect political effects of European incursions. The study of acculturation in Latin America has emphasized the initial effects of Hispanization, the destruction of indigenous Indian society, and the emergence of complicated new patterns of culture. These studies have taken a total system view of the societies in relation to overwhelming political, economic, and social power which were directly or indirectly applied to indigenous societies. The American Indian studies have illustrated how persistent indigenous patterns have been and to a large extent how effective American Indians have been in the face of often overwhelming pressure, in maintaining many of their indigenous patterns. In Africa by and large the studies indicate that in the political realm the Africans have adapted European institutions to their own political ends.

The societies of India offer a much different situation from that of the American Indian or the African to study long-term social change under colonial and post-colonial conditions. Indian society and political development were recognized by Europeans in the eighteenth century as being at relatively the same level as European society. In India there was settled agriculture and a variety of craft production on a large scale, political institutions of kingship, a legal system based partially on written law, taxation based on regular assessment, with record-keeping, and military forces roughly organized along lines similar to those of Europe. Many of the political and economic roles familiar to Europeans: clerks, judges, tax officials, generals, bankers, and traders, existed. In addition, there was a multiple cultural-religious system based on sacred texts, both Hindu and Muslim, with a wide range of ritual specialists and scholars.

Relatively speaking, British domination until the middle of the nineteenth century had little direct effect on Indian social, economic, and cultural life. As a result of British revenue arrangements, there was some circulation of personnel in the rural society as land became marketable and as new methods of acquisition of land through the use of British administrative procedures allowed nonmilitary groups access to control of land. New groups who tended to take advantage of the conditions established by the British fitted into the traditional structure or were placed on top of the existing structure and took over life styles well established by the eighteenth century.

THE STUDY OF INDIAN SOCIETY AND THE CASTE SYSTEM

There have been recorded observations on Indian society since the third century B.C. It is useful in considering more recent developments in the study of social change in India to sketch briefly the nature and content of the observations and assumptions which observers have made of the Indian social system.

CLASSICAL AND ARAB-PERSIAN ACCOUNTS

For the period 327 B.C. to 1498, there are scattered accounts of Indian society written by foreigners. These travelers included Greeks, Romans, Byzantine Greeks, Jews, and Chinese, and, increasingly from A.D. 1,000 onward, Arabs, Turks, Afghans, and Persians. Most classical accounts of Indian society follow Megasthenes, who had the advantage of direct observation of parts of India. But as Lach comments:

Although he was an acute observer, Megasthenes was handicapped by his ignorance of the native languages. Like many Europeans since his time, he was unable to penetrate deeply into the thought, literature and history of the country simply by looking and listening, or by using interpreters (1945, I: l, p. 10).

Megasthenes described Indian society as being divided into seven classes: (1) philosophers, who offer sacrifices and perform other sacred rites; (2) husbandmen, who form the bulk of the population; (3) shepherds and hunters; (4) those who work at trades and vend wares and are employed in bodily labor; (5) fighting men; (6) inspectors; and (7) counselors and assessors of the king (M'Crindle, 1901, pp. 47–53). Megasthenes also noted that each of these seven "classes" were endogamous and that one could not change his occupation or profession (M'Crindle, 1901, p. 53). From the context of his account it would appear, as with many subsequent observers, that Megasthenes' data came mainly from observation of urban political centers. It is also interesting to note that, at least in the materials of Megasthenes which have survived, he makes no reference to the varna theory.

Although there was regular and extensive contact between Rome and India through direct trade contact, Roman accounts, although fuller on geographic information, add little in the form of sociological information to our knowledge of the stratification system in early India.

The earliest Arabic accounts follow the classical view of Indian society in reporting the division of Indian society into seven classes (Elliot and Dowson, 1867, vol. 1, pp. 16–17, 77). Al-Biruni (973–ca. 1030) appears to have been familiar with Sanskrit sources and does mention the four-varna theory of the caste system (al-Biruni, 1962, pp. 132–40). In the seventeenth century many translations were made from the Sanskrit literature into Persian by Indo-Muslim scholars (Rehatsek, 1880; Sabah Al-Din, 1961). Abu'l Fazl 'Allami, the author of the *A'in-i-Akbari*, a late sixteenth-century gazetteer and description of Akbar's court, revenue, and administrative system, presents the view that the four varnas were produced from the body of Brahma at the creation of the world. He recognizes that there are internal divisions within the four varnas, but follows Brahmanic theory in attributing these divisions to the mixture of the original varnas through intermarriage (Abu'l Fazl 'Allami, 1786, vol. 3, pp. 82–84).

Functionally, as can be seen in the lists of military and revenue obligations given in the *A'in-i-Akbari*, the Mughals clearly recognized that the operational level of the Hindu social system was not at the level of the varnas but at the level of kin-based social categories such as we are familiar with in twentieth-century literature on the Indian caste system. The split view of Indian society, which we will see is so typical of nineteenth-century European views of India, of a theoretical varna-based society which sees the four major ideological based categories of Brahman, Kshatriya, Vaishya, and Shudra as being the system, existed functionally along with the necessity on the part of the Mughals to operate with localized kin-based caste groups.

The View of the Caste System of the Early European Travelers

The earliest direct observers of the Indian caste system in modern times were Portuguese adventurers, administrators, merchants, and priests, who began primarily on the Malabar coast to have direct experience with Indian society. Malabar at one and the same time was a highly cosmopolitan society, with enclaves of Arabs (Moplahs), Syrian Christians, Jews, and other foreign peoples, and an area in which the hierarchic principles of the caste system had been worked out in one of its most extreme forms. The Europeans were also fascinated in confronting matrilineal and polyandrous groups.

Early Portuguese observers like Duarte Barbosa (1866, 1918, 1921) naively but accurately reported major cultural features of the caste system which continue to be recognized as central today: the high position of the Brahmans (1866, p. 121), the significance of pollution in relation to untouchability (1866, p. 129), the bars to commensality among endogamous groups (1866, p. 136), the relationship of occupation to caste (1866, pp. 135, 137), the application of sanctions within castes to maintain caste customs (1866, p. 133), and the relationship between caste and political organization (1866, pp. 103–106).

Striking in Barbosa's description is his matter-of-fact and objective approach in trying to describe what he saw and what he was told; he presents his description of the caste system organized as a hierarchy with Brahmans on top and Untouchables on the bottom. There is no reference to the Hindu theory of the varnas and no moralizing about the benefits or evils of the system. In many respects European accounts for the next 250 years do not progress much beyond Barbosa's reporting. Unlike many of the Europeans who followed him to India, for shorter or longer periods, Barbosa knew an Indian vernacular well and was recognized by his contemporaries for his linguistic abilities (1918, p. xxxvi).

Although there were others over the next 250 years who became fascinated with Indian society, most accounts by Europeans which circulated in Europe tended to focus on the Mughal courts and on political and commercial matters rather than on Indian society itself. Jean Baptiste Tavernier, a French merchant and traveler who made six voyages to the Middle East, India, and Southeast Asia between about 1631 and 1667, wrote accounts of his travels that are typical of the works of this period (1889). He describes in detail the various routes and points of interest historically and commercially in his travels in India, much like a forerunner of Murray's guide to India (1889, vol. 1, pp. 1–318). He provides a history of the reign of Aurangzeb mainly based on oral evidence, and extensive discussions of commercial activities. Finally, Tavernier reports on various Hindu beliefs, rituals, and customs. This reporting is based on conversations with Brahmans and on eyewitness reports. The caste system receives very brief notice. Tavernier bases his views on what he "ascertained from the most accomplished of their priests" (1889, vol. 2, p. 182); that is, that although there are believed to be 72 castes, "these may be reduced to four principal [castes], from which all others derive their origin" (p. 182). Tavernier and other European travelers appear to have had little difficulty in finding Brahmans to discuss Hinduism with them.

Abraham Roger, the first chaplain at the Dutch factory at Pulicat in Madras, studied Hinduism from a Dutch-speaking Brahman, Padmanubha, in the 1630's. Roger's account of Hinduism was published in 1670, twenty years after his death, and contains Padmanubha's Dutch translation of Bhartrihari's *Satakas* (Yule and Burnell, 1903, p. xliii).

DEVELOPMENTS IN THE LATER EIGHTEENTH AND EARLY NINETEENTH CENTURIES

With the establishment of British suzerainty in the later eighteenth century, the rapid acquisition of knowledge of the classical languages of India by a few British officials, the need for administrative purposes of a knowledge of the structure of Indian society, and the intensification of missionary activities, systematic knowledge of Indian society began to develop very rapidly from 1760 onward. Three major traditions of approach to Indian society can be seen by the end of the eighteenth century: the orientalist, the administrative and the missionary. Each had a characteristic view, tied to the kinds of roles which foreign observers played in India and the assumptions which underlay their views of India.

THE ORIENTALIST

Although there was some knowledge of the learned traditions of India, both Hindu and Muslim, before the middle of the eighteenth century, it was not until the post-Plassey generation that a cumulative knowledge of Persian and Sanskrit and the vernacular languages began to develop which enabled the British to begin to comprehend the depth and range of texts and their contents through which the religion, philosophy, and history of India began to become known to Europeans. Alexander Dow, an officer in the East India Company's army, was one of the first to publish a translation of one of the standard Persian histories of India, *Tārikh-i-Firishtāhi*, which was published as *The History of Hindustan* in 1768–1771. As was typical for the period, Dow prefaced his translations with a number of essays, one on the nature of Mughal government, one on the effects of British rule in Bengal, and "A Dissertation Concerning the Customs, Manners, Language, Religion and Philosophy of the Hindoos." To Dow, customs and manners appear to have largely meant Brahmanic prescriptions derived from his study in Persian and "through the vulgar tongue of the Hindoos" of "some of the principal shasters." This he did with the assistance of a pundit from Banaras. Although Dow had tried to learn Sanskrit, apparently his official duties prevented him from mastering the language, but he was fully aware of the difficulties of understanding Hinduism through Persian translations. Matters which we would call sociological are treated in seven pages out of the fifty of his essay and cover the four varnas, which he sees as four great tribes, each of which is made up of a variety of castes; the tribes do not intermarry, eat, drink, or in any manner associate with each other. Dow presents the Brahmanical theory of the origin of the system as derived from parts of the body of Brahma. The caste system is treated in two pages. Other customs Dow thinks worth noting are astrological concerns at the birth of a child, early marriage, suttee, disposal of the dead, the privileged legal position of the Brahmans, the role of sannyasis as conveyers of Hinduism and types of penances which both sannyasis and the public sometimes perform.

The orientalists seem to have been convinced that the texts were indeed accurate guides to the culture and society of the Hindus. N. B. Halhead, who provided the first compilation and translation from the Dharmashastras under the title *A Code of Gentoo Laws, or, Ordinations of the Pundits. From a Persian Translation, Made from the Original, Written in the Shanscrit Language*, published in London in 1776, commented that from these translations "may be formed a precise idea of the customs and manners of these people" (Halhead, 1777, p. xi).

A view of Indian society which was derived from the study of texts and cooperation with pundits and *śāstris* (scholars of Hindu scriptures) had several consequences. In the first instance, it led to a consistent view that the Brahmans were the dominant group in the society. This was the function of the view which came from the texts themselves—a view which sees the Brahman as the center of the social order, which prescribes differential punishments for crimes based on one's varna status, which prohibits other varnas than Brahmans from learning certain texts, and which generally exalts the sacredness of the Brahman. The acceptance of this view is all the more odd in that it flew in the face of the evidence of the political structure of late eighteenth- and early nineteenth-century India, in which there were few Brahman dynasties, and political military power rested in the hands of other groups in the society.

The acceptance of a textual view of the society by the orientalists also led to a picture of Indian society as being static, timeless, and spaceless. Statements about customs which derived from third century A.D. texts and observations from the late eighteenth century were equally good evidence for determining the nature of society and culture in India. In this view of Indian society there was no regional variation and no questioning of the relationship between prescriptive normative statements derived from the texts and the actual behavior of individuals or groups. Indian society was seen as a set of rules which every Hindu followed.

THE MISSIONARY

The missionary view of India developed slightly later than the orientalist view. The first full expression of this view was contained in Charles Grant's *Observations on the State of Society among the Asiatic Subjects of Great Britain, Particularly with Respect to Morals, and on the Means of Improving It.* Grant, who was one of the early evangelicals, and who served as a commercial official in Bengal from 1774 to 1790, wrote the tract in 1792 for Henry Dundas, president of the Parliamentary Board of Control, the body responsible for the supervision of the East India Company's government.[1] Grant's view of Indian society and Indian character is summed up in the following quotation:

Upon the whole, then, we cannot avoid recognizing in the people of Hindostan, a race of men lamentably degenerate and base, retaining but a feeble sense of moral obligation, yet obstinate in their disregard of what they know to be right, governed by malevolent and licentious passions, strongly exemplifying the effects produced on society by great and general corruption of manners, and sunk in misery by their vices ... (Great Britain, House of Commons, 1833, vol. 14, p. 41).

Grant felt that the caste system, the legal system, government, and above all the despotic role of the Brahmans who control the society are the cause of the degraded state of the Hindus. Since society and culture are based, directed, and maintained by the religious system, the only hope for the improvement of Hindus and Hindu society lies in the elimination of Hinduism. This can be accomplished by government support of a highly effective campaign by Christian missionaries to convert the Indian population to Christianity.

The early nineteenth century saw a considerable literature by missionaries and by the evangelicals on Indian society. Claudius Buchanan, Sir John Shore, William Carey, and William Ward all produced extensive works in much the same tenor as Grant's *Observations*. In these later works, especially in William Ward's *Account of the Writings, Religion and Manners of the Hindoos*, originally published at Serampore in 1811 in four volumes, but subsequently republished with some changes in content and title in 1815 and in 1820, the nature and type of "documentation" of the condemnation of Hindu society changed. There is much more of an attempt to condemn Hindu society and to hold up the religion to ridicule with translations from the Sanskrit texts. In addition, increasing attention was paid on the basis of eyewitness and hearsay accounts of what the

---

1. For a full and valuable discussion of Grant, his ideas, and career, see Ainslie Thomas Embree, *Charles Grant and British Rule in India*, London, 1962. *The Observations* were published in the *Parliamentary Papers*, 1812–13, X, Paper 282, pages 1–112, and in *Parliamentary Papers*, 1831–32, VIII, Paper 734, General Appendix no. 1, pages 3–92.

missionaries took to be everyday examples of the depravity of the Hindu, suttee, purdah, sale of children into slavery, veneration of the cow, worship of idols, and the caste system. The caste system was described by William Ward (1820):

Like all other attempts to cramp the human intellect, and forcibly to restrain men within bounds which nature scorns to keep, this system, however specious in theory, has operated like the Chinese national shoe, it has rendered the whole nation cripples. Under the fatal influence of this abominable system, the bramhuns have sunk into ignorance, without abating an atom of their claims to superiority; the kshutriyus became almost extinct before their country fell into the hands of Musulmans; the voishyus are no where to be found in Bengal; almost all have fallen into the class of shoodrus, and shoodrus have sunk to the level of their own cattle (vol. 2, pp. 64–65).

The venom heaped on the caste system appears not to have been accidental, as the missionaries considered it necessary to destroy what they thought was the social basis of Hinduism. As long as those who converted to Christianity were merely another caste, as far as the rest of the Hindu population was concerned, and as long as an individual who converted cut himself off from the rest of society, there was little hope of diffusion of Christianity through normal channels of communication. As groups and individuals converted, the missionaries found themselves having to take on total economic and social responsibility for them as well as providing them with a different religion (Ingham, 1956).

The major thrust of the missionaries in their writing was to condemn Hindus and Hindu society along the lines indicated above; however, as a by-product of their proselytizing endeavors, they often made major contributions to the empirical study of Indian society. This partially came out of their need for translations of the Bible and religious tracts into the Indian vernaculars. Perhaps the first sociolinguistic study we have of an Indian language is William Carey's *Dialogues Intended to Facilitate the Acquiring of the Bengali Language*, published at the Press at Serampore in 1801. This work, which reads like a forerunner of modern language teaching materials for learning a language through the oral-aural method, is a series of dialogues between various types of Indians— zamindars and their tenants, zamindars and their officials, washermen and fishermen, cultivators, and various types of women. The different social and occupational groups are recorded as speaking presumably as they would in normal conversation.

William Adams, who came to Bengal as a Baptist minister in the early nineteenth century, was commissioned to do reports on indigenous education. These were highly laudatory of the nature of traditional vernacular education and reported in detail on the continued vigor of indigenous education in the 1830's (Long, 1868). In the middle of the nineteenth century Robert Caldwell spent fifty years of his life in South India. His study, *Comparative Grammar of the Dravidian or South Indian Family of Languages*, was one of the first systematic accounts of the Dravidian languages and was to have considerable indirect effect on the politics of South India. Stephen Hislop, a missionary in Central India, provided some of the earliest and most useful descriptions of the tribal peoples of Central India. In the twentieth century, Charles Freer Andrews and Edward Thompson were important interpreters of changing Indian society in relation to the rise of nationalism and were consistent defenders of India and Indians in the face of official British policy.

The orientalists and the missionaries were polar opposites in their assessment of Indian culture and society, but were in accord as to what the central principles and institutions of the society were. They agreed that it was a society in which religious ideas and practices underlay all social structure; they agreed in the primacy of the Brahman as the maintainer of the sacred tradition, through his control of the knowledge of the sacred texts. Both groups essentially accepted the Brahmanical theory of the four varnas and saw the origin of castes in the intermixture through marriage of the members of the four varnas. Neither group related what they must have known was the structure of the society on the ground to their knowledge of the society derived from textual study and discussions with learned Brahmans. There was little attempt on the part of either to fit the facts of political organization, land tenure, the actual functioning of the legal system, or the commercial structure into their picture of the society derived from the texts. Both the orientalists and the missionaries agreed that Hinduism as practiced within the realm of their observation in the late eighteenth and early nineteenth centuries was filled with "superstition" and "abuses" and that by and large the Hindus were debased and licentious. Their major differences lay in that the orientalists admired in theory the civilization and religion embodied in the texts and saw the difficulties of Indian society as being a fall from a golden age. The missionaries saw the society and culture as always having been corrupt, pernicious, and filled with absurdities.

The differences in view of the missionary and orientalist were related to their respective social backgrounds and their occupational roles in India. The orientalists tended to be better educated and from the upper classes of Great Britain; some, as Sir William Jones, were trained as scholars before their arrival in India and they wanted to treat Sanskrit and Persian learning with the same methods and respect as one would treat European learning. Their general political and social stance was conservative in that they accepted the status quo. They saw stability and order in the theory of caste. William Robertson, one of the Scottish moral philosophers, who, although not a Sanskrit or Persian scholar, was a disseminator of early studies of Indian tradition, argued:

The object of the first Indian legislators was to employ the most effectual means of providing for the subsistence, the security, and happiness of all the members of the community over which they presided. With this view, they set apart certain races of men for each of the various professions and arts necessary in a well ordered society, and appointed the exercise of them to be transmitted from father to son in succession. . . . To this early division of the people into caste, we must likewise ascribe a striking peculiarity in the state of India; the permanence of its institutions, and the immutability in the manners of its inhabitants. What now is in India, always was there, and is likely still to continue: neither the ferocious violence and illiberal fanaticism of its Mahomedan conquerors, nor the power of its European masters, have effected any considerable alteration. The same distinctions of condition take place, the same arrangements in civil and domestic society remain, the same maxims of religion are held in veneration, the same sciences and arts are cultivated (1828, appendix, pp. 52–53).

Many of the orientalists in India were concerned with judicial affairs of the East India Company, as were Halhead, Jones, and Colebrooke. In their role as judges they were confronted with Indians who by the nature of court action appeared to be litigious, purveyors of false testimony, dishonest, and cheats. On the other hand, they were studying Sanskrit legal treatises with pundits and were impressed with the learning and sophistication of Hindu law. They were trying to apply Hindu law to the cases they were hearing on the grounds that Indians would be best governed under their own law rather than under imported British law. The gap between the way Indians behaved in the courts and what the "orientalist" judges believed was the law and the theory of the society was seen as a fall from an older and better state of society caused by the intervention of foreign rulers, Muslim and European.

The missionaries with much the same perceptions and information interpreted the situation differently because of their differences in background. They largely came, particularly the Baptist missionaries, from lower orders in British society; they were committed to reform of their own society as well as of Indian society, and they were concerned with changing India rather than with maintaining the status quo.

THE GROWTH OF AN EMPIRICAL KNOWLEDGE OF THE STRUCTURE AND FUNCTIONING OF INDIAN SOCIETY

The period 1757 to 1785 was a time in which the officials of the East India Company in Bengal had to develop an administrative system capable of maintaining law and order and producing in a regular fashion income to support the administrative, military, and commercial activities of the company and to provide a profit for its owners. Through this period, the company officials had to learn from scratch a great deal about India, Indians, and how they had been governed. The assessment and regular collection of land revenue, it became clear by Warren Hasting's time, required considerable detailed knowledge of the structure of Indian society. As the East India Company in Madras, in Maharashtra, and in upper India came into contact with and had to establish relations with a wide range of states, a knowledge of Indian political history and a working knowledge of the internal political structure of Indian states became a necessity.

Persistently, inquiries into the nature of land tenure in Bengal were made, and collections of documents and records of previous rulers were assembled to determine what rights and duties various persons connected with the production of agricultural products had. Although it is clear that many of the efforts to learn the nature of Bengal rural society were confused and incomplete, none the less there were an increasing number of officials like James Grant and John Shore, who from documents and firsthand experience had considerable knowledge of the actual functioning of Bengali society. The misunderstandings leading to permanent settlement were as much a function of philosophical and social conceptions about the general nature of society and polity and the goals of British policy as they were a misunderstanding of the complicated facts of Bengali social structure.[2]

In addition to the duties which some British officials had to perform in collecting and studying information about Indian rural society, some British, official and nonofficial, out of interest and curiosity began to study and write on Indian society from firsthand observation in relatively objective fashion. William Tennant, a military chaplain, wrote a two-volume work, *Indian Recreations: Consisting Chiefly of Strictures on the Domestic and Rural Economy of the Mahommedans and Hindoos,* originally published in Edinburgh in 1804, which contains a collection of careful observations of agricultural practices in upper India (see vol. 2). Tennant's goal was to instruct himself about the "condition of a numerous people, living in a state of society and manners to me almost entirely new" (1804, vol. 1, p. 3). His information was based on personal observation, "conversations and writings of several intelligent natives of India, both Mussulmans and Hindoos," and "oral conversation with the most intelligent of the Honourable Company's civil and military servants" (1804, vol. 1, pp. viii, ix). In short, he applied the techniques which were typical of the earliest generation of anthropologists down to the beginning of the twentieth century: observation and interviews with key native informants and knowledgeable Europeans. Tennant describes a particular village, 36 miles from Banaras, of about a thousand acres and a population of a thousand. He briefly mentions the crops and the methods of cultivation and also gives a brief description of the occupations of the principal villagers. In addition to the zamindar, the patwari, and the Byah (grain weigher), he describes the carpenters, blacksmith, washermen, barbers, potters, Chamars, Ahirs, *bārhi* (leaf plate maker), *bhaṭ* (genealogist), shepherds, and the Brahman of the village. Tennant notes that the most numerous occupation (by implication irrespective of caste) is that of plowmen, of whom there were about 100 in the village, who received five seers of grain a day and one rupee for each of two annual plowing seasons (1804, vol. 2, p. 196).

Another example of careful description of rural society in relation to agriculture was provided by H. T. Colebrooke (1806), one of the early Sanskrit scholars. It is interesting that Colebrooke wrote *Remarks on the Husbandry and Internal Commerce of Bengal* before he was far along in the learning of Sanskrit. His work combines statistical material and summaries of official reports with his own observations and provides a good general description of the cultivation of most of the commercial crops, cotton, indigo, sugar cane, and opium. Colebrooke believed that by and large Bengal was relatively prosperous and was capable of becoming even more so as agriculture developed and manufacturing

---

2. For an excellent discussion of the relationship of eighteenth-century European social and economic theory to British revenue policy in Bengal, see Ranajit Guha, *A Rule of Property for Bengal: An Essay on the Idea of Permanent Settlement*, Paris, 1963. For a full discussion of the development of the policies and the growth of empirical knowledge of Bengali land system, see Walter K. Firminger, Introduction to *The Fifth Report . . . on the Affairs of the East India Company . . . 1812*, vol. 1, Calcutta, 1917.

increased. He was sure that the caste system and the religious systems were in no sense any bar to further development. After quoting an unnamed author who argued that there was a hereditary prohibition on undertaking other than one's father's occupation, and briefly summarizing the four-varna theory of caste, Colebrooke commented:

In practice, little attention is paid to the limitations to which we have alluded; daily observation shows even Brahmens exercising the menial profession of a Sudra. We are aware that every caste forms itself into clubs or lodges, consisting of the several individuals of that caste residing within a small distance; and that these clubs, or lodges, govern themselves by particular rules and customs, or by laws. But, though some restrictions and limitations, not founded on religious prejudice, are found among their by-laws, it may be received as a general maxim, that the occupation, appointed for each tribe, is entitled merely to a preference. Every profession, with few exceptions, is open to every description of persons; and the discouragement, arising from religious prejudices, is not greater than what exists in Great Britain from the effects of Municipal and corporation laws. In Bengal, the numbers of people, actually willing to apply to any particular occupation, are sufficient for the unlimited extension of any manufacture (1806, p. 174).

With the rapid expansion of the East India Company's territories in the last decade of the eighteenth century, leading up to the final defeat of the Marathas in 1818, the British became increasingly aware of the bewildering variety of peoples, histories, political forms, systems of land tenure, and religious practices which were to be found in the subcontinent. The mid and late eighteenth century western myth of "an undifferentiated Orient characterized by the rectilinear simplicity of its social structure, the immutability of its laws and customs, the primitive innocence of its people" (Guha, 1963, p. 26) could not be sustained in the face of the experience that the Wellesley generation had in India. Through their direct experience, such as Munro's in the land settlements in Salem District in Madras, Malcolm's in his diplomatic duties in Mysore and with the Marathas, Tod's in his diplomatic duties in Rajasthan, Elphinstone's in his diplomatic and administrative duties in Maharashtra, as well as dozens of other officials, the British now began to have fairly deep if somewhat unsystematic knowledge of Indian society. Coincident with the relatively haphazard collection and reporting of sociological information, usually embedded in revenue reports or in historical works, the company directly supported surveys part of whose goal was acquisition of better and more systematic information about the peoples of India. One of the earliest and most famous of these endeavors to collect information was that of Dr. Francis Buchanan.

Buchanan—who later in his life took his mother's name, Hamilton, on the inheritance of her family's estate in Scotland—was born in Scotland in 1762. He had an excellent education in Glasgow and Edinburgh and became a physician; he apparently made several trips to India as an assistant surgeon on an East Indianman, and then in 1794 joined the East India Company's service as an assistant surgeon (Prain, 1905). He initially served in what is today East Pakistan and began early to collect and report on botanical and zoological specimens.

His work caught the attention of William Roxburgh, the great student of Indian botany. It was Roxburgh who recommended Buchanan to Lord Clive, Governor of Madras, and Lord Wellesley, the Governor General, when late in 1799 they wanted a survey made of Mysore and the Company's territories acquired after the Fourth Mysore War. Buchanan's instructions from Wellesley were to collect information on agriculture, nature of tenures, natural products of the country, manufacturing, commerce, mines and quarries, and the climate. In addition, Wellesley said: "The condition of the inhabitants in general, in regard to their food, clothing and habitations, will engage your particular attention. . . . The different sects and tribes of which the body of people is composed, will merit your observance; you will likewise note whatever may appear to you worthy of remark in their laws, customs, etc . . ." (Buchanan, 1807, vol. 1, p. xii). Buchanan's report was published as a diary, in which he notes under a particular date what he observed or was told about the wide range of topics he was sent to obtain information about. He was obviously a keen observer, and his descriptions of technology, historic sites, and plants are excellent. He also obtained considerable data on what we would today call ethnographic accounts of the various castes, their subdivision, and occupations. Most of his information was obtained through interviewing members of various castes, and he is frequently careful in telling us of his sources and his guess as to their reliability.

Buchanan's great work, however, was his survey carried out on the orders of the court of director's of the Company of January 7, 1807. They wanted a statistical survey of the country, under the authority of the presidency of Bengal. If it had been completed it would cover what is today East and West Pakistan, parts of Orissa and Assam, most of present-day Bihar and Uttar Pradesh exclusive of Oudh, and the Bundelkhand districts. Buchanan was engaged in this work for seven years and completed 25 folio volumes of manuscript. The results of this work have never been completely published and were known in the nineteenth century largely from Robert Montgomery Martin's editing of the materials, which are contained in *The History, Antiquities, Topography, and Statistics of Eastern India* . . . , published in three volumes in London in 1838. Martin's volumes cover the northern part of Bengal, the Districts of Dinajpur and Rangpur, the southern part of Assam, and the portions of Bihar south of the Ganges, and Gorakhpur District in Uttar Pradesh. In the twentieth century the Bihar and Orissa Research Society and Bihar government undertook to edit and publish the full version of Buchanan's reports which related to Bihar. In all, five volumes on four districts were published, and in addition three volumes of Buchanan's field journal which give his itinerary and incidental notes were also published.

The Bihar materials differ greatly in quantity and quality from the Mysore survey of Buchanan. There are extensive statistics on various aspects of the society, estimates of the number of houses classified by general types of persons who occupied them (that is, gentry, traders, artificer, and plowman), health statistics, statistics on types of farm laborers, size of families, types of houses, attempts at statistically estimating standards of living and the numbers engaged in various trades and crafts in the cities and districts. In addition to the statistical material, there are extremely well-organized and detailed descriptions of education and land tenure, as well as normative descriptions of a wide range of customs. Buchanan organized his material under five main headings, Topography and Antiquities, The People, Natural Products, Agriculture, and Commerce, Arts, and Manufactures. Under the heading "The People," he discussed demography, his statistics usually being based on interviews with native officials and various registers, which he frequently spot-checked. He paid a great deal of attention to the standard of living of the people and constantly tried to measure income and consumption; he also gave materials on the form and content of education in the districts he covered. He described the various sects of the Hindus and Muslims found and their ritual and theological differences. His discussion of castes was weighted to description of their occupations. Much of what he wrote about the ethnography of Bihar was presented in comparison to Bengal, which apparently was more familiar to him and his readers.

THE DEVELOPMENT OF THE "OFFICIAL" VIEW OF CASTE

Buchanan's work in Bengal and Bihar was the forerunner of a continuing effort undertaken by the British in India to collect, collate, and publish for official as well as scholarly use detailed information about all aspects—physical, cultural, and sociological—of every district in India, which reached its high peak with the Imperial Gazetteer of India, published in the early twentieth century. The line of work stretches from Buchanan, through efforts in the 1840's to publish district manuals and histories, through the efforts of the 1870's such as the *Statistical Account of Bengal*, edited by Hunter, to the Provincial and Imperial Gazetteers of the early twentieth century. With the publication for the first time of the census of India on a systematic and all-India basis in 1872, a whole new body of material on Indian society became available, and in North India with the successive waves of revenue settlements which produced a great deal of material on the relation of people to the land and the organization of Indian rural society, an implicit view of the nature of Indian society and particularly the caste system began to emerge.

The "official" view of caste was very much related to how the British collected information about the caste system. In the first instance, a caste was a "thing," an entity, which was concrete and measurable; above all it had definable characteristics—endogamy, commensality rules, fixed occupation, common ritual practices. These were things which supposedly one could find out by sending assistants into the field with a questionnaire and which could be quantified for reports and surveys; or one could learn about the castes of a particular district by sitting on one's horse or in the shade of the village banyan tree as the adjunct of one's official duty. What was recorded could be collated so that the Lohars, or the Ahirs, or the Mahishyas, or the Okkaligas could be pigeonholed and one could then go on to the next group to be described. This way of thinking about a particular caste was useful to the administrator, because it gave the illusion of knowing the people; he did not have to differentiate too much among individual Indians—a man was a Brahman, and Brahmans had certain characteristics.

He was "conservative." His intelligence was "superior to that of any other Race." "His chief fault has been extreme exclusiveness" (Bingley and Nicholls, 1897, pp. 37–42). Not only could one know a "people" by knowing their caste and what its customs and rules were; what one "knew" could be reduced to hard facts. "The 1901 Census [of Bengal] found there were over 205 castes and tribes over 25,000 in population in Bihar and Orissa. In Bengal there were 450 groups from one to 22,000,000. Half of them did not have over 1,000 members" (O'Malley, 1913, p. 440). India was seen as collection of castes; the particular picture was different in any given time and place, but India was a sum of its parts and the parts were castes.

The "official" census-based view of caste therefore saw the system as one of separate castes and their customs. In order to understand caste one had to develop classifications to order the data. The most famous classification is H. H. Risley's, in which he reduced the 2,000-odd castes which the census had found in India to seven types: tribal, functional, and sectarian; castes formed by crossing; national castes; castes formed by migration; and castes formed by changing customs. After the castes had been counted and classified and their customs and characteristics recorded, the gnawing question remaining was why did this "caste" exist; what were its origins? Here origins were taken not as a direct historical question. Unlike the early orientalists, the "official" ethnographers of caste, although they recognized the Brahmanical theory as embodied in the texts, did not think the texts were documents in which could be traced the history of caste. By origin they rather meant a very broad functional question. Nesfield regarded caste as having its origin in the division of labor, and the occupation was the central determining factor in the system. H. H. Risley argued for a racial origin of caste. Ibbetson saw the major impetus to the formation of caste in "tribal origins." Crooke and others came out for more eclectic theories of origin. This eclecticism reaches its final form with the last of the British official ethnographers and census commissioners, J. H. Hutton. He compiled a list of fourteen "more obvious factors which have been indicated as probably contributing to the emergence and development of the caste system" (1946, pp. 89–90).

The administrative-official view of caste not only was an outgrowth of the way in which information was collected but also reflected anthropological interests and theories of the period 1870–1910. The reflection of contemporary anthropological theory can be seen both in the general theoretical books written about the caste system and in the data assembled and classified for the series of provincial "tribes and castes" books, for example, W. Crooke's *The Tribes and Castes of the North-Western Provinces and Oudh*, published in four volumes in Calcutta in 1896. In the accounts given of the castes, which are alphabetically arranged, a good deal of space is devoted to "marriage rules" and subdivisions of the caste, usually termed exogamous sections, which are listed by name with customs of particular sections, for example, whether they worship a particular deity or have a distinctive marriage ceremony. There are descriptions of life-cycle rites for most castes. If any mythological origin stories are known about the caste or the exogamous sections, these are recorded as well. There is usually a brief description of the occupation traditionally followed by the caste. Statistics on the geographic distribution of the caste and its major sections taken from the 1891 census are presented in tabular form.

The data and their organization implicitly reflect the work of Morgan, McLennan, Lubbock, Tylor, Starcke, and Frazer (see pp. clxi–ccvii of the introduction to volume 1 for Crooke's summaries of these Victorian anthropologists). These men were concerned with the use of "customs"—for example, marriage by capture, polyandry, or the levirate—to infer something about the origin of culture or, as they termed it, "civilization." Similarly, religious practices were utilized as disparate bits of information to develop stages of the development of religion. The "customs" were reported and studied out of their contexts as hard facts which could be compared and classified as to the stage of development. The compilers of the handbooks and gazetteers, the recorders of the proverbs, myths, and practices reported in *Panjab Notes and Queries* or in *North Indian Notes and Queries* were contributing not only to an antiquarian interest in Indian society but to the eventual solution of general anthropological problems.

In 1901 an official effort was made to establish an ethnographic survey of India, which would develop as part of the census of 1901. The expense and effort connected with the ethnographic survey were justified on the following grounds: "It has come to be recognized . . . that India is a vast store house of social and physical data which only need be recorded in order to contribute to the solution of the problems which are being approached in Europe with the aid of material much of which is inferior in quality to the facts readily accessible in India" (Government of India, 1901, p. 138). The need to collect this ethnographic information was considered pressing because the "primitive beliefs and usages in India" would be completely destroyed or transformed, another late Victorian justification for ethnography. Finally, the survey was justified on the grounds that "for purposes of legislation, of judicial procedure, of famine relief, of sanitation and dealings with epidemic disease, and almost every form of executive action, an ethnographic survey of India and a record of the customs of the people is as necessary an incident of good administration as a cadastral survey of the land and a record of rights of its tenants" (Government of India, 1901, pp. 138–39). One cannot help but wonder what use knowledge of marriage customs or a cephalic index would be to an administrator.

The final question connected with the "official" view of caste was what effect it had on Indian society. The history of British rule in India is to some extent to be seen in the unanticipated consequence of its actions. With the recent increasing work on eighteenth- and nineteenth-century social history, for example, the work of Ronald Inden on Bengali Kayasthas and Brahmans, Karen Leonard's work on Hyderabadi Kayasthas, and Robert Hardgrave's work on South Indian Nadars, a much different view of caste and the caste system is beginning to emerge. In some castes in the nineteenth century the effective unit, as in many rural areas today, was the endogamous unit, not the exogamous unit, which the administrators thought of as the effective unit in the system. Through changes brought about by literacy, aspirations for upward mobility, and new geographic and occupational mobility, the endogamous unit began to take on a wider importance. In the urban environment or in the modernized segment of the society, Indians increasingly identified themselves with endogamous groups and with the caste name "Brahman," "Kayasthas," "Nadar," etc. In this process of change, the census, the constant need for government applications to identify oneself by caste, the application of varying law to different castes, all seemed to have played a part.

In the census of 1901, H. H. Risley, who was census superintendent, classified castes on the basis of "social precedence as recognized by native public opinion" (1915, p. 111). Risley argued that, although this turned out to be very troublesome in terms of the amount of argument and petitions submitted by Indians claiming different status than had been granted by the provincial census commissioners, it indicated that this indeed was a successful classification. Risley also noted that most of the petitions were in English, indicating that the educated classes were still very much within the caste system (1915, pp. 112–14). The question remains, however, of what was cause and what was effect. Did the notion of social precedence on a provincial basis, the enshrining of the categorical level of the caste system as against any real social grouping known in the earlier part of the nineteenth century, in effect create that level? The answer, of course, is not a simple one. The census operations were only one of many changes affecting Indian society at the time. The changes which were being simultaneously recognized included the caste sabha movements, expansion of marriage networks, establishment of caste hostels at colleges, as well as the petitioning of census commissioners for changes in rank accorded a caste in the census tables.

The Village "View" of Indian Society

In the early nineteenth century another "official" view of Indian society developed alongside of and to a surprising extent not articulated with the official view of caste. This view was that India was a land of "village republics," of self-sufficient corporately organized villages. Professor Dumont has recently traced the development of the concept of the "village community" (1966). Dumont sees three connected but successive meanings in the term "village community." In the first phase, the village community is seen by British writers as primarily a political society, in the second phase as a body of co-owners of the soil, while in the third phase it becomes to Indians the emblem of traditional economy and polity, "a watch word of Indian patriotism" (1966, p. 67). Two documents contain the basic ideas and descriptions of the Indian village community, the Fifth Report of 1812 and Charles Metcalfe's minutes on the village of Delhi of 1830 (Dumont, 1966, pp. 38–70).

Although there is some variation in detail, through time the village community had certain unchanging components (Dumont, 1966; Srinivas and Shah, 1960; Thorner, 1966). The village consists of a body of co-sharers of the land and or its produce. It is not too clear if this included everyone in the village or just the dominant landholding group. This group made all decisions relevant to the village, social and economic. In the South this group is represented by a headman.

Decisions for and by the village are made in council (the panchayat). The economy of the village is self-sufficient, both in producing what it needs and thus needing little from the outside and in having all the crafts and services necessary for the functioning of the village economy. The village is relatively unconnected to other villages or other higher levels in the political system except that taxes are extracted by the government from the village. The village has existed in this form in unchanging fashion "from the days of Menu" (Mark Wilks, quoted in Dumont, 1966, p. 71), or, in the famous terms of Metcalfe: "They [the village communities] seem to last when nothing else lasts. Dynasty after dynasty tumbles down; revolution succeeds to revolution; Hindu, Pathan, Mughal, Mahratta, Sikh, English, are masters in turn; but the village communities remain the same" (quoted in Spear, 1951, p. 117).

In the middle of the nineteenth century Marx and Maine accepted the basic assumptions and the idea of the village community, and it was incorporated into general social and economic theory of the later nineteenth century. R. C. Dutt's important work, *Economic History of India*, originally published in 1902, seems to have been one of the principal sources used by twentieth-century scholars, publicists, and politicians for the continuation of the myth of the Indian village community, which became central to the Indian nationalists' view of their past. In this view, India was both economically well off in the pre-modern period and reasonably democratically governed at the village level, and it was the evils of British imperial rule which turned India from this idyllic state into the stagnated rural economy dominated by moneylenders and rapacious landlords.

B. H. Baden-Powell's massive compilation, *The Land Systems of British India*, published in three volumes by Oxford University Press in 1892, may be seen as the culmination of the empirical study of the social structure of rural India which grew out of the more than 100 years of British experience with attempting to assess and collect land revenue. In this work Baden-Powell gives a region-by-region summary of the leading legislation affecting land tenures in relation to the immediate history of the regions at the time of their acquisition by the British. He then tries to trace the general effectiveness of the land tenure legislation in terms of the collection of the revenue, discusses the protection of rights of various groups who were on the land during the nineteenth century, and makes passing reference to effects of British legislation on the distribution of land. Baden-Powell's work is based on a close study of the land revenue regulations, annual and special government reports, the settlement reports, and the district gazetteers and manuals. He rightly argues that the empirical basis for a study of rural India had greatly expanded in the twenty years since 1870, when Maine had published his *Village Communities East and West* (Baden-Powell, 1908, ch. III).

Baden-Powell's *The Land Systems of British India* was not just a compilation of data but contained a series of arguments about the nature of Indian village communities in relation to the state. Baden-Powell recognized in general that there were two claims on the produce of the soil, the state's and the landholder's. He postulated that the government derived its revenue "by taking a share of the actual grain heap on the threshing floor from each holding" (1892, vol. 1, p. 97).

In order to collect this share, a wide range of offices and intermediaries between the grain heap and the state developed through time. These were headmen and accountants recognized or appointed by the government, local and district officials, and other revenue officials of the state. Often these officials were remunerated by land grants, which were turned into permanent hereditary holdings, and at later stages revenue farmers converted their contracts to pay the land revenue into "ownership" of the land. In addition, rights over the land were established by conquest. Under this level of the system, that established by the government and conquest, existed the village, which was the result of a "natural instinct" (1892, vol. 1, p. 106).

Baden-Powell strongly disagreed with Maine, who saw only one type of Indian village, by arguing that there are two types of villages which were distinct in their origin. One type was variously called "ryotwari" or non-landlord (Baden-Powell, 1892, vol. 1, p. 128), or "severalty." In this type of village, the cultivators did not have any right as a joint or corporate body to the whole estate. "The land [estate] is divided amongst themselves and each man owns his own holding, which he has bought, inherited or cleared from the jungle. The holders are not jointly responsible to the state for revenue or other obligations" (1892, vol. 1, p. 107). This kind of holding, according to Baden-Powell, was closely connected with ideas and government. It was found in Madras, the central provinces, and Bombay. It originated, according to Baden-Powell, in Aryan times when a chief or raja was political leader and had no claim as a landlord but did have the right to grant to individuals the right to settle on waste land (1892, vol. 1, p. 128). The other type of village is termed by Baden-Powell a landlord or joint village. In these villages there is "a strong joint body, probably descended from a single head, or single family, which has pretensions to be of higher caste and superior title to the 'tenants' who live on the estate . . ." (1892, vol. 1, p. 107). Those who live and work in the village do so only by permission from the joint landholding body. This type was found in Uttar Pradesh and the Punjab. It took its origins from the break-up of raja's estates, grants made to courtiers by rajas, the conversion of land grants to revenue officials into a patrimony, the development of revenue farmers into landowners and "from the original establishment of special clans and families of associated bands of village farmers and colonists in comparatively later times" (1892, vol. 1, p. 130).

Baden-Powell combined what he thought of as direct history with evolutionary stages in the development of property, from a tribal stage in which land was held by a tribe, to family property, to individual property. The logic of the stages does not mesh with Baden-Powell's broad-scale history, as private property is found amongst the ryotwari villages, which derive from an earlier period in India history than do the joint or landlord villages, in which property is held by families or lineages.

Even though Baden-Powell thought of himself as attacking Maine, his arguments are of the same type as Maine's and lead in the same direction. The Victorian students of the Indian village were interested in the village as a type from which they could infer evolutionary stages and which could be used to compare similar developments or stages in other parts of the world. For the administrator the types and classifications of villages had the same kind of advantage that the official view of caste had: they reduced the need for specific knowledge. One could act in terms of categories. Latently, the categorical or conceptual thinking about villages directed attention away from internal politics in villages and from questions of the nature of actual social relations, of the distribution of wealth, of what was happening to agricultural production; in short, the Victorians were not concerned with what the actual conditions of life in the villages were but with general theoretical questions derived from social theory of the day.

STUDY OF THE INDIAN VILLAGE IN THE FIRST HALF OF THE TWENTIETH CENTURY

In the later decades of the nineteenth century, the British government became increasingly aware that there were widespread difficulties in the rural economy of India. The most obvious and tragic indicator of trouble were the famines, which appeared to be increasing in number, spread, and intensity. The Famine Commission of 1901 estimated there were twelve famines and four severe scarcities in the period 1765 to 1858. In the next fifty years famine or scarcity prevailed in one or another part of India, in twenty out of fifty years (see Bhatia, 1963, p. 8). There were widespread peasant riots in the Deccan in 1875 (see Catanach, 1966). In the Punjab the British officials became increasingly concerned with what they thought of as the alienation of land from peasants to moneylenders (Barrier, 1966). The famines, the riots, and the concerns over land alienation, as well as continuing concerns with tenancy legislation, resulted in a spate of official investigations by special commissions (for a listing see the bibliographies in Bhatia, Catanach, and Barrier).

The investigations accumulated extensive and important information, often of statistical nature, about rural India and recommended wide-scale administrative and legislative changes directed to correcting the faults or difficulties uncovered. The remedial action, whether it was aimed at securing better rights for tenants or protecting small landholders from moneylenders, or recommending cooperative societies or irrigation works, once again sent officials into the countryside to investigate local economic conditions. The methods adopted and the length of time spent in investigation of specific local conditions led to superficial results and were tied to the immediate political or administrative concerns which, once solved in the form of legislation or an administrative recommendation for action, were largely forgotten until the next crisis. The tendency in the reports and in the use made of the data by Indian and British critics was to aggregate the statistics and findings of specific studies, so that attention was directed to macro-economic and social problems. Once again, although some knowledge was accumulated, the actual working on the ground of the economic and social system was ignored.

In the early twentieth century Dr. Harold H. Mann, principal of the College of Agriculture at Poona, was responsible for directing two studies of the actual functioning of village economies in the Deccan (Mann, 1917, 1921). In these studies Mann and his collaborators wanted to collect data on "numerous economic and economic agricultural questions" by the "close study of a single village" (1917, p. iv). The table of contents of the two studies gives a good summary of the topics covered in the surveys: physical features of the village (rainfall, geology, soil, etc.); the land and its divisions (tenures, history of land revenue, landholdings); vegetation, crops, and cultivation (all the crops are noted with brief descriptions of methods of cultivation, amount of village land under the crops, value, etc.); agricultural stock of the village (number and kinds of animals and value); the people of the village (brief descriptions of the castes, their activities, and extensive discussion of their income and expenditures). Mann's assistants collected data by interviewing and observing over relatively long periods in the village and by a study of village records. According to Walter Neale, although questionnaires were used in the Mann surveys of the Deccan villages, much more reliance was placed on direct observation and the actual measurement by his assistants of all inputs and outputs in the village, "so that there was no dependence on the respondents' memory or willingness to tell the truth. Dr. Mann's survey quite literally took over and 'laid bare' the village and its life" (Neale, 1958, p. 398).

The rigor of Mann's study was rarely achieved in the subsequent village surveys done for other villages and small regions in India.[3] Even if their statistics were found to be unreliable and not comparable, the surveys did give in graphic fashion a detailed picture of the functioning of the village economies. Few, however, related the economies to social structure in any direct fashion. Two notable exceptions to this generalization are William Wiser, *The Hindu Jajmani System* (Lucknow, 1936), and S. S. Nehru, *Caste and Credit in the Rural Area* (Calcutta, 1932). In both these studies the authors related the social and political structure of villages to the distribution of wealth and income and were able to point out in a way that village surveys could show the dynamic relations between the organization of local societies and the functioning of the economy.

THE ETHNOGRAPHIC TRADITION IN
THE EARLY TWENTIETH CENTURY

The census operations of the twentieth century continued to have an ethnographic and physical anthropological component. The emphasis on race and physical anthropology of the 1901 census was repeated in 1931 when B. S. Guha directed an extensive study of physical types in India as part of the census. British officials connected with the census operations continued to produce books on the caste system as a result of their work on the census, notably L. S. S. O'Malley, E. A. H. Blunt, and J. H. Hutton. However, the major development in the first forty years of the twentieth century anthropologically did not concern the bulk

---

3. For a listing of the important surveys, see Neale, "The Limitations of Indian Village Survey Data," *Journal of Asian Studies*, vol. XVII, no. 3, 1958, note 3; the most ambitious set of village surveys was that carried out by the Board of Economic Inquiry, Punjab, under the general title of *Punjab Village Surveys*.

of the Indian population, as did nineteenth-century proto-anthropological studies, but concentrated on the tribal populations of India.

Some ethnographic study was done in the northeast of India under government auspices, by Hutton, Mills, and Hodson, who produced as government ethnographers extensive accounts of major Naga tribes. In the period before World War I, with some government encouragement, Seligman did a study of Vedda of Ceylon, Rivers did his famous study of the Todas, and Radcliffe-Brown his study of the Andaman Islanders. Grigson, an official assigned as a resident in Central India, studied the Gonds, and Fürer-Haimendorf, supported by the Hyderabad government, studied tribal peoples in Hyderabad. The most active ethnographer of the period was a civilian, Sarat Chandra Roy, who carried out a series of important studies in Chota Nagpur on the tribals of that region. It was through Roy's energy and skill that *Man in India* was founded and thrived. Verrier Elwin, whose career encompassed work as a missionary and a Gandhian worker, also carried out important work amongst the tribals of Central India. A. A. Aiyappan was the main exception to the generalization that professional anthropologists studied tribal peoples. Aiyappan, a student of Malinowski, carried out two important functionalist-oriented studies of castes in South India, the Nayadis and the Izhavas. In addition to their ethnographic importance, both studies paid close attention to social change in relation to the status and structure of the castes studied.

CONCLUSIONS

By the 1940's the study of Indian society cumulatively had the following components: (1) a broad-scale humanistically oriented tradition which emphasized the relationship between textual studies and a static model of contemporary Indian society; (2) an administrative tradition centered on the census for the study of caste which sought to see Indian society as a collection of discrete entities whose traditions and customs could be classified and studied; (3) a tradition of economic study which sought to describe the working of village economies, with some attention to the social structure of villages; (4) an anthropological tradition centered on the study of tribal peoples; and (5) an historical administrative strain which centered on the general theory of village organization in a broad comparative framework, but without an intensive ethnographic base.

One can go back to the eighteenth century and trace in a rough chronological fashion a changing view of Indian society as it relates to the two major institutions which contemporary students of Indian society concern themselves with—caste and village. Caste, which is a European word, has for the last 200 years been used to circumscribe analytically four distinct components of the social system of India, two structural and two cultural. The orientalist view of the caste system emphasized the broadest ideological category of the system of the varnas, which functionally provides the participants in the system with a very general explanation and a very rough set of categories to account for the hierarchy of castes. The varna categories in the last 100 years, with heightened opportunity for social mobility, may be taking on new meanings for the actors in the system. In addition to the varna categories, the system contains *jāt* categories, which are also cultural. A *jāt* is a named group usually spread over a wide territory roughly occupying vis-à-vis other such categories the same position in the caste hierarchy of a region. Members of a *jāt* roughly have the same traditional occupation and may have some rituals and myths in common. The *jāt* has no structural reality in terms of corporate activities nor does it directly affect the behavior of those who are classified in the category. In the last fifty years or so, however, for political and educational purposes there have been efforts to mobilize people around the cultural category of their *jāts*. It was the *jāt* which the administrative view of caste saw as one of the major parts of the system, and much of the data collected and published by the administrators related to the *jāt* category or level of the system. A *jāt* is still what is meant when someone uses the word "caste."

Jāts are composed of groups of people who are by kinship and marriage tied into endogamous sections, often named, with deities, rituals, myths, and stories in common and usually localized. In a very few instances they have formal headmen and temples, and may have accepted rules of behavior which can be enforced by the headmen. In North Indian terminology these units are called *jātis*, and in English they are usually referred to as subcastes. The administrators were aware of this level of the system and tried, generally unsuccessfully, to collect data about them. When after World War II social and cultural anthropologists began to do intensive field work in villages, they concentrated in their study of caste system on the lowest level of the system, the exogamous section, which in eastern Uttar Pradesh are called *birādarīs* (brotherhoods). A *birādarī* is a social group made up of males who believe they are descended from a common male ancestor: they are brothers. They occupy a known territory, a village or a group of villages usually of very limited range. Frequently there are headmen, common property, and effective means for controlling the behavior of members of the brotherhood. This grouping is exogamous. When one talks of caste ranking, intercaste relations in a village, vote banks in a caste, in fact almost any face-to-face actions in the rural social system in terms of caste, it is the brotherhood that is being talked about.

One way of looking at the history of the study of caste is as a history of the discovery of the levels of the system. This discovery is very much tied to the methods of study and presuppositions of those doing the study. In the Dharmashastras and Vedas studied by the orientalists one finds varnas. If one sends out assistants and surveys with questionnaires, as did the administrators, one finds *jāts*, and *jātis*; if one does long-term, intensive field work in one place, one finds brotherhoods.

The history of the study of the Indian village in an effective fashion began with the intensive survey work connected with British attempts to collect land revenue in the late eighteenth century. Paradoxically, the British began with collecting an extensive amount of detail about the structure of landholding in particular regions, for example, the Baramahals and the villages of Delhi. In order to make sense of these data, categories were developed and a theory of the Indian village emerged into which further observations continued to be compressed.

Through the nineteenth century both comparatively in terms of reconstructions of European village histories (Maine), and through more knowledge about Indian villages (Baden-Powell), the categories were refined. With the twentieth century and growing concern over the Indian economy on the part of the British officials and Indians, further development of the theory of the Indian village was ignored in favor of intensive empirical studies of the economy of the villages.

By the end of World War II, with extensive changes in the methods, theories, and subject matter of social anthropology, the independence of India, and wider availability in India, Great Britain, and the United States of funds for extensive field work, the stage was set for a new view of Indian society to emerge. Consciously or unconsciously much of the research in the period 1945 to 1955 by social and cultural anthropologists was based on the assumptions developed over the previous 200 years as reflected by the anthropological thinking which developed during the 1930's and 1940's.

These assumptions and methods can be summarized briefly. Anthropologists study isolated or circumscribed systems; such systems in India can be found in villages, in the self-sufficient Indian village community of Munro, Metcalfe, Maine, and Baden-Powell. The anthropologist's model of change is based on the assumption of a baseline or zero point of change. There was a time, anthropologists argue, when the systems we want to study were stable or static, and the anthropologist studies change by studying what happened from the postulated period of stability. In India this was to be found in villages where "traditional India" existed. This is the orientalist's assumption of the unchanging character of Indian civilization. Caste is the central institution of rural Indian society; it governs behavior and values. This is the official view of caste as a "thing," as a set of attributes. The way you study caste is to observe it in action and ask people about it.

The first publication in 1955 of two collections reporting the results of the "first round" of modern field work in India, *India's Villages* and *Village India*, reveals the shock of recognition that great correction was needed both in the anthropologist's assumptions about India derived from the traditions of study of India and in the transfer of interests in particular subject matter, methods, and theories from social and cultural anthropology as it existed in the late forties. The two collections also indicate the beginning of the new directions which anthropologists concerned with the study of India would travel in.

The present collection is one of many indications of the variety of directions we are going in. Politics, study of entrepreneurs, systematic study of cultural rules, history, sociolinguistics, and law, are all underlaid by new and more rigorous methods of quantification and model construction and are all tempered by wider comparative knowledge.

BIBLIOGRAPHY

ABU'L FAZL 'ALLAMI.
1786. *Ā'īn-i-Akbari*. Calcutta (no publisher).

AL-BIRUNI.
1962. *Alberuni's India*. Lahore: Government of West Pakistan.

BADEN-POWELL, B. H.
1892. *The land systems of British India*. Oxford: Clarendon Press.
1908. *The origin and growth of village communities in India*. London: S. Sornenschein.

BARBOSA, DUARTE.
1866. *A description of the coast of East Africa and Malabar in the beginning of the sixteenth century*. London: Hakluyt Society. Vol. 35.
1918, 1921. *The book of Duarte Barbosa: an account of the countries bordering on the Indian Ocean and their inhabitants*. (2 vols.) London Hakluyt: Society Series 2, vols. 54 and 59.

BARRIER, NORMAN G.
1966. *The Punjab alienation land bill of 1900*. Duke University Program in Comparative Studies on Southern Asia Monograph and Occasional Papers, Series No. 2.

BHATIA, B. H.
1963. *Famines in India*. Bombay: Asia Publishing House.

BINGLEY, A. H., and A. NICHOLLS.
1897. *Brahmans. Caste handbook for the Indian army*. Simla: Office of the Quarter Master General.

BUCHANAN, FRANCIS.
1807. *A journey from Madras through the countries of Mysore, Canara and Malabar. . . .* (3 vols.) London: T. Cadell and W. Davies.

CATANACH, I. J.
1966. Agrarian disturbances in nineteenth century India. *The Indian Economic and Social History Review*, 3: 65–84.

COLEBROOKE, HENRY THOMAS.
1806. *Remarks on the husbandry and internal commerce of Bengal*. London: Blacks and Parry.

DUMONT, LOUIS.
1966. The "village community" from Munro to Maine. *Contributions to Indian Sociology*, 9: 67–89.

ELLIOT, HENRY MEIRS, and JOHN DOWSON.
1867. *A history of India as told by its own historians*. London: Trubner.

GOVERNMENT OF INDIA.
1901. Extract Nos. 3219–3232. *Man*, i: 137–41.

GREAT BRITAIN, HOUSE OF COMMONS.
1833. *Report on East India Company affairs*. No. 14, General Appendix I.

GUHA, RANAJIT.
1963. *A rule of property for Bengal: an essay on the idea of permanent settlement*. Paris: Moutora and Co.

HALHEAD, N. B.
1777. *A code of gentoo laws, or, ordinations of the pundits from a Persian translation, made from the original, written in the Shanscrit language*. London: (n. p.).

HUTTON, J. H.

1946. *Caste in India: its nature, function and origins*. Cambridge: Cambridge University Press.

INGHAM, KENNETH.

1956. *Reformers in India: 1793–1833*. Cambridge: Cambridge University Press.

LACH, DONALD.

1965. *Asia in the making of Europe*. Chicago: University of Chicago Press.

LONG, J. (Ed.)

1868. *Adam's three reports on vernacular education in Bengal and Behar*. Calcutta: Home Secretariat Press.

M'CRINDLE, J. W. (Trans. and Ann.).

1901. *Ancient India: as described in classical literature*. Westminster: A. Constable and Co.

MANN, HAROLD H.

1917. *Land and labour in a Deccan village*. Bombay: Oxford University Press.

1921. *Land and labour in a Deccan village*. Study No. 2. Bombay: Oxford University Press.

NEALE, WALTER C.

1958. The limitations of Indian village survey data. *Journal of Asian Studies*, 17: 383–402.

O'MALLEY, L. S. S.

1913. *Bengal, Bihar, Orissa, and Sikkim, Census of India*, 1911. (vol. 5.) Calcutta: Bengal Secretariat Book Depot.

PRAIN, DAVID.

1905. *A sketch of the life of Francis Hamilton called Buchanan: Annals of the Royal Botanic Garden*. (vol. 10., Part 2.) Calcutta: Bengal Secretariat Press.

REHATSEK, E.

1880. Early Muslim accounts of the Hindu religion. *Journal of the Asiatic Society of Bombay*, 14: 418–38.

RISLEY, H. H.

1915. *The people of India*. (2d ed.) London: W. Thacker.

ROBERTSON, WILLIAM.

1828. *An historical disquisition concerning the knowledge which the ancients had of India . . .* (Originally published 1791.) London: Jones and Co.

SABAH AL-DIN 'ABID AL-RAHMAN.

1961. Study of Hindu learning and religion in Indo-Persian literature. *Indo-Iranica*, 14: 1–13.

SPEAR, PERCIVAL.

1951. *Twilight of the Mughals*. Cambridge: Cambridge University Press.

SRINIVAS, M. N., and T. M. SHAH.

1960. The myth of the self-sufficiency of the Indian village. *Economic Weekly*, 12: 1375–78.

TAVERNIER, JEAN BAPTISTE.

1889. *Travels in India by Jean B. Tavernier*. (Ed. by Valentine Ball.) (2 vols.) London: Macmillan.

TENNANT, WILLIAM.

1804. *Indian recreations: consisting chiefly of strictures on the domestic and rural economy of the Mahommedans and Hindoos*. (2 vols.) London: Longman, Hurst Rees, and Orine.

THORNER, DANIEL.
  1966. Marx on India and the Asiatic mode of production. *Contributions to Indian Sociology*, 9: 33–66.

WARD, WILLIAM.
  1822. *A view of the history, literature and mythology of the Hindoos.* (3 vols.) London: Kingsbury, Parbury and Allen.

YULE, HENRY, and A. C. BURNELL.
  1903. *Hobson-Jobson.* London: John Murray.

2. FAMILY, *JĀTI*, VILLAGE

DAVID G. MANDELBAUM

I. FAMILY: COMPLETING THE FAMILY CYCLE

THE GROWTH PHASE: THE REARING OF CHILDREN

THE FAMILY GROWS. The bride settles in and in time brings forth her child, the family's child. Within the family circle the child learns the fundamentals of his culture and society, is taught to become the kind of person who will, in his turn, fulfill the appropriate roles of family and society. We see something of how this is done in a study of child rearing in Khalapur village, some ninety miles north of Delhi. The authors observed family life in a sample of Rajput families, the dominant *jāti* of Khalapur (Minturn and Hitchcock, 1963). There, as elsewhere in village India, childbirth practices foreshadow the later lessons in cultural fundamentals. The notion of pollution pervades in these practices. The newborn infant arrives in a highly polluting state and must be carefully and gradually brought into a safer ritual and social condition. While physiological processes have produced the baby, only after the family performs the proper ritual does the infant become a member of society. Society, not nature, has the decisive word in adding a new person to its number.

The sharp difference between the status of male and female, a difference which runs through all social relations, is presaged by the kind of welcome which is given to a newborn infant son—with drumming, singing, and proud public announcements—while the advent of a daughter is much more quietly observed. One result of this differential interest is that far fewer girl babies survive, not because they are neglected but rather because much greater medical efforts are made to cure a baby boy when he falls sick than are usually made for an infant girl. The infant mortality rate for boys in one Khalapur sample was 25 per cent, for girls 41 per cent (Minturn and Hitchcock, 1963, p. 284).

As a Rajput child in this village begins to speak and can be trained, the most common form of punishment is scolding, and a usual form of scolding is to call the child by "a derogatory but not obscene name"; that is, by the name of either of the two lowest *jātis*, the Leatherworkers and the Sweepers (Minturn, 1963, p. 327). What he must not touch and who he should not be are inculcated into a child as soon as he can understand anything. The training repeatedly reinforces

---

This discussion of three of the main elements of village social organization in India is from a larger work on the subject. The passages given here deal with the structural principles of each and with some of their interrelations. The purpose is to sketch those principles for behavior that are generally shared by villagers and that underlie the variations of locality, social level, and action context.

the idea that there is a hierarchy of relations, inside and outside the family, and a proper child carefully observes the proprieties of subordinate and superior roles.

The domestic ecology drives home this lesson. In Khalapur as in many north Indian villages, men and women have virtually separate quarters; the women of the family do not usually enter into the platform where the men spend most of their leisure time, asleep and awake. The men come into the women's quarters for some specific purpose and, having met that purpose, leave. Young children scoot fairly freely between the two, but they early become aware of the women's quick covering of the face when an elder man of the family enters and of his warning cough before he comes into the women's side of the house. Social distance, respect avoidance, hierarchical calibration of action are daily made manifest to the child in his home.

The child, as junior in the household, must soon be taught deference and obedience. The virtues which Rajput parents in Khalapur most emphasized in interviews were obedience, politeness, peaceableness. But Rajputs pride themselves also on being a martial, dominant people, so that while obedience in the family is emphasized, dominance over social inferiors is tacitly encouraged. Perhaps because of these conflicting injunctions—that the child must be quite deferent to some and quite imperious toward others—the Khalapur children did not seem to the observers to be particularly well trained. They were not quick to obey their mothers, nor were they closely attentive to the orders of their fathers (Minturn, 1963, pp. 338–40).

The way in which adults discipline and reward children in Khalapur, as everywhere, varies not only by individuals but as between men and women and according to the adult's kinship relation to a child. But on one principle of child training all agreed: the belief that a child should never be praised to his face lest this make him disobedient. One Khalapur man summed it up in these words: "If we praise, the child will think that we love him too much, and then he will not be under our control" (Minturn, 1963, p. 325). This seems to mean, if we generalize from the Khalapur data, some position such as this: Control of the child is of paramount importance. He must be trained to be properly deferent, suitably observant of the hierarchy of family relations. Yet his deference and his adherence to the hierarchy cannot be taken for granted. They are jeopardized if the child hears himself praised, "loved too much," and so gets an overweening sense of his own importance. And a child, or anyone, who comes to feel so important will not easily accept subordinate status and the deferent demeanor that must go with it (Minturn and Lambert, 1964, p. 232). A child may indeed be praised and held up as a model for other children, but not in his presence. Nor should parents praise their own children in any company lest the evil eye be attracted. Excellence, immoderately flaunted, draws malevolence.

From quite a different part of India we get testimony of both these reasons for not praising children within their hearing. It is from a study of child rearing among the Nayars of Angadi village in Calicut district. Khalapur is within sight of the snowy peaks of the Himalayas, Angadi is on the tropical coastal strip of the southernmost state of Kerala. Yet the beliefs on this fundamental aspect of child rearing are quite similar. In Angadi all praise is suspect. It is taken either as untrue or, if true, as dangerous. The danger lies partly in encouraging the praised one to "take advantage." The latter explanation was given by everyone who was interviewed on this question. As one Angadi villager commented about praising children, "We won't say anything nice to them, feeling that if we say it out like that they will take advantage. So praise and affection will be in our mind only." All through a villager's life in Angadi, as Joan Mencher reports, this attitude prevails. People have a natural desire to be praised and also a fear of praising. It is almost impossible to accept praise easily as being well deserved (1963, p. 62).

There are other interesting parallels in child rearing between these two villages at opposite ends of the subcontinent. In the southern village as in the northern, a child "should, above all, be obedient and respectful to elders." The Nayar child in Angadi is not encouraged to assert himself, is not rewarded for being self-reliant or innovative; much the same expectations surround the Rajput child in Khalapur (Mencher, 1963, p. 57; Minturn, 1963, p. 359). Such parallels should not obscure the real differences in child rearing between different regions and social strata.[1] But there are similarities in child rearing which do point to a certain basis in personality development for the basic similarities in social relations across India. And it is well to add that in all these villages there are people who have grown up to be outgoing, independent, entrepreneurial persons, even though the prevailing push on young children seems to be more on passivity, dependence, defense.

The pressures on the Rajput boys of Khalapur change as they begin to spend more time in the men's area. When they are about twelve, they move out of the women's quarters entirely. This means that they are under stricter discipline and are exposed to masculine values which differ in emphasis from those of the women, particularly in respect to aggression and quarrels. Women do not try to pass on their personal quarrels to their children; a woman will usually allow her child to play with children of a mother with whom she is at odds or who are from a family antagonistic to her own. But the men must take care to instill their posture of loyalty or hatred. They warn their boys not to play with boys who belong to a hostile lineage. They are equally careful to point out the family's allies and the neutrals as well as the opponents. Men feel that they cannot afford to be passive about antagonisms. Each family has enemies in the village, any one of them may in a fit of temper, drink, or zeal decide to settle a grievance with a "conversation of sticks." A youth must be ready to defend himself and his family in physical combat (Minturn, 1963, p. 350).

1. For example, the taboo on praising children is not equally observed everywhere (see Kennedy, 1954, p. 7; Cormack, 1961, p. 62). Urban, educated mothers, possibly because of acquaintance with western child-rearing practices, do not regularly observe it. And yet in interviews with eighteen such women, mothers of children in the Baroda University nursery school, five said that a child should not be praised to his face because it would make the child "too proud," two that a child should not be praised at all, and two that a child should not be praised when others are present (Poffenberger, 1964).

The Dispersal Phase

The Rajput boys, like their sisters, experience a marked change in what is expected of them as they grow into adolescence. For the boys the shift is more gradual and occurs in the roles they have taken all their lives, as sons, nephews, and brothers. But the girls must change more abruptly from one set of roles to another, from being daughter and sister to becoming daughter-in-law and wife. These changes bring on a sharp stiffening of discipline after a relatively permissive childhood.

The whole constellation of family relations, in most levels of Indian society, shifts in this pattern as the children grow up. There comes the time when the daughter must be married and sent off, when the son must receive a wife. This necessary growth through incoming brides also guarantees eventual dispersal, because sooner or later thereafter the household becomes too cramped, psychologically and socially if not physically, to hold the brothers and their wives and children. Even if the brothers manage to stay together as one joint family, their sons almost certainly grow restive when they, in turn, become fathers, and then they separate to establish families of their very own.

Herein lies an inherent contradiction and continuing strain in family life. The partitioning of the joint family, typically the separation of brothers, is in fact inevitable. But the ideal belief is strongly held through the society that fraternal solidarity should not be breached and, when it is, some one is at fault and should be blamed. Hence family separation is frequently perpetrated in quarrel and accusation. Some amicable separations do occur, and, in any event, kinsmen and village elders usually try to restore friendly relations among brothers after a stormy parting (Kapadia, 1956, pp. 125–26). But quite often long echoes of recrimination leave a legacy of bitterness into another generation (see Mayer, 1960, pp. 241–42).

The more property there is to divide, the more protracted are apt to be the throes of parting; the more touchy each brother's honor (whether by *jāti* tradition or by personal bent), the more bitter the aftermath. Those whose education or job sends them forth from the household are often spared this fraternal fracas; so too is an only son spared. And among the poorer families of lower rank, the divisive quarrel tends to come earlier, usually between father and son. The son and his wife leave quickly, and whatever rancor flares then, generally dissipates before long.

But among families of some substance, of the middle and higher echelons of local rank, the division does not usually take place all at once, in a clean, decisive break. The strains mount, but at every stage there are countervailing forces and people urging continued cohesion. The first step in the process of family fission is usually that of establishing separate hearths within the household: all no longer eat from the same kitchen; food stores are divided; cooking and eating are separately done (see Sengupta, 1958, p. 384; Minturn and Hitchcock, 1963, p. 232). New walls may next be built inside the house; the physical partition portends the economic and legal partition to follow. The brothers may next separate their farming or craft activities and thereafter formalize the split in a legal act of joint family partition. At any of these stages, the presence of the father tends to slow the process; the death of the father and even more of both parents tends to hasten the legal division.

The causes of family strain are commonly said to be quarrels among the women. And commonly they do quarrel; theirs is a kind of accepted quarreling relation as other dyadic relations are accepted as joking or as solidary relations. Whatever may be the reasons for a particular argument, there are some general predisposing factors. Most village women spend a great deal of their lives within a narrow courtyard. The space is cramped, opportunities for friction abound. A woman, after she is a mother and a secure matron, does not hesitate to defend her rights in the household vigorously and loudly. She has come from another family, often from another village; she harbors no special loyalty or affection for her sister-in-law, who usually is from yet another village and family. Money in the common purse is always in short supply for each woman's needs. Food in the common larder runs low in the lean seasons, and doling out food to the children of the family can easily become a daily source of tension (see Karve, 1953, p. 79; Srinivas, 1952, pp. 29–31; Mayer, 1960, pp. 178–79; Minturn and Hitchcock, 1963, p. 261; Nicholas, 1961, p. 1059).

As each wife pours out her troubles to her husband when he comes home, he is apt to remember how one of his brothers or another has not done his proper share in getting the family's livelihood or has shirked a clear responsibility. A younger brother is then likely to find the elder more insufferably overbearing than before, the elder finds the younger more incorrigibly impertinent than ever. The brothers seek and usually find support in different directions, from their respective wives' relations. Both brothers find the idea of separation attractive, all the more so if a man's mother and his wife are constantly at each other, placing him in the uncomfortable and hopeless middle.

"As long as the brothers stay united, the social personalities of the younger brothers do not attain completion," Srinivas writes of Rampura in Mysore (1952, p. 30), and younger brothers elsewhere in India as well find this a constant irritant as they come into manhood. Each brother has an equal right, as legal co-parcener, to change this state of inequality by demanding the formal assignment of his share of the family's property. If the father is alive, vigorous, and forthright he brooks no nonsense about family separation. He can only lose by it, in power, comfort, prestige, and wealth. The mother, who may have helped set off the outburst, now tries to calm it; she scolds, reasons, weeps, bemoans her cruel fate and ungrateful sons.

The elders and leaders of the family's lineage and *jāti*-group counsel patience and unity. They too can only lose if their kinsmen and community come to be known as quarrelsome, irascible people. Parents will think twice before betrothing their daughters to a fractious lot. These elders point out to the brothers what they already know: that each will lose by the division. They will lose economically, by the immediate expenses of setting up a separate household, and in the long run by the dispersal of their land and labor. Then there is the danger—for which ample local precedents are usually quoted—of long lawsuits between brothers about property rights which sap energy and drain away resources.

They will lose socially. The name of each one in the family may be diminished by their separation. Even more, no man can hope to stand alone and defend himself singly in the village. Each will go down before their mutual enemies, for enemies are immanent, unless they can unite in strength of arms, of wealth, and of patrons and clients. Each will lose as an individual. Who will look after the children if the food-winner falls sick? Indeed, who will look after the sick man himself? The elders may suggest various healing moves. Perhaps one brother may go off to find work in a city (Ross, 1961, p. 47; Gould, 1961). Among some groups a younger brother is encouraged to find personal freedom in the army.

Brothers who cultivate their own land together, whose pride, strength, and security lie in their land, are usually ready to see the disadvantages of dispersing the ownership. Brothers whose income is in cash, or who can raise cash crops as well apart as together, are less likely to delay the parting (Bailey, 1957, p. 92; Epstein, 1962, pp. 176, 306). Yet whatever their economic circumstances may be, there is usually some delay after the first restless signs, because the parting goes against the grain of the ideal and is contrary to the pattern of domestic authority in which they have been reared. This keeps the restive ones quiescent for a time. But only for a time. The smoothing devices successfully repair cleavages only temporarily. Before long, other cracks in family solidarity appear, and the pacifying devices only paper them over, until finally no devices can hide or stop the split. The old family can no longer be maintained, and new ones are established to succeed it.

The Family as Module and as Model

Relations within a family are in certain important ways similar to relations within a *jāti* and in a community. We should scarcely expect it to be otherwise; no society can long endure a clashing incongruence between its smaller and its larger social groupings. But in India there is a particularly close nexus between family and *jāti*, so that it is necessary to understand family life well in order to grasp the nature of *jātis*.

What a villager does in his role as family member underlies his behavior as *jāti* member. His family serves both as module and as model for his *jāti* relations. It provides the matrix for the beginnings of his conduct and contains the ends, the purposes, of his social striving. It is his fundamental corporate group, the locale of much of his social action, and is also a main unit of attribution, by which expectations for his behavior are projected and judgments of his activities are made.

It is a module, a regular structural segment, of the *jāti*, just as the *jāti* is a module of the community. Every person is born into a family as into a *jāti*, and into one only. He cannot readily opt out of either family or *jāti*. As his *jāti* is the field of actual and potential kin, the family is the actual field of closest kin. All in a *jāti* are taken as ritual equals by the community primarily because they are considered to interact as equals in their family capacities.

Religious observances entail much participation by family groups. In Senapur village of Uttar Pradesh, for example, Opler found some forty calendrical rites being observed. Twenty-five of these revolve mainly around family needs and purposes, so that "a large part of the religious system is an elaborate apparatus for putting family members and family interests under the protection of benign supernaturals, and for defending the family from unfriendly supernatural attacks" (1959, p. 273). Priests do not have much to do with these rituals; they are usually planned, directed, and carried out by members of a family. And it is the women of the family who have the greatest responsibility for this sphere of religion (see Minturn and Hitchcock, 1963, pp. 273–74). Life cycle observances are mainly family affairs, each of them marking an occasion when the family, helped by its wider kin, delivers up to society a person in successive stages of social completion, from newborn baby to ancestral soul. It is in the name of his family and on their behalf as well as his own, that a man pays ritual homage to the ancestors, thus linking each person with the remembered and with the infinite past.

The village family is also the fundamental module of production and of reproduction. Most economic activities—cultivation, crafts, services—are performed by people operating in family groups or as representatives of their families. The interchange of goods and services according to *jāti* specialization is an interchange between families of different *jātis*. And the interchange among families of a *jāti* in marriage is the basis of *jāti* integration, of much of the cultural communication, and of a good deal of economic distribution.

As a reproductive, socializing group, the family provides the primary model of social relations for the child. The expectation of hierarchical order in society he first learns through the hierarchy of the family. Respect, deference, avoidance are all inculcated as part of family roles (see Dumont, 1957, pp. 7, 11; Carstairs, 1957, pp. 63–76; Sarma, 1951, p. 53). Inside the family, deference to elders is of the essence of family relations, yet in the two instances mentioned above, it seems that the subordination of child to parents is considered to be precarious unless it is constantly guarded. Among families, each must strive to keep up and, if possible, improve its prestige among other families of its *jāti*.

A child learns about pollution and purity in the round of household tasks, in the preparation of food, in the various degrees of purity of the separate precincts of the house, in the daily avoidances brought on by one's biological functions, and in the periodic avoidance brought on by his mother's menstrual cycle. The touch taboos observed between family members because of temporary pollution set the style for keeping permanent distance between members of different *jātis*. The household is the scene of stricter purity observance than is the village outside, as the women are the most careful guardians of domestic purity; hence the child's earliest experiences are with the more rigorous observances of the purity-pollution theme (see Mayer, 1960, pp. 51–52).

The importance of matching conduct to context, of switching role behavior as the social situation changes, is daily illustrated to the child in the household. Thus he feels the restraint which descends over his relations with his mother or father, who may have been playing gaily with him a moment before, when his grandfather enters the room. He sees his mother joking with his younger uncle, but withdrawing demurely from the presence of his elder uncle. Even while they quarrel, members of a family are likely to affirm the ideal of family solidarity, each charging the other with dereliction of family duty and loyalty. Both implicitly agree through their vehement disagreement that loyalty to family must be put above all other personal and social considerations.

The basic patterns of social control, of systematic counterchange, are learned and are used in family relations. Thus in one village of northern Mysore, as Alan Beals observed, the giving or withholding of food is a main means of control. In that village, Gopalpur, children soon learn the connection between social survival and social support. "The individual is brought to feel that the major securities and satisfactions of life are to be found in the acquisition of a large number of friends and supporters and in the control of them through the use of food. The most important supporters of the individual are the members of his family" (1962, p. 22).

In most of the day-to-day relations with his *jāti* fellows in his village, a person is commonly perceived by them as a member of a particular family. In all extraordinary situations of stress, a person's first loyalty inclines to his family, above all other considerations, even above *jāti* solidarity (see Cohn, 1961, p. 1055). It is scarcely possible to single out and deal with a single person in a village. As one man is called forth, his family comes with him; often enough this is physically so, typically it is symbolically and figuratively true.

Yet in the expansion of the family, cleavages regularly appear. It is part of the process of family growth, part of a family's natural, inevitable, yet disapproved development. The pattern of family fission, with each new segment setting up a living space and social space of its own, resembles the pattern of *jāti* fission.

A family can usefully be seen as a structure of roles and as a system of structure maintenance. So viewed, the similarities and recurrent crises of family life throughout a vast population can be formulated. But family life in any one real family is much more than role structure and counterchange, just as a house is much more than the set of blueprints and a home infinitely more than a dossier of behavior patterns. In an actual family there are decisions, choice points, exigencies, rewards, sorrows. A villager's emotions, motivations, conflicts, achievements are chiefly played out within his family and with other families. The central themes of traditional drama and story have to do with family affairs. The scenes from the *Rāmāyana* which are dramatized in the annual pageant of Ram Lila in northern India are mainly concerned with family problems. They show how a woman caused great difficulty by seeking to promote the interests of her own son above those of the others in the joint family. They depict the grief of a mother when her son is exiled, the devotion and virtue of a wife, the loyalty of a younger brother (Opler, 1959, p. 288).

Scenes from the other epic are also staged, told, and retold in villages of every part of the land. In Mrs. Karve's words, "It is simply the story of a huge, big joint parti-family and illustrates the interrelations, the personality development, the feuds, the strength, the weakness, the ethos of the joint family. . . . The Mahabharata family is found today all over India and a Mahabharata battle is being fought in most joint families" (1953, p. 21). Family battles there are in plenty, but their very intensity and interest testify to the importance of family to person and to society. For the family is at the core of a man's allegiance, his loyalty, his identification. It is his own gauge of his success in life, it is a main standard used by others to measure his achievement. All the more is it so for a woman. A man may have other interests and achievements; a village woman cradles them all in her family.

Yet caste society is not just the family writ large, nor is a family only a *jāti* in small. There are other groupings, other bonds, other traditions within a *jāti* and among *jātis* which together make up village society.

II. *JĀTI*: THE COHESION OF THE ENDOGAMOUS GROUP

A main variation on the general pattern by which villagers maintain their respective *jātis* is between *jātis* of higher and those of lower rank. There are usually more effective panchayats in the middle and lower blocs of a local system than in the highest bracket. Hutton reports that "It has frequently been observed that the lower the caste in the social scale, the stronger its combination and the more efficient its organization" (1961, p. 99). This is borne out by recent anthropological studies, as in parts of Uttar Pradesh, where the highest ranking *jātis* do not have intervillage panchayats, while all the others do (Sharma, 1956, pp. 298–301). So is it also in Totagadde in northwestern Mysore, "The formal caste organization—both intravillage and intervillage—of the Untouchables, who are repressed by all other castes, is more tightly knit than that of the Sudras, while the latter's is more highly structured than that of the Havik Brahmins" (Harper, 1959, p. 461). The lower groups have to unify against those who hold power, while the ruling Brahmans do not. The lowest in this village are still strong enough to maintain an organization.

But the very poorest can scarcely organize at all. The Untouchables of another Mysore village, Wangala, have no panchayat organization beyond the village (Epstein, 1962, p. 118). When a *jāti*-group—those of a *jāti* who live in the same village—is very poor and totally dependent, its people cannot afford to move about beyond the village. This holds true of whole villages also, if the inhabitants are under the tight domination of landowners. In those villages of West Bengal, for example, where the village lands were owned by a single landowner or by a few, the landowners imposed most decisions. Panchayats of any kind were rare and feeble. In those Bengal villages where land ownership was more widely shared, there was a corresponding increase in panchayat activity and effectiveness (Nicholas and Mukhopadhyay, 1964, pp. 36–38).

Rivalry, not poverty, contributes to the relatively loose cohesion of many high, dominant *jātis* as compared with their middle-ranking neighbors. Thus in Kumbapettai of Tanjore district the resident overlords had little *jāti* organization. Quarrels between Brahman families "drag on in a desultory manner for months, sometimes years, until both parties are weary or kinship or ceremonial obligations draw them together again" (Gough, 1955, p. 44). While they would gather in council to preserve a ritual norm or punish rebels of low *jāti*, this was not often necessary. As for other matters, a Brahman landowner did not particularly need to cooperate with his peers, either economically or socially. He was trained from childhood to value the dependent relation of son upon father rather than the cooperative relationship among brothers. In the low *jātis*, however, the authority of the father is relatively short-lived, broken shortly after a boy's puberty when the boy becomes an independent wage earner. Hence among them the main emphasis is on the equivalence and solidarity of peers and on the solidarity of the *jāti*-group and *jāti* (Gough, 1956, pp. 845–46).

Yet even in a loosely organized *jāti* there is joint, corporate response in certain situations. The people of a *jāti* do not march always as a close social company, hewing to a set direction, fulfilling given functions, and mechanically correcting deviations. There are often considerable differences within a *jāti* in wealth and power, in goals and ideals. In certain matters, modes of worship for example, there can be quite considerable deviation. But in other affairs, particularly in those which have to do with permanent pollution, *jāti* members impose sharp limits on deviation. Pollution affects the external relations of all in a *jāti*, and when they feel that they are collectively confronting others, they tend to act as a unified social group.

Why, then, does a villager feel so strongly identified with his *jāti*? Part of the answer is that he usually knows of no alternative groupings for his loyalty, but the more important reason is that he is daily and through all his life identified as a *jāti* member by others and he identifies himself as such. He does so because a very large part of all his social relations are within his *jāti*. It is, first of all, the harbor of his kin. All his kinsmen are of the *jāti*; none are outside it. The valence of kinship helps to hold a *jāti* together, despite the rivalries that beat at its unity. Men of one village may be at odds with their *jāti* fellows in another. Yet the wives of some and the mothers of others have come from that place, and affinal relatives are usually one's supporters, from whom a man is not usually long estranged. So it goes through the thick web of kinship, and thus is *jāti* disunity diminished, if not always and for everyone, still in many instances for many in the group.

There is further the bond of common interest in work and livelihood. A potter does not have the same economic concerns as does an astrologer, nor does a farmer find as close understanding with a merchant as he does with another farmer of his own *jāti*. Even if only a few in a *jāti*-group actually practice the traditional occupation, most are apt to be in a similar range of occupations. A man's friends in the village are most often of his *jāti*; all the more so for a woman, whose movements and social contacts are more restricted.

The great ritual events of the life cycle, marriages and funerals, bring together gatherings of kin, that is, of *jāti* fellows. Many of the major experiences of a person's life take place among those of his *jāti*. When he goes to other villages he usually goes to visit *jāti* fellows. Communication between villages is largely between people of the same *jāti*. *Jāti* fellows may even have a distinctive speech; in some localities there are dialectal differences in the language used by each of the principal blocs of *jātis* (Gumperz, 1958, 1961; Bright, 1960; McCormack, 1960).

A child learns quite early to discriminate between his own kind and those of other *jātis* who have different degrees of pollution and with whom his interplay must be more guarded. He absorbs the self-image of his *jāti* in countless ways. A boy of a Rajput *jāti* learns about the martial style and regal tradition of his group by the bearing of his elders, by their contemptuous references to those of other *jātis*, by the tales, proverbs, and ballads he hears frequently. He may later reject that ethos, but he is not often indifferent to it (see Hitchcock, 1958). Similarly, one who was raised as an orthodox Brahman in a Brahman stronghold may later deliberately leave behind his early training, but it does not usually leave him. He is likely to prize learning, to abhor overt aggression, to remain personally (if not ritually) fastidious, quite in the manner of his village *jāti* fellows.

It is not only the higher *jātis* who entertain flattering views of themselves and have heroic tales to prove it. One of the great folk-epics of northern India, the Lay of Lorik, is sung by Ahirs, traditionally herdsmen, about one of their forebears (Deva, 1958, pp. 87–89). Even the very lowest *jātis* have explanatory tales of how they fell from a higher state through no great fault of their own (see Reddy, 1952, pp. 334–41; Fuchs, 1950, pp. 235–37). The origin legend of the tribal Konds conveys a message which is duplicated in the origin myth of many lower *jātis*. "Konds belong to the same community as the rulers; Konds are a dominant caste; they have fallen because they are a little stupid and unlucky, and have had to come and live in the jungle, but in origin they are warriors and the associates of kings" (Bailey, 1960, p. 161).

A villager typically identifies closely with his *jāti* because so much of his social world is encompassed within it and because his idea of who he is cannot be separated from what his *jāti* is. He is continually identified by others as one of his *jāti*. *Jāti* is thus a leading reference category in village life. Villagers often deal with each other in terms of grosser categories, as *jāti*-cluster or varna, but *jāti* is nonetheless at the basis of reference. The villager's drive for higher status is tied to the status of his *jāti*. He cannot lift his family much higher than the level of his *jāti*, and if his *jāti* should fall in status, he is bound to suffer some status decline with it. From the inside view of the villager, his allegiance to *jāti* is inevitable, necessary, morally proper.

From the outside view of an observer studying the whole system, a *jāti* is both a social and a cultural unit. Yet for all that the endogamous group is the fundamental unit of the system, *jāti* boundaries are frequently quite fuzzy. There are, it is true, some numerically small *jātis* which are sharply demarcated, as those Tamil Brahmans who intermarry only among five villages, or the Gayawals of the town of Gaya, who have only some 120 families (Vidyarthi, 1961, pp. 53–57). But in some larger *jātis* the poorer families may take brides from an adjacent but lower group (see Mayer, 1960, pp. 155); among Rajputs and similar martial groups of North India, women are occasionally taken as wives from much lower groups, though few official ties are then admitted with their natal kinsmen. *Jātis* which are stratified into hypergamous sections may have little or no intermarriage between top and bottom sections, though all will be taken as ritual equals for certain purposes, as in interdining.

Such blurring of *jāti* boundaries does not impede *jāti* relations. A villager generally has the notion that his *jāti* is a quite firmly bounded group, and he can indeed point out the main lineages and *jāti*-groups with whom those of his own lineage have repeatedly intermarried. But a man of the same *jāti* in another village may give a somewhat different list of the lineages and villages in his endogamous circle, and both may choose to ignore certain marriages which are rare or disapproved. A *jāti*-group is a more clearly demarcated unit. Within a village there is usually little question as to who belongs to which *jāti*.

Beyond the geographic spread of actual marriages there may be people of similar name and status, with comparable customs and occupations, with whom marriages could possibly be arranged. As the families of a *jāti* prosper, and as means of communications improve, marriage affiliations tend to be extended to such putative *jāti*-fellows.

A measure of the *jāti* as a corporate unit is in the number and character of the leaders who gather for a large panchayat of the *jāti*. But precise measures of *jāti* boundaries are not very relevant to the operation of the system. Villagers believe and act as though their *jāti* were a firm, corporate entity, while at the same time they allow for some modification in its scope. As each *jāti* maintains its own group cohesion, its people also help maintain the local system of caste. The principles of *jāti* maintenance are also those used for system maintenance.

III. VILLAGE: THE EXTENT OF SOLIDARITY

A *jāti* cannot stand alone. Its people must cooperate with people of other *jātis*, and they commonly compete with some of them for power and status. The main locale of both cooperation and competition is the village. The groups involved are primarily families and *jāti*-groups of the same village, rather than whole *jātis* of a region. A village is far more than a locale, more than just a collection of houses, lanes, and fields. For a villager it is a prime social reality; for the observer it is a principal unit for the understanding of the society. Yet some observers have doubted the significance of the village either as a corporate group or as a useful unit for analysis (for example, Dumont and Pocock, 1957, pp. 25–32, and 1960, pp. 88–89).

These doubts arise, in part, as a reaction to the exaggerated notions of the independence of an Indian village that once were current. They also stem from the observer's problem of showing the relationship between the multi-*jāti* village and the multi-village *jāti*. And village discord is apt to strike the observer's eyes and ears more stridently than does village concord.

A classic quotation, often reprinted, on the Indian village as a monolithic, atomistic, unchanging entity is from a report by Sir Charles Metcalfe, one of the great founding administrators of British rule in India. The passage begins, "The village communities are little republics, having nearly everything that they want within themselves and almost independent of any foreign relations." It goes on to tell that wars pass over it, regimes come and go, but the village as a society always emerges unchanged, unshaken, and self-sufficient. Later writers of considerable influence, among them Sir Henry Maine, Karl Marx, and Mahatma Gandhi, reiterated this idea and suggested that the village was so perduring because it was so self-sufficient (Metcalfe, 1833, p. 470; Srinivas and Shah, 1960).

When modern field studies came to be made, however, they showed quite a different situation. An Indian village typically is hardly a republic; it had certainly changed from time to time; and it clearly was not and is not self-sufficient. The whole nature of traditional society militated against the independent isolation of a village. In earlier days there was a good deal of coming and going among villages, even though roads were poor and travel dangerous. Marriage affiliations were commonly made between families of different villages, and each marriage set in train a lifetime of visiting between the two families by the married couple and at least another generation of such visiting by their children. On the basis of this interchange in marriage, *jāti* ties among people of different villages are continually reinvigorated.

Economic needs send people in and out of the village. Few villages have a complete roster of resident specialists. Senapur, near Banaras, has quite a large number of *jātis*, 24, but a family will require services provided by 35 to 40 *jātis*. So there is constant movement by villagers of the local area for work and trade. Each local area is a kind of labor pool; some villages in it utilize the surplus labor of others, villagers with special skills circulate through the locality (Opler, 1956, p. 7). In former times and all the more now, some services are available only in the nearest towns. Bricklayers and limeworkers, goldsmiths and coppersmiths, florists and genealogists usually are found in towns or larger villages.

Movement between villages also occurs when a man acquires land through inheritance or purchase in another village and has to visit there regularly to look after it. Markets are also an important reason for travel to another village. Some in practically every village are outward bound for market weekly, unless the village is itself the seat of a market concourse. A good many villages have been involved in an interregional market economy for centuries, producing crops which were transported across regions and states (Srinivas and Shah, 1960, pp. 1376–77).

Added to the economic forces which necessitate travel, there long have been the religious attractions of going to other places. A ceremony staged by the people of a village often draws visitors from miles around. In every region of India there are holy places which people visit on special days or at any time when impelled by a pressing need. And there is the magnetic pull of the great centers of pilgrimage which draw millions yearly.

All these movements have been intensified and sped up in recent decades. New reasons for travel—education, administrative business, litigation—have augmented the traffic. Not every villager travels; many a village woman seldom leaves the village bounds, and some men rarely go beyond the limits of their fields, either because they cannot afford the expense of a few coins or because they are just not interested in what lies outside their village. But the village is not by any means an isolated unit; its people are closely bound into a larger social sphere and have long been so joined. Opler writes that the articulations of Senapur people with other communities and far-flung places are "not a recent development or a consequence of modern systems of communication or transportation. They rest on ancient practices and patterns" (1956, p. 8).

Just as a villager is bound to many other people with multiple strands—pick up one and a bevy of others follow—so his village is linked by many ties to other villages, towns, cities. A village is not a neatly separable social and conceptual package. Moreover, when an observer first comes to live in a village, the internal cleavages claim attention at once, in the very settlement pattern, in the daily avoidances, in the division of labor and of power, so that any signs of solidarity among the people of the village tend to be overshadowed.

Village Solidarity

Yet, solidarity potentially exists and villagers commonly show it on certain occasions, for certain purposes, under certain circumstances. Geography and government impose one kind of village unity. Villagers live close to each other, see each other, and interact more frequently than they do with people of other villages. They share the same familiar life-space and share also common experiences of famine or harvest bounty, of flood or epidemic, of village fast or festivals. By edict of governments, from those of early record to now, a village is an administrative and revenue unit. This in itself enjoins common experience, since all use and are are affected by the same institutions, as of school, post office, or revenue collection. Within his village a man commonly has his closest economic associates—patrons or clients or workers or customers—with whose help he makes his livelihood.

When a man goes outside his village, he is identified first of all by his village rather than by *jāti* or other reference category. As two strangers meet at a weekly market or in town and begin to talk, one of the first questions they are likely to ask of each other is, "To what village do you belong?" The word used is specifically village (Karve, 1958, p. 83). Long after a family has emigrated to a town, its members still know and can identify themselves by their ancestor's native village. In Maharashtra the village is also called by a term meaning "white mother earth," the habitation area being so distinguished from the black fields. A man uses this term in taking a solemn oath, and if he is excommunicated he must beg forgiveness of all in the village before he can be taken back (Karve, 1958, p. 87).

A village tends to get a reputation in its locality, and all in it are dubbed with a common label, whether as simple, or hard-working, or tightfisted. These stereotypes do not ordinarily have great effect on relations among villagers, though during quarrels between sisters-in-law each may belabor the other with the less complimentary epithets of their native villages. But sometimes the village reputation becomes a more serious matter. Carstairs tells (1961, p. 105) of an incident in a Rajasthan village in which a youth, egged on by companions as a dare, ate a bit of human feces. This became immediately known, with depressive results for the boy. Even more, all in the village came to be known as from the place "where they eat feces."

In the ranking of *jātis*, the immediate judges and enforcers are the people of one's village. They are indeed influenced by the standards held in the region and through the civilization, and they will not depart too widely from the regional and civilizational norms. Yet it is they after all who perform the acts and give the opinions which place a person and his *jāti* in a particular niche of the local hierarchy. And this varies from locality to locality. For example, in Bisipara village the washermen are ranked among the clean *jātis*, but in neighboring Boad, in the same district of Orissa, they are considered Untouchables.

Outside his own village, a person may find *jātis* ranked somewhat differently than in his home place. The people of Ramkheri in Dewas District, of Madhya Pradesh, for example, follow the customs of the places in which they are visitors, but within certain limits. A guest may adjust his conduct to suit the standards of his host to the extent that he may take food from a person from whom he would ordinarily accept only water. One villager cited the example of two men, of the Rajput and of the Farmer *jātis* in Ramkheri, going together in a wedding party to another village. The two could not eat in one line at home, but in the other village this was done. "We shall also eat in one line; and it will not be a matter for our Ramkheri caste councils, because it is the custom of that village." The author comments that a man going across the boundary to another village automatically sheds his status as a resident of his own village and can conform to the commensal rules of the host village. In this respect "the village is very much a reality" (Mayer, 1960, pp. 49, 159). In other parts of India as well, the village is, in limited but appreciable degree, the arbiter of its own ranking practices.

Out of these common standards, experiences, identifications, and practices comes an allegiance to one's village which may be shown in a range of activities, as in kinship, ceremonies, defense. There is in much of northern India the feeling that all in the village share something of a kinship bond. This feeling finds strong expression in fictive kin relations and village exogamy. In some regions, a bride may not be taken from any village into which any daughter of the village, no matter of what *jāti*, has previously been given in marriage. Sometimes, as in villages near Delhi, village exogamy is expanded so that a person may not take a spouse from any village whose fields touch one's own village boundaries (Karve, 1953, p. 119; Lewis, 1958, pp. 160–61).

In the south of India also, a marriage can be of concern to the village as well as to the family and the *jāti*. This is particularly true in a village like Gopalpur, where, Beals writes, a marriage is seen as a victory in the competition among villages. Every marriage of a child of Gopalpur activates more kinship ties and facilitates future alliances for the people of Gopalpur. "For this reason, the village as a whole must sanction any marriage that takes place between Gopalpur and any other village, and the village as a whole undertakes the responsibility of ensuring that people from other villages get value received when they arrange a marriage in Gopalpur" (1962, p. 28). Not all villages of south India, by any means, display this kind of interest; where there is a vast social distance among the *jātis*, those at the top could hardly care less how the Harijans mate. But even in such places the topmost are still concerned that no one in their village should bring an evil reputation on it, and they too find useful the kind of validating function which daughters of the village can perform. Thus when a Gopalpur man goes to another village in the local area, a woman from Gopalpur is apt to be there to recognize him and vouch for his status. Among other uses, this can facilitate economic transactions (Beals, 1962).

In the region of Gopalpur, village solidarity is explicitly demonstrated in festivals called *jātras* which are given by a host village to honor its village deity. The host families invite their relatives from other places and regale them with food and entertainment. Wrestling matches between teams from different villages are a principal feature of the festival. As each contestant grapples with his opponent, he is cheered on by his teammates and fellow villagers. Young men from all *jātis* except the very lowest and the Brahmans participate as teammates for their home villages, their usual differences and cleavages forgotten for the occasion. On one such team there were two men who had sworn to murder each other. "In the hand wrestling as in other aspects of the jatra, intra-village differences of status are minimized in order to create a representation of village unity" (Beals, 1964, p. 107).

A main purpose of staging the festival is to show the host village as a good, friendly, and cooperative place in which to live. Those who succeed in establishing a favorable reputation for their village through giving lavish festivals gain advantages in marriage negotiations as well as in trade and employment. Hence most people in a host village try hard then to please the guests as well as to honor the deity. Women visitors "exist inside happiness" at these occasions, in good measure because fathers and elder brothers provide a plentiful supply of drink to their daughters and sisters who have come back for the festival. Far into the night groups of women gather, sing, and pass the bottle.

Visitors, for their part, do not really want to be convinced that their hosts' festival is better than their own, so there is a great deal of criticism and fault-finding. "Visitors leaving a jatra talk about 'our village,' about how well 'our village' behaved, and about the superiority of 'our village jatra.'" This competition between villages occasionally leads to riots. And Beals notes that a village which actually is free of overt conflict hardly feels an imperative need to demonstrate that fact at great cost. Hence a village which advertises its state of harmony through holding a *jātra* may be one which is not particularly harmonious. But in the very process of holding the festival, there is affirmation and demonstration of loyalty of one's village (Beals, 1964, pp. 109–113).

These *jātra* festivals are more specifically directed toward solidarity than are festivals in most other parts of India, but village solidarity rites are not uncommon. In Ramkheri, for example, there is a ceremony at which all 44 shrines in the village are honored in succession as the concern of the entire village (Mayer,

1960, pp. 101–102). In many villages, a particular local deity is worshipped as the special tutelary spirit of the whole village. In Senapur and elsewhere in eastern Uttar Pradesh the village guardian is supposed to protect all its people and animals from external dangers. But the deity does so only "if they are willing to co-operate by obeying the accepted religious, moral, and spiritual discipline of the community." Each family must worship the local deity (Singh, 1956, p. 11). While village festivals are fading out in a good many places (see Nath, 1962) because modern circumstances make it difficult to arrange for them and alternative celebrations have become popular, they are still major events in some regions, as around Gopalpur. And even when the ritual manifestation of village unity diminishes, that unity may continue to be shown in other ways.

One common way is the repelling of incursions by outsiders. If the forces of government threaten all in a village, or if strangers attempt to harm a fellow villager, or if the people of another village assault one's own, the village neighbors may well spring to the joint defense. An example of this occurred in Rampura, near Mysore City, when the state agricultural department ordered that fishing rights in the village tanks should be auctioned off and thereafter only the successful bidder would be allowed to take the fish. The villagers had been fishing in these tanks whenever they wanted to, and they felt that this was an encroachment on their rights. So when a government official came to the village and opened the auction, there were no bids. The villagers had seen to it that no one from their village or from any other place could approach to buy their rights (Srinivas, 1955, p. 32).

A similar episode occurred in Wangala in Mysore when the revenue inspector announced the auction of an acre of good land because of delinquent taxes. The land belonged to a poor man of the dominant *jāti* who had suffered a series of misfortunes. Land is precious and scarce in Wangala, and eager bidders would not be lacking. The owner was a member of one of the two opposed alliances, yet when the leader of the other alliance heard of this, he declared that no one would attend the auction because "to bid at such an auction would be supporting the Government against a man of one's own village." This was decided at a panchayat meeting; the auction was later cancelled, and arrangements were made for the owner to borrow enough to satisfy the tax arrears. Village (and *jāti*) unity overrode factional differences (Epstein, 1962, pp. 143–45).

Two such incidents are told for Shamirpet, near Hyderabad. One day some soldiers from a nearby cantonment rode into the village in two army trucks and began loading firewood belonging to a villager. It was obvious that they did not intend to pay, and, when the owner remonstrated, they beat him up. Word of this spread quickly through the village, and men armed with staves came rushing up to stop the looting. At this, the soldiers retreated and threatened to come back with reinforcements to destroy the whole village. They did not.

On another occasion water for Shamirpet fields was diverted under cover of night to the fields of Aliyabad, a nearby village. Next morning an organized group from Shamirpet attacked Aliyabad. The Aliyabad people protested that it had been done by mistake; probably they had bribed the guards and had overreached themselves by not allowing any water at all to flow into Shamirpet. "But in the dispute itself the two villages had forgotten their internal differences and dissensions and each of them had acted as one body" (Dube, 1955, 210–11).

Shamirpet, Wangala, and Rampura are villages which appear to have had relatively little internal friction at the time when they were studied. So their people may have been readier to rally defensively than would those of a more deeply divided village. But most villages have a certain unity because each is a node for many activities central to the lives of the inhabitants. Typically, the village is where a man grew up, where his close kin live, where his work partners and helpers are, where his friends are found, where he worships, where he is known and placed. He shares with his village neighbors the lore of the village, that detailed inside knowledge which no others have. When he travels out of it, he is usually identified, in part at least, as a member of his village. It has been said that the village is a unity because of its extensions, not in spite of them (Singer, 1956, p. 4); that is, the villager's relations with other people take place so greatly in the context of his home village that he is socially and psychologically involved with the village as a whole. This is not to say that the village is always or even usually a unified community; it is to say that it is an entity of importance to its people.

The analogy is sometimes used that a villager participates in two kinds of unity, one "vertical," the other "horizontal"; the village is the vertical unit and is made up of horizontal layers, each of which is a *jāti*. But this tends to give too static a picture of a villager's affiliations. His support of one social entity or another can vary by social context and by his own circumstances. Thus in Rampura, Srinivas observes, there are occasions when many men of the village stand together, as they do occasionally in a fight against another village during a regional festival. Yet a Brahman of Rampura would not be likely to be attacked there by the enemies of his village because he has a special ritual position as a Brahman. An Untouchable or a Muslim of Rampura would be involved in the fight more because of his attachment to a particular patron who was also in the fray than because of village patriotism. The same three groups, Brahmans, Muslims, and Untouchables, are not given important formal roles in the annual village festival of Rampura, and yet their cooperation is sought in staging the ceremony (Srinivas, 1955, p. 33).

Just as the occasions for "vertical" unity do not necessarily engage every last man and group, so the occasions for "horizontal" unity do not necessarily bring in every man and family of the *jāti*-group. Loyalty to *jāti* sometimes conflicts with loyalty to village. An elder acting in village council must sometimes tread a narrow line between what is good for the village and what is to the advantage of his *jāti* kinsmen. The common suspicion is that kin ties prevail over all, but one test of an able leader is whether he can somehow reconcile the two, preserving the public good while not neglecting the cause of his kin.

The relations among *jātis* in a village are ways of "being together separately," as Beals puts it. That phrase indeed summarizes part of the human condition anywhere: each person is an individual in his family, a member of one group in a collocation of groups, a part of a local society in a larger social order. But for Indian villagers the togetherness and the separateness are carried on in the same locale, with much the same set of people and with the ritual separations pervasively significant. Separation often is a ruling concern, yet separation must always be mitigated by the fact that a *jāti* cannot live alone. In Gopalpur, as in many other villages, "The belief that jatis are related to each other, like brothers, and that all jatis provide essential services for each other creates a unity within the diversity of jatis" (Beals, 1962, p. 41).

A village is clearly an important and viable social entity, and its people also take part in the larger society and civilization. Hence the question which has been put by some students of Indian society, as to whether the village is an isolable unit for study, can lead to no absolute answer. In some ways it is, in others it is not. The people and culture of the village must be studied both in the local milieu and in wider perspective.

BIBLIOGRAPHY

BAILEY, F. G.
1957. *Caste and the economic frontier.* Manchester: Manchester University Press.
1960. *Tribe, caste, and nation.* Manchester: Manchester University Press.

BEALS, ALAN.
1962. *Gopalpur.* New York: Holt, Rinehart, and Winston.

1964. Conflict and interlocal festivals in a South Indian region. In E. B. Harper (Ed.), *Religion in South Asia.* Seattle: University of Washington Press.

BRIGHT, WILLIAM.
1960. Linguistic change in some Indian caste dialects. *International Journal of American Linguistics*, 26: 19–26.

CARSTAIRS, G. MORRIS.
1957. *The twice-born.* London: Hogarth Press.

1961. Patterns of religious observances in three villages of Rajasthan. *Journal of Social Research (Ranchi)*, 4: 61–113.

COHN, BERNARD S.
1961. Chamar family in a North Indian village. *Economic Weekly*, 13: 1051–1055.

CORMACK, M. L.
1961. *She who rides a peacock.* New York: Praeger.

DEVA, INDRA.
1958. *The sociology of Bhojpuri folk-literature.* Dissertation, Department of Anthropology, University of Lucknow.

DUBE, S. C.
1955. *Indian village.* Ithaca: Cornell University Press.

DUMONT, LOUIS.
1957. Hierarchy and marriage alliance in South Indian kinship. *Occasional papers of the Royal Anthropological Institute of Great Britain and Ireland*, No. 12.

DUMONT, LOUIS, and D. POCOCK.

1957. Village studies. *Contributions to Indian Sociology No. 1*, pp. 23–42.

1960. For a sociology of India: a rejoinder to Dr. Bailey. *Contributions to Indian Sociology No. 4:* pp. 82–89.

EPSTEIN, T. S.

1962. *Economic development and social change in South India.* Manchester: Manchester University Press.

FUCHS, STEPHEN.

1950. *The children of Hari.* Vienna: Verlag Herold.

GOUGH, E. KATHLEEN.

1955. The social structure of a Tanjore village. In McK. Marriott (Ed.), *Village India.* Chicago: University of Chicago Press.

1956. Brahmin kinship in a Tamil village. *American Anthropologist,* 58: 826–53.

GOULD, HAROLD A.

1961. Some preliminary observations concerning the anthropology of industrialization. *Eastern Anthropologist,* 14: 30–47.

GUMPERZ, JOHN J.

1958. Dialect differences and social stratification in a North Indian village. *American Anthropologist,* 60: 668–82.

1961. Speech variation and the study of Indian civilization. *American Anthropologist,* 63: 976–88.

HARPER, EDWARD B., and LOUISE G. HARPER.

1959. Political organization in a Karnataka village. In R. L. Park and I. Tinker (Eds.), *Leadership and political institutions in India.* Princeton: Princeton University Press.

HITCHCOCK, JOHN T.

1958. The ideal of the martial Rājpūt. *Journal of American Folklore,* 71: 216–23.

HUTTON, J. H.

1961. *Caste in India.* (3d ed.) Bombay: Oxford University Press.

KAPADIA, K. M.

1956. Rural family patterns: a study in urban-rural relations. *Sociological Bulletin,* 5: 111–26.

KARVE, IRAWATI.

1953. Kinship organisation in India. *Deccan College Monograph Series No. 11.* Poona: Deccan College.

1958. The Indian village. *The Bulletin of the Deccan College,* 18: 73–106.

KENNEDY, BETH C.

1954. *Rural-urban contrasts in parent-child relations in India.* Bombay: Bureau of Research and Publications, Tata Institute of Social Sciences.

LEWIS, OSCAR.

1958. *Village life in Northern India.* Urbana: University of Illinois Press.

McCORMACK, WILLIAM.

1960. Social dialects in Dharwar Kannada. *International Journal of American Linguistics,* 26: 79–91.

MAYER, ADRIAN C.

1960. *Caste and kinship in Central India.* Berkeley and Los Angeles: University of California Press.

MENCHER, JOAN.

1963. Growing up in South Malabar. *Human Organization,* 22: 54–65.

METCALFE, SIR CHARLES.

1833. *Appendix to the report from the Select Committee of the House of Commons on the affairs of the East India Company. Part III—Revenue.* London: House of Commons.

MINTURN, LEIGH.

1963. Child training. In Beatrice B. Whiting (Ed.), *Six cultures, studies of child rearing.* New York and London: John Wiley and Sons.

MINTURN, LEIGH, and JOHN T. HITCHCOCK.

1963. The Rājpūts of Khalapur, India. In Beatrice B. Whiting (Ed.), *Six cultures, studies of child rearing.* New York and London: John Wiley and Sons.

MINTURN, LEIGH, and WILLIAM W. LAMBERT.

1964. *Mothers of six cultures, antecedents of child rearing.* New York: John Wiley and Sons.

NATH, V.

1962. Village, caste, and community. *Economic Weekly,* 14: 1877–82.

NICHOLAS, RALPH W.

1961. Economics of family types in two West Bengal villages. *Economic Weekly,* 13: 1057–60.

NICHOLAS, RALPH W., and TARASHISH MUKHOPADHYAY.

1964. Politics and law in two West Bengal villages. *Bulletin of the Anthropological Survey of India,* 11: 15–39.

OPLER, MORRIS E.

1956. The extensions of an Indian village. *Journal of Asian Studies,* 16:5–10.

1959. Family, anxiety, and religion in a community of North India. In M. K. Opler (Ed.), *Culture and mental health.* New York: Macmillan.

POFFENBERGER, THOMAS.

1964. *The use of praise.* Unpublished manuscript, University of Baroda, Department of Child Development, Working Papers on Indian Personality.

REDDY, N. S.

1952. *Transition in caste structure in Andhra Desh with particular reference to depressed castes.* Dissertation, Department of Anthropology, University of Lucknow.

ROSS, AILEEN D.

1961. *The Hindu family in its urban setting.* Toronto: University of Toronto Press.

SARMA, JYOTIRMOYEE.

1951. Formal and informal relations in the Hindu joint household of Bengal. *Man in India,* 31: 51–71.

SENGUPTA, SUNIL.

1958. Family organisation in West Bengal, its nature and dynamics. *Economic Weekly* (Bombay), 10: 384–89.

SHARMA, K. N.

1956. *Urban contacts and cultural change in a little community.* Dissertation, Department of Anthropology, University of Lucknow.

SINGER, MILTON.

1956. Introduction, the Indian village, a symposium. *Journal of Asian Studies,* 16: 3–5.

SINGH, RUDRA DATT.

1956. The unity of an Indian village. *Journal of Asian Studies,* 16: 10–19.

SRINIVAS, M. N.

1952. A joint family dispute in a Mysore village. *Journal of the M. S. University of Baroda,* 1: 7–31.

1955. The social system of a Mysore village. In McK. Marriott (Ed.), *Village India*. Chicago: University of Chicago Press.

SRINIVAS, M. N. and A. M. SHAH.
1960. The myth of the self-sufficiency of the Indian village. *Economic Weekly*, 12: 1375–78.

VIDYARTHI, L. P.
1961. *The sacred complex in Hindu Gaya*. Bombay: Asia Publishing House.

3. A COMPARATIVE ANALYSIS OF CASTE: THE UNITED STATES AND INDIA[1]

EDWARD B. HARPER

ONE OF THE AIMS of social anthropology is to make meaningful cross-cultural comparisons of similar structural elements; but, when any aspect of social structure is examined in depth, it is found to be a rather complex phenomenon—so complex, indeed, that one does not find an exact correspondence of all components of the structure in any two societies. Caste, as one such structural element, may be broadly defined so as to be applicable to the relationships between two or more groups in many societies, or more narrowly defined so as to be relevant to such relationships in only one society. To paraphrase Kluckhohn and Murray's famous statement with respect to personality, any system of stratification is in some ways like all systems of stratification; any system of stratification is in some ways like some other systems of stratification; any system of stratification is in some ways like no other system of stratification (1949, p. 35).

Broadly stated, my question is this: To what extent does the fact that some social scientists apply the term "caste" to both American and South Asian societies indicate that they are referring to forms of structure which are analytically similar? This question is complicated by the fact that both the United States and India have regional and strata variations in their respective systems of caste, variations which make it difficult to generalize and pose the problem of what variants to compare. This lack of uniformity inevitably decreases the rigorousness with which a comparative analysis may be made. My use of the term "caste" in the case of the United States is restricted to relationships between Negro-white groups, and in that of India to relationships between those units of stratification in which intramarriage may take place, called *jātis*[2] in the modern anthropological literature.

Caste systems are but one of several types of social stratification. To be properly

1. I wish to thank John Atkins, Ernest A. T. Barth, and Raymond D. Fogelson, who read drafts of this paper, for their helpful suggestions. I am, of course, solely responsible for its shortcomings.

2. Although the term "*jāti*" is now used by social scientists with a rather specific connotation, it must be understood that its meaning in most Indian languages has at least as large a number of connotations as does the term caste in colloquial English. In Kannada, for example, "*jāti*" most simply means "kind." A man may say, for instance, that he prefers one *jāti* of cigarettes over another *jāti*. If an individual is asked "what is your *jāti*?" he may respond with the name of the unit within which he confines his marriage relations, with the name of a collection of these units that are similar (caste category or caste complex in anthropological jargon), with his varna affiliation, or even with the name of his religion, as for example, "Christian *jāti*."

understood caste should be compared with and distinguished from lineage and clan, groups which are composed only of real or putative kinsmen, are not necessarily ranked, are generally exogamous, and may form subunits within a caste; and castes should be further distinguished from tribes, which form complete societies that may be segmented internally into castes. Castes are similar to some ethnic and sect groups which define membership exclusively in terms of birthright, but neither are these necessarily hierarchically arranged nor is an entire society necessarily divided into such mutually exclusive groups; and rules of marriage for class groups are preferential rather than prescriptive. Caste systems more closely approximate the European "estate" system than they resemble modern class systems; in estate systems, however, some social mobility was legitimate, and intermarriage between estates was more a breach of etiquette than a sin (in Weber's words, a "mesalliance" rather than "absolutely and legally inadmissible" [1958, p. 40]). Class, estate, and caste systems are based upon groups of individuals who are ranked into some kind of hierarchical ordering, and such systems are in this way distinguished from systems of stratification which primarily rank individuals, as the societies of some Northwest Coast Indian tribes are reported to do (Drucker, 1939).

My concern is to compare in a general way the structure of the caste systems of the southern United States and India. My model for caste in both regions is best represented in their rural communities during the recent historical past (approximately 1900–1945 for the United States and 1900–1947 for India). I shall not consider the dynamics of modern change. In both societies I shall be concerned with the ideal models of the systems as well as with deviations from these models. I shall draw many of my Indian examples from the Malnad part of South India, where my wife and I did field work.

DUAL VERSUS MULTICASTE SYSTEMS

In both the United States and India there are regional differences in the rules, functions, and nature of the respective nation's caste systems. One of the most obvious differences between the two systems is the number of units composing their caste societies. Broadly speaking, the American ideal model can be thought of as consisting of endogamous moieties, whereas the Indian model contains within any region a large number of more or less differentiated but interdependent units which constitute that region's caste system; that is, the United States has a dual-caste system, whereas India has a multicaste system. This does not mean that more than two castes are never encountered in any southern United States town, or that less than three castes are never found in any Indian village, but only that the members of these societies conceive of their respective systems of caste stratification in these differing ways.

ENDOGAMY

Although the rules governing intercaste relations in the United States specify endogamy, they do not always do so in India, as is demonstrated by the Nayar and Nambudiri Brahman castes in Malabar, by the Kulin Brahmans in Bengal, and by the Patidars in Gujarat. Although castes in both societies are often associated with rules which require endogamy, and intracaste marriages are always approved of, when exogamy is not completely prohibited carefully defined rules exist stating the other castes from which one may or may not legitimately seek a marriage partner. Approved intercaste marriages or alliances are generally hypergamous. In some instances, hypergamy is primarily "an exchange of prestige for goods," as Risley and Dumont suggest (Dumont, 1961, pp. 30–31); but at least for Nambudiri Brahmans, more seems to be involved—possibly an exchange of prestige by Nambudiris for descent group stability, and for economic hegemony, by preventing the division of their estates.

Patterson (1958) has suggested that to characterize the Indian caste system predominantly as one in which intercaste marriages are prohibited is to underemphasize the individual's preference to marry within his own caste. It is my experience, however, that when the suggestion is made to an Indian that a fellow casteman of his marry someone of lower caste, the informant is more likely to prefer endogamy than when the suggested intercaste marriage is to a potential spouse of a caste higher than his own. It seems quite conceivable that if intercaste marriages were generally possible in India, the preferred norm of marriage would be to a higher caste person, as is suggested by the fact that, in those castes which permit hypergamy, the girl's family apparently prefers it to endogamy (Gough, 1962; Pocock, 1957).

But should we describe caste as a preference for marriage to a member of an appropriate or permissible group, we would be overlooking one of the major ways in which caste differs from social class. Americans frequently express the belief that intraclass marriages are more desirable than interclass ones—a rule of preference rather than of prescription. A caste ideology specifies that, even though a male from caste X and a female from caste Z are ideally matched in all other respects, the fact that they belong to castes between which marriages are prohibited is *ipso facto* sufficient reason for their not marrying. On the one hand we are dealing with rules of preferred behavior which statistically might be followed by most members of the society and on the other hand with rules of prescription which might be statistically observed considerably less than 100 per cent of the time in a given society. The two systems thus differ in the nature of their rules but not necessarily in the frequency of compliance with their rules. From this point of view, a caste system is not just a more rigid class system but differs from such a system in principle.

Although the American and Indian caste systems have rules prohibiting marriage between certain specific castes, they differ in the ways these rules relate to their respective cultural contexts. The explicit American ideology states that marriages should be arranged by the involved parties and based solely upon love, while the explicit Indian ideology states that marriages should be arranged by parents, who have the wisdom to make a more desirable marriage for their children than the children could make for themselves. The American ideal of mate-selection procedure flatly contradicts the principle of caste endogamy, while the South Asian point of view is more congruent with a caste system.

BOUNDED STRATA

Castes in both societies are *bounded* rather than ego-centered; or, as Nadel and Bailey have worded it, they are "exclusive and exhaustive" (Bailey, 1963, p. 109). In the ideal type all individuals clearly belong to one but to no other caste. This is unlike the American social class system, in which there may not be agreement even among social scientists as to the class position of a particular individual. A bounded stratum rests upon an either-or principle; American social classes are more like arbitrarily defined categories on a continuum along which individuals are placed according to their relative prestige. In both the American and the Indian ideal conceptions of caste, all residents of a locality know precisely to which caste they belong, and the one to which any other individual in their area belongs, while in the American class system certain individuals are not easily nor consistently assigned to one social class rather than another, by their own valuation, the community's, or the social scientist's. Surely the American social class system is much more difficult to analyze conceptually than is the Indian caste system. Not only are social classes more difficult to define rigorously, they are also more difficult to place definitely in the esteem hierarchy, since multiple criteria are used for the assignment of prestige. Problems in the analysis of social classes may be cut across caste boundaries.

HIERARCHY

A caste system is associated with societies sufficiently complex to allow the differentiation of a population into two or more hierarchically arranged strata; in its association with such societies, caste constitutes one type of social stratification. Hierarchy is a necessary feature of a caste system and this distinguishes it from ethnic groups in a plural society. Nevertheless, hierarchy cannot be used to distinguish caste from other forms of social stratification, such as class systems.

In the American dual-caste system, one group must be ranked directly above the other if the groups are to be stratified at all; otherwise they would be merely differentiated. In the Indian caste system the same logic would lead to the statement that some castes must be ranked above some other castes, but it would not follow that, in order to have stratification in a multicaste society, all castes in a given local region must fit neatly into a system of relative ranking vis-à-vis all other castes. One implication of a multicaste system is that any two castes may be approximately equal in rank, or some may occupy indeterminate positions in the hierarchy in respect to others. This is often the case in India: two castes may be isogamous, as are Divarus and Potters in the Malnad region of South India; or they may dispute their relative rank, as two Untouchable castes do in the Malnad and Lingayats and Brahmans in some parts of Mysore.

A caste system implies the existence of "a superiority-inferiority scale" (Williams, 1951, p. 79). Although group superiority is probably always obtained and maintained by the use of some form of power, it is justified and validated in these two societies by reference to a credo which expounds the notion of inherent and immutable differences and explains these differences by reference to philosophical, religious, or pseudoscientific principles. The belief that certain groups are intrinsically inferior to others is probably an inevitable accompanying rationalization for any hierarchically structured caste system in which there is differentially determined access to the culturally defined desirables.

In order for castes to be ranked sequentially in the hierarchy, there must be consensus as to what criteria are relevant to evaluating a stratum's relative worth. The American class system is based upon a multiple-criteria hierarchy, in which different individuals and social groups have different standards for evaluating relative esteem. When this is combined with the absence of a method to assign any given individual infallibly to one and only one group, a rather fuzzy hierarchy of hazily demarcated classes results, in which no one class is necessarily superior to all other classes in all respects. Attempts to clarify this problem have engaged the attention of American sociologists for the past several decades. In contrast, a caste system seems to have a single criterion by which to evaluate each caste's placement in the hierarchy. In the United States this criterion has generally been "race"; in India it has generally been ritual purity. In the United States, as long as the dual-caste system is the focus of our attention, there is no problem in sequentially ranking the castes (but if groups other than "Negro" and "white" are brought into our analysis of caste in the United States, the problem of hierarchy becomes less clear and seems to call for more than one criterion of evaluation).

A multiple caste system such as India's theoretically could use two or more criteria for caste evaluation, but, if a clear-cut hierarchy encompassing all castes were to result, there would have to be a near-perfect correlation among all criteria and each caste's relative standing with respect to each criterion. This would be cumbersome and extremely difficult to implement. In Hindu ideology, ritual purity or impurity constitutes the criterion generally accepted for justifying and explaining a caste's rank (Stevenson, 1954; Harper, 1964), although relative power is more likely to determine caste rank (Marriott, 1959); in the United States, on the other hand, "an innate difference between races" is the justification. If ritual purity, to the exclusion of wealth, "race," skill or knowledge, is the sole criterion for ranking Hindu castes along points of a continuum, then lack of agreement about the relative ranking of two castes is a dispute over which is more pure, not over what standard of evaluation is to be used. Although the Hindu caste ideology theoretically uses only a single "immutable" scale for evaluating a caste's intrinsic worth, in actual practice secular factors such as power derived from wealth are employed when castes compete for positions on this scale. In contrast, in the United States a Negro who is upwardly mobile usually does not jockey for position on the attributional caste scale, but instead attempts to obtain a different position within the class system. In both the United States and India, however, the respective caste ideologies are contained in a social milieu where many educated and influential persons profess a philosophy based more or less upon a principle of social equality. Thus in both societies attributional theories used to justify caste ranking are discordant with emerging modern national ethics.

REGNANT STATUS AND STATUS GROUPS

Caste is but one of many status positions, accompanied by culturally defined role behavior, which an individual occupies and which forms part of his social identity. In every interactional situation each interactant has at least several relevant statuses vis-à-vis the other(s): child-adult; aunt-niece; farmer-lawyer; stranger-stranger; Republican-Democrat; Negro-white; Brahman-Shudra; Rajput-Rajput; or upper class-lower class. Castes are composed of individuals of equivalent statuses and thus are *status groups* in which all members have the same "quality of social honor or lack of it" (Weber, 1958, p. 39) in respect to their being caste members. This "social honor" exists independently of such factors as wealth, education, age, or accomplishment. In the southern United States, any Negro, and in rural India any Untouchable, is just as unwelcome in a restaurant which caters to higher status groups as any other Negro or Untouchable. In a hierarchically ranked status group system there are culturally defined modes of interacting, based solely upon status group membership, which are symbolically expressive not only of differences but also of superiority, deference, or equality. Although hierarchy and consequent inequality are implied by the presence of two or more status groups within a society, social equality within a status group is also implied. All members of a caste are equal in their inherent worth because they are defined as having equal degrees of ritual purity (India) or genetic purity (United States). Certain behavioral expressions of equality are appropriate only between members of the same (or isogamously ranked) caste(s), while certain behaviors expressive of deference and superiority must be symbolically expressed when the interactants are members of different hierarchically ranked castes. In this way caste status in both the United States and India can be thought of as a *regnant status*—an overriding status that may take precedence over any other statuses the interactants may occupy. Within the Havik Brahman caste, equality is expressed by the willingness of any member to dine in a ceremonial situation with any other member, regardless of other differing statuses of the interactants (for example, male-female; rich-poor; elder-junior; enemy-enemy), while their superiority is shown by their complete unwillingness to interdine with members of any other caste, regardless of other statuses they may occupy (landlord-tenant; friend-friend). It would be almost as deviant for one Havik to refuse to interdine ceremonially with another Havik (provided his caste standing were not in question) as it would be for an Havik to interdine with a member of another caste. Untouchability is another expression of a regnant status: in the Malnad, a member of an Untouchable caste must be treated by members of all other castes as untouchable simply because of his caste affiliation. Ego, a member of any Shudra or Brahman caste, expects and can demand that any Untouchable show him deference, even though ego is poor, illiterate, and unmarried, and the Untouchable is older, married, educated, and financially successful. In the southern United States, the use of "Mister" as a form of address is expressive of equality when used within a caste but of inequality when used between castes. "Mister" is not supposed to be used by a white toward a Negro, but an upper-class Negro may be required to address a lower-class white male as "Mister." Although in some situations of interaction the higher caste individual may choose to hold in abeyance his regnant status in favor of other statuses which the two interactants occupy (for example, a white clerk may attempt to make a sale by addressing a Negro customer as "Mister," or a Rajput landowner may offer a place on his cot to an educated Chamar schoolteacher), he nevertheless may reactivate his regnant status by demanding the appropriate symbolic expressions of deference from the member of the lower-status group.

POWER, OCCUPATION, SEGREGATION, AND COMMENSALITY

Both systems of caste rest upon the unequal distribution of power between status groups occupying different positions in the prestige hierarchy. In any system of social stratification, the upper echelons face the problem of how to maintain their positions, which they or their ancestors at one time achieved, against the more socially disadvantaged segments of the population who desire a larger share of the rewards available to members of that society. To maintain their position of superiority, the higher strata must be able to control the mechanisms of coercion. Presumably the more rationalized and internally consistent a system of stratification becomes—the more all-pervasive and encompassing, the more integrated into other aspects of the culture—the easier it is to perpetuate it without resort to direct force. One could probably develop the thesis that caste in India is a more involute and smoothly functioning institution than it is in the United States (except possibly in the pre-Civil War slavery system), and therefore is less dependent upon the use of the available direct and bare power. As Allison Davis (1954) has pointed out, it is in those parts of the South where a substantial number of Negroes are economically better off than many whites, that is, where the correlation of caste and economic rank is furthest from being congruent, that force and violence are most likely to be used by members of the white caste to maintain their hegemony over the Negro caste. (Davis's thesis could be expanded to help explain why, in the present-day South, racial conflict is more characteristic of urban than of rural areas, for it is in the urban centers that the most incongruities appear in the caste system.) This thesis is also in accord with Sanskritization movements in India, which seem to be successfully implemented only by those castes whose economic position is discrepant with their ritual rank in the hierarchy.

As in any civilization, occupational specialization is elaborated both in the United States and in India, and in both countries it is related to social class (but more so in the United States) as well as to caste. These strands are difficult to separate. Caste and occupation in the modern industrial and entrepreneurial sectors of the Indian economy do not appear to be highly correlated (Morris, 1960, 1965), and in government service laws have been passed favoring previously underrepresented castes. In rural India, caste and occupation are more highly correlated; occupations may be both prescribed and proscribed according to caste affiliation. Almost all castes have a traditional occupation which their members may or may not follow, and some castes are simply known by their occupational name (for example, Potter). Some occupations are the special privilege of some castes (for example, priestcraft) and others are too ritually defiling to be performed by any but the very low castes (for example, sweeping). Certain occupations are open as primary or secondary occupations to the members of many castes (for example, agriculture), and other specialized artisan and service occupations are the monopolies of members of the appropriate castes (for example, oil pressing). In India the right to engage in some occupations is regarded as a property right, to be defended against encroachment; some labor unions in the United States treat occupational rights in the same way, but these unions most certainly are not castes.

The rural Indian system of many occupationally specialized castes is possible only in a relatively simple and stable economy where the occupations necessary to the society's continuance are limited in number and do not require a high degree of technical skill. For this reason the traditional Indian system of occupational specialization by caste ceases to work in a complex modern industrial economy. This consequence of industrialism, and the logical consequences of a dual-caste system, make occupational specialization by castes impossible in the United States.

Although the notion of "privilege" is much more firmly tied to low-status jobs in India than in the United States, we find in both countries that routine, menial, and degrading jobs tend to be filled by members of the lower castes. But this is basically no different, except in statistical frequency, from a class system in which residual occupations are filled by members of the lower classes, whose position in the class system is in turn partly derived from their performance of these jobs. In both societies, the upper castes apparently must exert or threaten force to get the lower to perform their menial jobs, as is indicated by the rapid social change now seen in both societies as members of the lower castes militantly attempt to shed these occupations (for example, Cohn, 1955; Harper, in press).

In the more traditionally oriented segments of each society, certain types of jobs are prohibited to the lower castes, not because of their prestige or lucrativeness but because of the authority vested in them. This is most clearly evident in the American South, where most Negroes have menial, low-prestige jobs for which they receive minimal wages. However, some few Negroes are high-status professionals; but while Negroes may become doctors, professors, lawyers, or undertakers (only for other Negroes), every impediment is put in the way of their becoming judges in courts of law, managers in retail stores employing white clerks, or teachers in white schools. Although some whites may accord respect in a manner consistent with social class to a Negro minister or lawyer or professor, the regnant caste status may be at any time invoked by the white, and thus reverse the flow of deference, making it consistent with the interactants' respective caste roles. Although prestigious high-status occupations are not entirely prohibited to Negroes, occupational statuses that give an incumbent authority over members of the higher caste tend to be prohibited to low-caste persons. This bias explains the opposition of white southerners to Negroes' occupying the lower middle class job of policeman.

In both systems, the two cardinal sins are caste insubordination and prohibited marriages. Inequality is symbolized and reinforced by patterns of deference and respect, and by social distance. Behavior symbolizing equality is tantamount to insubordination. Social distance is expressed in both these societies by rules of segregation regarding place of residence[3] and use of community facilities such as barbers or barbershops, temples or churches, wells or drinking fountains. In India untouchability is carried to a further extreme than in the United States, while segregation in public facilities is carried to greater lengths in the United States. As noted by Weber (1958, p. 397) "it has been impossible to introduce caste coaches on the railroads [in India] in the fashion of the American railroad cars or waiting rooms which segregate 'White' from 'Black' in the Southern States." Social distance is also expressed in both societies by rules governing commensality, and in neither society may members of different castes freely interdine. In both, an individual may be served by someone from a caste which he may not join for a meal; in the United States, the upper caste person may have his food cooked and served by the lower, while in India this order is reversed. In the United States the concept of "service" by a subordinate is the ruling principle, while in India the alternative principle of ritual purity takes precedence. In both societies, interdining is symbolic of an equality which is not attuned to the hierarchical ranking of castes.

In all these respects—power, occupation, segregation, and commensality—the caste systems of the two societies are broadly similar and can be interpreted as extraordinarily rigid class systems, for all these features appear in less full-blown form in class-stratified societies.

RECRUITMENT

Caste systems have been similarly described as being composed of groups in which "membership is hereditary and permanent" (Berreman, 1960, p. 120); as groups in which membership is "ascribed on the basis of birth" and from which "no change is possible because of personal qualities or achievements" (Williams, 1951, p. 89); as "closed social stratification" in which "everyone, in normal circumstances, is born into one or another caste and stays in it for life" (Bailey, 1963, p. 109); or simply as "closed status groups" (Weber, 1958, p. 39). Certain complexities arise when these statements are examined closely. The most relevant comparative questions we may ask are: How does an individual become a member of a caste? Is any effort required of an individual to maintain caste membership? Is it possible for a person to lose his caste affiliation? May caste affiliation be changed?

3. In the traditional South, Negro servants often lived interspersed throughout white residential areas and residential integration was common. Even in the modern South, residential segregation does not seem to be as important as in northern cities. As Ernest A. T. Barth has pointed out to me, this is true precisely because of the caste assumption that no Negro could be a threat to the social position of any white.

In India, when parents belong to the same caste, children almost invariably bilaterally inherit their caste affiliation. But, when Hindu parents who belong to different castes have entered into a socially acceptable intercaste alliance (for instance an hypergamous union with a spouse of an appropriate caste), several different principles of descent may be used to determine the progeny's caste. Between Nambudiri Brahmans and Nayars, and among the various Nayar castes, a matrilineal principle is used for ascribing caste to the progeny of hypergamous unions, so that the child belongs to the mother's caste (Gough, 1962). Among the patrilineal Patidars[4] the opposite appears to be the case (Pocock, 1957). A woman's children are added to her husband's descent group and thus are members of their father's caste. These systems are not mirror images, as in the Nayar situation the relative social rank of the hypergamously allied castes does not appear to be affected by such unions, whereas among the Patidars hypergamous marriages have an equalizing effect: each such marriage may slightly diminish the rank position of the husband's caste and slightly enhance the rank position of the wife's caste, creating a fluid situation in which different families, lineages, or localized village segments may strive to be included in a higher caste or may be expelled into a lower one. A patrilineal principle of ascribing status is also used in Swat, but here true intercaste marriages are allowed; that is, both the hypergamous and hypogamous types are possible (Barth, 1960).

So far we have referred only to prescribed or permissible types of marriage resulting in legitimate births, for which rules assigning caste affiliation to the offspring exist. In all societies, however, some unions take place between proscribed partners in defiance of customary or legal laws. Also, illegitimate births resulting from premarital and adulterous relationships occur. In all these instances, the offspring must be given some status, no matter how nebulous or degraded, within the social system. The literature on how this is accomplished in South Asia is meager in the extreme.

Methods of social control in rural India are sufficiently effective to make illegitimate intercaste common-law marriages infrequent occurrences. With one type of exception, the few participants in intercaste "marriages" I heard about in the Malnad, where all castes are strictly endogamous, were regarded as men and women of different castes who simply lived together, not as married couples. Indeed, it would have been impossible for these partners to have obtained either priests or guests for a wedding ceremony, and they were not sufficiently sophisticated or motivated to think in terms of a civil marriage. I will first discuss the exception.

Like many other very low castes in India, the two indigenous Untouchable

4. I prefer to conceptualize "Patidars" as a caste category (such as Chamars or Okkaligas) composed of numerous similar castes, rather than as a single caste. (For another point of view see Pocock, 1957.) According to this interpretation, the caste (*jāti*) units are the Patidar's ranked "marriage circles," which are ideally endogamous but which under some circumstances permit hypergamous marriages with other castes in their caste category, and occasionally outside of it. It is worth noting that in the Patidar castes, or marriage circles, if a family contracts an hypergamous marriage it is subject to a fine, but the fine is less for the family that marries a daughter "up" than for the family that marries a son "down."

castes in the Malnad, but no other castes, recruit by initiation as well as by birth. I have fragmentary case histories on several individuals, both Brahman and non-Brahman, who have applied for and gained admission into an Untouchable caste. In all these instances the initiate also married an Untouchable. I do not know whether an application for membership from a married couple belonging to another caste or castes would be favorably received. Similarly, the case histories reported by Fuchs in which non-Balahis were taken into the Untouchable Balahi caste also involved marriage with a male or female Balahi (Fuchs, 1950, pp. 18–19). Higher caste individuals who are motivated to enter a low caste are generally in some difficulty within their own caste, if indeed not already excommunicated. If one party in this intercaste marriage is already a birthright member of the lower caste which allows admission, and the other party changes his or her caste affiliation to that of the spouse, the situation is not technically an intercaste marriage, and the caste affiliation of children resulting from this marriage is bilaterally ascribed.

Of the few stable intercaste unions for which I have some information, children were not produced, and in each there were rumors of abortions. With the possible exception of the instance of a Havik Brahman and his Maleru concubine, children of these prohibited unions could not have been accepted as members of either parent's caste, even if the parents were not socially boycotted and thus incapable of passing on their caste affiliations. Should concubinage have become institutionalized in this area it would undoubtedly have involved only males of one or two wealthy castes and women of a few lower castes. In this event it is probable that a new caste or castes would have been formed for the descendants of these unions, as has happened in Rajputana (Karve, 1961, p. 16). Even in regions which have institutionalized concubinage, it is likely that situations could arise in which common-law marriage or concubinage could take place between members of castes which prohibited such alliances and for which there would be neither a third caste for the children to enter nor a way to incorporate them into either of their parents' castes.

Provided the parents were permitted to remain in the village, the child of a prohibited intercaste alliance in India could (1) emigrate from the area, (2) remain in the region where his ancestry was known but join an Untouchable caste, or (3) remain in the region and become a truly marginal man—an individual without caste affiliation. In the cases of either (1) or (3) and in the unlikely event that such a person could obtain a spouse, the choice would be to perpetuate the anomalous situation by having children or to resort to birth-prevention techniques. While it is sometimes possible for a couple from two indigenous castes proscribing intercaste marriage to live together and remain in a village in the Malnad, I would speculate that their chances of having a tolerable existence would be much more remote should they attempt to raise a family.

Illegitimacy resulting from premarital sexual relations also raises problems. Among non-Brahman castes in the Malnad, when an unmarried girl becomes pregnant (an infrequent occurrence), either the matter is hushed up and the girl married as if she were not pregnant or a husband for her and pater for her child from her own caste is eventually found by the subcaste[5] headman, and the child's caste is then bilaterally ascribed. But here the presumption is that the genitor's caste is the same or higher than the mother's. If it were "publicly proved" that the unwed mother's pregnancy was caused by a lower-caste man, I simply do not know what would happen to the mother's and bastard's caste affiliation, as I have no case histories to guide my analysis. In the Malnad it appears that such situations could not arise unless, as is quite unlikely, the unwed pregnant girl should choose to admit her hypogamous fornication. What usually happens, instead, is that in the final analysis evidence of such misdoing never seems to be proved; a fiction of innocence is maintained, and the mother and child remain in the mother's natal caste. If the girl flagrantly lived with an Untouchable she would be boycotted (socially isolated) by members of her own caste but could join the Untouchable caste and legally marry. If the lover with whom she openly lived was of a caste lower than hers, but one that did not give entrance to applicants from other castes, both would undoubtedly be boycotted and their children would bilaterally acquire their lack of caste affiliation.

Among Havik Brahmans, illegitimate births were said to have been previously nonexistent, as a result of the mandatory rule that a girl must marry before puberty, a rule now changing under the influence of legislation. The only instance known to my informants took place in a neighboring village, and, after an unsuccessful attempt was made to force the accused genitor to take her as his second wife, several young Havik males from the more progressive South Kanara area boldly offered to marry her. Although these events were concluded after we left India, I suspect that the child will be regarded as an Havik, but stigmatized in the eyes of less liberal members of the community. Had the genitor been indisputably and publicly proved to be a non-Brahman, I suspect there would have been no alternative but to outcaste the mother.

Intercaste adultery among all castes in the Malnad seems to be handled by methods other than outcasting, and children belong to the caste of their mother and her legal husband. Although Haviks say they would outcaste a woman who was publicly proven to have committed adultery with a non-Brahman, they could supply no case histories of such events. The few rumors of intercaste adultery committed by Havik women that were reported to me were classed by other informants as malicious and unfounded gossip, misconception of events, or true but neither admitted nor "proved." That outcasting for adultery does not occur is more probably due to the fact that public exposure would bring discredit to the entire caste and, for reasons of status honor, would compel representatives of the caste to mete out punishment of a more severe nature than the community apparently would feel warranted, than a complete absence of adulterous relationships.

One other situation does sometimes arise: among Brahmans but in no other castes of the area, widows may not remarry. Occasionally, a Havik Brahman

---

5. Following Cohn (1959) I use the term "subcaste" for the localized (village, hamlet, or ward) segment of a caste, which generally has a political structure.

widow gives birth to a child long enough after her husband's death to make it obvious that he was not the genitor. At the time of parturition, "public proof" is incontravertible and the Havik mother is punished by being outcasted. Her legitimate children remain Haviks who inherit their father's property, and the illegitimate child becomes a member of the Maleru caste, a relatively high but numerically small status group composed solely of illegitimate children of Havik widows and the descendants of such children. Again, I do not have data on the caste affiliation of these children should their genitor be publicly proved to be a non-Brahman.

Another partial case history is of interest here. A powerful and wealthy Rajput moneylender in a village in Chhattisgarh District in Madhya Pradesh had a male child by his Shudra maid servant. The child was raised by his legitimate wife, by whom he already had children. The maid continued to work for him but spent the nights in her own hamlet. The father claimed that the illegitimate boy was his son by his legitimate wife, although members of the community knew this to be untrue. Knowledge of this case history, supplied to me by Purnima Sinha (personal communication), ends when the boy was ten years old, so it is impossible to tell whether or not the father was able to make good his claim that this boy was a Rajput. The crucial test would come at the time of the boy's *upanayana* and marriage. Extrapolating from my personal knowledge of social relations in the Malnad, I can well imagine that the father might be able to import Brahmans from neighboring regions to perform these ceremonies, and even that the priests would continue them if informed of the true state of affairs, replying that they were acting on the only formal knowledge they had, their patron's statement. Furthermore, it even seems to me possible that a Rajput bride for the boy could be obtained from a remote village. However, a necessary ingredient for the successful completion of this deceit would probably be a wealthy father who was a patron and a man of influence. In analyzing this case hypothetically, I have utilized the approach that appears to me to be most frequently used in avoiding the problem of assigning caste affiliation when there are absolutely no rules to cover an unlikely contingency; that is, ignoring social facts in favor of convenient fictions, even when the real facts are commonly known. Only if the facts become publicly known and formally proved do they become relevant, and "proof" of cardinal sins is difficult to obtain.

In summary, the methods used in India to create boundaries around castes appear to be:

(1) To require endogamous marriages and to affiliate children bilaterally to the caste of their initial and/or adoptive pater and mater.

(2) To permit couples who belong to certain specific different castes to contract marriages or form recognized alliances and affiliate any resulting children to the caste of either their mater or their pater through one or the other principle of unilineal descent; or, if the child is not granted membership by either its mater's or its pater's castes and yet the type of intercaste alliance that brought it into existence is common, to affiliate the child to a third caste created for such a contingency, different from that of either its mater or its pater.

(3) If an unmarried woman of marriageable status becomes pregnant and the genitor is presumed to be of her caste or a caste recognized by members of her caste as higher than their own, her child is affiliated to her caste. (In this eventuality the woman is often appropriately married before her child is born.)

(4) If a woman of unmarriageable status (for example, a widow) becomes pregnant and the genitor is presumed to be of her caste or a caste recognized by members of her caste as higher than her own, her child may enter a caste different from its mother's, one specially created for such a contingency.

(5) Children derived from other possible combinations of publicly known intercaste unchastity are generally without caste affiliation. Their anomalous status is difficult, for they must live in a society in which all individuals are assumed to belong to a caste. The difficulties inherent in such births undoubtedly help to reduce the likelihood of their occurrence and to explain why they are often publicly overlooked when they do occur. The resulting individuals are without caste affiliation simply because the circumstances that brought them into being are so rare that other persons with a similar background with whom they could join to form a caste do not exist in their local region.

The basis for caste ascription in the southern United States is both more simple and more complex. In the United States, where both hypergamy and hypogamy are socially disapproved and sometimes legally prohibited, caste is bilaterally ascribed. Bounded strata are supposed to be visibly identifiable; but as this is not always the case, caste ascription is made according to culturally recognized principles of descent. It is when "race" and the most commonly presumed principles of descent are not congruent that complexities begin to arise in the system.

Skin color is evaluated in both countries. In India, light skin is a mark of beauty and may enhance the desirability of a bride or groom in the marriage market. Also, there appears to be some statistical correlation in any given region in India between the rank of a caste and the average degree of lightness or darkness of skin color of its members, but the range of variation within a caste is often so great that skin color by itself can seldom indicate much about an individual's specific caste affiliation. Skin color is not used as a basis for assigning caste affiliation —an extraordinarily dark Brahman does not become a Shudra any more than an extraordinarily light Untouchable becomes a Shudra. Race in the United States may identify an individual's caste regardless of dress, demeanor, or dialect,[6] whereas in India these cultural criteria are used to identify a stranger's background.

In the same way that the American kinship system is presumptively organized around a biological model which it does not in fact follow (examples of deviation being adoption or the distinction between genitor and pater), the American caste system presumes a biological model which is not always in accord with reality. Caste in the United States is popularly viewed racially. A member of the Negro caste is customarily thought of as an individual who has any known or presumed "Negro blood," even though in such small quantity as not to be pheno-

6. This would not necessarily apply to an African visitor to the United States.

typically expressed; this folk taxonomy approximates the legal definition in the laws of most southern states. Given this definition, the question of who is and who is not a member of the white or Negro caste is sometimes difficult to answer.

To understand the American caste system we need to start with the assumption that there were initially two physically identifiable "races" and that belonging to one or the other of these was the prime basis for ascribing caste; only then can we analyze caste recruitment in terms of descent. The American ideal-type caste system is thought to be composed of two racially differentiated and endogamous groups, and children resulting from these marriages bilaterally inherit their caste affiliation. Nonendogamous marriages go against customary law and sometimes statutory law; extralegal hypergamous alliances are permitted but not approved, and the rule for this contingency is that the children resulting from these unions belong to the mother's caste. As long as the "race" of all individuals is physically identifiable, and as long as the rule that marriages should not cut across caste boundaries is observed, the congruence of "race" and rules of descent combine to form a caste system of relatively little complexity. But when hypergamous alliances are permissible and children are assigned caste affiliation under the contingency rule, the unanticipated latent consequence is to create eventually a situation where some individuals' caste affiliation is no longer unambiguously identifiable from their physical features.

Although in the modern southern United States it is said that endogamy should prevail in all sexual relations, deviations from the rules prohibiting intercaste premarital, marital, and extramarital sexual relations do take place, and methods of ascribing caste affiliation to resulting progeny do exist. The approved method for ascribing the caste affiliation of children resulting from hypergamous and hypogamous intercaste sexual relations is simply to assign the child to the status group of the lower-ranking parent, even though it may "look" like a member of the higher status group. But in order for this comparatively simple rule of caste ascription to work, the presumed genitor sometimes must be also the real genitor, and the mater must be the same as the presumed genitrix. The following cases exemplify this: (1) a secret premarital hypogamous alliance results in the pregnancy of a white woman; in the absence of contrary facts the genitor might be presumed to be white and the expected child prematurely assigned to the white caste, but this "fact" would be abandoned in the face of sufficient evidence (a "black baby"); the bastard would then be assigned to the caste of its newly presumed genitor rather than its previously presumed genitor. (2) The critical case is that of hypogamous adultery. A white woman married within her own caste engages in an intercaste adulterous affair known only to the participating parties and gives birth to a child fathered by her lover. The child would, if it showed sufficient identifying features, belong to a caste different from that of its mater or pater: it would belong to the caste of its newly presumed genitor rather than its previously presumed genitor. (3) A woman of white caste marries a man of white caste who had previously been married to a woman of Negro caste by whom he had had children who are then adopted by his white wife. In this instance, the caste of the children is determined by their genitrix; their caste would be different from that of their mater, pater, and genitor, their caste affiliation having been inherited from their genitrix. Again, if a woman of white caste who had previously had children whose presumed genitor was white married a person sociologically defined as being of the Negro caste who became her children's pater, the children would remain white and be of the same caste as their presumed genitor but of a higher caste than their pater. However, children subsequently born to this woman while she was married to or living with her Negro husband would be Negro as long as he was the presumed genitor even though their actual genitor might be of the white caste.[7]

The principle for caste affiliation in the United States is, then, that the child is assigned to the lowest caste believed to be applicable to either its presumed genitrix or its presumed genitor, regardless of the caste of its mater or pater.

If we systematically examine the various contingencies under which caste affiliation might be assigned in the United States, we find a number of possibilities, the vast majority of which lead to assigning a child to the Negro caste.

1. If customary norms are followed, marriage and sexual relations are restricted to individuals of the same caste. In the case of marriage, children are of the same caste as their mater, pater, genitrix, and genitor, or, in the case of a premarital alliance, they are of the same caste as their mater, genitrix, and presumed genitor. (In this and the following diagram = symbolizes sexual activity resulting in progeny, whether or not legitimized by marriage.)

2. The most straightforward deviation from this norm is miscegenation. If the couple is married, the children belong to the status group of their mater-genitrix or pater-genitor, whichever is lower. If the children result from a premarital alliance, they belong to the status group of the mater-genitrix or that of the presumed genitor, whichever is lower:

7. In many instances, we have considered cases in which the social status of a member of the white caste is lower, in the eyes of both whites and Negroes, than that of members of the Negro caste. Although these individuals may be despised, socially boycotted, or called "nigger lovers," they remain members of the white caste. A rough ranking of social statuses in this hierarchy might go as follows: whites who act as whites should; Negroes who act as Negroes should; "uppity niggers"; and "renegade whites." As was pointed out to me by John Atkins, a similar hierarchy exists in the way we classify the sexes: males who act as males; females who act as females; lesbians; and homosexuals. But in the same way that a renegade white remains within the white caste, although he is considered to be of lower status than a Negro, a homosexual is still regarded as a male, although contemptuously so by many Americans. It is precisely because the highest status positions have the most "social honor" to lose that those who repudiate the way of life most symbolic of such positions are so heavily punished.

or, more simply diagrammed, using a square to denote either a male or a female,

3. In the event of adulterous relationships (symbolized by x), the resulting progeny belong to the status group of their lower-ranking presumed genitor or genitrix, and not to the status group of this individual's spouse if the spouse's caste differs from that of the presumed genitor or genitrix. (Here and below the symbol = signifies cohabitation or marriage.)

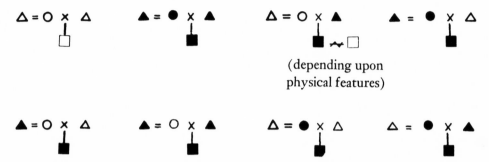

(depending upon physical features)

4. In the event of secondary marriages, children from either marriage are assigned to the status group of the lower-ranking presumed genitor or genitrix; their siblings may belong to a different caste. As in one of the contingencies under adulterous relationships, it is possible for children to belong to a caste different from that of both their mater and pater. (≠ symbolizes "divorced," "widowed," or "separated," and = symbolizes a secondary marriage.)

5. In the event of an adoption (symbolized by a broken line), a child takes the caste of its lowest presumed genitor or genitrix rather than that of its newly acquired pater and mater, and thus a child may again be of a caste different from that of either of its parents. Some of the examples, for instance that of a Negro couple adopting a white child, are hypothetical for the southern United States.

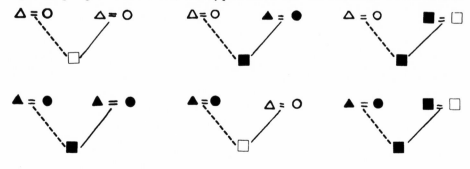

The rules of caste ascription are sociological rather than biological in both the United States and India. But in India matrilineal and patrilineal principles may be used in addition to bilateral ascription, and children may belong to a caste different from that of their pater, mater, genitor, or genitrix (as is possible in a multicaste system but not in the United States, insofar as the United States is believed to have a dual caste system in which all individuals belong to one or the other caste). In the United States, the only alternative to bilateral caste ascription is to place the child in the caste of the lowest-ranking person who could have been its genitor or genitrix. Correct application of the respective rules of descent may be more precisely implemented in the United States than in India; racial features may give a sharper criterion for applying the sociological rules of caste ascription than is available to a society in which caste membership and physical features are not so highly correlated.

While in the United States caste membership is believed to be permanent—it can be changed only by illegitimate means—in many Indian castes it is a privilege which may be withdrawn by one's fellow castemen. In South India an offender against caste honor may be boycotted by denying to him the privilege of interacting socially, ritually, and economically with other members of his caste. However, if the boycotted individual reforms and apologizes there generally exists a ceremonial means by which he may be reinstated to full caste ritual status. Boycotting, then, may become permanent, but only if the person who has violated sacred caste norms is unwilling to make restitution. Although among Havik Brahmans this temporary mechanism of social control (boycotting) is used, for the greatest "sins" true outcasting—permanent and irrevocable expulsion of the offender—may be applied. In an outcasting ceremony the individual's death rites are prematurely performed and his kinship ties are symbolically declared null and void. This conception of ceremonial outcasting does not fit the American scene any more than does the idea that some castes allow outsiders to join their ranks officially. In the Malnad, a Brahman may marry an Untouchable and *become* an Untouchable, whereas a man of white caste in the southern United States who marries a woman of the Negro caste may be socially ostracized but remains a renegade white who has married a Negro; only his wife's children become members of the Negro caste, not he.

In the United States there is a functional equivalent to being without caste in India. This is true because the United States does in fact have a multicaste system, although it is popularly conceived of as being composed of only two castes. Scattered throughout parts of the South and southeastern seaboard are numerous pockets of peoples who have mixed Indian, white, and Negro ancestry, graphically portrayed by Berry (1963), who are not classed as Indians by the governmental agencies that deal with Indian affairs, by Indians whose claim to this status is not in dispute, or by the local white populations. These marginal enclaves, known by such names as Brass Ankles, Lumbees, and Red Legs, refuse to identify themselves with Negroes, and are refused full white status by the locally dominant white populations. However, these "outcastes" form a social group and thus differ from those scattered individuals in India who do not form a viable social unit and are therefore without caste affiliation.

KINSHIP

Castes in India are sometimes said to be actual or potential kinship units, or it has been said that, although economic ties cut across caste lines, kinship relations exist only within a caste (Karve, 1961, p. 17). These statements apply fairly well to caste as it conventionally operates in both countries, but do not take account of special circumstances. In India hypergamous intercaste unions are exceptions to this generalization, since in such cases a child's matrilineal kinsmen are of a different caste than his patrilineal kinsmen.

Another Indian exception is exemplified by the case of an Havik widow who was outcasted after giving birth to an illegitimate child and was thus without caste affiliation herself. Her illegitimate child, however, entered the Maleru caste (which might be described as a degraded Brahman caste, composed solely of illegitimate children born to Havik widows and their descendants). Her legitimate children and natal kinsmen remained Haviks.

There are few comparable situations in the United States. One possible example is the fact that according to the constitution of South Carolina, an individual whose ancestry is one-eighth or less Negro is legally white (Berry, 1963, p. 119). To take the hypothetical example of an ego whose mother was "clear white" and whose father was one-eighth Negro and legally white, it would then be possible for ego's father's father, say, to be three-fourths white, and thus legally Negro. Nevertheless, I seriously doubt if local community norms for assigning caste affiliation would agree with this legalistic approach.

Other examples, although probably found only in the northern United States, involve half-siblings. For instance, a couple of one caste could adopt children of both castes, or a person of one caste could marry a person of the other caste and have children, but subsequently marry a person of his own caste and produce more children.

SOCIAL MOBILITY

Although the caste systems in both societies have been accompanied by an ideology that caste rank is immutable and a philosophy that harmony and justice result from acceptance of the ideal-type system, nevertheless attempts at upward social mobility have been a persistent feature of both societies. Upward social mobility may be attempted by a caste, a family, or an individual. The type of social mobility most often encountered in India is for the whole caste, or a segment of a caste, to claim higher rank than they had been previously accorded and to justify this claim by creating a mythology that the rank they aspire to was theirs in the distant past and they are merely attempting to recapture what is rightfully theirs (for example, Rowe, in press). At the same time they also manipulate religious and cultural symbols which they identify as connoting a higher-status way of life in order to validate ritually their pretended rank (Srinivas, 1955). Although much more frequently attempted than achieved, social mobility of a whole caste is possible over several generations, but, as many social analysts have pointed out, this strategy does not seem to be successful unless the caste also effects a rise in its economic status (for example, Gould, 1961; Pocock, 1957; Srinivas, 1955).

Caste mobility movements in the United States have been of a much more revolutionary nature in that they have attacked the caste system itself; their aim has been the total destruction of caste in favor of a merging of the separate class systems within each caste. Negroes in the United States do not generally attempt to "Sanskritize" their caste customs by emulating those of the higher caste, although they do attempt, as do whites, to appropriate the symbols of the higher *classes* they aspire to enter. When castes in India attempt to be socially mobile, they, in effect, support the system of caste but question their place in its hierarchy. In India, the rationale used to legitimize the desired change in the system of stratification is based upon the traditional philosophy that supports societal unity through caste separateness and caste inequality, while in the United States the revolutionary philosophy is drawn from the ideology of democracy and egalitarianism which lauds rewarding individual achievement without consideration of ascribed statuses. In India the aim of a caste's social mobility movement is to surpass in the hierarchy some previously higher caste or castes; in the United States the aim is to gain equality by doing away with caste distinctions.[8]

Both systems of caste have recently been under direct and persistent attack by the governments of the respective countries. These legislative bodies have attempted to undermine the principle of caste by doing away with privileges ascribed solely by caste. But in India this legal action does not have the same mass support as in the United States and is certainly not the aim of the majority of members of even the lower castes living in rural areas.

In the best oiled social systems there are bound to be some flaws. Although both caste systems assign membership at birth, it is possible in both societies for an adult to make good a claim of false caste identity. When upward individual caste mobility takes place in either country, the means must be illegitimate. Downward individual caste mobility, in the form of outcasting or joining a lower caste, can be legitimate in India, while in the United States it is always illegitimate, but neither heavily punished nor easily detected.

"Passing" in the United States is open to those who are socially defined as Negroes but who do not exhibit physical features which identify them as belonging to that status group. To pass permanently, the individual must move from the community in which he is known. Those who fulfill both these requirements— physical indistinguishability and altered residence—can then make the choice of being Negro or white. Although passing is generally accompanied by stress and

8. This does not apply to the Black Muslims, whose goal is to gain equality through separateness. The Black Muslim philosophy appears to be a reaction to the failure to obtain this end by conventional means.

insecurity from having to reject kin and kith, partially or fully, and from the fear of being detected, the rewards are evidently sufficiently great to motivate many Negroes to become white. Although social class affiliation does not have to be changed, a fair amount of learning of a new subculture—a new "life style" (Frazier, 1957; Davis, Gardner, and Gardner, 1941), new ways of raising children (Davis and Havighurst, 1953), a new type of family structure (Frazier, 1939), as well as new forms of speech (Pederson, 1964) and new meanings for a common English vocabulary (Barth, 1961)—must take place. Nevertheless, it is quite possible that the amount of change is no more, and possibly less, than that which many socially mobile whites and Negroes undergo when they change their class affiliation. But given the nature of American society, the stranger who enters a new social group and learns the new subcultural patterns has a good chance of starting a new life and even obtaining a spouse from the caste which he illegitimately entered.

Passing in India is open to nearly everyone in the sense that caste affiliation is not readily visible in physical features, and yet it is probably less frequent than in the United States. The difficulty in passing derives not from denying membership in one's birthright caste but from making good one's claim to belong to a caste of which one is not legitimately a member.

In the Malnad some artisans and unskilled laborers from other regions, regions which contain locally unknown castes, often temporarily, sometimes permanently, reside in a Malnad village. The ties these individuals have to indigenous members of the community tend to be economic rather than social. The caste status of these outsiders is considered by village members to be relatively unimportant, and any reasonable caste affiliation claimed by them may go unquestioned. Should they be outcastes, children of illegitimate intercaste unions, or even Untouchables claiming to be something else, their marginal position in the village would make this fact somewhat irrelevant. They could reside in the village without being a threat to the local standards of intercaste morality. The farther away they were from their home region, the less likely would it be that their trickery would be detected and that they would be treated in a significantly different manner should it become known. Attempts to establish intimate social relations, commensal or marital, would be rejected under any circumstances. The same ease of passing in this way would probably be true in urban centers. But in either case the price is social isolation—the same price as is paid by many Indians who make no pretense about their background but who leave their local area in search of employment.

Untouchables who move into the white collar sector of the urban Indian society are more likely to try to hide their caste identity, to attempt to treat the question as if it were irrelevant, than to claim a false caste affiliation (Isaacs, 1965). This is quite the opposite of passing in the United States, where by hiding their ancestry Negroes almost automatically claim to be white. Practical considerations rather than a morality against deceit probably explain these varying modes of coping with similar problems, for should an Untouchable employed in a business or government bureaucracy meet a legitimate member of the caste (*jāti*) in which he falsely claimed membership, a not unlikely event, he would be all too easily exposed.

Passing in India would, as in the United States, mean breaking ties with kin and kith, but it would mean doing so in a society where social support from kinsmen and fellow castemen is customary, and where new intimate social relations with neighbors and associates who are not also fellow castemen are more difficult for adults to form; in other words, the price might well be higher than in the United States, where supportive social ties sometimes are fairly easily formed in a new community. In India it is unlikely that the claim of the passing individual to be a member of a specific caste not legitimately his would be accepted without question, and his chance of marrying or finding spouses for his children in a falsely claimed caste is remote.

Both societies contain individuals who believe in the irrelevancy of caste. These people, who belong to social circles which now have political influence, reject the ideology backing up their societies' caste systems; they function in a social world in which intercaste marriages are possible, and their ethos does not see caste distinctions as a proper way for sorting human beings into groups of differing worth.

RELIGION

The caste system in India is sometimes said to be comprehensible only when viewed against the religious matrix of Hinduism. If this is taken to mean that the Indian caste system could not develop or operate without its philosophical or religious props, several difficulties arise. First, such a view does not explain the existence of essentially similar systems of stratification within non-Hindu groups on the Indian subcontinent; this difficulty, however, could probably be resolved by demonstrating that those beliefs of Hindus most relevant to the caste system are also held, to some degree, by similarly stratified non-Hindu groups, such as Christians and Muslims.

Second, and of far greater importance, is the question of which came first, the caste system or the philosophical principles upon which it is based. I must admit I am among those who assume that a society's philosophical justifications for an explanation of its social institutions are more likely to be formulated as rationalizations of self-interest than to be developed first by pure philosophers and then to influence the form that the society's social institutions take. Certain aspects of Hinduism most certainly do support a caste system, but other strands of Hindu philosophy can be used equally well to negate the institution, just as in the United States Christian doctrines have been used both to justify and to condemn the caste system. To say that caste in India rests upon and has developed out of religion is to be one-sided if not fallacious; but it approximates the truth to say that a religio-philosophical rationale develops around any important social institution and that this rationale in turn becomes a revered or sacred doctrine which is then interpreted by self-interest groups to support their desires to effect or to prevent social change.

CONCLUSIONS

Although the systems of caste in the United States and in India are similar in a great many respects, in two features—the importance of "race" and the number of castes which compose the respective systems—they differ fundamentally, and from these differences others follow.

Both countries have rules for affiliating the newly born to a caste. Various castes in India have matrilineal or patrilineal descent groups and thus have available to them principles of descent for ascribing caste affiliation not possible in the bilateral kinship system of the United States. "Race" is more relevant to caste in the United States than in India, and in the United States race may give silent physical evidence that allows sociological principles of caste ascription to be used with more precision than would otherwise be possible. But in the United States caste is not solely "race," as is most clearly exemplified by the fact that a member of the Negro caste may have members of the white caste as his actual genitor and genitrix, so long as his presumed genitor is Negro, as in

Multiple castes make possible (but do not determine) the occupational specificity of caste in India; the dual caste system of the United States precludes the development of a system in which hereditary occupational specialization takes place along caste lines. The multicaste system allows castes (*jāti*) to be small and localized and thus to have a greater degree of uniformity of customs within a caste than would be likely in a dual-caste system. A dual-caste system in a large-scale society facilitates the differentiation of social classes within the castes. The existence of small and somewhat homogeneous castes in India helps to prevent an individual from making good a falsely claimed caste identity, since proof of caste affiliation through kinship ties or mutual acquaintance is generally a prerequisite to full acceptance as a caste member or to a marriage alliance.

In both countries there are small localized caste-segments within which effective methods of social control exist and from which an individual may gain most of his social succor. Once an individual in the United States leaves the local community in which his social history is known, he does not have to prove membership in order to move into another localized and socially supportive segment of his caste or into that area of American society which is more impersonal and where intimate social support is less crucial to his welfare. This is not true of a society predominantly composed of "enforceably exclusive" small groups, each within a caste which has boundaries that close it effectively to illegitimate entrance. In this latter type of system, social boycott and outcasting become severe forms of punishment. It is precisely because these forms of punishment are so effective in Hindu society that they are used so judiciously; individuals are motivated to punish in less drastic ways breaches of rules by their kinsmen, friends, neighbors, and fellow castemen. When caste members feel that some rules are so important to their caste honor that the violation of those rules must be punished by complete ostracism, their only choices are either to mete out such punishment or formally to ignore the informally known facts and declare the defendant innocent. Outcasting in the United States would not have the same effectiveness, as those social needs that are met often only within a localized exclusive segment of a caste in India are in the United States generally met by other similar but nonexclusive social segments of a caste. This also explains why in the United States circumstances do not arise which would make it necessary for adults legitimately to change their caste affiliation and why such a change is possible in India.

In the United States the lack of numerous small bounded strata within which social relationships are personalized means that other methods, such as the presumed correlation between caste and "race," have to be employed to prevent illegitimate changes in caste affiliation. Also, distinctive physical features that usually identify caste membership make more effective the enforcement of prescriptive and proscriptive rules regulating intercaste interaction and social distance when individuals move outside the local region in which they are personally known than is possible within an Indian social class in an urban setting.

Perhaps the simplest manner in which caste may be defined so as to be applicable to both the United States and India is to say that it is a type of social stratification system in which all members of a society, regardless of age, sex, lineage, education, wealth, or political position, are clearly assigned to one or another bounded social stratum, initially through rules of descent. "Bounded" refers to a system in which each individual must belong to one and to only one such group. "Clearly assigned" means that there must exist a cultural rule that caste membership is based upon a "this-or-that" principle—individuals must classify themselves as do other members of the society who know their social history. Social stratification implies a hierarchy and specifies that at the minimum the society must be divided into two groups. By stating that caste affiliation is initially assigned through rules of descent we imply that some change, legitimate (India) or illegitimate (India and the United States), in caste membership may be made after original assignment.

The most widely used mechanism for maintaining caste boundaries, and the one most characteristic of India and the United States, is a prescriptive rule which confines marriage to partners from within the caste. A rule of preferential endogamy would not distinguish castes from social classes and ethnic groups. However, endogamy itself is not always prescribed in a caste system; instead, rules may exist, as in parts of India, that allow intercaste marriages to take place with certain specified other castes, under certain conditions, as in the case of hypergamy.

For caste boundaries to be maintained there must exist rules for status group assignment of any individual born into the society, whether or not the particular union which brought him into existence was in accord with or in defiance of the society's prescribed marriage rules. How then are these rules enforced when members of one caste have frequent contact with those who may or may not belong to their own caste?

It is doubtful if a simple "ethic of casteism," internally inculcated in the individual, would be sufficient to maintain boundaries around all castes in a society which is sufficiently large and complex so that every individual does not personally know every other individual and cannot easily find out the social history of any person with whom he has social contact during the course of a normal life. Even if an "ethic of casteism" were combined with a system in which each caste maintained its cultural identity by having distinctive customs, dress, and dialect, it is doubtful if this would be sufficient to maintain caste boundaries, especially if the rewards of belonging to a higher caste were great enough to motivate those who belonged to a lower caste to attempt to be upwardly mobile. The end result would probably be ethnic groups in a plural society, or a social class system, in which boundaries were imperfectly maintained over any length of time.

One method for maintaining boundaries is to base caste identity upon physical features. This method can be used in large, complex, and anonymous societies (but only in those which have the additional prerequisite of being divided into two or more physically identifiable groups). In this event, there need not be cultural differences between castes, as every stranger's caste is, in theory, identifiable, and appropriate intercaste and intracaste behavior can be brought into play in each interactional situation. In the long run such a caste system is inherently unstable, as the inevitable licit or illicit gene-flow from one caste to another undermines its foundation by producing some individuals whose caste affiliation cannot be accurately determined by their physical features, as may have happened in ancient India. A sufficient amount of genetic mixing would, *ipso facto*, make impossible the perpetuation of a caste system based solely upon "race."

Finally, if neither physical features nor cultural uniqueness are available to identify a stranger's caste affiliation in a complex society, the only other practical means for maintaining caste boundaries is to trace ties through kinsmen and known fellow caste members. Such a caste system is facilitated by dividing the society into a proportionately large number of small castes, as happens in many parts of India, but this is not a prerequisite for its continuance. In a complex society in which many social and/or economic contacts take place with individuals whose claimed caste cannot be readily substantiated, each caste must make a distinction between inviolable norms of intercaste behavior and secondary norms, creating a system such that if the secondary norms are broken the consequences are not irreparable, and such that there is little or no chance of anyone's breaking the primary ones. Inviolable norms must include those that deal directly with the maintenance of caste boundaries—rules of marriage and principles of descent. For these to operate efficiently in a large-scale society, individuals need to be able to determine with assurance, through kinship and friendship, that any individual with whom a marriage alliance is contemplated is of the appropriate caste. In such a system, boundaries are maintained by members of each caste checking the references of proposed mates for their members and excluding those whose caste is deemed to be lower than their own.

BIBLIOGRAPHY

BAILEY, FREDERICK G.
1963. Closed social stratification in India. *European Journal of Sociology*, 4(1): 107–124.

BARTH, ERNEST A. T.
1961. The language behavior of Negroes and whites. *Pacific Sociological Review*, 4(2): 69–72.

BARTH, FREDRIK.
1960. The system of social stratification in Swat, North Pakistan. In E. R. Leach (Ed.), *Aspects of caste in South India, Ceylon and North-west Pakistan*. Cambridge Papers in Social Anthropology, 2: 113–46.

BERREMAN, GERALD D.
1960. Caste in India and the United States. *American Journal of Sociology*, 66(2): 120–27.

BERRY, BREWTON.
1963. *Almost white—a study of certain racial hybrids in the Eastern United States*. New York: Macmillan.

COHN, BERNARD S.
1955. The changing status of a depressed caste. In McK. Marriott (Ed.), *Village India—studies in the little community*. Chicago: University of Chicago Press.

1959. Some notes on law and change in North India. *Economic Development and Cultural Change*, 8(1): 79–93.

DAVIS, ALLISON.
1945. Caste, economy and violence. *American Journal of Sociology*, 51(1): 7–15.

DAVIS, ALLISON, BURLEIGH B. GARDNER, and MARY R. GARDNER.
1941. *Deep South*. Chicago: University of Chicago Press.

DAVIS, ALLISON, and ROBERT J. HAVIGHURST.
1953. Social class and color differences in child-rearing. In Clyde Kluckhohn, Henry A. Murray, and David M. Schneider (Eds.), *Personality in nature, society and culture*. New York: Alfred A. Knopf.

DRUCKER, PHILIP.
1939. Rank, wealth and kinship in northwest coast society. *American Anthropologist*, 41(1): 55–65.

DUMONT, LOUIS.
1961. Caste, racism, and "stratification": Reflections of a social anthropologist. *Contributions to Indian Sociology*, 5: 20–43.

FRAZIER, E. FRANKLIN.
1939. *The Negro family in the United States*. Chicago: University of Chicago Press.

1957. *Black bourgeoisie*. Glencoe, Ill.: The Free Press.

FUCHS, STEPHEN.
1950. *The children of Hari*. Vienna: Verlag Herold.

GOUGH, KATHLEEN.
1962. Nayar: central Kerala. In David M. Schneider and Kathleen Gough (Eds.), *Matrilineal Kinship*. Berkeley: University of California Press.

GOULD, HAROLD A.
1961. Sanskritization and westernization: A dynamic view. *Economic Weekly*, 13(25): 945–51.

HARPER, EDWARD B.

1964. Ritual pollution as an integrator of caste and religion. In Edward B. Harper (Ed.), *Religion in South Asia*. Seattle: University of Washington Press.

In press. Social consequences of an "unsuccessful" low caste movement. In James Silverberg (Ed.), *Social mobility in the caste system of India*. Comparative Studies in Society and History, supplement 3.

ISAACS, HAROLD R.

1965. *India's ex-untouchables*. New York: John Day.

KARVE, IRAWATI.

1961. *Hindu society—an interpretation*. Poona: Deccan College.

KLUCKHOHN, CLYDE, and HENRY A. MURRAY.

1949. Personality formation: The determinants. In Clyde Kluckhohn and Henry A. Murray (Eds.), *Personality in nature, society, and culture*. New York: Alfred A. Knopf.

MORRIS, MORRIS DAVID.

1960. Caste and the evolution of the industrial workforce in India. *Proceedings of the American Philosophical Society*, 104(2): 124–33.

1965. *The emergence of an industrial labor force in India—A study of the Bombay cotton mills, 1854–1947*. Berkeley: University of California Press.

PATTERSON, MAUREEN L. P.

1958. Intercaste marriage in Maharashtra. *Economic Weekly*, 10(4, 5, 6): 139–42.

PEDERSON, LEE A.

1964. Non-standard Negro speech in Chicago. In William A. Stewart (Ed.), *Non-standard speech and the teaching of English*. Center for Applied Linguistics, Language Information Series, 2: 16–24.

POCOCK, DAVID F.

1957. Inclusion and exclusion: A process in the caste system of Gujerat. *Southwestern Journal of Anthropology*, 13(1): 19–31.

ROWE, WILLIAM L.

In press. The new Cauhāns: A caste mobility movement in North India. In James Silverberg (Ed.), *Social mobility in the caste system of India*. Comparative Studies in Society and History, supplement 3.

SRINIVAS, M. N.

1955. A note on Sanskritization and Westernization. *Far Eastern Quarterly*, 15(4): 481–96.

STEVENSON, H. N. C.

1954. Status evaluation in the Hindu caste system. *Journal of the Royal Anthropological Society*, 84: 45–65.

WEBER, MAX.

1958. *The religion of India*. Translated and edited by Hans H. Gerth and Don Martindale. Glencoe, Ill.: The Free Press.

WILLIAMS, ROBIN M., JR.

1951. *American society—a sociological interpretation*. New York: Alfred A. Knopf.

PART II:

The Structure
of Intercaste Relations

4. CASTE REGIONS OF THE NORTH INDIAN PLAIN

JOSEPH E. SCHWARTZBERG

INTRODUCTION

THIS PAPER PRESENTS what is probably the first attempt at regionalization of the pattern of caste for any large area of India. The specific area chosen is the North Indian Plain, that is, the continuous belt of Indo-Gangetic· alluvium within the present-day Republic of India, extending from the West Pakistan border 1,000 miles eastward to the border of East Pakistan and the Bay of Bengal. This area, with a 1961 population of around 155 million, was studied in detail both in the field and on the basis of the data of the census of 1931, the last Indian census to deal comprehensively with the subject of caste. The first part of this paper explains and illustrates some key variables associated with caste which were considered in the regionalization process and which are regarded as important in and of themselves. The section following is primarily descriptive, characterizing the several caste regions and subregions into which the study area has been divided. In a brief concluding section the utility and limitations of the study are indicated.

Figures 1 and 2 depict the study area. Figure 1 indicates the component traditional regions, more or less indefinite in extent, but generally recognized by the population on the basis of shared history and culture or, in some instances, physical distinctiveness (for example, the Sundarbans or the Terai). Figure 2 portrays the precisely delimited administrative sub-units—provinces, districts, and princely states—as they existed at the time of the 1931 census. With rather few exceptions, the districts portrayed on this map retain essentially the same borders today as they had in 1931.[1]

In studying the 1931 census the population of all castes and tribes comprising over one per cent of the total population of any district or princely state was computed as a percentage of the total population of that district or state. These castes and tribes were then rank-ordered by population and graphs were prepared for each district or princely state showing the ten most numerous castes in rank order (Figs. 3a-f).[2] For 27 of the most numerous castes or tribes of the North

---

1. The 1961 census, among other sources, provides maps showing contemporary boundaries for those who wish to compare the present situation with that of 1931. The princely states of 1931 no longer exist, of course; but their extent within the study area was exceedingly limited, except in Punjab. In any case, correlation of their former extent with the areas of present-day districts is not difficult.

2. In some cases to reach the figure of ten, it was necessary to calculate percentages for castes with less than 1 per cent of the population.

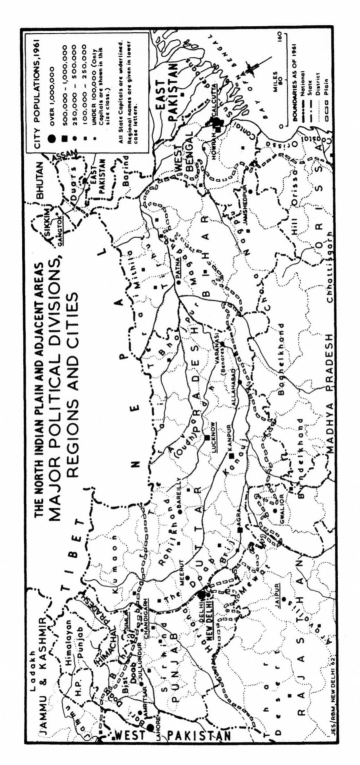

FIGURE 1

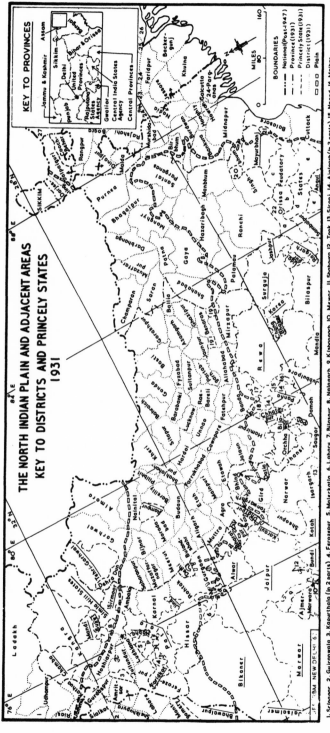

THE NORTH INDIAN PLAIN AND ADJACENT AREAS
KEY TO DISTRICTS AND PRINCELY STATES
1931

KEY TO PROVINCES

BOUNDARIES
—··—··— National(Post-1947)
————— Province (1931)
— — — Princely State(1931)
·········· District (1931)
▭ Plain

1. Srinagar 2. Gujranwala 3. Kapurthala (in 2 parts) 4. Ferozepur 5. Malerkotla 6. Loharu 7. Bilaspur 8. Nalagarh 9. Kishangarh 10. Mewar 11. Shahpura 12. Tonk 13. Sironj 14. Ajaigarh (in 2 parts) 15. Nagod 16. Maihar 17. Rest of Baghelkhand Agency 18. Rest of Bundelkhand Agency 19. Benaras (in 2 parts) 20. Saraikela & Kharswan(Chhota Nagpur States) 21. Niligiri 22. Orissa Feudatory States— a. Gangpur b. Bonai c. Keonjhar d. Bamra
e. Congeries of petty states (in 2 parts) 23. Pabna 24. Dacca 25. Tippera 26. Noakhali 27. Goalpara

J– Part of Jind   P– Part of Patiala   N– Part of Nabha   (PRINCELY STATES ARE UNDERLINED)

FIGURE 2

83

Indian Plain, maps were prepared showing, by district or state, what percentage they represented of the total population. For eleven of these, additional maps were made showing their rank by population among all castes and tribes of the respective districts or states.[3]

My field work was conducted in the academic years 1958–59 and 1962–63. In the former year the work was concentrated in, but not limited to, the North Indian Plain. Of 198 villages visited that year, 105 were in six study areas within the broad area of the present study. The focus of the research in 1958–59 was not on caste but on regional variations in the occupational structure of India. It was, however, obvious that the role of caste was a vital consideration in any such study and, from the beginning, systematic inquiries were made as to the caste structure of the villages visited. In 1962–63, the research focus was definitely on caste. Unlike the previous year's choice of areas, the selection of regions selected for study was primarily on the basis of their caste composition, as revealed by the study of the 1931 census. Duplication of previous coverage was, however, avoided. To obtain a more comprehensive coverage of the North Indian Plain, to which field work was then confined, the number of sample study areas was increased to seventeen; consequently, the number of villages visited per area was greatly reduced. The total number of villages surveyed was 121, making a grand total for the two years of 226 within the overall study area.[4]

In the field, sample villages were selected more or less at random, generally at three- to seven-mile intervals within any study area. An attempt was, however, made to include within the sample some villages close to large urban centers and some relatively remote from such centers (in some study areas this question did not arise, as no large urban center existed), some villages on or very near main

3. Examples of percentage and rank distribution maps are provided for ten castes in an earlier work of mine (1965, pp. 477–95, and folded map plate). The castes treated are Brahman, Rajput, Jat, Kurmi, Lodh, Ahir, Sheikh, Chamar, Pasi, and Nai (there was no rank map for the Nais). Together these castes comprised roughly 45 per cent of the total population of the study area in 1931. The figure would be somewhat higher today because of population changes attending the partition of India. It is desirable that the maps, graphs, and tables in that article be consulted in reading the article in hand. Reprints may be obtained from the author. The additional castes I have mapped but not treated in the article cited include: Baniya, Barhai, Bhangi, Dhobi, Dusadh, Gujar, Julaha, Kahar, Kayastha, Kewat, Kori, Kumhar, Lohar, Mahishya, Pathan, Santal (tribe), and Teli. The 27 castes named include all those which had over 1.25 million population within the study area in 1931 and together constitute roughly three-fourths of its total population.

While my study of the census data was primarily for the year 1931, supplementary data for the years 1881, 1921, and 1961 were consulted and partially mapped. The 1881 data were taken from the handy single volume by Kitts (1885). Nineteen of the most important castes were mapped on the basis of data in this volume. (The degree of stability in caste distributions between 1881 and 1931, as revealed by the maps made, is, on the whole, remarkable; but the pace of change has undoubtedly increased since 1931.) The 1921 data consulted related only to certain Muslim castes in Bengal, Bihar, and Orissa, since 1931 data for these groups are far from complete in these areas. The 1961 data consulted and mapped relate to "scheduled castes" and "scheduled tribes" only.

4. The precise distribution of the areas of field research in both years of study and the number of villages visited in each area is indicated in my map, "Areas of Field Work," (1965, map plate). By states, the number of villages studied and (in parentheses) the number of field areas are as follows: Rajasthan (Ganganagar District only), 5 (1); Punjab 47 (4); Delhi and environs (not counted in Punjab and U.P. totals), 9 (1); Uttar Pradesh, 97 (8); Bihar, 32 (4); and West Bengal, 36 (5).

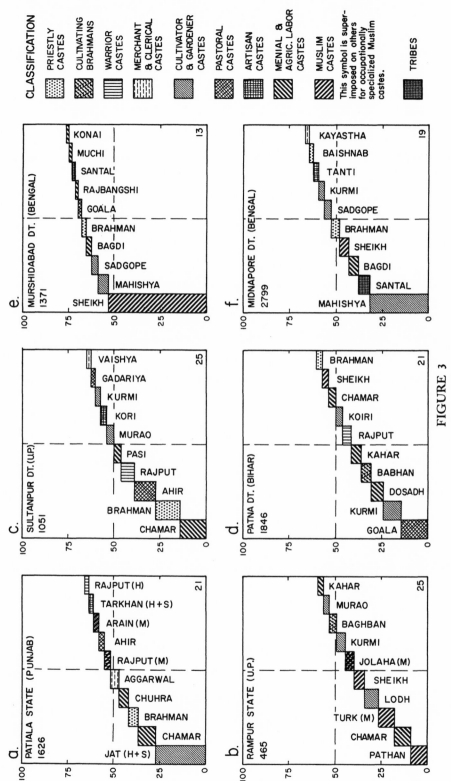

FIGURE 3

Size, Rank Order, and Nature of the Ten Most Populous Castes or Tribes with over 1.0% of the population. The castes are arranged or Tribes of Six Representative Districts or Princely States of the in rank order from left to right. The height of the bar representing North Indian Plain, 1931. The district or state names appear in each caste is proportional to its percentage to the total population. the upper left corner of each graph along with the 1931 population The figures at left relate to cumulative percentages. in thousands. In the lower right corner is the total number of castes roads and some relatively remote from such roads, some large and some small, some up on the doabs (interfluves), and some down in the flood plain (where applicable). Thus, while no claim can be made that the samples are truly representative in any statistical sense, it is probable that they are, for the most part, free from pronounced bias.

Figure 4 shows by way of example the area of field work in Central Uttar Pradesh (in November and December, 1958) and the distribution of the 48 villages surveyed therein, by far the largest sample of any area studied. The villages are indicated by circles scaled in proportion to the village population (in number of households). The key number of each village and a letter representing a subjective evaluation of its relative state of economic development are indicated in bold type. Below are indicated the number of households, the number of castes, the number of households in the principal castes, etc.[5]

The time spent in each of the villages surveyed was, in keeping with the nature of the investigation, rather short. The time actually spent in interviewing ranged from only around a half hour, in an exceedingly simple and small village of seventeen households, to nearly eight hours in another. All interviews were conducted through an interpreter.[6] The average interview lasted nearly three hours. Interviews were most commonly conducted with the village headman. Otherwise, some other prominent individual, usually a member of the panchayat, or the village patwari or schoolteacher, was selected. More often than not, prominent or knowledgeable members of various castes and the remarkably well-informed village chokidar were present, often being summoned expressly to aid in the interview. Their presence and assistance generally enhanced the accuracy and completeness of the responses. In a few large or dispersed villages the information sought was obtained by interviews conducted separately in different wards or hamlets. In general, the cooperation of the villagers was exceedingly gratifying, though in 1962–63 the disturbances on India's northern borders occasionally caused an attitude of suspicion which was not so apparent in 1958–59. Recalcitrance, however, was usually dispelled on presentation of an official letter soliciting cooperation signed by Asok Mitra, the Registrar General, India, and/or by assurances that we wished to know nobody's name, that we would not inquire about amounts of land owned, that we had no connection with the revenue authorities, and that after completing the interview we would have no cause to revisit the village. The total time spent in a village averaged less than a day.[7]

The interviews followed a standard format in both years of field work. A two-

5. A full explanation is provided on a master legend sheet for this and comparable maps of areas of field study in 1958–59, in my doctoral dissertation (1960).

6. A single interpreter (himself a villager and already experienced in village survey work conducted under the aegis of the Delhi School of Economics) was used throughout the North Indian Plain in 1958–59 and for all areas except Bengal in 1962–63. While he was fluent in Hindi and Punjabi, his Bengali was poor, and the data for the sample of five villages studied near Calcutta in the former year are, consequently, of little worth. A native Bengali interpreter was used for all work conducted in Bengal in 1962–63.

7. Nights were usually spent in some nearby city or town or in rurally situated government rest houses and only rarely in the villages surveyed. The pattern varied greatly with the areas and the available means of transport: mainly by bicycle in 1958–59, mainly by motor scooter in 1962–63. Travel between sample areas was by train, bus, or motor scooter.

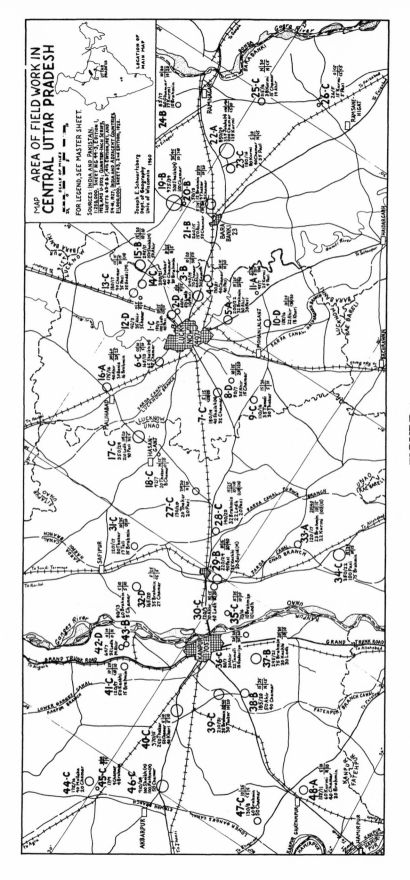

FIGURE 4

page printed schedule was used in 1958–59 and a six-page schedule in 1962–63, with additional pages appended in the relatively few cases of unusually complex villages. The questions asked sought, first, to learn something about the village in general (for example, available amenities, crops grown, and relationship to market towns), then to learn the number of households in each caste, and, finally, caste by caste, to learn something of the land tenure status, the occupations followed, adherence to the jajmani system, and ties beyond the village.[8] Subsequent to each interview a subjective reliability rating, ranging from "excellent" to "poor" was assigned.[9]

Two carefully considered decisions determined the field method outlined above. First, it was decided to sacrifice depth for breadth of coverage. While those anthropologists and other fieldworkers willing to devote a year or two of their lives to the study of a single village deserve great admiration, there is an equally great, and all too often unrecognized, need for the study, through sampling, of the broad regional contexts within which villages exist, and for comparative studies among regions. Given the first decision and the paucity of scholars willing and able to carry on broad-based regional research, it seemed advisable also, in this initial period of systematic work on the social and cultural geography of India, to sacrifice a measure of rigor and even of accuracy for speed. In both cases I am convinced that the gains derived from these two basic decisions far outweighed the sacrifices involved. What were sought, essentially, were ensembles of regional data sufficiently representative of reality to permit interregional comparisons and generalizations of the sort made in this essay. Judging from such limited comparisons of field and census data as are possible and from conversations and correspondence with knowledgeable individuals, it is felt that the stated ends were generally obtained.

SIGNIFICANT VARIABLES

The number of variables—of kind and of degree—which have potential utility in the study and delimitation of caste regions is quite large, and choices of those which are most significant are bound to be more or less arbitrary. Moreover, variables which appear to be of general significance may, in particular instances, turn out to be either unimportant or irrelevant. This makes the framing of a strictly logical scheme of classification exceedingly difficult, and no claim is made that the tentative regionalization of the area of the North Indian Plain presented in this study conforms, as regionalizations ideally should, to the canons of classifi-

8. The much longer schedule in 1962–63 is explained by (a) a greater number of questions being asked, particularly in regard to the village as a whole; (b) the inclusion of space for a rough sketch map of the village (made on conclusion of the interview, usually by memory, after a guided walk throughout the village); (c) a more generous space allowance for answers; and (d) the inclusion of a tabular form for summarization of results.

9. "Excellent" was assigned in 45 cases, "very good" in 75, "good" in 72, "fair" in 21, and "poor" in only 11, including 4 of the 5 villages studied in the environs of Calcutta (see note 6). An "excellent" interview, it is felt, should be of a reliability comparable to that of the census itself; "very good" signifies that accuracy is generally within a range of 5 per cent to 10 per cent, "good" within 10 per cent to 15 per cent, "fair" within 15 per cent to 25 per cent, and "poor" commonly worse than 25 per cent. These, of course, are only estimates. There is no way to verify them short of detailed resurvey.

cation laid down by formal logic.[10] The variables used were not assigned particular weights or priorities and were not all consciously considered for each of the regions and subregions portrayed. Nevertheless, it may be well, prior to presenting the map of caste regions, to itemize and discuss those factors which were considered significant.

Possibly no single variable is quite as important in determining the character of a caste region, over much of India, as is the specific dominant caste in these areas where one may be said to exist. Related to this variable of kind is another of degree, that is, the degree of dominance of a particular caste in a particular area. In discussing the phenomenon of the dominant caste, the functional aspect of Srinivas' definition is generally followed. The dominant caste is taken to be one which "wields predominant economic and political power." In practice, as Srinivas correctly observes, "A large and powerful caste group can more easily be dominant if its position in the local caste hierarchy is not too low" (1955a, pp. 17–18).[11]

Unfortunately, the dominant caste of a given area cannot be determined with certainty from numbers alone (see note 11). This will be apparent from Figure 5, which shows for each of the districts and princely states of and around the study area the most numerous caste or tribe in 1931. It will be seen that there are a large number of districts of Uttar Pradesh where the formerly untouchable, now "scheduled," caste of Chamars were (and still are) the most numerous group, as they were, in fact, in the state as a whole. But nowhere, it is safe to assume, are they considered the dominant caste. Nevertheless, using the data of the census in combination with that derived from field sampling and a general knowledge of the caste system, one can frequently discern, or infer with reasonable confidence, the dominant caste of a region. This is not always the case, however; in some areas, most notably in Uttar Pradesh, the dominant caste of a given tract may not be at all clear if, in fact, there is a dominance transcending control at the individual village level.[12] It is noteworthy in this context that there are a number of districts

10. For a discussion of the logic of taxonomic classifications and of regionalization as an analogous process, see Grigg (1965). For more general discussions of the nature of regions and the problems of regionalization see Richard Hartshorne (1939), especially "The Concept of the Region as a Concrete Unit Object," pp. 250–85 (in which the notion implicit in the title is refuted) and "Methods of Organizing the World into Regions," pp. 285–364; Hartshorne (1959), especially "Is Geography Divided Between 'Systematic' and 'Regional' Geography?", pp. 108–45, and Whittlesey (1954).

11. In the same passage (pp. 17–18) Srinivas makes two additional points I reject on the basis of my field data and the findings presented in this article: "The concept of the dominant caste is important for understanding intercaste relationships in any [sic] local area . . . ," and "A caste may be said to be 'dominant' when it predominates numerically [sic] over the other castes . . ." In a later (1962) discussion of the concept, however, he abandons these two positions, noting that "dominant castes exist in many [sic] parts of India" and that "Traditionally, numerically small [sic] castes owning land in rural areas, or wielding political power, or inheriting a literary tradition were able to dominate the rural scene." (See also his introduction to *India's Villages*, 1955b, especially pp. 7–8; and his analysis of the functional attributes of a dominant caste, 1959, pp. 1–16.)

12. My maps of the distribution, by percentage and rank, of selected castes (1965, pp. 477–95) will help clarify this point with regard to areal dominance. With regard to dominance at the village level, the distribution graphs in the same article and Table 1 in this article will be instructive. Mayer (1958, pp. 407–427), distinguishes between village and regional dominance and shows how a numerically weak caste may become regionally dominant through its central position in an implicit multicaste alliance (pp. 418–19).

in and outside the North Indian Plain where the most numerous caste or tribe comprised only 10 per cent or less of the total population (for example, Rampur, 9 per cent). With regard to the existence of clear-cut regional dominance, the contrast between most of Uttar Pradesh, on the one hand, and most of East Punjab and Bengal, on the other, is striking. Bihar is in an intermediate position (see Fig. 3).

There is probably no empirical justification for a belief that a region will have but one dominant caste. Particularly in those districts or regions in which religious groups are intermixed or in which tribals form a large part of the population, there may well be a sort of dual or multiple dominance: one caste is dominant within the Hindu population, another among the Muslims, and so forth. Within the North Indian Plain, as defined for this study, areas of greater than usual community admixture in 1931 included the whole of Punjab (for which that situation no longer exists), Rohilkhand, in Western Uttar Pradesh, and virtually the whole of West Bengal. As Figure 5 shows, one or another Muslim caste was the largest single group not only in most of the districts of West Bengal but also in adjoining Purnea (Bihar), Rampur (U.P.), Delhi, and Kapurthala (Punjab).

In the areas just mentioned and in areas in which scheduled caste groups or, south of the plains, tribal groups were numerically the most important group, Figure 5 affords no clue as to the probable dominant caste within the community of "clean" caste Hindus. Figure 6, however, helps overcome this deficiency, insofar as the admittedly fallible criterion of numbers alone may be taken as a guide. (It will be noted that, for the purposes of this map, Hindus and Sikhs are treated as a single community.) An interesting picture emerges from this map, the broadening of the several areas of Hindu caste dominance already discernible from Figure 5, of the Brahman area in most of Uttar Pradesh, of the Mahishya area in West Bengal, and so forth. In general, the pattern has become much simpler than that of Figure 5 and in some ways more meaningful.

The degree of ramification of the caste system is a variable of considerable importance in comparative regional study. Despite its obvious social and political implications, this ramification does not appear to have received much attention in the literature.[13] A simple count of the number of castes represented in a given area or population is not, unfortunately, a reliable guide to caste ramification. Many districts contain representatives of literally hundreds of castes. But what is of importance is the number of castes which are present in significant numbers, that is, those that are recognized as entering corporately into the life of the local community. This, however, begs objective determination and could only be ascertained with some sense of confidence after protracted field work. A simple, objective, but not wholly satisfactory index of ramification, however, would be provided by the number of castes (or tribes) with over n per cent of the population of each district or other unit of study, n being taken as some arbitrary

13. A happy exception is provided by Marriott (1965). Marriott explicitly recognized the number of "ethnic groups," including both castes and tribes, as the first of four principal determinants of the "degree of elaboration" of hierarchical caste structure (pp. 3–4, 7, and *passim*) and provides an interesting graph of the number of local caste groups plotted against village population for an all-India sample of 151 villages (p. 23).

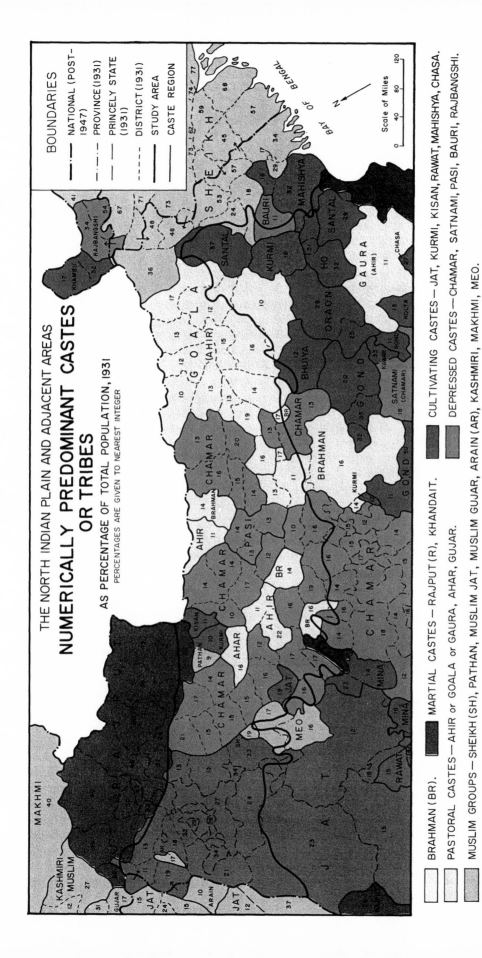

FIGURE 5

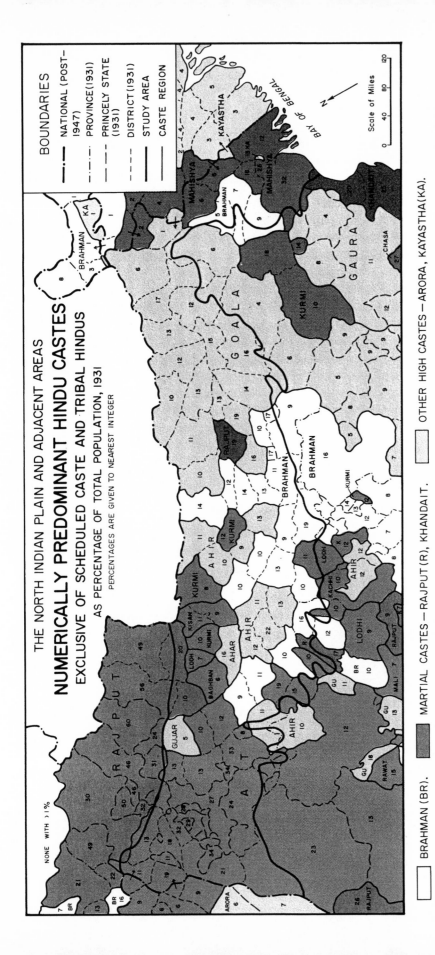

THE NORTH INDIAN PLAIN AND ADJACENT AREAS

NUMERICALLY PREDOMINANT HINDU CASTES

EXCLUSIVE OF SCHEDULED CASTE AND TRIBAL HINDUS

AS PERCENTAGE OF TOTAL POPULATION, 1931

PERCENTAGES ARE GIVEN TO NEAREST INTEGER

BOUNDARIES

NATIONAL (POST-1947)
PROVINCE (1931)
PRINCELY STATE (1931)
DISTRICT (1931)
STUDY AREA
CASTE REGION

BRAHMAN (BR).

MARTIAL CASTES — RAJPUT (R), KHANDAIT.

OTHER HIGH CASTES — ARORA, KAYASTHA (KA).

CULTIVATING CASTES — JAT, KURMI, LODH or LODHI, KISAN, BAGHBAN, RAWAT, KACHHI (K), MALI, MAHISHYA, CHASA.

PASTORAL CASTES — AHIR or GOALA or GAURA, AHAR, GUJAR (GU).

FIGURE 6

small number. Ideally, the study units should be standardized by area or population; but the available data render standardization difficult. If, however, one is willing to accept the district or princely state as a unit area (specific caste data are not available for smaller units) and n as 1, then Figure 7, depicting the number of castes or tribes with over 1 per cent of the total population in 1931, serves as a rough guide to the regional variations in the degree of ramification in the caste system. (In counting castes, Hindu and Muslim segments of a single caste, such as Jats or Rajputs, were counted separately, while Sikhs were counted as if they were Hindus.)

In Figure 7, the area of greatest ramification appears to be northwestern Uttar Pradesh (excluding the tribal zone in the Orissa Feudatory States, which are outside the study area), while within the plains portion of the present Republic of India, the tier of districts bordering what is today East Pakistan seems to be least ramified.[14] East Punjab, which appears, by and large, to be only slightly less ramified with regard to caste than Uttar Pradesh as of 1931, would today probably be shown to have an appreciably less ramified caste structure. While a large proportion of the emigrant Muslim population at the time of partition was in a wide variety of cultivating, artisan, menial, and other caste groups large enough to be counted in Figure 7, the Hindus and Sikhs who replaced them were drawn overwhelmingly from a few castes.

An alternative index of degree of ramification might be the average number of castes per village in a given area. But, as the average village size varies considerably from one part of India to another (in some areas of dispersed settlement, it is even difficult to ascertain just what the village is), the computation of such an index might entail considerable bias, since the larger the village the more castes, in general, it will contain. Thus it is possible that in a region of large villages, in which relatively few castes have over 1 per cent of the total population of a given district, a representative sample of villages might suggest a more ramified caste structure than in another area in which there were many small, dissimilar villages and many castes with over 1 per cent of the total district population. Meaningful comparisons, then, will have to be in terms of specific village-size categories. This necessitates a rather large sample of villages from which to draw data and leads not to a single index number but to a series of numbers, one for each size-category considered.

Figure 8 is relevant in the above context. It shows the rate of rise in the average number of castes per village with increasing village size for a sample of 48 villages in Central Uttar Pradesh (see Fig. 4 and Table 1) as against 33 for Punjab.[15] The size categories are even intervals as plotted on a semi-logarithmic

14. The fact that the map and the method are somewhat arbitrary is borne out by the case of Bijnor District in Rohilkhand, which had no fewer than eleven castes with a population of between 1.0 per cent and 1.5 per cent of the total. Had the cut-off point for counting the degree of ramification been 1.5 per cent rather than 1.0 per cent the relative standing of this and a number of other districts would presumably be significantly altered. Similarly, if the cut-off point were lowered, say to 0.75 per cent, comparable, but unpredictable, alterations would also be obtained.

15. A map of the villages in the Punjab sample is found in my dissertation (1960, map appendix, map 31). Descriptions of the caste structure of the two areas are on pp. 333–38 and 455–63 respectively.

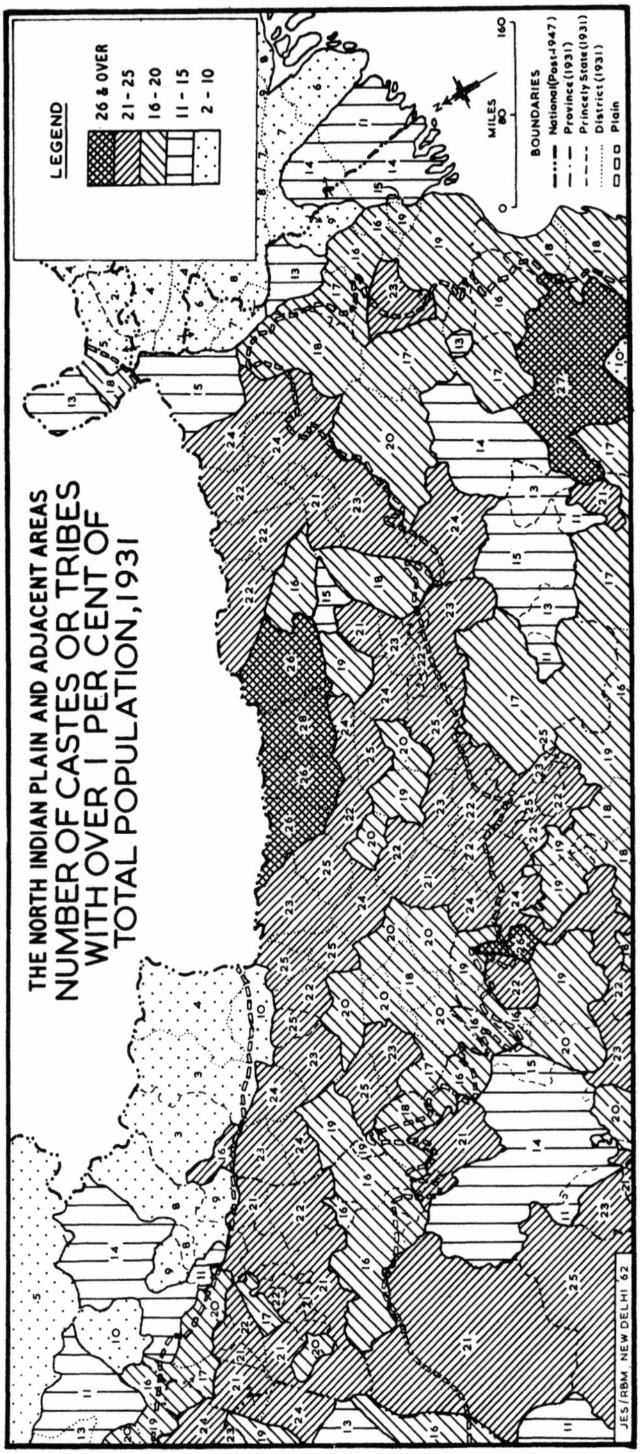

THE NORTH INDIAN PLAIN AND ADJACENT AREAS
NUMBER OF CASTES OR TRIBES
WITH OVER 1 PER CENT OF
TOTAL POPULATION, 1931

LEGEND

26 & OVER
21 - 25
16 - 20
11 - 15
2 - 10

BOUNDARIES
National (Post-1947)
Province (1931)
Princely State (1931)
District (1931)
Plain

MILES
0   80   160

JES/RBM NEW DELHI 62

FIGURE 7

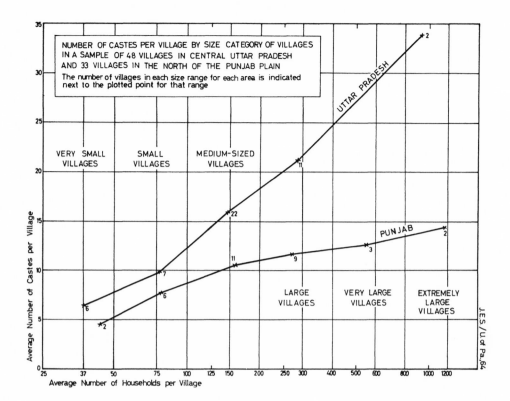

FIGURE 8

graph. There is, it will be noted, a significantly greater rate of increase in the former area than in the latter. On the basis of a still incomplete analysis of the available field data, it is felt that steep rates of increase are indicative of relative rural poverty while gentle rates betoken relative prosperity. The reason appears to be related to the persistent, if not absolute, determination of occupation along caste lines. Briefly, in the more prosperous areas, such as Punjab, even small villages can afford a relatively large number of such goods and services as are available in the general region, the provision of each of which is the traditional monopoly of a particular caste. Thus, one or a few households of a number of such specialized castes, finding a ready clientele at hand, are willing to remain in or, if need be, move to small but prosperous villages. Often, in fact, they are given considerable inducement to come. By contrast, in small villages in poor areas there would be little custom for many specialized castes and, as poverty forced a severance in the jajmani ties on the part of their patrons or as persons withheld their cash purchases of goods and services, the representatives of such castes would drift away, usually to the larger villages, towns, or even cities where wealth is apt to be concentrated and where they would very often find kin or, at least, other members of their caste. Thus, the larger villages would gradually gain new castes at the expense of the smaller ones and the curve as shown on Figure 8 would steepen.[16]

It is apparent that the degree of homogeneity of caste structure varies greatly from one region to another. To a certain extent this follows from the preceding discussion. Other things being equal, relatively prosperous areas ought to have a more homogeneous structure than relatively poor ones, that is, the caste structures of individual villages should conform more to a modal type or vary less from the average caste composition of the area itself. But factors other than relative prosperity enter the picture. In areas and villages where the population is largely tribal (for example, near the Chota Nagpur) or Muslim (for example, near the border of East Pakistan) village patterns are often quite simple. While Hindus and non-Hindus are commonly intermixed in the same villages, there are apt to be, in villages at a given size range, substantial differences in caste structure (counting tribes as castes for present purposes) between those villages which are predominantly made up of caste Hindus and those predominantly inhabited by tribalists or Muslims. Among other factors which may disrupt local patterns are dislocations caused by flood, famine, or other natural catastrophes; the implantation of colonies of a particular alien caste in a select number of villages in an area; and selective emigration.

Tables 1 and 2 illustrate the wide range of variation in local homogeneity of caste pattern as revealed by two of the field samples: one, of five villages, drawn from Hoshiarpur District in Punjab, the other, of nine villages, from Midnapore District in West Bengal. While a glance shows that the Hoshiarpur sample is far more homogeneous than that of Midnapore, where no two villages appear to be very much alike, an attempt to quantify the differences has been made. At the bottom of each column appears an "index of deviation" indicating for each village the degree to which its caste composition deviates from the average composition of the entire group, on a zero to 100 scale, and, for the sample as a whole, a weighted average deviation.[17] If these figures be accepted as mean-

16. For a graph similar to that of Figure 8, relating to 175 villages in eight regions of India (including five outside the North Indian Plain, see my dissertation (1960, p. 510). The relevant discussion is on pp. 509–515. No comparable work has as yet been done with the data collected in 1962–63. Because of the small sample size in the several areas of field work in that year, it may not be worth the effort unless some satisfactory method of aggregation can be devised. Even for the data gathered in 1958–59, sample sizes appear to be adequate for only four areas. It should not be supposed that households of specialized castes leaving small villages invariably drift to larger villages (though the *net* shift should normally be in that direction). If, by chance, there is a nearby village, of whatever size, which has well-established members of the same caste as the households feeling it necessary to move, those households may well gravitate to that place in hope of securing whatever assistance may be forthcoming.

17. The figures for the individual villages are derived by: (a) totaling the caste-by-caste membership of all the villages in the sample and computing the average caste composition of the total sample in percentage terms; (b) computing for each village the percentage of the total village population in each of the castes represented therein; (c) obtaining the differences, irrespective of sign, between the percentages derived in (b) and those derived in (a); and (d) totaling the differences. The average deviation for the entire sample is the average of each of the village deviations duly weighted for village size. If all villages were identical in caste makeup, in percentage terms, the deviation index of each of the entire sample would be zero. If, on the other hand, no two villages had any household of any caste found in another village the individual village indices would approach the theoretical maximum of 100, being less only

ingful and the samples as representative, one might say that the caste structure of Midnapore, with an average index of deviation of 65.4, is more than two and a half times as heterogeneous as that of Hoshiarpur, with an index of but 25.6. In fact, no claim is made either that the method of computing homogeneity is perfectly adequate or that the two samples used are truly representative of the districts named. On the contrary, they were selected to demonstrate the wide range in variability which might be obtained in a presumably unbiased sample. When we aggregate the data from the several sample areas, state by state, however, it does appear reasonably certain that localities of a given size (say, twenty miles square) in Punjab typically have more homogeneous caste structures than is true anywhere else on the North Indian Plain. For West Bengal the opposite is probably true. Bihar and Uttar Pradesh appear to occupy intermediate positions, with the latter probably slightly the more heterogeneous of the two, but closer to Bengal than to Punjab.

CASTE REGIONS

Figure 9 presents a preliminary synthesis of the census and field data discussed above in the form of a map of the caste regions and subregions of the North Indian Plain. But prior to any discussion of the deviations portrayed on this map it would be well to consider to what degree the entire area of study is itself a meaningful entity with regard to caste. At the outset of the second year of field work, confined, unlike the first, solely to this area, I had no intimation either that it was or that it was not such an entity.[18] The choice of the area, then, was not dictated by any a priori notions as to its caste structural unity. It was felt, however, that this broad region warranted study on other important grounds. First, in the broad expanse of the continuously settled plain, where natural obstacles to movement ceased centuries ago to be of great consequence, it was felt that the regional peculiarities in caste structure could not be simply attributed to variable and divergent development in relative physical isolation, as might well be the case, for example, in the Vale of Manipur, in the Chhattisgarh Plain, or in Kerala. Rather, regional and subregional differences would have to be explained in terms of the socioeconomic mechanics of the caste system itself or of that system in interaction with other forces not of a basically physical nature. Second, the sheer importance of the Plain as the core and culture-hearth of the subcontinent and the home of a third of India's people commended it to study. Finally, considering the good beginning I had made in studying parts of this area in 1958–59, it appeared that, with an additional concentrated research effort in this area

---

in proportion to the degree to which their own population contributed to the average composition of the entire sample. For truly adequate interregional comparisons, samples should have the same number of villages (much larger than those illustrated) and the indices should be village size-specific; that is, multiple indices should be used.

18. Ideally, this question should have been resolved, in a general way, from the 1931 census data prior to beginning field work. But a set of unforseeable circumstances brought me back to India a year earlier than I had hoped to go and, because of the exigencies of time, field work had to begin as early as possible and proceed concurrently with the necessary tabulations and ordering of census data by assistants working in Delhi.

TABLE 1

Castes in a sample of five villages in Hoshiarpur District, Punjab.

Key Number of Village	0–1	0–2	0–3	0–4	0–5	Total	Average
Number of Castes	10	8	6	9	10	17	8.8
Number of Households	105	71	63	137	331	707	141.4
Brahman (Priests)	1	2	8	1	10	21	4.2
Rajput (Warrior-Landlords)		1				1	0.2
Arora (Merchants)	1					1	0.2
Khatri (Merchants)				1	1	2	0.4
Jat (Cultivators)	13	10	2	48	130	203	40.6
Bhati (Cultivators)		15	12	1		28	5.6
Saini (Gardener-Cultivators)	13					13	2.6
Sonar (Goldsmiths)					1	1	0.2
Rangaria (Carpenters)	5	8	2	17	40	72	14.4
Sareri (Cotton-carders)	6					6	1.2
Kumhar (Potters)					3	3	0.6
Jhinwar (Water-carriers)	1	1	2	1	7	12	2.4
Mahsi (Basket-makers)	3					3	0.6
Nai (Barbers)				2	4	6	1.2
Ramdasi (Leather-workers and Agric. Laborers)†	2	4	37	6	15	64	12.8
Ad-Dharmi (As above)†	60	30		45	120	255	51.0
Balmiki (Scavenger)				16		16	3.2
Index of deviation from average for total sample	39.8	25.6	75.8	19.0	14.2	—	25.6*

Castes (with traditional occupations) arranged by functional categories on a roughly hierarchical basis.

* The average deviation is for all five villages, weighted for village size.

† Ramdasi and Ad-Dharmi represent local schisms within the Chamar caste.

96

TABLE 2

Castes in a sample of nine villages in Midnapore District, West Bengal.

Key Number of Village	B-1	B-2	B-3	B-4	B-5	B-6	B-7	B-8	B-9	Total	Average
Number of Castes	9	9	9	3	4	19	6	6	6	28	7.9
Number of Households	23	48	122	33	40	169	67	50	53	605	67.2
Brahman (Priests)	1	2	1		1	10	2			18	2.0
Kayastha (Scribes)	5	3				12				21	2.3
Baniya (Merchants)				2						2	0.2
Solanki (Cultivators)	7	8	19		32	11		34		77	8.6
Sadgop (Cultivators)	2					8				42	4.7
Mahishya (Cultivators)			7			2	50		42	103	11.4
Dalui (Cultivators)						2				2	0.2
Ghorui (Cultivators)								5		5	0.6
Tambuli (Betel Growers)						1				1	0.1
"Hindustani" (?) (sic)						1				1	0.1
"Oriya" (?) (sic)				1						1	0.1
Sheikh (Muslims)			65							65	7.2
Kamar (Blacksmiths)			1			1				2	0.2
Malakar (Garland-Makers)						1				1	0.1
Sinha Tanti (Weavers)		3								3	0.3
Pather Tanti (Weavers)		6				1				7	0.8
Kumhar (Potters)						1				1	0.1
Nai (Barbers)	1	3	1			1	3		1	10	1.1
Baishnab (Beggars)	1	1				5	1		3	11	1.2
Bagdi (Agric. Laborers)	3	2		30						35	3.9
Dhobi (Washermen)	2						1	2	1	6	0.7
Muchi (Cobblers)						1		3		4	0.4
Bhumij (Tribe)		20				63				83	9.2
Santal (Tribe)	1		18		5	1	10	5	5	45	5.0
Bhuiyan (Tribe)			5							5	0.6
Kora (Tribe)			5							5	0.6
Bagal (Tribe)						1				1	0.1
Mahali (Tribe-Basket-Makers)					2	46				48	5.3
Index of deviation from average for total sample	63.0	63.8	65.8	93.7	72.4	53.8	68.4	75.4	69.2	—	65.4*

Castes or Tribes (with traditional occupations for Hindus) arranged by functional categories on a roughly hierarchical basis

* The average deviation is for all nine villages, weighted for village size.

97

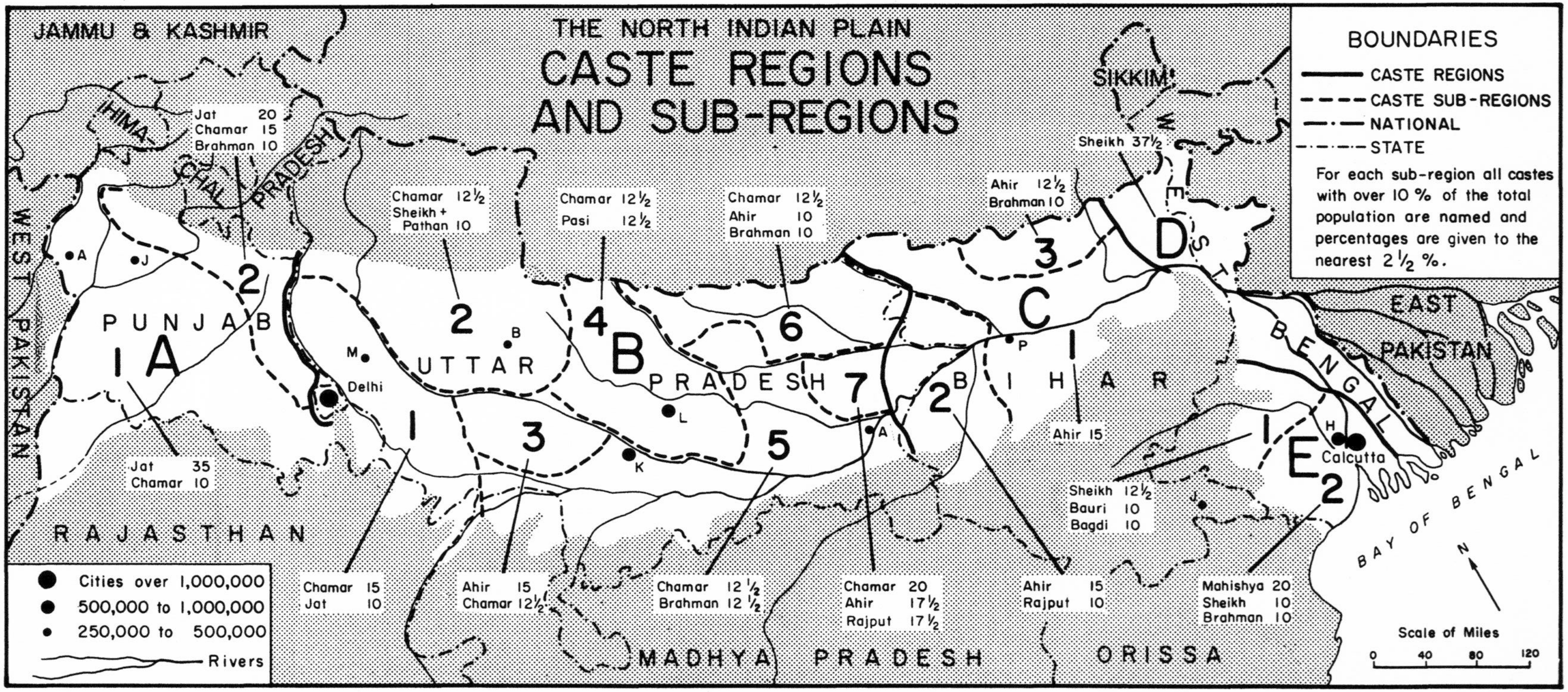

JAMMU & KASHMIR

THE NORTH INDIAN PLAIN
CASTE REGIONS
AND SUB-REGIONS

BOUNDARIES

CASTE REGIONS
CASTE SUB-REGIONS
NATIONAL
STATE

For each sub-region all castes
with over 10% of the total
population are named and
percentages are given to the
nearest 2½%.

Scale of Miles
0   40   80   120

WEST PAKISTAN

EAST
PAKISTAN

BENGAL

BAY OF BENGAL

Calcutta

ORISSA

MADHYA PRADESH

RAJASTHAN

PUNJAB

HIMA.
CHAL
PRADESH

UTTAR PRADESH

BIHAR

SIKKIM

Delhi

Jat   20
Chamar 15
Brahman 10

Jat   35
Chamar 10

Chamar 15
Jat   10

Chamar 12½
Sheikh+
Pathan 10

Chamar 12½
Pasi   12½

Chamar 12½
Ahir   10
Brahman 10

Sheikh 37½

Ahir   12½
Brahman 10

Ahir   15
Chamar 12½

Chamar 12½
Brahman 12½

Ahir   15
Chamar 12½

Chamar 20
Ahir   17½
Rajput 17½

Ahir   15

Sheikh 12½
Bauri 10
Bagdi 10

Ahir   15
Rajput 10

Mahishya 20
Sheikh   10
Brahman 10

Cities over 1,000,000
500,000 to 1,000,000
250,000 to 500,000
Rivers

FIGURE 9

in 1962–63, a reasonably comprehensive view of the whole could be obtained.

In the light of what has been learned since 1962 it appears that the study area is, in fact, rather well differentiated from neighboring areas along most, but not all, of its perimeter. The differences between it and both West and East Pakistan, especially the former, have, of course, been heightened and sharpened by partition and subsequent population movements. To the north there is a marked break as one leaves the complicated pattern of the plain for the simpler Hindu society of Himachal Pradesh, Himalayan Punjab, and Kumaun, or the ethnically quite different societies of Nepal and Sikkim. In the southeast, the change from the plain to the largely tribal society of the Chota Nagpur is also great, though a distinct, if not very wide, transitional belt appears to exist. West of the Chota Nagpur, however, as one goes south into Baghelkhand, Bundelkhand, and the desert of Rajasthan—but not into Mewar (see Fig. 1)—the caste structures of the plain appear to undergo no very marked transformation. In fact, the differences between Hindustan and Bengal or within Bengal between the southwestern districts and the remainder appear to be significantly greater than those between the central and western parts of the Plain on the one hand and the hill and desert areas to the south in Madhya Pradesh and Rajasthan on the other. How far southward in the latter areas the broad pattern of the plain persists has not yet been determined. Conceivably, there is no major break in pattern up to the Vindhya-Kaimur escarpment. While it is thus evident that the North Indian Plain is, to some degree, an arbitrarily defined study area so far as caste is concerned, it in no way follows that it may not be meaningfully regionalized. In the following pages are presented a tentative regionalization and an analysis of the five major regions and fifteen subregions recognized.

The major caste regions recognized are identified by letters A through E in Figure 9 and the subregions by suffixed Arabic numerals. Indicated for each subregion are those castes estimated to contain 10 per cent or more of the total population, based on aggregation of district-wide totals given in the 1931 census (with prior proportional division of the totals in those cases where districts are split by subregional or regional boundaries) and inferences as to population movements since 1931, and especially subsequent to partition. These inferences were facilitated both by the field study and by the published census data on religious composition of the population in 1951 and 1961.[19] No attempt was made to refine estimates through hypothesizing or projecting differential growth rates. Population estimates are given only to the nearest 2.5 per cent. In view of the age and limitations of the data and the method of estimation, any attempt at greater refinement would have been specious.

REGION A

Region A is roughly coterminous with the plain portion of the state of Punjab plus the adjacent irrigated portion of Ganganagar District in Rajasthan.

19. Data on the location and origin of displaced persons in both India and Pakistan are available in the 1951 censuses of both countries. I have not yet studied them, however. It is probable that, with careful study, they will permit more refined estimates of the movement within particular caste groups.

The area is characterized most strikingly throughout by the high proportion of the total population in the cultivating caste of Jats (mainly Sikhs, but also including numerous Hindus, especially in the southeast). This caste led all others in 1931 in every district and princely state except for Kapurthala, and today almost certainly leads there as well. Typically, the Jats were two or more times as numerous as the second most populous caste (over six times as numerous in Ludhiana) and, because of the exodus of Muslims (Jats, Rajputs, Gujars, and numerous other castes) and the return of Sikh Jats from the Canal Colonies of West Punjab to their ancestral homeland, their proportions have considerably increased since partition. There is currently, however, probably a considerable net emigration of Sikh Jats to other parts of India in search of a wide variety of jobs, largely military and mechanical, to which they gravitate (Gosal, 1965, pp. 119–24). In view of the ubiquity and pronounced dominance of the Jats within Region A, the unusual homogeneity of the sample villages of the several areas studied therein is hardly surprising; but the wide and fairly even diffusion of such artisan and serving castes as are represented, as discussed in connection with Figure 8, also contributes significantly to this trait.

The great majority of villages in Region A are clearly dominated by a single agricultural caste, constituting rarely less than a quarter and about as often as not over half the total population. Most commonly, of course, the leading group are Jats, but Rajputs, Sainis (a gardener caste), Kambohs, and Ahaluwalias all lead in certain villages. So too did Muslim cultivator groups, quite commonly, prior to partition. The degree to which these cultivating (or landowning) castes mutually exclude one another is truly remarkable; yet the phenomenon of mutual exclusivity does not appear, to my knowledge, in the literature on the area. Thus, in a typical Jat village there will be not a single household of Rajputs, Sainis, etc., while in a Rajput village Jats, Sainis, etc. will normally be absent. Among the villages sampled, exceptions were usually attributable to the arbitrary granting of formerly Muslim-owned lands to displaced persons from West Pakistan. In no other area of the North Indian Plain does the tendency toward mutual exclusion (that is, village-wise monopolization) among castes of roughly equivalent functional status manifest itself to the degree that it does in Punjab.

There is also a pronounced tendency toward almost complete mutual exclusivity among those scheduled caste groups constituting the chief agricultural labor groups of Punjab, one or another of which is, in a majority of cases, the second most numerous caste in a given village. Throughout most of the area the principal such group are the Chamars, traditionally leather workers. Those following the Sikh faith are usually called Raidas or Ramdasis, but were not counted as constituting a separate caste from their Hindu counterparts. In and around Amritsar District, however, the Majabhis (Sikh Bhangis), traditionally sweepers, are far more numerous. Since neither of these two groups will do the lowly traditional work of the other, it is highly desirable, if not absolutely essential, that at least one or a few households of each caste be present. Typically, then, a village of around 250 households, let us say, may have around fifty families of Raidas and but two or three of Majabhis, or, alternatively, the proportions may be reversed. While each group would tend to its specialized calling, one or the other would have a near monopoly as well on the performance of agricultural labor, either on a casual basis or attached to specific patron households in jajmani-type relationships.

Among the more widespread professional artisan and serving castes of the region, other than those just discussed, the priestly Brahmans, the carpenter-*cum*-blacksmith caste (Tarkhans), the potters (Kumhars), the water-carriers (Chuhras, Jhirs, Jhinwars), the barbers (Nais), and the goldsmiths (Sonars) are all worthy of note. There are several merchant castes, largely urban, of considerable strength, Khatris and Aroras, both very similar and sometimes intermarrying, and Aggarwals. The strength of all three of these groups was considerably augmented after partition. Among Muslim artisan groups, formerly well represented, the blacksmiths (Lohars), weavers (Julahas), tailors (Darjis), and shoemakers (Mochis) deserve mention. One effect of partition was to leave a less ramified caste structure than had previously existed, but even more important was the major blow dealt to the functional integration of castes within the general framework of the jajmani system.

The characteristic features of Region A are most clearly present in its core area, Subregion A-1. There, for example, the ascendancy of the Jats is most evident. In Ludhiana District, and probably a few others, they approach or exceed half the total rural population. The fringe belt, Subregion A-2, is largely transitional to Caste Region B. While Jats are still predominant, Chamars and Brahmans are relatively more numerous than in area A-1, the former especially so toward the northwest, the latter toward the south. Probably no other caste has as much as 5 per cent of the total population; but Rajputs, Gujars, Sainis, and Chuhras may all approach that figure.

The transition along the boundary of Region A is sharp toward the north and west, only moderately sharp toward the east, and more or less arbitrary toward the south, as has already been intimated. The western boundary with Pakistan was, of course, much less sharp prior to partition than it has become since.

Region B

Region B is roughly coterminous with the plains portion of Uttar Pradesh except for a small area in the east, with the addition of Delhi and other small tracts of adjoining territory in the southwest. It is by far the largest and most populous of the five major divisions of the study area, is probably the most extensive area of India without a clearly dominant caste, and possibly has a more highly ramified caste structure than any other part of the subcontinent. The lack of clear-cut regional dominance is quite commonly iterated at the level of the individual village. In the sample the most numerous caste in the village averaged only 40 per cent of the total population in Region B as against 53 per cent in Region A. But while the most populous caste in Region A was almost always one of cultivators, with the second caste well behind in numbers and even further behind in power, most often a scheduled caste group, in Region B it was not uncommon for the most numerous caste to be in the scheduled category (in 24 cases out of 106), and quite commonly two or more cultivating castes coexisted in significant numbers in a single village. As has already been demonstrated (Fig. 8), there tend to be great differences in the caste composition of large and small villages, greater by far than in Punjab, for example. There is also much greater local heterogeneity of caste structure within any given locality. The district indices of deviation in the sample ranged from a low of 36.2 (in Allahabad District) to a high of 61.4 in Rampur District, and averaged 53.5 as against 39.7 in Region A.

Much of the ramification of the caste structure in Region B can probably be attributed to the prolonged interaction of Muslims and Hindus in this area. Certain Muslim groups are of distinctly foreign origin (for example, Pathans, Mughals, Saiyids, and Turks); others are probably of mixed foreign and local provenance (for example, Sheikhs); and numerous others, which are occupationally specialized counterparts of Hindu artisan and serving castes (for example, Julahas [weavers], Telis [oil-pressers], and Nais [barbers]), are probably predominantly derived from Hindu converts. While the number of Muslims who left this area for Pakistan at the time of partition was by no means small, though probably drawn overwhelmingly from the higher caste groups, the number who remained behind was larger by far. In 1961 Uttar Pradesh was still 14.6 per cent Muslim, and the district-wise proportion ranged as high as 45.0 per cent in Rampur District in the core of Rohilkhand, the most heavily Muslim tract. By and large, the Muslims of Uttar Pradesh are relatively concentrated in larger villages, towns, and cities (for example, Lucknow), but, according to the sample data, nearly three-fourths of all villages have one or more Muslim castes represented.[20] The most diffuse of all Muslim castes appears to be the beggar caste of Faqirs, though Sheikhs, Pathans, and Julahas in that order, are far more numerous. In rural areas the integration of Muslims into the village polity, economy, and society appears to be remarkably good, despite their being regarded as ritually unclean by their Hindu neighbors. Villages dominated by Muslims are by no means uncommon.

The most numerous caste of Region B are the lowly Chamars, who lead all others in six of the seven subregions recognized and rank second in the seventh. Nowhere, however, is their plurality very large, and over no extensive tract do they constitute over a fifth, or less than an eighth, of the total population. The distinctive local flavor and the internal areal differentiation are, then, invariably imparted by other castes: the Brahmans, for example, who, though of considerable importance throughout the area, are particularly well represented in Subregions B-5 and B-6; the Ahirs, who are most numerous in B-3 and second only to the Chamars in B-6 and 7; the Jats, who are important in B-1, the Upper Doab, adjacent to their Punjabi hearthland; the landed Rajputs, in western Bhojpur, Subregion B-7; various landed Muslim castes, especially Sheikhs and Pathans in Rohilkhand, Subregion B-2; and, in western Oudh, Subregion B-4, even the

---

20. Since the villages in the sample were somewhat more populous on the average than villages in the area as a whole, it is probable that the proportion of all villages in which Muslim castes are represented is slightly less than the sample data would suggest.

low-status, allegedly aboriginal Pasis, traditionally a caste of toddy tappers, but generally agricultural laborers in practice.

Within Region B, the transitions between pairs of adjacent subregions are, for the most part, not very sharp. The most pronounced exception is Subregion A-2, which, largely because of its high concentration of Muslims, is the most distinctive of the seven subareas. If considerations of caste composition had been the sole criterion for classification, it might have been desirable to single this area out as a region unto itself rather than as a subregion within Region B; but, in view of the total range of significant variables discussed, it appears to have enough in common with the other subregions to justify being placed on a par with them. Also fairly well set off from neighboring areas are Subregions B-1 and B-7. Subregions B-3, B-4, B-5, and B-6, on the other hand, appear to grade into one another without a sharp break, yet are sufficiently different in their core areas to warrant individual recognition. The seven subregions are discussed in numerical order in the following paragraphs.

Subregion B-1, generally corresponding to the area known as the Upper Doab, between the Jumna and the Ganges, is, in some ways, transitional between Subregion A-2 and the remainder of Region B. An eastward extension of the great area over which Jats are the dominant landowning caste, this subregion is apparently a frontier of relatively recent Jat expansion, with noticeably lower proportions of that caste in the total population than in Punjab or Rajasthan (Mukerji, 1961, pp. 41–53).[21] Chamars, in fact, are considerably more numerous. Among the traditional landowning and cultivating castes, the Rajputs also appear to outnumber the Jats in certain tracts, especially toward the east, while in the infertile, sandy riverain along the Jumna, the traditionally pastoral caste of Gujars, largely cultivators in practice, is locally dominant. The tendency noted in Region A for the three main and other landowning and cultivating castes to be mutually exclusive at the village level is probably more marked in this subregion than anywhere else in Region B.

After Chamars and Jats, Brahmans are the third most numerous caste. Like the Chamars, the Brahmans are ubiquitous, but are particularly important toward the south, where they, too, outnumber the Jats. The only other castes of particular note are the merchant caste of Vaishyas (Baniyas), whose greater than average concentration in this intensively irrigated area presumably reflects its high productivity and commercialized agriculture; and the largely urban Sheikhs, who in 1931 were by far the leading caste in the city of Delhi and presumably in certain other cities as well. The exodus of Muslims from the area at the time of partition was probably not so great as to displace this caste from its leading position in certain cities, numerically speaking; but the loss of many prominent individuals and the great urban influx of displaced persons has undoubtedly reduced their relative power position, especially in the greater Delhi area.

Subregion B-2 corresponds generally to the area known as Rohilkhand, which

21. Mukerji dates the major Jat penetration of this area from only the late eighteenth century.

was the last part of what is now Uttar Pradesh to fall under the sway of the British (though Oudh did maintain nominal independence for several more decades). It is hardly surprising that in this lingering stronghold of Muslim resistance to British domination, Sheikhs and Pathans should be the two dominant castes, though, as is usually the case in Region B, Chamars are the most numerous group. Of the two leading Muslim castes, the Sheikhs are more numerous toward the west and the Pathans toward the east, each approaching or exceeding a tenth the total population in its area of concentration. In Rampur District, which was a Pathan-ruled princely state prior to independence, Pathans, with 9.4 per cent of the population, actually ranked first. But in no other district of the North Indian Plain did the first-ranking caste have so low a proportion of the total population, and in no other subregion was this characteristic of caste structure quite so pronounced. Given the ruling position of the Muslims of Rohilkhand and the fact that the dominant Muslim groups were better represented in the villages there than in other parts of Hindustan, it is only natural that Muslim representation in the artisan and serving castes should be rather greater than usual. The Muslim components of these specialized castes (counted separately from the Hindu components) not infrequently exceeded 1 per cent of the population, especially among the weaving caste of Julahas. The peculiarly widespread Muslim beggar caste or Faqirs are probably better represented in this subregion than in any other part of India. (They were encountered in six of the nine villages surveyed in Rampur District.)

Of the clean Hindu castes, Rajputs were the most numerous, ranking third among all castes in the subregion, with particular strength toward the west. Although Brahmans ranked fourth, they comprised less than 5 per cent of the total population, a lower percentage than in any other subregion or region of the study area, save Region D in West Bengal. These two castes increase in strength outward from Rampur, the core district of Subregion B-2, where both reach their nadir in the state of Uttar Pradesh. Among the cultivating castes, Kurmis, Ahars (an offshoot of the pastoral Ahirs), Kisans, Bhumihars (cultivating Brahmans) and Lodhs, in that general order of importance, are worth noting. While each is of local importance in one or a few districts, none is even as numerous as the Brahmans in the subregion as a whole. Their pronounced localization contributes measurably toward a greater degree of internal heterogeneity within Subregion B-2 than in any other part of Region B.

Subregion B-3, with its core in Mainpuri District, constitutes the only extensive tract within Region B in which Chamars are not the most numerous caste. Even here, however, they rank first in two districts and second in the area as a whole. On the basis of numbers alone, the traditionally pastoral caste of Ahirs (in practice mainly cultivators) would clearly appear to be the dominant group; but it may well be that both the Brahmans and the Rajputs possess more land and power, despite the fact that each is only around half as numerous. More populous than these two groups are the cultivating castes of Kachis, who specialize in garden crops, and Lodhs, both of whom are presumably dominant in a number of villages, if not in any distinct multivillage tracts. The shepherd caste of Gadariyas is probably more numerous in this area than any other. Last, we may note the Vaishyas, whose relative importance here may be explained in the same way as for area B-1.

The two most numerous castes of Subregion B-4 are the Chamars and the almost equally depressed Pasis. The combined strength of these two groups is chiefly responsible for the fact that this area probably has the highest proportion of the population in scheduled castes of any in the North Indian Plain, close to 30 per cent of the total. (Subregion E-1 has roughly the same percentage.) Pasis, traditionally toddy tappers, but mainly agricultural laborers and petty cultivators in practice, are allegedly the aborigines of this part of the plain. They are the most numerous of all castes in the three southeastern districts of this area, while Chamars are slightly more numerous to the northwest. The former group falls off very sharply in numbers beyond the Ganges to the southwest and also northwestward toward Rohilkhand, but declines more gradually in strength toward the south and east into Subregions B-5 and B-6.

Ahirs, Brahmans, Kurmis, and Rajputs are, in that order, the next most numerous castes, their strengths ranging from close to 10 per cent to not much over 5 per cent of the population. In terms of property ownership, power, and status, however, Ahirs probably fall behind the others. The Kurmis are particularly strong toward the northeast and the Rajputs toward the southwest of the subregion. The Lodh cultivating caste is fairly well represented in the southeast. Ahirs and Brahmans are, characteristically, rather evenly dispersed. The only other caste of note are the Sheikhs, who, though not especially numerous in the area as a whole, have a considerable concentration in and around the city of Lucknow, the capital of Uttar Pradesh and formerly of the Muslim kingdom of Oudh.

Subregion B-5 is the largest, most populous, most typical, and, in a sense, most nebulous of the seven under review, being the residual area remaining after the delimitation of the more exceptional areas to the north, northwest, and northeast. The first five castes in order of size, Chamars and Brahmans, each with over a tenth the population, and Ahirs, Rajputs, and Kurmis, with less, duplicate the rank order within Region B as a whole. All these castes are fairly evenly spread over the area, except the Kurmis, who are concentrated in the south center and southeast portions. No other caste has as much as 5 per cent of the total population. But those worthy of mention include the gardening castes of Kachis, Koeris, and Muraos, the Kachis being fairly strong toward the southwest and stronger still beyond the plain in Bundelkhand; the Pasis and Lodhs, near Subregion B-4; the Sheikhs, especially in the cities of Allahabad and Kanpur; and the Gadariyas. This area, like most of Region B, probably has few large tracts over which there is a clearly dominant caste, and even at the village level, the dominant caste is often not obvious.

Of all the subregions depicted in Figure 9, Subregion B-6 along the Nepalese border probably has the most ramified caste structure. As Figure 7 shows, the districts comprising this area average 27 castes with over 1 per cent of the total population. For an admittedly small sample of eight villages in Gorakhpur and Deoria districts, within this area, an average of 18.25 castes was found per village, the average village in this sample containing 189 households. This appears to be slightly higher than for the Central Uttar Pradesh sample in the same size ranges, judging from the curve depicted in Figure 8. Apart from this singularity, which may or may not be significant, the subregion does not appear to be markedly different from Subregion B-5. The proportion of Ahirs is somewhat higher and that of Brahmans somewhat lower, and no caste has a population in the range 5 to 10 per cent of the total. Of the traditionally cultivating and/or gardening castes, Kurmis are most numerous, especially toward the west, while Koeris are more prominent toward the east. Also, of note in the east are the Kewats, a caste of agricultural laborers, petty cultivators, and fishermen. The only other castes deserving mention are the Rajputs, who are, however, proportionately fewer and relatively weaker in this area than in any other subregion of Region B, and the Pathans, who were locally (as of 1931) the most numerous group among the Muslim population.

Last, least populous, and in some ways the most distinctive among the subregions of Region B is area B-7, centering on Azamgarh District in Western Bhojpur. This area is quite different from Subregion B-6 just across the Gogra River to the north, but gradually blends in other directions into Subregions B-5 and C-2. Here the three most numerous castes, Chamars, Ahirs, and Rajputs, in that order, together account for approximately 55 per cent of the total population, a figure attained, presumably, in no other subregion of the North Indian Plain. The dominance of the Rajputs, the leading caste in power and landholding, is not at all apparent from their numerical strength. Two other castes each have over 5 per cent of the population, the Brahmans, who are virtually nowhere weak in numbers in areas of Rajput strength, and the Bhars, allegedly the indigenous population of this tract. There is also a sizeable group of Bhumihars, cultivating Brahmans, who dominate a number of villages in the area. And, finally, the traditional lime- and salt-making caste of Noniyas is better represented here than any place else in northern India, which fact is probably related to the unusually widespread occurrence in this area of *kankar* (nodular limestone) concretions in the soil and of the prevalence of *reh* (saline efflorescences) at the soil's surface.

REGION C

Region C comprises the northern plains portion of the state of Bihar, minus most of Purnea District in the northeast, plus Ballia District of Uttar Pradesh in the west. Throughout, this region is characterized by a numerical predominance of Ahirs, locally called Goalas. In the core area, Subregion C-1, comprising a majority of the total area and population, this group far surpasses any other; and, at its strongest, in Bhagalpur, it was over three times as numerous as the second ranking group. Yet, even in Bhagalpur, Ahirs were only 16.8 per cent of the total population in 1931. It follows, then, that none of the remaining castes is very strongly represented, except in the peripheral Subregions C-2 and C-3, where Rajputs and Brahmans respectively are estimated to comprise around a tenth of the total. On the basis of numbers alone, one might assume that the Ahirs are clearly the dominant caste, at least in Subregion C-1. While they probably do dominate more villages than any other single group, they do not, however, lead in nearly as many villages as might be supposed. This stems from the fact that they are a relatively evenly distributed caste, whereas a number of other groups, to be discussed below, tend to be much more concentrated in fewer localities or villages in which they enjoy ascendancy. In practice, then, the pattern of local caste dominance in Region C resembles Region B more than Region A, which also has a uniform numerical preponderance of but a single caste. Regions B and C are also similar in having high degrees of ramification of overall caste structure, in their fairly steep average rises in the numbers of castes per village with increasing village size and in their degree of heterogeneity of caste structure at the local level.

In terms of the relative strengths of specific castes, however, there are a number of noteworthy differences between the two regions. Region C, except in the specially delimited peripheral areas, has relatively fewer Brahmans and Rajputs than Region B and far fewer Chamars. On the other hand, Dusadhs, a caste of petty cultivators and agricultural laborers scarcely found in Region B, occur in significant numbers throughout Region C, where they have slightly over 5 per cent of the total population and are second only to the Ahirs in total numbers. Very close behind are the Koeris, also found throughout the region.

A peculiar feature of Subregion C-1 is that after the Ahirs, who, as indicated, lead substantially in every district, the second ranking caste is not the same in any two districts. After the more or less ubiquitous Dusadhs, who rank second in the area as a whole and in Muzaffarpur, and the third-ranking Koeris, the castes of some numerical importance are: the Brahmans, who rank second in Darbhanga (but whose main strength lies in the northern part of the district within Subregion C-3); the Rajputs; the Kurmis, who rank second in Patna; the Sheikhs, who rank second in Bhagalpur and who were concentrated in Tirhut, on the north bank of the Ganges and in and near Patna; the Bhumihars, a caste of cultivating Brahmans, concentrated in Magadha on the south bank of the Ganges and second-ranking in Gaya; the fairly evenly spread Muslim weaving caste of Julahas; the Kahars, Hindu water-carriers and domestic servants; and, finally, the depressed pig-rearing caste of Musahars, who are generally more numerous toward the east and who rank second in Monghyr.

Somewhat transitional in nature between Subregions C-1 and B-7 is Subregion C-2, where, despite their second-place position numerically, Rajputs are almost surely the regionally dominant caste. Ahirs, however, probably dominate a larger number of villages, especially those of smaller than average size. The third ranking caste are the Brahmans, with Koeris and Chamars following fairly closely behind, all three with between 10 and 5 per cent of the population. Of the remaining castes only the Bhumihars and Dusadhs are sufficiently numerous to be worthy of mention. Muslims are quite poorly represented in this subregion.

The existence of a distinct Subregion C-3 could not have been reasonably inferred from the district-wise data of the 1931 census alone. While Darbhanga District does stand out from other districts as an area with a peculiarly high concentration of Brahmans (10.1 per cent, over double that of any neighboring district), this anomaly in itself would not have warranted its separation from the rest of Subregion C-1. It was only in the field that I discovered that there was a distinctive belt of territory in Mithila, extending across the grain of administrative district boundaries through most of northern Bihar, in which the Maithil Brahman community was established in sufficient strength to warrant mapping that area, tentatively, as a distinct subregion. The Maithil Brahmans are said to have fled into Nepal before the advancing Muslim power on the plain and reestablished themselves in the northern part of their home area only after Muslim power there had waned. Apart from Brahmans, the castes significantly represented are, by and large, the same as those mentioned for Subregion C-1, except that the water-carrying caste of Kahars are almost totally absent, while a boatman caste, Mullahs (this area is particularly subject to flooding) takes their place.

REGION D

Extending southward from the Nepalese border all along the border of East Pakistan to the Bay of Bengal is Region D, marked throughout by an unusually high percentage of the population in but a single caste, the Sheikhs, who comprised almost the whole of the resident Muslim population. Prior to partition this group would have comprised close to 50 per cent of the total population of the area depicted, but an outflow of modest proportions to East Pakistan and an inflow of Hindus in much larger numbers have considerably reduced their relative strength. (The figure of 37.5 per cent in Figure 9 is a rougher than average estimate; but local percentages may run much higher. Murshidabad District was 55.9 per cent Muslim in 1961.) Were the Sheikhs Hindu, rather than Muslim, their dominant position, regionally, would be assured, since no other group even approaches them in numerical strength. But as members of a communal minority the Sheikhs presumably find their strength somewhat vitiated, since there is always the risk that in situations of potential conflict the otherwise factious Hindu community would unite against them. Yet, within their own hamlets or villages or clusters thereof, where they tend to constitute a very large proportion of the total population, it is probable that they exercise authority much as they did before Indian independence. Villages or hamlets tend to be, on the whole, clearly Muslim dominated or clearly Hindu dominated, Muslim villages having far fewer castes in general than those dominated by Hindus.[22] The non-Muslim groups who are most commonly found in large numbers in Sheikh villages are depressed Hindu castes or tribal or semitribal people, who are, for the most part, petty cultivators, fishermen, and agricultural laborers. Insofar as these groups interact socially and economically with their Muslim neighbors, questions of ritual pollution and traditional jajmani relationships probably have little or no importance. This, however, is not to say that between Hindu and Muslim no jajmani ties exist. The caste structure of the area as a

22. The only single-caste village among the 223 surveyed was a Sheikh village of 52 households in the environs of Calcutta, just west of the boundary of Region D. Presumably, all-Sheikh villages and certainly single-caste hamlets are not particularly rare in Region D itself. The closest approach in the sample, however, was a two-caste village in which non-Sheikhs were represented by but four depressed Hindu (Hari) households out of a total of 89.

whole is not highly ramified; but the intermixing of Hindu and Muslim communities commonly yields a local caste pattern with a very high level of heterogeneity.

In two not very desirable, but fairly extensive, tracts of land, only recently becoming densely settled, there are non-Muslim groups of rather appreciable strength. To the north there is the so-called Barind Jungle Tract (very little jungle still remains) in the districts of Dinajpur and Malda and for some distance across the border in Pakistan. Here the aboriginal Rajbanshis, often in small, simple villages almost exclusively their own, constitute up to a fifth of the total population. Today the group is split into a more tribalistic group, the Deshi Rajbanshis and an upward-aspiring (Sanskritizing, to use the well-known term of Srinivas) group, who style themselves Paliyas. In the same general region, moving northeastward from the Santal Parganas of Bihar, are the tribal group of Santals, who for generations have been reclaiming jungle throughout much of West Bengal and who are becoming particularly well established in the Barind tract, where conceivably they may now constitute as much as a tenth of the population.

The second area in which a non-Muslim group registers particular strength lies on the prograding portion of the Ganges delta in the swampy terrain known as the Sundarbans, which, like the Barind Tract, extends well into East Pakistan. There the depressed Hindu fishing-laboring caste of Pods (currently styled Paundra-Kshatriyas) has a position much like that of the Rajbanshis to the north, except that they are more apt to be found as laborers on lands owned by Sheikhs or various clean Hindu castes. In 1931 they constituted a fourth of the total population of the district of 24 Parganas and may even have been a majority in the southernmost sub-divisions, where they provide most of the labor involved in poldering and reclaiming the prevalent mangrove swamp, often on tracts held by absentee landlords. Other groups have been specifically recruited or have immigrated spontaneously for this work. These have been tribals, for the most part, particularly Santals, from the Chota Nagpur.

Of the clean Hindu castes, the cultivating Mahishyas are the most numerous particularly toward the south, where they may today constitute over an eighth of the total population. To the north, near Region C, the Goalas (Ahirs) are of note. Not nearly so numerous as the Mahishyas, but with rather similar general distributions, are the Brahmans and the clerical or scribe caste of Kayasthas. In practice, these two groups are often landlords. Their holdings in East Pakistan, where Kayasthas constituted the most numerous clean Hindu caste, were considerable. Most of these two groups have now immigrated to India, and it is probable that their strength in Region D is now well above what it was in 1931.

REGION E

Region E comprises the portion of Bengal extending west from Region D to the Chota Nagpur Plateau and the narrow coastal plain of Orissa. Here, regional dominance, insofar as it can be recognized, resides throughout in one or another clean Hindu caste. Among these castes, only the Brahmans are found in really significant numbers throughout the region, though they are outnumbered by the not quite so ubiquitous Mahishyas. Though the Muslim caste of Sheikhs are also important over all of this area, their numbers and influence are far less than in Region D. Here, their dominance is presumably limited to a relatively small number of villages, generally larger than average in size and located along more important roads or near the border with Region D. Almost as numerous as the Muslims, but much more diffuse, are the tribal groups, overwhelmingly Santal, who are generally Hinduized in varying degrees. While Santals constitute the largest group in a number of villages, in some cases even an absolute majority, they do not normally enjoy much power.

The caste structure of Region E is not as ramified as that of Regions B, C, and, probably, A, though it is more so than in Region D. This is true whether one analyzes particular localities or individual villages. In the sample of seventeen villages in Birbhum and Midnapore Districts, the average number of castes per village was not quite eight. Even after making allowances for the relatively small average village size, this was much less than one finds, typically, in Uttar Pradesh and Bihar. On the other hand, the degree of local heterogeneity of caste structure, as evidenced by the data for Midnapore (Table 2) is probably greater than for any other major caste region of northern India. (At the subregional level, area B-2 may well be comparable.)

Very few villages of Region E appear to have the broad complement of artisan and serving castes (such as blacksmiths, carpenters, potters, barbers, and leather workers) which characterizes most villages in Punjab and Uttar Pradesh. Insofar as these castes exist locally, each tends to be found in a relatively small number of villages, rather than to be highly diffuse, and to provide its services over a more or less broad area, rather than in one or a very few villages. Brahmans, however, are an exception, being found in most villages; but even the barbering caste, so widely and evenly spread in most sample areas, is here found in only around half the sampled villages. Certain artisan castes (for example, potters, weavers, metalsmiths, oil-pressers, and confectioners), are believed to be particularly concentrated in but a few centers, from which they provide their wares over a rather extensive area, largely via the weekly or bi-weekly outdoor markets (*hāṭs*), which are more important in Bengal than in other parts of northern India, where customary exchange within the traditional Hindu jajmani system is better developed. Greatly facilitating market exchange in Bengal is the fact that population densities are exceedingly high. Thus, in an area with a population density of 1,000 per square mile (a figure commonly reached in Regions D and E) a group of artisans clustered in a single village will have a potential clientele of nearly 80,000 persons within a radius of five miles (that is, within two hours' walking time where no natural obstacles are interposed).

Of the two divisions recognized within Region E, Subregion E-1 to the north is much the smaller and the more heterogeneous from one locality to another. Throughout the area, however, there is a remarkably high proportion of the population in scheduled castes and tribes, who together constitute around a third of the total population, more than in any other subregion of the North Indian Plain. The principal such groups are the Bagdis and, especially toward the south, the Bauris, both agricultural laboring castes, and the recently immigrant Santals. When the Muslim population, predominantly of Sheikhs, is added to these groups, not much more than half the total population remains in "clean" caste Hindus. Of these, the two principal groups are the Brahmans, whose numbers have presumably risen as a result of heavy emigration from East Pakistan and immigration into the rapidly developing industrial area along the Damodar River (extending on into the Chota Nagpur), and the Sadgops, the most numerous and wealthiest of the cultivating castes. No other group has as much as 5 per cent of the total population. Goalas, however, come close to that figure and surpass it in Bankura District. The only other castes worthy of note are the Tilis and Telis (also called Kalus), actually two subcastes of oil-pressers found in unusually large numbers in this area, and the relatively prosperous Kayasthas, who, though not especially numerous, are quite widespread in the area and presumably on the increase since partition.

Subregion E-2, with its core in Midnapore District, straddles the Hooghly River in the east and includes Calcutta and the great Hooghlyside conurbation, which is among the largest metropolitan clusters in the world. The largest caste by far within the subregion is the dominant cultivating caste of Mahishyas, who numbered not quite a third of the total population of Midnapore in 1931 and who may now constitute a clear majority of the total population in the eastern part of that large and very populous district. Formerly Sheikhs were clearly the second most numerous caste, and possibly first east of the Hooghly; but a certain relative reduction in their numbers since partition, and the immigration of various Hindu groups, may have displaced them from that position. It would appear that Brahmans today are nearly as numerous, if not more so, with a particularly heavy concentration in the Calcutta-Hooghlyside complex. A third group, particularly well represented in the city of Calcutta itself, are the Kayasthas, who slightly outnumbered the Brahmans there in 1931, and who can be presumed also to have gained notably in strength since partition. In the subregion as a whole they may now exceed 5 per cent of the total population. Apart from the castes already mentioned, the only other noteworthy groups of clean Hindus are the Goalas and Sadgops and possibly a newly emergent group styled Solankis.[23] Of the depressed groups, the Bagdis, who constitute the fourth most populous caste, and the Santals are most important.

SUMMARY AND CONCLUSIONS

That there are distinct regional variations in the caste composition and caste structure of India is obvious. This article presents what is thought to be the first systematic attempt at a holistic mapping of those variations in the important,

23. The field sample reveals a totally unanticipated result in that in two out of nine villages surveyed in western Midnapore the most numerous (and most powerful) caste were Solankis, who are not even mentioned in the 1931 census and who were unknown to Professor Ralph Nicholas, who did field work in the eastern part of the district (personal correspondence, dated October 13, 1964). Conceivably they are a schismatic group among either Mahishyas or Bagdis who are aspiring to higher corporate status than the remainder of the caste, whom they no longer recognize as caste fellows. The lower than anticipated numbers of both Mahishyas and Bagdis in the sample lend plausibility to this hypothesis.

but arbitrarily delimited, area of the North Indian Plain. The mapping is a synthesis, based on a detailed study of the caste data of the 1931 census and of a large number of maps of individual caste distributions made therefrom, of graphs showing the ten most numerous castes in each district and princely state, as computed from the 1931 census, and of the data from a sample of 223 villages studied in two years of field research. No claim is made that the field sample data are perfectly accurate or truly representative of reality, but it is believed that they are sufficiently accurate and representative to afford a sound basis for regional generalizations about a number of variables relative to local caste structure which cannot be made on the basis of the census data alone. These variables and others, which can be studied directly from the census data, have been explained and illustrated. Among the variables, the locally dominant caste, the degree of dominance, the degree of ramification of the system as a whole, the rate of rise in the number of castes with increasing village size, and the relative heterogeneity of caste structure within the villages of a particular locality are considered of special importance.

The map presented, depicting five major caste regions and fifteen subregions, cannot be considered as definitive. Inevitably it incorporates certain subjective decisions, particularly where regional and subregional boundaries do not closely follow district boundaries and where more or less intelligent guesses had to be made relative to major changes since partition. Inferences and assumptions as to the nature of the local caste structure inbetween the areas of sampling may not always turn out to be correct. There is a definite need for densification of the field sample. One might argue that the number of regions or subregions recognized should have been greater or less. The decision not to recognize certain singular areas of particularly small population or size as separate subregions (for example, Saharanpur District in Uttar Pradesh, which was split between Subregions B-1 and B-2, but which fits neither really well, or the highly cosmo-politan metropolitan areas of Delhi and the Calcutta-Hooghlyside conurbation) is admittedly arbitrary. Somewhere, however, a line must ultimately be drawn. Although the map has shortcomings, it seems reasonably certain that for its scale it provides an essentially correct picture of the regional variations in caste structure and composition within the area of purview.

So long as the institution of caste retains a fundamental role in contributing to the character of Indian society—and the evidence suggests that this will be the case for some time to come—there will be a need for understanding it in its regional dimension. The almost frightening complexity of the caste system and the paucity of interested scholars with the requisite geographic skills and inclina-tions and the resources to carry out the necessary work have, however, too long delayed any attempt to map and describe that dimension in a systematic manner. It is hoped that the present contribution will provide an impetus to other scholars to conduct further investigations of the geography of caste, aimed both at improving what is offered here and at extending the work throughout the area where caste exists.

BIBLIOGRAPHY

GOSAL, GURDEV SINGH.
1965. Religious composition of Punjab's population changes, 1951–61. *Economic Weekly*, 17(4): 119–24.

GRIGG, DAVID.
1965. The logic of regional systems. *Annals of the Association of American Geographers*, 55: 465–91.

HARTSHORNE, RICHARD.
1939. *The nature of geography*. Lancaster, Pa.: Association of American Geographers.
1959. *Perspective on the nature of geography*. Chicago: Rand McNally.

KITTS, EUSTACE J.
1885. *A compendium of the castes and tribes found in India compiled from the census reports for the various provinces and native states of the empire*. Bombay: Education Society's Press.

MARRIOTT, McKIM.
1965. *Caste ranking and community structure in five regions of India and Pakistan*. Poona: Deccan College Postgraduate and Research Institute.

MAYER, ADRIAN C.
1958. The dominant caste in a region of central India. *Southwestern Journal of Anthropology*, 14: 407–427.

MUKERJI, A. B.
1961. The migration of the Jats—a study in historical geography. *Indian Geographer*, 6: 41–53.

SCHWARTZBERG, JOSEPH E.
1960. Occupational structure and levels of economic development in India: a regional analysis. Ph.D. dissertation, University of Michigan. Ann Arbor: University Microfilms.
1965. The distribution of selected castes in the north Indian plain. *Geographical Review*, 15: 477–95.

SRINIVAS, M. N.
1955a. The social system of a Mysore village. In McK. Marriott (Ed.), *Village India*. Chicago: University of Chicago Press.
1955b. Introduction. In M. N. Srinivas (Ed.), *India's villages*. Calcutta: Development Department, West Bengal.
1959. The dominant caste in Rampura. *American Anthropologist*, 61: 1–16.

WHITTLESEY, DERWENT.
1954. The regional concept and the regional method. In *American geography: inventory and prospect*. Syracuse: Syracuse University Press.

5. TOWARD A GRAMMAR OF DEFILEMENT IN HINDU SACRED LAW

HENRY ORENSTEIN

C ULTURE IS "CODED"; all of its subsystems are structured in much the same manner as is language. This is almost certainly true of the legal subsystem. The frequent coupling of the words "code" and "law" may not be wholly accidental, although its significance is not, perhaps, completely apprehended; the coded quality of culture is probably more evident and its philosophic implications are surely more striking in this than in most other aspects of culture. In a previous paper (1965) I began an analysis in these terms of one legal—more properly, quasilegal—subsystem, the sacred laws of Hinduism, or Dharmashastras.[1] That analysis covered regulations regarding caste, usually rendered in sacred law as "varna." Here I will carry the analysis further. I will summarize briefly the results of my earlier inquiry and then show that the "grammar" holds, not only for caste but also for many other conditions of Hindu life.

A GRAMMAR OF CASTE AND DEFILEMENT

Hindu sacred law contains an implicit opposition of pollution (defilement, impurity) and purity. Pollution signifies involvement with life substance and process, which is to be avoided so far as is possible and proper. Polluting things or processes include birth, death, sexual intercourse, bodily excretions, harmful actions, and so on. Purity means, perhaps "spiritually," in any event the absence of biological involvement. Polluted things defile pure ones, and exposure to the latter removes the effects of the former.[2]

Pollution in the Dharmashastras falls into a number of implicit types, to which

Cora Du Bois and J. A. B. Van Buitenen were kind enough to read my paper with much care and give me their constructive criticisms and helpful suggestions. I have taken their advice in some matters. Some others which called for fairly marked alterations in my trend of thought are indicated in the notes to this paper. At present I am considering these suggestions while working on the final version of this study. In the meanwhile I should like to thank Professors Du Bois and Van Buitenen for their time and effort in behalf of my work.

1. Two references are given to each code. The numbers of the relevant subdivisions of a code are placed after the name of the code-writer, and this is followed by the kind of reference usual in anthropology, naming the translator. The translators insert parentheses in the texts, presumably to convey accurate meaning. I retain these and and use square brackets for my own insertions or substitutions. I have used two rather different versions of one code, Apastamba, a recenssion from Bengal, I refer to as Apastamba-B. For discussion of the codes and the manner in which I use them, see my earlier paper (1965, pp. 1–3, 13–14).

2. In regard to matters that concern us, the main goal of the shastras, as I see it, was the avoidance of pollution. Living was a battle against life, a constant struggle to put aside engagement with things of the body and, as Robert Miller has pointed out to me, in this way

I have assigned what is largely my own nomenclature. (1) When a birth or death occurs in ego's kin group he is subject to *relational pollution*. He is defiled for a stipulated period of time varying with his genealogical distance from the deceased or newborn. Defilement is believed to "spread" through the kin group, which is conceived, in the words of the Mitakshara, as "connected by particles of the same body." Relational pollution is incurred neither through ego's actions nor through the actions of others upon him; he is simply the recipient of defilement by virtue of his biological connection with others. (2) *Act-pollution* is brought about by some form of contact with biological phenomena. It is subdivided into (*a*) *internal pollution*, in which ego, as subject, acts upon objects, and (*b*) *external pollution*, in which ego is the object. One is defiled internally by injuring living things. External pollution is brought on if one contacts biological substance or process, for example, by touching or eating bodily secretions, one's own or another's.[3]

Each of these types of pollution is associated with distinctive "paradigms," by which I mean orderly variations on rules not unlike the declensions of grammar. The paradigms for internal and external pollution are fairly obvious and easily explained. The amount of internal pollution ego incurs is proportionate to the purity of his victim's varna; for example, the penance for killing a Kshatriya is less than that for killing a Brahman, and so on down in varna rank. Defilement is simply dependent upon the magnitude of the crime, which depends, in turn, upon the purity of the victim. The extent of ego's external pollution is proportionate to the defilement of the varna he contacts; for example, a Vaishya's corpse defiles more than does a Brahman's. Pollution here simply involves "catching" defilement from someone or something; the more defiled the source, the greater the pollution.

The explanation of act-pollution and relational pollution is more complex. Ego's relational defilement is inversely proportionate to his caste rank; that is, the higher the rank the less the defilement in case of a birth or death. Brahmans are usually said to be polluted for ten days, Kshatriyas for twelve days, Vaishyas for fifteen, and Shudras for thirty. In contrast, the amount of act-pollution is pro-

---

to achieve moksha, the ultimate "not-so." Van Buitenen dissents from this emphasis on the negative side of the codes; if I understand him correctly, he views the central aim of the shastras as the attainment of a positive state of purity, which, in turn, gives spiritual power. He may be correct in this, but for the time being I think it best to hold to my original position. Obviously the difference is one of emphasis and does not substantially alter the conclusions of this paper.

3. This classification is preliminary; it is intended to cover only the regulations discussed in this paper and will later be elaborated. On the advice of Du Bois, Van Buitenen, and others, I have changed the nomenclature employed in my earlier paper, adopting in part a suggestion of Du Bois'. For "relational pollution" I formerly used "intransitive pollution," for "act-pollution," the term "transitive pollution." Though they serve to describe fairly well the kinds of pollution involved, I am not yet fully satisfied with the new terms and may alter them in the final version.

I retain the words "external" and "internal," although when I first chose them I had forgotten that they had been used earlier by Stevenson for very different kinds of pollution (1954, pp. 56–58). However, my distinction is one of kind, Stevenson's is one of degree; his "internal pollution" is more severe than his "external," and one can, it seems to me, simply refer to them as more or less severe. Nevertheless, I would yield on this small matter were it not for the fact that my usage is based on that of Baudhayana (*circa* 500–200 B.C.), which gives it precedence.

portionate to rank; if one touches a corpse or kills a cow, one's pollution is greater if one's caste is higher.

To explain this reversal, we must assume, first, that in the minds of the sacerdotal lawyers, all human beings, all living things, were conceived as to some extent polluted, and, second, that the amount of pollution "normally," "naturally" associated with each caste was believed to vary with its rank; that is, low castes were conceived as naturally more deeply implicated with life substance and process than high ones. Any deviation from normal pollution requires a purifying process or period of time to return to the normal state. Since the latter differs among the castes, a different amount of purification is required of each.

Relational pollution was taken to be something that happens to a kinship group (people "connected by particles of the same body"), something that "spreads" throughout the group. "Spreading" affects pollution in a manner analogous to multiplication. Holding constant such factors as degree of relationship, birth or death results in a "multiplication" of normal pollution by the same amount for each caste. Because the normal condition of lower castes is to be more defiled, the increase in relational pollution for them is greater than for higher castes.

Act-pollution was conceived as impinging on the individual from without. Its extent was seen as determined, other things being equal, entirely by the phenomena with which ego interacts. To recover a normal state after act-pollution, a member of a high caste, hence, must rid himself of more defilement than someone of low caste, for his normal state involves less defilement.

In order to make this position as clear as possible, I represent the distinction between relational and act-pollution graphically, exaggerating the precision of the rules.

Act-Pollution		Normal Condition	Relational Pollution		
Remainder	Object (= Abnormal Condition)		Event	Abnormal Condition	Remainder
		(Brahman)			
8	10	2	(x5)	10	8
		(Kshatriya)			
7	10	3	(x5)	15	12
		(Vaishya)			
5	10	5	(x5)	25	20
		(Shudra)			
2	10	8	(x5)	40	32

Of course, multiplication and subtraction did not take place in this precise fashion. The penances vary from code to code, and many of the paradigms are not given numerically. I suggest not an arithmetical model but rather a linguistic one.

TOWARD A GENERAL GRAMMAR OF DEFILEMENT

This, in broad outline, represents the essential features of a grammar of defilement in Hindu sacred law. However, it has been referred only to differences and variations in pollution associated with caste rank, and there are other relevant matters. For example, while each caste was thought of as having a normal amount of defilement inextricably associated with it, the impurity of individuals was believed to be changeable. Changes could be temporary, such as the additional purity that accrues to persons engaged in religious rites. In many cases there are permanent alterations in natural pollution; that is, the polluted condition to which the individual is expected to return after defilement is, itself, altered. Thus, when an individual becomes learned in the Vedas he is elevated; when he refrains from doing his religious duty, he is "degraded," *nirguṇa*. If our grammar is valid, it should be applicable to conditions of this kind as well as to caste. I will now show that it is.

RELATIONAL POLLUTION

Some of the codes classify Brahmans according to the number of sacred "qualifications" they possess; those classified as more sacred (hence less polluted) are less subject to relational pollution. Atri (83) and Parashara (iii:5), for example, put in one group Brahmans who know the Vedas and keep the sacred fire, in another group those who know the Veda but do not keep the sacred fire, and in a third those who are "without either the Veda or the fire." The most sacred group attains purity, in the event of a birth or death, in one day, the second group attains it in three days, while the last must wait out the full ten-day period (Dutt, 1907; p. 296; Bhattacharyya, 1887, p. 13). Ushanas (vi: 7, 34) puts forward different qualifications, implying four groups, of which the most "qualified" is pure in one day, the next in three days, the third in four days, and ordinary Brahmans in ten days (Dutt, 1907, pp. 239, 243). Ushanas (vi: 4–5, 23–25, 51, 55–57) and Parashara (iii: 19–20)[4] make other statements, more general but of the same type, which allow immediate purification or curtailed pollution for those given to religious study, for those who give daily charity, and so on (Dutt, 1907, pp. 238–39, 241–42, 245–46; Bhattacharyya, 1887, pp. 15–16). Gautama (xiv: 1), Baudhayana (i, 5, 11: 1), Yajnavalkya (iii: 28), and Shankha (xv: 21) also exempt from relational pollution individual Brahmans who have undergone special purificatory rites, such as the *śrauta* sacrifice, or who perform highly sacred duties, such as

---

4. The reference to Parashara in Bhattacharyya's version, which I have used here, apparently corresponds to sloka 28 in Dutt's recension, where the statement is not relevant to this topic (Dutt, 1907, p. 549).

those of the sacrificial priest (Bühler, 1879, p. 246; 1882, p. 177; Dutt, 1907, pp. 122, 641).[5]

On a number of occasions one is in a temporarily heightened state of purity. The rules here are consistent with others. One should not perform marriage ceremonies, vows, sacrifices, or other religious rites when in relational pollution; this would defile the deities involved in the rites. But once such ceremonies have begun, one is temporarily elevated to a highly spiritualized plane, and one is, hence, immune from relational pollution. Codes that provide for exemptions of this kind are Manu (v: 93), Vishnu xxii: 49–53), Yajnavalkya (iii: 28–29), Ushanas (vi: 23–25), Atri (84, 97–98), Katyayana (xxiv: 5), and Apastamba-B (x: 16). Parashara (iii: 20–21) mentions it only in regard to birth pollution (Bühler, 1886, p. 185; Jolly, 1880, pp. 92–93; Dutt, 1907, pp. 122, 241–42, 296, 298, 407, 749; Bhattacharyya, 1887, pp. 15–16).[6]

The king is usually thought to be in a highly sacred state and is, hence, not subject to relational pollution. Thus Manu (v: 93–94, 96–97): "For a king, on the throne of magnanimity, immediate purification is prescribed. . . . Because the king is pervaded by [the eight guardian deities of the world], no impurity is ordained for him" (Bühler, 1886, pp. 185–86).[7] Vishnu (xxii: 48) exempts kings from impurity, but he specifies that this holds for them "while engaged in the discharge of their duties" (Jolly, 1880, pp. 92–93). Gautama (xiv: 45) also relieves monarchs of the burden of impurity but adds that this is "lest their business be impeded" (Bühler, 1879, p. 251).[8] This is difficult to interpret. It is possible that Gautama and Vishnu release kings from such necessities in order to facilitate affairs of state, that is, as a matter of simple practicality, which would place this regulation among a number of others that I will consider in later publications. The ruling may be interpreted as one of practicality *and* increased purity, for the two principles, in this instance, obviously do not clash. Other codes, such as

5. A śrauta sacrifice is one prescribed in the Vedas. There were a number of different kinds (see Kane 1930–62, iii, Ch. 29). An additional ruling by Gautama may be interpreted as exempting very pure Brahmans from pollution. See note 9.

6. See note 5.

7. Van Buitenen has been good enough to give me a more accurate translation of this passage. The most important discrepancy with that given by Bühler is in the words "pervaded by," which can be rendered as either "inhabited by" *or* "governed by."

Van Buitenen believes that the king is a unique, singular case, not comparable with, for example, ordinary Kshatriyas or even unusually pure Brahmans, who comprise aggregates or groups of persons. The king's immunity from pollution is, therefore, not comparable with others; he is exempt because of his unique position, and, if I understand Van Buitenen correctly, because of the importance of his work, because of practicality. This is quite possibly correct, for, as I recall, the king is exempted from other forms of pollution in some texts. I will take up this problem at a later date. Meanwhile, I would argue that his exalted secular condition, however unique, was believed to bestow on him greater purity, even if he was seen to be only "governed by" and not "inhabited by" deities; hence, both explanations apply.

8. In the sutra immediately following the one on kings, Gautama exempts a Brahman from pollution "lest his daily study of the Veda be interrupted." I conjecture that Gautama was employing a turn of phrase here, knowing that his reader would understand his meaning as "A Brahman who daily studies the Vedas is never impure," much as Manu and other codes put it. I think this interpretation may also apply to the preceding sutra, referring to kings. However, I am not equipped to resolve problems such as this and must leave their resolution to those who are.

Manu, exempt the king without qualification: Parashara (iii: 19–20), Yajnavalkya (iii: 27), Ushanas (vi: 55–57), Atri (184), Daksha (vi: 5), and Shankha (xv: 21); Bühler (1879, p. 251), Bhattacharyya (1887, pp. 15–16), Dutt (1907, pp. 122, 246, 296, 450, 641).

One shastra writer, Yajnavalkya (iii: 22), makes special provisions for Shudras in birth and death pollution. He first gives the usual paradigm prescribing thirty days of impurity for Shudras and then adds, "and half of that for well behaved (Shudras)" (Dutt, 1907, pp. 120–21).[9]

This paradigm was applied, at least in part, to the ashramas, the orders or stages of life through which the high-born Hindu should pass. The orders, of course, differ in purity. The householder, or grihastha, was most polluted, the student, or brahmacari, less so, the forest hermit, vanaprastha, yet less, and the wandering ascetic, *yati* or sannyasi, least. Many of the codes mention the effect of birth or death on students. Vishnu (xxii: 85–87) says that a student may, if necessary, perform the funeral of his deceased guru and implies that this holds for a deceased parent as well. If he does so, he undergoes the regular ten-day pollution. However, the student is not polluted if he does not actually perform the funeral rites and he is not polluted at the death of other sapinda (close kinsmen, primarily patrilineal) unless he offers them water libations after his studentship ends, in which case he is impure for three days. The recent commentator Nandapandita is consistent with this when he exempts the student from impurity on the demise of all kinsmen but his parents (Jolly, 1880, pp. 92, 96). According to Katyayana (xxiv: 6), a religious student does not become impure even at the death of his father; the impurity takes place after his studies cease "or [and?] lasts for three days" (Dutt, 1907, p. 407). The remainder of the codes that mention the matter state, without qualification, that the religious student is exempt from relational pollution: Gautama (xiv: 1), Baudhayana (i, 5, 11: 1), Parashara (iii: 17), Yajnavalkya (iii: 15), Ushanas (vi: 55–57), Atri (97), Shankha (xv: 21); Bühler (1879, p. 246; 1882, p. 177), Bhattacharyya (1887, p. 15), Dutt (1907, pp. 119, 246, 298, 641).

Vasishtha (x: 27), Jajnavalkya (iii: 28),[10] Shankha (xv: 21), and Atri (97) assert that ascetics are not affected by birth or death (Bühler, 1882, pp. 48–49; Mandlik, 1880, p. 247; Dutt, 1907, pp. 298, 641). There are no further statements on ascetics and none whatever on hermits. This lack is comprehensible; if students are said to be subject to little or no pollution, then the immunity of these orders, which are considerably purer than that of student, may have been considered too obvious for much discussion.

Those who consistently fail in their religious duties are thereby degraded; in case of birth or death they are more polluted than others. Ushanas gives a number of rules of this type (vi: 6, 9, 15). If a very young child dies or an abortion occurs, he prescribes no impurity for sapinda, but if the sapinda is "*Nirguna* (unmeritorious)," then he is polluted for one day or one day and a night. Ushanas

9. Van Buitenen: Shudras "who abide by the rules."
10. Reference is to Mandlik's version of Yajnavalkya. Dutt's rendering differs, as a result either of a difference in translation or of the recension used (1907, p. 122).

states that on the death of an adult the period of impurity of the unmeritorious extends over the usual ten days, and then later adds: "The period of impurity of those who do not perform religious rites, who do not read in the Veda, and who suffer from leprosy,[11] etc., terminates with their death." According to Atri also (102–103) perpetual impurity is the lot of the unmeritorious (Dutt, 1907, pp. 198, 239–41).

A nearly complete paradigm for relational pollution, taking in most of the conditions we have mentioned, is given in a highly systematic manner by Daksha (vi: 1–11). He begins by asserting that impurity can cease immediately; it can last for one day, two, three, four, ten, twelve, fourteen, or thirty days; or it can terminate with death. He then goes on to describe those who are "immediately pure," such as kings, sacrificial priests, and those engaged in religious rites. Next he adds, "One day is spoken of for him who maintains the Sacred Fire and studies the Vedas. Two, three, and four days are for those who are inferior and more inferior." He then gives the usual paradigm for the varnas, concluding with the thirty-day period of pollution for Shudras. He ends with those for whom "perpetual impurity" is ordained, such as people who do not bathe or give gifts, the illiterate, and those who do not do shraddhas (ancestor propitiation rites) (Dutt, 1907, pp. 450–51).

ACT-POLLUTION

The anticipated regularity also holds for act-pollution; the normally less polluted require more purification. If one is bitten by a dog, a wolf, or a similar animal, a penance is required. Parashara gives several penances (v: 1–5). If a man, "whether religious or not," is bitten he need merely salute a number of Brahmans, who purify him by looking at him. If a "superior Brahman" is bitten, he must wash and recite the highly sacred Gayatri mantra inaudibly, while a Brahman sanctified by knowledge of the Vedas must wash with water touched by gold and eat clarified butter. If one is bitten while engaged in a religious rite, one must fast three nights, take clarified butter, and drink sanctified water (Bhattacharyya, 1887, p. 24). In Atri (66, 68) we find a paradigm like this one, involving animal bite, but with different details (Dutt, 1907, p. 294).

Manu gives a special rule on self-defilement (for example, after urination) for superior Shudras. First he asserts that one must sip water three times in the ritual and adds that a Shudra should do so only once (v: 139). Then he modifies the rule (v: 140), saying that for "Shudras who live according to the law . . . their mode of purification (shall be) the same as that of Vaishyas." A number of commentators interpret living "according to the law" as "who serve Aryans" (Bühler, 1886, p. 193). It is possible that the idea in regard to sipping is not that by serving Aryans the Shudra's normal defilement is decreased, necessitating greater purification, but rather that they must keep themselves in a purer condition than other Shudras because they are in contact with the twice-born. Baudhayana (i, 5, 10: 20) asserts that Shudras serving the twice-born should sip water according to the

11. Many diseases, especially leprosy, were thought to be the result of grave sins committed in former lives.

same rule as the latter, and Apastamba (ii, 2, 3: 5) prescribes that Shudras who prepare food for the ceremonies of the twice-born must follow the same rules for sipping as their masters (Bühler, 1882, pp. 174–75; 1879, p. 103). However, the two explanations are not inconsistent; I believe both apply.

In the eyes of the code-writers women differed from men in natural pollution. To be sure, there was ambivalence on this topic. As Yalman has shown (1963), the purity of women is of extraordinary importance among Hindus, for it is through them that "blood" is perpetuated, hence through them that caste purity is preserved. In some contexts this attitude is reflected in the codes. One finds statements such as "women are free from all stains," "pure in all limbs." They "never (become) entirely foul." Agni (fire) gave them "perfect purity." They can no more be sullied by impure substances than a river. For examples of such statements, see Vasishtha (xxviii: 5–6, 9), Baudhayana (ii, 2, 4: 4–5), Yajnavalkya (i: 121), and Atri (139, 189); Bühler (1882, pp. 133, 223), Vidyarnava (1918, p. 137), Dutt (1907, pp. 303, 308).

However, women were simultaneously conceived of as impure, perhaps because they were believed to be more intimately involved with life process. Women are permitted no exposure to the sacred mantras according to Manu (ii: 66), seconded by the commentator Balambhatta (Bühler, 1886, p. 42; Vidyarnava, 1918, pp. 102–103). Others allow them but one exposure to mantras, at the time of their wedding. Apart from this occasion, their samskaras (rites intended to rid the body of defilement) are devoid of mantras. See, for example, Vishnu (xxvii: 13–14), Vyasa (i: 16), and Yajnavalkya (i: 13); Jolly (1880, p. 114), Dutt (1907, p. 503), Vidyarnava (1918, p. 54). As Manu has it (ix: 18), "women[,] (who are) destitute of (the knowledge of) Vedic texts, (are as impure as) falsehood (itself), that is a fixed rule" (Bühler, 1886, p. 330). The commentator Balambhatta directly compares women with Shudras in matters pertaining to religion (Vidyarnava, 1918, p. 144), and, indeed, as will shortly be seen, they are often grouped with Shudras when penances and purification are put forward.

The impure condition of women is reflected in some of the rules. According to Apastamba-B (iii: 6) and Angiras (i: 33), it is a general rule that a woman's penance is half that of a man. A number of commentators agree (Dutt, 1907, pp. 272, 730; Bühler, 1879, p. 84; Vidyarnava, 1918, p. 138). Children of outcastes could be readmitted to caste if they underwent a penance; Baudhayana (ii: 1, 2, 24–25) requires a milder penance for women (Bühler, 1882, p. 221). Parashara (v: 2, 5, 7) and Atri (66–67) require lighter penances for women in cases of dog bite. Vasishtha (xxvlll: 7) attests that only major crimes, such as the murder of Brahmans or of their own husbands, justify outcasting women (Bhattacharyya, 1887, p. 24; Dutt, 1907, p. 294; Bühler, 1882, p. 133).

Some of these regulations might be interpreted as concessions to the "weakness" of women, as matters of practicality, for the sacerdotal lawyers were not insensitive to such problems. However, I doubt that this holds for all the rules, for women are frequently linked with Shudras in regard to the quantity of water required for purification; the expression often employed is "a woman and a

Shudra." Like Shudras, but unlike men of higher caste, they are purified, in Vishnu's words (lxii: 9), "by water which has once touched their palate." Statements akin to this are made by Vasishtha (iii: 34), Baudhayana (i: 5, 8: 22–23), Manu (v: 138–39), Yajnavalkya (i: 21), Shankha (ix: 4), and a number of commentators (Jolly, 1880, p. 199; Bühler, 1882, pp. 21, 167; 1886, p. 193; Vidyarnava, 1918, pp. 60–61; Dutt, 1907, p. 627). As will be seen in connection with internal pollution, women are also sometimes grouped with Shudras when penances for murder are given.[12]

Clearly the paradigm holds for the ashramas, the ideal stages of life. Vishnu first gives the rules for cleansing oneself after voiding excrement—one cleans the left hand ten times, the right seven, etc.—and then adds (lx: 25–26), "Such is the purification ordained for householders; it is double for students; treble for hermits; quadruple for ascetics." Other instances of this paradigm, with minor variations, are in Vasishtha (vi: 19), Manu (v: 137), Daksha (v: 8–9), and Shankha (xvi: 22); Jolly (1880, p. 196), Bühler (1882, pp. 36–37; 1886, p. 193), Dutt (1907, pp. 448–49, 644). According to a recension of Angiras not available to me, this paradigm also holds for internal pollution; when householders, students, hermits, or ascetics inflict injury on living things, their penances are increased in the order given. Angiras' rule is seconded by the Mitakshara (Gharpure, 1942, p. 1739; see also Kane, 1930–1962, iv, 83).

The rule for act-pollution is applied not only to people of different degrees of pollution but also to different parts of the human body, for these are believed to differ in the extent of natural pollution. A rough classification, as given, for example, by Baudhayana (i, 5, 10: 19) and Manu (v: 132), is that the portion of the body above the navel is pure, while that below is impure (Bühler, 1882, p. 174; 1886, p. 192). In fact, this is a simplification, for the classification of the body is sometimes further refined, the head being purer than most other parts, the mouth the purest, and so on. For illustrations, see Manu (i: 92; iv: 82) and Vishnu (lxviii: 83); Bühler (1886, pp. 24–25, 141–42), Jolly (1880, p. 220). It is understandable, then, that we should find in a number of codes, including Apastamba (i, 5, 16: 14), Vasishtha (iii: 38), and Manu (v: 145), that water must be sipped after sleeping in order to purify the body. This is explained by Daksha (ii: 8) as due to the fact that the body secretes substances in sleep, and "the superior organs thereby come to be level with the inferior ones" (Bühler, 1879, pp. 58–59; 1882, p. 22; 1886, p. 194; Dutt, 1907, p. 435).

The rules of act-pollution applied to the body follow those we have previously discussed. Yama (45) and Apastamba-B (i: 10) assert that if one is "sullied" by impure substances below the navel, one must wash the particular spot and rub it with earth, but if one is defiled above the navel, one must bathe the entire body (Dutt, 1907, pp. 282, 743). The Mitakshara refers to Devala (a code unavailable to me) in agreement on this point, and the commentator Govinda's interpretation

12. Women are not mentioned as subject to longer periods of relational pollution despite their greater natural impurity. As Irawati Karve pointed out at the conference at which this paper was given, such lengthening of the pollution period would present an impossible situation, for women must prepare food for the household and could not do so if in an abnormal state of defilement.

of Baudhayana, which specifies being touched by a dog, also gives this rule (Vidyarnava, 1918, p. 286; Bühler, 1882, p. 183). The same idea is given in other law texts, sometimes with refinements. Thus Vishnu (xxii: 77–80) gives a similar rule for defilement with liquor or bodily excretions but adds that pollution above the navel necessitates cleaning the spot with earth and water as well as bathing. He then states that if the mouth or lip is likewise defiled, one must fast, bathe, and drink pañcagavya (cow urine, milk, dung, curds, and clarified butter); Jolly (1880, p. 95). According to Ushanas (ix: 81–82), if a man is bitten by a dog below the navel, he must drink only milk in the evening for three days; if the bite is above the navel, "threefold is the penance." If he is bitten on the head, the penance is fourfold. Atri ignores the grosser division of the body and asserts (206): "The head, neck, thighs, and feet being contaminated with spiritous liquor, one should fast, in order, for ten, six, three, and one day" (Dutt, 1907, pp. 264, 310).[13]

The paradigms for act-pollution make sense of the extent to which things perceived as supernatural in India are shielded from contacts with things of this world. They are the purest of things; hence they are highly susceptible to defilement and, therefore, require elaborate defense against polluting influences. The Vedas are the most sacred of all phenomena in Hinduism; the codes abound in strictures regarding them. For example, one may not study the Vedas within the hearing or sight of Shudras or other low castes; according to some, not even in a village inhabited by a "vile caste." One should not study the Vedas when a dog, jackal, or ass emits a noise, or in the vicinity of such animals. Study is prohibited for three days after one is invited to a shradda, or for that matter, anywhere in the vicinity of death or when in any way affected by it. It is obviously prohibited when one is defiled by food leavings, excrement, or the like. Some codes require that one should not even think of the Vedas when impure. Rules of this kind can be found, for example, in Apastamba (i, 3, 9: 6–10, 17; i, 3, 10: 2–5, 10), Vasishtha (xiii: 11–16, 20–29), Baudhayana (i, 11, 21: 4, 8, 15, 21), Manu (iv: 108–11, 127), Vishnu (xxii: 6; xxx: 10–14; lxviii: 38), Yajnavalkya (i: 144, 146, 148–49), Ushanas (iii: 65–69, 74, 78; vi: 1–2), and Shankha (iii: 4–7); Bühler (1879, pp. 34–37; 1882, pp. 64–66, 208–11; 1886, pp. 146, 149), Jolly (1880, pp. 87, 124, 220), Vidyanarnava (1918, pp. 251–54), Dutt (1907, pp. 210–12, 238, 614–15).

Deities and other supernatural beings and phenomena are also conceived of as highly susceptible to pollution, although, probably because they are not considered so pure as the Vedas, the codes do not give as much attention to them. One must not pronounce the name of a deity when "unclean." There must be no blemish on one's clothing during a sacrifice to a god. While performing a religious rite one must not touch oneself below the navel. One cannot step on the shadow of a god's image. It is forbidden to look at the sacred celestial bodies, the sun, the moon, etc., while unclean. A cow must not be touched while one is unwashed. Indeed, one must not approach a fire too closely when defiled, for fire is a deity. Even when pure, one should not blow on a fire with one's breath for fear that

---

13. Van Buitenen suggests that this may be a metaphorical way of referring to degrees of drunkenness rather than to distinctions between parts of the body.

saliva will pollute it. Eating is prohibited in a house wherein a sacred fire is preserved. One should not urinate in a river or in any body of water and not in the direction of a fire or the sun. No bodily impurities should be thrown into water. Regulations of this type are present, for example, in Apastamba (i, 5, 15: 18–20; i, 11, 30: 19–20; i, 11, 39: 4), Vasishtha (xii: 11–12), Baudhayana (i, 5, 10: 18; i, 6, 13: 4), Manu (iv: 130, 142–43), Vishnu (xxii: 6; lx: 15, 18–19, 21–22; lxviii: 37, 47), Yajnavalkya (i: 134–35, 137, 152, 155), and Ushanas (ii: 36–38, 41–42; ix: 85–86, 89, 96–99); Bühler (1879, pp. 56, 93–94; 1882, pp. 60, 174, 186; 1886, pp. 149, 151), Jolly (1880, pp. 87, 195–96, 220–21), Vidyanarva (1918, pp. 246–48, 255–56, 257), Dutt (1907, pp. 201, 264–66).

INTERNAL AND EXTERNAL POLLUTION

Paradigms pertaining to variation from normal pollution occur not only when the subject but also when the object of action is involved, that is, in regard to internal and external pollution. Internal defilement is not difficult to document. When an individual is killed while in an unusually pure state, the murderer is more polluted than otherwise. If one kills a Brahman, the usual penance lasts twelve years; however, according to Apastamba (i, 9, 24: 7, 20, 24–25), if the Brahman was a student of the Vedas or had completed a Vedic sacrifice, the murderer must perform the same penance for the remainder of his life (Bühler, 1879, pp. 79–81). Yajnavalkya (iii: 252) and Shankha (xvii: 7) assert that if one kills a Brahman while he is engaged in an important religious ceremony, the normal penance is doubled, requiring 24 years of austerity (Dutt, 1907, pp. 153, 645).

Similar principles are applied to Kshatriyas and Vaishyas. Vishnu (1: 11) prescribes a 24-year penance for the murderer of a king, which is much more than that for the murder of an ordinary Kshatriya (Jolly, 1880, p. 158). Apastamba (i, 9, 24: 6–7) holds that the murder of a Kshatriya or a Vaishya "who had studied the Veda, or had been initiated for the performance of a Soma-sacrifice" is equivalent to Brahmanicide. Manu (xi: 88) says the same, but applies the rule only to those from these castes who are engaged in or have completed a Vedic sacrifice (Bühler, 1879, p. 79; 1886, p. 448). Vasishtha (xx: 34), Vishnu (xxxvi: I; 1: 6–7), Yajnavalkya (iii: 251), and Shankha (xvii: 4) give rules of much the same kind, pertaining to Kshatriyas or Vaishyas who are engaged in ceremonies (Bühler, 1882, p. 107; Jolly, 1880, pp. 133–34, 157; Dutt, 1907, pp. 152, 645).

A woman being less pure than a man, her murder requires a lesser penance in most of the codes that mention the subject. According to Vasishtha (xx: 37–40), the murder of a Brahman woman requires the penance appropriate for killing Kshatriya men, the murder of a Kshatriya woman that appropriate for Vaishya men, while killing a Shudra woman requires but one year of the penance for Brahmanicide (Bühler, 1882, p. 108). Gautama (xxii: 16–17), Baudhayana (ii, 1, 1: 10–11), and Yajnavalkya (iii: 269) assert that the penance for killing a woman is the same as that for killing a Shudra (Bühler, 1879, pp. 281–82; 1882, p. 212; Mandlik, 1880, p. 267). Atri (164–67) also prescribes a lighter penance for killing a woman (Dutt 1907, p. 306). According to Parashara (xii: 74), the murder of a woman engaged in a sacrifice, that is, one who is in an unusually pure state, is equivalent to the murder of a man (Bhattacharyya, 1887, p. 73). Apastamba (i, 9, 24: 5) is, in part, an exception regarding women. He asserts that the penance for murdering women of the Kashatriya, Vaishya, or Shudra castes is the same as that for murdering men of those castes. He makes no unqualified statement about Brahman women but does say that the murder of a Brahman woman "during her courses" is a major sin, like the murder of a Brahman man. The murder of a menstruating woman is always classed as a much graver sin than the murder of a woman under ordinary circumstances (a subject I will discuss in a later publication), thus a lighter penance is implied for killing Brahman women than for killing Brahman men (Bühler, 1879, p. 79).

The murder of persons "degraded" for one or another reason requires a milder penance. Atri (278) prescribes that, if one kills a deceitful Brahman, the penance is that for Shudra murder (Dutt, 1907, p. 320). Yajnavalkya (iii: 268–69), as I have mentioned, equates the murder of a woman with that of a Shudra, but he asserts that, if the woman be unchaste, the killer need merely give a gift; in the case of a Brahman woman, this gift would be a leather vessel; of a Kshatriya, a bow; and of a Vaishya, a goat and a lamb (Mandlik, 1880, p. 267).[14] Manu (xi: 139) makes a similar statement regarding unchaste women, but does not mention the penance for killing the chaste among them (Bühler, 1886, p. 458). Gautama applies the same principle (xxii: 16–17, 26–27) but mentions only Brahman women and adds that there is no penance for killing harlots (Bühler, 1879, pp. 281–83).

I have found but little data on external pollution involving permanent variations in normal defilement, although—more likely because—it is one of the most obvious features of the grammar of defilement that pollution is "contagious," that the more polluted the source, the more polluting will be the contact. One case is from Vasishtha (xxi: 16–17), who requires a severe penance of a Brahman for adultery with a Brahman woman but a yet more severe penance if the woman's husband is debased, negligent in his religious duties (see xxiv: 2, for penance) Bühler (1882, pp. 113, 123–24).[15] The defilement of sinful persons is "catching." According to Parashara (iv: 7–11), if a Brahman associates, even unintentionally, with someone degraded by sin, "he becomes as degraded as they." The length of the association determines the severity of the penance required to free him from degradation. Indeed, Parashara asserts that one should not even approach a degraded sinner (xii: 53); Bhattacharyya (1887: 20, 71). Much the same idea is conveyed by many other codes; association with one who has committed a *mahāpātaka* (the gravest sins) is itself a *mahāpātaka* and requires the appropriate penance in order to restore purity; association with an outcaste similarly results in loss of caste; see, for example, Gautama (xx: 8–9; xxi: 3) Manu (xi: 55, 182), Vishnu (xxxv: 2–5), Yajnavalkya (iii: 227), Ushanas (viii: 1), and Atri (164); Bühler (1879,

---

14. Mandlik's version of Yajnavalkya refers to women "not greatly misbehaving," while Dutts' (lll: 270) refers to women "who have gone a little astray" (Dutt, 1907, p. 55). I believe that the difference is one of translation and that Mandlik is closer to the intent of the original. Van Buitenen corroborates this.

15. In some cases adultery was conceived of in terms of internal pollution, for example, see Gautama (xxii: 29–30); Bühler (1879: 283).

pp. 275, 277; 1886, pp. 441, 468), Jolly (1880, p. 133), Dutt (1907, pp. 149, 250, 306).

While there are relatively few rulings on external pollution incurred through contact with persons whose normal condition of pollution is permanently altered, there are numerous cases involving pollution through contact with the temporarily defiled. That this is polluting is well known to anyone familiar with Hinduism and does not require heavy documentation here. People of twice-born caste, ordinarily not polluting, pollute on contact when they have the remains of food in their mouths; people with whom contact ordinarily pollutes but little pollute more when they are unwashed after having eaten. This kind of rule can be found in, among other codes, Angiras (i: 8–9, 11), Yama (281), Atri (283), Apastamba-B (v: 12–13), and Parashara (iii: 21); Dutt (1907, pp. 269, 281, 283, 743), Bhattacharyya (1887, p. 38). Additional illustrations of this type were given in my earlier paper (1965, pp. 6, 9–10).

CONCLUSION

Some of the data of this study lend greater plausibility to the wording of one rule of our "grammar." It was suggested that relational pollution differed among the varnas because it was considered to affect the individual in a manner analogous to multiplication; the event itself, the birth or death, was of equal "potency" in all groups, but the differences in their natural defilement resulted in varying durations of pollution. Contrary to this, one might argue plausibly that the event was thought to have different "potencies" in different varnas; thus, because a Brahman is believed to be purer than a Shudra, his corpse might be thought to pollute his kinsmen less than the Shudra's defiles his. We see now that this is probably not what was in the minds of the *śāstris*. The condition of the living kinsmen was taken to be of greatest importance. Without special reference to the condition of the deceased, impure Brahmans, for example, were said to be more defiled by a death, and especially pure Brahmans to be less defiled.

Most important, the "codified" system of rules that in my earlier study was shown to be relevant for caste we now see applies, as well, to many other facets of Hindu life. It applies to, among other conditions, the life history of the individual, the extent to which man is dutiful, differences between the sexes, different parts of the human body, and the distinction between man and the supernatural. Even in this as yet incomplete study, we find that structured regulations subsume a very large slice of life indeed. At a later date I will take up other aspects of this grammar of defilement, some of which involve modifications—structured modifications—of the rules thus far discussed. For the present I should like merely to mention some of the implications of this approach for the study of law and ethics.

To start, I would point out that my data are not peculiar. A cursory glance at traditional Chinese law gives hints of the possibility of similar regularities there (Ch'ü 1961, pp. 16–18, 65–70, 72–74, 128–29, 186–87, 196–98). Clearly this approach is not to be conceived of as applicable only to this one case or even to this one kind of cultural subsystem. A number of studies of kinship systems show that these are highly structured, more so, or in any event more plainly so, than legal systems (for example, see Goodenough, 1951, pp. 92–110; 1956; Lounsbury, 1956; 1964; Buchler, 1964). Folk medical concepts and practices are probably similarly structured (Frake, 1961; Yalman, 1964). The outlines of this kind of coding are being discerned in a native system of color perception (Conklin, 1955). Aesthetics is not excluded; Jacobs has applied something of this method to the study of an oral literature (1959). Lévi-Strauss, who pioneered the approach represented here, has, in one of many studies of this kind, depicted totemism in broad strokes as part of a larger system of categories probably involving innate tendencies of thought (1963).

Working from a perspective far different from ours, some legal theorists are reaching conclusions having interesting parallels to our own. Lon Fuller (1958, 1964), for example, has maintained that some of the very characteristics entering into the definition of law involve an element of what we usually consider to be justice. There is a "morality that makes law possible," which includes such features as a degree of generality in most laws and a lack of contradiction among them. A completely chaotic, self-contradictory, constantly shifting agglomeration of commands, Fuller makes clear, would be utterly unjust in its demands and correspondingly remote from law as that term is normally understood.

Fuller (1964, ch. 4) and other jurists go beyond these purely formal criteria. Thus Roscoe Pound has shown that the legal order inescapably contains moral ideals of a more substantive character (for example, 1926, 1952, 1958). He writes:

It is futile to reject wholly an ideal element in legislation, administration and adjudication. Men are governed consciously or unconsciously in what they do by assumptions as to what it is that they are doing and of purposes of their doing it. The words "idea" and "ideal" are derived from a Greek word which may be rendered as picture. What is done is done to a picture of what is being done and this picture is shaped to why it is being done (1952, p. 132).

F. S. C. Northrop (1946, 1959) holds a view akin to this, although the direction of his analysis differs.

To put Pound's position in our own terms, we might say that the legal order involves a quasi-deductive procedure; laws (and, I would add, ethical rules in general) are framed for particular circumstances, but the manner in which they are framed is "deduced" from generally shared, though usually not consciously formulated, abstract moral and cognitive principles. Preserving at least a part of the meaning of a venerable expression, one may conclude that there are "natural principles of justice" necessarily implicated in any given body of law, if it is to be law, "properly so-called."[16]

16. A summary as brief as this of Pound's highly complex legal theory runs into danger of distortion. To my knowledge, the fullest discussion of the aspect of his theory relevant here is his *The Ideal Element in Law* (1958), which I recommend to those interested. I recognize, of course, that a legal or ethical system cannot too closely approach complete consistency without violating other principles, for example, what I call practicality. Fuller has observed (1964, pp. 41–44) that most of the essential characteristics of law are part of a "morality of aspiration" rather than a "morality of duty"; that is, no legal system is ever perfectly legal. I expect to discuss this problem more thoroughly at another time.

One implication of Pound's theory and of the approach to law and ethics taken here is that legal or ethical rules, even if one considers them to be wholly relative to the culture in which they are embedded, may be objectively judged and perhaps condemned by nonparticipants in the culture. The orientation of the members of a society to a norm is not significant in this regard; they might, one and all, display deep emotional attachment to a rule and carry out its injunctions fully; yet the rule could, by reference to the general principles they themselves implicitly hold, be censured as unjust and illegal.

This does not exhaust all of the implications of the grammatical approach to law and ethics. I give my conjectures on one more. It is becoming increasingly evident through recent developments in linguistic theory (Chomsky, 1957; Lees, 1960) that languages are not learned in a simple inductive fashion; a child seems almost to deduce the grammar of its language from pre-existing general principles —probably, in fact, to assimilate very rapidly such principles and then readily, although largely unconsciously, to fit in or deduce particular applications. In brief, man may be innately prone to be grammatical (see, for example, Lees, 1957, pp. 406–408; Chomsky, 1959; Berko, 1958). It is possible that this holds, not only for language but for all or most of the other subsystems of culture; a genetically determined, quasi-deductive process may be involved in their acquisition. While it is not proved that the legal or ethical subsystems are as fully and complexly structured as is the linguistic, this study, however preliminary, demonstrates similarities too great to be set aside. Contrary to the claims of the relativists, there may be at least one sense in which man can be said to have a moral sense: he may be innately prone to be just.

BIBLIOGRAPHY

BERKO, J.
1958. The child's learning of English morphology. *Word*, 14: 150–77.

BHATTACHARYYA, K.
1887. *The institutes of Paras'ara*. Calcutta: Asiatic Society of Bengal, n.s., 567.

BUCHLER, I. R.
1964. A formal account of the Hawaiian- and Eskimo-type kinship terminologies. *Southwestern Journal of Anthropology*, 20: 286–318.

BÜHLER, G.
1879. The sacred laws of the Aryas, Part I: Apastamba and Gautama. In F. Max Müller (Ed.), *The sacred books of the East*. Oxford: Clarendon Press.

1882. The sacred laws of the Aryas, Part II: Vâsistha and Baudhayana. In F. Max Müller (Ed.), *The sacred books of the East*. Oxford: Clarendon Press.

1886. The laws of Manu. In F. Max Müller (Ed.), *The sacred books of the East*. Oxford: Clarendon Press.

CHOMSKY, N.
1957. *Syntactic structures*. The Hague: Mouton and Co.

1959. Review of B. F. Skinner, Verbal Behavior. *Language*, 35: 26–28.

CH'Ü, T.
1961. Law and society in traditional China. The Hague: Mouton and Co.

CONKLIN, H. C.
1955. Hanunóo color categories. *Southwestern Journal of Anthropology*, 11: 339–44.

DUTT, M. N.
1907. The Dharma S'a'stras (text and translation of the twenty Samhita's). (2 vols.) Calcutta: Elysium Press (printers).

FRAKE, C. O.
1961. The diagnosis of disease among the Subanun of Mindanao. *American Anthropologist*, 63: 113–32.

FULLER, L. L.
1958. Positivism and fidelity to law—a reply to Professor Hart. *Harvard Law Review*, 71: 630–72.
1964. *The morality of law.* New Haven: Yale University Press.

GHARPURE, J. R.
1942. Yâjñavalkya Smrti with Mitâksarâ, Virâmitrodaya and Dîpakalikâ, Part VIII: Parâyaśchittadhyâya. The *Collection of Hindu Texts*, Vol. II. Bombay: V. J. Gharpure.

GOODENOUGH, W. H.
1951. *Property, kin, and community on Truk.* Yale University Publications in Anthropology, no. 46. New Haven: Yale University Press.
1956. Componential analysis and the study of meaning. *Language*, 32: 195–217.

JACOBS, M.
1959. *The content and style of an oral literature.* New York: Wenner-Gren Foundation for Anthropological Research. Viking Fund Publications in Anthropology no. 26.

JOLLY, J.
1880. The institutes of Vishnu. In F. Max Müller (Ed.), *The sacred books of the East.* Oxford: Clarendon Press.

KANE, P. V.
1930–62. *History of Dharmaśāstra.* (5 vols.) Poona.

LEES, R. B.
1957. Review of N. Chomsky, syntactic structures. *Language*, 33: 375–408.
1960. *The grammar of English nominalizations.* Indiana University Research Center in Anthropology, Folklore, and Linguistics, Publication No. 12. Bloomington: Indiana University Press.

LÉVI-STRAUSS, C.
1963. *Totemism.* (Trans. by R. Needham.) Boston: Beacon Press.

LOUNSBURY, F. G.
1956. A semantic analysis of Pawnee kinship usage. *Language*, 32: 158–94.
1964. A formal account of the Crow- and Omaha-type kinship terminologies. In W. H. Goodenough (Ed.), *Explorations in cultural anthropology.* Philadelphia: McGraw-Hill.

MANDLIK, V. N.
1880. *The Vyavahara Mayukha and the Yajnavalkya Smriti.* Bombay.

NORTHROP, F. S.
1946. *The meeting of East and West.* New York: Macmillan.
1959. *The complexity of legal and ethical experience.* Boston: Little, Brown.

ORENSTEIN, H.
1965. The structure of Hindu caste values: a preliminary study of hierarchy and ritual defilement. *Ethnology*, 4: 1–15.

POUND, ROSCOE.
1926. *Law and morals.* (2d. ed.) Chapel Hill: University of North Carolina Press.

1952. Natural law and positive natural law. *The Law Quarterly Review*, 68: 330–36.

1958. *The ideal element in law.* Calcutta: University of Calcutta.

STEVENSON, H. N.

1954. Status evaluation in the Hindu caste system. *Journal of the Royal Anthropological Institute of Great Britain and Ireland*, 84: 45–65.

VIDYARNAVA, S. C.

1918. *Yâjñavalkya Smriti, with the commentary of Vijñânesvara, called the Mitâksarâ and notes from the gloss of Bâlambhatta, Book I: the Achâra Adhayâya.* Allahabad: The Panini office.

YALMAN, N.

1963. On the purity of women in the castes of Ceylon and Malabar. *Journal of the Royal Anthropological Institute of Great Britain and Ireland*, 93: 25–58.

1964. The structure of Sinhalese healing rituals. *The Journal of Asian Studies* (Aspects of Religion in South Asia), 23: 115–50.

6. CASTE RANKING AND FOOD TRANSACTIONS: A MATRIX ANALYSIS

McKIM MARRIOTT

THIS PAPER REPORTS an attempt to understand a local caste hierarchy in village terms, and more particularly an attempt to connect local ideas and opinions about caste rank with a model of this hierarchy as a system of symbolic interaction, also local. The attempt is experimental, the results are incomplete. The paper is written somewhat autobiographically, not because a science of such things does not exist, but because I hope to set out in some detail the problems as they arose and the solutions attempted. I do not here say much about similar work by others because, at the time this attempt began, not much other work on local caste systems existed; I reserve for discussion elsewhere the rather large amount of such work which has developed since.

I did not begin in a vacuum, of course. I had read Hutton's summary (1946) and other large-scale theories, and was aware that scholars had held, variously, that castes are related and ranked by ancient law, by royal decree, by the value of their contributions to the division of labor, by Brahmanical convenience, by magical contagion of impurity, etc. I was pledged, however, as a field ethnographer, to build my understanding upon what I could learn in the village.

THE DIFFICULTIES OF AN ATTRIBUTIONAL INDEX

This experiment began for me in predominantly Hindu villages of Aligarh District, Uttar Pradesh, where I was trying to make meaning out of the verbalizations of villagers concerning the highness and lowness of the many castes present. At first I was touring, making rough local census tabulations in many villages in order to decide where to settle for a year's study. The principal local castes were usually listed in an order which began with the castes that my high-caste respondents regarded as higher and ended with the castes that they regarded as lower. Very often, adjectives like "high" and "low" were attached to the names of castes or sets of castes in the lists supplied. My inquiries as to why some were regarded as high, others as low, were answered with many other kinds of expressions: the castes at the top—Brahmans, Jats, Baniyas, and so on—were said to live in fortresses and mansions, to require service by the other castes, to lead a pure life, to feed

The data of this paper were gathered with the help of an Area Research Training Fellowship granted by the Social Science Research Council during 1950–52. The central formulations of the analysis were developed with support by a Public Health Service special fellowship award (MF 17, 311 of the National Institutes of Health) for work at the Center for Advanced Study in the Behavioral Sciences, Stanford, California, during 1961–62.

upon *pakkā* foods—those prepared in the finest manner. The castes below were said to serve their betters, to eat ordinary, *kaccā* preparations of food, to consume "dirty" things like garbage, beef, pork, etc. Brahmans were the top caste especially because they purified the world by performing rituals of worship. Other reasons for the low castes' being low, my explainers thought, should be obvious to me simply from a description of their occupations: Barbers shaved people, Potters drove donkeys, Leatherworkers flayed carcasses and made skin buckets, and Sweepers collected garbage and swept the streets.

Much of this verbalization was of a sort that I should have expected to hear according to those theories of caste rank which hold that objects, persons, and states of being are ranked by the inherent qualities or attributes of relative purity or pollution which they possess, or by the impurities which they absorb in the course of carrying on their traditional work (for example, the theory of Blunt, 1931, pp. 87–103, or of Stevenson, 1954). If such theories were correct, I supposed that I might predict caste rank by methods like those used by sociologists of the United States for the quick estimation of individual social class position (for example, Warner, Meeker, and Eells, 1949, pp. 121–85). I might first sample local opinion to get an overall ranking of the units (here castes rather than individuals), and then gather opinions on the ranking of the various attributes or qualities associated with those units. I assumed that such attributes would serve villagers as criteria for ranking the units. By regression analysis, I would be able to determine the relevance of various criteria to ranking and would be able to assign relative weights to those criteria. Finally, I would combine the most weighty attributes to form a predictive index of caste ranks.

The kinds of statements I had heard repeatedly from villagers left me no doubt that opinions as to the relative ranks of at least some castes were clear enough to yield a reliable and sharply delineated hierarchy. Six months later I was to begin to collect samples of such opinions, as reported later in this paper. At the outset, I could see that some opinions about rank were held strongly enough to lead directly to action. As soon as I began residing in the village called "Kishan Garhi," I found that persons of different castes were struggling to assert and establish a caste-ranked order of social relationship around me, governing the activities of my employees, and affecting my personal uses of food and water, house, furniture, automobile, household rubbish, and so on.

Yet the alleged attributes of castes which villagers had adduced for me as explanations of the highness and lowness of castes began to seem less and less likely to prove satisfactory as correlated predictors of opinion. Manpower, a conceivable determinant of rank, was diffused widely among castes other than Brahman. Landed wealth was highly concentrated, three-quarters of it being in the hands of members of three castes; but this fact could be of little help in explaining the relative ranks of the 21 other castes represented in the village (see Table 1). Observing at close range members of the 24 different castes, I could see nothing about their persons, their households, or their habits in which I could find objective referents for the common ascription of relative "cleanness" or "dirtiness." Occasionally they exhibited certain differentially valued features of diet and occupation. However, these features did not contrast among all castes, and neither dietary nor occupational features as such seemed to possess any order of rank among themselves that could be readily stated.

In diet, for example, the contrasting superior (*pakkā*) and inferior (*kaccā*) types of food could not as attributes distinguish the ranks of any castes, for all castes prepared and consumed food of both types on the same sorts of occasions. In this now generally vegetarian "Brahman village," certain dietary contrasts did constitute differential attributes of castes: certain meats and eggs were currently and publicly proclaimed as desirable foods only by the four Muslim castes (numbers 26–30 in the following tables), the Hunters (35), the Sweepers (36), and the Saheb. But these seven castes did not occupy any uniform rank, for the Saheb (to the extent that I came to have a caste rank) stood next to the Jat Cultivators (2), just below the top of the hierarchy; the Muslims certainly ranked in the midst of the "lower" castes (19 to 36); the Hunters and Sweepers, respectively, came at the very bottom. The eating, respectively, of vermin and of filth-fed pork might keep the Hunter and Sweeper at the bottom, one could grant, given pop-

TABLE 1

KISHAN GARHI: CASTES, FAMILIES, AND LAND RENT (1952).

Caste			No. of Families	Land Rent	
Verbal Class	Code No.	Name		Total	Average per Family
"Highest"		1. Sanadhya Brahman	43	Rs. 2362	Rs. 55
		2. Jat Cultivator	15	404	27
		3. Barahseni Merchant	1	0	0
		4. Kulasrestha Scribe	2	40	20
		6. Maithil Carpenter	8	0	0
		9. Jogi Devotee	3	0	0
"High"		11. Phulmali Gardener	1	0	0
		12. Kachi Cultivator	3	147	49
		13. Baghele Goatherd	6	589	98
		14. Turai Waterman	4	20	5
		15. Thakur Barber	6	12	2
		19. Gola Potter	12	0	0
		20. Darzi Tailor	1	0	0
		21. Karhera Cottoncarder	5	0	0
		24. Koli Weaver	6	0	0
		25. Khatik Cultivator	9	84	9
"Low"		26. Muslim Faqir Devotee	11	140	13
		27. Muslim Mirasi Singer	1	0	0
		29. Muslim Manihar Bangleman	1	0	0
		30. Muslim Teli Oilman	1	0	0
		33. Jatav Leatherworker	16	206	13
		34. Mathuriya Washerman	6	112	19
"Lowest"		35. Kanjar Hunter	1	0	0
		36. Bhangi Sweeper	4	5	1
	Total		166	Rs. 4121	Rs. 25

ular repugnance against such foods. But self-styled non-meat-eating castes (3 through 25, 33, 34) were interspersed at intervening ranks among these confessed meat-eaters. The Washermen (34), recently mutton-eating and now becoming vegetarian, were ranked as equal to the recently beef-eating Leatherworkers (33); Leatherworkers were ranked as superior to Hunters (35) and Sweepers (36), whom none accused of having ever eaten beef; Washermen, Leatherworkers, Hunters, and Sweepers were all ranked as inferior to the potentially still beef-eating Muslims. Even if one mentally removed the beef diet ascribed to Muslims and allowed that their position is a special one connected with a previous political status; even if one turned back, in one's mind, the growth of sectarian Vaishnavism and other vegetarian movements through several past centuries; even if one re-versed the recent filip to claims of vegetarianism given by Mahatma Gandhi's personal precept and example during the struggle for national independence— even if one removed all of these recent disturbing, unorthodox influences, one still would not have found meat-eating closely correlated with low rank, for near the top and politically controlling the village 100 or 500 years ago one would have found Rajput or Jat gentry sponsoring the annual sacrifice of young buffa-loes, certainly themselves consuming at least eggs, chickens, and liquor, as most Jat and Rajput landlords of adjacent villages do today. Reputation held that mutton was regularly eaten by Jats in past generations. Not improbably at earlier times one would have found many others among today's non-meat-eating castes following the carnivorous lead of the then local aristocracy. Vegetarians would then, too, have been found standing below meat-eaters. A dietary index for pre-dicting caste ranks would thus have been as difficult to construct for any known past era as it seemed to be for the village of 1951.

The job of constructing an occupational index of caste rank seemed to pose problems as formidable as those of a dietary index, but more complex because the number of occupational differentia is so much larger than the number of nutritional differentia. An index might be constructed along the lines implied by Hocart (1950, pp. 7–12) and later by Stevenson (1954) for a series of personal service occupations which deal with bodily contacts, exuviae, or emissions, or perhaps for a series of trades dealing with more or less pure things, provided that the relevant occupational attributes could themselves be specified and ranked reliably and consensually by villagers. But could one elicit meaningful opinions as to the relative impurity of saliva-polluted food and hair (removed by the Barber), feces (removed by the Sweeper), and menstrual blood (removed by the Washerman)? Most people have no common context in which to compare the degrees of impurity inherent in these substances. There would seem to be a vast number of questions to ask about differences in occupational purity as among, say, Scribe, Potter, Oilman, and Leatherworker. Granting that some attri-butes of these occupations may be influential in their rank, just which are the attributes? The materials (paper, earth, oil, skins)? The animals associated (horse, donkey, ox, etc.)? The processes (writing, animal driving, seed pressing, tanning, etc.)? Or perhaps all of these and others, too? Next, presuming that I could isolate the important features, I would have had to scale each relevant occupational attribute in relation to all the others, comparing villagers' relative distaste for mustard oil and human hair, saliva and donkeys, contact with menstrual blood and the sin of killing plants, etc. This seemed in prospect a very doubtful and difficult operation, requiring me to obtain and to combine heterogeneous judgments of an abstract and hypothetical nature in which I could have little confidence and even less assurance of a predictively useful result.

Furthermore, there remained in Kishan Garhi a substantial number of hard cases of ranking and nonranking for which no person and no idea suggested any consistent justification in terms of occupational attributes. Why in terms of occupational purity were Carpenters felt to rank above Gardeners, Gardeners above Kachi Cultivators, Kachis above Watermen, and Watermen above Tailors? All seemed equally free of polluting attributes. On the other hand, Goatherds, Barbers, and Watermen, while differing quite markedly in occupational purity, I supposed, did not seem to differ in their ranking by local opinion. The question, "How are Goatherds, Barbers, and Watermen alike in occupational purity?" sounds something like a conundrum and probably is capable of being answered only as a conundrum is—by *ad hoc* or specious rationalizations. My impression grew that much of the patchwork of explanatory talk which one could elicit from high-caste persons by such leading questions represented *ex post facto* ingenuity rather than any actual, local process of judgments arising from systematically applied criteria.

A variety of other kinds of attributes were mentioned by villagers in their casual remarks on highness and lowness of caste. Wearing the sacred thread was ennobling. Customs such as permitting the remarriage of a widow, allowing divorce, or receiving bridewealth rather than paying dowry were regarded as lowering. Having wealth made a caste high, some said, while begging made it low, etc. Many more good and bad attributes were cited and argued by villagers. As long as their discussions concerned the judgment of castes by single attributes, however, the relative ranks of the castes seemed to shift disconcertingly, both from person to person and within a single person's conceptions. The style of life of the Jat Farmers of the village would be called "very low" by a Brahman when speaking of the Jat tolerance of widow remarriage, but "very high" when speaking of the present Jat trend toward a vegetarian diet. A Jat would not accept widow remarriage as a relevant criterion for ranking; he would admit the superiority of both his own and the Brahman caste in their purity of diet; he would go on to declare the Brahmans a miserable lot for living on religious alms (*bhīk*), as some of them do. The possibility of discovering much consensus in such judgments of castes by their styles of life thus seemed quite remote from my grasp.

My desideratum had been an index which could accurately predict the caste ranks of a locality while revealing the values by which highness and lowness of caste are locally judged. It appeared to me that previous attributional theorizing about caste rank would ultimately stand or fall by the test of producing a satisfactory index of this kind for some locality. Of course, no list of my doubts and difficulties can rule out the possibility that an attributional index of caste rank for Kishan Garhi—probably an index of great complexity—might ultimately be constructed by combining dietary, occupational, and other traits in numbers beyond the mind's ready reckoning. But the failure to date of any ancient law-giver or modern ethnographer to produce such an index adequate to explain caste ranking in any multicaste locality further discouraged me from believing that such an index could be made at all. (For further doubts, see Marriott, 1959; Dumont and Pocock, 1959.) At the same time, other evidence close at hand in the immediate concerns of villagers in Kishan Garhi suggested that more profit might be found in setting aside the effort to interpret village culture through the foregoing kind of logic which assumes the operation of criteria through attributes and contagions.

LOCAL CONCEPTIONS OF RANKING

It was a return to the intended first step of my method, following six months of study in Kishan Garhi, that presented the local logic of social relationships most forcefully to my attention. Whatever might be the criteria, if any, by which ranks are ascribed to castes, I felt that I would first need direct judgments about the caste ranks themselves. Using a technique of moveable cards suggested in an American community study by Hollingshead (1940, pp. 29–40), later described by Freed (1963) as it was subsequently applied to Indian castes in another village, I sought to elicit a sample of local opinions. I now asked simply, "Which caste is high, which is low?" repeating this question for each pair of castes. Villagers found this a natural kind of questioning and often responded with grave interest. They seemed to take care in answering, sometimes shifting ranks as new castes were introduced and cross-checked, but maintaining and justifying their opinions in the face of final inquiry on a long regional list of 36 castes. Twenty-four male villagers belonging to ten different castes were individually interviewed about the local castes. The way they placed the cards for each caste is recorded in Table 2.[1]

From the preceding discussion of chaos in attributional thinking about the local castes, one might have expected to find little clarity in conceptions about ranking, no more than a few generalized rank levels distinguished, and little consensus among various respondents. In fact, a contrary state of affairs was discovered. Each respondent was found to have a quite clear notion of how he thought most people would rank the castes. Each arranged the 24 local castes in from 11 to 24 different ranks, the average number of ranks stated being 18.5 (Table 2, last line). Consensus was also quite high: 93 per cent of all 6,463 opinions given were in agreement with each other (Table 3). After contemplating all 552 possible pairs of castes among the 24, two-thirds of the respondents independently agreed on which caste is higher in 516 of the pairs. When these two-to-one (and in most pairs much stronger) majorities in the 516 cells were placed in one total configuration, they were found to form a collective caste

1. A full statement of the method of ranking by opinions, with resulting data from this and a dozen other villages, is given in the forthcoming book by Marriott, Freed, and Nicholas.

TABLE 2. OPINIONS ON CASTE RANK HELD BY TWENTY-FOUR RESPONDENTS IN KISHAN GARHI VILLAGE.

Respondent

Caste Code.* Individual Serial Number

Rank of Caste — Higher ←——————————→ Lower

Rank of Caste	1.1	1.2	1.3	1.4	1.5	1.6	1.7	1.8	1.9	1.10	1.11	2.1	2.2	9.1	13.1	14.1	14.2	14.3	19.1	21.1	25.1	26.1	26.2	33.1
	1	1	1	1	1	1	1	1	1	1	1	1	1	1	1	1	1	1	1	1	1	1	1	1
	6	2	6	3	3	3	2	2	6	3	4	2	2	6	3	6	2	3	6	3	6	2	4	6
	4	4	3	4	4	2	3	3	2	6	2	4	3	9	4	3	4	4	2	2	11	3	3	9
	9	3	9	2	6	11	6	9	3	11	3	3	4	4	2	4	3	2	3	6	3	4	2	2
	2	9	4	6	9	4	4	4	4	4	11	13	6	2	9	2	6	6	4	4	9	6	6	4
	3	6	2	9	2	6	9	6	11	9	13	6	11	13	6	9	11	11	9	9	2	9	9	3
	11	11	11	11	12	12	11	15	12	2	14	11	12	11	11	11	12	12	12	12	4	12	12	11
	14	12	12	12	11	13	12	14	9	12	12	12	9	12	13	12	14	13	15	15	12	11	11	12
	15	13	13	13	13	9	13	12	13	13	9	15	14	14	12	15	15	9	11	11	13	14	14	15
	12	14	14	14	14	14	14	13	15	15	27	14	15	15	14	13	13	14	13	13	14	15	15	14
	13	15	15	15	15	15	15	21	14	14	6	9	13	3	15	14	9	15	20	14	15	26	13	15
	19	19	20	19	19	20	20	11	20	19	15	20	19	20	19	19	20	19	19	21	25	27	21	19
	24	21	21	20	24	24	21	19	24	20	19	25	20	21	20	20	21	24	24	19	21	29	19	20
	20	24	24	21	25	19	24	24	21	21	29	21	21	24	21	21	19	20	15	25	19	30	25	25
	21	20	19	24	20	21	19	25	25	24	26	24	24	19	24	25	24	25	21	20	20	19	20	30
	25	26	25	25	26	25	25	20	19	25	30	19	26	25	25	24	29	21	27	24	24	21	24	21
	34	27	26	33	29	26	33	34	26	26	21	34	25	33	26	26	26	26	26	26	33	24	34	24
	26	29	27	26	30	29	26	33	34	29	25	30	27	26	27	27	30	27	29	27	34	26	26	26
	27	30	30	27	21	30	27	26	30	30	20	26	29	29	30	29	25	29	30	29	26	25	27	27
	29	25	29	29	34	34	30	27	29	34	33	29	30	27	29	30	34	30	33	30	27	34	29	29
	30	33	33	34	33	33	34	30	33	33	24	33	34	30	33	33	33	33	34	33	29	35	30	35
	33	34	34	30	35	35	29	29	35	35	36	35	33	34	34	34	35	34	25	34	30	33	33	34
	36	35	35	35	36	36	35	36	36	36	34	36	35	35	36	35	36	35	35	35	35	35	35	36
Lower	35	36	36	36			36	35			35		36	36	35	36		36	36	36	36	36	36	36
Ranks	20	17	23	13	15	20	15	24	22	21	19	22	15	22	17	11	19	15	24	19	12	17	21	11

*For the meaning of caste code numbers, see Table 1.

139

hierarchy with thirteen agreed ranks (Table 4). Opinion was overwhelmingly consistent, transitive; a single instance of intransitivity occurs over the question as to whether the Muslim Mirasi Singer (27) is superior or equal to the Muslim Manihar Bangleman caste (30).

Naturally, my inquiries were directed now toward discovering the sources

TABLE 3

MATRIX OF OPINIONS ON CASTE RANK IN KISHAN GARHI VILLAGE.

(Caste Code Number)

	(2)	(3)	(4)	(6)	(9)	(11)	(12)	(13)	(14)	(15)	(19)	(20)	(21)	(24)	(25)	(26)	(27)	(30)	(29)	(34)	(33)	(35)	(36)
(1)	24 0	24 0	24 0	23½ ½	24 0	24 0	24 0	23 0	24 0	24 0	24 0	24 0	24 0	24 0	24 0	24 0	18 0	24 0	24 0	24 0	24 0	24 0	24 0
(2)		13 11	12 12	14 10	17 7	22 2	23½ ½	23 0	24 0	24 0	24 0	24 0	24 0	24 0	24 0	24 0	18 0	24 0	24 0	24 0	24 0	24 0	24 0
(3)			14 10	15 9	20 4	22 2	23 1	22 1	23 1	23 1	24 0	24 0	24 0	24 0	24 0	24 0	18 0	24 0	24 0	24 0	24 0	24 0	24 0
(4)				12 12	18 6	20 4	22½ 1½	23 0	24 0	24 0	24 0	24 0	24 0	24 0	24 0	24 0	18 0	24 0	24 0	24 0	24 0	24 0	24 0
(6)					18 6	20½ 3½	21½ 2½	21 2	23½ ½	23 1	24 0	24 0	24 0	24 0	24 0	24 0	17 1	24 0	24 0	24 0	24 0	24 0	24 0
(9)						14 10	16 8	18 5	21½ 2½	20½ 3½	24 0	24 0	24 0	24 0	24 0	24 0	18 0	24 0	24 0	24 0	24 0	24 0	24 0
(11)							16 8	18½ 4½	21 3	22 2	24 0	24 0	23 1	24 0	24 0	24 0	18 0	24 0	24 0	24 0	24 0	24 0	24 0
(12)								18½ 4½	20½ 3½	20 4	24 0	24 0	24 0	24 0	24 0	24 0	18 0	24 0	24 0	24 0	24 0	24 0	24 0
(13)									13 10	13 10	22½ ½	22½ ½	23 0	23 0	22½ ½	23 0	17 0	23 0	23 0	23 0	23 0	23 0	23 0
(14)										13 11	23 1	23 1	24 0	23 1	23½ ½	24 0	17 1	24 0	24 0	24 0	24 0	24 0	24 0
(15)											24 0	24 0	24 0	24 0	23½ ½	24 0	18 0	24 0	24 0	24 0	24 0	24 0	24 0
(19)												15 9	13½ 10½	17½ 6½	20½ 3½	23 1	16 2	23 1	23 1	24 0	24 0	24 0	24 0
(20)													15½ 8½	18½ 5½	16 8	22 2	16 2	22 2	22 2	24 0	24 0	24 0	24 0
(21)														16 8	17½ 6½	20 4	15½ 2½	20 4	20½ 3½	24 0	23½ ½	24 0	24 0
(24)															16 8	20 4	14½ 3½	20 4	20 4	23 1	21½ 2½	24 0	24 0
(25)																17½ 6½	13½ 4½	18½ 5½	19 5	23 1	23 1	24 0	24 0
(26)																	11 7	16 8	16½ 7½	18½ 5½	18 6	24 0	24 0
(27)																		12 6	11½ 6½	13½ 4½	12 6	18 0	18 0
(30)																			12½ 11½	16½ 7½	18½ 5½	24 0	24 0
(29)																				17½ 6½	18 6	24 0	24 0
(34)																					13½ 10½	23 1	22½ 1½
(33)																						23 1	24 0
(35)																							18 6

NOTES: Caste names corresponding to code numbers of row and column headings are given in Table 1.

Row caste is ranked higher by majority in cell, column caste by minority.

Cells showing a majority-minority ratio of 2:1 or better are separated by a line from other cells.

of this amount of precision and consensus in ranking. Spontaneous remarks during the ranking interviews offered strong clues to an explanation. While deciding where to place the caste cards and while responding to my further probes after all cards had been placed, villagers in almost every difficult case referred to ranked transactions in food and sometimes also to ranked relationships of service as bases for their decisions. Some examples of these contextual remarks are the following:

Brahmans are higher than any other caste—everybody takes their inferior (*kaccā*) food.

Previously we [a Brahman family] had the Carpenter M. L. working for us. But he wouldn't work at our house, or take food here, so we left him.

Barbers are lower than Watermen because the Barber takes inferior bread from the Waterman's house after shaving him.

The Waterman has no religious preceptor (guru), so he must be lower than the Barber.

TABLE 4

COLLECTIVE CASTE HIERARCHY OF KISHAN GARHI VILLAGE.

(Based on opinions given in Figures 2 and 3)

Castes

Code
No.   *Name*

1. Sanadhya Brahman
2. Jat Cultivator
3. Barahseni Merchant
4. Kulasrestha Scribe
6. Maithil Carpenter
9. Jogi Devotee
11. Phulmali Gardener
12. Kachi Gardener
13. Baghele Goatherd
15. Thakur Barber
14. Turai Waterman
19. Gola Potter
20. Darzi Tailor
21. Karhera Cottoncarder
24. Koli Weaver
25. Khatik Cultivator
26. Muslim Faqir Devotee
27. Muslim Mirasi Singer
30. Muslim Teli Oilman
29. Muslim Manihar Bangleman
34. Mathuriya Washerman
33. Jatav Leatherworker
35. Kanjar Hunter
36. Bhangi Sweeper

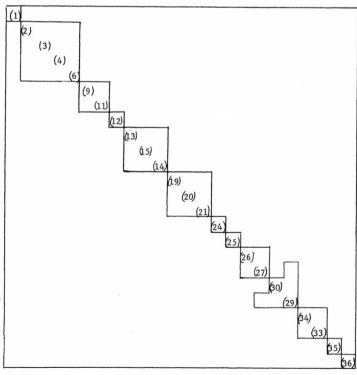

Goatherds are higher than Watermen, because Watermen pick up the dirty plates of Goatherds.

Barbers, Watermen, Goatherds, and Jat Cultivators are all equal because they all take each other's feasts.

Barbers are better than Potters because the high castes will take the Barbers' superior (*pakkā*) food, while they won't take it from Potters.

We musicians [Muslim Faqir Devotees] will not play for any caste below Barber. We serve only where we can eat.

Brahmans and Thakurs [Jat Cultivators] won't use a Barber who shaves Leatherworkers.

The Leatherworker is very low because he is everyone's servant—he eats from every house.

A cardinal assumption of ranking in such statements about food could be formulated very simply: givers are higher; receivers are lower. If a member of caste A gives food to a member of caste B, then the whole of caste A must be regarded as higher than caste B. If a member of the receiving caste B also gives food to a member of caste A, then castes A and B are of the same rank once more. Concern for transitivity is evident wherever three or more units are involved: if A gives to B and B gives to C, then A is higher than C even if there is no direct transfer of food from A to C. Arithmetic computations are also implied: if A gives to C while B does not, A is higher than B; if A gives to C and D while B gives to D but not C, then A is higher than B.

Food and services are closely linked in the above statements, as in everyday life, for food is often the pay of servants. Giving a service implies a readiness to receive some kind of food, and giving food implies an expectation that service will be rendered. The logic for deriving rank from service is the exact inverse of the logic for deriving rank from food transfers. If a member of caste A serves a member of caste B, then caste A must be regarded as lower than caste B. If caste A serves many other castes and B serves few, A is lower. Transitivity and arithmetic computations occur, as with foods, and so does the possibility of equalizing ranks through reciprocity. Statements made about services and about foods further seem to refer to the same domain of discourse, as they are readily introduced into the same utterances, or are substituted for each other.

A part of such village thinking about caste rank may be understood as expressing the value of avoiding pollution, for some of the food transferred— garbage and feces—is regarded as polluting, while certain personal services are thought to remove impurities. Garbage (*jūṭhā*), that is, food left on plates after eating, is felt to have been polluted by saliva flowing from the mouth of the eater. Such garbage is to be handled in the family only by persons such as wives, whose status is thereby marked as inferior to the eater; it may be fed to domestic animals, but among humans outside the family can be given only to Sweepers. Human feces, commonly deposited at night in the doorways of their houses by high-caste women, are also extremely polluting to other castes. Outside the family, they can be handled only by Sweepers, and will be consumed only by those animals which are therefore low, such as the Sweeper's pigs and chickens, perhaps the Potter's donkey. The services of the Sweeper, like those of the Leatherworker, of the Washerman, and some of those of the Barber are employed with the explicit aim of removing certain kinds of bodily or household pollution, thereby creating a relatively purer, higher condition for the master and his caste. Hocart's Ceylon-based understanding of caste rank as an order of pollution-transfer (1950, pp. 8–20), fits this part of Kishan Garhi's transactional hierarchy very well.

Yet in itself, as an attribute of the person or caste, self-induced fecal, salivary, or other pollution is not dreaded as an absolute evil: instead, it may be manipulated or even enjoyed, may be used as a state from which to undertake the domination of inferior persons or castes, or may be removed ostentatiously before approaching superiors in order to show respect for them. Superiors, whether gods or men, are generally best reverenced or supplicated when they are in a polluted condition, and when one is oneself recently purified. Others whom one does not desire to exalt excessively over oneself are better approached without purifying oneself too much. So it comes about through frequent confrontations between higher and lower castes that most villagers, including Brahmans, prefer to remain ordinarily in a protected, impure state. Brahmans come to eat feasts directly from working in the fields, washing only their hands and faces; servants begin their morning's labors directly after defecating, without an intervening bath. Purity is not, cannot be, should not be practiced to the exclusion of pollution. Seen in the contexts of daily transactions, values of purity and pollution appear to be necessarily complementary, as Dumont and Pocock (1959, p. 34; also Dumont, 1966, pp. 76–81) have insisted on other theoretical grounds.

Even understood in their relativistic uses, considerations of pollution and purity do not seem to underlie all or most of the several kinds of transactions on which villagers say that caste rank is based. Values such as independence or power and luxurious display are also prominent in villagers' talk about the main kinds of food transfer other than transfers of garbage and feces. Thus the best state of food is raw (*sīdhā*). Raw flour, sugar, ghee, or whole fruit, or a set of such foods forming the materials for a complete meal is sent as a gift to the house of a Brahman or other higher-caste patron for him to prepare in his own house. Such a gift is honorific, my respondents emphasized, for the recipient may "enjoy it at will" without the necessity of lowering himself by appearing to eat a cooked meal at any particular time and place, in who-knows-what company. Such a gift earns diffuse spiritual merit (*pūn*) for the donor. The simple sugar confections (*batāsā*) which are distributed by the hundreds to all comers and to passers-by on auspicious occasions in the family of the donor share with raw foodstuffs the virtue of being freely combinable as ingredients in whatever the receiver may choose to eat and are similarly productive of merit. Unground grain and nonfoods such as land, animals, and money are prized even beyond foodstuffs for the same sorts of transactional reasons: they are convertible at will into food, or service, or into many others among the desired things of life. Accepting them involves a clear gain along with only the slightest degree of subordination.

Somewhat less freely convertible, and therefore less honorific than raw food-stuffs, is *pakkā* food. This is the superior category of cooked food, the only kind of meal which can be offered in feasts to gods, to guests of high affinal status, to those who provide honorific services, and generally to persons of other castes. Villagers save and borrow heavily toward the costs of giving large feasts to such persons in order to earn both religious merit and individual social prestige. The *pakkā* food of feasts, according to the definitions given to me repeatedly, is not food that is free from the impurity of water or salt, for it may contain both of these ingredients; rather, it is food containing ghee as an extra inducement to attendance and eating. Ghee (clarified butter) is the costliest of the fats known locally. It is prized for building health, strength, and virility. It is especially welcomed when applied to the preparation of fried cakes of wheat, wheat being the costliest and most desired of grains grown in the area and itself the prime grain of feasts. Preparations of relatively expensive vegetables, such as red squash or potatoes, are also included in the *pakkā* menu. With *pakkā* food, the subordination involved in any situation of being fed is qualified by the high value placed on the food itself.

Third comes inferior cooked food (*kaccā*), typically the dry-baked cakes of barley which are used as ordinary family fare or as daily payment for dependent artisans and servants. Some kinds of pickles, and also the cheaper curries of home-grown, dried pulses are also regarded as *kaccā* and are eaten with *kaccā* bread. The inferiority of this category of food is defined by villagers as deriving from the absence of the honorific ghee or other highly valued contents, not from the presence of pollutants. To accept inferior food is to accept one's lack of honor, one's more intimate, routine dependence upon the food-provider. Such dependence carries with it also a degree of security resembling that of family members. A servant may go to the "mother-and-father" who provides him with *kaccā* food and legitimately beg help in any personal emergency. Loud acknowledgment of his nutritive dependency is generally effective in getting some additional payment or a loan from the flattered employer.

Placing garbage and feces at the end of this series of food categories, one sees that the lower role of these materials is consonant with their small monetary and nutritional worth, and with the extremity of domination which their transfer involves, as well as with the attribution of impurity to their nature.

If a theory of pollution offers an incomplete understanding of the values involved in food transfers, it also fails to account fully for the hierarchy of services. While some services are declared by their practitioners to be concerned with the removal of pollution from the employer, others are not. Many purveyors of services emphasize what they contribute to the refinement, aristocracy, good fortune, and commanding appearance of the employer. The Carpenter's, Jogi Devotee's, Gardener's, Waterman's, Cottoncarder's, Mirasi Singer's, and Hunter's ritual services, as well as part of the Barber's, Potter's, Faqir Devotee's, and Brahman's services, are explicitly intended to exalt the master and his caste, not by avoiding or subtracting negative qualities, but by adding proof of his honor, religious merit, liberality, or power. Without any necessary conveyance of pollution through the nature of the service, an order of relative highness and lowness can be asserted simply through the transactional idiom: honorific acts are performed; payment is given and received.

, Villagers often seem to apply a strictly transactional logic, treating all foods, objects, services, and persons as if they were substantially equivalent. Their main concern is to see that a previously enacted order of castes is currently re-enacted. Thus with foods, although persons of castes above the lowest two refuse to accept food in any form, not even in the pure form of whole grain, from a Sweeper as gift or payment, they will nevertheless accept grain which was actually harvested or threshed by a Sweeper if he worked as an employee under a landowner of a caste higher in rank. Not the substance, or the Sweeper's touch, but his rank in the transaction is what matters. Similarly, flour ground by a Leatherworker woman in her own house and sold or given away by her is regarded as inedible by Brahmans, while flour ground by her working as an employee in a Brahman house is quite acceptable to the same consumers. Not touch or house, but control of the work defines purity or pollution in this case. Again Sweepers and Leatherworkers, for reasons of "pollution," should avoid casual trespass upon even the exterior platform of a house belonging to a person of high caste, yet they may enter the same house and have a purifying rather than a polluting effect on it, provided that they come on the owner's command to do their respective jobs of cleaning and repairing. Obviously the maintenance of rank, not pollution by proximity, is the issue on which action turns in such instances. A Brahman may walk into a Leatherworker's house to call him for work without incurring any pollution dangerous to the standing of the Brahman caste, but a Leatherworker may not enter a Brahman's house to call him without exciting anger, and possibly suffering a beating to redress the disturbed pecking order. The Potter caste's rank as such, rather than the danger of pollution to porous vessels, seems most at issue in the ban on a Potter's serving food to high-caste persons in feasts: although the earthenware vessels are made and delivered by the Potter's hand, and are accepted by all castes as pure, they may not be taken up by him in the role of feeder, villagers say, simply because "his caste is low." Even when any chance of pollution is technically circumvented, the suppressed issue of high and low may still be felt and be acted upon. Thus a wealthy person of low caste who wishes to demonstrate his power is not forbidden to feast high-caste persons, so long as he hires high-caste caterers to cook and serve, and does not attempt to feed the guests with his own hand; but in no such case which I investigated were the high-caste invitees pleased to attend (and thereby to accept even indirect, financial dominance) unless they were assured that some member of the host's caste would acknowledge that caste's inferiority unambiguously on the same occasion by gathering up the garbage-laden plates of the high-caste diners.

If there is one master conception on which village thinking about caste rank constantly focuses, this appeared to me to be the idea of the intercaste transaction. In their transactions with each other caste, the members of a caste take either higher rank through giving or commanding, or lower rank through receiving or serving. From an economical viewpoint, they may attempt to take a higher rank as hosts or masters, expecting some material loss through payment of costs; or they may settle for a lower rank as receivers or servants, rewarded by material gain in the form of gifts, feasts, or payments. Social rank and material gain stand in a relation of complementarity, as do purity and pollution at the level of values. While a variety of other values, such as power, health, luck, and piety, also stimulate apologies for and rationalizations of caste ranking, I was persuaded that village opinions depend both immediately and ultimately upon transactions.

PROBLEMS OF REPRESENTATION: THE MATRIX

Given a clear picture of opinion on the ranks of castes in Kishan Garhi and given the above understanding of the idiom of relationships on which opinions were said primarily to depend, I strove for an additional six months to accumulate further data on intercaste transactions in food and services. Directly connected with the gathering of these data were many problems of how best to represent and analyze the great number of relevant relationships.

The unit which I would need for this analysis was now quite sharply defined: it had become the symbolic transaction of highness and lowness between two castes, represented by any members of those castes. Any publicly exhibited transaction between any members would be equally relevant to ranking, since caste ranks are the corporate property of the whole membership. Corporate liabilities and powers of corporate representation are vested in every adult member of the caste: everyone gains, loses, or retains the same caste rank in consequence of the transactions made by every other caste member. Frequencies of uniform, individual activity within the same intercaste pair-relationship seemed unlikely to prove relevant, but coverage of all possible pairs of castes would be crucial, I thought, for testing the conceptions developed above. The kind and extent of data gathered are described in the section following this one.

While still in the field, I endeavored for a short time without success to devise a system for scoring transactions based on a rating of the several types of food transferred and on the differing degrees of honor or pollution implied in the many kinds of services rendered. I was puzzled then as to how to cope with ambiguous problems of measurement like the one implied in the statement, typical of previous analyses of intercaste relations, that a Brahman caste might occupy a low position in food taking (for example, Blunt, 1931, pp. 90–94)—that a caste might not be demeaned by taking food from another caste below itself if the receiving caste were sufficiently high, the giving caste not too far below, the food and vessel of the proper sort. The simple rule derived above that receiving is lowering would have to have an appendix of corrections in the case of certain castes, certain vessels, etc. At the very least, there would have to be differing weights assigned to transactions in different food media.

Among the service transactions I saw similar difficulties: are Brahmans not lowered by giving priestly services to other castes, as Barbers are by giving their services? Is a kingly caste which commands many services not therefore higher than a Brahman caste which commands fewer? (For Dumont, 1966, p. 121, such considerations invalidate the attempt to derive ranks from service transactions.) Also, services are of a great many more kinds than foods are and might not have identical values. A Barber, for example, does not merely provide one face-shaving and hair-cutting service for all men. He does this for some, but not for others. For some he additionally provides manicure, pedicure, massage, surgery, fanning in hot weather, perfume for the ears, valet and messenger service, cooking, dishwashing, and various kinds of ritual assistance at ceremonies of the life cycle. The Barber's wife has an analogous range of offices to perform for females in the same households. Both Barber and Barber's wife graduate and ration their many services according to the caste, economic status, and generosity of their employers. Like the attributional index which I had considered at the beginning of my field work, this qualitatively differentiated system for scoring transactions which I was now contemplating would have required an elaborate preliminary interviewing and probably precise testing of opinions about hypothetical situations in order to devise a single, and then probably uncertain weighing or scaling of the many variables to be combined.[2] Yet the structure of opinions on caste rank which I had found seemed at once simpler and more sharply delineated than any such multivariate index of foods and services which I could hope to design.

At this point, I listened once more to the simple logic used by villagers in responding to my questions on caste rank. Suppose this logic were literally and consistently true—suppose that any transfer of food *always* makes the giver higher, the receiver lower; suppose that any rendering of service *always* makes the master higher, the servant lower. If such logic were to be trusted, then a weighting or scaling of degrees of importance to be applied to different media, distances, castes, etc., would not be required. I determined therefore to postpone the attempts to construct such a weighted index, and proceeded instead to gather data on transactions of all types equally. I observed several hundreds of such transactions.

After leaving the village, my first attempts to represent the observed food transactions took the form of sociograms like the one for *pakkā* food reproduced in Figure 1. A general impression of the preponderantly downward direction of food transfers may be apparent to some viewers from such a sociogram. But just how a precise order of ranking might be derived from this picture is not at all clear to the eye. A long list of graphic conventions about the discovery and representation of rank would have to be adopted and explained; such explanations would reduce the sociogram's apparent initial advantage of immediate intelligi-

2. My earliest efforts in 1951 were based on a questionnaire eliciting opinions on "social distances" or "interdictions" closely resembling those used by Mahar (1959) and Orenstein (1965, pp. 326–30), respectively. I abandoned this technique on realizing that I could more directly deal with an objective, multilateral system of relationships than with subjective reports of unilateral distastes and avoidances.

FIGURE 1

SOCIOGRAM OF TRANSACTIONS IN SUPERIOR (*Pakkā*) FOOD.

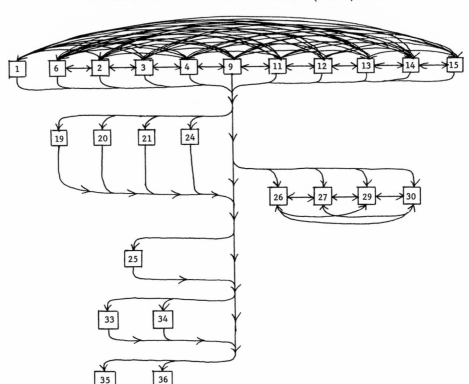

bility. Clarity of representation conflicts with full presentation of such data. Finally, my attempt to combine in one sociogram all data on the several kinds of food transactions led me to a tangled, multicolored result (not shown) which I could not readily interpret myself, and which even the most expert other viewers found unintelligible.

A suitable, more complete means of representation already widely used and understood in the field of sociometry was suggested to me by Harrison C. White in 1961, as exemplified in the text of Kemeny, Snell, and Thompson (1957, pp. 307–315). This is the mathematical matrix of binary numbers. Such a matrix permits a concise, orderly, and exhaustive statement of all data on dichotomous transactions among many participants.[3] The use of binary numbers facilitates rigorous analysis of simple propositions and makes explicit provision for such mathematical manipulations of groups as may later be required. An example is the matrix given in Table 6, which represents the same data on *pakkā* food that

3. The naturalness, one might say the inevitability, of matrix-like, if not of binary numerical representations, is implied by their adoption by Wiser (1936, pp. 12–13), by Mathur (1964, p. 130), by Orenstein (1965), p. 330), and as this book is in press, by Dumont (1966, pp. 116–17).

are represented in the sociogram of Figure 1. Avoiding the question of assigning different weights to the different foods, I proceeded to set up a separate matrix for each of the five types or states of food discussed above, namely, raw food-stuffs (*sīdhā*), superior (*pakkā*) cooked food, inferior (*kaccā*) cooked food, garbage (*jūṭhā*), and feces (*gū*). These five matrices are given as Tables 5 to 9.

In these matrices, the rows represent the 24 castes as givers, while the columns represent the same 24 castes as receivers. The sequence of listing the castes' code numbers along the main diagonal is the approximate order of ranking as sub-sequently determined from the results of the present analysis. Any such set of 24 units can form 276 pairs arranged with the giver first and another 276 pairs with receiver first. Hence each 24 × 24 matrix provides 552 cells in which trans-actions of food may be displayed.

Each cell of one of the matrices in Tables 5 to 9 represents a type of encounter between two castes, a potential giver and a potential receiver. Wherever a transfer of food is known to occur, the digit "1" is written. Wherever no transfer is believed to occur, a zero is written instead.

There are two cells and four possible outcomes of confrontations between any pair of two castes, A and B, as in the diagrams below. The asymmetrical

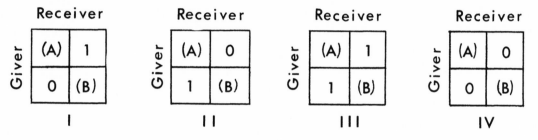

outcomes of types (I) and (II) set up orders of ranking between castes A and B, while the symmetrical outcomes (III) and (IV) do not set up any order of rank. In outcome (I), caste A gives to caste B as shown by the "1" in A's row as giver and in B's column as receiver; B does not reciprocate, and shows a "0" in B's row as giver and A's column as receiver. In outcome (II), there is ranking, but in a reverse order which makes caste B higher than caste A. Outcome (III)—reciprocal giving and receiving by both A and B—leaves the two castes equally ranked. By outcome (IV), where no giving or receiving occurs, the two castes are left in a not unequal state of unrelatedness.

Each of these logical possibilities occurs among the castes considered in the matrix of *pakkā* food transactions (Table 6), excepting outcome (II), which is eliminated by the perfect transitivity of the data. Outcome (I) occurs between Thakur Barbers (caste 14) and Gola Potters (caste 19), with the effect that these two are ranked in the order (14) over (19). The positive equality of outcome (III) occurs in the reciprocating subsets (2) to (14) and (26) to (29), the members of each subset ranking as equals. Unrelated equality of type (IV) occurs throughout the subset (19) to (24), as well as within the pairs (1)–(6) and (35)–(36).

To make the matrices more readable, zones of identical entries are outlined with a solid line. Wherever a balanced zone of either zeros (IV) or of digits (III) cuts symmetrically across the main diagonal of the matrix, the zone is emphasized by a dotted-line boundary.

THE DATA ON INTERCASTE TRANSACTIONS

The occurrences and nonoccurrences of transactions represented by the digits and zeros in these matrices are actual behavior for the most part and expectations of actual behavior for the rest. In the course of fourteen months' residence in Kishan Garhi, I observed and recorded instances of encounters in perhaps 30 per cent of all the cells. I obtained verbal reports on specific transactions in about 25 per cent more of the cells. I have completed the remaining cells according to villagers' general statements as to what would normally be expected to occur between those pairs of castes.

That raw foodstuffs—grain, flour, sugar, etc.—may be transferred among all castes above (35) and (36) as shown in Table 5 is well attested by information on specific transactions in about 300 cells. Most information on grain transfer

TABLE 5

MATRIX OF RAW FOODSTUFFS (*Sidhā*)

(Giver Castes) / (Receiver Castes)

																							Given	Received	Net
(1)	1	1	1	1	1	1	1	1	1	1	1	1	1	1	1	1	1	1	1	1	1	1	23	21	2
1	(6)	1	1	1	1	1	1	1	1	1	1	1	1	1	1	1	1	1	1	1	1	1	23	21	2
1	1	(2)	1	1	1	1	1	1	1	1	1	1	1	1	1	1	1	1	1	1	1	1	23	21	2
1	1	1	(3)	1	1	1	1	1	1	1	1	1	1	1	1	1	1	1	1	1	1	1	23	21	2
1	1	1	1	(4)	1	1	1	1	1	1	1	1	1	1	1	1	1	1	1	1	1	1	23	21	2
1	1	1	1	1	(9)	1	1	1	1	1	1	1	1	1	1	1	1	1	1	1	1	1	23	21	2
1	1	1	1	1	1	(11)	1	1	1	1	1	1	1	1	1	1	1	1	1	1	1	1	23	21	2
1	1	1	1	1	1	1	(12)	1	1	1	1	1	1	1	1	1	1	1	1	1	1	1	23	21	2
1	1	1	1	1	1	1	1	(13)	1	1	1	1	1	1	1	1	1	1	1	1	1	1	23	21	2
1	1	1	1	1	1	1	1	1	(15)	1	1	1	1	1	1	1	1	1	1	1	1	1	23	21	2
1	1	1	1	1	1	1	1	1	1	(14)	1	1	1	1	1	1	1	1	1	1	1	1	23	21	2
1	1	1	1	1	1	1	1	1	1	1	(19)	1	1	1	1	1	1	1	1	1	1	1	23	21	2
1	1	1	1	1	1	1	1	1	1	1	1	(20)	1	1	1	1	1	1	1	1	1	1	23	21	2
1	1	1	1	1	1	1	1	1	1	1	1	1	(21)	1	1	1	1	1	1	1	1	1	23	21	2
1	1	1	1	1	1	1	1	1	1	1	1	1	1	(24)	1	1	1	1	1	1	1	1	23	21	2
1	1	1	1	1	1	1	1	1	1	1	1	1	1	1	(25)	1	1	1	1	1	1	1	23	21	2
1	1	1	1	1	1	1	1	1	1	1	1	1	1	1	1	(26)	1	1	1	1	1	1	23	21	2
1	1	1	1	1	1	1	1	1	1	1	1	1	1	1	1	1	(27)	1	1	1	1	1	23	21	2
1	1	1	1	1	1	1	1	1	1	1	1	1	1	1	1	1	1	(30)	1	1	1	1	23	21	2
1	1	1	1	1	1	1	1	1	1	1	1	1	1	1	1	1	1	1	(29)	1	1	1	23	21	2
1	1	1	1	1	1	1	1	1	1	1	1	1	1	1	1	1	1	1	1	(33)	1	1	23	21	2
1	1	1	1	1	1	1	1	1	1	1	1	1	1	1	1	1	1	1	1	1	(34)	1	23	21	2
0	0	0	0	0	0	0	0	0	0	0	0	0	0	0	0	0	0	0	0	0	0	(35) 1	1	23	-22
0	0	0	0	0	0	0	0	0	0	0	0	0	0	0	0	0	0	0	0	0	0	1 (36)	1	23	-22

Received   21 21 21 21 21 21 21 21 21 21 21 21 21 21 21 21 21 21 21 21 21 21 23 23 was obtained incidentally in the course of systematic observation and interviewing on agricultural sales, employment, and credit. Observations of and reports on instances of meritorious alms-giving in raw foodstuffs to Brahmans, to collection agents for charities, and to beggars add nearly a hundred further cells of information. Observed distributions of sugar on auspicious family occasions—births, wedding ceremonies, dowry payments, etc.—nearly complete this first matrix, while interviews indicate a general expectation that the remainder of the cells will be filled ultimately as marked.

The matrix of superior cooked food and water (Table 6) is based to the extent of about 60 per cent on observation at some thirty large feasts "to the whole village" given mostly on the occasion of weddings by members of eight castes. It is based also on observation of payments at fourteen annual festival days to members of six of the eight jajmani serving castes. The transactions occurring at a single wedding feast in one of the higher castes often approximate what is symbolized by a solid row of digits in this matrix, while a single low-caste servant's tour of his clients' houses on a festival day often exhibits what is shown as a long column of digits. *Pakkā* transfers thus provide some of the most comprehensive and public dramatizations of caste rank. Intercaste transfers of water, on

TABLE 6

MATRIX OF TRANSACTIONS IN SUPERIOR (*Pakkā*) FOOD.

(Giver Castes) ↓ / (Receiver Castes) →

c1	c2	c3	c4	c5	c6	c7	c8	c9	c10	c11	c12	c13	c14	c15	c16	c17	c18	c19	c20	c21	c22	c23	c24	Given	Received	Net
(1)	0	1	1	1	1	1	1	1	1	1	1	1	1	1	1	1	1	1	1	1	1	1	1	22	9	13
0	(6)	1	1	1	1	1	1	1	1	1	1	1	1	1	1	1	1	1	1	1	1	1	1	22	9	13
1	1	(2)	1	1	1	1	1	1	1	1	1	1	1	1	1	1	1	1	1	1	1	1	1	23	10	13
1	1	1	(3)	1	1	1	1	1	1	1	1	1	1	1	1	1	1	1	1	1	1	1	1	23	10	13
1	1	1	1	(4)	1	1	1	1	1	1	1	1	1	1	1	1	1	1	1	1	1	1	1	23	10	13
1	1	1	1	1	(9)	1	1	1	1	1	1	1	1	1	1	1	1	1	1	1	1	1	1	23	10	13
1	1	1	1	1	1	(11)	1	1	1	1	1	1	1	1	1	1	1	1	1	1	1	1	1	23	10	13
1	1	1	1	1	1	1	(12)	1	1	1	1	1	1	1	1	1	1	1	1	1	1	1	1	23	10	13
1	1	1	1	1	1	1	1	(13)	1	1	1	1	1	1	1	1	1	1	1	1	1	1	1	23	10	13
1	1	1	1	1	1	1	1	1	(15)	1	1	1	1	1	1	1	1	1	1	1	1	1	1	23	10	13
1	1	1	1	1	1	1	1	1	1	(14)	1	1	1	1	1	1	1	1	1	1	1	1	1	23	10	13
0	0	0	0	0	0	0	0	0	0	0	(19)	0	0	0	1	0	0	0	0	1	1	1	1	5	11	- 6
0	0	0	0	0	0	0	0	0	0	0	0	(20)	0	0	1	0	0	0	0	1	1	1	1	5	11	- 6
0	0	0	0	0	0	0	0	0	0	0	0	0	(21)	0	1	0	0	0	0	1	1	1	1	5	11	- 6
0	0	0	0	0	0	0	0	0	0	0	0	0	0	(24)	1	0	0	0	0	1	1	1	1	5	11	- 6
0	0	0	0	0	0	0	0	0	0	0	0	0	0	0	(25)	0	0	0	0	1	1	1	1	4	15	-11
0	0	0	0	0	0	0	0	0	0	0	0	0	0	0	0	(26)	1	1	1	0	0	1	1	5	14	- 9
0	0	0	0	0	0	0	0	0	0	0	0	0	0	0	0	1	(27)	1	1	0	0	1	1	5	14	- 9
0	0	0	0	0	0	0	0	0	0	0	0	0	0	0	0	1	1	(30)	1	0	0	1	1	5	14	- 9
0	0	0	0	0	0	0	0	0	0	0	0	0	0	0	0	1	1	1	(29)	0	0	1	1	5	14	- 9
0	0	0	0	0	0	0	0	0	0	0	0	0	0	0	0	0	0	0	0	(33)	0	1	1	2	16	-14
0	0	0	0	0	0	0	0	0	0	0	0	0	0	0	0	0	0	0	0	0	(34)	1	1	2	16	-14
0	0	0	0	0	0	0	0	0	0	0	0	0	0	0	0	0	0	0	0	0	0	(35)	1	1	23	-22
0	0	0	0	0	0	0	0	0	0	0	0	0	0	0	0	0	0	0	0	0	0	1	(36)	1	23	-22
Received: 9	9	10	10	10	10	10	10	10	10	10	11	11	11	11	15	14	14	14	14	16	16	23	23			

the other hand, give more frequent, pair-by-pair repetition to many scattered cells of the same matrix.

Transfers of inferior cooked food (Table 7)—payments for the routine services given by the Waterman, Barber, Potter, Washerman, Leatherworker, and Sweeper —are known from scattered observations, and are more generally confirmed by a comprehensive survey of all employers and employees. Alms consisting of *kaccā* food were observed in transfer between many pairs of castes. They were reported as having gone from many castes to Muslim Faqir Devotees (27) in the recent past. Muslim castes feed each other reciprocally in both *kaccā* and *pakkā* food and clear away each other's garbage. Brahmans, when asked or hired to do so by persons of lower caste, may provide either *kaccā* or *pakkā* meals to out-of-village wedding guests of caste too high to take *pakkā* food from their hosts, according to several observations and specific reports. The remaining unobserved 73 cells of this matrix are completed according to a few reported cases plus general assertions by members of both giving and receiving castes to the effect that they expected to act in similar fashion should the need arise.

The entries concerning the disposal of food-soiled plates in Table 8 are based largely on statements of expectations held by both hosts and diners, and on verbal reports of past occurrences, since activity in most of the cells in which garbage

TABLE 7

MATRIX OF TRANSACTIONS IN INFERIOR (*Kaccā*) FOOD.

(Giver Castes, rows) × (Receiver Castes, columns)

Giver	1	6	2	3	4	9	11	12	13	15	14	19	20	21	24	25	26	27	30	29	33	34	35	36	Given	Received	Net
1	(1)	0	1	1	1	1	1	1	1	1	1	1	1	1	1	1	1	1	1	1	1	1	1	1	22	0	22
6	0	(6)	0	0	0	0	0	0	0	1	1	1	1	1	1	1	1	1	1	1	1	1	1	1	15	0	15
2	0	0	(2)	1	0	0	0	0	0	1	1	1	1	1	1	1	1	1	1	1	1	1	1	1	16	2	14
3	0	0	1	(3)	0	0	0	0	0	1	1	1	1	1	1	1	1	1	1	1	1	1	1	1	16	2	14
4	0	0	0	0	(4)	0	0	0	0	1	1	1	1	1	1	1	1	1	1	1	1	1	1	1	15	1	14
9	0	0	0	0	0	(9)	0	0	0	1	1	1	1	1	1	1	1	1	1	1	1	1	1	1	15	1	14
11	0	0	0	0	0	0	(11)	0	0	1	1	1	1	1	1	1	1	1	1	1	1	1	1	1	15	1	14
12	0	0	0	0	0	0	0	(12)	0	1	1	1	1	1	1	1	1	1	1	1	1	1	1	1	15	1	14
13	0	0	0	0	0	0	0	0	(13)	1	1	1	1	1	1	1	1	1	1	1	1	1	1	1	15	1	14
15	0	0	0	0	0	0	0	0	0	(15)	1	1	1	1	1	1	1	1	1	1	1	1	1	1	14	10	4
14	0	0	0	0	0	0	0	0	0	1	(14)	0	0	0	0	0	1	1	1	1	1	1	1	1	9	10	-1
19	0	0	0	0	0	0	0	0	0	0	0	(19)	0	0	0	0	0	0	0	0	1	1	1	1	4	10	-6
20	0	0	0	0	0	0	0	0	0	0	0	0	(20)	0	0	0	0	0	0	0	1	1	1	1	4	10	-6
21	0	0	0	0	0	0	0	0	0	0	0	0	0	(21)	0	0	0	0	0	0	1	1	1	1	4	10	-6
24	0	0	0	0	0	0	0	0	0	0	0	0	0	0	(24)	0	0	0	0	0	1	1	1	1	4	10	-6
25	0	0	0	0	0	0	0	0	0	0	0	0	0	0	0	(25)	0	0	0	0	1	1	1	1	4	10	-6
26	0	0	0	0	0	0	0	0	0	0	0	0	0	0	0	0	(26)	1	1	1	0	0	1	1	5	14	-9
27	0	0	0	0	0	0	0	0	0	0	0	0	0	0	0	0	1	(27)	1	1	0	0	1	1	5	14	-9
30	0	0	0	0	0	0	0	0	0	0	0	0	0	0	0	0	1	1	(30)	1	0	0	1	1	5	14	-9
29	0	0	0	0	0	0	0	0	0	0	0	0	0	0	0	0	1	1	1	(29)	0	0	1	1	5	14	-9
33	0	0	0	0	0	0	0	0	0	0	0	0	0	0	0	0	0	0	0	0	(33)	0	1	1	2	16	-14
34	0	0	0	0	0	0	0	0	0	0	0	0	0	0	0	0	0	0	0	0	0	(34)	1	1	2	16	-14
35	0	0	0	0	0	0	0	0	0	0	0	0	0	0	0	0	0	0	0	0	0	0	(35)	0	0	22	-22
36	0	0	0	0	0	0	0	0	0	0	0	0	0	0	0	0	0	0	0	0	0	0	0	(36)	0	22	-22
Received	0	0	2	2	1	1	1	1	1	10	10	10	10	10	10	10	14	14	14	14	16	16	22	22			

disposal can occur is infrequent. Feasts testing the behavior of the castes from (1) to (15) and (26) are frequent enough and could be observed. Feasts sponsored by members of ten castes showed the Sweeper disposing of the scrapings from all the diners' plates. Actually, among the high castes just below the Brahman, there is reluctance on the part of guests to insist that their hosts pick up the garbage-soiled plates; it is polite for each guest, even if he is of higher caste standing, to do his own disposal; that is, carry his plate to the waiting Sweeper. However, relatively few instances were observed or remembered in which castes from (19) through (35) sponsored feasts (with a high-caste cook, of course) for members of castes (1) to (15). About 100 cells of this matrix are thus based on statements of precedent and willingness to follow the precedent.

The professional disposal of feces by the Sweeper alone (Fig. 10) is a matter of daily observation to all who rise early enough to witness that event.

This review of some of the many contexts in which food transactions continually occur—trade, agricultural work, credit, religious merit-seeking, feasting, private celebrating, domestic service, visiting, etc.—suggests also the pervasiveness of caste-rank-defining activity in village life.

Variations occur within castes, of course. Most Jats eat *pakkā* from any caste of the subset (1) through (15), but a few Jat families would not eat the feasts

TABLE 8

MATRIX OF GARBAGE (*Jūṭhā*) DISPOSAL.

(Giver Castes) — rows; (Receiver Castes) — columns

1	6	2	3	4	9	11	12	13	15	14	19	20	21	24	25	26	27	30	29	33	34	35	36	Given	Received	Net
(1)	0	1	1	1	1	1	1	1	1	1	1	1	1	1	1	1	1	1	1	1	1	1	1	22	0	22
0	(6)	0	0	0	1	1	1	1	1	1	1	1	1	1	1	1	1	1	1	1	1	1	1	19	0	19
0	0	(2)	0	0	1	1	1	1	1	1	1	1	1	1	1	1	1	1	1	1	1	1	1	19	1	18
0	0	0	(3)	0	1	1	1	1	1	1	1	1	1	1	1	1	1	1	1	1	1	1	1	19	1	18
0	0	0	0	(4)	1	1	1	1	1	1	1	1	1	1	1	1	1	1	1	1	1	1	1	19	1	18
0	0	0	0	0	(9)	0	0	0	1	1	1	1	1	1	1	1	1	1	1	1	1	1	1	15	5	10
0	0	0	0	0	0	(11)	0	0	1	1	1	1	1	1	1	1	1	1	1	1	1	1	1	15	5	10
0	0	0	0	0	0	0	(12)	0	1	1	1	1	1	1	1	1	1	1	1	1	1	1	1	15	5	10
0	0	0	0	0	0	0	0	(13)	1	1	1	1	1	1	1	1	1	1	1	1	1	1	1	15	5	10
0	0	0	0	0	0	0	0	0	(15)	0	1	1	1	1	1	1	1	1	1	1	1	1	1	13	9	4
0	0	0	0	0	0	0	0	0	0	(14)	1	1	1	1	1	1	1	1	1	1	1	1	1	13	9	4
0	0	0	0	0	0	0	0	0	0	0	(19)	0	0	0	0	0	0	0	0	0	0	0	1	1	11	-10
0	0	0	0	0	0	0	0	0	0	0	0	(20)	0	0	0	0	0	0	0	0	0	0	1	1	11	-10
0	0	0	0	0	0	0	0	0	0	0	0	0	(21)	0	0	0	0	0	0	0	0	0	1	1	11	-10
0	0	0	0	0	0	0	0	0	0	0	0	0	0	(24)	0	0	0	0	0	0	0	0	1	1	11	-10
0	0	0	0	0	0	0	0	0	0	0	0	0	0	0	(25)	0	0	0	0	0	0	0	1	1	11	-10
0	0	0	0	0	0	0	0	0	0	0	0	0	0	0	0	(26)	1	1	1	0	0	0	1	4	14	-10
0	0	0	0	0	0	0	0	0	0	0	0	0	0	0	0	1	(27)	1	1	0	0	0	1	4	14	-10
0	0	0	0	0	0	0	0	0	0	0	0	0	0	0	0	1	1	(30)	1	0	0	0	1	4	14	-10
0	0	0	0	0	0	0	0	0	0	0	0	0	0	0	0	1	1	1	(29)	0	0	0	1	4	14	-10
0	0	0	0	0	0	0	0	0	0	0	0	0	0	0	0	0	0	0	0	(33)	0	0	1	1	11	-10
0	0	0	0	0	0	0	0	0	0	0	0	0	0	0	0	0	0	0	0	0	(34)	0	1	1	11	-10
0	0	0	0	0	0	0	0	0	0	0	0	0	0	0	0	0	0	0	0	0	0	(35)	0	0	11	-11
0	0	0	0	0	0	0	0	0	0	0	0	0	0	0	0	0	0	0	0	0	0	0	(36)	0	22	-22

Received: 0 0 1 1 1 5 5 5 5 9 9 11 11 11 11 11 14 14 14 14 11 11 11 22 of Brahmans on the theory that this would be taking something away from those who should themselves be receivers of religious charity. One Jat would not attend any local tenant's feast, not even one given by a local Brahman, in order to avoid suffering possible insult to his personal status as the resident landlord. Not all Sweepers would take food, let alone feces, from Khatik Cultivators (caste 25), and so on. But by the conception of caste ranks as corporate and vested in each member, no such variation should alter or create ambiguity in deciding on a caste's rank in food transactions. Insofar as it is known that any member takes or gives food, the caste is considered to take and give food. The caste thus takes the lowest position which any lowering transaction by any member can demonstrate, and also the highest position which any elevating transaction by any member can demonstrate.

SCORING IN THE MATRIX

The matrix form of representation encourages one to look upon the set of intercaste transactions in any kind of food in Kishan Garhi as a kind of tournament among the 24 teams which make up this village's society. As in most ordered

TABLE 9

MATRIX OF FECES DISPOSAL.

(Giver Castes) / (Receiver Castes)

																								Given	Received	Net
(1)	0	0	0	0	0	0	0	0	0	0	0	0	0	0	0	0	0	0	0	0	0	0	1	1	0	1
0	(6)	0	0	0	0	0	0	0	0	0	0	0	0	0	0	0	0	0	0	0	0	0	1	1	0	1
0	0	(2)	0	0	0	0	0	0	0	0	0	0	0	0	0	0	0	0	0	0	0	0	1	1	0	1
0	0	0	(3)	0	0	0	0	0	0	0	0	0	0	0	0	0	0	0	0	0	0	0	1	1	0	1
0	0	0	0	(4)	0	0	0	0	0	0	0	0	0	0	0	0	0	0	0	0	0	0	1	1	0	1
0	0	0	0	0	(9)	0	0	0	0	0	0	0	0	0	0	0	0	0	0	0	0	0	1	1	0	1
0	0	0	0	0	0	(11)	0	0	0	0	0	0	0	0	0	0	0	0	0	0	0	0	1	1	0	1
0	0	0	0	0	0	0	(12)	0	0	0	0	0	0	0	0	0	0	0	0	0	0	0	1	1	0	1
0	0	0	0	0	0	0	0	(13)	0	0	0	0	0	0	0	0	0	0	0	0	0	0	1	1	0	1
0	0	0	0	0	0	0	0	0	(15)	0	0	0	0	0	0	0	0	0	0	0	0	0	1	1	0	1
0	0	0	0	0	0	0	0	0	0	(14)	0	0	0	0	0	0	0	0	0	0	0	0	1	1	0	1
0	0	0	0	0	0	0	0	0	0	0	(19)	0	0	0	0	0	0	0	0	0	0	0	1	1	0	1
0	0	0	0	0	0	0	0	0	0	0	0	(20)	0	0	0	0	0	0	0	0	0	0	1	1	0	1
0	0	0	0	0	0	0	0	0	0	0	0	0	(21)	0	0	0	0	0	0	0	0	0	1	1	0	1
0	0	0	0	0	0	0	0	0	0	0	0	0	0	(24)	0	0	0	0	0	0	0	0	1	1	0	1
0	0	0	0	0	0	0	0	0	0	0	0	0	0	0	(25)	0	0	0	0	0	0	0	1	1	0	1
0	0	0	0	0	0	0	0	0	0	0	0	0	0	0	0	(26)	0	0	0	0	0	0	1	1	0	1
0	0	0	0	0	0	0	0	0	0	0	0	0	0	0	0	0	(27)	0	0	0	0	0	1	1	0	1
0	0	0	0	0	0	0	0	0	0	0	0	0	0	0	0	0	0	(30)	0	0	0	0	1	1	0	1
0	0	0	0	0	0	0	0	0	0	0	0	0	0	0	0	0	0	0	(29)	0	0	0	1	1	0	1
0	0	0	0	0	0	0	0	0	0	0	0	0	0	0	0	0	0	0	0	(33)	0	0	1	1	0	1
0	0	0	0	0	0	0	0	0	0	0	0	0	0	0	0	0	0	0	0	0	(34)	0	1	1	0	1
0	0	0	0	0	0	0	0	0	0	0	0	0	0	0	0	0	0	0	0	0	0	(35)	0	0	0	0
0	0	0	0	0	0	0	0	0	0	0	0	0	0	0	0	0	0	0	0	0	0	0	(36)	0	-22	-22

Received   0 0 0 0 0 0 0 0 0 0 0 0 0 0 0 0 0 0 0 0 0 0 0 22 competitions, transitivity is assumed as a principle and is expected to occur in any confrontations in the future. Game-like scorings of the relative ranks of the castes could be made in several different ways. If a minimal number of intercaste transactions occurred in a straight, diagonal (upper-left-to-lower-right) chain of paired confrontations, such as might occur in a perfect series of hypergamous alliances, then a purely positional, nonparametric statement would constitute the only suitable method for counting the ranks resulting from the game. If a minimal number of intercaste transactions occurred by successive eliminations according to a pyramidal pattern, as in most large sports tournaments, then either a positional or an arithmetic scoring might be meaningful. But the actual occurrences of inter-caste food transactions in Kishan Garhi are maximal, not minimal; they form a highly redundant pattern in which transitivity is not merely assumed, but often comprehensively realized. While a sports competition may have a brief duration and a definite end signaled by the announcement of scores and the award of prizes, intercaste food transactions in the village are embedded in most of the essential, recurrent social encounters of Hindu community life. Old victories and defeats are continually and inevitably reenacted in sales, gifts, feasts, and payments of many kinds. Given such a pattern and accepting a literal interpretation of the logic expressed by village respondents, the most suitable system of scoring seemed to me to be an arithmetic and additive one which includes and counts all types of transactions which are felt to be important, however redundant they may be with respect to each other.

I therefore adopted the following system of scoring for determining the overall ranks of single castes. The total of encounters (out of 23) in which a caste domi-nates or "wins" over other castes is the total number of digits in its row. The total of the encounters (out of 23) in which a caste is dominated or "loses" is the total number of digits in its column. The net rank position of each caste in each matrix is computed to the right of each matrix by subtracting each caste's total of losses from its total of wins. For example, in Table 6 of *pakkā* transactions, Brahmans dominate in their encounters with 22 of the other 24 castes (row total at the right) and are in turn dominated by 9 of the same castes, who feed the Brahmans recipro-cally (column total, lower left). The net position of the Brahmans is 22 minus 9, leaving a positive balance of 13 net wins to the Brahmans' credit. At the lowest extreme, take caste (36), Bhangi Sweepers, in the same matrix: they dominate in only one encounter; that is, they are able to persuade members of only one other caste, the Kanjar Hunters (35) to attend a *pakkā* feast at their houses, yet they themselves receive *pakkā* food at the houses of all 23 of the other castes. The Bhangi Sweepers' net position in *pakkā* food is thus 1 minus 23, leaving them with a net score of negative 22. Each other caste earns a net score equal to that of the Brahman or that of the Bhangi, or another score of some intermediate value.

The matrix for each type of food thus yields three series of scores by which every caste may be ranked in relation to every other caste: a series of giving (dominating, winning, credit) scores in the row totals; a series of receiving (sub-ordinating, losing, debit) scores in the column totals; and a series of net scores as the balance between the giving and receiving series. Generally, a caste's rank by the giving scores agrees closely with its rank by the receiving scores, but reversals can occur: the four Muslim castes (castes 26–30) stand higher as givers than they do as receivers in Tables 6, 7, and 8; the Maithil Carpenters (6) stand higher as receivers than they do as givers in Tables 7 and 8. Since both giving and receiving are mentioned (often separately) by villagers as being relevant in their thinking about rank, both need to be included in any general analysis. Net scores thus seem preferable as representing the two ways of thinking in combination.

FIVE TYPES OF FOOD TRANSACTIONS COMPARED

The matrix for each type of food also differs somewhat from the matrix for every other type of food. A comparison of the five matrices in Tables 5 to 9 by the Guttman scaling technique employed by Mahar (1959) would reveal that transactions in the differing food media are in fact scaled at four steps, moving from many transactions to few transactions in the order: (a) raw foodstuffs, (b) pakkā food, (c) kaccā food and garbage disposal together, and (d) feces disposal. In this series of steps, each later step implies all earlier steps. This finding that the five systems of food transaction are scaled solves the problem initially felt in trying to rank or weight the types of food by direct questioning. Differential weightings of the several media would be justified and necessary if one were dealing with each medium in isolation; identical weightings are retained here, as the several media are themselves all retained in the aggregate analysis.

As between eating another caste's kaccā food and disposing of its garbage, there is no clear overall scaling: some high castes (those from 9 to 13) shrink from receiving kaccā food from castes (2) to (6), yet willingly clear away the same castes' dirty plates at feasts. On the other side, the Waterman caste (14) and three lower castes (33 to 35) refuse to pick up the garbage-soiled plates of certain castes (15 and 19 to 25 or 34, respectively) from whom they willingly accept kaccā food. Had the high and low castes in this contrast both reversed their choices of medium, their overall ranks would not have been altered in any apparent way. One might say that these higher castes take more pride in their independence in matters of food supply, while more readily conceding to the top castes a strictly symbolic superiority; these lower castes, on the contrary, realistically accept their own dependence in food, yet jealously resist any further, mannered subordination to their nearer competitors for rank.

The net effects of the five kinds of food transactions upon the rankings of all castes may be compared by inspecting their respective series of net scores. These are brought together in Table 10. Here one notes that no two media of transaction yield exactly the same series of net scores or the same distinctions of caste rank. Nevertheless, since these transactions are related systems within one small community, they are to a very high degree mutually compatible, as one would expect them to be. Only one set of reversals occurs between media: the Khatik Cultivators (25) stand slightly below the four Muslim castes (26 to 30) in pakkā transactions, rather than being equal to or slightly superior to Muslims, as they are in all other kinds of food transactions. One might anticipate a corresponding divergence in opinion at such a point of incongruity.

That *pakkā* and *kaccā* food-handling distinctions are more useful in ranking the lower castes while garbage-handling distinctions are more useful in ranking the upper castes is also demonstrated by the comparison of net scores in Table 10. More than one type of food transaction would be needed to differentiate the whole range of castes, it seems.

In some ways, the five types of transactions are redundant, as some of the same distinctions recur in more than one of them. Net caste scores in three of the food media in particular—*pakkā*, *kaccā*, and *jūthā*—spread out over wide ranges and afford many distinctions of rank, while scores in the other two media—raw food-stuffs and feces—spread over smaller ranges and afford few distinctions of rank. Furthermore, the two last-mentioned media repeat distinctions made in one or more of the first three, without adding any new distinctions peculiar to themselves.

TABLE 10

DISTINCTIONS OF CASTE RANK CONTRIBUTED BY TRANSACTIONS IN FIVE TYPES OF FOOD.
(Net Scores by Caste from Tables 5 to 9)

Caste	Raw Foodstuffs	Superior (Pakkā) Food	Inferior (Kaccā) Food	Garbage (Jūthā) Disposal	Feces	Total
1.	2	13	22	22	1	60
6.	2	13	15	19	1	50
2.	2	13	14	18	1	48
3.	2	13	14	18	1	48
4.	2	13	14	18	1	48
9.	2	13	14	10	1	40
11.	2	13	14	10	1	40
12.	2	13	14	10	1	40
13.	2	13	14	10	1	40
15.	2	13	4	4	1	24
14.	2	13	− 1	4	1	19
19.	2	− 6	− 6	−10	1	− 19
20.	2	− 6	− 6	−10	1	− 19
21.	2	− 6	− 6	−10	1	− 19
24.	2	− 6	− 6	−10	1	− 19
25.	2	−11	− 6	−10	1	− 24
26.	2	− 9	− 9	−10	1	− 25
27.	2	− 9	− 9	−10	1	− 25
30.	2	− 9	− 9	−10	1	− 25
29.	2	− 9	− 9	−10	1	− 25
33.	2	−14	−14	−10	1	− 35
34.	2	−14	−14	−10	1	− 35
35.	−22	−22	−22	−11	0	− 77
36.	−22	−22	−22	−22	−22	−110
Ranks	2	6	9	8	3	12
Range	25	36	45	45	24	171

This suggests a way of simplifying the present analysis. Since an equally differentiated ranking may be had without recourse to transactions in raw foodstuffs or feces, I here eliminate those two types of transactions from further part in the experiment. Were they to be retained at this point, their effects would substantially disappear later in the final matrix of scores anyway: in the final matrix, they would affect only the last two columns, and would affect all of the scores evenly, raising each value in column (35) by 1 and each value in column (36) by 2. The existence and importance of transactions in raw foodstuffs and in feces should not be forgotten in other contexts, however: the first qualifies most other distinctions of rank by its large area of untrammelled mutual exchange, while both severely reiterate the low status of the Sweepers.

The remaining three types of transactions—*pakkā*, *kaccā*, and garbage—all seem necessary for developing a complete picture of the distinctions of rank afforded by transactional systems generally. The hierarchy of *kaccā* food, with its nine ranks, is the most differentiated of the three: if one had to choose a single transactional medium as an indicator of rank, *kaccā* food would be the medium to choose in Kishan Garhi. However, such a simple index would be quite incomplete, for transactions in garbage add two further distinctions to these nine, and transactions in *pakkā* food add still one more distinction, bringing the total number of distinctions by food transfer to twelve. In narrowing consideration to these three most differentiated media, I am also selecting those three sorts of transactions in foods which are most often mentioned by villagers in explaining their opinions about caste rank.

Does study focused on just these three types of food transfer provide enough of the full actuality for the purpose at hand? Or must additional kinds of transactions be considered in order to construct a model that will be fully true to village thought as well as to action? I would be happy here to incorporate for consideration any further systems of ranking that emerge out of serving or other relationships, but I am not satisfied that I yet know just what these systems are. Ranked behavior occurs in the transfer of other consumables, such as that found in the drawing of water from wells, the use of metal and pottery vessels, the grinding of flour, processing of milk, etc. There are further media of interactional ranking in forms of greeting, sitting, etc. However, none of these other media was mentioned by any respondent as affecting his decisions about ranking, and, as far as I know, none would add any further distinction of rank to those already present. Intercaste usages surrounding the smoking of tobacco were occasionally mentioned as providing current information on close points of reciprocal dominance between equal castes; they seemed, however, to add nothing to an already comprehensive scheme of stratification. Since smoking involved only small groups, often located out of public view, its usages were difficult to know and seemed susceptible to a greater amount of individual variation than transfers of food. I therefore ignore them until evidence meriting their consideration appears. The three types of food transactions seem likely to provide as full a series of rankings as can be developed from the data at hand.

THE SUMMARY MATRIX (TABLE 11)

To consider the food transactional system as a whole, I now wish to combine the data of the three most relevant matrices in some fashion. Maintaining my earlier postulate that a transaction in any type of food is equal to a transaction in any other type of food, I now *add* the matrices of transactions in *pakkā, kaccā,* and garbage (Tables 6, 7, and 8) to form the summary matrix of Table 11. Here the patterns of the earlier matrices overlap each other transparently, so that one can readily perceive the scaling of the several types of transactions as values rise toward the upper righthand corner.

The constant meaning of a unit in this matrix is "a transaction in (any one of the three types of) food." Where "1" appears, the type of food is always *pakkā,* as in Table 6. Where "2" appears, two types are transferred, either *pakkā* and *kaccā* (in the lower right and in row 15), or *pakkā* and garbage (in the upper left). Where "3" appears, all three types of food are transferred.

This summary matrix yields in its righthand column a series of summary net scores for all the castes. These are scores by which the castes may be set in a

TABLE 11

SUMMARY MATRIX OF TRANSACTIONS IN THREE TYPES OF FOOD—SUPERIOR, INFERIOR, GARBAGE.

(Sum of Tables 6, 7, and 8)

(Giver Castes) / (Receiver Castes)

1	6	2	3	4	9	11	12	13	15	14	19	20	21	24	25	26	27	30	29	33	34	35	36	Given	Received	Net
(1)	1	3	3	3	3	3	3	3	3	3	3	3	3	3	3	3	3	3	3	3	3	3	3	67	10	57
1	(6)	1	1	1	2	2	2	2	3	3	3	3	3	3	3	3	3	3	3	3	3	3	3	57	10	47
1	1	(2)	2	1	2	2	2	2	3	3	3	3	3	3	3	3	3	3	3	3	3	3	3	58	13	45
1	1	2	(3)	1	2	2	2	2	3	3	3	3	3	3	3	3	3	3	3	3	3	3	3	58	13	45
1	1	1	1	(4)	2	2	2	2	3	3	3	3	3	3	3	3	3	3	3	3	3	3	3	57	12	45
1	1	1	1	1	(9)	1	1	1	3	3	3	3	3	3	3	3	3	3	3	3	3	3	3	53	16	37
1	1	1	1	1	1	(11)	1	1	3	3	3	3	3	3	3	3	3	3	3	3	3	3	3	53	16	37
1	1	1	1	1	1	1	(12)	1	3	3	3	3	3	3	3	3	3	3	3	3	3	3	3	53	16	37
1	1	1	1	1	1	1	1	(13)	3	3	3	3	3	3	3	3	3	3	3	3	3	3	3	53	16	37
1	1	1	1	1	1	1	1	1	(15)	2	3	3	3	3	3	3	3	3	3	3	3	3	3	50	29	21
1	1	1	1	1	1	1	1	1	2	(14)	2	2	2	2	2	3	3	3	3	3	3	3	3	45	29	16
0	0	0	0	0	0	0	0	0	0	0	(19)	0	0	0	1	0	0	0	0	2	2	2	3	10	32	-22
0	0	0	0	0	0	0	0	0	0	0	0	(20)	0	0	1	0	0	0	0	2	2	2	3	10	32	-22
0	0	0	0	0	0	0	0	0	0	0	0	0	(21)	0	1	0	0	0	0	2	2	2	3	10	32	-22
0	0	0	0	0	0	0	0	0	0	0	0	0	0	(24)	1	0	0	0	0	2	2	2	3	10	32	-22
0	0	0	0	0	0	0	0	0	0	0	0	0	0	0	(25)	0	0	0	0	2	2	2	3	9	36	-27
0	0	0	0	0	0	0	0	0	0	0	0	0	0	0	0	(26)	3	3	3	0	0	2	3	14	42	-28
0	0	0	0	0	0	0	0	0	0	0	0	0	0	0	0	3	(27)	3	3	0	0	2	3	14	42	-28
0	0	0	0	0	0	0	0	0	0	0	0	0	0	0	0	3	3	(30)	3	0	0	2	3	14	42	-28
0	0	0	0	0	0	0	0	0	0	0	0	0	0	0	0	3	3	3	(29)	0	0	2	3	14	42	-28
0	0	0	0	0	0	0	0	0	0	0	0	0	0	0	0	0	0	0	0	(33)	0	2	3	5	43	-38
0	0	0	0	0	0	0	0	0	0	0	0	0	0	0	0	0	0	0	0	0	(34)	2	3	5	43	-38
0	0	0	0	0	0	0	0	0	0	0	0	0	0	0	0	0	0	0	0	0	0	(35)	1	1	56	-55
0	0	0	0	0	0	0	0	0	0	0	0	0	0	0	0	0	0	0	0	0	0	1	(36)	1	67	-66
Received																										
10	10	13	13	12	16	16	16	16	29	29	32	32	32	32	36	42	42	42	42	43	43	56	67			

summary order of rank. Each of these summary scores has the meaning of "the net number of wins or losses in encounters with other castes concerning the three food types." Since the maximal possible number of encounters for each caste in the three matrices together is 138 (3 times 23 other castes, each met once as giver, once as receiver), a caste's summary net score could reach as high as a positive 69 or as low as a negative 69. The actual values approximate these maxims: the Brahmans show a net score of positive 57, while the Sweepers show a net score of negative 66. (The Brahmans may be said to spend a few of their credits by taking feasts from others.) The range of the net scores for transactions in the three types of food is therefore large in proportion to the possibility—123 out of 139. Half of the possible ranks, 12 out of 24, are evenly distinguished in the scores of giving, in the scores of receiving, and in the net scores. Transactions in the three types of food taken together are thus rather highly discriminating of gradations in rank. These are the gradations that are to be compared below with the rankings obtained independently through a sample of collective opinion.

THE MATRIX OF NET SCORES (TABLE 12)

The summary matrix of Table 11 depicts the whole of the essential transactional system and yields a summary net ranking of the castes. From the summary matrix one can further extract a report on the net score obtaining finally within all pairs of castes. One does this by taking the summary matrix and subtracting its reciprocal, negative values (all the values in the lower left triangle) from its positive values (all the values in the upper right triangle). The values remaining after this subtraction appear in the matrix of net scores (Table 12). All mutual relationships have been removed; only distinctions of rank remain. The numbers of Table 12 are no longer code symbols for certain food media, as are the numbers in Table 11; instead, they are abstract values expressing the ultimate differences to be found within each pair of castes. One here confronts the final balance sheet of intercaste dominance.

This matrix of net scores displays more clearly than any preceding matrix the total configuration of ranks. It exposes (within dotted lines) those blocs of castes whose final positions in food transactions are mutually undifferentiated in rank by direct transactions. The visual configuration of ranks (castes and blocs of castes) will be seen now to agree precisely with the continuities and discontinuities in the series of net scores at the right of the matrix.

From this matrix of net scores, one also obtains confirmation of the reality in action of that basic division into "high" and "low" which villagers initially expressed to me through their approximate, absolute uses of these broad terms. Among themselves, both the high subset of castes and the low subset of castes show little transactional dominance—the low castes least of all—but a superbloc of high castes (1 to 15) preponderates strongly over a superbloc of low castes (19 to 36).

CASTE ROLES IN THE DIFFERENTIATION OF RANKS
(TABLE 13)

The matrix form of representation makes possible a separate analysis of the distinctions of rank made by each caste in its vector of transactions with the others. Table 13 presents this final, caste-by-caste analysis. In this table, the castes of one rank or bloc are classed together in one column, since their roles in interaction with other castes are by definition identical. As there are twelve ranks in the transactional system, there are twelve columns, each column accommodating one of the twelve transactional role types that are found to exist among the 24 castes.

The values entered in this table are extracted from the matrix of net scores (Table 12) simply by reading down the column to find what, if anything, the caste receives, then across the row to find what, if anything, it gives. Negative signs are prefixed where it gives.

Table 13 is best read column by column, starting each column from the top.

TABLE 12

MATRIX OF NET SCORES OF TRANSACTIONS IN THREE TYPES OF FOOD—

SUPERIOR, INFERIOR, GARBAGE.

(Summary matrix, Table 11, less inverse values)

(Receiver Castes)

```
                                                              Given  Received  Net
(1) 0  2 2 2 2 2 2 2 2  3 3 3 3 3 3 3 3 3 3 3 3 3 3 3          57      0     57
   (6) 0 0 0 1 1 1 1 2 2 3 3 3 3 3 3 3 3 3 3 3 3 3 3           47      0     47
      (2) 0 0 1 1 1 1 2 2 3 3 3 3 3 3 3 3 3 3 3 3 3 3          47      2     45
         (3) 0 1 1 1 1 2 2 3 3 3 3 3 3 3 3 3 3 3 3 3 3         47      2     45
          0 (4) 1 1 1 1 2 2 3 3 3 3 3 3 3 3 3 3 3 3 3 3        47      2     45
                (9) 0 0 0 2 2 3 3 3 3 3 3 3 3 3 3 3 3 3        43      6     37
                  (11) 0 0 2 2 3 3 3 3 3 3 3 3 3 3 3 3 3       43      6     37
                     (12) 0 2 2 3 3 3 3 3 3 3 3 3 3 3 3 3      43      6     37
                        (13) 2 2 3 3 3 3 3 3 3 3 3 3 3 3 3     43      6     37
                          (15) 0 3 3 3 3 3 3 3 3 3 3 3 3 3     39     18     21
                            (14) 2 2 2 2 2 3 3 3 3 3 3 3 3     34     18     16
                              (19) 0 0 0 1 0 0 0 0 2 2 2 3     10     32    -22
                                (20) 0 0 1 0 0 0 0 2 2 2 3     10     32    -22
                                   (21) 0 1 0 0 0 0 2 2 2 3    10     32    -22
                                     (24) 1 0 0 0 0 2 2 2 3    10     32    -22
                                       (25) 0 0 0 0 2 2 2 3     9     36    -27
                                         (26) 0 0 0 0 0 2 3     5     33    -28
                                           (27) 0 0 0 0 2 3     5     33    -28
                                             (30) 0 0 0 2 3     5     33    -28
                                               (29) 0 0 2 3     5     33    -28
                                                 (33) 0 2 3     5     43    -38
                                                   (34) 2 3     5     43    -38
                                                     (35) 0     0     55    -55
                                                       (36)     0     66    -66

Received   0 0 2 2 2 6 6 6 6 18 18 32 32 32 32 36 33 33 33 33 43 43 55 66
```

(Giver Castes) — left margin label

TABLE 13

CASTE ROLE TYPES DISTINGUISHED BY TRANSACTIONS IN THREE TYPES OF FOOD.

(Net Scores by Caste from Table 12)

Code No. Name	(1)	(6)	(2)(3)(4)	(9)(11)(12)(13)	(15)	(14)	(19)(20)(21)(24)	(25)	(26)(27)(30)(29)	(33)(34)	(35)	(36)	Total Net Scores
1. Sanadhya Brahman	—	0	2	2	2	2	3	3	3	3	3	3	57
6. Maithil Carpenter	0	—	0	1	2	2	3	3	3	3	3	3	47
2. Jat Cultivator	-2	0	—	1	2	2	3	3	3	3	3	3	45
3. Barahseni Merchant	-2	0	—	1	2	2	3	3	3	3	3	3	45
4. Kulasrestha Scribe	-2	0	—	-1	2	2	3	3	3	3	3	3	45
9. Jogi Devotee	-2	-1	-1	—	2	2	3	3	3	3	3	3	37
11. Phulmali Gardener	-2	-1	-1	—	2	2	3	3	3	3	3	3	37
12. Kachi Cultivator	-2	-1	-1	—	2	2	3	3	3	3	3	3	37
13. Baghele Goatherd	-2	-1	-1	—	2	2	3	3	3	3	3	3	37
15. Thakur Barber	-2	-2	-2	-2	0	0	2	2	3	3	3	3	21
14. Turai Waterman	-2	-2	-2	-2	-3	-1	2	2	3	3	3	3	16
19. Gola Potter	-3	-3	-3	-3	-3	-2	—	-1	0	2	2	3	-22
20. Darzi Tailor	-3	-3	-3	-3	-3	-2	—	-1	0	2	2	3	-22
21. Karhera Cottoncarder	-3	-3	-3	-3	-3	-2	—	-1	0	2	2	3	-22
24. Koli Weaver	-3	-3	-3	-3	-3	-2	-1	0	0	2	2	3	-22
25. Khatik Cultivator	-3	-3	-3	-3	-3	-2	0	0	-1	2	2	3	-27
26. Muslim Faqir Devotee	-3	-3	-3	-3	-3	-3	0	0	-1	0	2	3	-28
27. Muslim Mirasi Singer	-3	-3	-3	-3	-3	-3	0	0	-1	0	2	3	-28
29. Muslim Manihar Bangleman	-3	-3	-3	-3	-3	-3	0	0	-1	0	2	3	-28
30. Muslim Teli Oilman	-3	-3	-3	-3	-3	-3	0	0	0	0	2	3	-28
33. Jatav Leatherworker	-3	-3	-3	-3	-3	-3	-2	-2	-2	-1	2	3	-38
34. Mathuriya Washerman	-3	-3	-3	-3	-3	-3	-2	-2	-2	-1	2	3	-38
35. Kanjar Hunter	-3	-3	-3	-3	-3	-3	-2	-2	-2	-2	-1	0	-55
36. Bhangi Sweeper	-3	-3	-3	-3	-3	-3	-3	-3	-3	-3	0	—	-66
Ranks { Realized	3	4	5	5	3	4	6	6	4	5	3	2	12
Ranks { Possible	4	5	6	7	7	7	7	7	7	6	5	4	24

Caste Role Types

Within each column, a blank space occurs where a caste role type's constituent castes are related to themselves. A neutral "0" occurs where a caste role type is related to the castes of other role types without distinction of rank, that is, without a net balance of transactions in either direction. A high-ranking caste role type such as that of Carpenter (column 6) may be related to castes below itself by getting the lower castes to accept food in one, two, or three media, thus according them from one to three negative degrees of inferiority. The role types of lower-ranking castes, such as Khatik Cultivator (column 25), show positive net scores of from one to three, representing the degrees of superiority accorded through food transactions to the higher castes listed at the left margin of the table.

No more than seven ranks (scored as 3, 2, 1, 0, —1, —2, —3) can possibly be distinguished by means of any one caste's dealings in the three types of food. Yet there are at least twelve ranks collectively distinguished through transactions by the whole hierarchy of castes in Kishan Garhi. As Table 13 shows in its penultimate row, no one of the castes of Kishan Garhi achieves even as many as the seven possible distinctions, although five castes (19 through 25) manage to realize distinctions among as many as six ranks. That these five more discriminating castes stand near the middle of the hierarchy is not surprising, since such middle castes will have more opportunities to engage in all kinds of transactions, both receiving from castes above and giving to castes below.

The old notion (cited by Hutton, 1946, pp. 62–63, and by many others) that the Brahman's transactions in food provide the most complete guide for conduct in any local transactional system seems from Table 13 to be both untrue for this village and impossible generally. The reason for this impossibility is that castes at the upper and lower extremities of any such hierarchy have comparatively restricted opportunities to engage in rank-defining transactions, as is indicated by the lower "possible" values for the top and bottom castes in the last row of Table 13. The Brahman is not in a position to receive all media of foods, while the Sweeper is not in a position to give them. The castes whose own practices will in fact provide the most discriminating guidance are likely to be those castes discussed above which stand near the middle of the hierarchy. To be sure, some of the middle castes, such as Barber or Waterman, make only half of the maximum number of distinctions in food, apparently because too many refusals would interfere with their work as domestic servants. In fact, however, no one or two castes' transactions can exhibit all the distinctions of the collective system: at least four caste role types out of the twelve would have to be taken into account in order to comprehend all twelve of the ranks found. The hierarchy of transactions is not a unilateral but a multilateral structure.

That persons or groups in any social system tend to make finer distinctions close to themselves and cruder distinctions at a greater distance from themselves appears to be borne out by the distribution of distinctions which emerges in Table 13. The higher castes' transactions seem to discriminate better among the high castes, the lower castes' among the low; each seems to deal with castes at the opposite end of the hierarchy as a relatively undifferentiated bloc. I shall return to this observation later in comparing transactions with opinions.

A striking fact in Table 13, as in the net and summary matrices (Tables 11 and 12), is that nearly every caste by its transactions makes a distinction of rank between the Waterman (caste 14) and the Potter (caste 19). (Only for the Sweeper's transactions is this distinction unimportant.) The same point of distinction is observed in each of the three principal food types (Table 10). Here again is the grand contrast between the castes verbally categorized as "high" and "low," marked now by a gap of 38 points (the largest gap in this series of scores) in the transactional scores of the castes above and below it. At this same gap a distinction occurs between the high castes whose scores make them net winners or creditors in food transactions (they give to more castes than they receive from) and the low castes whose negative scores make them net losers, or debtors in food transactions (they receive from more castes than they give to). An aggregate scoring of transactions thus yields an objective understanding of the epithets "clean" versus "dirty," which are occasionally applied to the higher and lower castes, respectively. A lower caste aspiring to become "clean" or "high" by crossing the (14/19) line faces the task of negotiating changes in possibly 38 of its transactions with other castes.

MOBILITY AND CONSERVATISM: THE CASE OF THE GOATHERDS

The formidable barrier in the middle of the hierarchy of food transactions in Kishan Garhi appears to have been crossed during the past two generations by one caste group—the Baghele Goatherds. The Goatherds are now caste 13, but are said once to have been at a level with the Potters and other castes in the bloc of castes from (19) to (24). Their case is instructive when examined in terms of food transactions.

The Goatherds became one of the richest groups per capita in Kishan Garhi during the 1930's when they bought cheaply at governmental auction one of the best plots of land from an insolvent Jat landlord. Playing the persuasive roles of employer and moneylender, the Goatherds began trying to increase their standing as donors of *kaccā* food to their near-equals, who are now the Goatherds' servants. Before their gain of wealth, some Goatherds provided honorific services at weddings and at the harvest for ten of the higher castes; they used to receive payment, it is said, in *kaccā* as well as in raw and *pakkā* food. With new wealth in hand, one large Goatherd family dissuaded the others from accepting *kaccā* food payments and thus drew the caste up to the level of the Kachi Cultivators in their lessened intake of subordinating food. Specialists in the Waterman and Barber castes were richly paid by the Goatherds to provide their fullest services at feasts; both would soon have been waiting at the Goatherds' doors for loaves of inferior bread, but for the jealousy of the Kachis and their allies, who included certain Brahman debtors-to-the-Kachis. Brahmans then threatened to discharge Barbers from their work in Brahman homes and feasts if the Barbers picked up the garbage-soiled plates at Goatherd feasts; Goatherds continued to employ Barbers at high rates while excusing them from the garbage-connected duties. Some time later, the Goatherds began to succeed in making *kaccā* payments to both Waterman and Barber, however.

The Goatherds' next move was to drop their former local Brahman priest, who would not take their *pakkā* food. In his place, they called a priest of a neighboring village in which the Brahman group was of separate and somewhat doubtful status within the caste. The new priest had no concern about the local Barber and was himself willing to eat the Goatherds' feasts. But an outside, dubious Brahman feaster was not as good as a local one. The Goatherds therefore aimed their suasion at the most impecunious members of the oldest Brahman lineage of Kishan Garhi, and, by a secret codicil to a liberal loan, arranged for these Brahmans to come and dine. One result was a near-split in the Brahman caste group of Kishan Garhi. Another result was the Goatherds' gain of enough *pakkā* credits to insure their standing in that food medium along with the "high" castes 2 through 12. The Goatherds finally completed their *kaccā* food-giving scores in relation to the lower castes, aided by the transitive logic that they were givers of *kaccā* food to castes such as Barber and Waterman, who were themselves established as givers of *kaccā* to the lower castes. At last, some members of other Brahman lineages began to attend the Goatherds' feasts.

The case of the Goatherds illustrates both of the two basic tactics for upward mobility: give food to more other castes (that is, increase one's row sums) and receive from fewer (that is, reduce one's column sums). Other castes in Kishan Garhi have been known, on a smaller scale, to apply just one or the other of these tactics—Jats and Leatherworkers the giving tactic, Carpenters, Potters, and Faqir Devotees the tactic of refusing to receive.

The Goatherds' initial difficulties also illustrate the interconnectedness of the system of food transactions as a whole. What happened in one cell of the matrix between Goatherds and Barbers affected relations in other cells and other matrices between Barbers and Brahmans, Brahmans and Kachis, etc. A great many reciprocal controls are apparent in all those zones of equal values which cut across the main diagonal. In the largest reciprocal zone, the Carpenters once refused to continue taking *pakkā* food from Sanadhya Brahmans, the Carpenters being launched on a campaign for recognition as "Maithil Brahmans" themselves; the established Sanadhya Brahmans could then simply reply by a reciprocal act of refusal. The Carpenters therefore gained no net score by their unilateral withdrawal from a bilaterally reciprocal pair.

The more promising spots for upward mobility by refusal to accept food would appear to be those cells (pairs of castes) where there is initially no such reciprocal transfer, but rather simple dominance. The Carpenters did gain two points at such spots by ceasing to accept *kaccā* food and to dispose of soiled plates coming from the Sanadhya Brahmans. Certain other cells in the matrix of *kaccā* food (Table 7) also seem ripe for change by the lower partner: (1/2), (6/2), and (15/14). But the structurally similar rank of Goatherds over Barbers, (13/15), is, of course, firmly stabilized by the Goatherds' great economic power. In the *pakkā* matrix (Table 6), most situations of this structural type similarly appear to be buttressed against change by the superior wealth of the higher partner.

Withdrawal by the lower partner would cost him not only a portion of his food, but loss of a diffuse status of patronage and favor, as richly detailed by Wiser (1936, pp. 61–123). One such cell (24/25), nevertheless seems unstable, given an ambitious and newly wealthy Khatik Cultivator pushing up from below.

Two kinds of structural openings to upward mobility have been implied above: (a) one in which, unlike the (14/19) line, relatively few castes make the distinction or make it in few types of food, and (b) one in which reciprocal penalties may not be invoked. Such apparent openings might be listed and the intercaste relations around them examined systematically. Conversely, where many castes are concerned in many distinctions, or where ritual, economic, or other retribution is possible, a stable order should prevail. If food transactions form a kind of "economy" with a rationality of its own, that economy nevertheless overlies other analogous economic matrices having more material or political content. As in the instances described above, castes seem often to alter or to maintain their positions in food transactions according to the advantages and disadvantages available in the corresponding cells of other, nonritual matrices. Many further investigations seem desirable on these matters.

RANKINGS BY FOOD TRANSACTION AND OPINION COMPARED
(FIG. 2)

In all the hypothetical reasoning about food transactions that goes before, I have neglected to apply one of the best available tests of that reasoning's validity —a comparison of the rankings obtained here through observation and logic (Table 12) with those obtained separately through the sampling of opinion described earlier (Tables 3 and 4). This comparison is represented diagrammatically in Figure 2.

The two sets of rankings might be expected to agree on the order of ranking the castes, especially at the major lines of division in the matrix of transactions. They should agree on the grouping of castes at equal ranks and on areas of uncertainty or change of rank. In general, the two sets of rankings do agree in all these ways.

The food ranks are twelve, the opinion ranks are thirteen, and among these the ranks common to both are nine. One may therefore say that gross agreement between the two is about 75 per cent. While each set of rankings distinguishes at certain spots where the other fails to distinguish, neither reverses the order of ranking of any pair of casts.

Where transactions in foods distinguish ranks by the largest gaps (ten points or more) between the scores of adjacent castes (1/6, 13/15, 14/19, 29/33, 34/35, and 35/36), one might expect that opinions would also make a sharp distinction. In five of the six cases they do, failing only to distinguish the Goatherd-Barber (13/15) ranking, which is very strong in transfers of both *kaccā* food and garbage.

Deviant opinions might be expected to occur in greater numbers at locations where food transfers are ambiguous in their meanings for rank, and in the minds of persons occupying such ambiguous positions. Although a thorough testing of these propositions is not attempted in this paper, they seem likely to prove correct.

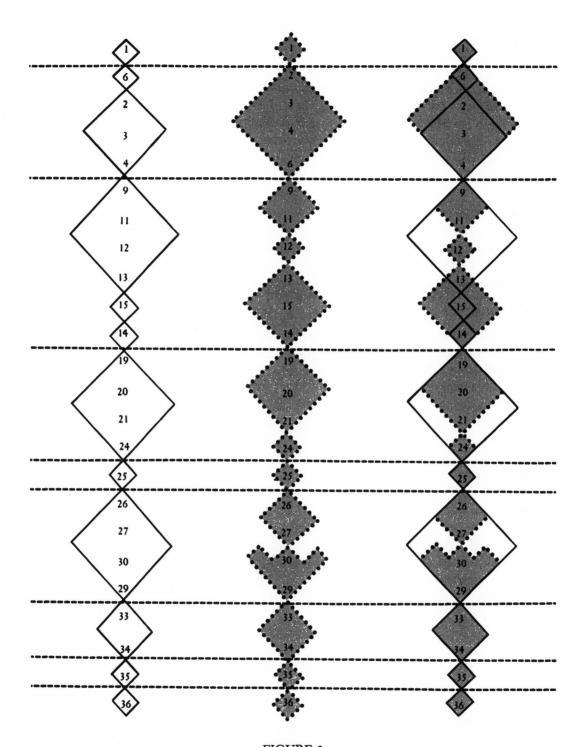

FIGURE 2

FOOD TRANSACTIONS AND OPINIONS OF RESPONDENTS: RANKINGS BY TWO METHODS COMPARED.

Only one caste occupies a different rank in two types of food transactions—the Khatik Cultivators (25). This is the one caste concerning which respondents' opinions are most divergent. Among the 3 respondents out of 24 whose opinions about caste rank are most deviant from the community norm, one respondent is a Khatik (25.1 in Table 2).

According to the comparison of caste roles in transactions (Table 13), the castes at the upper and lower extremities of the list are directly involved in fewer transactional discriminations among the castes standing farthest from themselves in rank. Do opinions parallel transactions here, too? Do high-caste respondents fail to distinguish ranks among the low castes and vice versa? The data given in Table 2 provide an answer: despite the fact that their own castes engage in fewer direct transactional discriminations, those respondents who are themselves located in castes at either extreme nevertheless make at least as many distinctions as any other respondents located elsewhere in the hierarchy. High-caste respondents drawn from four castes (1, 2, 9, 13) above the Potters distinguish an average of 10.7 ranks among the thirteen castes from Potters on down. At the other extreme, three low-caste respondents from castes (26) and (33) distinguish an average of eight ranks among the eleven castes above the Potters. Both compare favorably with the general rate of rank discrimination throughout the sample of opinions. Evidently the perspective provided by membership in a high or low caste does not much impair knowledge of the larger system by which all castes are ranked. Indeed, a broad knowledge of transactions far removed from one's own caste's roles may be important to persons of all castes, since transactions form a connected system in which each may affect all. As during the rise of the Goatherds, changes begun within one or two pairs may have consequences for the ranks of a majority of castes in the village.

What are the effects, if any, of caste mobility upon opinions of rank? Carpenters and Goatherds have made higher standings for themselves in the system of food transactions than they have yet achieved in community opinion. Actual mobility in these cases seems to have run ahead of what opinion is prepared to concede. Opinion is built not only upon actuality but also upon memories, which in the competitive matter of caste rank are often long. Many villagers claimed to know of, or to have heard of, a time when or a place where neither Carpenters nor Goatherds were so high as their present positions in food transfer assert.

The remaining small differences between the two sets of rankings find no general explanations but dissolve on examination into cases of variant practice or disputed precedent. For example, Kachi Cultivators and Baghele Goatherds, being in dispute with each other over garbage disposal at feasts, have avoided accepting each other's invitations for many years, a fact which leaves public opinion wondering; by transactional scoring of their invitations to each other, and by their actual feeding relations with other castes, the two are now equal, yet the Kachis' earlier, higher position remains effective in many minds. Sometimes there are peculiarities of history and myth ("The Koli Weavers are really Leatherworkers who changed their occupation," some say) and ambiguities attending special religious roles ("The Faqir Devotees are the Brahmans among Muslims") that may complicate the distinctions of food transfer which are otherwise systematic and pervasive.

CONCLUSIONS

The approximate correctness of the transactional model of caste ranking developed in this experiment appears to be validated by its resemblance to the picture of caste rankings developed through a sampling of opinions. But perhaps I should rather say, with villagers, that the rankings stated as opinions are validated by their resemblance to the realities and presumed potentialities of the rankings established by food transfer. Opinions are often explicitly based upon known transactions in food. "Known transactions" are not only those local, current ones scored in the 1952 matrices, but also nonlocal or earlier ones recalled and described by travelers and by elders. Opinions are based not only upon the person's own caste's transactions with other castes but also upon his observations of remote pairs of castes within the whole multilateral system of transfers. The system is an objective fact for all, so that differences of caste participation and individual membership are generally unimportant in their effects on opinions.

The multilaterality of interests in food transactions appears to be a principal reason for the conservatism of the system. A change in the transactions of any one caste may affect the relative standing of any other caste, and a change of relative rank can never be in the interests of everyone. Reciprocating features of the system seem likely to restrain change between castes in many pairs. The large amount of redundancy in the system as a whole—the actual occurrence of many transitive transactions, the repetition of the same transactional rankings in several different media—also tends to buttress many distinctions against change. Wealth and power may be applied congruently outside the system so as to restrain change in certain transactional pairs or may be applied incongruently so as to stimulate change.

Gaining dominance over others through feeding them or securing dependence on others through being fed by them appear to be comprehensive goals of actors in the system of transactions. Purity and pollution, among other values, are used as expressions of achievement toward these goals. Dietary or occupational purity and pollution, regarded as attributes of the castes, do not correlate well with the rankings found either in transactions or in opinions. However, major distinctions in verbalized opinion among higher and lower blocs of castes correlate closely with large distinctions in the transfer of food, pollution, and other symbols of dominance and subordination. The distinction of "high" versus "low" corresponds with a shift from net creditor to net debtor status in food transactions. Styles and tactics used in managing these transactions vary with high and low rank, and differ from caste to caste.

The transactional model developed here uses a many-layered matrix form of representation which permits both concise summation of all transactions and reduction of that summation to its most essential components. Separate analysis of the five layers (media of transaction) initially thought relevant shows that just three—*pakkā* food, *kaccā* food, and garbage—are essential to the distinctions of rank made locally. Separate analysis of the vectors of the three-layered matrix reveals that the roles of 24 castes in ranking can be reduced to twelve distinct role types, of which not all, but at least four are essential.

This model is based on an implicit local postulate of the symbolic equivalence of transactions in any medium between any two castes, high rank always deriving from the giving, low rank from the receiving of foods. Serving relationships, here represented only through their payments in food, appear to create rank by complementary logic: givers of services are lower than receivers, whatever the nature of the service. Services themselves seem likely to yield to a similar, but more complex, transactional analysis involving a much larger number of media.

While this model of stratified transactions attempts to represent a ranking of castes in the local cultural terms of a particular Indian village in a region of some peculiarity, I believe that variants of its matrix forms of representation may help in analyzing and comparing caste hierarchies in other communities and regions of South Asia as well. Such forms of representation can be adapted to the study of actual systems of stratification effected through gift or potlatch; Mauss (1954) notes many such systems. Similar representations may help to examine systems of tribute, hypergamy, games, and competitive behavior generally. They can be used to examine corporate or noncorporate, transitive or intransitive, redundant or nonredundant competition, so long as outcomes of confrontations among the competitors may be scored dichotomously. They may help to discover the essential features of complex, actual systems, to generate and test hypothetical alternatives (as proposed by Barth, 1966), or to create wholly hypothetical systems for theoretical study (as is done by White, 1963, pp. 31–93).

BIBLIOGRAPHY

BARTH, FREDRIK.
 1966. *Models of social organization.* Royal Anthropological Institute Occasional Paper No. 23.

BLUNT, SIR EDWARD ARTHUR HENRY.
 1931. *The caste system of northern India with special reference to the United Provinces of Agra and Oudh.* London: Oxford University Press.

DUMONT, LOUIS.
 1966. *Homo hierarchicus.* Paris: Gallimard.

DUMONT, LOUIS, and DAVID F. POCOCK.
 1959. Pure and impure. *Contributions to Indian Sociology,* 3: 9–39.

HARPER, EDWARD B.
 1964. Ritual pollution as an integrator of caste and religion. In Edward B. Harper (Ed.), *Religion in South Asia.* Seattle: University of Washington Press.

HOCART, ARTHUR MAURICE.
 1950. *Caste: a comparative study.* London: Methuen.

HOLLINGSHEAD, AUGUST B.
 1949. *Elmtown's youth.* New York: John Wiley.

HUTTON, JOHN HENRY.
1946. *Caste in India.* Cambridge: Cambridge University Press.

KEMENY, JOHN G., J. LAURIE SNELL, and GERALD L. THOMPSON.
1957. *Introduction to finite mathematics.* Englewood Cliffs, N. J.: Prentice-Hall.

MAHAR, PAULINE MOLLER.
1959. A multiple scaling technique for caste ranking. *Man in India,* 39: 127–47.

MARRIOTT, McKIM.
1959. Interactional and attributional theories of caste ranking. *Man in India,* 39: 92–107.

1960. *Caste ranking and community structure in five regions of India and Pakistan.* Deccan College monograph series 23. Poona, India.

MARRIOTT, McKIM, STANLEY A. FREED, and RALPH W. NICHOLAS.
n.d. *Hindu caste ranking.* The Lewis Henry Morgan Lectures, 1967, The University of Rochester. Chicago: Aldine Publishing Company. (In press.)

MATHUR, KRIPA SHANKAR.
1964. *Caste and ritual in a Malwa village.* Bombay: Asia Publishing House.

MAUSS, MARCEL.
1954. *The gift; forms and functions of exchange in archaic societies.* (Trans. by Ian Cunnison.) Glencoe, Ill.: Free Press.

MAYER, ADRIAN C.
1960. *Caste and kinship in central India.* Berkeley and Los Angeles: University of California Press.

ORENSTEIN, HENRY.
1965. *Gaon; conflict and cohesion in an Indian village.* Princeton, N. J.: Princeton University Press.

STEVENSON, HENRY NOEL COCHRAN.
1954. Status evaluation in the Hindu caste system. *Journal of the Royal Anthropological Institute,* 84: 45–65.

WARNER, WILLIAM LLOYD, MARCHIA MEEKER, and KENNETH EELLS.
1949. *Social class in America.* Chicago: Science Research Associates.

WHITE, HARRISON C.
1963. *An anatomy of kinship: mathematical models for structures of cumulated roles.* Englewood Cliffs, N. J.: Prentice-Hall.

WISER, WILLIAM HENRICKS.
1936. *The Hindu jajmani system.* Lucknow: Lucknow Publishing House.

7. CASTE AND WORLD VIEW: THE APPLICATION OF SURVEY RESEARCH METHODS

JOSEPH W. ELDER

THOSE USING SURVEY METHODS in India have occasionally questioned whether the assumptions underlying the use of such techniques in the West apply in the Indian context. Lloyd and Susanne Rudolph, for example, have asked whether most people in India have opinions they can articulate on a broad range of issues and whether the individual in India is a relevant unit of opinion (1958, pp. 235–44). Members of the Cornell Cross-Cultural Methodology Project in India, while not challenging the underlying assumptions of survey techniques, have shown that the interviewers' affiliations can markedly bias their results, even when they ask questions with identical wording (Ralis, Suchman, and Goldsen, 1958, pp. 245–60). The purpose of this paper is to describe certain limitations and problems, as well as advantages, I have found in using survey research techniques in India.

SURVEY RESEARCH AS A SUPPLEMENT TO FIELD OBSERVATIONS

From November, 1956, to March, 1958, I gathered data in a small village in Uttar Pradesh for my Ph.D. dissertation on industrialism and Hinduism. The techniques I used were essentially those of anthropology: participant observation, interviews with the better-informed or at least more talkative members of the village, lineage-tracing, census-taking, map-making, and taking of copious field notes.

Two months before the end of my stay I added a type of data-gathering not generally included in an anthropologist's kit. With the aid of a structured schedule, I interviewed over 200 respondents selected as random samples of five groups I considered important for my research topic. Following are some of the main conclusions I drew from these interviews.

1. Such interviewing helps counteract the "self-selection" of respondents so familiar to field workers. Before I started the interviews, my best informants had been a tailor of the Dunha caste, a Bhangi boy, the Brahman village priest, and two or three of the younger Jat and Chamar farmers. My systematic

The overseas portions of the research described in this paper were conducted with the aid of a fellowship from the American Institute of Indian Studies and a grant from the University of Wisconsin Office of International Studies and Programs. The computer time for processing the data was made possible by a grant from the Wisconsin Alumni Research Foundation.

interviews forced me to talk with categories of villagers I had missed in my less structured interviews, for example, village women (especially the new brides), men who were out of the village much of the time, and persons from some of the less numerous castes. From the respondents' point of view the fact that their name was "on the list" appeared to justify their dropping what they were doing to talk with me.

2. An interview schedule that needs to be filled out can "legitimize" quite a lengthy, far-ranging discussion. My questions included views on reincarnation as well as attitudes toward urbanization and industrialism. The structured nature of the question, furthermore, permitted me to cover a wider range of topics in forty minutes than if I had been having a more informal conversation.

3. Asking the same questions from 200 people permits comparisons of their replies according to caste, age, income, religious belief, and other broad categories. For certain questions, such as "How many *pakkā* houses were there in the village before the sugar mill was built?" or "What happened to the Muslims in the village at the time of partition?" three or four good informants are all one needs. But for other questions, such as, "On the whole, would you say that the mill has brought more benefit or more harm to the village?" some people will say "benefit" and others "harm." From the researcher's point of view, the relevant question is *who* says "benefit" and *who* says "harm" and what proportion of the total population each group represents.

As a matter of fact, the tabulations of my interview results forced me to change some of my tentative conclusions based on other discussions with respondents. For example, my general impression was that the poorer villagers looked back with nostalgia on the days of the British; whereas the richer villagers were glad that India was independent. When I had totaled my interview returns, however, I saw that the rich-poor distinction was not as important as the caste distinction, with the highest and lowest castes feeling things had become better since independence while the middle castes felt things had been better under the British. Unless I had systematically interviewed a sizeable sample of the population, I would not have been able to correct my initial error.

By the time I had completed my analysis of the interview data, I was convinced of the advantages of supplementing standard field work methods with systematic interviewing. However, with only 200 people in my sample, there were all kinds of interesting questions that I was unable to pursue. For example, the nature of the group I interviewed was such that the higher castes were also highly educated and had spent a considerable length of time in cities, whereas the lower castes were largely illiterate and had lived most of their lives in the village. When the two groups differed in outlook, as they frequently did, there was no way in which I could attribute their attitude difference to caste, education, or urbanization. I could only note that, if my sample size had been larger and my respondents more heterogeneous, I could have separated caste from education and urbanization and have seen which of these factors correlated most closely with the attitude difference.

SURVEY RESEARCH AS AN INDEPENDENT
DATA-GATHERING TECHNIQUE

Four years after completing my industrialism and Hinduism study, I was back in India on another project, this one dealing with changes in attitudes from "traditional" to "nontraditional." Stimulated by the findings of my first study as well as by the work of such writers as Everett E. Hagen, David McClelland, and W. W. Rostow, I had decided to conduct a large-scale study of such attitudes as mobility aspirations, universalistic versus particularistic identities, causality consciousness, empathy, authoritarianism, caste orthodoxy, and political awareness. I was concerned that writers describing the attitudes of persons in nonexpanding economies tended to lump all sorts of opinions under the general rubric of "traditional attitudes" (see, for example, Hagen, 1962, pp. 83–84). They then occasionally concluded that, as one part of these "traditional attitudes" changed, all other parts also changed.

My own experience in India suggested that the picture was more complex than this. I myself had met highly emancipated social reformers who were still orthodox, pure vegetarians. I had met religiously conservative and devout parents who insisted their children should have the highest university degrees possible. And I had met innovative farmers who still insisted that man proposes but God disposes. To my way of thinking, these people were full of contradictions. But, after meeting enough of them, I began to wonder how much of what I was seeing was contradiction and how much was merely different from some implicit notions of a priori western logic I was carrying about with me. One purpose of my research project was to determine the frames of reference being used by people themselves within a society undergoing change.

THE RESEARCH DESIGN

In order to be able to control for a sizeable number of variables (something I had been unable to do in my first study), I set up the following research design:

1. My sample would consist of a minimum of 600 11-year-old boys, plus their fathers, their mothers, and any resident grandparents. I chose 11-year-old boys hoping that they would be young enough to reconstruct the child-rearing patterns in their homes yet also old enough to answer the attitude questions. Generally this hope was realized. One reason for selecting boys, their parents, and their grandparents was that I would have three generations for comparison.

2. Half my sample would come from one section of India and the other half from another. This would make it possible to determine to what extent patterns of responses were regional and to what extent they might be the same throughout India. For example, do Harijans in all of India have the same attitude toward the caste system, or do Harijans in the South view the caste system differently from Harijans in the North?

3. My sample would be divided equally between villagers, townsmen, and city

dwellers. This would allow comparisons of differences between relative degrees of urbanization. In order to make the towns roughly comparable, I decided their populations would have to be approximately the same size and they would have to be tahsil (taluk) headquarters, similar to county seats in the United States. To make the cities more comparable, I decided they would have to be political-administrative centers, either state capitals or large district headquarters.

4. In each of the designated areas, my sample would be a random cross section of the population. This would provide me with a variety of religions, castes, occupations, and levels of education and would allow internal comparisons.

SELECTING THE SITES

Having set up my overall research design in terms of more or less carefully thought-out criteria, I selected the actual sites according to conveniences of time, place, and previous acquaintance. My three North Indian sites and three South Indian sites were as follows:

Uttar Pradesh (North India)

City: Lucknow, population 656,000, capital of state of Uttar Pradesh.

Town: Malihabad (15 miles west of Lucknow), population 8,000, headquarters for Malihabad tahsil.

Villages: Utraitia and vicinity (8-12 miles east of Lucknow), population of each less than 2,000.

Madras State (South India)

City: Madurai, population 425,000, headquarters for Madurai district and partial headquarters for Ramanathapuram (Ramnad) district.

Town: Melur (20 miles east of Madurai), population 15,000, headquarters for Melur taluk.

Villages: Chittampatti and vicinity (9–11 miles east of Madurai), population of each less than 1,000.

DRAWING THE SAMPLES

In the towns and villages my teams of census takers went from door to door finding 11-year-old boys. If the parents weren't sure of the boy's age (as was often the case), the census-taker was instructed to guess. If the boy passed muster as being (more or less) 11 years old, and neither his father nor his mother proved to be dead or away on an extended trip, the census-taker recorded the boy's name, his father's name, and some form of neighborhood address. In the towns and villages we used as house addresses the orange malaria-control numbers the public health people had painted by each doorway. Despite these efforts to specify the location of given families, we still "lost" a few of our respondents between the initial census-taking and the interviewing that took place a few weeks later.

In the originally enumerated villages in both North and South India we literally ran out of eleven-year-old boys before the interviewers reached their quota of 100. In both cases we had to make a hasty additional census of several more villages to meet our quota.

In the cities we faced considerably greater difficulties. It was obvious from the size of both Lucknow and Madurai that a door-to-door census was out of the question. In Madurai I was able to obtain street maps of the 33 census zones plus information as to the percentage of total city population living in each zone. On the basis of this information I determined how many of my 100 Madurai families should come from each zone. Then I measured with a string the total street frontage on that zone's map, divided with knots the measured length of string into as many parts as there were to be families drawn from that zone, and measured the street frontage again, placing an "x" on the map whenever I reached a knot. I then sent a census-taker to those "x's" and instructed him to obtain the name of the 11-year-old boy living closest to the "x." Occasionally the census-taker found the "x" to be in the middle of a paddy field or a factory compound, but on the whole the system worked effectively in providing us with a random cross section of the Madurai population of 11-year-old boys. As for recording the addresses in Madurai, we often had street names and house numbers by which to go, although we were occasionally reduced to such addresses as "house over grain shop beside water tap."

Lucknow posed even more serious problems than Madurai. The recent Chinese invasion had swept most maps and census information out of public circulation for security reasons. In fact, the only way I was able to obtain a map of Lucknow district was to borrow the relevant district planning book from a local library and trace the map in the back of the book myself. At any rate, we were unable to carry out as reliable a system of randomization in Lucknow as we were able to carry out in Madurai.

Since Lucknow has a compulsory education bill, I decided to use school registers as my population source. After obtaining the names of as many primary and secondary schools as we could from the education offices, the Lucknow telephone directory, and general information of Lucknow residents, the census-takers went to the schools, perused the school registers, and recorded the names and addresses of every fifteenth boy born in 1952. By this method we obtained names and addresses for about 400 11-year-old boys in Lucknow. We were aware that our sampling procedure automatically ruled out any boys not enrolled in schools (despite the compulsory education bill) or enrolled in private tuition "sidewalk schools," and probably skewed our sample toward the higher castes and occupations. Nonetheless, we could think of no better way of working it.

One of the most serious deficiencies in our Lucknow census concerned street addresses. The school register might carry something like "Ram Lal son of Roshan Singh, Aminabad Park." Several thousand people lived in the area known as Aminabad Park. How one was to find Ram Lal son of Roshan Singh was a neat problem. In the end we were forced to abandon nearly three-fourths of our Lucknow sample pool because we could not trace the addresses.

THE INTERVIEW SCHEDULE

The interview schedule presented unusual methodological problems. Certain English concepts do not translate into Hindi or Tamil. For example, one question asking whom people trusted more and providing paired alternatives had to be dropped after the schedule pretest because there was no well-known Hindi synonym for "trust," and the roundabout explanation of "trust" that I had devised simply confused the respondents. Because of translation problems, I almost dropped another question about adults "standing together" or not "standing together" when one of them punished a child. The best I could do was to ask if all adults in the house should punish a guilty child with a "common mind," or should one adult protect a child from the punishment of the others, which was hardly a smooth way of handling it.

Another wording problem arose regarding the three questions dealing with willingness to abandon caste orthodoxy. For example, should the question read, "Would you be able to eat food prepared by someone from *a low caste?*" or "Would you be able to eat food prepared by someone from a caste *lower than yours?*" A high-caste respondent might be willing to eat food cooked by some other relatively high-caste person while objecting to eating food cooked by a lower-caste person. If I held to the "caste lower than yours" form, respondents were apt to ask "which castes" and "how much lower." If I held to the "low caste" form, a low-caste respondent might think, "I'm a low-caste person, and I eat my own cooking; hence I should answer 'yes.'" In the end I chose the "low caste" form of the question, hoping that the context would imply that the "low-caste" person was intended to be lower than the respondent.

In both the Hindi and the Tamil translations of the schedule, I went to considerable effort to have the questions put in normal, conversational language, so that a minimum of reinterpretation would be necessary in the field. Only those familiar with the gulf between the spoken and written languages in most of India can fully appreciate how difficult it was to convince both translation assistants and printers that I wanted to *write* the language *spoken* in normal conversations.

The final phrasing of the interview schedule brought a few additional problems. The lack of a generic term for "you" in both Hindi and Tamil (see *"tum"* and *"āp"* in Hindi and *"nī"* and *"ningaḷ"* in Tamil) meant that the same pronouns and verb endings could not be used in the parents' and sons' interview schedules. The difference in male and female forms meant that changes had to be made between the fathers' and the mothers' schedules. Entire working days went into proofreading the schedules in order to eliminate "carryovers" from one schedule to another.

THE RESEARCH TEAM

In order to observe the local proprieties, I had female interviewers talk to the boys, their mothers, and their grandmothers, while male interviewers talked to the fathers and grandfathers. In both North and South India my advertisements in the local papers and my inquiries in local colleges and universities brought a large enough pool of experienced candidates so that I could eliminate those with questionable talent, motivation, or energy. At the peak of operations, my North

Indian team included nine females and five males (all of whom were high-caste Hindus except for one Muslim). My South Indian team contained five females and four males (who represented a range of Hindu castes and included one Christian).

After an initial training session, I required all candidates to complete two practice interviews with the trial interview schedule. These trial interviews served two purposes: they helped eliminate a few more candidates, and they provided a pretest of the interview schedule. In neither North nor South India did I send the final schedule copy to the printer until I had added modifications recommended from the pretest.

To check against dishonest reporting in both north and south, I hired one person as "back checker." His job was to take completed interview schedules, return to the respondent, and to find out if the respondent had really been interviewed and whether the date and length of interview time described by the respondent corresponded with the date and time recorded by the interviewer on the schedule. The "back checker" also asked the respondent what questions he remembered and re-asked half a dozen questions to see if the respondent's answers the second time tallied with the answers he was reported to have given the first time.

I described in advance to all the interviewers how the process of "back checking" worked and informed them that they would be paid only for their "satisfactorily completed" interviews. On the whole, the knowledge that there was a "back checker" discouraged dishonest reporting. However, in South India the "back checker" uncovered one interviewer who had "coffee-housed" two dozen interviews. The offender was promptly sacked, and the other members of the team completed the interviews he reported he had done.

THE FIELD OPERATIONS

The field operations in the Lucknow area began in late May and continued into early June. In Malihabad and the Utraitia village area we used public works department and irrigation department inspection bungalows as our base, the male interviewers remaining in the bungalows throughout the period while the females commuted from Lucknow every day by hired taxi. Public eating facilities were unavailable in these areas; so I had to hire cooks and arrange for utensils and food supplies to be transported to the bungalows. In both Malihabad and Utraitia the interviewers frequently had to walk miles between interviews. Special arrangements for bicycles and horse-drawn *ikkās* alleviated, but did not solve, the problem.

In South India, where we interviewed in July and August, the logistics were considerably simpler. Melur contained numerous satisfactory "hotels" for meals, and buses were constantly plying between Melur, Chittampatti, and Madurai. In the Chittampatti area there were still many miles between villages, but even here the problem was easier to deal with than in the North, since one could rent bicycles for a nominal sum near the bus stand.

THE INTERVIEWS

Periodically, before going into the field, the interviewers received the names of respondents they were supposed to interview. Their instructions were to locate the person at the given address and conduct the interview with as much privacy as possible. As a matter of fact, from the moment they arrived in the neighborhood they were frequently surrounded by children eager to tell them where the given respondent lived. Often after the interview began the audience expanded to include relatives and neighbors. At times the interviewers had to use considerable tact to discourage members of the audience from interjecting their own answers to the questions being asked.

Occasionally the interviewers met resistance. In Malihabad in North India a Chamar neighborhood insisted that after Independence they did not have to perform favors for anyone; therefore they would not answer questions unless they were paid. No amount of discussion or explanation dissuaded the Chamars. In the end, we were forced to abandon their neighborhood. In the town of Melur in South India the rumor started that the interviewing was part of a government program to recruit 11-year-old boys into the army to train them to fight the Chinese. In this case the interviewer set an 11-year-old boy in the midst of the questioning townsmen and asked them if they seriously believed the government wanted boys this size in the army. The townsmen had to agree it was unlikely, and there were no further objections to the study.

The field team was instructed to explain that the interviews were part of a large attitude study being done in two parts of India. However, it quickly turned out that people wanted answers about other aspects of the survey as well. Furthermore, upon checking one interviewer's answers against another's, they sometimes discovered discrepancies. For example, some of the interviewers, in their eagerness to elicit cooperation, promised that after the survey the neighborhood would receive schools, roads, and electricity; other interviewers denied it. The static began almost immediately. I called the interviewers together and insisted that they make no promises of government largess. The survey had to sell itself on its own merits.

Even more touchy was the matter of the interviewers' salary. Early in the survey, some villagers overheard two interviewers totaling their day's interviews and figuring how much they had earned. The word was out. Respondents demanded that they receive part of the interviewers' pay. It took weeks for these demands to die down. In the meantime, I informed the interviewers that, if questioned, they were to state that they were receiving subsistence and expenses. Beyond that, they were never to discuss their salary while in the field.

The most effective way of eliciting support for the project was to describe it as an effort by university students to meet degree requirements. As most of the interviewers were university students, this explanation seemed plausible. We were surprised at how much sympathy there was for the plight of students trying to meet professors' demands and how much recognition there was of the neutrality of academic research. In a few places, especially in the South, we met respondents who had been polled as part of earlier biscuit and soap surveys. Such respondents seemed even more willing than the others to be part of the survey.

In order to keep morale high, in both North and South India I held periodic all-expenses-paid celebrations. These included such events as a special bus trip to a newly built dam, movies, dinners at a good restaurant, and mango and litchi feasts. Within the contexts of Madurai and Lucknow, this "big daddy" approach seemed appreciated.

THREE EXAMPLES OF RESULTS FROM THE SURVEY

A major drawback of survey research methods is that one loses the clarity of detail and the supplementary interpretive information that one obtains in a case study. A major advantage of the survey research method is that one typically deals with sufficiently large numbers of respondents (in this case over 2,500) so that one can control for several variables. Below are three illustrations of how the use of such controls can radically alter the conclusions one draws from one's data. In the first illustration, an apparently significant association proves to be no association at all. In the second illustration, an apparent non-association proves to be "hiding" some association. And in the third illustration an apparent association proves to apply only to a portion of the population.

1. *An Apparent Association:* Apparently a significantly greater proportion of lower-caste people believe that events occur because of fate; a significantly greater proportion of high-caste people believe that events occur because of discoverable reasons (see Table 1).

Question: One learned man says, "Most things that happen like disease and poverty are caused by fate. As it is written, so must it happen." Another learned man says, "There are many other reasons besides fate for why these things happen. If we can discover the reasons, we can change what will happen." Which of these learned men do you think is correct?

TABLE 1

	Mothers and Fathers		
	Twice-Born Castes	Intermediate Castes	Scheduled Castes
"Caused by Fate"	53%	64%	73%
"Caused by Discoverable Reason"	47%	36%	27%
	100%	100%	100%
	n = 353	n = 520	n = 337

(Chi² for difference between "Twice-Born Castes" and "Intermediate Castes" = 10.4, significant at the 0.1 level. Chi² for difference between "Intermediate Castes" and "Scheduled Castes" = 6.03, significant at the 0.02 level. Chi² for difference betwween "Twice-Born Castes" and "Scheduled Castes" = 27.19, significant at the 0.001 level.)

With an association such as this, we might set out to discuss the "fatalism" engendered by the caste system, the way in which this "fatalism" is most thoroughly concentrated at the bottom of the system, how the stability of the system through time may have depended on this concentration of fatalism at the bottom, etc.

However, before starting off on a chain of plausible conclusions, it may be wise to control for other variables. Controlling for sex, we separate the fathers from the mothers. The association remains in both groups. Controlling further for North India and South India, the association remains for North and South Indian fathers but disappears for all mothers. And finally, controlling for "No Education" and "Some Education," the pattern of caste association disappears entirely, to be replaced by a consistent pattern of association of "Caused by Fate" with "No Education" and "Caused by Discoverable Reason" with "Some Education."

Had we plunged ahead with our initial statistically significant association, we might have come up with plausible explanations of why low status generates certain types of "world view" fatalism. The only trouble would have been that our explanation would have been based on a spurious association.

2. *An Apparent Non-Association:* Apparently there is no significant association between caste position and unwillingness to eat food cooked by a low-caste person (see Table 2).

Question: Would you be able to eat food prepared by someone from a low caste?

TABLE 2

	Mothers and Fathers		
	Twice-Born Castes	Intermediate Castes	Scheduled Castes
"Would be able to eat"	11%	12%	16%
"Would *not* be able to eat"	89%	88%	84%
	100%	100%	100%
	n = 353	n = 516	n = 335

(Chi^2 for difference between "Twice-Born Castes" and "Intermediate Castes" is negligible. Chi^2 for difference between "Intermediate Castes" and "Scheduled Castes" is 2.75, not significant at the required 0.05 level. Chi^2 for difference between "Twice-Born Castes" and "Scheduled Castes" is 3.41, still not significant at the required 0.05 level.)

Although there is a tendency for lower-caste respondents to be more willing to eat such food than higher-caste respondents, the difference between the highest and lowest categories (5 per cent) is too small to be statistically significant. With this absence of any significant association, we might be tempted to write an essay on the equal penetration of pollution taboos on all caste levels. We might even be tempted to expand on this and describe how the equal support of caste-avoidance taboos on all levels reveals the strength of the present caste hierarchy. However, before starting off on this or some other chain of plausible conclusions, it may be useful to control for other variables.

Controlling for sex, we separate the fathers from the mothers. The slight trend of differences between the "Twice-Born Castes" and "Scheduled Castes" appears on both tables, but continues not to be statistically significant. Controlling further for North India and South India, two markedly different patterns suddenly emerge, each statistically significant (see Tables 3 and 4. To simplify the tables, I have again combined the fathers and mothers).

TABLE 3

	Northern Mothers and Fathers		
	Twice-Born Castes	Intermediate Castes	Scheduled Castes
"Would be able to eat"	11%	3%	6%
"Would *not* be able to eat"	89%	97%	94%
	100%	100%	100%
	n = 245	n = 149	n = 211

(Chi² for difference between "Twice-Born Castes" and "Intermediate Castes" = is 6.3, significant at the 0.02 level. Chi² for difference between "Intermediate Castes" and "Scheduled Castes" is negligible. Chi² for difference between "Twice-Born Castes" and "Scheduled Castes" = 3.42, not significant at the 0.05 level.)

TABLE 4

	Southern Mothers and Fathers		
	Twice-Born Castes	Intermediate Castes	Scheduled Castes
"Would be able to eat"	10%	15%	33%
"Would *not* be able to eat"	90%	85%	67%
	100%	100%	100%
	n = 108	n = 367	n = 124

(Chi² for difference between "Twice-Born Castes" and "Intermediate Castes" = 1.23, not significant at 0.05 level. Chi² for difference between "Intermediate Castes" and "Scheduled Castes" = 17.23, significant at the 0.001 level. Chi² for difference between "Twice-Born Castes" and "Scheduled Castes" = 16.06, also significant at the 0.001 level.)

Controlling for "No Education" and "Some Education," we discover that the above association pattern remains firm. Therefore, quite unlike our original conclusion that there is no association between caste position and unwillingness to eat food cooked by a low-caste person, it now appears that there *are* patterns of association by caste, but the patterns differ in North and South India.

Where in North India the most impressive break with tradition appears among the "Twice-Born Castes" (a "rebellion from above"), in South India the most impressive break appears among the "Scheduled Castes" (a "rebellion from below"). However, eating food cooked by a low-caste person is only one form of unorthodoxy. To see if the pattern is general, one needs to look at the other two caste orthodoxy questions in the schedule: "Would you be able to be friends with someone from a low caste?" and "Would you be able to marry your son or daughter to a boy or girl from a low caste?" Sure enough, the same pattern does appear to hold. One is then free to spin plausible links between the "Twice-

Born," Gandhianism, and the struggle against caste injustices in the North, and the Justice and Dravida Munnetra Kazhagam Parties and the struggle against caste injustices in the South. One is also free to look for parallels between the Indian data and comparable data on the social and ideological correlates of "rebellions from above" and "rebellions from below."

3. *An Apparent Association:* Apparently a significantly greater proportion of South Indians than North Indians feels that India needs an autocratic ruler.

Question: One man says, "Our country needs a strong leader who will take over the government and make everybody obey him." Another man says, "Our country needs leaders who have been chosen by the people and who will act in accordance with the people's wishes." Which of these men do you think is correct? (see Table 5).

TABLE 5

| | Sons, Mothers, and Fathers | |
	South India	*North India*
"Pro-Autocracy"	46%	26%
"Pro-Democracy"	54%	74%
	100%	100%
	n = 1152	n = 1390

(Chi² for difference between "South India" and "North India" = 106.4, significant at the 0.001 level.)

With an association as high as this one, we might begin looking for roots of autocratic preference in the power structure of South India. Perhaps the long centuries of Brahman domination have produced a general pattern of subservience to power figures. Or perhaps the more recent anti-Brahman struggles in the South have generated pro-autocracy sentiment. Before following these possible chains of reasoning, however, it may be useful to control for other variables.

Controlling for religion, caste, and residence in city, town, or village, the difference between North and South India remains. Then, controlling for sons, mothers, and fathers, a different pattern suddenly emerges (see Table 6).

TABLE 6

| | South India | | |
	Sons	*Mothers*	*Fathers*
"Pro-Autocracy"	56%	54%	25%
"Pro-Democracy"	44%	46%	75%
	100%	100%	100%
	n = 364	n = 360	n = 345

(Chi² for difference between "Sons," "Mothers," and "Fathers" = 81.3, significant at the 0.001 level.)

Interestingly enough, the North Indian pattern does not change when controlled for sons, mothers, and fathers (see Table 7).

TABLE 7

	North India		
	Sons	Mothers	Fathers
"Pro-Autocracy"	25%	29%	22%
"Pro-Democracy"	75%	71%	78%
	100%	100%	100%
	n = 431	n = 433	n = 403

(Chi² indicates no significant association between "Sons," "Mothers," and "Fathers.")

As Table 6 shows, in South India the support for autocracy appears to come from the sons and mothers. The association that seemed to hold between North and South India now needs to be refined, for the Southern fathers are very similar to the North Indians in this response. To discover why this is so requires further questions: In South India what access to mass media do sons and mothers have, and does their access differ from that of the fathers? Does the sons' and mothers' pattern of political participation differ from the fathers'? In what other ways do the Southern sons' and mothers' perceptions differ from those of the Southern fathers? Can these help explain the association? To find answers to these questions, one turns to other questions on the schedule and one tries to control additional variables. Such steps do not necessarily provide explanatory hypotheses for phenomena; however, they do from time to time permit certain hypotheses to be discarded, such as the one suggesting that long centuries of Brahman domination in South India have produced a general pattern of submissiveness to power figures. If such were the case, one would hardly find such a dramatic difference between the mothers and fathers in South India.

Survey research methods, then, appear to have some use in the Indian context. I myself prefer to use them as one of several methods of gathering and analyzing data so that the strengths of one might be supplemented by the strengths of another. Yet even by themselves, survey research methods can permit the identification of relevant associations and, depending on the nature of the questions asked, even permit a certain amount of checking of alternative explanations for a given finding. One of their greatest contributions comes in the fact that, by dealing with sufficiently large numbers of people to permit controls, field survey methods help direct the search for explanations to focus on genuine, rather than spurious or accidental, associations.

BIBLIOGRAPHY

HAGEN, EVERETT E.
   1962. *On the theory of social change*. Homewood, Ill: Dorsey Press.
RALIS, MAX, E. A. SUCHMAN, and ROSE K. GOLDSEN.
   1958. Applicability of survey techniques in northern India. *Public Opinion Quarterly*, 22: 245–60.
RUDOLPH, LLOYD, and SUSANNE RUDOLPH.
   1958. Surveys in India: field experience in Madras State. *Public Opinion Quarterly*, 22: 235–44.

PART III:
Is the Caste System Changing?

8. MOBILITY IN THE CASTE SYSTEM

M. N. SRINIVAS

WHILE TRADITIONAL, that is, pre-British, Indian society was stationary in character, it did not preclude the mobility, upward as well as downward, of individual castes in the local hierarchy. This fact, however, has not received sufficient emphasis nor have its implications been commented upon by analysts of caste.

The two most potent sources of mobility were the fluidity of the political system, especially at the lower levels, and the availability of marginal land which could be brought under the plow, itself the result of a static demographic situation. I shall consider each of these sources briefly.

It was the establishment of British rule over the Indian subcontinent that closed the door finally to families and bigger groups achieving mobility through resort to warfare. Until then, it was always possible, though not easy, for an official or soldier, or the head of a locally dominant caste, to acquire political power and become a chief or king. Thus, even during the heyday of the Mughal empire, Shivaji (1627–1680), the son of a jagirdar or fiefholder of the Muslim kingdom of Bijapur in South India, was able to found a large and powerful kingdom (Majumdar, 1963). Shivaji's was no doubt an exceptional case, but it illustrates, though somewhat exaggeratedly, the fluidity or openness of the pre-British political system. Recent detailed studies of this system in such different parts of the country as eastern Uttar Pradesh (Cohn, 1962) and Central Gujarat (Shah, 1964) make clear how ambitious and unscrupulous tax collectors and officials could take advantage of periods of confusion to found their own chiefdoms or kingdoms.

Political fluidity in pre-British India was in the last analysis the product of a pre-modern technology and institutional system. Large kingdoms could not be ruled effectively in the absence of railways, post and telegraph, paper and printing, good roads, and modern arms and techniques of warfare. A ruler, however able, had to delegate his authority to his subordinates. Succession to political office followed the rule of primogeniture, and this posed a problem to kings who had uncles (father's younger brothers) and younger brothers who had to be kept out of mischief. Fratricide and parricide were deemed to be great sins, and a man was indeed expected to show affection for his brothers and his father's brothers who stood in the social relationship of fathers. Appointing uncles and younger brothers to posts was one way of solving the problem, though it was not without its risks. Where the kingdom was big, they could be posted to jobs far away from the capital.

The life of ordinary folk was regulated by such institutions as caste and village community, and the elders of the locally dominant caste punished violators of the social and moral code. This suited the rulers, even Muslim rulers, excepting those whose proselytizing zeal was stronger than their political wisdom. Warfare was endemic, and frontiers as well as loyalties changed frequently. A great ruler brought a brief period of order to the kingdom. The death of a great king was often followed by efforts on the part of tribute-paying chiefs to declare themselves free and stop paying tribute.

Opportunities for seizing political power were more likely to be available to the leaders of the dominant castes, and even tribes, than to others. This is why in South India dominant peasant castes such as the Marathas, Reddis, Vellalas, Nayars, and Coorgs have been able to claim Kshatriya status. Numerical strength and the prestige and power coming from ownership of land put them in a strategic position for capturing political power in periods of uncertainty, which were only too frequent. This situation, however, does not seem to have been confined to South India. The medieval Pala dynasty of Bengal was "Shudra" in origin (Pannikar, 1955, p. 9). The Patidars of Gujarat, in origin a peasant caste, became politically powerful in the eighteenth century, when they claimed to be Kshatriyas. Arvind Shah has written: "The Pātidārs were the principal local supporters of the Gaekwads [Maratha rulers of Central Gujarat]. Some Pātidārs had taken to arms, and a couple of them had established petty principalities. All this had led the Pātidārs to claim the status of the Kshatriya *varna* and to adopt many 'kingly' customs and manners" (1964, p. 94).

Historically, the Kshatriya varna was recruited from a wide variety of castes all of which had one attribute in common, that is, the possession of political power. According to Athelstane Baines: "There is, in fact, no section of the Brahmanic hierarchy into which recruitment from the outside has been more extensive or to which the claims to membership have been more numerous" (1912, p. 30). The historian K. M. Panikkar has stated that ever since the time of Mahapadma Nanda in the fifth century B.C., every known royal family has come from a non-Kshatriya caste (1958: 8). Even the upper levels of tribes, such as the Bhumij, Munda and Gond, established their claims to be Kshatriyas (Sinha, 1962).

When a leader of a dominant caste or small chieftain graduated to the position of a raja or king, acquiring, in the process, the symbolic and other appurtenances of Kshatriyahood, he in turn became a source of mobility for individuals and groups living in his domain. A necessary concomitant, if not precondition, of such graduation was Sanskritization, that is, the acceptance of the rites, beliefs, ideas, and values of the great tradition of Hinduism as embodied in the sacred books. For instance, a king who did not have the requisite number of Brahmans for performing an important ceremony did not hesitate to raise members of a lower ranking group to the status of Brahmans (Baines, 1912, p. 27). Where, however, there was an entrenched group of Brahmans, the king had to recognize their power and make the necessary adjustments.

By virtue of his position as the head of the social order, the Hindu king had the responsibility to settle all disputes with regard to caste and the power also to raise or lower the ranks of castes as reward or punishment. Muslim kings, and even the British in the early days of their rule, exercised at least the first function. Most of the Hindu maharajas ruling over the larger "native" states during the British period allowed their jurisdiction in caste matters to lapse only at the beginning of the twentieth century (Smith, 1963).

I shall now consider the second source of mobility, that is, the "open agrarian system" of medieval India. According to Burton Stein, a historian of medieval South India, "marginally settled lands suitable for cultivation" were always available, and this "permitted the establishment of new settlements and even new regional societies" (Stein, in press). This situation was not, however, confined to South India, but was true of the country as a whole. Irfan Habib has written: "The *Ain-i-Akbari* and Rennel's Atlas (1780) show that down to the 18th century large cultivable tracts still lay behind the forest-line. The mediaeval governments attempted to encourage extension of cultivation and improvement in cropping by grant of revenue concessions and loans to finance [the] purchase of seeds, cattle, or excavation of wells by the cultivators themselves" (1962, p. 62). In other words, there was a premium on human labor, initiative and skill, and rulers offered incentives to individuals to open up new frontiers. Such a situation imposed a check on the authority of chiefs and kings, who had to treat their rural subjects reasonably well in order to keep them. The ability of citizens to flee to frontier areas provided a sanction against excessive oppression by rulers.

Burton Stein has argued that the modern phenomenon of competition among castes for enhanced status within a narrow, localized ranking system is inappropriate for understanding medieval mobility. Social mobility in medieval India involved spatial mobility, and the units of mobility were individual families; the need as well as the facilities for "corporate mobility" did not exist. Stein has pointed out that the various subdivisions which now exist among the Tamil peasant caste of Vellalas arose out of their former mobility. (Stein, in press). Similar subdivisions also exist among several other peasant castes.

While the sources of mobility lay in the political and economic systems, Sanskritization provided a traditional idiom for the expression of such mobility. This is not to say, however, that all cases of Sanskritization in traditional India were always preceded by the possession of political or economic power, or even that Sanskritization always had a mobility aspect.

THE BRITISH PERIOD

The establishment of British rule resulted, on the one hand, in closing the traditional avenues to mobility and, on the other, in opening several new ones. More important, it set forces in motion which altered fundamentally the overall character of society; Indian society ceased to be stationary and became mobile, and the quantum of mobility increased as the years went by.

I shall now mention briefly, and in a grossly oversimplified form, the factors directly bearing on the new mobility which came into existence as a result of British conquest. For the first time in Indian history there was a single political power straddling the entire subcontinent, and this was made possible by the new technology as well as by certain forms of administrative and military organization which the British brought with them to India. The land survey and settlement work of the nineteenth century, the introduction of tenurial reforms, the application of British concepts of ownership to land which made it saleable, and the availability of new economic opportunities in the port cities and capitals, all had far-reaching effects on mobility. Land could be sold to anyone who had money, even members of "low" castes (Bailey, 1957, p. 49). There came into existence a class of men, recruited generally from the upper castes, who resided in urban areas but who had a *pied-à-terre* in villages. Land ownership was a symbol of security as well as high social status even for them, and there was, in addition, a sentimental attachment to ancestral land and village. But gradually the high cost of urban living, including the education of sons, and later, daughters, celebrating expensive weddings, performing funeral and other rituals, and fulfilling obligations to a large number of relatives, forced this class to sell their land to peasant and other rural castes.

The British were instrumental in bringing modern knowledge to India and Indians and also such new values as the equality of all citizens before the law, the right of every man not to be imprisoned without resort to due legal processes, and the freedom to practice as well as to propagate one's religion. So also there was a new humanitarianism or, rather, the extension of humanitarianism to new areas, resulting in the abolition of suttee, human sacrifice, and slavery. Western rationalism appealed quite early to the Indian elite, and by 1830 there was a small but articulate body of rationalists in Calcutta (O'Malley, 1941, pp. 70, 309, 314).

I should make it clear that I am not concerned here with the argument that the British belief in the equality of all human beings was far from being un-equivocal, and that some of them were indeed racists; that in their desire to remain in power they supported such reactionary sections of Indian society as princes and landlords, and indeed, even resorted to the time-honored principle of divide and rule. My main concern here is with the understanding of the changes in social mobility brought about by British rule and their implications for Indian society as a whole.

European missionary effort was a significant factor in the modernization of India. Spurred by an evangelizing zeal, missionaries highlighted the evils of indigenous society, quite unmindful of the bitter hostility which their criticisms roused among Indians. One of the causes of the Indian Mutiny was "a genuine fear that government intended to Christianize Hindus and Muslims alike. This idea seems to have been entertained chiefly in North India, where missionary propaganda was active and recent" (O'Malley, 1941, p. 78). Untouchability, suttee, human and animal sacrifice, idolatry, ritualism, polytheism, polygyny, infant marriage, and the ban on widow marriage among the higher castes, all were subjected to sharp and persistent criticism.

The missionary onslaught was particularly significant inasmuch as it threw the new, Western-oriented Indian elite on the defensive and made them address themselves to the immense task of reforming their society and reinterpreting their religion. This reaction was more prominent among Hindus than among others for a variety of reasons which are not relevant here.

Missionaries were also active in humanitarian work and education. They ran hospitals, orphanages and schools, concentrating their attention on the poor and lowly, that is, Untouchables and others from the low castes, tribal folk living in remote areas, and women behind the purdah (Spear, 1962, pp. 290–91; Tangri, 1961, p. 377). They stimulated the growth of regional literatures by setting up printing presses, cutting types for various Indian scripts, printing books and founding journals, writing dictionaries and grammars, and translating classics in the regional tongues into English.

New economic opportunities came into existence as a result of the establishment of law and order, removal of internal customs barriers, and the extension of communications linking, first, the different parts of the country into a single economy and, second, the country with the world outside. The building of railways, digging of canals and roads, introduction of such plantation crops as indigo, tea, cotton, coffee, and jute, and the growth of towns and factories, provided employment for thousands all over the country. However, for an Indian to take advantage of the better-paid and more prestigeful occupations such as the higher levels of the administration and commerce, and the professions, English education was indispensable. The new opportunities, at least at the higher levels, were usually taken advantage of by the high castes, resulting in a considerable overlap between the traditional and new elites. This had the twin effect of increasing the cultural and ideological distance between the high and low castes, as well as making the new opportunities doubly desirable. In the first place, they were well paid and prestigeful, and in the second, only the high castes had access to them. Eventually, this gave rise to the Backward Classes Movement.

Less frequently, and in some areas, a few low castes had access to new trading or employment opportunities. Bailey mentions how the prohibition policy of the government of Bengal (of which Orissa was then a part) resulted in relative prosperity for the Ganjam and Boad Distillers (1957, pp. 160–61). Oilmen (Telis) all over eastern India benefited from the enlarged market for trade in oil and pressed oilseeds brought about by improved communications and population growth. The Noniyas of eastern Uttar Pradesh, Kolis of the Surat Coast in Gujarat and members of several other groups also benefited from the new employment opportunities resulting from railway, road, and canal construction. In all such cases, the wealthier families or sections became possessed of a desire to move up in the caste hierarchy by acquiring the symbols and ritual of the higher castes. The absence, in British India, of legal barriers to donning the sacred thread and chanting Vedic hymns (mantras) on ritual occasions, both symbolic of "twice-born" status, was certainly an important factor in this process. But everywhere the locally dominant castes were antagonistic to the mobility aspirations of the low castes, and they used physical violence as well as economic boycott to prevent the low castes from Sanskritizing their style of life. They did not always succeed, however. An ambitious low caste had a new remedy at its disposal: it could appeal to the police and law courts against dominant caste violence. The twentieth century has indeed witnessed a great increase in the quantum of mobility in the caste system, and Sanskritization played an important role in this mobility by enabling low castes to pass for high.

The mobility of a few low castes had a "demonstration effect" on all the others in the region. The latter felt that they were no longer condemned to poverty, oppression, and lack of esteem. They could also move up if they tried hard enough. Social horizons suddenly expanded for the low castes. It is probable that this widening of social horizons contributed to the vigor and strength of the Backward Classes Movement of the twentieth century.

The Backward Classes Movement was widespread in the Indian subcontinent as a whole and was particularly strong in peninsular India, where it had a distinctive ideology and pervaded every area of social life. The importance of the movement is beginning to be appreciated by Indianists, particularly in the context of the significant changes occurring among Harijans. But it is necessary to stress that the movement affected not only the Harijans but a wide variety of castes and, in South India, all castes except the Brahman.

The conversion of the so-called low castes to Islam and Christianity in many parts of India, and to sects such as Sikhism and the Arya Samaj in the Punjab and western Uttar Pradesh, was often motivated by a desire to shed the odium attached to being low. But the converts found that it was not at all easy to shake off their caste and that, in fact, they carried it with them to their new faith or sect. Indian Islam and Christianity are both characterized by caste; this is not to say, however, that caste among Indian Christians and Muslims is the same as caste among Hindus.

THE BACKWARD CLASSES MOVEMENT

Speaking broadly, the Backward Classes Movement passed through two stages; in the first the low castes concentrated on acquiring the symbols of high status, whereas in the second the emphasis shifted from the symbols to the real sources of high status, that is, the possession of political power, education, and a share in the new economic opportunities. The leaders of the Backward Classes Movement realized clearly that all three were interrelated and that one could not be secured in full measure without the others. Thus political power was necessary to introduce the principle of caste quotas for jobs in the administration and seats in technological, medical, and science courses, and, later, to secure the licenses and permits necessary for trading in a variety of goods and for undertaking other economic enterprises. Education, on the other hand, was indispensable for obtaining the higher categories of posts in the administration and even for the effective exercise of political power.

It is this emphasis on power that led to such seeming inconsistencies as a caste claiming to be "backward" in official and political contexts and of high rank in traditional contexts. Classification as "backward" enabled the members of a caste to obtain preference as a matter of right in the matter of seats in educational institutions, scholarships, and jobs in the administration, and this was not counted against it in evaluating its rank in the traditional hierarchy.

The "low" castes realized clearly that, once they had the necessary power, the acquisition of the symbols of high ritual rank would be easy and also meaningful. It also meant that they were aware that a new prestige system had emerged, in which education, political power, and a Westernized style of life were important ingredients. Otherwise, the high castes, which had a head start over the others with regard to the new sources of power and prestige, would continue to remain on top. The kind of situation depicted by Harold Gould for a few villages in eastern Uttar Pradesh for the mid-1950's (1961), belongs, properly speaking, to the first phase of the Backward Classes Movement and not to the more sophisticated second phase.

In the first phase, the traditional aspects of the caste system were still strong and the high castes resented the appropriation of the symbols of high rank by the low. It is true that they could no longer rely on the political authority to punish the parvenus who dared to appropriate those symbols. The latter, however, had to overcome their own resistance to such appropriation, and, even when they did, the high castes had enough "moral authority," if that is indeed the proper term, to ostracize and even physically punish them. As important was the fact that the new opportunities thrown up by British rule were taken advantage of mainly by the high castes: Brahman, Baniya, Vaidya, and Kayastha. It was in this context that the institution of the decennial census, introduced by the British, came unwittingly to the aid of ambitious low castes. Sir Herbert Risley, the commissioner of the 1901 census, decided to make use of the census investigations to obtain and record the exact rank of each caste. Not unnaturally a number of castes decided to seize this occasion to claim high rank. They seem to have felt that, if they succeeded in getting themselves recorded as high in the census, an official document of the government of India, no one would indeed be able to dispute their rank. In other words, the census became the equivalent of the traditional copper-plate grants of Indian kings declaring the rank and privileges of a caste, incidentally highlighting the role of the political authority in the caste system. There was a widespread move among castes to assume new and high-sounding Sanskritic names generally ending with suffixes indicating "twice-born" rank; and mythology, traditions, and particular customs were also cited in support of the claim to high rank. (No distinction was made between mythology and history.) Not infrequently, the different sections of a single *jāti* living in different areas claimed to belong to different varnas, and ambitions also changed from one census to another. Over the years, an increasing number of castes assumed new names in their desire to be recorded as high castes, and this was one of the factors which made intercensus comparisons of particular castes impossible.

The coming into existence of caste sabhas or associations was an important factor in the spread as well as the acceleration of mobility. Initially, their aims were to reform caste customs in the direction of Sanskritization, to lay claim to high rank, to undertake such welfare activities for caste fellows as building hostels, houses on a cooperative basis, and even colleges and hospitals in some areas, and to found journals and endow scholarships. With the gradual transfer of power from the British to Indians, caste associations tended to become political pressure groups demanding for their members electoral tickets from the principal political parties, ministerships in state cabinets, licenses for undertaking various economic activities, jobs in the administration, and a variety of other benefits. I may add here that castes performed these functions even where they were not organized into formal sabhas or associations.

CASTE AND CLASS

According to Burton Stein, the modern phenomenon of competition among castes for enhanced status within a narrow, localized, ranking system is inappropriate for understanding medieval mobility (Stein, in press). The need as well as the facilities, such as the printing press, for "corporate mobility" did not exist in medieval India. The units of medieval mobility were individual families, and the "open agrarian system" favored spatial mobility, which, in turn, facilitated social mobility. Burton Stein has certainly enhanced our knowledge of Indian society, but in his analysis of mobility processes in medieval South India he has ignored the need which has always existed in the caste system to translate familial mobility to caste mobility. Otherwise mobility does not obtain public recognition. Whom will the sons and daughters of the mobile family marry? Marriage within the old caste group, the most natural solution, would be the negation of such mobility. Another solution would be hypergamy, by which the parent group continues to give its girls in marriage to the mobile family, while the girls born in the latter either marry into a higher caste or remain unmarried. The connubial drag on mobility was far less severe in South India where cross-cousin and cross-uncle-niece marriages were, and are, more preferred than elsewhere. Ideally, in South India a simple, nuclear family could in the course of two generations achieve connubial self-sufficiency. However, in every part of India it was necessary for the mobile family or section of a caste to break with the parent caste and claim a new identity. To that end it was necessary to form a separate endogamous unit. Having hypergamous relations with the parent caste was only a second best. Further, even apart from marriage, a mobile family or section had to become a caste, for only then could its relations with other castes be defined.

The new opportunities created by British rule resulted in greater spatial mobility and increased economic disparity among members of the same local caste group. These two effects became heightened as the Indian economy developed and political power was gradually transferred to the people from the rulers. An important feature of social mobility in modern India is the manner in which the successful members of the backward castes worked consistently for improving the economic and social condition of their caste fellows. This was due to a sense of identification with one's caste, and also to a realization that caste mobility was essential for individual or familial mobility. Thus a rich

Distiller or Butcher had to get the name, customs, and style of life of his caste changed in order to shed *his* identity as Distiller or Butcher and acquire another that was more esteemed. Herein came the enormous usefulness of the traditional avenue to mobility, Sanskritization. However, it had now to cope with a far greater number of castes than before.

The kind of mobility I have described above may be regarded as typical. There was, however, another, much less common, but which might become more common in the future. In the big cities of India there are small numbers of rich people who are educated and have a highly Westernized style of life. These may be described as living minimally in the universe of caste and maximally in class. The occupations practiced by them bear no relation to the traditional occupations of the caste into which they were born. They ignore pollution rules, their diet includes forbidden foods, and their friends and associates are drawn from all over India and may even include foreigners. Their sons and daughters marry not only outside caste but occasionally also outside region, language, and religion.

The introduction, in independent India, of universal franchise at all levels of the political system has placed before vast sections of the populace new opportunities of mobility through the acquisition of political power. This is particularly true of the dominant peasant castes and even nondominant castes which are numerically strong. There are highly influential political leaders from Harijan and other backward castes. In these cases, there exists a wide cultural and economic gulf between the leaders and their castes. The leaders' style of life tends to be Westernized, and their associates and friends are not restricted by caste and regional considerations. But political leaders have to maintain their links with their castes and regions if they wish to stay in power, whereas members of the professional elites need not.

COMPETITION AMONG CASTES

Edmund Leach recently stated that "wherever caste groups are seen to be acting as corporations in competition against like groups *of different caste*, then they are acting in defiance of caste principles" (1960, p. 7). Again, "People of different castes are, as it were, of different species—as cat and dog. There can therefore be no possibility that they should compete for merit of the same sort." According to him, in a caste system as distinct from class, only the dominant castes, who are always numerically in a majority, compete for the services of individual members of the lower castes (1960, p. 6). There is also competition between members of different *grades* of the same caste: "the grades would not exist unless their members were constantly in competition one against the other" (1960, p. 7). According to Leach, then, the position of each caste is fixed, while the *grades* within each caste are in a relation of competition with each other. If such competition results in mobility, the position of the mobile *grade* ought not to be higher than that of the caste of which it was a *grade*, for that might result in competition between different castes.

I have tried to show earlier that the traditional or pre-British political and economic systems favored the mobility of particular castes, especially the dominant peasant castes. Several of them claimed, some successfully, to be Kshatriyas. Indeed, as many observers of the Indian scene have noted, the Kshatriya category has been a very popular one, and all kinds of castes have claimed to be Kshatriyas. This would run counter to Leach's statement that there can be no possibility that different castes "should compete for merit of the same sort."

Again, it is a commonplace of observation that the caste system, in any given area, is not a clear-cut hierarchy with the position of each caste defined precisely, but that vagueness characterizes the position of many castes. This is the position today, and there is no reason to think that the situation was radically different in pre-British India. This lack of clarity is not accidental but an essential feature of the system, inasmuch as it makes for the mobility of individual castes (Srinivas, 1962). It is relevant to note here that during the traditional period the ultimate authority for settling disputes with regard to the rank of a caste was the king, who could also, incidentally, raise or lower the rank of castes. All this is not consistent with a situation in which different castes are in a noncompetitive relation with each other.

If Leach's "principles" are not applicable to the caste system in traditional or pre-British India, they are even less applicable to the situation today. In independent India competition between different castes seems to be the normal situation. With the passing of political power to the people, castes have become pressure groups and are competing for power and for the fruits of power.

Burton Stein's characterization of mobility in modern India as "corporate," in distinction from medieval mobility, which was familial, is important. While the existence of modern means of communication facilitates "corporate mobility," the motive force for corporateness comes from the prospect of obtaining political power and using that power to benefit caste fellows. This tendency has become stronger in independent India, where every adult has the vote, and the government pursues the policy of providing special facilities and concessions to backward castes with a view to enabling them to catch up with the advanced castes in education and economic position. Numbers mean strength, and divisions which previously seemed important are now ignored. As Beteille has pointed out, "Competition for power and office requires a certain aggregation of segments. The thousands of minimal segments in a given region cannot compete individually in the struggle for power. When they come together they follow alignments inherent in the traditional structure of caste. That is why the larger segments which compete for power today regard themselves as castes or *jātis* and are so regarded by others" (1964, p. 134). However, the political need for aggregation is so great that sometimes distinct caste groups occupying different positions in the regional hierarchy manage to come together. As an example, I may mention the Gujarat Kshatriya Sabha, in which Rajputs are admitting the populous but low-status Kolis to the rank of Kshatriyas in order to capture power in Gujarat State. The Yadavs of North India provide an even more egregious instance of a large number of castes from different linguistic areas coming together and trying to form a single caste-category in order to strengthen their political power

(Rao, 1964). It is likely, however, that aggregations attempting to span great social and cultural distances are apt to be less stable than those which only bring together the different segments of the same caste or even structurally neighboring castes.

The situation may be summarized by stating that mobility in medieval India was based on *fission* and, in modern India, on *fusion*. But the fusion of like units has had consequences for the entire system; for instance, it contributes to the weakening of pollution ideas, and it is also a result of such weakening. The unit of endogamy is beginning to widen to include adjacent segments or *grades*. In other words, in the process of exploiting the new opportunities, significant changes are occurring in the caste system. This is why Bailey's formulation that "Castes still exist: but they are used as building blocks in a different kind of system," is unsatisfactory inasmuch as it ignores the changes which have occurred in the individual "building blocks" (1963, p. 123).

BIBLIOGRAPHY

BAILEY, F. G.
   1957. *Caste and the economic frontier*. Manchester: Manchester University Press.
   1963. Closed social stratification in India. *European Journal of Sociology*, 4: 107–124.
BAINES, A.
   1912. *Ethnography*. Strassburg.
BETEILLE, ANDRÉ.
   1964. A note on the referents of caste. *European Journal of Sociology*, 5: 130–34.
COHN, BERNARD S.
   1962. Political systems in eighteenth century India: the Banaras region. *Journal of the American Oriental Society*, 82: 312–20.
GOULD, HAROLD A.
   1961. Sanskritization and westernization: a dynamic view. *Economic Weekly*, 13: 945–50.
HABIB, IRFAN.
   1963. An examination of Wittfogel's theory of 'oriental despotism.' *Enquiry*, 6: 54–73.
LEACH, E. R. (Ed.).
   1960. *Aspects of caste in South India, Ceylon and North West Pakistan*. Cambridge: Cambridge University Press.
MAJUMDAR, R. C., H. C. RAYCHAUDHURI, and K. DATTA.
   1963. *An advanced history of India*. London: Macmillan.
O'MALLEY, L. S. S. (Ed.).
   1941. *Modern India and the West*. Oxford: Oxford University Press.
PANIKKAR, K. M.
   1955. *Hindu society at the crossroads*. Bombay: Asia Publishing House.
RAO, M. S. A.
   1964. Caste and the Indian army. *The Economic Weekly*, 16: 1439–43.
ROWE, W. L.
   In press. The new Chauhans, a caste mobility movement in North India. In J. Silverberg (Ed.), *Social mobility in caste in India*.

SHAH, A. M.

1964. Political system in eighteenth century Gujarat. *Enquiry*, 1: 33–95.

SINHA, S.

1962. State formation and Rajput myth in tribal Central India. *Man in India*, 42: 75–77.

SMITH, D. E.

1963. *India as a secular state*. Princeton, N.J.: Princeton University Press.

SPEAR, P.

1962. *India: a modern history*. Ann Arbor: University of Michigan Press.

SRINIVAS, M. N.

1962. Varna and caste. In *Caste in modern India*. Bombay: Asia Publishing House.

STEIN, BURTON.

In press. Social mobility and medieval South Indian Hindu sects. In J. Silverberg (Ed.), *Social mobility in caste in India*.

TANGRI, S. S.

1961. Intellectuals and society in nineteenth century India. *Comparative Studies in Society and History*, 3: 368–94.

9. MOBILITY IN THE NINETEENTH-CENTURY CASTE SYSTEM

WILLIAM L. ROWE

IT IS POSSIBLE to discern a variety of problems which demand investigation if we are, in general terms, to reach a more sophisticated, cross-culturally valid understanding of social mobility processes, and if, in particular terms, we are to understand the cultural content of mobility movements in India. One area which has received relatively little attention so far, although a number of papers prepared for this conference allude to it (see Srinivas, Lynch, and Singer in this book), is the question of intragroup processes by which patterns of choice are made among available alternative models for social emulation. While there is considerable evidence concerning intergroup conflict in the process of re-stratification, we should also look rather closely at intragroup struggle, particularly since, with the growth of many Indian mobility movements, increasing heterogeneity and breadth of membership occur. Struggles for precedence among subcastes over ranking and intragroup relations at the state and national levels also need examination.

Srinivas' formulation of the concepts "Sanskritization" and "Westernization" (1952, 1955) has been utilized, qualified, and discussed by a number of anthropologists in varied settings. Marriott's use of universalization and parochialization (1955) has also contributed to the discussion. Singer, in discussing some of the limitations of the typological approaches, calls our attention to the compartmentalization of styles typical of persons occupying roles in both "modern" and "traditional" sectors, while both Damle (in press) and Lynch stress the aptness of reference group theory.

In an earlier paper (in press), I discussed the emergence of the Chauhan Rajput movement among the Noniya (saltmakers) caste of North and Central India, pointing out that in its earliest phases (roughly from the 1890's to the 1940's) the aims of Chauhan leadership had been almost classically those of Sanskritization. However, the more recent developments within the movement, emphasizing class and secular aims, were seen largely as a result of impinging sociocultural change from outside the movement. Leaders seemed to stress this factor themselves during interviews (1955–57) in Bombay and in North Indian cities. In Bombay, caste associations seemed very concerned with politics as such (Rowe, 1964a), while in rural areas in the north, the emphasis was more solidly on Sanskritization.

Preliminary analysis of caste history materials obtained in London in 1964 indicates more intracaste struggle in mobility movements than was evident solely on the basis of contemporary information. F. G. Bailey and Max Gluckman have recently and forcefully stated their positions on the "boundaries" which social anthropologists should maintain (Gluckman, 1965) in their studies. Bailey's principal argument against the anthropologist's stepping into Indology ("to lump a lot of disciplines together-Indology," page 59) seems to be that such ventures will not help us to "better understand our own problems" (as distinct from being more knowledgeable). Of course all inquiries about social mobility implicitly utilize a time dimension ("What *was* your father's occupation?" seems to be the standard question) and indeed, in Bailey's own major contributions, history is explicit (Bailey, 1957, 1960, 1963).

One of the attributes of group rather than individual mobility in India is that groups, for a variety of reasons, are more likely to publish accounts of their activities. Records of caste associations, at least in some instances, tell us things which do substantially *alter* our understanding of mobility. The resultant insight should allow us to formulate more meaningful questions which then can be asked in the field situation.

Specifically, in the materials available (dated 1890–1915) on both the Kayastha (writers) and the Khatri (Punjabi merchants) castes, we find descriptions of conflict and accommodation over both the choice of symbols for emulation and the relative ranking of competing intracaste groupings. Paradoxically, a closer examination of written history serves not to enshrine historical *causation* but rather to pinpoint processes to be examined in the contemporary struggle for mobility.

KAYASTHA CLAIMS AND THE COUNTERATTACK

The Kayasthas of Bombay, Bengal, and the United Provinces claimed the rank of Kshatriyas (warriors) in a forceful and persistent manner over many decades. While these people were steadily improving their secular status during the late nineteenth century, British courts ruled that they were Shudras (K. C. S. Varma, 1904, pp. 86–90). Their proverbial literary talents were widely utilized in a flood of pamphlets, books, caste histories, family histories, and a monthly journal, all directed toward (1) exerting pressure on the government for recognition as Kshatriyas in the census reports, (2) reformation of caste practices, frequently in *both* the Sanskritic and Westernized directions, and (3) creation of a powerful all-India high-status endogamous caste of Kayasthas (see Basu, 1911; Chowdry, 1913; Gupta, 1912; Joshi, 1914; Krishna and Narain, 1877; C. K. N. Varma, 1893; K. C. S. Varma, 1904; Sinha, 1899–1915).

Undoubtedly, to the Kayasthas and to other castes attempting to change varnas at the turn of the century, the villain for a long time was Mr. H. Risley, who had instituted a ranking of castes in order of their social precedence for the 1901 census. Many of the caste publications are specifically addressed to Risley and to other officials, ranging from district level census officers to the King Emperor himself. As supplicants before authority, castes follow traditional procedure (see Srinivas' paper in this book, also Rowe, 1964b) in validating "lost" status, as in the following petition presented to the king by the Hindu Mair and Tank Kshatriya Rajput Sabha of Lahore (a caste of Sonars or goldsmiths) on the occasion of the Coronation Durbar at Delhi in 1911:

In early times we occupied the same high position in society as our brother-Rajputs. But under pressure of many vicissitudes we were driven to making our living by some handicraft. We generally preferred working in precious metals. Hence we came to be called Sonars (or jewelmakers) by the populace—Today, by the grace of the Almighty *and the help of the British Officers*, we have regained what we had almost lost, our *Rajput* prestige and title (quoted with italics by K. C. S. Varma, 1904 [note xv]).

Although the recording of caste claims by census officials and the attempt in 1901 to rank castes in the census gave an opening to the socially mobile, many if not most groups failed to be accorded the right to claim membership in a higher varna. This is partially explained by the decentralization, in many cases, of the procedure by which claims were judged. A portion of the intra-caste conflict was caused by inconsistent judgments of the district-administered "committees" appointed by the government census officials to evaluate claims. While in one district a claim was approved, it might well be denied elsewhere. One response to this was to claim that one's own subcaste was superior. Hence, Chowdry attempts to place the Barendra Kayasthas on the highest step within the Bengali Kayastha fold. And in the Punjab there was considerable conflict between the Khatris and the Arora Khatris, the latter being considered inferior to the former; both groups were claiming Kshatriya rank. Arora petitions to the government specifically mention the Khatri leaders as their enemies, while some Khatri writers take pains to explain the lower status of the Aroras. This illustrates a general tendency to deny relationship with "backward" sections if the socioeconomic level or special circumstances of the case make general mobility of the total caste unlikely.

In many cases, specific castes of Brahman *purohits* (frequently low-ranking Brahmans) seem to have a symbiotic relationship with a mobile caste, thus explaining something of the nexus behind Brahman support. Both the Khatris of the Punjab and the Pathare Kayasthas of Bombay had such relationships, and in each case had *gotras* identical to those of their Brahmans rather than to Kshatriya divisions. Brahmans who supported low-caste claims in the form of learned opinions (*vyavasthās*) were subject to attack. K. C. S. Varma calls them "hired mercenaries," and other commentators point out the shaky scholarly grounds of the opinions as such.

Beyond the suspicion and reaction to harassment by government officials, there were the rival claims of sections within the caste, as well as the considerable hostility of caste groups adjacent in rank to the mobile group. Finally, there was the ire of the "real" Kshatriyas (K. C. S. Varma, 1904; Krishna and Narain, 1877). Varma partially directed his ire at Risley, but largely at the Kayasthas, Khatris, and Jats. It seems clear, however, that he blames much of the opportunism on British influence, although he finds it contradictory that "it is even found that modern education and enlightenment are made, by certain sections of the country, to serve the purpose of advancing their respective claims" (Varma, 1904, p. xv).

Both the claimants and critics, such as Varma, point to "actual native opinion" and to actual rules of social interaction as the best guides to status. Varma writes (p. xx): "The Khatri who would fain rank himself with the Sesodias of Meywar, with the Jadus of Karauli, or with the Bhatis of Jaisalmere, still remains a Panjabi Bania; and no species of argument will ever transform the quill-driving caste of Kayasthas into a Rajput clan. It is rather late in the day for these would-be Kshatriyas to claim a higher status than that which for centuries past they have been entitled to, and have accepted without question."

A detailed record of the development cycle of a caste association is available in the volumes of the *Kayastha Samachar* of Allahabad, which began as an Urdu language monthly in 1873, converted to an English monthly in 1899 (under the editorial guidance of a "modern" barrister), and became *The Hindustan Review and Kayastha Samachar* in 1905. In the 1899–1904 period the journal is entirely taken up with caste agitation, the question of Risley's ranking of castes, monthly installments of the "Kayastha Ethnology," and reports of district-level caste meetings. By 1905, the specifically "caste" matters have been relegated to the rear section of the journal, with an increasing number of articles on national and political questions. Parsi, Muslim, and foreign writers also appear in the journal for the first time. By 1915 the Kayastha section has been reduced to a few pages.

Yet, even in the 1899 issues, a number of potential conflicts have already appeared, for all the elements of (1) Sanskritization, (2) Westernization, and (3) national political integration are present as styles for emulation. Little direct guidance is given the reader in making choices, but the editor becomes increasingly bold in urging the essential unimportance of much of the caste-ranking agitation. In "Caste Conferences and National Progress" (unsigned, June, 1901, pp. 428–36) the author reports that, as a result of the nefarious attempt by the census officials to rank castes, the columns of the *Pioneer* (an English-language Allahabad daily) are filled with fighting over caste precedence. While deploring the "many dangers" of caste conferences, he points out that this is the only form of organization currently available as a vehicle for social reform. Caste feeling is seen to hinder the growth of "true national feeling," and finally the author suggests that instead of the eight or ten annual province-wide caste meetings, all caste conferences should be combined into the Indian Social Conference, each caste sending its own group of delegates.

The journal was still entirely devoted to caste matters, yet in July, 1901, the editor writes (following a report of the agitation on census ranking): "At the same time, we cannot help thinking that all these grand demonstrations . . . [referring to Kayasthas, Khatris, Kurmis, etc.] seem to us to display a morbid anxiety which is by no means commendable." Although not *directly* criticizing the Kayastha movement, he states: "In fact it has come to be that any caste as soon as it rises in the social scale in the Hindu community claims for itself a Kshatriya origin, and the poor old Kshatriya caste is thus made the stocking-horse on which each community rides its hobby to death."

In almost each issue, alongside articles expressing pious hopes of attaining Kshatriya status for Kayasthas, items appear which are critical of such attempts. In March, 1902, in an article by Alfred Nandy, "Caste as a Factor in Indian Politics," the author makes the following charges:

1. The (caste associations) betray a retrograde tendency in that the forces at work are scattered and thereby enfeebled.
2. They foster a spirit of selfishness, and antagonism to the other communities.
3. The unnecessary waste of time, money and energy by the holding of separate meetings (of the various associations).
4. They foster within the narrow limits of caste itself strife, jealousy and uncharitable feelings.
5. They are antagonistic and destructive of national movements like the National Congress and the Social Conference.

By 1908, the entire tone of the journal has changed. The "modernists" seem to have won, yet at the back of the journal in the reports on Kayastha conferences one reads of a meeting at which the proposal for a resolution favoring an end to subcaste endogamy is met by the suggestion that perhaps there should *first* be an attempt at interdining among the various subcastes! The resolutions passed by the Kayasthas in 1899 and 1915 are strikingly similar, combining elements of reform in emulation of Kshatriya ritual and caste regulations, as well as "modern" reforms such as the education of women.

This is not a process limited to the Kayasthas or to a specific period. Reporting on an Orissa-wide conference of Oilmen held at Puri in May, 1959, Patnaik and Ray (1960, pp. 69–79) describe a similar combination of elements, which in this case centered about a question of the priority of claims: to build a caste dharmsala (rest house for pilgrims of the caste worshipping at the famous Jaganath Temple) or to build a caste hostel for college students? Significantly, at the conclusion of the three day conference, resolutions were passed on *both* education and construction of a dharmsala, so that both "conservative" and "progressive" demands were met.

Another important theme which appears in many caste publications is the attempt to create the widest possible caste endogamy, to extend effectively the boundaries of the marriage network. I have discussed elsewhere (1963) the necessity of new marriage networks for the elites who must maintain and strengthen the new standards, whatever the style or combination of life styles characteristic of the group. Although resolutions such as the 1959 Orissa Oilmen's: "There should be complete freedom (of arranging marriage) without any prejudice among all sub-castes . . . ." are common, we know little of the extent to which such marriages occurred. This type of resolution appears at the turn of the century in Kayastha literature, and the journal even publishes notices of inter-subcaste marriages at this time. But this question might well be investigated for a state-wide caste such as the Kayasthas in Bengal or Uttar Pradesh, or

Khatris in the Punjab. To the extent that state-wide resolutions on caste reforms have been uniformly translated into custom over time, the possibility exists for broadening the area of the marriage network and hence strengthening, building, the solidity of a caste on a regional or national basis.

Finally, the caste association functions as a political interest group, a problem taken up elsewhere in this volume. This mechanism is also evident in activities of the Kayasthas early in the century, when the economic basis of their mobility was threatened by a United Provinces government decree on limiting numbers of Kayasthas to be hired in government service. Organized response through the caste association was effective in countering this attack on the fundamental basis of mobility.

BIBLIOGRAPHY

————.
1888. *A short ethnographical history of Aror Bans. According to Question No. B, prepared by the Consultation of many Panchayats and Many leading Members of Lahore, Dera Ismail Khan, Gurjanwala, Multan, Jhang, Fayazabad, Etc.* Lahore.

————.
1904. *A petition in form of a Brief history of the Acharjya, Sakadvipi and Sarajupari Brahmans of Bengal.* Calcutta.

AGNIHOTRI, PANDIT RAMBHAROSA.
1925. *Bans Prabodhni.* Kanpur.

BAILEY, F. G.
1957. *Caste and the economic frontier.* Manchester: Manchester University Press.

1960. *Tribe, caste and nation.* Manchester: Manchester University Press.

1963. *Politics and social change: Orissa in 1959.* Berkeley: University of California Press.

1964. Two villages in Orissa (India). In Max Gluckman (Ed.), *Closed systems and open minds.* Chicago: Aldine Publishing Company.

BASU, SARAN CHANDRA.
1911. *The Bengal Kayasthas (their Sastric status and social position with quotations of authorities).* Calcutta.

BHANDARI, TODAR MAL
1908. *Thoughts on the origin of present day Khatris and its morals.* Amritsar.

BHATTARCHARJEE, K. M.
1901. *The social status of the Baidya caste.* Calcutta.

BOSE, NIRMAL KUMAR (Ed.).
1960. *Data on caste: Orissa.* Memoir no. 7, Anthropological Survey of India. Calcutta.

CHOWDRY, K.
1913. *The traditional history of my family (an attempt to trace the Kshatriya origin of the Bengal Kayasthas).* Rajshahi.

DAMLE, Y. B.
In Press. Reference group theory with regard to mobility. In J. Silverberg (Ed.), *Social Mobility in Caste in India.*

GLUCKMAN, MAX (Ed.).
1964. *Closed systems and open minds: the limits of naivety in social anthropology.* Chicago: Aldine Publishing Company.

Gupta, B. A.
1912. *The Kayastha Prabhus of Bombay, Baroda, central India and central provinces.* Calcutta.

Gupta, R. C.
1916. *Brief family accounts of Rai Sahib Kanta Gupta.* Sylhet.

Joshi, Rao Bahadur P. B.
1914. *History of the Pathare Prabhus and their gurus and spiritual guides.* Bombay.

Krishna, Pandit Hari, and Pandit Lakshmi Narain.
1877. *Kayastha Kshatriyatva Drum Kuthar (an axe at the root of the Kayastha claim to Kshatriya origin).* Banares.

Marriott, McKim (Ed.).
1955. *Village India.* Chicago: University of Chicago Press.

Nayacker, T. A.
1891. *Vannikula Vilakkam, a treatise on the Vanniya caste.* Madras.

Patnaik, Niyyananda, and Ajit Kishore Ray.
1960. Oilmen or Teli. In N. K. Bose (Ed.), *Data on caste: Orissa.* Memoir no. 7, Anthropological Survey of India. Calcutta.

Ray, Durga Mohan.
1913. *A report on the origin and progress of the social movement of the Rajbansya Kshatriyas.* Rangpur.

Rowe, William L.
In press. The new Chauhans: a caste mobility movement in north India. In J. Silverberg (Ed.), *Social mobility in caste in India.*
1964a. Caste, kinship and association in urban India. In E. Bruner and A. Southall, (Eds.), *Urban anthropology.* In press.
1964b. Myth as social charter: Hindu caste origin stories. (Unpublished.)

Seal, Nemeje Chand.
1888. *A brief history of the Mondal family of Balasore.* Calcutta.

Silverberg, James (Ed.).
In press. *Social mobility in caste in India.*

Sinha, Sachchiananda (Ed.).
1899–1915. *Kayastha Samachar, Hindustan review and Kayastha Samachar.* English monthly. Allahabad.

Srinivas, M. N.
1952. *Religion and society among the Coorgs.* London.
1955. A note on Sanskritization and Westernization. *Far Eastern Quarterly,* 15(4): 481–96.

Varma, C. K. N.
1893. *Criticisms on Mr. Risley's articles on Brahmans, Kayasthas, and Vaidyas as published in his Tribes and castes of Bengal, on behalf of the Arya Kayastha Samiti.* Calcutta.

Varma, H. D.
1901. *An account of Khatris, as a race of ancient Kshatriyas, fully proving the high origin of Khatris.* Lahore.

Varma, K. C. S.
1904. *Kshatriyas and would-be Kshatriyas: a consideration of the claim of certain Hindu castes to rank with Rajputs, the descendants of the ancient Kshatriyas.* Allahabad.

10. THE POLITICS OF UNTOUCHABILITY: A CASE FROM AGRA, INDIA

OWEN M. LYNCH

THE PROBLEMS DISCUSSED in this paper are two. The first was posed by M. N. Srinivas in the discussion of the concept of Sanskritization: "To describe the social changes occurring in modern India in terms of Sanskritization and Westernization is to describe it primarily in cultural and not structural terms" (1962, p. 55). Employing materials from a study of Chamars in Agra City, India, this paper attempts to give a solution to the problem of how structurally to analyze Sanskritization.[1] Discussions of Sanskritization often mention another process called Westernization. Srinivas notes that, with the advent of the British, Westernization began. Westernization involves the acceptance of Western dress, diet, manners, education, gadgets, sports, values, etc., though this varies from region to region in India (Srinivas, 1962, pp. 49–62).

The net result of the Westernization of the Brahmans was that they interposed themselves between the British and the rest of the native population. The result was a new and secular caste system superimposed on the traditional system, in which the British, the new Kshatriyas, stood at the top while the Brahmans occupied the second position, and the others stood at the base of the pyramid (p. 51).

This latter quotation from Srinivas and the former one in the second sentence of this paragraph tell us two things about Westernization as conceived by Srinivas and as used by those who follow him on this point. First, the former quotation tells us that Westernization, too, has been defined in cultural and not structural terms. Second, the latter quotation tells us that Westernization does not necessarily mean a structural change in the society. Note that Srinivas says, "the result was a *new and secular caste system*"; that is, it was not the caste system as a structural system which changed but rather the cultural symbols which identified those at the top of the hierarchy changed. The British were "the new Kshatriyas," while the "pyramid" of caste remained. It is for this reason that we do not use

For critical comments and help in writing this paper I am grateful to Conrad M. Arensberg, Robert Murphy, Ainslie Embree, Bernard Barber, and John Lally. The paper's weaknesses and misunderstandings are wholly my own. The field work on which this paper is based was carried out for fifteen months during 1963–64. This field work was sponsored in part by the National Defense Fellowship and in part by project number MH 06227-03 of the National Institute of Mental Health. Time for writing of this paper was wholly sponsored by the latter project.

1. I consider social structure to be composed of statuses and their counter statuses, the roles that relate them, and the analytical properties that such structures may possess.

the term "Westernization" when we refer to basic structural changes in post-independence Indian society. For the same reason, our discussion of Sanskritization in this essay applies equally to Westernization.

To make the analysis, I have relied heavily on reference group theory as developed by Merton (1957) for the purposes of defining both the social situation in which mobility takes place and the structural positions from which mobility begins. Such a discussion necessarily includes some answer to the problem of *why* such reference group behavior occurs. Once a social situation has been defined, organized action for social mobility may take place. This action may lead to conflicts with other groups in the system. For the structural analysis of such conflict, I have relied on status theory as developed by Merton (1957) and role theory as developed by Nadel (1957).

The second problem to which this paper addresses itself was posed by Gould in 1961 (p. 949). He noted:

By the time they [the low castes] reach their destination [of Sanskritization], however, they will discover that the Brahman has himself vacated the spot and moved on [to] the higher hill of Westernization where he still gazes contemptuously down upon them from an elevated porch. . . . No doubt it will be at this point that the lower castes also commence abandoning their craze for Sanskritization and then the book will have to close on this concept, as the resultant new Indian society comes to grips with the problem of hierarchy in *radically different and at this juncture hardly forseeable terms* (italics added).

This paper considers that the point of which Gould spoke has been reached, at least in Agra, and that, though the terms may be radically different, they are now to some extent foreseeable. Such a consideration necessarily examines the utility of the concept of Sanskritization, especially in its application to post-independence India.

THEORY AND DEFINITION OF TERMS

The sociological aspects of reference group theory have been summarized by Merton (1957, p. 234):

That men act in a social frame of reference yielded by groups of which they are a part is a notion undoubtedly ancient and probably sound. Were this alone the concern of reference group theory, it would merely be a new term for an old focus in sociology which has always been centered on the group determination of behavior. There is, however, the further fact that men frequently orient themselves to groups *other than their own* in shaping their behavior and evaluations, and it is the problems centered about this fact of orientation to non-membership groups that constitute the distinctive concern of reference group theory.

.   .   .   .

In general, then, reference group theory aims to systematize the determinants and consequences of those processses of evaluation and self appraisal in which the individual takes the values and standards of other individuals and groups as a comparative frame of reference.

In using this theory, the data have forced me to identify three, among many possible types of reference groups, as follows:

1. Reference group of *imitation*. This is a group whose values and/or norms and/or ways of behavior are accepted as right and proper and therefore to be imitated in behavior and belief by the group making the reference.

2. Reference group of *identification*. This is a group to which an individual refers when identifying himself; it is usually a nonmembership group to which he claims to belong or seeks to belong.

3. *Negative* reference group. This is a "general concept designed to earmark that pattern of hostile relations between groups or collectivities in which the actions, attitudes and values of one are *dependent* upon the action, attitudes and values of the other to which it stands in opposition" (Merton, 1957, p. 301). It is, then, a group rejected by or in opposition to ego's own group; it is "the enemy."

These three types of reference group are analytical types and may be overlapping in a concrete case; that is, they may all be located in one concrete group. Yet this is not always so; for example, the Jatavs of Agra now identify with Buddhists throughout the world; they are, however, imitating other Indian political parties such as the Congress and the Jan Sangh, and their negative reference groups are the orthodox Brahmans and the rich upper castes and class.[2] What these three reference groups do, then, is to answer three questions basic to the definition of the social situation in which a group attempts to rise in status. These are: (a) Who are we (or who do we claim to be)? (b) How must we behave in order to validate who we are (or claim to be)? (c) Who is blocking our way or rejecting our claim?

The usefulness of this theory is that it enables the analyst to identify the socially structured frame of reference which defines for a group or individual its or his social situation vis-à-vis other groups or individuals. In terms of this definition of the situation, a group or an individual may compare or evaluate itself or himself relative to other groups or individuals. Such a comparison in structural terms involves the identification of ego's status as it compares with alter's status. This is so because:

some *similarity in status attributes* between the individual and the reference group must be perceived or imagined, in order for the comparison to occur at all. Once this minimal similarity obtains, other similarities and differences pertinent to the situation will provide the context for shaping evaluations (Merton, 1957, pp. 242–43; italics added).

The identification of these statuses is important because, once they are defined, a mobile group can engage in the appropriate social interaction.

Reference group behavior occurs within a social structure, and in the society under consideration the caste system is paramount. I consider caste to be an involute system or a system based upon mutually exclusive status-sets or subsets.

2. What Srinivas says of the caste system may just as well be applied to interaction within it. "Caste is an institution of prodigious strength and it will take a lot of beating before it will die. The first lesson to be learnt here is to not underestimate the strength of your 'enemy.'" (1962, p. 72).

The most recent statement of this model is that of Bailey (1963), who follows Barth (1960) and Nadel (1957). Bailey lists six criteria for defining a caste system: (1) exclusive—everyone is in only one group; (2) exhaustive—everyone is included in a group; and (3) ranked—groups are hierarchically ordered. The first three criteria are considered to define any system of stratification; therefore, three additional criteria are added to define a caste system: (4) closed—recruitment to a group is ascribed by birth; (5) involute—relations between groups are organized by role summation;[3] (6) cooperative—groups in the system do not compete.

To these six criteria I would make the following qualifications. First, I believe there can be competition in the system so modeled. To allow for this, I make use of Bailey's own distinction between conflict and contradiction.

"Contradiction," as distinct from "conflict," is primarily an heuristic device used to diagnose the presence in a social situation (or social "field") of more than one structure. . . . Conflict appears at the level of dynamic analysis; and it can only be recognized as a contradiction by the absence of self-regulating factors. . . . If a man follows rule A and deviates from rule B, and if there is a third rule or institution designed to settle such situations on the grounds that *in this particular situation* one or the other rule is appropriate, then this is not a contradiction. . . . If the group which comes into action is not neutral between A and B but is in fact one of the sanctions of B (or A, as the case may be), and if it is effective, then there is a contradiction between the two allegiances and not merely a conflict (Bailey, 1960, p. 239; see also p. 7).

Contradiction is taken as "symptomatic of social change" (Bailey, 1960, p. 7).

Second, for the term "involute" I prefer to substitute the term "mutually exclusive status-sets or subsets" to designate the organizing mechanism of relations between groups.[4] This means that each caste is defined by at least a subset of statuses which are idiosyncratic to it and which are the basis of its identification, ranking, and interaction within a caste system. Were this not so and were all the statuses in the status-set cross-cutting, that is, open to all levels of the hierarchy, we would have a class system. Third, I consider these criteria for a caste system to be an ideal type of the system and therefore not an exact replica of any particular system in reality. The difference between a real caste and a real class system, then, is based upon which end of the continuum, that is, mutually exclusive versus cross-cutting status sets, they approximate. In this paper the terms "mutually exclusive" and "cross-cutting status sets" rather than "involute" versus "non-involute systems" will be used.

Three other structural concepts remain to be defined. The first is the notion of "dominant" status, which is the status that ego asserts ought to take normative

3. By role [read "status"] summation is meant that in a particular society an individual occupies a set of linked or mutually exclusive statuses which in another society may be found separately. Thus in society A, a "family head" also occupies the statuses of wise man, priest, and estate manager. However, in society B the status of "family head" and "estate manager" are linked together and are mutually exclusive of the linked statuses of "priest" and "wise man." Society A would therefore be more *involute* than society B, since in society A statuses are summed up in one individual while in society B they are not (see Nadel, 1957, for further explanation).

4. For the ideas of mutually exclusive and cross-cutting status sets as well as the ideas of "dominant" and "salient" status, I am indebted to the stimulating lectures of Dr. Robert Merton. Any misunderstanding or misuse of these terms is, however, my own responsibility.

and behavioral precedence in interaction with alter. The second notion is that of "salient" status, which is that status from a number of possible statuses of ego that alter imputes to him. It may thus be an accorded "dominant" status or a non-accorded "dominant" status, in which latter case "conflict" or "contradiction" is present. For example, an Untouchable (ego) asserts that he is a Kshatriya. A Brahman (alter) activates ego's "salient" status of Untouchable and thereby fails to accord to him the claimed Kshatriya "dominant" status. This is a situation of "conflict," since neither ego nor alter is questioning the legitimacy of caste statuses as such. It is only a question of whether ego may occupy or be accorded the status he is trying to assert. However, when ego claims a "dominant" status of citizen and alter accords him the "salient" status of Untouchable, then in our terms "contradiction" is present. This is true because there is in this case a rejection not only of the asserted "dominant" status but also of the legitimacy of that status and the social system of which it is a part. It is, in effect, an attempt to change not only ego's status but also alter's; that is, both would be citizens. In the former case, alter, who is a Brahman, can interact with both a Kshatriya and an Untouchable, while in the latter case a Brahman cannot interact with ego as a citizen, since neither is a counter-status of the other in any logical way.. Third, there is the notion of "observability," which

is conceived as a property of groups, it directs attention to the ways in which the structure of the group affects the input of information and the output (of response) which thereupon works to exert social control.

. . . .

[It] is a name for the extent to which the structure of a social organization provides occasion to those variously located in that structure to perceive the norms obtaining in the organization and the character of role-performance by those manning the organization. It refers to an attribute of social structure, not to the perceptions which individuals *happen* to have (Merton, 1957, pp. 321, 350).

BACKGROUND

The City

Agra City is situated in the state of Uttar Pradesh at a distance of about 120 miles south of New Delhi. For some time it was the capital of the Mughal Empire and afterward it was the capital, under the British, of the Northwest Provinces and Oudh until 1868. Today Agra is mainly a commercial and cottage industry city, although there are the beginnings of power industrialism, especially in small-scale industries. Today, however, Agra's reputation lies in the fact that it is the home of the famous Taj Mahal. According to the 1961 census, the population of Agra is 462,020 (Census of India, 1962, p. 237). As a city, it has a complex of institutions that distinguishes Agra from the village, so that it approximates Weber's "urban community" (Weber, 1962, p. 88). There is a law court as well as an administrative headquarters for the district; there has been for some time, though with interruptions, a local municipal government; there is a school system, including colleges and Agra University; the city has a market-type economy; and, finally, Agra is a communications center, as a major railway depot, a telegraph and postal center, a newspaper and book publishing center, and since 1945 the site of a major airport.

THE CASTE

The particular caste with which this paper is concerned is a Scheduled Caste known as Jatav.[5] Formerly, as leatherworkers, Jatavs were polluting to upper castes and were, therefore, known as Untouchables. At present they form about one-sixth of the city's population and are the city's largest single caste. The residential wards, neighborhoods, or *mahallās* of the Jatavs tend to be dominated by or completely occupied by them. The Jatavs are, therefore, segregated residentially into caste blocs. Furthermore, these *mahallās* tend to be in low-lying areas of the city, near drainage ditches or in former villages on the outskirts of the old city but now, because of growth and expansion, they are included within the municipal boundaries of the city. The case study presented here is limited to the spatial unit of Agra City and the social unit of the Jatav caste.

PRE-INDEPENDENCE PERIOD

The first change in the Jatav caste for which there is some evidence before 1900 was in the economic status of some of its members. In Agra some Jatavs had become contractors for stone cutting, for construction work, for obtaining hides and skins, and for scavenging in the city. The most famous of these were the Seth brothers, Sita Ram and Man Singh, who were able to open a number of cotton-pressing mills before their deaths in the 1890's. These occupations, except for cotton pressing, were merely elaborations of the various occupations the Jatavs had performed in the villages and were, therefore, left to them by default of the upper castes, for whom they were polluting or degrading, although profitable.

These various types of occupations continued to be the main employment of the Agra Jatavs until about the 1920's, when a shoe and leather industry, which had begun about the turn of the century, blossomed into a full-fledged industry. Shoemaking has, since 1920, become virtually the only occupation of the Jatavs and has involved them in a market system that is not only national but also international in scope. Again, this was a work with which the Jatavs, as Chamars, were traditionally associated, and, because of its association with pollution, it was a work which they virtually monopolized and controlled.

The sociological effects of these economic changes were many. To the early contractors there came some leisure time as well as economic independence and security. They were not bound to upper castes by jajmani-type relationships (though it is possible that the contractors had such relationships with members

5. The term "scheduled caste" derives from the fact that the government has listed certain castes on a schedule. These castes are considered to be Untouchables within the context of the caste system. The purpose of the schedule was to make available to those castes on it special privileges to help them improve their social and economic position. This is known as the government's "protective discrimination" policy.

of their own caste). With leisure, independence, and security, these wealthier Jatavs had the time to engage in activities other than breadwinning. The advent of the shoe industry added a significant dimension to this situation. Since the making of shoes was initially completely in their hands, the Jatavs became not only residentially but also occupationally segregated. Thus, interaction with other castes was reduced to a minimum. In other words, the "observability" of the Jatavs' role performance was reduced and thereby control of them by other castes was also reduced. In temporal terms, this also meant that patterns of socialization could develop which were, as far as the upper castes were concerned, deviant or nonconforming to the traditional Chamar place in the caste system.

These factors of residential and occupational segregation, social isolation, economic independence, and leisure time were, however, only conditions, perhaps necessary conditions, for mobility within the caste system. There was at this time a similarity of status attributes, that is, wealth and the wealthy way of life, which provided a basis for reference group behavior vis-à-vis upper and wealthier castes. "Once this minimal similarity obtains, other similarities and differences pertinent to the situation, will provide the context for shaping evaluations" (Merton, 1957, pp. 242–43). This "assumes that individuals comparing their own lot with that of others have some knowledge of the situation in which these others find themselves" (Merton, 1957, p. 247). It is precisely this knowledge of similarities and differences *pertinent* to the situation which most of the earliest Jatav contractors and shoemakers did not have, though they were somewhat wealthy. The opportunity structure, which could be opened to some extent by education, was closed because of the "dominant" status in their mutually exclusive status subset, that is, their status of Chamar, which included the status of Untouchable. This "dominant" status precluded "observability" and therefore knowledge of the situations in which other castes found themselves.

A significant change in the opportunity structure itself, however, was the growth of the mission schools in Agra and more importantly the growth of the Arya Samaj. It was the Arya Samaj that taught to the Jatavs not only the three R's but also knowledge of Sanskrit symbols, rites, and beliefs necessary for identification of similarities and differences pertinent to effective reference group behavior in the caste system. This began before 1900 with Seths Sita Ram and Man Singh, who came under the influence of a Nepali Brahman named Swami Atma Ram.

Swami Atma Ram wrote a book called *Gyān Samudra* (Ocean of Knowledge) dated about A.D. 1887. In this book it was said:

Indra, Shiva, Varun, Yam, Surya, Agni, Ashvani, etc. These ten gods are counted as belonging to Kshatriya varna. If, according to the Lomash and other Ramayans, the origin of the Jatav race [*vaṃś*] is traced from Shiva's gotra, then how can there be any doubt that it [Jatav race] is from among the Kshatriyas (quoted in Yadvendu, 1942, p. 98).

The *Lomaś Rāmāyan* was supposed to be found only in Nepal, whence came the Swami. Nevertheless, this was the first claim to Kshatriya status on the part of the Agra Jatavs. The Seth brothers organized a Jatav Committee of Agra City which had the purpose of bringing about social reform among the Agra Jatavs. It is said that an all-city panchayat of the Jatavs was held at this time, in which it was resolved that the eating of beef and buffalo should henceforth be prohibited.

During the first two decades of 1900, a number of these early contractors' sons received some education in the mission, Arya Samaj, and government schools. In 1917 these men banded together and formed the *Jātav Vīr Mahāsabhā* (Jatav Men's Association) and, in 1924, the *Jātav Pracārak Maṇḍal* (Jatav Propaganda Circle).

The purpose of these societies was to enlighten the Jatavs as to who they "really" were, as well as to stimulate them to get education and to Sanskritize their way of life. Education was considered of primary importance, because without *pertinent knowledge* effective reference group behavior and a claim to higher status were impossible. At first, the problem was to create an awareness and acceptance among the Jatavs themselves of a new definition of their status and the means to legitimize it. Thus, one of the leaders of this early period writes: "But there are some Jatavs also who being crushed by them [upper castes] think it to be a great sin to educate their children. They do not understand that it is learning and education which makes mankind above all creation" (Sagar, 1924).

In 1924 a book called *Jātav Jīvan* was written to prove the claim to Kshatriya status. This was followed in 1942 by a more sophisticated book by a Jatav lawyer called *Yaduvaṁś kā Itihās* (History of Yadu Race). The earlier book notes: "Through this book we want to tell other castes that the Jatav race is one of the *sacred* and *highest* races and is not untouchable" (Sagar, 1924; italics added).

What, then, is the structural definition of this movement for upward mobility? In the first place it must be noted that there was not a single reference group. The Arya Samaj was a reference group of *imitation*, since it was the Vedic practices of this group that the Jatavs tried to imitate in behavior, rite, and belief. This meant that meat-eating and scavenging were to be eschewed, and the practice of the Vedic samskaras, especially the sacred thread ceremony, was to be adopted. It is significant that the Arya Samaj taught not only the Vedic way of life but also that an individual's caste status was achieved, not ascribed. This was translated by the Jatavs into group action for a change of status for the whole group. The notion of individual achievement and its legitimacy had been planted in the Jatav mind as an awareness of a potential alternative form of social structure and social mobility. The manifest function of the Arya Samaj was to convert or bring back the scheduled castes to the fold of Hinduism. This it did by a process of socialization that included an anticipated rise in status. The latent function of the Arya Samaj was to undermine the caste system itself by those traditionally associated with its immutability, the Brahmans, though they were Arya Samajists. In other words, the idea of achievement was dysfunctional at that time but eufunctional as anticipatory socialization for the future. At that time, however, the Jatavs accepted the notions both of achievement and of a caste system based on Hinduism.

However, the reference group of *identification* was the Kshatriya varna, which is not really a group but rather a social category. The aim of this identification was not assimilation and intermarriage; rather, it aimed at a change of "dominant" status and therefore of status rank. The crucial factor here was to prove an acceptable genealogy and thereby to legitimize their claim. It was claimed that the Jatavs were really of Yadav *vaṃś* (clan) and that they were really Kshatriyas. The legend of the Brahman Parashurama[6] was pressed into service, and it was said that Jatavs were really survivors of the ancient war between this mythological Brahman who attempted to kill all Kshatriyas: "The main reason for the non-availability of our complete history is the jealousy of Parashuram and his disciples towards the Kshatriya [warrior] race" (Sagar, 1924). The condition of being shoemakers and contractors was rationalized as a defense and disguise to which they were reduced to escape the wrath of Parashurama. Proof of Kshatriya ancestry was found in a series of correspondences or status similarities between Jatav and Yadav *vaṃś*. These included identical gotras, and such Kshatriya-like ceremonies as shooting a cannon at weddings and the use of the bow and arrow at the birth samskara. These similarities of status attributes were the basis on which identity of status was claimed and taken as proved, at least for the Jatavs.

Finally, there was a *negative* reference group in the *sanātanī* (orthodox) Brahmans, who were the enemy both in fiction, as the descendants of Parashurama and, in fact, as the significant others who were rejecting the Jatav claim. While other castes also rejected the claim, it was the Brahmans who, in Jatav eyes, were responsible for the behavior of these other castes. It was, then, these three reference groups which defined the social situation for upward mobility of the Jatavs.[7]

The "conflict" in this situation was between the Jatavs with their definition of them*selves*, as Kshatriyas, and the *others*, who were higher in the caste hierarchy and who rejected this claim to a position higher in the caste hierarchy. In structural terms, the Jatavs were laying claim to a new "dominant" status, that of Kshatriya, which the other castes would not accord to them. In making this assertion, I am trying to consider the structurally intended consequences of the Jatav's social action. That is, were the claim to Kshatriya status accepted by other castes, two things would structurally result:

(1) All those statuses which are normatively and behaviorally ascribed to and open to achievement by Kshatriyas would be open without "conflict," of the mobility-induced type, to the Jatavs. In effect, this would mean that the oppor-

6. Parashurama is a legendary Brahman whose hostility to Kshatriyas was so great that he is alleged to have cleaned the earth of them 21 times. His story is told in the *Mahābhārata* and the Puranas (Dowson, 1961, pp. 230–32).

7. "Sanskritization does not automatically result in the achievement of a higher status for the group. The group concerned must clearly put forward a claim to belong to a particular *varna*, Vaishya, Kshatriya, or Brahman. They must alter their customs, diet, and way of life suitably, and if there are any inconsistencies in their claim, they must try to "explain" them by inventing an appropriate myth. In addition, the group must be content to wait an indefinite period, and during this period it must maintain a continuous pressure regarding its claims" (Srinivas, 1962, p. 57).

tunity and power structures would be both normatively and behaviorally open to them and, therefore, the benefits of power, prestige, education, and wealth that flow therefrom.

(2) The newly acquired statuses of rich men and educated men would not elicit sanctions from other castes, because such statuses are legitimately part of the status-set of one who occupies the status of Kshatriya, while they are traditionally illegitimate for one who occupies the "dominant" status of Untouchable.

Such "conflict" as the Jatavs engendered by their mobility-oriented behavior was not "contradictory" to the caste system. It was, in our terms, "conflict," since it accepted the caste system as such and did not aim at its destruction. This is proved by the fact that those Jatavs who were most committed to the position already outlined rejected a claim of certain other Chamars, called Guliyas, to be Jatavs and therefore Kshatriyas. It was said that the Guliyas were really Chamars and not Jatavs. Another incident might also be adduced. During the 1930's there was a low-caste swami named Achhut Anand, who led a movement named the *Ādi Hindū Āndolan* (Original Hindu Movement).[8] This movement had followers throughout Uttar Pradesh and some in Agra, where the swami taught for some time. However, he was driven out (some say he was stoned out) of Agra by the leaders of the Jatav-Kshatriya movement because of his teachings. The swami taught that the scheduled castes were really the original inhabitants of India and that the caste system had been imposed upon them by foreign conquerors. He taught that the caste system was wrong, and he advocated the abolition of caste differences and caste endogamy. He furthermore advocated accepting help from the Christian missionaries in the form of education but not of conversion. His Christian sympathies made him objectionable and *persona non grata* to the Arya Samaj-leaning Jatavs. His advocacy of caste intermarriage, especially with other castes, went contrary to their claims of Kshatriya status and made him more objectionable. A Jatav leader of the Kshatriya movement had earlier written:

We do not want to be absorbed into others [castes and religions] and thereby lose our identity as some of our Jatav brothers have done by accepting Christianity, after being tortured by false and proud castes.

. . . .

Would not India brighten her face if the highest qualities of the Jatav race are given the *highest place* (Sagar, 1924; italics added).

The second result of the Jatav-Kshatriya movement was the rise of a parallel leadership to the nereditary caste *caudharīs* (headmen), called the *baṛe ādmī* ("influentials"). These men were either rich men or sons of rich men who were organized into the *Jāṭav Yuvak Maṇḍal* (Jatav Youth League) in 1930 or the old *Jāṭav Pracārak Maṇḍal*. Many of these men were literate, though not necessarily

---

8. The extent of this movement, as well as other scheduled caste movements of this time, is a strategic research site that has not as yet been explored in North India. Why all these movements did not gain the strength that they did in South India is a question that needs to be answered. The roots of these northern movements and their possible relations to the southern movements are, as yet, unknown and significant questions for the social historian.

well educated. Structurally they had added to their status-sets the statuses of rich man (*seṭh, byohār*) and literate man (*paṛhe-likhe ādmī*). These statuses were not involute or mutually exclusive to their Chamar or Untouchable status; rather they had become cross-cutting statuses, since they were part of the traditionally mutually exclusive status-set of the upper castes, but not of the lower castes. It is such a structural change and inconsistency which is one of the possible determinants of upward mobility within the caste system.

The *baṛe ādmī* were "influentials" both within the caste and without it vis-à-vis other castes and the local administration. They functioned as translators and problem solvers and attempted to exert political influence.

The functions of translation and problem solving were internal to the caste. As translators these leaders tried to make intelligible and desirable to other Jatavs Sanskritic values, rituals, and behavior patterns which they had absorbed from the Arya Samaj. Since they were also literate and some were engaged in politics, they also communicated to their caste mates other values and ideas of a Western type. As problem solvers, it was they who took over many of the problems of the caste with other castes and with the administration. They were in a sense a link between the caste and the world outside.

The caste-external function of these big men centered on political influence in legitimating their claim to Kshatriya status.[9] Vis-à-vis the British Raj this took the form of "advice (consisting of opinions and recommendations but not commands)" and "manipulation (when the influencer's objectives are not made explicit)"; and vis-à-vis the upper castes, influence occasionally took the form of "coercion (force, violence)" when court action was threatened (Merton, 1957, pp. 419–20). Yadvendu (1942) said of the actions of the *Jāṭav vīr Mahāsabhā*: "In the villages landlords used to treat the farmers with all possible atrocities, and the situation is the same today. Legal actions were taken with the oppressors and they were made to undergo punishment" (p. 140).

One of the first actions of the *Jāṭav Vīr Mahāsabhā* was to lobby for the inclusion of one of their members in the State Legislative Council. Thus, in 1920, a Bohare Khem Chand was appointed member of the legislative council of Uttar Pradesh, where he served two terms. Bohare Khem Chand then made the proposal that one member of his community[10] be appointed to each district board in Uttar Pradesh. The motion was admitted, and Bohare himself was appointed to the district board of Agra from 1922 to 1930. He further proposed that one member of his community be appointed to every municipal board, town area, and notified area committee in the state of Uttar Pradesh. The motion was admitted and passed. Bohare was appointed to the municipal board of Agra, where he served from 1926 to 1928. In 1926 he further proposed that Jatav (or Untouchable) students be given scholarships in all schools. He withdrew this motion, however, on the assurance of the government that it would consider the matter

9. This would seem to confirm Weiner's hypothesis that "the economic improvement of ritually low status groups is likely to stimulate the political organization of such communities" (1962, p. 70).

10. The word used in the text is *samudāy*. The exact referent is unclear, but that the Jatav community was meant or included is certain.

favorably. He also became a member of the Agra Central Jail Committee, the Excise Committee, and the Housing Committee of the district board. More significantly, in 1928, he gave testimony before the Simon Commission Electoral Committee.

The structural significance of all these added statuses of a man whose "salient" status was Chamar, as far as *other* castes were concerned, was that, while it may not have given him much direct power, it did give him (a) a voice to make his community's demands known, that is, he performed the function of "interest articulation" (Almond, 1960, pp. 17ff.) and (b) "observability" over the actions of other castes both in terms of their decisions and in the ways the decisions were made. This "observability" was translated into communication to the other big men and ultimately to the rest of the caste. Thereby the caste itself became more aware of its position in the power and opportunity structures, as well as of the political instrumentalities that would influence a change in caste position. The communication function was formally organized through annual meetings of the *Jātav Vīr Mahāsabhā*. These meetings were held up until 1925, when the organization dissolved because of internal factionalism. Before its dissolution, however, the movement had spread from Agra City to all of Agra District and had branches in neighboring districts.

Education in the community steadily increased and the first B.A. degree was awarded to a Jatav in 1926. As a consequence, other men were able to move into statuses previously closed to them, such as clerks and tahsildars, and one man also became a deputy superintendent of police. These more educated men also formed in 1930 a new organization known as the *Jātav Yuvak Maṇḍal* (Jatav Youth League). In these newly added statuses, they increased the structural pressure for a "dominant" status, that is, Kshatriya, concordant with these new statuses. Pressure was also increased upon members of their own caste to adopt Vedic (Arya Samajist) ways and ritual. From time to time newspapers were published to spread this message as well as more general information useful to the caste. The growing political consciousness of the caste was evident in the annual resolutions of this organization, which by 1941 had branches in other states such as Rajasthan, the Punjab, and Madhya Bharat (now part of Madhya Pradesh). The following resolutions were passed in 1937 and 1938 respectively:

The conference takes a decision that the aim of the League in the future will be to attain *political freedom* by suitable constitutional and verbal means.

This conference would impress upon the Jatav members of the Provincial Legislative Assemblies that regardless of the political party to which they personally belong, *they should vote unanimously on any issue concerning the interests of their community* (Yadvendu, 1942, p. 163; italics added).

It should be noted, however, that the whole movement was not against the caste system as such. The object was merely to raise themselves in the caste hierarchy by changing their "dominant" status. This is clear from the *Jātav*

Yuvak Maṇḍal's resolution in 1939 against the Adi Hindu movement, which had as its express aim the end of the caste system and caste endogamy.[11]

This conference declares that Jatavs have no connection with the "Adi Hindu Movement" and considers the Adi Hindu Movement to be harmful for the Jatav race. Therefore, the workers of the League, the members of the League and the Jatav people should not take part in the Adi Hindu Movement otherwise the League will take disciplinary action against them (Yadvendu, 1942, p. 167).

During the 1930's, when the *Jātav Yuvak Maṇḍal* was organized, the Round Table Discussions were taking place in England. As far as the Scheduled Castes were concerned, there were two protagonists, both of whom claimed to be "the" leader of the Untouchables: Mahatma Gandhi and Dr. B. R. Ambedkar. Of these two, Ambedkar alone was an Untouchable and one of exceptional qualifications and accomplishments. The struggle between Ambedkar and Gandhi over the issue of separate elections was not unknown to the Agra Jatav "influentials." They, along with other Untouchable groups, sent a telegram to London asserting that Ambedkar was their leader. The significance of this move was that it brought their problems and activities into national focus by a process of analogical identification, that is, the problem, insofar as it was a matter of the Agra Jatavs, was local and different; but, insofar as it was a matter of untouchability, the problem was national and similar.

Further political action of the Jatav "influentials" during the 1930's involved lobbying for acceptance of the name of Jatav by the government. A first attempt to have the caste listed separately in the census was made in 1931 in the form of a letter to the Viceroy and the Census Commissioner. However, when in the 1936 list of scheduled castes the Jatavs were not listed separately, the movement went into full operation with three demands: (a) that in all government papers the caste be listed as Jatav and not as part of the Chamar group of castes, (b) that the caste be listed separately as Jatav in the census, and (c) that the U.P. government recommend to the British government the acceptance of the Jatav community as a separate caste in the list of scheduled castes. The Jatavs again in this case took the position that they were not Chamars and that they should not be included under such a status group. In a letter addressed to the Secretary of State for India in London, dated December, 1938, the position taken was that Jatavs were by force of circumstances in a depressed condition and that they were not really like other scheduled castes or Untouchables. The letter says:

It is needless to mention that the Jatavs, as constituted at present, form *the most prominent class* of the community styled as Scheduled Castes. . . .
. . . We desire to make it plain that we, as Jatavs, claim to be recognized as a *separate caste amongst the Scheduled Castes* without being amalgamated with other castes under the list of Scheduled Castes with which we have no endogamous connection (All India Jatav Youth League, 1938; italics added).

The technique was an effort to get the government to recognize their claim to

11. The story of this movement can be found in Jigyasu (1962). See also text above at note 8.

being Jatavs in name, which they connected with Nesfield's assertion that they were possibly an offshoot of the Yadu tribe from which Lord Krishna came. Once this was done, their claim to Kshatriya status would be recognized, at least by the government.

The political machinations involved in the problem of name recognition were not unsophisticated for a previously totally depressed and powerless caste. A deputation of "influentials" went to present their claims to Govind Vallabhai Pant, then Premier of the U.P. government. One of the two Jatav members of the U.P. Legislative Assembly, elected in 1936, pressed the U.P. Minister of Education with questions on this problem in the Assembly. A memorial, supposedly with 6,000 Jatav signatures, was sent to the Secretary of State for India in London. As a result, all the demands were accepted by the government. However, World War II intervened, so that a follow-up on these actions was not forthcoming. Nevertheless, the conclusion that the Jatavs had an effective organization for "interest articulation" and political influence is inescapable. The structural fact on which these actions were based is the expansion of their status-sets, which by 1942 included educated men with college degrees, members of the assembly, *nāyab tahsildārs*, inspectors of police, and clerks. Occupants of these statuses further helped to open the power and opportunity structures. Slowly the Jatavs were entering these structures by moving into statuses previously closed to them. The Jatavs, themselves, did not seem to be willing to grant these new statuses to other Untouchables because of the Jatav claim to a Kshatriya "dominant" status.

Two significant anomalies remained, however. The first was that the occupation upon which they based much of their economic independence, that is, shoemaking, was still part of their status-set, and as such it was very visible and therefore easily identified them as Chamar and as Untouchable. Had they been able to leave this polluting occupation, their claim to a new dominant status might more easily have been achieved and legitimized. The point is that the Jatavs were not trying to add new statuses to the mutually exclusive status subset of Chamar; rather, they wanted to supplant the Chamar subset with the mutually exclusive subset of Kshatriya, which did not include the status of shoemaker. They could not easily do this because of the economic need to retain the profitable but visible occupational status of shoemaker.

The second anomaly was that involved in opting to include themselves under the list for scheduled castes. This option brought them very real benefits from the government, but it also included them under the Untouchable groups in fact. This was inconsistent with their position in claiming Kshatriya status.[12]

One further point might be noted. None of this action on the part of the Jatavs can be considered as "contradiction"; it was "conflict" within the caste system. The calling upon the British to validate their claim is in accord with the "self-sealing mechanisms" for dealing with conflict within the caste system. Such was formerly the duty of the king, whom the British had supplanted. The

---

12. For this very reason the Kolis of Agra did not want to be included on the list of the scheduled castes, though Kolis elsewhere were so included.

Jatavs themselves, unlike the Adi Hindus, were attempting to rise within the system, and, in doing so, they accepted it. The intended consequence of their social action, at this time, was not to destroy the caste system; it was to rise within it.

TRANSITIONAL PERIOD

During the 1930's and early 1940's the attention of the Jatav elite centered upon a new problem. This was the independence movement and the position of the Jatavs in an independent India, though the latter issue was overshadowed to some extent by World War II. However, two things happened. First, the more liberal concepts of the independence leaders, such as democracy, individual freedom, and achievement were not lost on Jatav ears. These ideas were already familiar to them through the Arya Samaj. Second, the notion that India was to be free was translated into "if India is to be free, then the Jatavs too must be free in an independent India."

In 1944–45, these political undercurrents crystallized into the foundation of the Scheduled Castes Federation of Agra, which was linked to Dr. Ambedkar's All-India Scheduled Castes Federation. This was a major turning point. The Jatav's reference group of *identification* now became the scheduled castes, which considered them*selves* the oppressed, unenlightened, and deprived section of the country. These status attributes were the basis of Jatav identification. Such an identification, however, was an about-face, in that the Jatavs now identified with those groups considered Untouchable by the *other*, that is, upper, castes.

This about-face might be explained to some extent by the reference group of *imitation*. This group contained the liberal leaders of the independence movement in India and, for some of the elite, leaders of other independence movements of the oppressed, such as the French and American revolutions. These were the groups to be imitated both as activists who advocated liberation of the oppressed and the poor and as idealists who would build the new society that independence was to usher in to India.

Finally, the reference group of *negation* was still the Brahmans, those who were seen as oppressing and causing the misery of the Untouchables through the instrument of their repression, the caste system. It was these three groups that defined for the Jatav his position in the society at this time.

The Jatavs had definitely become antagonists of the caste system. Much of this is due to the influence of Ambedkar, who was both the ideologue and the leader of the new movement. The elite were cognizant of his ideas and his objectives, which he summed up in the phrase "Liberty, Equality, and Fraternity." Ambedkar's experiences as a student in America, where he took a Ph.D. in economics, and in England, where he became a barrister, must have colored the interpretations he gave to this phrase.

The years of "political socialization" that had preceded now became years of "political recruitment" (Almond, 1960, pp. 17 ff.) into a united Jatav front. Leadership moved steadily from political influence to political participation. These shifts solidified into three acts. The first was the Scheduled Castes Federation satyagraha at Lucknow, in which the Agra Jatavs claim to have taken a leading part both in numbers and in leadership. The satyagraha presented to the state government in Lucknow eleven demands including that of reservation of government jobs for the scheduled castes.[13] Those, including women, who participated in this march and were subsequently held in prison still claim it as a mark of honor. Gandhi's technique for getting independence was *imitated* and turned into a technique for procuring the "rights" of the scheduled castes, and the use of this powerful political tool is not forgotten to this day.

The second act taken at this time was a parade through the streets of Agra. The main symbol in this parade was a wolf representing the Poona Pact. The Poona Pact was the wolf of the Brahmans which went around devouring the scheduled castes. Ambedkar's interpretation of the pact as a betrayal of the scheduled castes by Gandhi was publicly accepted and displayed by the Agra Jatavs, who still hold to this interpretation. The wolf was publicly burnt, and the significance of the event was not lost upon Agra upper castes, who were symbolically destroyed.

The third event of this time was the election for the reserved seats in the Legislative Assembly. It was this election which crystallized a split in the Jatav front, a split which remains today. The split was between the Congressites and the Scheduled Caste-ites; originally the Congressites were in favor, but they have steadily decreased in influence to the point that today the tables have completely turned. In the 1946 election the Jatav Scheduled Castes Federation candidate, who was a former Congressman and M. L. C. (Member of the Legislative Council), was defeated by a Jatav Congress candidate. It was said that he won because of the joint electoral system, in which upper castes gave votes to the Scheduled Caste Congress candidate. No doubt, too, the prestige of the Congress Party was still high at this time and contributed to the success of the Congress candidate. The same thing happened again in 1952 and 1957. However, some of the defeat was due to internal factionalism, lack of organization, and lack of money in the Scheduled Castes Federation group.

INDEPENDENCE PERIOD

The transitional period quickly came to a close with the achievement of independence in India. This brought with it parliamentary democracy, a constitution whose basic values included democracy and the freedom of the individual, and, more important, the universal franchise. This created a basic change in the status-set of the Jatavs, who now occupied the status of citizen, equal to other individuals, and also the status of voter, holding an important tool, the vote. It is on

---

13. A leading English language newspaper of Lucknow, the *National Herald*, gave little publicity to this satyagraha except to note in inner pages that groups of sixty to seventy, etc., were put in prison for defying Section 144 Cr. P.C. of the law. Most of these notices were of about four or five lines, and none tells of the aims of the movement. This news blackout seems significant, especially when a fairly reliable recorder of the movement told me that a total of 3,023 persons were, at one time or another, in prison.

these structural terms that the Jatavs are now trying to open the opportunity and power structures. So, too, they are attempting to make the politically ascribed status of citizen, and not the religiously ascribed status of caste, the "dominant" status which takes precedence over other statuses in cases of conflict. The social situation is that "in which both caste and open class norms obtain in a society, with a resulting widespread ambivalence toward the *de facto* class *and* caste mobility of those assigned to a lower caste" (Merton, 1957, p. 192).

Untouchability was abolished legally under Article 17 of the Constitution as well as other forms of discrimination. Two further pieces of legislation, the Acts of 1955–56, unifying Hindu law on marriage, inheritance, etc., and the Untouchability Offenses Act of 1955, further strengthened the position and safeguarded the rights of the scheduled castes.[14] What these pieces of legislation did, in effect, was to make caste illegal as a "dominant" status and replace it by the "dominant" status of citizen. The appointment of the Commissioner for Scheduled Castes and Tribes to safeguard the rights of the scheduled castes brought in the state as the third party to observe the role performance of persons occupying these statuses.[15] This third party, who at the local level becomes the Harijan Welfare Officer, is, publicly at least, no longer neutral between the statuses of caste and citizen and the systems in which they operate. "Contradiction" is now possible, since the state is legally bound to settle cases in favor of equality of status as citizens, though informally caste does continue to operate.[16] Furthermore, the possibility of "bridge actions"[17] is now introduced into the Indian social system. An individual may now activate as "dominant" either his caste or his citizenship status to obtain certain goals.

These changes in the structure of Indian society are basic to the redefinition of the social situation by the Agra Jatavs. First of all, in 1956, most of the Agra Jatavs followed Dr. Ambedkar into Buddhism. They claim to be the original Buddhists of India, who were forced underground by the Brahmans through the instrument of Brahmanical oppression, the caste system. *Identification* with the ancient Buddhists as a reference group, however, was more than a religious move. Four factors might be noted: (a) Buddhism was an indigenous Indian religion and therefore could not be treated as foreign, as were Christianity and Islam. (b) It was strongly anti-caste, at least in Ambedkar's version of it. It therefore appealed to an indigenous but *alternative* Indian tradition. Buddhism presented an alternative system to the caste system in which attempts at social mobility were not successful enough for the Jatavs. The Buddhists are counter-moralists in that they

14. This legislation and the problems involved therein are admirably summed up in Galanter (1963).

15. This is a good example of the politicization of roles under the principle of *dichotomization* of roles (Nadel, 1957, pp. 85, 88).

16. It is a constant complaint of the Jatavs, especially of the members of the Republican Party, that the Harijan Welfare Officer really does not want to assist them, since he is a member of an upper caste. They want a scheduled caste person to hold this position. In other words, they feel that, while publicly he activates his status of Harijan Welfare Officer, privately he acts in accord with his upper caste status. I was not able to observe any acts to justify this complaint.

17. ". . . the actor may play upon the roles which he has in different systems of social relationships, so as to win for himself the support of more efficient allies" (Bailey, 1960, p. 251).

consider themselves to represent the true values of the new India. (c) Buddhism exists in countries outside India. A number of informants have told me that it was their hope that non-Indian Buddhists would take up the cause of the depressed and "persecuted" Buddhists of India in an international forum. There was in 1964 a strong identification with the persecuted Buddhists in South Vietnam just before the downfall of the Diem regime. (d) The "we are the original and ancient Indians" theme gave an ideological and moral justification to underpin the political demands of "give the land back to the tillers and give the government back to the people." Such demands, incidentally, have more than a local and communal appeal.

The Buddhist movement now has very few publicly avowed members, though privately most Agra Jatavs will identify themselves as Buddhists. The reason is that, in the U.P., scheduled castes are defined as Hindus.[18] Therefore, in order not to cut themselves off from the government benefits of scholarships and job reservations, most Jatavs will publicly say that they are Hindus. However, the demand for extending these benefits to the Buddhists is one of the most important in the Republican Party's list of demands (see below).

The second element in the redefinition of the social situation by the Jatavs is the location of a *negative* reference group, and this continues to be the Brahmans. Now, however, the Brahmans have become the Congress and the Jan Sangh Parties, the capitalists such as Birla and Tata, and the *baṛe petvālās* (the rich men), a caste-anomalous class of the bourgeoisie. This lack of differentiation between religious status and social class is indicative of the operation of both caste and class status attributes in a changing Indian society.

Closer to home, the so-called Punjabis are the negative reference group against whom the Jatavs are pitted. The reason for this is that after independence a number of Hindu Punjabi merchants from Pakistan came to Agra and took over the stores of the middlemen in the Agra shoe market. This position was formerly held by Muslims. These middlemen are now resented because it is they who make the major share of the profits in the shoe trade, and, furthermore, they are now trying to set up or buy shoe factories of their own. This is seen as an intrusion on the ownership of means of production, which Jatavs had held for some time. What aggravates the situation is that Punjabis have capital, while the Jatavs have little or none of it. A Jatav writes in a local newspaper:

Formerly we were slaves of the Mohammedans. We enjoyed great profit by wearing felt caps for some time. Our brothers who have come from the Punjab have obligated us to them in one way; they have freed us from the slavery of the Muslims, and put us in their own slavery. They have provided for many of our brothers by opening shoe factories in Agra and Delhi.

.   .   .   .

The day is not far away, when not a single Jatav factory owner will be visible, and all the factory owners will have turned into shoemakers. . . . Have the Jatav factory

18. "The courts found this religious classification a reasonable one in view of the fact that Scheduled Castes are intended to include those who suffer under the stigma of disabilitties of untouchability, a condition which supposedly exists only within Hinduism and which change of religion supposedly effaces, at least in part" (Galanter, 1961, p. 63).

owners seriously considered the consequences of the policy they are following? (*Nau Jāgṛti*, Oct. 22, 1956).

The sarcasm in this passage is most evident in the word "brothers."

The third element in the redefinition of the situation of the Jatavs was the formation of the Republican Party of Agra in 1958. This is a branch of the All-India Republican Party and is the successor of the Scheduled Castes Federation of Agra. The reference group of *imitation* upon which this is based is the other political parties of India, especially the Congress Party. In another sense, the party is, on the part of those castes who followed Ambedkar, an adaptive response to a political structure in which their interests are not being articulated in the way that they want. Structurally, it is an organization based on the statuses of citizen and voter in a parliamentary democracy. The difference between the party and the Buddhist movement is that the party emphasizes the "exoteric" issues, the harsh here and now, the economic, political, and social plight of the Jatavs as they live with the other castes, while the Buddhist movement emphasizes the "esoteric" issues, the sweet by-and-by, when the Buddhists will inherit the land and caste will no longer be. Buddhism provides both a psychological justification and an ideological rationalization for the Jatav position.[19]

The relationship of the party to the Buddhist movement also lies in the fact that Dr. Ambedkar, in effect, founded both. Many of the ideals of the Buddhists may also be found in the Constitution of India. It is not insignificant that much of the Republican Party literature is concerned with the fact that Dr. Ambedkar, the now-apotheosized (as a *bodhisatva*) culture hero of the Jatavs, was the major architect of the Constitution of India. Because of this, there is a strong attachment to the Constitution and the parliamentary system as envisioned by Ambedkar, who is affectionately called "*Bābā Sāheb*."

Bābā Sāheb framed the constitution. . . . *Bābā Sāheb* placed in it the highest principles of justice, equality, freedom and fraternity. If the 90% of the people of India, who are oppressed, backward, exploited, and deprived, want to take these rights by constitutional means, they can do so. And if they want, they can also acquire control of the whole administrative machinery. The Republican Party of India is the most valuable and proper means for achieving the objectives of the Constitution (Jigyasu, n.d., p. 7).

Under conditions of a political and social structure based upon the cross-cutting statuses of citizen and voter, it is easy to see why the Jatavs have given up claims to a "dominant" status of Kshatriya and Sanskritic cultural behavior, and have become antagonists of caste and the caste system; in effect, they have reversed their old position against the Adi Hindu Movement. The change is due to the fact that Sanskritization is no longer as functional as is political participation for achieving a change in style of life and a rise in the Indian social system, now composed of both caste and class elements. The object of Sanskritization was ultimately to open and legitimize a place in the opportunity and power structures of

19. The distinction between esoteric and exoteric teachings was taken from Essien-Udom (1964, p. 22).

the caste society. The same objects can now be better achieved by active political participation. It is no longer ascription based on caste status, but rather achievement based on citizenship status that, manifestly at least, is the recruitment principle for entrance into the power and opportunity structures.[20] It would appear that caste and the caste system are now illegitimate but do continue to function latently and, no doubt, efficiently (Gould, 1963).

The Republican Party is an organized response to a changed sociopolitical environment. It bids for a share in the opportunity and power structures of post-independence India. While it is the upper castes which now resent and label the Jatavs as troublemakers and nonconformers, it must be noted that "it is not infrequently the case that the nonconforming minority in a society represents the interests and ultimate values of the group more effectively than the conforming majority" (Merton, 1957, p. 367).

The relationship of the party to its negative reference group (Congress, to which the Republicans will not conform) can be summed up in the words of Tangri:

Increased intergroup contacts are raising the levels of aspiration without increasing the levels of achievement. Consequently, the sense of *absolute deprivation* is increasing among urbanites. Closer contact with upper classes and their modes of living increases the sense of *relative deprivation*. At the same time, urban political and social ideologies are sensitizing the norms whereby people evaluate "social injustice," thus increasing the intensity of resentment and hostility. . . . Indian motion-pictures and literature, platforms of political parties and political speeches, and the sermons of preachers and social reformers often reflect as well as stimulate this emergent social ethos (Tangri, 1962, p. 208).

As an adaptive organizational response of the caste to the changing political and social structure of Indian society, the Republican Party performs four functions: It provides power, programs, integration, and leadership.

1. Power. The Jatavs through the Republican Party seek to place their own men in status positions that help them in (are functionally relevant to) their attempt to hold power; such placing assists them in changing their own position in the economic and opportunity structures. They now have the opportunity to do this through the statuses of citizen and voter in a political system which has institutionalized the universal franchise and the parliamentary system of government. Thus elections to legislative posts assume great significance, since they are the structural (and legitimate) means for entering the power structure, at least the formal power structure, of Indian society.

In 1959 Agra City became a municipal corporation under the new Municipal Corporation Act of the State of Uttar Pradesh. This same year elections were held for 54 corporators of Agra City. The Republican Party won seventeen seats, six of which were reserved for the scheduled castes. Of these seventeen, eleven

---

20. Long ago Bailey (1957, p. 227) noted that the Boad outcastes were tending to separate themselves from the rest of the village and to order their relationships with other castes in the village not by the village structure but through the administration. The reason is similar if not identical with that given above.

were Jatavs. Four of the seventeen (non-Jatavs) were really candidates supported by the party, but soon after the election they severed any connection with the party, thus bringing the total down to thirteen members. However, there were also three independent Jatav candidates who periodically associate themselves with the party and derive support from it. Thus, there were sixteen effective members of the party. To this number, one other Jatav was co-opted, bringing the party membership up to seventeen. Of this total one is a Muslim, who is now peripherally associated with the party, and another is a member of a merchant caste, or Vaishya.

The Jatav member who was co-opted as a municipal corporator is the only really educated man among them, except for the Vaishya, who is a doctor. This co-opted Jatav corporator was later elected to the status of member of the legislative assembly of U.P., from a general, not from a reserved seat, since he is an avowed Buddhist and therefore ineligible for a reserved seat. The fact of his election from a general seat is considered a great victory for the party. This man is now trying to add to his status-set the status of lawyer because he feels that he can then operate more effectively in behalf of his caste.[21] In addition to this man, there are also two other Jatav members of the legislative assembly resident in Agra, bringing the total to three. The first of these, who is also a municipal corporator of Agra and a Republican, was elected as a member of the legislative assembly from Fatehabad District on a reserved ticket. The second was elected from a reserved seat on the Congress ticket. He receives much of his support from the Jatav "big men." In this election he won by about 1,100 votes (21,912) over the Jatav Republican candidate (20,865). In this defeat three factors might be noted. First, there was a third Jatav in the contest, who entered it, he says, because he had a grudge against the Republican candidate and wanted to defeat him. This he did by taking away 2,852 votes. Second, this constituency is also a rural one, and the Republicans are not as effectively organized in rural areas as they are in the city. And third, the Congress activated the "salient" status of Untouchable against the Republicans, since most Republicans are Jatavs who are considered to be Untouchable.

The third seat was a reserved seat and from it a Congress candidate from the Scheduled Castes won because the caste [savarṇa] Hindus felt that they could defeat the Republican Party's Jatav candidate by making the Congress Jatav candidate win. Like all other parties, the Congress candidates did not get even 1% of the votes in the name of socialism or informed opinion. Of the votes which were won, 70% were gotten in the form of influence [sattā], money and communalism or anti-communalism. The primary and most effective reason for the success of the two Congress candidates for the Legislative Assembly was that nowhere was there more evident the feeling of the communalism of the caste Hindus than against the Republican Party candidates. "Let not a Mallah win, let not a Muslim win," this slogan raised such a storm in 48 hours, that nobody could stand up against it (Sainik, May 14, 1962).

21. There is only one Jatav lawyer in Agra today, though there are a number of law students. He is not a very good lawyer, as the Jatavs themselves admit, and his clients are therefore few.

Significantly, this statement was written by a well-informed and experienced Brahman politician who has recently joined the Congress.

Some of the success of the Jatavs in these two elections is due to a number of factors which may be peculiar to Agra. As already mentioned, the Agra Jatavs form about one-sixth of the city's population, and they are concentrated into segregated caste wards of the city. These two factors of numbers and segregation are sociological facts that, given an enlightened electorate, are powerfully adaptive in a political system with the universal franchise. Added to these two factors was the political socialization and enlightenment (it is spoken of as *jāgṛti*) of the pre-independence years. In this socialization process might be included the fact that the Jatavs had a literate elite and to some extent a literate public, who could and did make effective use of the communications media available in the city, such as newspapers and leaflets.

In the 1962 election, already mentioned, there was a union between the Muslims and the Republican Party. A Muslim was nominated for the parliament seat, and three Republicans, including the Vaishya doctor, ran for the state legislature. The point I wish to underline is that, while caste as a "dominant" status is no longer legal and publicly asserted, it does continue to function illegally and informally. The Jatavs, as well as the other castes, can activate it as "salient" in any situation in which it is eufunctional for them, though it is not necessarily the status which is formally appropriate to the situation, that is, citizenship. Thus, after this election, two leaders of the Republican Party published a public denunciation of a slogan which accused them of communalism and therefore would implicitly put other castes in opposition to them and their party. The Republican leaders said it was false that their party had used such a slogan as:

> Jatav Muslim Brotherhood
> Where did these Hindus come from, anyway?
>
> *Jātav Muslim Bhāi bhāi*
> *Hindū kaum kahāṃ se āye*)

. . . This slogan was raised by other parties when they feared their defeat (*Amar Ujālā*, March 27, 1962).

Another instance of this occurred in the elections for the deputy mayor of Agra. When the Republican Party put up as their candidate the B.A. graduate of their own caste, he received only sixteen votes, all from his own party. This took place in an elective body where the Republican Party is the second largest, next to the congress, which does not have a clear majority in the corporation. On the other hand, when the Republicans subsequently put up the Vaishya doctor as a candidate for this post, they were able to form a coalition with the Jan Sangh and some Independent members. As a result, the Republican Vaishya won and is deputy mayor today. In such situations, the Jatavs activate their "dominant" status as citizens, while the other castes activate their (the Jatavs') "salient" but illegal status as Chamar or Untouchable. This is an instance of engaging in "bridge actions," that is, acting in terms of the caste system or the democratic system, as the situation demands.

The Jatavs, too, do the same thing when they activate as "dominant" their status of scheduled caste. Such a status is "dominant" when it is a question of government privileges granted to such castes. It is in these situations that the upper castes attempt to activate citizenship as the "salient" status and claim that there should be equality for all and special privileges for none. In such cases, however, the government is not neutral between the two parties. It decides in favor of the scheduled caste status. Such action is "contradictory" to the caste system.

2. Programs. The program of the Republican Party, in general, is set out in its election manifesto, whose major demands are concerned with improving the lot of the poor and "downtrodden" of India. More recently a charter of ten demands was presented to the late Prime Minister Shastri. These demands were:

1. Portrait of Baba Saheb Dr. B. R. Ambedkar "The Father of the Indian Constitution" must be given a place in the Central Hall of Parliament.
2. Let the land of the Nation go to the actual tiller of the land.
3. Idle and waste land must go to the landless labourers.
4. Adequate distribution of Food Grains and Control over Rising Prices.
5. Lot of Slum Dwellers be improved.
6. Full implementation of Minimum Wages Act, 1948.
7. Extension of all privileges guaranteed by the constitution to such Scheduled Castes as embraced Buddhism.
8. Harassment of the Depressed Classes should cease forth-with.
9. Full justice be done under the untouchability (Offenses) act, to them.
10. Reservation in the Services to Scheduled Caste and Scheduled tribes be completed as soon as possible not later than 1970. (Republican Party of India, 1965, p. 1.)

In addition to such resolutions as these, the state units of the party generally make their own annual resolutions. The U.P. Party generally includes in its resolutions that (1) Urdu should be taught in the schools on a par with Hindi, if it cannot be made the official state language, and (2) taxes on shoemakers should be rescinded. The first is a concession to the Muslims, with whom the party has close relations, especially in the neighboring city of Aligarh. The second reflects the prominence that the Chamar group of castes, especially those of Agra and Kanpur, has in the U.P. Republican Party. The seventh resolution shows again the relationship between the party and the Buddhists, just as the first resolution shows the primary place Dr. Ambedkar holds in the minds of both the party and the religion.

The ten resolutions noted above are instructive for many reasons. All of them are of immediate concern to the Agra Jatavs and are part of daily conversation. These resolutions might be summed up as the "Politics of Scarcity."[22] They are the demands of a party that feels it has too little of the scarce economic, social, and political resources of the country. All these demands are iterated and reiter-

22. "The gap between government plans and decisions and the many demands of organized groups is so great that the danger is ever present that neither democratic institutions nor effective policy will survive" (Weiner, 1962, p. xiv).

ated at rallies and meetings throughout the year. Politics, among the Agra Jatavs, is not just a matter of elections; it is, on the contrary, involved in the basic issues of day-to-day life and conversation.

The tenth resolution is a subject of debate within the party itself. There is one group that feels all reservations should be continued for some time. There is another group that feels that, as a minimum, reserved elected posts, such as M.L.A. and M.P., should be abandoned. As a maximum, members of the latter group hold that all types of "protective discrimination" should be abandoned. This second group reasons that it is because of reservations that Congress "yes men" are elected from the scheduled castes, and not men who will represent and fight for the "real" interests of the scheduled castes. Those who feel that all "protective discrimination" should be abandoned say that then the scheduled castes will be forced to act in the status of citizen and not be kept in their "conforming" and dependent status as scheduled castes through congressional handouts. The policy of protective discrimination is, they say, a Congress trick to divide and rule the scheduled castes; if it is abandoned these castes will be forced to unite.

These demands are made known not only through formal presentations and public meetings but also in parades and satyagrahas. In 1963, a parade of Jatavs marched through the streets of Agra to the commissioner's residence. On the way they shouted *"roṭi, rozī aur makān"* (food, work and shelter). The parade presented sixteen demands to the commissioner, similar to the ten already stated above. At this time, too, there was also much discussion on whether to go to Lucknow once again and conduct a satyagraha for the release of B. P. Maurya, who, as a Republican member of parliament, had been imprisoned under the Defense of India Rules (D.I.R.). An abortive attempt was made to do so, but it was postponed due to lack of leadership and organization. Maurya was subsequently released, and the project was abandoned.

3. Integration. The integrative function of the party follows a double pattern. It is uniting castes on a regional and interregional scale, so that the Jatavs of Agra are in contact with Jatavs of the rest of the U.P., as well as with other castes of Chamars in Eastern U.P. Strong links with the Mahars of Maharashtra also spread down to Mysore. There was also hope that a party unit would grow in Bengal under Jogendranath Mandal, former Law Minister of Pakistan. However, he was imprisoned under the D.I.R. before any effective action could take place. Identification in the Buddhist movement is also linking these castes together into a common group for concerted social action.

Integration is taking place not only horizontally between castes but also vertically. Politics and the whole governmental structure of patronage and development have integrated various individuals of the caste into higher levels of state and national organization. The same is true of the schools, the administrative structure, and the market system of economy. A direct effect of this has been a gradual replacement of the hereditary caste *caudharīs* by the *netā log* (see below) or politicians as the leaders of the caste and a disintegration of the urban panchayat system (Lynch, 1967).

All these movements may be seen structurally as the movement of the Jatavs into status positions actually or normatively closed to them in the past because of their "dominant" status of Chamar. These expanded status-sets exert a structural pressure, or a strain toward status-set consistency, for the Jatavs to occupy a "dominant" status that is not as incongruent with these new statuses as is their Untouchable caste status. Once occupying these new statuses, the Jatavs attempt to exert political pressure to open the opportunity and power structures still more, so that the status system will be open to all. This pressure is ultimately toward a system that is "cross-cutting" and based on citizenship as the "dominant" status, rather than one that is "mutually exclusive" and based on caste as the "dominant" status.

4. Leadership. The rise of the Republican Party of Agra has brought forth a new type of leader called the "politicians" (*netā log*). These men are distinct from the old "influentials" (*baṛe ādmī*), who still continue to exist but who are now primarily the wealthier entrepreneurs of the Jatav caste. The "influentials" are mostly Congressmen and do not on the whole engage in direct political participation. They consider membership in the Congress Party as a matter of survival because it is Congress which largely controls the financial resources upon which they to some extent depend. Their aims and sympathies are with their caste, but their tactics are somewhat different and might be summed up in the saying "Why bite the hand that feeds you?"[23]

The "politicians" (*netā log*), on the other hand, though they all have some independent means of support, are primarily engaged in politics. They are no longer merely "influentials" as in pre-independence days. These men deal in patronage, power, and influence. They can conveniently be discussed under the headings of structural position and functions.

1. Structure. While some of these politicians—for example, some of the party leaders and officers—do not occupy elected offices, most of them do, and it is these elected men who are the *de facto* caste elite. Included in this group are the municipal corporators and/or the members of the state legislative assembly. They therefore occupy these statuses on the basis of achieved, not ascribed, criteria. As members of these assemblies, they are also members of various committees and thus they have structural "observability" over the actions and decisions of these committees. The power of these committees is formally little, but informally it is not inconsiderable. Committee members in the Agra Corporation are able to reduce assessments on house taxes and to decide on development projects, etc. The importance of this is twofold. First, structural "observability" is translated into communication to the members of the caste in such a way that its members are aware of the decisions being made as well as of the substance and effect of these decisions upon them. Second, the Jatavs occupy these positions on a basis of equality with members of other castes. In these status positions, therefore, relations are manifestly coordinate, not sub-

23. The parallels in the development of these two types of leadership with the development of the leadership among the Eta of Japan are so striking as to seem more than coincidental (Cornell, 1963).

ordinate. Thus other castes are forced to bargain and work with them in ways not possible in a caste system.

One example of this is the pact, already mentioned, between the Republicans, the Jan Sanghis, and some Independents, to elect a mayor and deputy mayor of the Agra City Municipal Corporation. Through this pact, an Independent is now the mayor and a Republican is now deputy mayor, though he is not a Jatav. This coalition succeeded in defeating the Congress candidates.

It is interesting to note how the Congress in the 1962 elections responded to this pact by playing caste politics, that is, by activating caste as a "salient" status. Through its scheduled castes mouthpiece, the *Dalit Varga Sangh* (Depressed Classes League), a handout was circulated, which read as follows:

We humbly request all the downtrodden people and especially the Jatavs to seriously consider in casting their vote in the General Election on March 12th, with which party candidates their good lies. Some persons of the Scheduled Castes, who are in positions of power [that is, the *netā log*] and who call themselves policy makers and leaders of the Jatavs, want to sell their Jatav brothers for their selfish ends. It is because of this that they have entered into a contract with the Jan Sangh; those communal, narrow-minded and primitive sloganeers of the Brahmanical Hindu State. These leaders have not even consulted the voters, their Jatav brothers.

We cannot understand how there can be a union of straw with fire. These devotees of Brahmanism, these priests, these primitive Jan Sanghis and their kind have continually been inflicting all sorts of tyranny, injustice, insults and disrespect upon us, according to the Laws of Manu Smriti (*Dalit Varga Sangh*, n.d.).

The position of the Republican Vaishya who was elected deputy mayor is interesting. First of all, in order to get elected, he needed the support of the Jatavs in his electoral ward. This he got by joining the party and contributing financially out of his not-inconsiderable wealth.[24] Second, the Jatavs use his upper caste status to assert that they are not a communal party. Third, and most important, his higher caste status, wealth, and influential connections allow him a structural "observability" over informal situations where untouchable caste status is "salient" and Jatavs cannot tread. Thus, he is a valuable liaison with the informal structures of power and influence where one's caste is important. And fourth, he is a man of experience and wealth and, as such, he is the virtual leader of the "politicians" (*netā log*) in the Republican Party of Agra. He is, in effect, the "outside leadership" which Weiner has so aptly described as characteristic of many secondary organizations in India.

Generally by reason of their income, education, family background, land ownership, or caste, they are of higher social status than the groups they lead. Of the various hypotheses, status is perhaps the most persuasive, and most adequately explains the general phenomenon. Although India has a hierarchical social system in which subservience to authority and acceptance of one's role, no matter how onerous, are important values, people have not been reluctant to protest through political organization. But in organizing politically, they turn to those of higher status for their leadership (or at least are organized by them) (Weiner, 1962, p. 99).

24. He is also a real estate speculator and developer. During the election there was a rumor that his mother was really a secret Chamar. Just how many votes this rumor actually won or lost will probably never be known.

2. *Functions.* The functions of the *netā log* or politicians may be grouped into three: (a) goal achievement, (b) "interest articulation," and (c) organization. By the goal-achievement function is meant that the *netā log* through political participation and representation have made substantive gains for their party and caste. The first and most important of these involves the decision on the allocation of development funds for their electoral wards of Agra. In many of the Jatav *mahallās* one can now find electricity, brick-paved roadways, and additional water outlets. The municipal corporators have the right to decide which *mahallā* should receive these development projects, and in making their decisions they do not forget their own caste. Second, there now hangs in the meeting hall of the corporation a picture of Dr. Ambedkar, along with other national and local notables. This picture would not have been there unless the Republicans had fought for it. Also resolutions are now pending to install a statue of Ambedkar at a place called Tikonia Bazar in the center of the city and also to rename a road Ambedkar Marg. Symbolically, this is forcing public recognition of the achievements of a citizen of the Indian Union, because vis-à-vis upper castes Ambedkar's "salient" status is Untouchable. Third, the fact of these office holders' election and positioning in the local power structure is considered by other members of the caste to be no mean achievement. As one informant answered, when I chided him provocatively, saying that the corporators are scoundrels, "No matter what they do, we'd elect them again, just to show the Hindus that we can do it." Note again how the Jatavs do not consider themselves Hindus.

The function of "interest articulation" involves presenting the Republican Party's demands and views in the local, state, and national legislatures, as well as before the administrative authorities. Furthermore, men in status positions of some power, and with public forums from which to make grievances known, are able to intercede for their caste mates and for other scheduled castes in the courts and with the administration. In fact, as already noted, they have taken over many of the functions of the hereditary caste *caudharīs*. An omnicompetency to solve all problems of the caste and individuals in the caste is imputed to them as *netā log*, whether or not they actually possess it.

Finally, the function of organization involves joint action of the party and the caste in specific actions. Thus the various satyagrahas, *āndolans* (campaigns), and meetings throughout the year depend upon the decision and organizational skills of the *netā log* to make these events successful. A striking example of this was the First All-India Buddhist Conference at Agra in 1963. The party supplied the leadership and organizational skills to make this meeting a success, after the Buddhist leadership had proved unable to do so.

CONCLUSIONS

The analysis presented in this paper leads to the following conclusions.

1. The concept of Sanskritization is of limited utility for the appraisal of social mobility in India. It would be more useful to subsume Sanskritization under

the more general theories of reference groups and of status and role. The reasons for this conclusion are:

a. Under the frame of analysis provided by reference group and status-role theories, Sanskritization can be defined not only culturally but also structurally. That is to say, it can be seen as more than a borrowing of status attributes or as more than a change of behavior of a particular caste, whereby it substitutes the ritual, pantheon, and practices of an upper caste for that which it previously held. Sanskritization can now be seen as a structured relation between groups or castes. Thus a Sanskritizing caste defines the social situation in which its mobility is to occur (reference groups) and thereafter interacts with members of other castes. In such interaction particular statuses are activated (dominant and salient statuses). Such social action has the intended consequence of a rise in status within the caste hierarchy and an opening of the power and opportunity structures to members of the Sanskritizing caste. More often than not, such social action has the unintended consequence of "conflict" or "contradiction."

b. A structural analysis of Sanskritization also points out a major difficulty of the concept, that is, *it is culture-bound*. In this paper a frame of analysis has been proposed which uses generalized types of reference groups (identification, imitation, negation) and generalized types of statuses (dominant and salient) which can be applied cross culturally. Sanskritization subsumed under such a generalized frame of reference might then be compared to other mobility movements in other societies with the expectation of revealing significant similarities and dissimilarities.

c. The analysis of Sanskritization under such a general frame of reference might help to avoid the growing proliferation of terms now arising on the Sanskritization analog, such as Kulinization (Prasad, 1957), Kshatriyaization and Desanskritization (Srivastava, 1963), and Brahmanization.

d. Sanskritization as a process is not applicable to all movements for social mobility in post-independence India. When a caste, such as the Jatavs, rejects Sanskritization and the caste system and opts for political participation and parliamentary democracy, the term does not apply. Nor does the term "Westernization" apply, which, as defined by Srinivas, designates a replacement of Sanskritic symbols, rites, etc., by Western ones and, at the same time, a replacement of a religious caste-hierarchy by a secular one (Srinivas, 1962, p. 51). Westernization so understood is both a way to maintain position in the caste system and a way to preserve the system itself. The frame of analysis provided in this paper is applicable to mobility based on political participation and parliamentary democracy as well as to Sanskritization. In this sense our frame is not only cross cultural but is also cross temporal and allows for the analysis of significant differences of mobility movements under different or changing social structures.

2. The second of our introductory problems as posed by Gould (1961, p. 949) may now be answered. Having realized the point where reference group behavior on the Sanskritic model is no longer eufunctional, some castes, such as the Jatavs, have turned to political participation. Structurally this shift is due

to the fact that these castes now occupy and activate the "dominant" status of citizen and also the status of voter. Conflict is now within the field of politics, in terms of attempting to make citizenship and achievement the recruiting principles to the structures of opportunity and power, on the one hand, and, on the other, to destroy caste and caste-ascribed rank as the recruitment principle to these structures. However, since both these statuses can now be asserted as "dominant," there is "contradiction" within the social structure as well as the possibility of "bridge actions."

Scheduled caste status, when activated, vis-à-vis non-scheduled castes, brings in a third party, that is, the state, which has structural "observability" over the role performance of both. This third party is not neutral in the matter of the precedence of citizenship-and-equality over caste-and-inequality. In addition, scheduled castes, such as the Jatavs, by activating their status as voters, have been able to elect and place their own people in statuses of power within the power structure. Scheduled caste "observability" over the role performance of other castes is not only made possible but also sanctioned by the law of the land. Such reverse "observability" is impossible in a caste system.

3. One further point has been implicit in the analysis, and it now needs to be made clear. We have considered Sanskritization as a *means* to social mobility. Yet political participation has now become one of the alternative means to the same *end*, such as revolution and passing. If, then, we were to construct a list or typology of means to social mobility, we would find that political participation, revolution, passing, etc., are concepts sufficiently generalized as to be applicable cross culturally. Not so Sanskritization, which is as culture bound as "keeping up with the Joneses," though they seem to be alike in some ways. Under what more generalized concept can we consider Sanskritization and "keeping up with the Joneses?" For want of a better term we might call this more generalized means to social mobility "elite emulation," of which Sanskritization and "keeping up with the Joneses" are but specialized cases. "Elite emulation" appears to be of the same level of generality as the terms "revolution," "passing," etc., and is also capable of cross-cultural application. In this sense, then, our frame of reference for the analysis of Sanskritization has led us to a structural definition of the general process of elite emulation.[25]

4. I would hazard the prediction that the model of political participation, as presented in the preceding section of this paper, is the direction that movements for social mobility will increasingly follow in India. The danger lies in whether the more conscious and vociferous demands of these movements can be met in an economy of scarcity without jeopardizing the goal of democratic socialism that India has set for itself (see Weiner, 1962).

5. I would hypothesize that the ideas of Frazer (1963) and Friedl (1964) can be located theoretically in reference group theory and the notion of "observability." These two theories of "lagging emulation" and "one-way visibility" attempt to explain the Sanskritization of lower castes and the concurrent

25. I am indebted to Dr. Herbert Passin for pointing out this fact to me.

Westernization of upper castes in peasant society through the notion of differential observability of imitative reference groups. The lower peasant castes have opportunity to observe only village models, while the upper castes, with greater mobility and urban contacts, imitate the urban prestige model. These two theories, when located in reference group theory and observability, eliminate the need for three theories rather than one. Thus what is happening in villages can be seen and located theoretically as identical in process with what is happening in cities.

BIBLIOGRAPHY

I. Works in English

ALMOND, GABRIEL A.

1960. Introduction: A functional approach to comparative politics. In Gabriel A. Almond and James S. Coleman (Eds.), *The politics of the developing areas.* Princeton, N.J.: Princeton University Press.

BAILEY, F. G.

1957. *Caste and the economic frontier.* Manchester: Manchester University Press.

1960. *Tribe, caste and nation.* Manchester: Manchester University Press.

1963. Closed social stratification in India. *Archives Européennes de Sociologie,* 4(1): 107–124.

BARTH, FREDRIK.

1960. The system of social stratification in Swat, North Pakistan. In E. R. Leach (Ed.), *Aspects of caste in South India, Ceylon and North-West Pakistan.* Cambridge: Cambridge University Press. (Cambridge Papers in Social Anthropology no. 2).

BERREMAN, GERALD.

1964. Aleut reference group alienation, mobility, and acculturation. *American Anthropologist,* 66: 231–50.

CORNELL, JOHN B.

1963. From caste patron to entrepreneur and political ideologue: Transformation of nineteenth- and twentieth-century outcaste leadership elites. Unpublished paper presented at Conference on the Nineteenth Century Elites, University of Arizona, Tucson.

DOWSON, JOHN.

1961. *A classical dictionary of Hindu mythology and religion, geography, history and literature.* London: Routledge and Kegan Paul.

ESSIEN-UDOM, E. U.

1964. *Black nationalism.* New York: Dell Publishing Co. Also Chicago: University of Chicago Press, 1962.

FRAZER, THOMAS MOTT.

1963. *Directed change in India.* Unpublished Ph.D. dissertation, Columbia University.

FRIEDL, ERNESTINE.

1964. Lagging emulation in post peasant society. *American Anthropologist,* 66: 569–86.

GALANTER, MARC.

1961. Equality and "Protective Discrimination" in India. *Rutgers Law Review*, 16: 42–74.

1963. Law and caste in modern India. *Asian Survey*, 3: 544–559.

GOULD, HAROLD A.

1961. Sanskritization and Westernization. *Economic Weekly*, 13(25): 945–50.

1963. The adaptive functions of caste in contemporary Indian society. *Asian Survey*, 3: 427–38.

INDIA, REPUBLIC OF, CENSUS COMMISSIONER.

1962. *Census of India 1961: Paper no. 1 of 1962–final population total*. Delhi: Manager of Publications.

LYNCH, OWEN M.

1967. Rural Cities in India: Continuities and Discontinuities. In Philip Mason (Ed.), *India and Ceylon: Unity and Diversity*. London: Oxford University Press.

MERTON, ROBERT K.

1957. *Social theory and social structure*. Glencoe, Ill.: The Free Press.

NADEL, S. F.

1957. *The theory of social structure*. London: Cohen and West.

PRASAD, NARMADESHWAR.

1957. *The myth of the caste system*. Patna: Samjna Prakashan.

REPUBLICAN PARTY OF INDIA.

1964. *Charter of demands*. New Delhi.

n.d. *Election manifesto*. New Delhi: Ganga Printing Press.

SRINIVAS, M. N.

1962. *Caste in modern India and other essays*. Bombay: Asia Publishing House.

SRIVASTAVA, S. K.

1963. The process of desanskritization in village India. In Bala Ratman (Ed.), *Anthropology on the March*. Madras: The Book Center.

TANGRI, SHANTI.

1962. Urbanization, political stability and economic growth. In Roy Turner (Ed.), *India's urban future*. Bombay: Oxford University Press.

WEBER, MAX.

1962. *The city*. (Trans. and ed. by Don Martindale and Gertrude Neuwirth.) New York: Collier Books.

WEINER, MYRON.

1963. *The politics of scarcity*. Bombay: Asia Publishing House.

II. WORKS IN HINDI

a. Books and Pamphlets

JIGYASU, CHANDRIKA PRASAD.

1960. *Sri 108 Svāmi Achūtānadji* Harihar. Lucknow: *Hindū Samaj Sudhār Kāryālay*.
n.d. *Bhāratīya Ripablikan Pārti hi kyoṃ āvaśyak hai*. n.p. Bahujan Kalyāṇ Prakāśan.

SAGAR, PANDIT SUNDARLAL.

1924. *Jāṭav Jivan*. Agra: *Jāṭav Pracārak Maṇḍal*.

YADVENDU, RAMNARAYAN.

1942. *Yāduvaṃś kā Itihās*. Agra: *Navyug Sāhitya Niketan*.

b. Newspapers

Amar Ujālā (Agra Daily)
Nau Jāgṛti (Occasional)
Sainik (Agra Daily)

III. Documents

ALL INDIA JATAV YOUTH LEAGUE.
  1938. *Memorial to the Most Honourable Marquess of Zetland.* Agra.
DALIT VARGA SAṄGH.
  1963. Letter to Jatav brothers. Agra: Janata Press.

PART IV:

Caste in Politics, Economics, and Law

11. STRUCTURES OF POLITICS IN THE VILLAGES OF SOUTHERN ASIA

RALPH W. NICHOLAS

INTRODUCTION

WHAT ARE the objectives of political activity in Indian villages? Can the concepts used to analyze Indian village politics be employed in the analysis of other kinds of political systems? By a detailed comparison of political events in two villages, this essay attempts to reveal some major objectives of political activity in rural Southern Asia. In the course of examining the kinds of prizes, privileges, and obligations for which village politicians compete, and the objective circumstances which surround this competition, something is discovered about how villages come to be organized as they are during political events. In order to derive generalizations about Indian village politics, the findings from my detailed comparison are set against those of other social anthropologists who have written on village politics in Southern Asia. The only hope I have for wider generalities, however, lies in having a good theory about politics in society. Therefore, the paper begins with consideration of some of the terms which seem essential in a general theory of politics, and with the place of politics in the structure of society.

David Easton (1959, p. 210) has said that there is not yet a full-fledged "political anthropology," and that such a subdivision of social anthropology cannot "exist until a great many conceptual problems are solved." This essay does not solve many of these problems, nor does it develop any elaborate models of village political structure; it remains too close to ethnographic accounts to permit genuine model construction. My efforts at generalizing are to be understood as progressing only part way to the goal of either the theorist or the model-builder. I stay primarily in the two methodological realms most common in social anthropology: analysis and comparison.

A number of people have read earlier versions of this paper and commented helpfully upon some of the ideas contained in it. I would like to thank particularly F. G. Bailey, Bernard Cohn, Henry Hart, Marc J. Swartz, and my wife, Marta. The field research which was the basis for the discussion of politics in the two Bengal villages was carried out in 1960 and 1961 under a Ford Foundation Foreign Area Training Fellowship. The Ford Foundation is, of course, not responsible for any of the statements made here. I am very grateful to the Asian Studies Center at Michigan State University and to Mrs. Amy Lee for assistance in the preparation of the manuscript. The names of the two Bengali villages, Radhanagar and Chandipur, are pseudonyms, as are the names of all persons mentioned in the discussion of the two villages.

POLITICAL ANTHROPOLOGY

In attempting to analyze the structures of South Asian village society, I have been impressed by the inadequacy of unitary conceptions of social systems to deal with the diverse facts of actual social life. Anthropologists who concern themselves with societies in which most social relations of all kinds are among kinsmen may be able to make some statements about social structure which comprehend a large proportion of a society's relations, whether these are relations of kinship and affinity, or legal, political, and ritual relations. However, recent anthropological attention to the complexity of actual societies seems to represent a step beyond the view that social structure is a system of invisible trolley tracks guiding social actors in their every motion. As Nadel (1957, pp. 153–54) has put it: "It seems impossible to speak of social structure in the singular."

It is impossible even to articulate the different "sectors" of social structure (or the several social structures of a society) with one another; at least, it cannot be done within the same logical framework, using only one set of terms. Rather, we need at least three different terms—recruitment, interpersonal command, and relative command over resources and benefits. Only the second set of terms corresponds to the conventional criterion of social structure, relationships in virtue of direct interaction; the first indicates only the mechanics (or 'organizational' factors) underlying the assumption of positions and relationships; and the third introduces an extraneous reference point, defining relationships indirectly. Finally, the two command criteria demonstrate little more than the distribution of power and authority, so that social structure coincides with power and authority structure.

Exhaustive analysis of social action in terms of recruitment and command does not tell all that needs to be said about a social structure. But recruitment and command seem to be of overriding importance in the political "sector" of a society, what Nadel might have called the "political social structure."

Anthropologists and other social scientists have frequently dealt with the problem of defining the terms and scope of research necessary to comprehend political structure. The most common terms—power, authority, politics, and government—have received the most numerous and most confusing definitions. I have selected a few existing definitions and distinctions which seem most useful for the purposes of this research. Bailey (1963b, p. 223) defines "the political" as "that aspect of any act which concerns the distribution of power, providing that there is competition for this power, and provided, secondly, that the competition takes place under a set of rules which the competitors observe and which ensure that the competition is orderly." It is helpful to specify that the "power" sought by contending politicians or groups is "public"; neither political action nor any other kind of activity ever involves all social power. Where public power is used without competition, the action is not politics but administration or government, seen here as a process rather than as a structure. M. G. Smith (1960, pp. 18–19) conceives of "power" in the context of administration or government as "authority."

The distinction between political and administrative action . . . derives from the distinction between power and authority. Authority is, in the abstract, the right to make a particular decision and to command obedience. . . . Power, in the abstract, is the ability to act effectively on persons or things, to take or secure favourable decisions which are not of right allocated to the individuals or their roles.

David Easton, a political scientist who has given thoughtful attention to the work of social anthropologists on politics, objects to the conceptual approach to politics through power and the conflict over power. He is concerned with the development of a coherent set of concepts which facilitates research; he finds that the use of "power" as a central idea does not serve his purposes, though it is superior to the concept of the "state" as a focus for political research (Easton, 1953, pp. 115 ff.). The difficulty in the "power approach" to politics, at least as it has been practiced, is that it:

omits an equally vital aspect of political life, its orientation toward goals other than power itself. Political life does not consist exclusively of a struggle for control; the struggle stems from and relates to conflict over the direction of social life, over public policy, as we say today in a somewhat legal formulation (p. 117).

I indicate this objection to the approach which I take to my subject in order to make it clear that, for the time being, I am talking only about the conflict over power, not about administration, government, or the direction of public policy in South Asian villages.

Power and Conflict

A convenient, brief definition of political activity is "organized conflict over public power."[1] A good deal of political conflict is of a perfectly ordinary variety, as when two candidates stand in opposition to one another for election. Conflict of this kind is controlled by a socially recognized set of rules and is generally regarded as "competition." In other circumstances, particularly where political change is under way, conflict is not regulated by a single legitimate order. This kind of conflict is of primary importance in contemporary South Asian villages. Political conflict frequently occurs not between individual actors but between groups—corporate groups, such as political parties or lineage segments, and non-corporate quasi-groups (Mayer, 1965), or factions (Nicholas, 1965).

Occasionally, councils or committees of certain kinds are thought to make consensual decisions over which there is no conflict. We may be tempted to regard decisions of this kind as part of the "process of government" not involving the "struggle for power," since conflict does not appear to be an essential part of governing. In many oligarchic regimes ("elite councils," Bailey, 1965)

1. Although I have employed this definition as a guide in the present research, I do not regard it as distinguishing between all important political phenomena and all other social activity. In his discussion of this paper, Professor Henry Hart argued that this definition deprives politics of some of its most important ingredients. I have stayed with this more restricted definition for the time being because I think it is more fruitful to cast a smaller net at this stage of research, and because of my interest in all forms of social conflict. The recent volume on *Political Anthropology* (Swartz, Turner, and Tuden, 1966, p. 7) offers a more comprehensive and more useful definition of politics than this one. Unfortunately, the present analysis was completed before the introduction to that book was written.

where decisions are reached through consensus, no overt conflict within the regime can reasonably be expected, since the dominant political cleavage in the society does not run through the council, as it does in the British Parliament, for example, but between the council and the public. Thus, even where consensus is the normal method of decision-making, conflict occurs as a regular and essential part of political activity. The problem for the investigator lies in locating the cleavage across which conflict occurs, since it is this cleavage which organizes the political arena. The rules of politics in a society organize the activity of politicians and political groups; the political cleavage orients them to one another and defines the extent of political activity in the society.

Before discussing the procedure employed to detect the dominant cleavages in South Asian village politics, I shall examine in a little more detail the kind of conflict not regulated by a single legitimate order. Bailey (1960, pp. 7–8) distinguishes between "conflict," such as that which occurs between the roles of a single actor who is both a father and a mother's brother, and "contradiction," irresolvable conflict which "indicates that the total situation cannot be understood within the framework of a single omnicompetent structure." Conflict of the simple kind is governed by rules contained within a single structure and "will even play a crucial part in maintaining the structure." Contradiction, on the other hand, is to be understood through the assumption that "there are two or more structures," each with its own set of rules, "operating in a single social field." Contrasting with equilibrium-maintaining conflict, contradiction "is symptomatic of social change." Observing this distinction, we shall find, in most cases, conflict within and maintaining the "older" political structures of South Asian peasant communities, while contradictions occur between "old" and "new" political structures. Conflict and contradiction cannot be distinguished from one another in individual empirical instances; one of the chief tasks of this essay is to perform the analysis which distinguishes between them.

The concepts elaborated above—power and authority, conflict, and contradiction—are comparatively high-order abstractions. They do not facilitate research by themselves but can be put to work easily when they are combined with the concept of the "political arena," or "field" (Bailey, 1960, pp. 243–48). A difficulty in comparative political research is to determine what it is that should be compared. At the highest level, politics of national states can be, and frequently are, compared. States fulfill certain minimal functions which guarantee that some aspects of their political life will be comparable. Clearly, there are many political arenas below the level of the nation: in federal systems there are component states; elsewhere there are constituencies, counties, cities, and other units which have political structures of their own. But it is well known that certain American cities, for example, have ancient political boundaries which do not include modern suburbs, each of which then has a miniature middle-class political life of its own; whereas the boundaries of other cities extend to include their middle-class populations for miles around the center of the city. Two such units are clearly not comparable, or need contrastive analysis primarily on account of their fundamental differences.

Looking not at the struggle for power, for the moment, but at the process of policy formulation, we may say that parliaments and legislatures are arenas or fields of conflict for political parties. More frequently than is expected, however, parties themselves compose arenas, often to the virtual exclusion of multiparty competition. In the state of Louisiana there is, for practical purposes, only one party, but it is divided into two factions; "bifactionalism has injected clarity and order into the confusion of one-party politics" (Sindler, 1955, p. 662). An unprepared comparativist from Ohio might observe the Louisiana legislature in operation for some time before discovering that the important arena of political conflict in that state was located not in the legislative chamber but in the Democratic Party caucus room, where the actual decision-making was under way.

In short, there is nothing to tell one beforehand that a particular social unit or governing body is significant for political research. The arena of political conflict must be identified "on the ground," so to speak, and a handy guide to its identification is the location of the breach across which most conflict passes. The nature of the conflict itself is determined by the rules of the system; it may be blood feud, sub-homicidal violence, invective, or peaceable voting. Knowing something of the rules, the student may quickly identify the sides which the various participants take, thereby detecting the dominant political cleavage. And by identifying the group to which all of the participants belong, one detects the arena in which political conflict occurs. It goes without saying that no society of any scope has only one important political arena. Bailey (1963b) has recently examined politics in Orissa by looking down the wrong end of a telescope at progressively less-encompassing arenas, from the state, to the constituency, to the individual village. This essay is concerned only with arenas of the minimal sort, villages.

For the most part I shall be discussing South Asian villages in the post-Independence period. Here and there, however, historical examples are used to show what is meant by a particular form of political organization or political conflict. When discussing systems of land tenure, I utilize nineteenth-century materials in order to explain how these systems existed *de jure*. Reforms in independent India have worked major changes in the legal land tenure positions of many cultivating families, but, when the contemporary situation in South Asian villages is examined, I am more concerned with the effective than with the legal landholding system.

POLITICAL CLEAVAGES IN TWO BENGAL VILLAGES

Radhanagar, an agricultural village of nearly 600 persons, is located in the low-lying eastern portion of Midnapore District, West Bengal, about sixty miles southwest of Calcutta. Chandipur village has a population of nearly 1,000 persons; it is situated on the bank of the Bhagirathi River in Murshidabad District, about 120 miles north of Calcutta. There is a fundamental difference between the kinds of cleavages across which conflict passes in these two villages; I hope to reveal this difference by contrasting the forms of political organization found in these communities. The most obvious difference between them, as I shall show in more detail later, is that the dominant political cleavage in Radhanagar is vertical, while that in Chandipur is horizontal.

Vertical political cleavages are characteristic of the ideal unstratified society, while horizontal cleavages are characteristic of the ideal stratified society. This is a statement about political systems in the most general and abstract terms; it is applicable to the analysis of political systems in societies of all scales at all times. In contemporary South Asian peasant villages, vertical political cleavages appear most frequently in the form of factions, and within certain castes, in the form of divisions between segments of patrilineal descent groups. Horizontal political cleavages in South Asian villages are found most frequently between caste groups and between ruling autocrats and their subjects. Elements of all of these sources of cleavage are found at work structuring the political arenas of Radhanagar and Chandipur.

POLITICS IN RADHANAGAR

Though there has been human habitation in Midnapore District for many centuries, most of the villages in the eastern part of the district are probably not old. It is likely that some of the most ancient towns in the eastern area—Tamralipti, Ambikanagar, and Ghatal—were centers of a population which gradually expanded into the less attractive interior deltaic areas (Mukerjee, 1938, p. 127). The earliest known kings of the area were Kaibarttas, members of the same caste which is today dominant in the district. They were Buddhists until perhaps the tenth century (Hunter, 1868, p. 100); traces of ancient Buddhist village institutions are still found in villages of eastern Midnapore and in Tamluk town, successor of the classical port of Tamralipti. Midnapore, in the southwestern corner of Bengal, escaped most of the impact of Muslim rule and was not hard hit by the Maratha invasions. The area became important early in the British period, however, as a source of salt, as well as for land revenue.

As in most of Bengal proper, the parganas into which Midnapore was divided by the Mughal land revenue system were intertwined and sometimes wholly or partially enclaved in one another. This situation was not simplified by the Permanent Settlement of Revenues in 1793. On the contrary, divisions of estates among joint heirs, and numerous auctions and re-auctions of tax-collecting rights, brought on by the inability of zamindars to pay fixed revenues on an agriculturally fickle area, lent additional complexity to the land tenure system.

Radhanagar village is a part of a *mauzā* (revenue village) located in Mandalghat pargana, which, in turn, was formerly part of a small domain subordinate to the Maharaja of Burdwan. The village contiguous with Radhanagar on the east paid its taxes "directly" to the Burdwan Raj. The village of Govindapur, which is physically and in many respects socially contiguous with Radhanagar on the west, was part of the little zamindari "kingdom" of the Kashijora Raja of Raghunath Bari, Midnapore District. In the Kashijora pargana the standard unit of land measurement is a bigha, equal to 0.52 acre. In the Mandalghar pargana, to which Radhanagar belongs, the standard bigha is 0.33 acre. The boundary between the two parganas cuts through the middle of a cultivated field directly south of the inhabited area of Radhanagar village. Kashijora pargana was styled a *kāmcā mahal*, on which revenue was not collectable in years when the annual flood was too deep for the local variety of rice. In Mandalghat, however, taxes were not remitted on any account, which may explain in part why Radhanagar is today a comparatively poorer village (1.31 acres of land per family) than Govindapur (1.87 acres of land per family). Traditionally, when the marriage of a son of a Radhanagar cultivating family was arranged, in addition to bride wealth, the groom's father had to contribute a *bāb* (rural Bengali form of Arabic *abvāb*, an additional cess) of Rs. 11/8 to the zamindar (which now goes to the village fund). If the bride came from another pargana, however, the *bāb* was Rs. 12/8, including a rupee for the zamindar from whose domain the bride came.

Beneath this complex set of interlocking little kingdoms, there is a pleasing simplicity. Each village is very much like the others in the area. Even in the nineteenth century, apparently, the zamindars did not concern themselves much with the affairs of individual villages in eastern Midnapore. The area is low-lying and generally regarded by outsiders as one of the most unhealthy parts of Bengal. Some members of the Burdwan Raj family once donated a *Siva linga* to the Radhanagar village temple. And once the zamindar is said to have ridden through Radhanagar on a horse and left a *pāṭṭā* (literally, "information," "whereabouts") stuck in the thatch of a village house; the inhabitants were required to cultivate the land described in the *pāṭṭā*. Although no one is quite certain when this event took place, the land gained in this way is still regarded as somehow "special" by the family which cultivates it. For the most part, however, cultivating families simply paid their taxes each year after the winter harvest to the zamindar's agents, who came around in the company of the village headman.

The tahsildar and *gomastā*, the local agents of the zamindari system, interposed themselves in the affairs of Radhanagar largely in pursuit of their tax-collecting duties and their personal financial schemes. It was apparently a custom of minor zamindari officials in rural Bengal to levy illegal cesses in their own interest on villages within their control. The village headman was reduced by developments in the zamindari system during the British period, from an independent, hereditary spokesman for the peasants to the lowest rung in the tax-collecting apparatus. He took as his reward one-fourth of the amount collected and, in addition, had a portion of his own taxes remitted on account of his service to the zamindar. It seems likely that he colluded with the zamindar's agents in the collection of *abvābs*, of which he took a share. The standard *abvābs* paid by villagers when they held auspicious ceremonies were supposed to go to the zamindar. However, in a large zamindari like that to which Radhanagar belonged, news of such events rarely passed up through the hierarchy to the zamindar, so that the tahsildar appropriated many of the fees for himself. If the headman succeeded in keeping a marriage or first-rice ceremony from the tahsildar, he might retain the *abvāb*, announcing that it would go into the village fund.

When I worked in Radhanagar, the headman was thought by villagers to line his own pockets at the expense of the village fund and of individual villagers at every opportunity. An example is the following description of a land transaction, which was told me by Dhiren, the man who served as witness:

> The maternal grandfather of Basanta Das owned much land in this village. He had no sons, so Basanta's father, who was poor, became a *ghar jāmāi* [son-in-law in the house], but he died before his father-in-law, so Basanta became heir to the land. Now his maternal grandfather kept a mistress. Perhaps she lived in Calcutta—I don't know. She purchased three bighas [one acre] of land in this village, but when her lover died he had the title to the land. Basanta decided to obtain the land without paying for it. The woman was in financial distress shortly after her lover's death and offered to sell the land to Basanta. He said he would not give any money for it. So she made a visit to Radhanagar to try to find another villager who would buy her land. She told some people that if they could arrange the sale she would make a contribution to the village fund. Suren Mukhya, the headman, privately told her that he would buy the land without title for Rs. 600, though the current price was nearly Rs. 6000 [probably an exaggeration]. Suren Mukhya called for me to witness the transfer, because I did not know the details of the affair.
>
> After the title had been registered in the Subdivisional headquarters, he told me what he had done. No one was sorry for Basanta, but everyone was angry that Suren Mukhya had taken the opportunity to buy the land for so much less than it was worth. Villagers asked that Suren Mukhya at least make a contribution to the village fund, but he refused. Everyone is happy when Suren does not appear at village litigation because this means that the fine which is collected can be used for an all-village affair, rather than going into the headman's box.

The final sentence of this testimony can be taken as a gratuitous bit of propaganda. Moreover, it is likely that Dhiren knew quite well what was under way when he witnessed the transaction, but at the time of the event he was a member of the pro-headman faction in Radhanagar politics. By the time he told me this story, however, he had become an opponent of the headman. He was not as strong an opponent as Basanta Das, however, who often drank heavily in the evening and went around the village vilifying the headman's name and telling tales, true and fictitious, about his misdeeds. Basanta even had the nerve to stand as a candidate against Suren Mukhya in a village election, an act regarded as irresponsible by most opponents of the headman. This election provided an event which "crystallized" all of the lines of political cleavage in the village and made clear the alliances and oppositions of almost every family. Before examining these cleavages, however, it will be necessary to explain some relevant features of Radhanagar's social structure.

As in most South Asian villages, the population of Radhanagar is divided into a number of distinct, named, ranked caste groups, which are indicated in Table 1. The six castes of the village are clearly divided by public opinion into five ranks. Looked at in one way, Radhanagar might be said to have a very elaborate form of social stratification for such a small community. However, compared to other South Asian peasant villages, Radhanagar appears to be remarkably unstratified by caste: a great majority of Radhanagar villagers are members of the single large group of Mahishya (*māhiṣya*) Cultivators. The Vaishnava (*baiṣnab*) caste, comprising about 9 per cent of the population, is deviant for reasons connected with the facts that it is, strictly speaking, a religious sect rather than a caste and that virtually all descendants of illegitimate unions are regarded as members of the group. Thus, the Vaishnavas of Radhanagar (with the notable exception of Basanta Das, who was mentioned earlier) generally have no agricultural land as a consequence of having no patrimony. The Muslim Weavers are also poor (with the exception of one man who has become prosperous as a cloth merchant). The houses of all of the Muslim Weavers stand upon a small plot of land which formerly belonged to a Radhanagar village temple. The Weavers purchased this land after zamindari abolition, though very little agricultural land is owned by members of the group.

The Brahmans of Radhanagar earn their livelihood by performing religious ceremonies in Mahishya households and in the village temples. Most of their small plots of agricultural land are on usufructuary mortgage to the headman. The Washermen are village servants who live far from the main part of Radhanagar, on the edge of a large tank belonging to the village. The Fishermen are residents of another distant corner of the village, near the point where the borders of three villages meet. A small neighborhood of their caste-fellows straddles the three village boundaries.

A village affair in Radhanagar means a Mahishya affair. The headman is a Mahishya. All the important political leaders of the community are Mahishyas. Differences in caste rank and caste power do not serve to distinguish among village politicians in Radhanagar. Yet there is political conflict in the village, so there must be cleavages of some sort.

A natural inclination for a person from Western industrial society is to look

TABLE 1

THE SYSTEM OF CASTE STRATIFICATION IN RADHANAGAR VILLAGE.

	Caste	% of total population
A	Mahishya Brahman	1.5
B	Vaishnava	9.1
C	Mahishya Cultivator	76.7
D	Kaibartta Fisherman	1.5
E	Washerman	1.5
F	Muslim Weaver	9.7
		100.0%

Note: The method employed to rank the castes of Radhanagar is closely similar to that described by Freed (1963). Differences between Freed's method and that employed here, as well as the method for preparing the "block diagram" shown above, were described by Marriott, Freed, and Nicholas (1963).

for these cleavages in "social class" differences. Indeed, in the reckoning of Radhanagar villagers, differences of social class do exist. There are men who own enough agricultural land to support their families without outside work. There are men who are landless or own so little agricultural and garden land that they must get most of their incomes by hiring themselves out as daily laborers. Finally, there are a few men who own more land than they can conveniently cultivate themselves and give it to others who share-crop it for a 50 per cent share of the produce. There are no Radhanagar landholders who engage in this practice on a consequential scale. But the difference between those who have enough and those who must work for others in order to earn a living is the basis of a distinction between "big men" and "small men" in the village. Big men, independent Mahishya Cultivators, have the right to participate fully in village decision-making. Small men may talk, and even dispute, when the affairs of the village are under discussion; but the big men may take just as much account of the opinions of the small men as they like.

To a small man who has no land except his house plot, the gap between himself and Suren Mukhya, who has a little more than five acres of agricultural and garden land, appears quite large. Yet a man can gain or lose five acres in a lifetime. Alternatively, we may say that the economic power represented in five acres carries with it political power for the holder, but not very much more power than several other men in the village have. Compared with peasant societies elsewhere in India, Radhanagar has a relatively equitable distribution of land. The dispersal of economic power among various families in the community implies a dispersal of political power also.

One of the most obvious ways of dividing Radhanagar, and all the other villages in its area, is into geographical units, which I shall call "neighborhoods" (Bengali, *pāṛā*). The villages of eastern Midnapore and other parts of the active delta of Bengal are settled in a dispersed pattern. It is about a mile from one side of Radhanagar to the other. Because of the routes of the principal paths through the inhabited area and the location of important households, the village is divided, in the conception of villagers, into three parts: the east, north, and west neighborhoods. Each neighborhood has a degree of autonomy in the settlement of local disputes and an acknowledged leader or set of leaders, the big men of the neighborhood, whom I call neighborhood elders. Further, each neighborhood is exogamous, though village endogamy is permitted. These and other features serve to define the neighborhoods of Radhanagar and, thereby, the primary spheres of influence of the political leaders of the village. Even Suren Mukhya, though he is recognized as the headman of the entire village, settles most disputes and otherwise exercises his authority largely in his own east neighborhood.

The east neighborhood is the most populous of the three major divisions; about 37 per cent of the population resides in it. Besides the members of the Brahman, Fisherman, and Washerman castes, and most of the poor Vaishnavas, this neighborhood includes three large groups of Mahishya kinsmen, one of them the headman's kin group. The headman may intimidate members of minority castes, but he must form political alliances with the major groups of kinsmen if they are to respect his authority and give him political support. This he has done with moderate success. The north and west neighborhoods are largely alien to the headman, however, and he has only a few supporters in them.

The west neighborhood, the smallest of the three, contains about 29 per cent of the village population. The acknowledged leader of this neighborhood is Dhiren, my informant for the story related earlier. Dhiren's family was much wealthier and more powerful before 1942. That year brought flood and famine to the village and ruined the fortunes of Dhiren's family. Dhiren learned the elements of what the villagers regard as "homeopathic medicine" and earns a small income from his medical practice. He owns only about 2.4 acres of land, but part of that is a relatively large, valuable betel garden. Thus, while Dhiren Doctor is not wealthy, he is still one of the wealthiest men in his very poor neighborhood, where most men are agricultural laborers. He seriously reduced his influence in the village when he came into sharp conflict with the largest landholder in the north neighborhood, but his younger brother has maintained good relations with the families alienated from Dhiren.

Thirty-four per cent of the villagers live in the north neighborhood, which is the most rebellious against the headman's authority. One Mahishya kin group and the senior of two Muslim Weaver descent groups support Suren Mukhya; the remainder, two important Mahishya kin groups and the junior lineage of Muslim Weavers, support the most skillful and successful of the headman's rivals, a 40-year-old Mahishya named Gopal. Gopal, with only 3.4 acres of land, is not unusually wealthy. He is a member of a large kin group: six separate households, each headed by one of Gopal's brothers or classificatory brothers. Two of these men are older and wealthier than Gopal, but he was informally chosen as political spokesman for the group and for the neighborhood. He has had a few years' more education than the others and is regarded as an excellent speaker. During the 1942 Bengal famine, Gopal, his two elder brothers, and an east neighborhood man built their little fortunes by smuggling rice from Orissa. Gopal acquired a special reputation for cunning during this period.

I may now summarize some outstanding features of political organization in Radhanagar before turning to an important recent political event. Radhanagar was a part of a large zamindari before the abolition of this system of tax-collecting. The zamindar had little occasion for intervening in the affairs of the village, though his agents probably plagued the villagers frequently with illegal extra cesses. The village headman was pivotal under the zamindari system. He had hereditary authority as the only spokesman for the entire village and also acquired authority as the lowest rung in the zamindar's tax-collecting apparatus. Village political and legal activities seem to have been largely internal matters before 1947, and the headman enjoyed a preeminent position in these affairs. The abolition of the zamindari system deprived the headman of some of his authority, but the economic power which he had accumulated under the old order remains. At the same time, the village is weakly stratified by caste and by something like economic classes. These cleavages do not divide Radhanagar families sharply or thoroughly for political purposes. Much clearer lines of cleavage divide the geographical neighborhoods of the village, with residents of different neighborhoods supporting their local leaders.

There has long been in Radhanagar something called a "panchayat," or village council. Whenever a serious dispute arises or a crime is committed, the neighborhood elders and other big men who care to consult with them are invited by the headman to meet in the common village pavilion to settle the dispute or punish the offense. The panchayat continues to exist in Radhanagar, but on top of it the government of West Bengal has superimposed a new statutory panchayat with powers limited by law and members chosen by universal adult franchise.

Universal adult franchise was known and vaguely understood in the village before the autumn of 1959, when the elections for the statutory panchayat were held. In both 1952 and 1957, Radhanagar residents had voted in national general elections, had been courted by representatives of the Congress and Communist parties, and had been taught the value of their votes. But the result of the vote was invisible to them. A member of the West Bengal Legislative Assembly was far removed from their lives, and this was particularly true of theirs, who was a Minister. A member of the Lok Sabha in Delhi was an even more distant figure. All an uneducated man might realize was that by voting in one way or another he could please or displease his neighborhood elder, the village headman, or a stranger from a political party. That his vote had some value was clear from the fact that he was offered money for it, but by the peculiar rule of secrecy, the purchaser could never see what he had bought.

The election of the new panchayat was almost entirely different; villagers were choosing among men whom they knew. This time there was no one to offer money for votes, though the political party workers came around again. There were, however, acquaintances and authority figures from each villager's everyday life who were vitally concerned with how he voted, who told him what he must do and what he must not do. The secret ballot was no longer strange; what seemed strange in this election was that important differences in the village were momentarily erased. Not only was there no difference between big men and small men inside the voting booth but there was not even a difference between men and women. Perhaps only a big man could be a candidate, but all adults could vote. The full impact of this change is still to be realized in rural India.

I need not give details of how the election was run, as I have written about this elsewhere (1963). Very briefly, the village was divided into two constituencies, with two members of the panchayat to be elected from each. Candidates allied with and opposed to the headman were nominated for each position; those supporting the headman were elected from the east constituency; opponents of the headman won in the west constituency. The headman himself did not run for a position because he was waiting to be elected to a higher-level intervillage panchayat. He was opposed for this seat by his enemy Basanta Das, but the headman was able to defeat this "upstart" easily. It is much more important for present purposes that I explain how the votes were organized.

At the time of the panchayat elections there were seven factions, or would-be factions, in Radhanagar. Elsewhere, I have defined factions as "noncorporate" political conflict groups, the members of which are recruited by a leader on the basis of diverse ties (1965, pp. 27–29). At the time of the panchayat elections, only two political leaders were successful in recruiting supporters on the basis of all the kinds of ties possible in the village. Suren Mukhya and Gopal, the north neighborhood elder, organized large groups comprising 36 and 22 per cent, respectively, of the village population. Both were senior men in large kinship groups, both had a number of economic dependents, both held a kind of hegemony over low and subordinate castes living near them, both were neighborhood elders and thus had strong neighborhood support, and both served as rallying points for disaffected followers of opposed leaders.

However, many votes lay outside these two key factions in smaller independent groups. Suren Mukhya was allied with the leaders of two large kinship groups which together comprised 16 per cent of the village population. Gopal brought some votes to himself and his supporters from Basanta Das's small family and his one economic dependent. Dhiren Doctor and the west neighborhood stood somewhat outside this polarization of factions, as did a large east neighborhood (with 33 members and over seventeen acres of land) and a few of its neighbors, who, for various reasons, opposed the headman. The election strategies pursued by these two groups baffled me for some time. In the west constituency, Dhiren Doctor stood for election in the headman's camp; his younger brother stood with Gopal's opposition group. Similarly, an elder brother from the large east neighborhood family stood for election on the headman's slate, while a younger brother stood with the opposition. It was later explained to me that they were merely protecting their family interests. Uncertain which way so unintelligible a thing as a universal adult secret ballot would go, these families decided to be winners either way. Now that the election has made the tendencies in the village clear, the east neighborhood family seems to have thrown in strongly on the side of the headman, while Dhiren Doctor, evidence indicates, is insinuating himself into a stronger position in Gopal's opposition group.

When I witnessed political activity in Radhanagar, there seemed to be room for a great deal of movement of this sort. A big man might pursue his self-interest in a variety of ways within the village. The goal toward which politicians were aiming, it seems, was the expansion of their personal authority. Public power in the village is very limited: there is a relatively stable number of men over whom one can expect to exercise command and very restricted resources which one could conceivably control. Within these limits, however, any man might rise to supreme authority.

POLITICS IN CHANDIPUR

Chandipur village was the site of a flourishing bazaar in 1757 when Clive defeated Siraj-ud-daula at Plassey, four miles south of the village. Clive stayed the night of his victory in Chandipur, where he found provisions for his troops. The village stands alongside the old high road, which ran from the Mughal capital of Murshidabad and the trading center of Kasimbazar to the now-useless port of Saptagram. The road once constituted the eastern embankment of the

Bhagirathi River, the first distributary of the Ganges in the Bengal delta. Now the river has moved its course about a mile to the west, so that Chandipur stands at a distance from the channel. But the river no longer carries the bulk of commerce in western Bengal, and Murshidabad is no longer the capital of the province nor even of the district that bears its name; the British built their headquarters south of the Mughal city in Berhampur.

The villages surrounding Chandipur, and those directly across the river from it, were divided among three different parganas: Fatehsing, Beldanga, and Mahisar. Chandipur itself, early in the nineteenth century, became the headquarters of an indigo plantation which supplied a refinery located a few miles downstream from the village. Judging from the disposition of the former indigo lands, the planter must have built up, with government assistance, a zamindari of several square miles almost exclusively in the rich river bottom. The zamindars around him were high-caste Bengalis. The Raja of Kandi, chief zamindar in Fatehsing pargana, was a Kayastha. During the latter part of the nineteenth century, zamindari rights in the village north of Chandipur were purchased by Kalipada Chakladar, a Barendra Brahman who had made his fortune as a barrister in Patna courts.

Also at the end of the nineteenth century, German synthetic dyes began to destroy the indigo market. The roots of the present political order in the village lie in the ruin of the Chandipur indigo plantation. I shall relate here a narrative of the rise of the Pradhan family of Bhumihar Brahmans, more or less as it was told to me by a Vaishnava religious man of the village. This man, who had few partisan interests in the village, was about 55 years old when he told me this story, so some of these events occurred before he was born or when he was a young boy. Other villagers have confirmed various parts of this story, so I feel confident that this is how events are remembered, whether they are true or not.

The last indigo planter was Smith Sahib. His land was yielding less of the "blue stuff" each year, so he pressed harder on the cultivators. He kept 150 horses and a gang of tribal *lāṭhiyāls* [hired clubmen] to ride them. He also had an automobile. Chittaranjan Pradhan was his *gomastā*. Toward the end of his life Smith Sahib went heavily into debt in Calcutta, bringing fodder for his horses, gasoline for his automobile, wine, and food in tins. When he died, the lands and the business passed to his son in England, who did not even care to find out what was happening. In the meantime, even when Smith Sahib was alive, Chittaranjan Pradhan had been getting plenty of money by selling rice from the Company's stores, by falsifying the records, and I know not what other ways. Soon after Smith Sahib died Chittaranjan set fire to the Indigo House, and all of the records were destroyed. Chittaranjan said that much paper money was burned in the fire, but no one believes that.

It was some time before Smith Sahib died that Kalipada Chakladar purchased the old Maniknagar zamindari for Rs. 50,000. Kalipada came from an unimportant family. He wanted to live like a nawab, and he built the great house which now stands ruined in Maniknagar. He used to have big parties which went on for days, with plenty of wine and dancing girls. He went into debt and began to sell to Smith Sahib inferior tax-collecting rights on some of his land located in the uninhabited *mauzā* along the river west of Maniknagar. When Smith Sahib died in debt the court gave temporary tax-collecting rights over his own land and much of Kalipada's land to two creditors, who were to take turns collecting the taxes until they were paid off. The first creditor to get this right had difficulty in collecting from the peasants. So he promised that if they would pay one year's tax, he would write off the taxes for three years. The next creditor could offer nothing less, so he said he would write off four years' taxes for one payment. With the taxes for seven years gone, the land reverted to Kalipada Chakladar.

Kalipada was desperate and prepared to get whatever he could from the land. He announced that he would auction it off. The cultivators sold their gold, silver, brass, and everything else they had, expecting to purchase the land for Rs. 30 to 40 per bigha. The night before the auction Chittaranjan went to Kalipada and convinced him that the land would bring him nothing if he sold it at auction. Kalipada's financial position worsened, and he finally sold almost all of his zamindari to Chittaranjan for Rs. 8 per bigha. That was the end of Smith Sahib and the Chakladar family. It was the beginning of the Pradhans and the Bhumihar Brahmans.

Chittaranjan was already rich when he purchased most of the Maniknagar zamindari. He gave both money and rice on loan to cultivators. He got 75 per cent interest per annum on cash loans, and 100 per cent on loans of rice—more if he collected in cash rather than rice. He died soon after zamindari abolition, and most of his zamindari was seized by the government. People say he left Rs. 300,000 and 1000 bighas of land when he died. His brother, Ramnarayan Pradhan, who is headman now, is trying to get back some of the land by saying it was private property, not zamindari. But that family already owns more than the legal ceiling; they say they have divided their joint family into three separate families, but it is still Ramnarayan's family.

In all these transfers of zamindari rights, it is worth noting that the right to collect taxes on Chandipur village itself was never transferred. This is because the village was a *khās mahāl*, an area over which the government, rather than a zamindar, had the tax-collecting rights. I am not certain why these rights were resumed by the government; the village was once part of the great Burdwan zamindari. The resumption of Chandipur may have been connected with the "Indigo disturbances" of 1859–60, following which the right of the peasants not to plant indigo, if they so chose, was recognized by the government. At any rate, when I worked in Chandipur, the tahsildar of the village was a classificatory brother (FaElBrSo) of the late Chittaranjan Pradhan and of the present headman, Ramnarayan Pradhan. As I shall attempt to show in more detail later, although Chandipur was a *khās mahāl* for several generations, it is more like the domain of a powerful zamindar than is Radhanagar, which was actually a zamindari village. One bit of evidence for this statement concerns the standard *abvāb* of Rs. 22 collected whenever a Chandipur girl of one of the higher castes is married. The *abvāb* is a feature of zamindari tax-collecting systems; if the actual zamindar of Chandipur—the government—were to be the recipient of this cess, the tahsildar would be expected to collect it. The *abvāb* being illegal, the revenue minister could scarcely ask that it be paid, though the tahsildar might try to collect it in his own interest. In fact, *abvābs* in Chandipur are collected by Ramnarayan Pradhan and, before him, by his brother Chittaranjan.

Ramnarayan's lineage, which includes the tahsildar's family, also includes two less powerful Bhumihar families headed by men from other villages affinally connected to the headman; presumably these marriages were arranged to strengthen the Pradhan family relative to the other Bhumihar lineage groups in

Chandipur. One of the other two lineages, the Tewaris, is small and less wealthy than either the Pradhans or the headman's chief rivals, the Dubes. Altogether, there are 21 Bhumihar families, 160 members of the caste, in Chandipur.

The Bhumihars are a prominent landholding caste in the neighboring state of Bihar, their prominence extending at least as far into North India as Banaras (Cohn, 1961a, p. 619). During the last seventy or eighty years they have moved into northwestern Bengal. Although the group claims Brahman status, it may have been Rajput in origin (Hutton, 1961, p. 276). The Chandipur Bhumihars migrated into the village about sixty years ago, from the village directly across the Bhagirathi. Their previous home was washed away by the westward movement of the river channel. Much of the agricultural land which they own is still located in riparian villages on the west bank of the Bhagirathi and in other villages of Kandi subdivision, where the caste is more strongly represented than it is on the eastern side of the river. In view of their relatively short career in Chandipur, the rise of the Bhumihars is somewhat spectacular. They have acquired most of the land and have virtually erased all traces of the old authority system.

The Chandipur caste hierarchy, shown in Table 2, is obviously quite elaborate. There are eleven distinct ranks among the nineteen castes represented in the community. Both social and ritual interaction among these nineteen castes, and several other castes resident in nearby villages, is complex. I shall consider here only those relations between members of different castes which most obviously involve power: economic and political relations.

Members of most castes either own agricultural land or work on it as laborers or sharecroppers. Members of some artisan castes own a little land, which is ordinarily cultivated by sharecroppers. The Confectioners, Merchants, and Oil Pressers are primarily shopkeepers and likewise depend upon others to farm their lands. Most of the land which is owned by Chandipur residents, however, is owned by Bhumihar Brahmans; they comprise 16 per cent of the population but own over 62 per cent of the land. The significant feature of the sharecropping system is that, because land is scarce, the landholder has considerable authority over his sharecroppers, servants, and employees; and these economic dependents or clients are almost invariably members of castes ranking lower than the castes of their patrons. Thus, most patron-client ties are between Bhumihars and members of other, lower castes. And the artisan and trading caste members who give land to sharecroppers usually give it to members of groups ranking lower than themselves. In other words, the system of economic stratification in Chandipur corresponds in a general way to the system of caste stratification.

There is an important set of patron-client or employer-employee links in the village which do not concern the land. The Carpenters have a thriving industry in the manufacture of bullock cart wheels. Their wheels have a good reputation over a wide area, and the demand for them has grown at a faster pace than the natural rate of population increase in the caste. As a consequence, the Car-

TABLE 2

THE SYSTEM OF CASTE STRATIFICATION IN CHANDIPUR VILLAGE.

	Catse	% of total population
A	Bhumihar Brahman	16.3
B	Funeral Brahman	0.2
C	Vaishnava	2.8
D	Confectioner	3.0
E	Herdsman	11.4
F	Garland-maker	2.8
G	Barber	8.2
H	Potter	3.1
I	Hindu Weaver	7.8
J	Carpenter	11.5
K	Goldsmith	1.9
L	Merchant	4.2
M	Jugi Weaver	0.9
N	Oil Presser	3.7
O	Rajbanshi	2.2
P	Chandal Fisherman	5.5
Q	Patuni Boatman	0.6
R	Scavenger	9.0
S	Leatherworker	4.9
		100%

Note: See note to Table 1.

penters have had to begin employing members of other castes, teaching them the skills of woodworking. The workers thus employed include most of the men of the Chandal and Jugi Weaver caste groups in Chandipur. The Carpenters have invested the profits from their business in agricultural land, and one young man from the group, Jagannath Mistri, spends most of his time and energy in village political affairs: he sits in the "politically important" tea stall, where most discussion goes on. This tea stall is patronized by several Bhumihar men, including the anti-headman Dube brothers, and by Lalchand Chakladar, the Communist grandson of the old Maniknagar zamindar.

Patron-client ties in Chandipur are readily converted into political ties. Jagannath Mistri and Lalchand Chakladar are close friends; together they organized the employees of the Carpenters and some Herdsmen who live nearby to vote for the Communist candidates in the 1957 general election. The Dube brothers organized friends and dependents to vote for the Revolutionary Socialist Party. Ramnarayan Pradhan contented himself with turning out a majority of the village for the Congress Party. To this extent, there were significant factions in Chandipur politics. Higher-caste political leaders organized lower-caste dependents, as well as kinsmen and friends, into politically opposed groups. Their ability to do this, however, was directly dependent upon Ramnarayan Pradhan's inaction.

Ramnarayan owns about 117 acres of land, much more than any other villager, 16 per cent of the total land held by all villagers, and 27 per cent of the total owned by Bhumihars. Ramnarayan operates a modest cloth shop in the Chandipur bazaar, in a small brick building of very solid, fireproof construction. He does not sell as much cloth as one or two other shopkeepers in the bazaar, and his shop is rarely crowded. Most of those who come are men seeking loans or making payments on loans which Ramnarayan has made to them. Village rumor says that he sometimes has as much as Rs. 10,000 in his shop at a time. He rarely leaves the shop, and when he does, on some financial or political errand, he is always accompanied by two or three of his gang of *laṭhiyāls*, strongarm men recruited from among his dependents in the Muslim village south of Chandipur.

Ramnarayan holds village trials at his own convenience in the open courtyard beside his shop. He beats accused thieves or adulterers until they confess, then fines them and pockets the proceeds. Refusal to accede to one of his decisions may mean a visit from the *laṭhiyals*, who might accidentally beat a man to death. There is, without doubt, much I do not know about events in Chandipur because Ramnarayan decided that no one should tell me about them. Only two villagers spoke to me freely on political subjects: a religious mendicant who had already renounced the material world, and the head of the small, independent Bhumihar lineage. Ramnarayan is an autocrat who cares little about the distinction between legitimate and illegitimate power.

The example of the village panchayat election is instructive here, as it was for Radhanagar. Early in 1960 the Block Development Officer and Panchayat Secretary informed Ramnarayan that members should be elected to the village panchayat, and that those chosen should select a member for the higher inter-village panchayat. He called a village meeting, attended largely by the tea stall politicians and family heads from the Brahman and middle-ranking caste groups. Ramnarayan named the members of the panchayat, all Brahmans save the secretary, who is a young man from a Hindu Weaver household. The young Weaver's father is a prosperous cultivator loyal to the headman; the young man himself is an ally of the Dubes. He is apparently meant to represent the lower castes and the insurgents in village politics. The Carpenters and their faction received no such concession, however. Ramnarayan chose himself as member of the inter-village panchayat and easily became president of that body. He now favors the appellation "President" more highly than his old titles of "Pradhan" and "Zamindar."

When I interviewed Ramnarayan Pradhan, he gave his age as 75 years. This was probably somewhat too high an estimate; he feels that he is aging. He has made all the preparations necessary to die, including "adopting" two of his elder brother's grandsons to light his funeral pyre and to inherit his share of the property (he had no children of his own, though he was twice married). He feels no compulsion to settle all the disputes in the village nor to make decisions about everything that affects the community.

Jagannath Mistri, under the tutelage of Lalchand Chakladar, managed to get funds from the local Community Development Block to construct a night school, ostensibly to give basic literacy classes for the Carpenters' scheduled caste employees. Ramnarayan could have interfered with this project, either by using his influence with the Block Development Officer to prevent the Communists from receiving money or simply by forbidding it. He took no action, however, and the Communists constructed the night school, which serves as a social center for the neighborhood and a credit to the "social work" of the Communist leaders in the village. The Dube brothers got a similar grant from the Community Development Block to construct a combination library and clubhouse, which serves as a social center for the politically minded young men of middle castes and the anti-headman Bhumihars. In this case also, Ramnarayan's political interest would seem to have dictated that he intervene to prevent his opponents gaining organizational advantage. Yet he did not interfere.

In his declining years, Ramnarayan seems to see political events which do not represent an immediate threat to his sovereignty as representing no threat at all. He will be dead before these projects bear their seditious fruits in the community. Thus, there is room for maneuver in Chandipur politics, based upon the age of the headman. In other tyrannies the leeway might be built into other characteristics of the tyrant's personality—his love for sports, for women, and for drink; his distaste for administration; or even his poor way with figures. But a political system of this kind, based upon unique individual personality differences, cannot be extensive nor can the tyrant's idiosyncrasies be great, or the system will fall.

SOURCES OF CLEAVAGE IN SOUTH ASIAN
VILLAGE POLITICS[2]

The point of the descriptions of political activity and political change in the preceding section is to indicate, by detailed comparison, some major differences among varieties of cleavage found in Indian and Pakistani village politics. The principal task of this section is to draw the general conclusions from the specific events. This will be done by contrasting the forms of political organization in Radhanagar and Chandipur and comparing them with forms found in other South Asian communities. In this section I consider, first, contrasts in the direction of political cleavage; second, the relation between landholding and political cleavage; and finally, the relation between caste and cleavage. Under each of these headings recent changes in village politics are examined.

The Direction of Political Cleavage

As I stated earlier, two ideal types of political conflict can be constructed: conflict between groups which are structurally equal and conflict between groups which stand in a relation of super- and subordination to one another. This is a statement in political terms of the differences between stratified and unstratified societies, between societies in which solidarity is "mechanical" and those in which solidarity is "organic." The characteristic unstratified society is a tribal or "folk" society, in which differences of wealth among economic units are not great and in which, ideally, there is little scope for individual accumulation. In such a society, political cleavages are vertical; conflict groups recruit members of descent groups to fixed genealogical depths or utilize some similar principle. The characteristic stratified society is urban and industrial; it is divided into social classes by differential relations to the means of production. Political cleavages in a stratified society, ideally, follow the horizontal lines of stratification; political conflict is between social classes. I hardly need to say that such a pair of polar types grossly oversimplifies any known political system, but this form of characterization is helpful in explaining very large contrasts between different political systems.

Peasant societies are "simpler" in some sense than stratified, urban, industrial societies; but they are also clearly more "complex" than the ideal folk society. They do not fit well into either of the ideal categories. Whatever else it may be, the caste system of South Asian villages is a system of social stratification. Given the ideal types of political conflict posited above, we might expect that political conflict in a caste-stratified peasant community would arise between castes, not between the more or less "equivalent" factions which predominate in Radhanagar and which play an important but smaller role in Chandipur. However, Bailey (1963a, p. 118), in analyzing the fundamental features of the caste system,

---

2. The line of thought implicit in this analysis, that conflict is an important part of much social action, and that dynamic features of social structure emerge from conflict, owes a great deal to the writings of Max Gluckman (for example, Gluckman, 1956), F. G. Bailey (1960), V. W. Turner (1957), and Lewis Coser (1956).

points out that structurally "the system does not allow of competition between castes." There is an important political implication contained in this characteristic of the caste system.

The absence of competition between castes is connected with the direction of political and economic relationships. All castes are corporate groups so far as ritual is concerned. But (. . . stating the rules of the game and not the way it is played nowadays) political cleavages (i.e., competitive relationships) are between vertical groups, not social strata: co-operative relationships run up and down between families in the dominant caste and families in the service castes. Only the dominant caste has an autonomous political existence, not as a corporate political group, but as a field for political competition. Certainly no subordinate caste is a corporate political group.

I shall discuss the role of caste in village politics at greater length later. The point to be made here is that, on structural grounds, caste ought not to appear as a principle organizing political conflict. The structure is more complicated than it is ideally represented, however; and, more important, it has been subjected to powerful agents of change in the recent past. To return to the question of social stratification and political cleavage: peasant societies are not tribal societies with structural equivalence between individuals or between segments. Social stratification in its less readily identifiable but more familiar form of "social class" is present, even in so equalitarian a community as Radhanagar. The difference between big men and small men is of considerable importance in the running of village affairs. The big men do not constitute a corporate group, though all or most of them may come together to compose a traditional village panchayat for the purpose of making legal or governmental decisions. The difference between big and small is clearly marked when decision-making is underway; Radhanagar society is divided by a definite horizontal line. But this horizontal division, significant for public decision-making, is not an important political cleavage in the village. The important cleavage runs through the category of big men, not between it and the category of small men.

In Chandipur, by contrast, horizontal divisions in the society are the most significant political cleavages. The clearest division is that between the headman and the remainder of the village. His authority is greater than that of the aggregate of other responsible villagers. He is the ruler; they are the subjects. There are, however, marked differences in the degrees of subjection among the villagers. Loyalty, fear, and complacency are mixed with sedition, courage, and involvement among the various factions and caste groups in the village. Many Bhumihar families have a great deal of authority over the lower-caste families which are economically dependent upon them. The Carpenters, horizontally demarcated from the Brahmans by difference in caste rank, have made significant efforts to increase their power, which implies a reduction in the scope of Brahman influence.

A clear way of bringing out the relative importance of horizontal and vertical cleavages in the politics of Radhanagar and Chandipur is by contrasting the roles of factions in the two villages. In political activity, factions resemble certain kinds of corporate conflict groups, such as lineage segments in acephalous political systems, in the important characteristic of "structural equivalence"—or perhaps I should call it quasi-structural equivalence. I mean that, although in any particular instance one faction may have more or fewer members, greater or less power than another, the factions in any arena are not functionally different from one another, as are political parties, for example. Factions, in other words, are divided from one another by vertical rather than horizontal cleavages. These divisions may originate in one social stratum and be extended to others, or they may internally divide a single group or category which is united in its external relations; but factions do not represent the interests of superordinate against subordinate or other counterpoised, stratified groups.

In Radhanagar, factions correspond rather closely to this idealized representation. Faction leaders are big men; followers are small men. Corporate group affiliations, chiefly of kinship and caste, are important but do not go far toward explaining loyalties in the community. Taken together, economic relations, residence locality, kinship, caste, and enmity dating from past conflicts can identify the factional affiliation of any follower and the position of any leader vis-à-vis the headman. Further, almost every adult male is somehow involved in a faction, thus determining the position of almost every household in village politics.

The two principal factions in Chandipur originate in competition between two Bhumihar kinship groups. The structural equivalence between these two groups is largely an anthropological fiction, since one is so much more wealthy and powerful than the other. The third faction has originated in the recent economic independence of the Carpenter caste group, which, according to structural principles, ought to be dependent and subordinate. These three factions do not come near exhausting the population of Chandipur; many families are able to avoid identifying themselves with one or another faction because the factions are of only secondary importance in the running of village affairs. Thus, while there are factions in Chandipur, they do not represent the dominant political cleavage in the community.

Another way of looking at the contrast between Radhanagar and Chandipur is to examine what happens when power is to be distributed, as occurred in connection with the establishment of the statutory panchayats in the two villages. In Radhanagar many villagers went to work organizing support, assessing relative strengths, and calculating advantages; the outcome was uncertain until all the votes were counted. In Chandipur the only person who took effective action concerning the new panchayat was the village autocrat, who held court to announce his nominees. This view of the political situations in Radhanagar and Chandipur suggests another ideal distinction between types of society, parallel to, but not the same as, the contrast between unstratified and stratified societies. The distinction here is between the conditions of maximum concentration and maximum dispersal of power in political communities. What would politics in Chandipur be like if the headman held absolute power, controlled all the land, and set all policy for village society—if all public decisions were made in his court? What would politics in Radhanagar be like if each householder in the village had equal power?

A society in which all power is concentrated in a single individual or role—a barely imaginable situation—would not constitute an arena of political conflict at all, since competition for power with an absolute tyrant is impossible. This conclusion suggests that Chandipur is not an important political arena for the headman; most of his political activity is outside the village with others of his own kind rather than inside the village, where there is little for him to gain. A society in which no person had any political advantage (a sort of Weberian classless society) would also, ideally, be free from politics, since no enduring leader-follower groups, in which leaders received greater rewards than followers, could be established. This conclusion directs attention to the shifting alignments of villagers and faction-leaders, which, in Radhanagar, accompany even minor changes in the path of personal interest.

Looking at the cleavages in Chandipur politics, then, we may say that they are primarily horizontal, running between the headman and the public, and between the Brahmans and other castes, particularly the rebellious Carpenters. There is also a major vertical cleavage, however, running between two Brahman descent groups and continuing between members of various other castes organized by them. The principal cleavages in Radhanagar, by contrast, run vertically between the various factions, both major and minor. The horizontal cleavage between "big men" and "small men" appears only when weight is given to various opinions presented to the traditional village panchayat.

LAND, POWER, AND POLITICAL CLEAVAGE

The title of this essay speaks about "South Asian villages," not only about two villages in West Bengal. This implies that there is a way of making sensible and moderately realistic statements about village political organization in all of southern Asia. In fact, there are probably several ways of making statements of this kind. Some of the most informative anthropological accounts have attempted to make generalizations about the linguistic and cultural regions into which the subcontinent is divided. Here I shall attempt to formulate general propositions in a different way: I shall divide the villages of India and Pakistan into several types based upon major features of social structure.

Recalling Nadel's criteria of social structure—"recruitment, interpersonal command, and relative command over resources and benefits"—I can now formulate a few central questions about politics in rural southern Asia. (1) How is relative command over resources and benefits allocated in a particular village? The principal resource in a peasant society is, of course, agricultural land; it is not too great a simplification to say that most benefits flow, directly or indirectly, from agricultural production. Therefore, I ask: Is control over agricultural land and its products centralized in the hands of a single individual or caste, or is this control dispersed widely throughout the society? The answer to this question has a direct bearing upon the direction of political cleavage in a society. (2) What are the locus, nature, and extent of interpersonal command in the political system of a particular village? For the villages I discuss here, the answer to this question is closely related to the way in which resources are allocated. Village politicians convert control over resources and benefits into interpersonal command; wealthy, high-caste men tell poor, low-caste men what to do and how to do it. (3) How are persons recruited into political groups in a society? Where castes or descent group segments are the principal political conflict groups in a village, recruitment is largely by birth. But politics in most South Asian villages are organized by factions which recruit their members through many and various channels.

There are two kinds of information about Indian village politics which appear to go at least part way toward answering these questions. Data about systems of land tenure, which, of course, tell us most about the answer to the first question, also shed light on the answers to the second and third. Data about individual forms of village political organization provide answers primarily to the second and third questions but also direct our attention, in answering the first question, to the importance of *de facto* rather than *de jure* interpretations of local land tenure systems.

There are two approaches to systems of land tenure which permit generalizations about the relations between landholding and political organization. The most productive approach relies on information about the distribution of holdings in the villages actually under analysis. Unfortunately, information of this kind is still not consistently reported in social scientists' accounts of Indian village politics. The second approach, which is taken here, relies upon information about land tenure which covers large portions of the South Asian subcontinent. Information of this kind has the advantage of giving breadth to generalizations about land and political organization, but it is of little use in the consideration of politics in any particular community.

Two of the three "classical" systems of land tenure found in India give us names for polar-opposite situations: the zamindari system ideally implies perfect concentration of land in the hands of a single individual; the ryotwari system is ideally characterized by a set of socially equal, independent cultivators, each the owner of the land he farms. The clarity of the ideal distinction disappears when cases are considered, however. Under both zamindari and ryotwari tenures, as well as in joint villages, all degrees of concentration or dispersal of landholdings may be found. And, in a cyclical process whereby wealthier families get more heirs and less land when they are at the pinnacle of success, a village marked by high concentration of landholding at one time may appear very equalitarian a generation or two later. Part of the difficulty in using the classical labels for land tenure systems is connected with the fact that each of these systems is concerned with a slightly different set of rights in land: the right to collect taxes or rents, the right to sell, the right to cultivate but not to sell, etc. What is important for political relations about rights in land is whether these can be made to serve political ends, whether possessing a certain set of rights makes a difference in one's interpersonal command. Clearly, where land is scarce, almost any right in land can be used to improve the command position of the holder. In looking at the three systems of land tenure which existed prior to modern changes in rural India, my concern is to show how the rights vested by these systems may be employed in village politics.

1. *Zamindari villages.* Properly speaking, zamindari is not a system of land tenure but of tax-collecting. Thus, Baden-Powell, in *The Indian Village Community* (1896), does not treat villages in which *de facto* political power is held by a zamindar, though he does examine some village systems with "traces of over-lord right" (pp. 380ff.). The reasons for this omission are multiple, but basically Baden-Powell was concerned with *de jure* rights. The East India Company, from its earliest efforts at revenue administration in Bengal, attempted, by and large unsuccessfully, to protect the legal rights of the cultivators from the great *de facto* powers of the zamindars (Baden-Powell, 1892, I, p. 393). I cannot here follow the entire historical argument showing that zamindars, who became agents of revenue under the British, were, in pre-Muslim times, "chiefs" whose original authority was primarily political rather than economic or administrative (see Moreland, 1929, p. 8). What is important is that even to the last under the British, zamindars held preponderant political power in their domains.

The term "zamindar" is misleading in that it covers such a variety of figures. A man with tax-collecting rights over only one or two villages was a zamindar; a self-styled maharaja whose domain, though a million acres in extent and including a thousand villages, was part of British India was also a zamindar. *De jure*, the two-village "zamindar" might be one of a long series of intermediaries standing between the tax-paying peasants and the man actually responsible for handing the taxes to the government. This complex picture is greatly simplified if we look at the zamindar from the point of view of the cultivator. Villagers characteristically regarded as "their zamindar" the most powerful landholder on the local scene, whether he was a true zamindar, an intermediary, or a powerful independent owner of *khās* land like the Chandipur headman. A million-acre zamindar, such as the Maharaja of Burdwan, who held ultimate tax-collecting rights over Radhanagar, could not intervene in the everyday political affairs of any individual village within his domain. Thus, paradoxically, Chandipur, a *khās mahāl*, was structurally a zamindari village, while Radhanagar, in which *de jure* zamindari rights existed, was very much like a ryotwari village.

Perhaps the best description of zamindar-peasant relations in nineteenth-century Bengal comes from a realistic novel set in a village of Burdwan District (Day, 1878, pp. 259–61):

The zamindár was a large-built man, taller than ordinary Bengalis, and proportionately corpulent. He was sitting like a lion couchant. . . . Jayachánd Ráya Chauduri (for such was the name of the zamindár of Kánchanpur) was, strictly speaking, not a zamindár, but a middle man, for he held a *Pattanitáluk* under his Highness the Maharaja of Vardhamána; but though he was only a *Pattinidár*, he was usually called the zamindár of Kánchanpur and of scores of other villages lying round about. He paid 2,000 rupees a year to the Mahárájá for the village of Kánchanpur: but it was generally believed that he himself realised in rents about three times that amount. For the whole of his zamindári, or rather *pattani*, he gave eighty thousand rupees to the Raja, but he himself has admitted that after paying the *Sadar Jamá*, his own net profit amounted to the round sum of two lakhs, or £20,000 a year. Such immense profit could only be obtained by a system of rack renting, of illegal extortion, and cruel oppression.

The activities of this evil zamindar would be of less interest if the author did not also portray the futile attempt of the peasants of Kanchanpur to organize a strike against an *abvab* being collected by him. The representation of the discussion among the peasants (significantly titled "Politics at the Smithy"), the fact that the discussion was reported to the zamindar by a spy, the shoe beating that the zamindar gave to the principal protagonist, and the subsequent burning of his house by two of the zamindar's gang of *lāṭhiyāls* all strike me as extremely realistic—they might easily be duplicated in the life history of the Chandipur headman (cf., Neale, 1962, pp. 203–205).

Chandipur and Kanchanpur are both small-scale autocracies backed up by private police forces and only vaguely sanctioned by external authority. The history of the Chandipur headman illustrates another important principle of politics under zamindari or pseudo-zamindari land tenure. The extension of the Chandipur headman's little domain had to be carried out at the expense of neighboring zamindars, particularly the Chakladar family in Maniknagar village. While the ordinary citizens of the community can direct their political ambitions only against the superordinate zamindar, the zamindar himself is involved in competition with others equal and opposed to himself, people from whom he might conceivably gain something. From the point of view of the zamindar, his domain is largely an administrative concern; extending it is a political and economic concern. In terms of a pair of ideal types established earlier, zamindari land tenure approaches the condition of the maximum concentration of power in society.

In general, the larger the domain of the zamindar, the more extensive his authority. At the same time, the larger his domain, the further removed he is from individual village political affairs. Thus, for present purposes, small-scale zamindars, intensely involved in local affairs, are the most significant. The principal political cleavage runs between the zamindar and the taxpayers, and is thus strictly horizontal. When a zamindar is not present on the local political scene, either because his domain is large or because he is an absentee landlord, the direction of political cleavages will be determined by other considerations, as has occurred in Radhanagar.

Of the multitude of changes which are being wrought in South Asian villages, I shall concern myself here with only two: land reform and voting. In general understanding, the expression "land reform" refers to a governmental attempt to alter the relation between land and cultivator in the interest of some social objective. Particular local conditions give concrete meanings to this term, so that the abolition of the zamindari system of tax-collecting is a special aspect of land reform in rural West Bengal, East Pakistan, and other parts of South Asia. Similarly, government efforts to prevent fragmentation of fields into uneconomically small units is another aspect of land reform. In both West Bengal and East Pakistan, where rural population density is exceedingly high, the goals of equalization and prevention of fragmentation are mutually contradictory.

I cannot examine here all of the details of land reform laws passed state-by-state in India and for the two wings of Pakistan.[3] The land ceiling laws, which are very significant for local power structures in rural areas, still permit individuals to hold amounts of land sufficient to guarantee their continued hegemony over individual villages. The abolition of zamindari tax-collecting deprives zamindars of a great deal of their former power. However, the fact that zamindars have been able to retain most or all of the agricultural land which they owned outright obviates some of the expected democratizing force of zamindari abolition. And there are many loopholes in the laws passed thus far which allow large landholdings to remain intact. Nonetheless, the general direction of the influence of land reforms on zamindari villages is away from autocracy. There is a contradiction between the rules for local politics implied in land reform laws and those upon which zamindari systems are based.

The effect of universal adult suffrage upon autocratic political systems is potentially very great. Elections which are of most concern to villagers are, of course, elections to local office: village panchayats in India and the bottom tier of Basic Democracies in Pakistan. The Basic Democrats in Pakistan seem to have been uniformly elected by secret ballot, which gives some substance to the voting right. In Radhanagar, voting was done by secret ballot, which affirmed the relatively great degree of political equality which existed in the community before the statutory panchayat. In Chandipur, however, the election of members to the village panchayat was not conducted by secret ballot. The "consensual" procedure for selecting panchayat members is justified in some Indian government circles by the strange assumption that villages which put on a show of unanimity in political decisions will not be split by factions.[4] Thus the Chandipur headman was given an opportunity to continue the administration of village affairs in his own way. A compulsory secret ballot in local government elections would undoubtedly hasten the devolution of political power into the hands of a larger number of villagers. Like effective land reforms, effective voting rights are contradictory to the principles of zamindari political systems.

2. *Ryotwari villages.* I have only the slimmest personal experience with villages under the ryotwari system of land tenure as it was developed under the British. Most of what I know about the political organization of these villages I have gained from reading between the lines in Volume III of Baden-Powell's *Land Systems of British India* (1892), his *Indian Village Community* (1896), and from the numerous anthropological accounts of Mysore villages where I

3. Neale (1962, pp. 211–78) examines much of the background relevant to zamindari abolition in Uttar Pradesh, including factors in the structure of village society, prior to analyzing the "accomplishments" of the legislation.

4. The lack of justification for this assumption is borne out in numerous recent accounts of village politics. For example, K. Ranga Rao (1965, p. 1375), reporting on an Andhra village in which politics are patently organized by factions, says: "Currently the village is known to be faction-ridden. . . . The present Panchayat was unanimously elected early in 1964. But it is very inactive."

believe ryotwari tenure prevailed before independence. What I say here, therefore, is tentative; I am anxious to receive further information on the kind of
political activity which characterizes ryotwari villages.

Ryotwari land tenure is, in one sense, the exact opposite of zamindari tenure.
Under the latter form, one individual is responsible for the payment to the government of all the taxes from one or more villages; under the former system,
each cultivator is individually responsible for the payment of his taxes directly
to the government. If zamindari tenure places great *de facto* power in the hands
of the zamindar, ryotwari tenure would seem to disperse power widely among
cultivating families. The effect of ryotwari revenue settlement on the village
of Namhalli in Mysore, for example, was to take control of much village land
out of the hands of the former proprietor of the village and give it to individual
cultivating families (Beals, 1955b, p. 84).

Baden-Powell's figures (1892, III, p. 142) for the old Madras presidency suggest that an average ryotwari village might have about 100 tax-paying cultivators. Besides the peasant families there would, of course, also be a number
of village servants, priests, etc., but recent accounts suggest that a majority of
the population would be made up of members of a single large cultivating caste,
or occasionally a block of such caste groups. There is no evidence that members
of these castes reckon kinship deeply, as would be expected in a segmentary
lineage political system, yet indigenous political activity seems to have been
based upon a competition of equals within the village. If this is so, then we
may presume that village councils, in one form or another, were probably significant. And perhaps from very early times these councils were divided by
what we would recognize as vertical, factional political cleavages.

This is a grossly idealized and simplified picture; I could begin to make it
more realistic by taking account of the effect of demographic factors (see Beals,
1961, pp. 31–33) or the number of village officers, either traditional or government appointed, present in the community. However, this would lead me away
from the point, which is to indicate how much like Radhanagar this ideal picture is. Baden-Powell (1896, p. 34) suggests that the indigenous tenure system
of Bengal proper (before the Mughals, and then the British, extended zamindari
tenure throughout) was ryotwari. I have no idea what evidence led Baden-
Powell to this conclusion; but, historical continuity aside, I would assign Radhanagar village without hesitation to the ryotwari type on grounds of political
structure.

Compared with the effect on zamindari villages, neither land reforms nor
voting would be expected to have a great impact upon the political systems of
ryotwari villages. Where a majority of villagers already hold agricultural plots
of limited size and no one owns a great deal more than anyone else, as is true
in Radhanagar, land reform is not an occasion for the redistribution of economic
or political power. Because no one is extremely wealthy, the relatively more
prosperous cultivators would continue to maintain dominant positions, to be
the "big men" of the community. The extension of political rights, in the form
of voting, to "small men" and to members of minority castes which previously

counted for little in village affairs might intensify old lines of cleavage between factions. Whereas under the traditional political structure the big men might fight out decisions affecting the entire community among themselves, now they are required to recruit supporters and to consciously organize factions or parties. A group of ablebodied men was previously of value to a leader only in physical conflict; given universal adult suffrage, however, followers become essential in nonviolent political conflict. Increased social and political functions for factions imply that leaders must be more attentive to the needs of their followers—that they must, in at least a marginal way, become "representatives."

3. Joint villages. From the point of view of land tenure, jointly held villages are more complex than either zamindari or ryotwari tenures. From the point of view of political structure, however, thanks to the thorough study given to acephalous segmentary political systems in Africa, joint village politics are quite intelligible to social anthropologists. And, in addition to the accounts of joint land tenure systems (Baden-Powell, 1882, 1896), we also have several recent anthropological accounts of joint villages which explicitly or implicitly make the connection between land, power, and politics (Opler and Singh, 1948; Cohn, 1959b; Barth, 1959a, 1959b; Lewis, 1958). As with the other systems described above, I am forced to present the political structure implied by joint village tenure in idealized outline here.

Two castes of northern India and West Pakistan, Jats and Rajputs, do not, or did not in the past, ordinarily partition their agricultural lands. Land was the collective property of a patrilineal descent group and was apportioned on some equalitarian principle to all household heads. On the peripheries of quasi-feudal Rajput states in medieval India (Ghoshal, 1929, pp. 234–36; Thorner, 1956, 133–43) and even within the dominions of the Muslim conquerors of northern India (Opler and Singh, 1948, p. 468) were relatively extensive estates, called mahals, held jointly by members of Jat or Rajput patrilineal descent groups. The British encouraged the continuation of these joint holdings by settling the revenue on entire mahals or upon individual villages, but making the dominant caste "brotherhood" collectively responsible for payment. Responsible men were named *nambardārs* (number-holders) and were charged with the responsibility of collecting and handing over the taxes; but these men seem to have been no more than lineage elders, *primi inter pares* (Baden-Powell, 1892, II, pp. 30, 101).

Within the dominant proprietary caste, politics seems to have functioned rather strictly on the principle of the opposition of equal lineage segments. Thus, the Thakurs or Rajputs of Senapur (also known as Madhopur; Opler and Singh, 1948, pp. 468–69; Cohn, 1961b) were divided into six structurally equivalent lineage segments, each reckoning its descent from one of the sons of the founder of the village (who was also founder of the mahal of which it was part). Three lineages compose a moiety in opposition to the other three. Several villages compose a mahal; in the taluk there are twelve mahals, each of which was originally the domain of one of the sons of the sixteenth-century apical ancestor of the group.

An interesting question is raised by the persistence of such a "tribal" form of social and political organization in a peasant society. First, it should be remembered that this description fits only the dominant caste, not any of the subordinate castes. If we follow Bailey's proposal that the dominant caste be regarded as a "field for political competition," then we may say that the Rajput and Jat unilineal descent groups serve to organize the dominant caste of a village into vertically divided segments for political conflict. This principle does not in any way obviate the subordination of lower castes to the dominant caste as a whole, nor does it hamper the development of patron-client ties between families in the dominant caste and lower artisan and serving castes.

In view of the widespread tendency for patrilineal families to partition their property within a very few generations, the persistence of joint property or joint rights of any kind over two or three centuries is remarkable. The explanation for this system may lie, initially, in the fact that the groups in which such joint holdings persist are notable militarists. The Rajputs and Jats expanded to become dominant over large parts of northern and western India by warfare. Sahlins (1961, pp. 341–42) has argued convincingly that, while segmentary lineage systems "appear at the tribal level of general cultural evolution," lineality is a principle of social structure under ecological circumstances requiring "repetitive, long-term use of restricted resources," and "a segmentary lineage system develops in a tribe that intrudes into an already occupied habitat rather than a tribe that expands into an uncontested domain." These conditions were undoubtedly met in ancient and medieval northwestern India. One effect of the British settlement of land revenue under the *mahālvāri* system in the 1820's may have been actually to strengthen lineage organization among the proprietary castes by giving the lineages legally recorded corporate property in perpetuity. This step contributed to the development of deep lineages and, thereby, fostered the system of politics which brings lineage segments into conflict with one another (Marriott, 1955a, pp. 185–86).

In many joint villages, land reforms would undoubtedly imply the distribution of land to lower castes whose members had tilled it for generations as servants. A joint village was joint only for the dominant caste, and, as Baden-Powell (1896, p. 26) has expressed it, "The idea that, *e.g.*, a body of proud Rājput co-sharers would acknowledge their cultivating tenants, and *a fortiori* the potter, the carpenter, or the *camār*, as a part of their brotherhood . . . is something quite grotesque." Thus, an expected effect of an utterly contradictory new structural rule—rights in land for subordinate castes—would be the creation of new horizontal cleavages between castes in village politics where there had been only vertical cleavages between lineage segments in the past. Similarly, voting suddenly gives political rights to members of all castes, where these had belonged previously only to dominant-caste landholders. The general consequence of recent changes in joint village political systems is a weakening of the authority of the dominant caste and a strengthening of subordinate castes. Cohn's (1955) account of the difficulties and defeats sustained by the Madhopur Chamars at the hands of their Thakurs when the Chamars attempted to take advantage of land reforms, legal protection, and voting rights is an indication of the marked disparity between expected and realized political and economic change in rural India. However, looking beyond the immediate situation to the long-term consequences of recent legislation, Cohn (1959a) forsees the development in India of something like the kind of peasant society which existed in medieval Europe.

The Dominant Caste and Political Cleavage

In his original definition of the concept of a "dominant caste" in a South Asian village community, Srinivas (1955, p. 18) emphasized four criteria of dominance: (1) numerical preponderance, (2) preponderant economic power, (3) preponderant political power, and (4) relatively high caste rank. The latter two criteria seem to me to be derivative from the first two: a village caste group is, ideally, the only caste which "has an autonomous political existence," and as the chief recipient of services from other castes, has high caste rank as a consequence of direct interaction. Later, Srinivas (1959, p. 15) added Western education and occupations to his list of criteria, but these accomplishments are directly dependent upon economic position and are not relevant to the many South Asian villages still largely unaffected by Western education. The concept of the dominant caste, as Mayer (1958, p. 425) points out, is a descriptive rather than an analytic one. But there seem to be only two essential terms contained in it: the dominant caste must be more populous than any other caste in a village,[5] and it must be economically the most powerful of the village castes; it must have these properties, that is, if it is to exercise "decisive dominance" (Srinivas, 1959, p. 15). In the absence of a numerical majority and perfect control over wealth in a village, we might say that a caste exercises "relative dominance," which implies that, in fact, most communities are characterized by several castes exercising various degrees of "relative dominance" and attempting to expand their control at the expense of other "relatively dominant" caste groups.

Bailey's structural analysis of the caste system, predicated upon the existence of an "absolutely dominant" caste at the head of a village society, suggests that the "rules" of the system preclude the possibility of competition between castes within the system. It is not necessary to construct a second model of the caste system here, basing it upon a structure of relative dominance; it seems sufficient to indicate that even in pre-British India there was undoubtedly competition for position among castes, and considerable change in rank and power between established and expanding or emerging caste groups. In the latter part

---

5. In the ideal model of a village caste system, dominance derives from a superior power alone; numbers play no necessary part in the establishment of a dominant caste. As I have suggested at various points in my argument, the significance of numerical strength is not great until the introduction of universal adult franchise elections. There may have been occasions in the past when the numerical size of a caste group was of importance, but, for the most part, the legitimacy of the rule of even a small dominant caste was rarely questioned. In the words of a Senapur Chamar leader who had received a beating from "his Thakur": "I was capable of taking revenge, but I thought BBS was my Thakur and therefore equal to my mother and father and he should not be insulted" (Cohn, 1959b, p. 87). This same village became the scene of intense Thakur-Chamar conflict as early as 1938 (Cohn, 1955, p. 70).

of the nineteenth century, intercaste competition became, in certain regions and in certain kinds of villages, a regular feature of local politics. One effect of the anti-Brahman movement in Madras, a movement related, at the village level, to the provision of economic opportunities that would make low castes independent of former Brahman patrons, may have been to solidify caste groups, healing former factional cleavages and making intercaste competition the dominant mode of political conflict (see, for example, Gough, 1955).

Bailey (1963, pp. 122–23) considers the fact that, nowadays, castes are frequently found in competition with one another, even within a single village, not to say in the wider society with which I do not deal here. In *Tribe, Caste, and Nation* Bailey (1957, pp. 211–27) examines in detail the political assertion of the Boad Outcastes of Bisipara village in Orissa. In the decline of the old order, under which the Boad Outcastes were clients of patrons in the dominant Warrior caste of the village, the Outcastes found that new economic opportunities, legislative favors, and increasing population had created the possibility for the caste group to act as a corporate political unit. "They are no longer content with the position of ritual and political subservience, which formerly the village offered them" (p. 227).

Political affairs in Chandipur village are primarily the business of the dominant Bhumihar Brahman caste group and, within that, of the powerful headman. But the economically mobile Carpenters have recently taken on a distinct political role in the village, irritating to both in- and out-of-power Bhumihar Brahman lineages. Like the Boad Outcastes of Bisipara, the Chandipur Carpenters have removed themselves from relations in which they acknowledged subordination to the dominant caste and, instead, have themselves become patrons for several families in the still lower-ranking Chandal and Jugi Weaver caste groups.

In comparing Chandipur with Bisipara, I am struck with another similarity. The Bhumihar Brahmans of Chandipur constitute 16 per cent of the village population and are the most numerous single caste in the village; the Carpenters are the second most numerous, with 12 per cent of the population. The most populous group in Bisipara is the Boad Outcastes, who constitute 22 per cent of the population; they are closely followed by the dominant Warriors, with 20 per cent. The caste demographies of these two villages, in which intercaste conflict figures importantly in local politics, contrast markedly with Radhanagar, where the dominant Mahishya cultivators constitute 77 per cent of the population. In Radhanagar it is the factions of the dominant caste which really participate in village politics; non-Mahishyas are in no position to upset the balance.

It would be a mistake to attempt to characterize politics in Radhanagar, Chandipur, or Bisipara as exclusively "factional affairs" or "caste affairs." Political leaders in Radhanagar were sufficiently concerned with the possible alignments of the small (10 per cent of the population) Muslim Weaver caste group to offer the senior man of the group a place on the Congress panchayat ticket (Nicholas, 1963, p. 28). Factional alignments in Chandipur are still almost exclusively determined by competition between different lineages in the Bhumihar Brahman caste group. And Bailey (1957, p. 194) says of Bisipara: "Division into factions starts within the Warrior caste group . . . [and] is extended into other castes mainly through attachments of individuals to the heads of two Warrior caste factions. . . ." For the Indian peasant villages considered here, politics appears to be something of a mixture of conflict between horizontally divided social strata and conflict between vertically divided factions.

There is a range of demographic patterns among village caste populations. The proportions of conflict between horizontally and vertically divided groups which go together to compose the structure of politics in any community seem to be directly related to the proportions of various castes in the population. In Bisipara and Chandipur, where intercaste conflict has political importance, the dominant caste is clearly a minority of the total village population—the Bisipara Warriors are not even the most numerous caste in the village. In Radhanagar, where there was no intercaste conflict, the dominant caste is a distinct majority of the population.

In Table 3, I have arranged information about nineteen South Asian villages according to the ratio of the dominant caste population to the population of the most numerous nondominant caste. Thus, the first village in the list is the My-sore village of Haripura, where the dominant Peasant caste composes 93 per cent of the population and the second most populous caste, the Potters, make up only 3 per cent. The final village in the list is the Madhya Pradesh village of Ramkheri, where the dominant Rajputs compose only 13 per cent of the population while the Khati Farmers make up 20 per cent.

Some villages do not fall easily into the categories established in Table 3. For example, no intercaste conflict is possible in a village like Pul Eliya, in Ceylon, where all the inhabitants are members of the Buddhist Goyigama caste, although members of other castes come into the village, both to work in the fields and to participate in rituals (Leach, 1961, p. 25). The U.P. village of Kishan Garhi was formerly dominated by a descent group of Jat landlords, who, in 1952, made up 9 of 160 village households. In recent times, however, Brahmans, composing about one-quarter of the village population, have become tenants of half the village lands. The Jats are clearly no longer dominant, but the Brahmans, when Marriott observed them, were still "trying to organize their own effective dominance over the village." In this ambiguous situation, there are both intercaste conflicts between Brahmans and Jats and sharp factional conflicts which cross-cut caste lines (Marriott, 1955a, pp. 174–85, and 1955b, pp. 103–5).

An even more elaborate story of political succession is implied in an account of the West Bengal village of Ranjana. In 1820 one of the great men of nine-teenth-century Bengal was born of a poor Brahman family in this village. Evidently, Ranjana was, at that time, dominated by the Sadgop Cultivator caste. During the lifetime of the Brahman "giant," the new wealth which came into the hands of Ranjana Brahmans evidently brought about a change in the bal-ance of power: Brahmans became, for a time, the dominant caste. During the twentieth century, control has gradually passed back into the hands of the Sad-gops, especially since the descendants of the great Brahman have left the village.

However, the numerical superiority of the low-ranking Bagdi Laborer caste has begun to be felt as a result of the elections which have been held over the past fifteen years, so that, although the village council is made up exclusively of Sadgops, there is reportedly no significant factionalism within this caste. The dominant cleavage is between the Sadgop and Bagdi castes (Chattopadhyay, 1964, pp. 35–36, 46–49, 56).

Recent changes in the situation of the dominant caste in the Mysore village of Gopalpur have resulted in a fluid and ambiguous factional system. There are fifteen castes in the village, ranging from Brahman to Leatherworker. The head-manship of the village is hereditary in the single Brahman family (less than 1 per cent of the village population). Traditionally, the headman was lord of the village, arbitrator of disputes, and spokesman and representative for the village in external relations. The grandfather of the present headman had control over seventeen villages, and his father was also very powerful. The family fortunes have dwindled, however, and at the same time the headman's political interests have shifted from the village to a wider political arena. He has established a house for his family in a nearby town "where he lives for a good part of the year" (Beals, 1962a, pp. 59–63).

Nowadays in Gopalpur, "nearly all" village families "own land and nearly all wish to own more land." "Dominance" is shared among three castes of "approximately equal status": Saltmaker (10 per cent), Farmer (45 per cent), and Shepherd (21 per cent). When a group of relatively low-caste Stoneworkers (12 per cent) bought a plot of rice land, they were attacked by a group of Farmers and Shepherds. In the post-headman era, most major political conflict is between factions, locally known as "parties." On the whole, Gopalpur politics are now very much like politics in Radhanagar, with the difference that the dominant 75 per cent of the population in Gopalpur is made up of three castes instead of one. An entry could be made in Table 3 for Gopalpur showing the Saltmaker, Farmer, and Shepherd castes as jointly dominant. I have not done this, however, because I am not certain of the meaning of "dominance" in this case (Beals, 1962a, pp. 36–44).

There is, likewise, no clearly dominant caste in the Mysore village of Namhalli; rather, 70 per cent of the villagers were of "middle class" castes, and 75 per cent of the villagers possessed enough agricultural land to live on. When Beals first studied Namhalli in 1952 and 1953, factional cleavages cross-cutting caste lines were clearly dominant in the village; a caste *cum* sectarian conflict developed, however, over the attempted reassertion of Jangama Lingayat precedence in the village (Beals, 1955a, pp. 133–39; 1955b, pp. 88–95; and 1962, pp. 262–63).

Some villages formerly held under joint, or *mahālvāri*, tenure pose special problems for the simple categories I have used in Table 3. Political cleavages in these villages, as I indicated earlier, characteristically follow the lines of seg-mentation between dominant caste descent groups (Marriott, 1955a, p. 186), especially as this segmentation is institutionalized in the formal division of the village into *tolas* (Lewis, 1958, pp. 22–26) or *paṭṭis* (Opler and Singh, 1948, p. 468; Smith, 1955, pp. 148–50; Inayat Ullah, 1958, pp. 174–76). Conflict in villages

TABLE 3

RELATIONSHIP BETWEEN CASTE COMPOSITION AND DIRECTION OF POLITICAL CLEAVAGE IN NINETEEN SOUTH ASIAN VILLAGES.

Ratio d/f[a]	Region	Village	Population (a)	No. of Castes (b)	Dominant Caste (c)	% (c) of (a) (d)	Principal Nondominant Caste (e)	% (e) of (a) (f)	Factional Conflict	Intercaste Conflict	Source
31	Mysore	Haripura	c750	3	Peasant	c93	Potter	c3	A	U	India, 1955
17	Pahari U.P.	Sirkanda	384	5	Rajput	87	Drummer	5	A	B	Berreman, 1963
9	Mysore	Morsralli	504	8	Peasant	74	Washerman	8	A	U	McCormack, 1956, 1959
8	Mysore	Dalena	707	10	Peasant	c80	Untouchable	c10	A	U	Epstein, 1962
8	West Bengal	Radhanagar	597	6	Peasant	77	Muslim Weaver	10	A	U	Nicholas and Mukhopadhyay, 1962
7	Andhra	Ratnagiri	1400	14	Peasant	c67	Harijan	c9	A	U	Ranga Rao, 1965
6	Delhi	Rampur	1080	12	Jat	60	Brahman	10	A	B	Lewis, 1958
5	West Bengal	Govindapur	677	11	Peasant	63	Potter	13	A	B	Nicholas and Mukhopadhyay, 1962
5	Mysore	Wangala	958	12	Peasant	c66	Untouchable	c14	A	B	Epstein, 1962
4	Uttar Pradesh	Khalapur	5117	31	Rajput	42	Chamar	12	A	A	Retzlaff, 1962[b]
3	Mysore	Rampura	1523	18	Peasant	42	Shepherd	15	A	B	Srinivas, 1955
1+	Mysore	Totagadde	479	8	Havik Br.	40	Cultivator	29	A	A	Harper, 1959
1+	West Bengal	Chandipur	980	19	Brahman	16	Carpenter	12	A	A	Nicholas, 1963
1-	Madras	Kumbapettai	962	18	Brahman	30	Laborer	32	U	A	Gough, 1955, 1960
1-	Orissa	Bisipara	685	22	Warrior	19	Outcaste	22	B	A	Bailey, 1957
1-	West Bengal	Ranjana	985	10	Peasant	32	Laborer	40	U	A	Chattopadhyay, 1964
1-	Maharashtra	Gaon	1421	16	Rajput	25	Maratha	34	A	B	Orenstein, 1965
1-	Uttar Pradesh	Madhopur	1852	23	Rajput	24	Chamar	34	A	A	Cohn, 1955
1-	Madhya Pradesh	Ramkheri	912	27	Rajput	13	Cultivator	20	A	A	Mayer, 1960

Notes: [a] Figures rounded to the nearest whole number.
[b] Population figures from Cornell India Project, 1955.

Key: A Conflict of this kind is reported and appears to be important.
B Conflict of this kind is reported but is apparently of secondary importance.
U Conflict of this kind is not reported.

of this kind frequently took the form of blood feud (Darling, 1934, especially pp. 95–97; Inayat Ullah, 1958, pp. 182–85). Exclusively on the basis of present caste composition, one might expect most political conflict in the West Punjab village of Tararwala to occur between the dominant Tarar zamindari caste (8 per cent) and the low-ranking but numerous Musalli (18 per cent). However, conflict is primarily between two *paṭṭī*-based factions, with a third small faction in development. Three factors seem responsible for the reported pattern of cleavage in Tararwala: (1) Land is actually held by members of several different zamindari castes, collectively termed "Jat" (probably *jāṭ*), comprising 38 per cent of the village population and occasionally intermarrying with one another. (2) Most families of subordinate *kāmīn* castes are individually tied to households of zamindari castes and, thereby, to *paṭṭīs* rather than to their village caste group. (3) Before 1947 the village was 30 per cent Hindu. The Hindus inhabited a major *paṭṭī* of the village; their departure must have worked a great change in village political alignments (Inayat Ullah, 1958, pp. 172–81).

If we can assume for a moment that the nineteen villages listed in Table 3 are somehow representative of the villages of Southern Asia, then there seem to be three major implications of the findings contained in it. (1) The dominant mode of political conflict in Indian villages is between factions. (2) Intercaste conflict is important in village politics only where the dominant caste makes up less than half of the total village population. (3) Intercaste conflict can be the dominant mode of political conflict in a village only where a subordinate caste is more numerous than the dominant caste.

To elaborate on these conclusions: (1) The dominant mode of political conflict in Indian villages is between factions. I have defined a faction as a noncorporate political conflict group, the members of which are recruited by a leader on the basis of diverse ties. Careful study of a few cases of Indian village politics has recently led Bailey to conclude that all political conflict groups in these villages are factions; that is, in no case can all leader-follower ties be accounted for on the basis of a single structural principle or a single kind of recruitment. In this study I aim not at generalizing about the nature of political conflict groups in Indian villages but rather at making a gross distinction between conflict groups which are divided from one another by horizontal cleavages, either conflicting castes or autocrats and their subjects. The frequency with which factional conflict appears in the table as an important form of political conflict suggests that, despite the distinctions among Indian villagers based upon differences in caste and wealth, villagers are more "like" than "unlike" one another, that "mechanical" prevails over "organic" solidarity in most village societies.

(2) Intercaste conflict is important in village politics only where the dominant caste is less than half of the total village population. Examination of the cases in which intercaste conflict seems to be important reveals that most of this conflict is not between castes which are in adjacent hierarchical positions but between high-ranking dominant castes and populous low-ranking castes. While competition for rank position between adjacent castes may have been an important feature of village life before the twentieth century, direct conflict

between low- and high-ranking castes, challenges to political and economic supremacy seem to be primarily features of the new order. Explanations for this change in the character of intercaste relations revolve around several changes instituted by the Indian government: (a) universal adult franchise, giving low-ranking but populous castes an element of power in the village; (b) legal privileges for members of scheduled castes; reserved seats on panchayats, in legislative assemblies, in schools, and in government offices; (c) legal protection for all villagers, which, ideally, provides recourse to the police and courts for individuals illegally punished or threatened by the dominant caste.

(3) Intercaste conflict can be a dominant mode of political conflict only in a village where a subordinate caste is more numerous than the dominant caste. This conclusion is a corollary to proposition 2 above and simply states that, where the threat from a subordinate caste under the new order is sufficiently great, where the subordinate caste has been able to realize the strength in its numbers, the dominant caste may draw together into a cohesive unit at least long enough to deal with the external danger.

SUMMARY

I have proceeded by two steps in this essay. The first was to treat, in some detail, two contrasting forms of political organization in Indian villages. In this contrast I saw some simple principles which are applicable to politics in other South Asian peasant communities. On the basis of the assumption that political activity is most fruitfully conceived of as organized conflict over public power, I began by locating the social cleavages which organize political conflict in villages. The simplest and most obtrusive contrast between types of political cleavage is seen in the opposite directions and effects of vertical cleavages, which divide structurally equivalent political groups, and horizontal cleavages, which divide super- and subordinate groups from one another.

The second step in this paper was to show the relationship between some crucial features of village social structure, found generally in South Asia, and the direction of political cleavage. The findings from this procedure can be summarized in the form of three propositions:

1. There are two factors, found repeatedly in Indian villages, which are conducive to the development of vertical political cleavages: (a) considerable dispersal of agricultural lands among cultivating families as is found, ideally, under ryotwari land tenure, and (b) a dominant caste group that is a majority of the village population. A combination of these two factors is ordinarily associated with political conflict between factions.

2. A second set of factors, often closely associated with one another, also frequently leads to vertical political cleavages; these are joint, or *mahālvārī*, land tenure, by a dominant caste group organized on segmentary lineage principles. Each of the vertically divided political groups in this case is generally composed of a patrilineal segment of the dominant caste group, often localized in a "quarter"

of a village, and its servants and dependents among the subordinate castes. Although the dominant caste in joint villages is often decisively dominant, having both economic and numerical preponderance in a village, it is not rare to find villages in which the dominant caste is less numerous than a low-ranking, traditionally dependent caste. In such instances, nowadays, horizontal cleavages between the dominant caste and low-ranking rebels are frequently found to be organizing political conflict in joint villages.

3. Political conflict between stratified groups, horizontally divided from one another, is the least frequent form in contemporary South Asian villages. Such conflict is most often associated with concentration of agricultural lands in the hands of one or a few individuals as is found, ideally, under zamindari land tenure, and/or dominance of a village by a minority caste.

In most villages there is a combination of horizontal and vertical forms of political cleavage at work at the same time. This combination of cleavages is an expression of two facts: (a) In addition to the frequently recurring structural features which permit vertical cleavages, even a small local caste group can have a significant political influence, promoting a horizontal cleavage. (b) There are economic class differences, not directly dependent upon caste, which also favor the development of horizontal cleavages. Furthermore, the variables considered under the three propositions listed above are not always interdependent, so that, for example, dispersed landholdings and a relatively small "dominant" caste may be associated in one village, while concentrated landholding and a large dominant caste may be found in another.

Of the changes which have been brought about in rural India by social and economic reform, the effects or potential effects of two seem most important. Universal adult franchise generally has a great impact upon the political systems of villages in which the dominant caste is a minority of the population. Land reforms, when they become effective, will bring major changes in the political systems of villages in which control over land has been concentrated in a small number of hands.

BIBLIOGRAPHY

BADEN-POWELL, B. H.

1892. *The land systems of British India.* (3 vols.) Oxford: Clarendon Press.

1896. *The Indian village community.* London: Longmans, Green.

BAILEY, F. G.

1957. *Caste and the economic frontier.* Manchester: Manchester University Press.

1960. *Tribe, caste, and nation: a study of political activity and political change in highland Orissa.* Manchester: Manchester University Press.

1963a. Closed social stratification in India. *Archives of European Sociology,* 4: 107–124.

1963b. *Politics and social change: Orissa in 1959.* Berkeley: University of California Press.

1965. Consensus as a procedure for taking decisions in councils and committees. In

Political systems and the distribution of power. Association of Social Anthropologists Monograph no. 2. London: Tavistock Publications.

BARTH, FREDRIK.

1959a *Political leadership among Swat Pathans.* London School of Economics Monographs on Social Anthropology no. 19.

1959b. Segmentary opposition and the theory of games: A study of Pathan organization. *Journal of the Royal Anthropological Institute,* 89: 5–21.

BEALS, ALAN R.

1955a. Change in the leadership of a Mysore village. In *India's villages.* [Calcutta] Development Department, West Bengal.

1955b. Interplay among factors of change in a Mysore village. In McKim Marriott (Ed.), *Village India.* Chicago: University of Chicago Press.

1961. Cleavage and internal conflict: An example from India. *Journal of Conflict Resolution,* 5: 27–34.

1962a. *Gopalpur: A South Indian village.* New York: Holt, Rinehart and Winston.

1962b. Pervasive factionalism in a South Indian village. In Muzafer Sherif (Ed.), *Intergroup relations and leadership.* New York: John Wiley and Sons.

BERREMAN, GERALD D.

1963. *Hindus of the Himalayas.* Berkeley: University of California Press.

CHATTOPADHYAY, GOURANGA.

1964. *Ranjana: A village in West Bengal.* Calcutta: Bookland Private Limited.

COHN, BERNARD S.

1955. The changing status of a depressed caste. In McKim Marriott (Ed.), *Village India.* Chicago: University of Chicago Press.

1959a. Madhopur revisited. *Economic Weekly,* 11: 963–66.

1959b. Some notes on law and change in North India. *Economic Development and Cultural Change,* 8: 79–93.

1961a. From Indian status to British contract. *Journal of Economic History,* 21: 613–28.

1961b. The pasts of an Indian village. *Comparative Studies in Society and History,* 3: 241–49.

CORNELL INDIA PROJECT.

1955. *The population of Rankhandi [Khalapur], Spring 1954, by caste and patti.* (Mimeographed sheet.)

COSER, LEWIS A.

1956. *The functions of social conflict.* London: Routledge and Kegan Paul.

DARLING, MALCOLM L.

1934. *Wisdom and waste in the Punjab village.* London: Humphrey Milford, Oxford University Press.

DAY, LAL BEHARI.

1878. *Bengal peasant life.* (2d ed.) London: Macmillan.

EASTON, DAVID.

1953. *The political system: An inquiry into the state of political science.* New York: Alfred A. Knopf.

1959. Political anthropology. In Bernard J. Siegel (Ed.), *Biennial Review of Anthropology.* Stanford: Stanford University Press.

EPSTEIN, T. SCARLETT.

1962. *Economic development and social change in South India.* Manchester: Manchester University Press.

FREED, STANLEY A.

1963. An objective method for determining the collective caste hierarchy of an Indian village. *American Anthropologist,* 65: 879–91.

GHOSHAL, U. N.

1929. *Contributions to the history of the Hindu revenue system.* Calcutta: University of Calcutta.

GLUCKMAN, MAX.

1956. *Custom and conflict in Africa.* Oxford: Basil Blackwell.

GOUGH, E. KATHLEEN.

1955. The social structure of a Tanjore village. In McKim Marriott (Ed.), *Village India.* Chicago: University of Chicago Press.

1960. Caste in a Tanjore village. In E. R. Leach (Ed.), *Aspects of caste in South India, Ceylon and North-west Pakistan.* Cambridge Papers in Social Anthropology no. 2.

HARPER, EDWARD B., and LOUISE G. HARPER.

1959. Political organization and leadership in a Karnataka village. In R. L. Park and I. Tinker (Eds.), *Leadership and political institutions in India.* Princeton, N.J.: Princeton University Press.

HUNTER, W. W.

1868. *The annals of rural Bengal. Volume I, The ethnical frontiers of lower Bengal with the ancient principalities of Beerbhoom and Bishenpore.* London: Smith, Elder.

HUTTON, J. H.

1961. *Caste in India: Its nature, function, and origins.* (3d ed.) Bombay: Oxford University Press.

INAYAT ULLAH.

1958. Caste, patti and faction in the life of a Punjab village. *Sociologus,* 8: 170–86.

INDIA. PLANNING COMMISSION. PROGRAMME EVALUATION ORGANISATION.

1955. *Leadership and groups in a South Indian village.* Delhi: Manager of Publications.

LEACH, E. R.

1961. *Pul Eliya: A village in Ceylon.* Cambridge: Cambridge University Press.

LEWIS, OSCAR.

1958. *Village life in Northern India.* Urbana: University of Illinois Press.

McCORMACK, WILLIAM.

1956. *Changing leadership of a Mysore village.* Unpublished Ph.D. dissertation, University of Chicago.

1959. Factionalism in a Mysore village. In R. L. Park and I Tinker (Eds.), *Leadership and political institutions in India.* Princeton, N.J.: Princeton University Press.

MARRIOTT, MCKIM.

1955a. Little communities in an indigenous civilization. In McKim Marriott (Ed.), *Village India.* Chicago: University of Chicago Press.

1955b. Social structure and change in a U. P. village. In *India's villages.* [Calcutta]: Development Department, West Bengal.

MARRIOTT, MCKIM, STANLEY A. FREED, and RALPH W. NICHOLAS.

1963. *Rank and caste in India.* Symposium presented at the annual meeting of the American Anthropological Association. (Unpublished.)

MAYER, ADRIAN C.

1958. The dominant caste in a region of central India. *Southwestern Journal of Anthropology,* 14: 407–427.

1960. *Caste and kinship in central India: A village and its region.* London: Routledge and Kegan Paul.

1965. The problem of the quasi-group. In *Anthropological approaches to the study of complex societies*. Association of Social Anthropologists Monograph no. 4. London: Tavistock Publications.

MORELAND, W. H.

1929. *The agrarian system of Moslem India*. Allahabad: Central Book Depot.

MUKERJEE, RADHAKAMAL.

1938. *The changing face of Bengal: A study in riverine economy*. Calcutta: University of Calcutta.

NADEL, S. F.

1957. *The theory of social structure*. London: Cohen and West.

NEALE, WALTER C.

1962. *Economic change in rural India: Land tenure and reform in Uttar Pradesh, 1800–1955*. New Haven: Yale University Press.

NICHOLAS, RALPH W.

1963. Village factions and political parties in rural West Bengal. *Journal of Commonwealth Political Studies*, 2: 17–32.

1965. Factions: A comparative analysis. In *Political systems and the distribution of power*. Association of Social Anthropologists Monograph no. 2. London: Tavistock Publications.

NICHOLAS, RALPH W., and TARASISH MUKHOPADHYAY.

1962. Politics and law in two West Bengal villages. *Bulletin of the Anthropological Survey of India*. 11: 15–40.

OPLER, MORRIS, and RUDRA DATT SINGH.

1948. The division of labor in an Indian village. In C. S. Coon (Ed.), *A reader in general anthropology*. New York: Henry Holt.

ORENSTEIN, HENRY.

1965. *Gaon: conflict and cohesion in an Indian village*. Princeton, N.J.: Princeton University Press.

RANGA RAO, K.

1965. Leadership in a community development village. *Economic Weekly*, 17: 1375–79.

RETZLAFF, RALPH H.

1962. *Village government in India: A case study*. Bombay: Asia Publishing House.

SAHLINS, MARSHALL D.

1961. The segmentary lineage: An organization of predatory expansion. *American Anthropologist*, 63: 322–45.

SINDLER, ALLAN P.

1955. Bifactional rivalry as an alternative to two-party competition in Louisiana. *The American Political Science Review*, 59: 641–62.

SMITH, MARIAN W.

1955. Social structure in the Punjab. In *India's villages*. [Calcutta]: Development Department, West Bengal.

SMITH, M. G.

1960. *Government in Zazzau 1800–1950*. London: Oxford University Press.

SRINIVAS, M. N.

1955. The social system of a Mysore village. In McKim Marriott (Ed.), *Village India*. Chicago: University of Chicago Press.

1959. The dominant caste of Rampura. *American Anthropologist*, 61: 1–16.

SWARTZ, MARC J., VICTOR W. TURNER, and ARTHUR TUDEN (Eds.).

1966. *Political anthropology*. Chicago: Aldine Publishing Company.

THORNER, DANIEL.
   1956. Feudalism in India. In Rushton Coulborn (Ed.), *Feudalism in history*. Princeton: Princeton University Press.

TURNER, VICTOR W.
   1957. *Schism and continuity in an African society: A study of Ndembu village life.* Manchester: Manchester University Press.

12. CASTE AND MERCHANT COMMUNITIES

LEIGHTON W. HAZLEHURST

INTRODUCTION

THERE APPEARS to be a growing consensus among those engaged in South Asian studies that the institution of caste is now, more than ever before, undergoing some fundamental changes, especially as caste is increasingly exposed to conditions generally associated with modernization. Among the more obvious factors expected to shape the future of caste in India, one must include urbanization, greater economic and political opportunity, and the implementation of both national and state policies engineered to minimize the inequities of the caste system. While it is relatively easy to delineate the factors which can be expected to shape the role of caste in the future, it is much more difficult to assess the manner in which these factors will bear upon the actual functioning of the caste system. Indeed, one might suspect from the outset that the very complexity of Indian society confounds any effort to develop general theories which would give us clear indications of the implications and direction of social change in India.

On the other hand, it is clear that progress in the fields of both anthropology and South Asian studies depends upon the development of general theories to explain otherwise unrelated facts and, further, that an important step in this direction can be gained by a systematic study, focused upon a number of communities in different regions of India, of the relationship between caste and those factors generally associated with modernity. While such an ambitious project is far beyond the scope of the discussion here, one objective of this paper is the preliminary analysis of the impact of these factors upon the structuring of caste relations among merchant communities in a single North Indian city.

The study of merchant communities might be looked upon as particularly relevant for our undertaking of the impact of modernity upon the caste system and social change in India, especially since the merchants' interest in the occupations of moneylending, banking, and trading have for centuries brought them into contact with urban centers and the ideas which emerge from such centers. Further, these occupations have long been associated with a wide range of cross-cutting social and economic relationships and, at a minimum, some form

This paper is based upon research conducted in India in 1962–63 and supported by a Research Training Fellowship from the Social Science Research Council. I wish to thank the Council for its support during both the initial period of field research in India and the subsequent period devoted to writing.

of local regulation. At the same time, the impact of these factors upon the functioning of caste among merchants is difficult to evaluate. At best, the study of merchants suggests that we should not expect uniform results, or a single response, from the interaction of caste and factors associated with modernity. In this regard, I suspect that there are few persons in the field of Indian studies who have failed to notice that, although merchants have repeatedly been exposed to an environment conducive to social change, they appear, as a whole, to be among the most conservative elements within Indian society. This would again suggest that it is important to pay close attention to the differential impact of modernity upon the structuring of caste relations among different communities and in different regions of India.

At least part of the apparent ambiguity arising from the juxtaposition of modernity and tradition among merchant communities stems from the failure on the part of the observer to differentiate between the cultural and the structural dimensions of caste. Culturally, the merchant castes might appear from without (that is, appear to non-merchants) as well as from within (that is, appear to themselves) as separate, autonomous, clearly differentiated social units. From this perspective, their distinctiveness is expressed in principles which the anthropologist has long identified with the Hindu caste system: *jāti* endogamy, considerations of ritual purity and pollution, dependence upon Brahmans for the proper performance of religious rituals, and the like. While merchants differ in the intensity with which they adhere to these principles, we are still able to identify an individual as belonging to a particular merchant caste and to arrange the castes themselves in some kind of hierarchical order on the basis of these principles. In this context, caste is most easily understood in terms of the cultural dimensions which enable us sharply to differentiate one merchant caste from another.

Beyond the acceptance and recognition of caste principles, there is a sphere of relationships reflected in the structural composition of merchant castes which appears to be in conflict with the notion that merchant castes are homogeneous social units, or isolates. What we observe among merchants in structural terms is a wide range of relationships elicited not by caste principles but by the demands of certain political and economic situations. The behavioral goal in these situations is not necessarily incompatible with maintaining the integrity of caste as defined by cultural dimensions. Yet, significantly, the situations themselves often demand the structural fragmentation of caste.

In the discussion which follows, caste will be considered in its cultural dimensions against a background of certain economic and political situations which require that decisions be made, and which seem, in some instances, to confound caste loyalties. Ultimately, our goal is to assess the significance of these situations for an understanding of the role of caste among merchant communities.

THE SETTING

The discussion in this paper is limited to a number of merchant castes of North India, representatives of which are to be found within the confines of a single city. The city itself, which we call Ram Nagar (pseudonym), is located some 130 miles northwest of Delhi, in District Ambala, Hariana (until recently a part of Punjab). Prior to the partition of India in 1947, Ram Nagar was sparsely populated and relatively insignificant. In spite of the existence of a sugar mill, paper mill, and timber market in this area, Ram Nagar was little more than a bazaar situated alongside the railroad. The significance the area did have was derived from its proximity to another town which had long been an important center for North India's small-scale brass industry.

During the years following partition, Ram Nagar took on a new shape and significance. Most notable was a rapid increase in its population. According to the census of India, the population of the city in 1961 had grown to some 51,000 persons, representing an increase of 36,000 persons during the period 1951–61. The large influx of persons into Ram Nagar was primarily the result of the resettlement of refugees, that is, Hindus and Sikhs who fled from West Pakistan following partition.

By and large the refugees who settled in Ram Nagar were businessmen, traders, and moneylenders from West Pakistan who found that their new status as refugees entitled them to certain compensations for the losses suffered in the process of emigrating from their previous homes in West Pakistan. These compensations took the form of government grants and loans intended to re-establish the refugees as shopkeepers, businessmen, and small-scale industrialists in, among other places, Ram Nagar. The most successful of these individuals, both historically and in the present context of Ram Nagar, have been members of the Khatri and Arora castes. Although they claim a traditional status of warrior (Kshatriya) in the varna hierarchy, both the Khatris and Aroras have long been engaged in commercial pursuits. Amongst Punjabi peasants, their cleverness in matters pertaining to business is proverbial. Thus, as local legend has it, "Even if a Khatri puts ashes on his head (i.e., even if he becomes a religious holyman), he will make a profit," and again, "Even if they sleep, do not trust a crow, a *kirar* (Arora) or a dog" (Darling, 1925, p. 177).

No less skillful in business matters are those I shall here identify as local merchants, individuals belonging to the Aggarwal Baniya and Sud castes who settled in Ram Nagar prior to partition and the arrival of the refugees. Perhaps the earliest and most enduring description of these local merchants can be attributed to Jean Baptiste Tavernier, whose early travels and adventures in India were recorded in an account published in 1889. According to Tavernier,

The members of this caste [Baniyas] ... accustom their children at an early age to shun slothfulness, and, instead of letting them go into the streets to lose their time at play, teach them arithmetic, which they learn perfectly, using for it neither pen nor counter, but the money alone, so that in a moment they will do a sum, however difficult it may be ... (quoted in Darling, 1925, p. 177).

Prior to partition, the local merchants had enjoyed a virtual monopoly over the occupations of moneylending, shopkeeping, and trading in both the rural and the urban areas surrounding Ram Nagar. In Ram Nagar itself, the Aggarwal Baniyas were primarily engaged as shopkeepers and commission agents, while the Suds exercised almost complete control of the timber market, in which they had invested considerable amounts of capital.

Following partition, the local merchants suddenly found themselves in competition with the equally astute, and in some cases more vigorous, members of the refugee community. The sudden confrontation of local with refugee merchants, and the ensuing economic competition, were intensified by sociocultural factors which tended sharply to differentiate the two merchant communities. Here we may mention the fact that the refugees had already begun to exhibit characteristics of social mobility, partly as the result of the influence of religious reform movements such as the Arya Samaj, and partly because partition had de-emphasized the already diminished importance attached to such elements of Hindu orthodoxy as sub-caste (*jāti*) distinctions and obeisance to Brahmans. On the other hand, the local merchant's life continued to be permeated by the strictures of Hindu orthodoxy and caste proprieties. A reflection of the confrontation of these two communities is nowhere more apparent than in the spatial arrangement of houses within the city, where one finds well-differentiated neighborhoods consisting of refugee and local households respectively. This spatial separation of the communities is complemented by a considerable degree of social exclusiveness.

SOURCES OF CREDIT

In Ram Nagar there is a further mechanism, economic in nature, which is related in an important way to the differentiation between local and refugee communities. I am speaking here of the phenomenon of credit and its impact upon the structuring of relations among merchants. Joseph Schumpeter once remarked, in a statement full of meaning for our understanding of the role of the entrepreneur in Ram Nagar:

The entrepreneurial function is not, in principle, connected with the possession of wealth, as analysis and experience equally teach, even though the accidental fact of wealth constitutes a practical advantage. . . . [an individual] can only become an entrepreneur by previously becoming a debtor (1934, pp. 101–102).

Credit has always been an important economic tool for Indian entrepreneurs, but the function of credit in the city of Ram Nagar is significantly different from that historically associated with the activities of merchants in rural areas, in respect both to the individuals involved in creditor-debtor roles and to the kind of security which enables one to enter creditor-debtor relationships. In contrast to rural areas, where one finds merchants lending money, with farmers as their principal debtors, in Ram Nagar, just as for Schumpeter's entrepreneur, it is *the merchant himself* who wishes to become a debtor (that is, to gain the use of another's capital).

Both refugee and local merchants find credit essential to the entrepreneurial function. Yet the conditions which enable a merchant to establish credit in Ram Nagar are not so obvious. In large part this is due to the fact that many of the objective measures of wealth and status, such as land and property, are not reliable indices of real security, without which one is unable to receive credit. The diminished value of land and property as objective measures of security has come about as the result of basic legislation, such as land reform in the rural areas and tenancy regulations in regard to urban property holdings.

Legislative acts, historical circumstances, and sociocultural differences all contribute to creating divergent sources of credit for the merchants in Ram Nagar. Generally speaking, it is possible to isolate two forms of credit in the city, *legal* credit and *social* credit. The ability of an individual to exploit these forms of credit is largely dependent upon his ability to manipulate the structural features of his own community. Legal credit is based upon the fact that refugee merchants enjoy certain benefits as a result of their special status as refugees. The benefits, as we have seen earlier, have come in the form of specific economic incentives introduced by the government to rehabilitate the refugee population and to give impetus, at the same time, to the development of small-scale industry in Ram Nagar. It was an acceptance of this status of refugee, rather than the caste status of Khatri or Arora, which helped one to secure "electric connections, quotas for raw materials, import and export licenses, railway priorities, etc." (Ministry of Rehabilitation, 1949–1950, pp. 4–5). Small-scale industry in Ram Nagar, as elsewhere in Punjab, became "a means of employment of displaced persons" (Punjab Government, 1957, pp. 1–2). The allocation of government loans, raw materials, machinery, and shops was offered by the government, acting in the role of creditor. To qualify as a debtor, one had to be a refugee, a status which, as we have already seen, is accompanied by a particular historical experience and "style of life."

For local merchants, as for refugees, the determinants of credit are to be found in adherence to a particular status. But unlike that of the refugees, which is defined by relationships with an external governmental bureaucracy, the local merchants' status is derived from relationships with others of their own community. These relationships are inextricably related to the phenomenon of social credit, which, for the local merchant, is neither *ad hoc* nor based upon security provided by the possession of land and property. Rather, the local merchant's access to social credit is derived from his ability to manipulate the internal features of the social structure of his own community.[1]

Social credit provides a basis for the local merchant to secure loans at low rates of interest and also to obtain certain concessional privileges within the local community which are not available to refugees. An example of concessional privileges is found in the common practice by which a local merchant of good standing will bid at auction for a quantity of raw materials being sold on the "open" market but will actually pay considerably less than the amount he publicly bids. A local merchant is considered to be entitled to such concessional rates from the local capitalist whose raw materials he buys on credit, while the

---

1. For a more detailed account of the determinants of legal and social credit for the merchants of Ram Nagar, see my *Entrepreneurship and the Merchant Castes in a Punjabi City* (Monograph no. 1, Programs in Comparative Studies on Southern Asia, Duke University, 1966).

refugee is not. Thus, while such economic transactions are theoretically open to all, they are in fact closed to those who, by virtue of their status, fail to qualify for social credit and concessional rates.

The phenomena of social credit and concessional rates are probably widespread among merchants throughout India. Thus the author of one of the few studies of Indian merchants reports:

The cotton traders of Indore, who are also bankers, kept with them a piece of cloth, and whenever a trader wishes to transact some business with another, he spreads the cloth over his hands and brings the other party's hands also under the same cloth. Then the two proceed to talk in a quaint language, the actual offer of a transaction is made under the secrecy of the cloth, while the rejection or acceptance is made verbally. So that even if one is hearing the conversation near by, he can have no idea as to the size or price of the bargain (Jain, 1929, p. 91).

The significance of legal credit, social credit and concessional rates, then, is that they serve the function of selectivity among the merchants in Ram Nagar and further strengthen the cleavages between local and refugee communities.

My objective thus far has been to set forth characteristics of the city of Ram Nagar and to cite the significant features which differentiate the two merchant communities within the city. In focusing attention upon these features, I have purposely limited the scope of analysis to the broad lines of community affiliation, while excluding from analysis the equally important cleavages within both the local and the refugee communities. This internal fragmentation of merchant communities is brought about by occupational specialization and by the fact that individuals within a single community experience varying degrees of success in their attempts to obtain credit from a common source. The implication of these factors can best be seen if we turn our attention at this point from the broad lines of community affiliation to a closer look at the internal composition of a given merchant community. The purpose in the next section of this paper is, first, to examine in more detail the make-up of a specific merchant community, in this case the local community of Aggarwal Baniyas and Suds, and, second, to set forth the relatively unstable points of articulation and discord within the community which become apparent in the light of specific situations requiring economic and political decisions.

CULTURAL AND STRUCTURAL DIMENSIONS OF THE LOCAL MERCHANT COMMUNITY: AGGARWAL BANIYAS AND SUDS

The Aggarwal Baniyas of Ram Nagar are orthodox Hindus who view others in terms of a rigid interpretation of the concepts of purity and pollution. As is customary among orthodox Hindus, the Baniyas are strict in their commensal relationships and marry only within the confines of their own caste, or *jāti*. Among the more important exogamous *gotras* (clans) in the area of Ram Nagar are the Goyel, Garg, Bansal, Kansal, Mittal, Singal and Kaushal. In addition, the Jains fall into the category of an Aggarwal *gotra*, as they provide eligible marriage partners for other Aggarwal Baniyas.

There are also low-caste Aggarwals known as *gaṭṭas* with whom the others will not marry and with whom high caste Aggarwals will neither eat nor smoke. Individuals are relegated to this status for having committed one of the following violations of kinship and caste rules: (1) incest; (2) marriage of a younger brother to the wife of a deceased elder brother; (3) selling a daughter for prostitution; and (4) marriage of a daughter into a lower caste.

It is generally accepted by others that the Aggarwal Baniyas are of Vaishya (merchant) status in terms of the traditional varna hierarchy. Thus they are ranked below the Brahmans and Kshatriyas but above the Shudras. Legendary history does not confirm a ritually high status for the Baniyas; in fact, some origin myths indicate a common ancestry with Chamars (Untouchable leatherworkers). Regardless of legendary history, the fact remains that the Baniyas do occupy a ritually high status in the area of Ram Nagar. In large part, this status is derived from Brahman-Baniya relationships. Traditionally, the Baniyas, as village money-lenders, traders, and urban merchants, contributed to the material welfare of the Brahmans in their pursuit of the priestly profession; that is, the Baniyas provided land and food for Brahmans in exchange for the Brahmans' validation of a ritually elevated status for the Baniyas.

The principles just outlined above, of *jāti* endogamy, recognition and acceptance of the *gotras* within the *jāti*, and a sense of common historical origins and ritual status, all contribute to defining the boundaries of the Baniya caste on the basis of cultural dimensions. So, too, does the status of *gaṭṭa*, to which one is relegated for transgressing these boundaries.

Yet from another perspective, a structural one involving occupational organization, the Baniyas cannot be considered as an isolate, for members of the caste are, in fact, engaged in a number of different occupations. Basically these occupations fall within the categories of shopkeeping and employment as timber merchants. As shopkeepers within the city of Ram Nagar, the Baniyas are largely self-employed grain merchants, general merchants, and cloth merchants. On the other hand, Baniya timber merchants are engaged as middlemen between the forest lessees (the Suds; see below) and those, such as saw millers and paper millers, who utilize wood or wood products in the manufacturing of specific items.

The occupational differentiation between Baniya shopkeepers and Baniya timber merchants is based primarily on differences in relative wealth and the volume of credit to which one has access; that is, Baniya shopkeepers are, as a whole, less wealthy and have fewer opportunities to obtain credit than do Baniya timber merchants. In other terms, all Baniyas would like to be timber merchants, but only some have managed to become merchants in fact.

As the distinction between refugee and local merchants is reflected in separate residential areas, so Baniya shopkeepers and timber merchants also live apart from one another. While Baniyas reside within a single ward of the city, each group of occupational specialists maintains its own residential area within the ward, with shopkeepers living less ostentatiously than timber merchants.

This sketch of the cultural and structural dimensions of the Aggarwal Baniya caste illustrates two points of equal importance: First, we can observe the manner in which Baniyas are considered an isolate within the local community, on the basis of the recognition and acceptance of, and adherence to, certain caste principles which differentiate members of this caste from members of all other castes. Second, we can observe that when we specify an economic context, neither the Baniyas themselves nor outsiders (that is, non-Baniyas) regard caste principles, as reflected in the concept of Baniyas as an isolate, as the primary motivation for economic decision-making. In situations involving economic decisions, it is not the fact that one is recognized simply as a Baniya that is of primary importance, but rather whether one is, in fact, a Baniya shopkeeper or a Baniya timber merchant. The distinction becomes clearer if we now consider the role of the Suds, the other caste which is a part of the local merchant community.

The Suds are, numerically speaking, a caste minority in Ram Nagar. Members of the caste settled in the city some fifty years ago, when they helped to initiate the development of the timber market there. Prior to that time they were engaged in mercantile pursuits and agricultural moneylending, primarily in the area of Hoshiarpur, Punjab. The Suds are proverbially acute and prosperous businessmen who have traditionally occupied a socio-ritual status inferior to that of the Aggarwal Baniyas.

In Ram Nagar, the Baniyas continue to perpetuate, amongst themselves, stories of the low-caste origin of the Suds. Popular among the Baniyas is the myth which portrays the Sud as the bastard offspring of a Baniya woman who, in her quest to have a son, had sexual relations with an unknown man. Later, the man was revealed to be a Muslim, and the Baniyas, on hearing this, refused to accept the offspring into the caste, calling it simply a Sud. It should be noted, however, that the Baniyas are not eager publicly to confront the Suds with this account, while the Suds themselves claim to be Kshatriyas, and therefore of a higher status than the Baniyas.

The Suds, while numerically insignificant, are generally acknowledged to be the wealthiest persons in Ram Nagar. Much of their capital has been invested in the timber business through the process of obtaining government leases to forest areas. While the Suds do not actually "own" the forests, they do lease the rights to the timber. They have been successful in this business for two very simple reasons: first, they have enough capital to outbid their competitors at government auctions, and, second, they are wealthy enough to survive the risks involved in the timber business, including forest fires and losses incurred in the process of transporting timber from the hill regions of northern India to Ram Nagar by a series of rivers and canals.

Baniya timber merchants, in turn, obtain the timber from the Suds on the basis of social credit and concessional privileges, to which they are entitled as members of the local merchant community, and then sell it to others who utilize timber or wood products in their businesses. In their capacity as middlemen, the Baniyas are dependent upon the Suds for the success of their business, and together they monopolize the timber market in Ram Nagar. It is this relationship between the Suds as forest lessees and the Baniyas as timber merchants that unites these two local merchant castes in a mutually satisfactory economic network.

In addition to common economic interests in the timber market, the Baniyas and Suds are spatially united by the fact that the houses of Sud forest lessees are located within the same residential area, or ward, of the city adjacent to those of Baniya timber merchants and thus separate from the dwellings of Baniya shopkeepers. The fact that both Suds and Baniyas reside within the same ward has important implications in terms of the structuring of political power within the local merchant community, and indeed within the entire city. The implications can best be seen if we take a close look at a situation which demands both political and economic decision-making, as, for example, the election of a member to the Ram Nagar Municipal Committee from within the ward inhabited jointly by Suds and Baniyas.

The Election of a Committeeman from the Local Merchants' Ward

Three candidates were nominated from the merchant ward during the Ram Nagar municipal election, held in January, 1961. One was to be elected to represent the ward on the municipal committee. The caste affiliations of the three candidates were respectively Sud, Aggarwal Baniya, and Sikh.

The Sud candidate was a forest lessee who resided in an area of the ward inhabited by others engaged in the timber business. The Baniya candidate was a grain merchant (shopkeeper) who resided in an area occupied by other local shopkeepers. The Sikh was in many respects an uninfluential marginal candidate, employed in service, who also resided with the shopkeepers. Both the Baniya shopkeeper and the Sud claimed to be political independents, while the Sikh backed his candidacy with claims of allegiance to the Congress Party.

The conspicuous absence of a Baniya timber merchant from among the candidates is significant, as was the absence of a candidate from among a small group of Harijans who cast their votes in municipal elections along with the merchants. The former group could have offered a candidate but declined, while the latter group was apparently unable to offer any candidate. However, both Baniya timber merchants and the Harijans played a significant role in the outcome of the election.

The Sud was the victorious candidate from within the merchant ward. He was supported by, in addition to other Suds, two segments of the ward; the Baniya timber merchants and the Harijans. Both voted for the Sud for what were, apparently, purely economic reasons. The particular Sud who was elected, and who is, incidentally, the wealthiest of the small group of forest lessees, was elected on the basis of the economic power which rested in his hands, both as an individual and as a representative of other Sud forest lessees.

The Suds in their capacity of forest lessees determine both the rate of sale and place of sale of the timber which the Baniya merchants depend upon for their business. In addition, as we have seen earlier, Baniyas depend upon the concessional rates and social credit which the Suds extend to Baniya timber merchants during the auction of timber in the Ram Nagar market. It was thus clearly in the interests of the Baniya timber merchants to support the Sud candidate rather than to nominate a candidate of their own or to support the Baniya shopkeeper, even though the latter was a member of their own caste. This decision of the Baniya timber merchants was encouraged by a rumor circulated by the Suds and interpreted by the Baniyas as an economic ultimatum: "Elect the Sud, or prepare yourselves for a financial disaster." The fact that a large auction of the Sud's timber was scheduled for shortly after the election encouraged the open support of the Sud candidate by Baniya timber merchants. The point to be emphasized is that the sense of loyalty to one's caste fellows was clearly nonoperative. More precisely, the notion of the Baniya caste as an isolate, defined on the basis of cultural dimensions, seemed relatively unimportant when certain members of the caste were faced with a situation requiring a decision which they were convinced would affect the future of their economic relationships with the Suds.

On the other hand, the Sud exercised no comparable control over Baniya shopkeepers, as the pursuits of shopkeepers are, for the most part, independent of the activities of forest lessees. This factor was apparently responsible for the large number of votes captured by the Baniya grain merchant from other shopkeepers. Had the Baniya timber merchants voted for their own caste member, he would easily have won the election. However, since they did not, the election was closely contested and the deciding votes were cast by the Harijans, who found themselves in the position of arbiters and who, correspondingly, sought their share of the campaign wealth. The Sud managed to capture the votes of the Harijans purportedly with the help of cash bribes. The Baniya shopkeeper, a man of modest means, could offer no comparable inducement to gain the votes of the Harijans.

Finally, the Sikh candidate was for all practical purposes defeated at the outset, having no substantial support and receiving far fewer votes than either of the other two candidates.

IMPLICATIONS OF THE ELECTION

The Sud, as the elected member to the municipal committee from the merchant ward (and also, incidentally, the committee chairman does, in a broad sense, represent the interests of the timber market and, to a lesser extent, the interests of the entire local merchant community. Yet the fact that a Sud was elected to represent the merchant community, rather than a Baniya, reflects not consensus on the part of the local community but the cleavages within it. The Sud required the support of the Baniya timber merchants not only as a means of expressing the structural bonds which unite individuals engaged in the timber business as opposed to others, but also as a means of expressing the basic distinction between Baniya timber merchants and Sud forest lessees as separate cultural units within the timber business itself. The former were implicitly coerced by the latter to support the Sud candidate, rather than a member of their own caste, on the threat of economic reprisal. In this regard, the election results reflect most clearly an act of entrepreneurship rather than an attack upon the caste system. Structural networks of interpersonal relations which cut across caste boundaries in this case have not appreciably altered caste principles as defined by cultural dimensions. The Baniya caste remains a cultural isolate, while at the same time situations demanding economic and political decisions have brought about the structural fragmentation of the caste.

CONCLUSIONS

One of the objectives of this paper has been to make clear a basic, but often neglected, distinction between the cultural and structural dimensions of caste. The distinction is a crucial one for an understanding of the role of caste among the merchants of Ram Nagar and is reflected in the fact that merchants participate in numerous cross-cutting social relationships and pursue diverse economic interests while still maintaining the cultural boundaries of caste.

When discussing the cultural dimensions of caste I was primarily concerned with the principles of the Hindu caste system, and as such my task was one of classification. For example, I was interested in the criteria which enable one to distinguish between Baniyas and Suds and, further, to differentiate members of the local merchant community from refugee merchants. In this connection it was seen that the status of "merchant" is, in a broad sense, associated with what Barth (1962) has called a "summation of part-statuses." Thus Baniyas and Suds, while separate cultural units for some purposes, are also able to align themselves as a local merchant community in opposition to the refugee community composed of Khatris and Aroras. Further, we saw that certain economic factors, such as the sources of credit available to merchants, tend to reinforce the broad cleavage between refugees and locals. The former are granted access to what I have termed legal credit, derived from their status as refugees, while the latter rely almost exclusively upon social credit, derived from status achieved within the local community and associated with certain concessional privileges.

But in shifting attention to the structural dimensions of caste it was found that caste is, in fact, a network of "substructures" (Bailey, 1960), rather than a number of self-contained caste isolates or cohesive communities. When attention was focused upon specific contexts, or situations, it was seen that members of a caste find themselves confronted with events which give rise to cleavages within a single caste as well as to alliances between members of different castes. This was illustrated by reference to the local merchant community, within which structural fragmentation is brought about by occupational specialization and differential access to a common source of credit. Here we found that Baniyas do not respond to economic and political situations as a single entity but are, rather, drawn apart by different, if not conflicting, interests. This is clearly the case in the structural alliance which developed between Baniya timber merchants and Sud forest lessees and which was perhaps best reflected during the municipal election held in Ram Nagar.

The distinction between structural and cultural dimensions of caste might help to clear up some of the confusion which consistently accompanies the discussion of social change in India. Generally, our understanding of change is clouded by the tendency to fuse different levels of analysis and to consider caste as a whole rather than as a composite of tenuously articulated parts. As a result, our picture of the process of social change is distorted: we tend to equate social change with the dramatic leap to Westernization, Sanskritization, modernization, and the like; otherwise, we are not convinced that there has been any social change.

This leads back to a second objective of this paper, which was to assess the significance of the relationship between factors of "modernity" and the functioning of the caste system among merchants. Earlier, I delineated some of the more obvious factors expected to shape the role of caste: for example, urbanization, greater economic and political opportunity, and the implementation of legislation engineered to minimize the inequities of caste. I would conclude that the impact of such factors has been far from uniform. Further, while these factors do create structural relationships which reach across caste boundaries among merchants, there is no comparable evidence to suggest that the caste principles which define these boundaries have been altered. To assume that such alteration should occur is again to confound the structural and cultural dimensions of caste.

On the other hand, it is equally clear that cross-cutting social and economic relationships do indeed alter the structure of caste among merchants. As new economic and political opportunities arise in Ram Nagar, members of the merchant castes continue to express what they consider to be appropriate responses to meet the exigencies which accompany these opportunities. As a result, new structural alignments continue to form within and between the merchant castes of Ram Nagar. These alignments reflect the results of entrepreneurship rather than attempts to subvert the caste system. The evidence which I have presented suggests that this process bears little relationship to the broadening of horizontal bonds between castes, or *jātis*, and corresponding loss of caste consciousness, such as would be reflected, for instance, in the frequent occurrence of inter-*jāti* marriages. Quite to the contrary, the process is accompanied by a persistent cultural gulf between newly found allies. What is of significance in terms of cultural change is that the process of structural change creates corresponding cultural gaps between caste fellows, as occupational specialization, differing degrees of success in obtaining credit, and intensified entrepreneurial efforts on the part of merchants in Ram Nagar further emphasize the cleavages within caste. For example, amongst the Aggarwal Baniyas, while all unmarried members of the opposite sex who meet the qualifications for marriage as defined by kinship principles and *jāti* endogamy are eligible marriage partners, some are, in fact, "more eligible" than others. The factor of selectivity in matters pertaining to the selection of marriage partners, to the performance of religious rituals, and to the interpretation of caste precepts within the Baniya caste is becoming more obvious as greater individuation becomes associated with entrepreneurial skills. In fact, we might postulate that this process follows rather closely Durkheim's (1933) notion of the transformation from mechanical to organic solidarity. Rather than a general process of cultural inclusiveness which extends across caste boundaries, we witness a greater degree of exclusiveness within these boundaries.

In concluding, I would hasten to add that the method of analysis used in this paper may not be applicable to the data collected by others who have worked with different castes and in different areas of India. It may well be that my conclusions are unique to Ram Nagar, or to merchant castes, or that they are characteristic of urban life as contrasted to village life. In this regard, it is apparent that only through a comparison of a number of unrelated communities in different regions of India can we arrive at any meaningful general theories concerning the processes of cultural and social change in India. What I have done in this paper represents no more than a step in that direction.

BIBLIOGRAPHY

BAILEY, F. G.
1960. *Tribe, caste and nation.* Manchester: Manchester University Press.

BARTH, FREDRIK.
1962. The system of social stratification in Swat. In E. R. Leach (Ed.), *Aspects of caste in South India, Ceylon and Northwest Pakistan.* Cambridge: Cambridge University Press.

DARLING, MALCOLM.
1925. *The Punjab peasant in prosperity and debt.* Oxford: Oxford University Press.

DURKHEIM, EMILE.
1933. *The division of labor in society.* Glencoe, Ill.: The Free Press.

INDIA MINISTRY OF REHABILITATION.
1949–50. *Report on the working of the Ministry of Rehabilitation.* New Delhi: Government of India.

JAIN, L. C.
1929. *Indigenous banking in India.* London: Macmillan.

PUNJAB GOVERNMENT.
1957. *Financial assistance for the development of small-scale industries in the Punjab.* Publication no. 2, Chandigarh, Punjab.

SCHUMPETER, JOSEPH A.
1934. *The theory of economic development.* New York: Oxford University Press.

13. CHANGING LEGAL CONCEPTIONS OF CASTE

MARC GALANTER

IT IS A COMMONPLACE that the Constitution of India envisages a new order as to both the place of caste in Indian life and the role of law in regulating it. There is a clear commitment to eliminate inequality of status and invidious treatment, and to have a society in which government takes minimal account of ascriptive ties. Beyond this the Constitution is undetailed and in some respects unclear about the posture of the legal system with respect to role of the caste group in Indian life.

In this paper I hope to elucidate some features of the relation between caste and law by considering the ways in which the law conceives of the caste group. The legal characterization of caste is of some interest as a reflection of the views of an important and influential group in Indian society. Second, it is of some historical importance, since there is evidence that the legal system is a powerful disseminator of notions about the various groups in Indian society and may affect their self-image and the image others have of them.[1] Finally, it is of great practical importance, for, on the one hand, the Indian government is committed to the abolition of certain features of caste[2] and the legal system places restrictions on the powers of caste groups, on governmental recognition of caste, and on claims that can be made in the name of caste standing; on the other hand, religious groupings and voluntary associations enjoy constitutional protections, and government is committed to allowing them free play within broad limits.[3] The extent to which caste groups are legally characterized as religious or voluntary groups may have considerable practical import. And, to the extent that these legal notions influence behavior, the legal characterization of the caste group may be an influential factor in the contemporary reform and reorganization of Hinduism and of Indian society.

In order to describe the judicial conceptualization of the caste group, I propose to use four models. These models represent different ways of visualizing caste groups and their mutual relations.[4] All of them are employed by courts

An earlier version of this paper was prepared for a seminar on Religion and Politics in South Asia held in Colombo in July, 1964, and has appeared in D. E. Smith (Ed.), *South Asian Politics and Religion* (Princeton, N.J.: Princeton University Press, 1966).

1. For example, McCormack (1963) suggests that the notion of a unitary Lingayat group with a single distinctive culture appeared as a result of the application of the Anglo-Hindu law and British judicial administration.
2. Constitution of India, Arts. 15(1), 15(2), 16(2), 17, 23, 29(2).
3. Constitution of India, Arts. 19, 25, 26, 29, 30.
4. This paper does not address itself to the question of the geographical spread and boundaries of the units that are called castes; for example, whether they are village groups, local

in dealing with concrete issues. Often the judicial response to an issue may employ more than one of these models of approaches. It is probably unnecessary to emphasize that the "models" discussed here exist in the eye of the present beholder. Courts do not often speak explicitly in these terms. It is my contention that the models are demonstrably but implicitly present in the work of the courts (and legislatures). The models point to different ways of visualizing the caste group and prove useful in describing recent changes in the legal view of caste.

The first model sees the caste group as a component in an overarching sacral order of Hindu society. Hindu society is seen as a differentiated but integrated order in which the different parts may enjoy different rights, duties, privileges and disabilities; these are determined by the position of the caste group in relation to the whole. We may call this the *sacral* view of caste.

In contrast to this is what we might call the *sectarian* view, which sees the caste as an isolable religious community distinguished from others by idiosyncratic doctrine, ritual, or culture.[5] It is a self-contained religious unit, disassociated from any larger religious order. The rights and duties of the group and its members follow from its own characteristics, not from its place in a larger order. Where the sacral view visualizes castes as occupying the various rooms, shrines, courtyards, and outbuildings of the great labyrinthine temple of Hinduism (to each of which is attached special prerogatives and disabilities), the sectarian view visualizes castes as a series of separate chapels under independent management. In the sacral view, the rights and duties of a caste (or its members) can be determined by its relation to the whole (or at least to its surroundings); in the sectarian view, they can be described by reference to its own internal order. It is the difference between a ward in a great and dense city, and a self-sufficient small town.

Both these views characterize caste in terms of religious factors.[6] The second pair of views is secular, not in the sense that they omit religion entirely, but because they do not give it a central place. The first of this second pair might be called the *associational* view of caste. Here, the caste is seen as an autonomous association with its own internal order and rule-making powers, but characterized neither by a fixed place in some larger religious order nor

---

endogamous groups, regional networks, whether they contain endogamous subgroups, etc. My general impression is that the courts have made little distinction between these kinds of "castes." I suspect that there may be some differences in the kind of groups involved in different sorts of cases, a suspicion that I hope to confirm upon a recheck of the cases. I have followed the designation and spelling of the courts in referring to castes, tribes, and sects.

5. In employing the term "sectarian" it is necessary to resist both the connotation that such groups have been "cut off" from some larger body and the implication that such groups are associated with a distinctive and precise doctrine.

6. Western and Indian writers alike disagree about the "religious" character of caste groups. To some they are the very units of Hinduism; to others they are "purely social," with only an accidental relation to Hinduism. I shall not attempt any reconciliation of different views of "religion," I have not attempted to define "religon" or "religious," but have been content to call "religious" those characterizations of caste that involve such rubrics as religion, worship, sacred, denomination, Hinduism, impurity, pollution, etc. References to castes in terms of clubs, associations, corporations, economic and educational level, political influence, etc., I have deemed nonreligious.

by distinctive and idiosyncratic religious beliefs or practices. It is a body with its own principles of affiliation and its own internal order. These may be in some respects like those of a corporation, a club, a dissenting church (in English law), or some other voluntary association, but they render the caste a form of association *sui generis*. The nature of the tie is not characterized solely or conclusively by religious fellowship. The bonds of association may include religious ones, but the religious tie is only one among a constellation of affinities. As is the case with the sacral view of the caste group, the associational view avoids characterization in terms of specific religious factors. And in common with the sectarian view, it does not identify the caste by its standing in a differentiated religious order of society. The sacral view regards the caste group in terms of its relation to the larger body of Hinduism; the sectarian view sees it in terms of its own religious distinctiveness; the associational view defines caste in terms of its associational bonds, which may include religious features, although they are not conclusve in identifying or characterizing it.

Recently, we find evidence of a fourth view of caste, which I call the *organic*. Here, the caste group is seen as occupying a particular place in a social order made up of many such groups. This place is determined by a certain level of resources and attainments relative to other groups in the society. As does the sacral model, this view characterizes the caste group in terms of its relative standing in a larger whole. But this organic view sees the standing of a caste as determined, not by its possession of Hindu ritual values as does the sacral view, but by its share of mundane accomplishments and resources. It does not take religious factors as the sole or primary determinant of the nature of the caste group; in this respect it resembles the associational view. But, this organic view, in contradistinction to both the associational and the sectarian views, does not see the caste as an isolated or idiosyncratic entity.

These models may be schematized as on the following chart:

		Characterization of the group in terms of its position in the larger society		
		Yes	*No*	
Conclusiveness of religious factors in characterizing the group	Yes	SACRAL View	SECTARIAN View	Religious Views
	No	ORGANIC View	ASSOCIATIONAL View	Secular Views
		Holistic Views	Segmental Views	

In order to trace the changing judicial conceptualization of caste, I propose to examine several kinds of cases in which caste comes before the courts. The matters I have chosen are (1) the administration of "personal law"; (2) the recognition of claims for precedence and for the imposition of disabilities; (3) the recognition of castes as autonomous self-governing groups. After briefly suggesting the judicial characterization of caste that prevailed in each of these fields in the latter days of British rule[7] in India, I shall attempt to trace developments since independence to show the emerging judicial view of caste.[8]

THE OLD REGIME

Personal Law

The Hindu law applied by the courts in matters of "personal law"[9] did not address itself to the multitude of caste groups, but recognized only the four varnas (and occasionally the intermediate classes of classical Hindu legal theory).[10] This law contained a number of instances in which different rules were to be applied to members of different varnas—in most cases one rule for the three twice-born varnas and a different rule for the Shudras. The most notable of these differences were in the law of succession, the law of adoption and, the law of marriage.[11] With limited exceptions, marriages and adoptions among members of different varnas were not valid at all. In order to apply these rules which differed according to varna, it was necessary for the courts to determine which castes and individuals were included within which varna. The assignment of standing in the four-varna system to actual castes presented an opportunity for eliciting legal recognition of the ceremonial status of the group and certification of its claims for higher status.

The courts developed several kinds of tests to determine the varna standing of particular castes. One was the listing of certain diagnostic customs, for example, admission of illegitimate sons to commensality and marriage within the group and the prevalence of second marriages for widows, marked the group

7. By this I mean the period since the consolidation of the modern legal system, which can be dated about 1860.

8. The developments described here are at the higher and more authoritative levels of the legal system. In describing the development and application of doctrine by legislatures and higher courts, it is not intended to imply any one-to-one correspondence between the pronouncements of these higher authorities and the day-to-day operations of magistrates, officials, and lawyers, and much less the lay public. In the long run, however, the higher courts' pronouncements not only tend to reflect what the officials and the public are doing but are uniquely influential, first, by disseminating influential "official" conceptions of caste which have an impact on the caste system and, second, by deflecting behavior toward conformity with the doctrines they promulgate.

9. Under the legal system which the British established in India, all persons were subject to the same law in criminal, civil, and commercial matters. However, a group of matters that might roughly be described as "family law"—marriage and divorce, adoption, joint family, guardianship, minority, legitimacy, inheritance and succession, and religious endowments—was set aside and left subject to the laws of the various religious communities. The applicable law in these fields was "personal" rather than territorial. In these family and religious matters, Hindus were ruled by Dharmashastra—not by the ancient texts as such, but by the texts as interpreted by the commentators accepted in the locality.

10. The judicial treatment of the relation between varna and caste was plagued by confusion, engendered in part by the use of "caste" to refer both to the four great classes or varnas into which Hindu society is theoretically divided by the Sanskrit lawbooks and to the multitude of existing endogamous groups or *jātis*. In the sequel, unless the context indicates otherwise, caste is used only in the latter sense.

11. These differences are concisely summarized by Derrett (1958).

as Shudras.[12] Another line of cases developed an alternative approach of testing the varna standing of a caste group by its own consciousness of its status and by the acceptance of this self-estimate by other castes in the locality.[13] These tests involve reliance on widespread conventional notions of purity and pollution; they emphasize orthodox and prestigious practice rather than refinements of doctrine or ritual.[14] These notions of differential purity are used to assign castes to their proper varna.[15] It is assumed that the castes are components of the varnas, which in turn comprise Hinduism. It is assumed that all groups within Hinduism are subsumed under one or another varna. Although there are some instances of judicial departures from the symmetry of this scheme,[16] generally the picture of Hinduism found in the administration of personal law is one which regards caste and varna as coextensive with Hinduism. Castes, therefore, have certain religious characteristics; they occupy their respective places in an overarching sacral order of ranks which embraces all groups within Hinduism. Positions in this order could be assigned by certain widely shared notions about the relative standing implied by certain practices.

The textual law recognized varnas but not castes. But the textual law was to to be modified by prevailing custom; the doctrine that "clear proof of usage will outweigh the written text of the law" was early accepted as part of the Hindu law.[17] The custom proved might be that of a family, a locality, or a caste. The latter was most commonly pleaded. William McCormack suggests that "most of the alleged 'caste customs' which came before the courts were in fact regional customs" (McCormack, 1966, p. 30). The strategy of pleading caste customs tended to associate the caste group with a distinctive set of customs, providing models for patterning social behavior, serving to maintain caste identity in new settings and facilitating the transformation of local caste

12. See, for example, *Gopal v. Hanmant*, I.L.R. 3 Bom. 273 (1879).

13. See, for example, *Subrao v. Radha*, I.L.R. 52 Bom. 497 (1928).

14. Mere performance of ceremonies associated with higher castes will not elevate lower classes to that station, though "where caste is doubtful, the performance of Vedic or Puranic ritual may be important evidence as to caste. . . ." *Maharajah of Kolhapur v. Sundaram Ayyar*, A.I.R. 1925 Mad. 497 at 553.

15. On pollution as a differentiating and integrative factor in caste systems, see Orenstein (1965) and Harper (1964).

16. Thus it is possible to have varna standing without belonging to a caste group. *Sunder Devi v. Jheboo Lal*, A.I.R. 1957 All. 215 (convert to Hinduism); *Upoma Kuchain v. Bholaram*, I.L.R. 15 Cal. 708 (1888) (daughter of outcaste); cf. *Ratansi v. Administrator General*, A.I.R. 1928 Mad. 1279 (convert to Hinduism). For some purposes at least, Hindu caste groups may fall outside of or below the four varnas. *Sankaralinga Nadan v. Raja Rajeswara Dorai*, 35 I.A. 176 (1908). Possibly one can be a Hindu without caste or varna. See *Ratansi v. Administrator General, supra*. Caste and varna may apply to persons who are not strictly Hindus, *Inder Singh v. Sadhan Singh*, I.L.R. (1944), 1 Cal. 233 (Sikh Brahmans). Caste groups have been recognized for some purposes which have no varna nor are Hindu in any sense. *Abdul Kadir v. Dharma*, I.L.R. 20 Bom. 190 (1895). Again members of the same caste may hold different varna statuses. *Subrao v. Radha*, I.L.R. 52 Bom. 497 (1928).

17. *Collector of Madura v. Moottoo Ramalinga Sathupathy*, 12 M.I.A. 397 at 436 (1868). However, the application of stringent common law requirements for proving a valid custom makes it difficult to prove variation from the rules of the lawbooks and had the effect, it appears, of extending the rules of the classical lawbooks to sections of the population which had previously been strangers to them. The British period then was marked by an attrition of local customary law at the expense of the written and refined law of the texts (Galanter, 1964a).

groups into wider congregations (McCormack, 1966). Thus the caste group was seen as a carrier of a distinctive set of cultural traits. When these traits were employed in assessing varna standing they implied the sacral view of caste; when employed to vary the textual law they implied a view of the caste group as a corporate body culturally distinct from its neighbors.

PRECEDENCE AND DISABILITIES

Prior to British rule, some Indian regimes had actively enforced the privileges and disabilities of various caste groups. Indeed, such enforcement of the caste order is urged by Hindu legal tradition as the prime duty of the Hindu king. During the latter part of the British period the prerogatives and dignities of castes received only limited support by active governmental sanctions. This limited support was undertaken on the basis of upholding customary rights, but these rights were often conceptualized in terms of the religious characteristics of caste groups.

With respect to the use of religious premises, caste groups did enjoy the support of the courts in upholding their claims for preference and exclusiveness. Courts granted injunctions to restrain members of particular castes from entering temples—even temples that were publicly supported and dedicated to the entire Hindu community.[18] Damages were awarded for purificatory ceremonies necessitated by the pollution caused by the presence of lower castes; such pollution was actionable as a trespass to the person of the higher caste worshippers.[19] It was a criminal offense for a member of an excluded caste knowingly to pollute a temple by his presence.[20] These rights to exclusiveness were vindicated by the courts not only where the interlopers were "Untouchables" but also against such "touchables" as Palshe Brahmans and Lingayats, whose presence in the particular temple was polluting.

In these cases the courts were giving effect to the notion of an overarching, differentiated Hindu ritual order in which the various castes were assigned, by text or by custom, certain prerogatives and disabilities to be measured by concepts of varna, of pollution, and of required ceremonial distance. Thus, in *Anandrav Bhikaji Phadke v. Shankar Daji Charya* the Court upheld the right of Chitpavan Brahmans to exclude Palshe Brahmans from worshipping at a temple, on the ground that such an exclusive right "is one which the Courts must guard, as otherwise all high-caste Hindus would hold their sanctuaries and perform their worship, only so far as those of the lower castes chose to allow them."[21]

In 1908 the Privy Council upheld the exclusion of Shanars from a temple and granted damages for its purification after a careful scrutiny of their social

---

18. *Anandrav Bhikiji Phadke v. Shankar Daji Charya*, I.L.R. 7 Bom. 323 (1883); *Sankaralinga Nadan v. Raja Rajeswara Dorai*, 35 I.A.C. 176 (1908); *Chathunni v. Appukuttan*, A.I.R. 1945 Mad. 232.

19. See cases cited, note 18 *supra*. Cf. *S.K. Wodeyar v. Ganapati*, A.I.R. 1935 Bom. 371, where damages were awarded although the parties agreed there should be no finding on the question of pollution.

20. *Atmaram v. King-emperor*, A.I.R. 1924 Nag. 121.

21. 7 Bom. 323 at 329. On the origins of this dispute, see Joshi (1913).

standing. Finding that "their position in general social estimation appears to have been just above that of Pallas, Pariahs, and Chucklies (who are on all hands regarded as unclean and prohibited from the use of Hindu temples) and below that of the Vellalas, Maravars, and other cultivating castes usually classed as Shudras, and admittedly free to worship in the Hindu temples," the Judicial Committee of the Privy Council concluded that the presence of Shanars was repugnant to the "religious principles of the Hindu worship of Shiva" as well as to the sentiments and customs of the caste Hindu worshippers.[22] As late as 1945, Nair users of a public temple were granted damages for pollution for the purificatory ceremonies necessitated by Ezhuvas' bathing in tanks.[23] These exclusionary rights were supported by criminal as well as by civil sanctions. Untouchable Mahars who entered the enclosure of a village idol were convicted on the ground that "where custom . . . ordains that an untouchable, whose very touch is in the opinion of devout Hindus pollution, should not enter the enclosure surrounding the shrine of any Hindu god, . . ." such entry is a defilement in violation of Section 295 of the Penal Code.[24]

While Hinduism is seen as a unified and overarching order, it is also seen as differentiated. The religious obligations and prerogatives of groups differ according to their standing in this whole. Where Brahmans tore the sacred thread from the neck of an Ahir who had lately taken to wearing it, the Court ruled that, since he was a Shudra, the wearing of it was not "part of his religion" vis-à-vis other Hindus. To them it was an assertion of a claim to higher rank. Therefore the injury was not to his religious susceptibilities—an offense—but only to his dignity.[25] Had it been torn by non-Hindus, it might have been an insult to his religion itself.

In these cases the courts clearly express their notion of a rank ordering of all Hindu groups in a scheme of articulated prerogatives and disabilities. One looks to the position of the caste in the whole—its position on the scale relative to the other groups—to ascertain its rights. This approach did not always work to the disadvantage of the excluded class. In *Gopala v. Subramania*, members of the Elaivaniyar community obtained a declaration of their right to enter the outer hall of the temple and an injunction restraining other worshippers from ejecting them. The court declared that each group enjoyed a prima facie right to enter that part of the temple assigned their caste (that is, varna) by the Agamas (texts on use of temples), that these texts authorized the entry of Shudras in this part of the temple, and that the plaintiffs were "at least Sudras." Their right could be overcome only by proof of a special custom of exclusion.[26] Similarly, where Moothans were convicted for defiling a temple by entering the part open to "non-Brahmans," the court reversed the conviction on the

22. 35 I.A.C. 176 at 182.
23. A.I.R. 1945 Mad. 232.
24. A.I.R. 1924 Nag. 121.
25. *Sheo Shankar v. Emperor*, A.I.R. 1940 Oudh 348. For another instance in the same neighborhood and time of a lower caste adopting (and relinquishing) the sacred thread, see Sinha (1960).
26. A.I.R. 1914 Mad. 363.

ground that Moothans are Shudras, no lower or more polluting than the Nairs, who were allowed to enter the temple.[27]

Again we see the notion of a single articulated Hindu community in which there are authoritative opinions (supplied by custom and accepted texts) which determine the respective rights of its component groups. The effect of this conception of the overarching Hindu order is revealed clearly in the case of *Michael Pillai v. Barthe*. Here a group of Roman Catholic Pillais and Mudalis sued for an injunction to require the Bishop of Trichinopoly to re-erect a wall separating their part of the church from that entered by "low-caste Christians" and to declare plaintiffs' exclusive right to perform services at the altar. The court characterized the claim as one for "a right of freedom from contact which can have but one origin . . . that of pollution,"[28] but refused to recognize pollution as either a spiritual or a temporal injury among Christians. Nor could Christians constitute "castes" with rights based on their respective purity. Not being Hindus, plaintiffs "cannot . . . invoke the authority of accepted sacerdotal texts for perpetuating the distinction between touchables and untouchables during a particular life solely by reason of birth."[29] When individuals have placed themselves by conversion outside the sacral order of Hinduism, their caste groupings are not invested with those rights which follow only upon their occupying a place in that order.[30]

Exclusionary practices did not enjoy the same judicial support in regard to "secular" public facilities such as schools, wells, and roads. The courts declared that no right could be maintained to exclude other castes or sects from the use of streets and roads.[31] The situation is more complicated regarding the use of water sources. The Lahore Court held other users had no right to prevent Chamars from drawing water from a public well.[32] However, other courts conceded that a right to exclude might be upheld if a custom of exclusive use by higher castes could be proved. Such customs were in fact difficult to prove. In *Marriappa v. Vaithilinga*, Shanars obtained an order allowing them to use a large tank on the ground that no custom of exclusion was proved (a right of exclusion was upheld in regard to one well in the dispute where such a custom was proved). What is interesting for our purpose is that even in denying the exclusionary claims of the higher groups, the court reveals an implicit view of an integrated Hindu community with graded rights. The absence of a custom of exclusion from the large tank, as distinguished from the well, is indicated by textual passages to the effect that precautions for impurity may be less intense in a body of water of this size.[33] Again, in *N. D. Vaidya v. B. R. Ambedkar*, the court found it unproved that there was any longstanding custom of exclusion. Textual provisions indicating that no elaborate precautions against pollution are

27. *Kutti Chami Moothan v. Rama Pattar*, A.I.R. 1919 Mad. 755.

28. A.I.R. 1917 Mad. 431 at 433.

29. *Id.*, at 442.

30. For a similar unwillingness to enforce exclusion in regard to Parsis, since there was no defilement, see *Saklat v. Bella*, 53 I.A. 42 at 56–7 (P.C., 1925).

31. For example, *Sadogopachariar v. Rama Rao*, I.L.R. 26 Mad. 376, aff'd 35 I.A. 93.

32. *Kazan Chand v. Emperor*, A.I.R. 1926 Lah. 683.

33. 1913 M.W.N. 247.

required in a tank of that size rendered it "doubtful whether any attempt would have been made to secure exclusive use of the water until such time as the tank came to be surrounded by houses of caste Hindus."[34]

In dealing with exclusionary rights, the courts tried to confine themselves to claims involving civil or property rights as opposed to claims merely for standing or social acceptance. Thus the courts refused to penalize such defiance of customary disabilities as failure to dismount from a wedding palanquin or failure to concede another caste an exclusive right to ceremonial deference.[35] The prevailing notion was that social and religious matters did not give rise to legal rights unless the right was the sort of thing that could be possessed and made use of. Thus we find gradation from the temple cases, where there was ready enforcement of exclusionary rights, to water sources, where it seems enforcement might be forthcoming if difficult technical requirements were met, to customs in no way connected with the use of specific property, where there was no enforcement at all.[36] But where government intervened, it upheld custom and this custom was evaluated and rationalized by the courts in terms of notions of ceremonial purity and pollution—existing in different degrees among different groups of Hindus.

It should be emphasized that prescriptive rights and disabilities received their greatest governmental support not from direct judicial enforcement but from the recognition of caste autonomy, that is, from the refusal of courts to interfere with the right of the caste group to apply sanctions against those who defied its usages or contested its claims. Members of a caste could be outcasted, and outsiders could be boycotted for violations of customary privileges and disabilities.[37] The broad sphere of autonomy enjoyed by caste groups permitted effective enforcement of their claims without resort to the courts and with immunity from governmental interference.

Caste Autonomy

Castes were early recognized as juridical entities with the right to sue and be sued, to sue on behalf of their members, and to acquire, hold, and manage property. More important for our purposes here, the caste was recognized as a group having the power to make rules for itself and to constitute tribunals to enforce these rules.[38] While caste power was limited by the official courts, which

34. A.I.R. 1938 Bom. 146 at 148.

35. *Jasani v. Emperor*, A.I.R. 1936 All. 534; *Govinda Amrita v. Emperor*, A.I.R. 1942 Nag. 45.

36. While there was no support for these usages at the high court level, there is evidence of widespread local acquiescence in and enforcement of such practices. See, for example, the actions of the local officials described in *Kazan Chand v. Emperor*, A.I.R. 1926 Lah. 683, A.I.R. 1927 Lah. 430; *Jasani v. Emperor*, A.I.R. 1936 All. 534; *Govinda Amrita v. Emperor*, A.I.R. 1942 Nag. 45.

37. Assertion of caste superiority by members of one caste over another and withdrawal of social intercourse does not amount to criminal defamation. *Venkata Reddi* (Mad. High Court, 1885), reported in I Weir 575. Cf. *Salar Mannaji Row v. C. Herojee Row*, I Weir 614 (Mad. High Court, 1887); *Babulal v. Tundilal*, 33 Crim. L. J. 835 (Nag., 1932). Refusal of villagers to have social intercourse with members of an unpopular sect or allow them to use a well is not criminal annoyance or nuisance. *Ramditta v. Kirpa Singh*, 1883 P. R. (Criminal) 3.

38. For detailed analysis and references in the area of caste autonomy, see Kikani (1912); Ramakrishna (1918); Mulla (1901). The only legislation directly impinging on caste autonomy

had exclusive jurisdiction over many matters (for example, criminal law), on most matters the caste could make, modify, and revoke its rules. The majority, or the established authorities within the caste, could not be overruled by the civil courts on these "caste questions." Caste questions were said to include all matters affecting the internal autonomy and social relations of a caste.[39] A caste then might make whatever rules it wished about these matters. It might forbid the wearing of European clothing, departure from customary headdress, crossing the sea; it might prohibit intercourse with members who participated in widow remarriage; it might excommunicate those who failed to observe customary avoidance of lower castes.[40]

The right to have a fellow caste member accept one's food, gifts, or invitations; the right to receive invitations from him; the right to have precedence in leading one's bullock in a procession—in all these cases of dignity, acceptance, or precedence within the caste, the civil courts would not entertain a suit. Again, claims to leadership of a caste, claims to a caste office, claims to enjoy privileges and honors by virtue of such office, and claims to officiate as priest were held to be caste questions. Even if the dispute resulted in the expulsion of one person or faction, the courts would take no cognizance in such cases. Unwarranted attribution of loss of caste was defamatory. But so long as publication was not more extensive than necessary to effect the purpose of informing the caste,[41] announcement of a duly pronounced sentence of excommunication to other caste members was privileged, that is, immune from a claim for defamation as tending to protect the public good.[42]

But the courts were willing to take jurisdiction where they found that the claim was not merely for social acceptance or dignities but involved enforceable civil or property rights, which included rights in caste property, the right to offices with pecuniary emoluments, and the right to reputation. Even here, the courts were wary about the extent of intervention and set up standards that emphasized procedural rather than substantive supervision. The courts would

---

was the Caste Disabilities Removal Act (Act XXI of 1850, also known as the Freedom of Religion Act), which provided that there was to be no forfeiture of civil or property rights "by reason of renouncing, or, having been excluded from the communion of, any religion, or being deprived of caste. . . ."

39. But they did not include the economic interests of the group, where these conflicted with the property right of a member. See *Pothuraju Setty v. Padda Poliah*, 1939 (1) Mad. L. J. 116.

40. *Sri Sukratendar Thritha Swami of Kashi Mutt v. Prabhu*, A.I.R., 1923 Mad. 587. Cf. *Khamani v. Emperor*, A.I.R. 1926 All. 306.

41. See *Queen v. Sankara*, I.L.R. 6 Mad. 381 (1883), where the use of a postcard to inform the excommunicant was found to be a "wanton excess of privilege." Cf. *Thiagaraya v. Krishnasami*, I.L.R. 15 Mad. 214 (1892) (circulation of accusation against Brahman to persons of all castes in bazaar not privileged).

42. See the Exceptions to Section 499 of the Indian Penal Code (Act XLV of 1960). Generally courts were well disposed toward caste tribunals and paid high regard to the beneficent qualities of caste discipline. See, for example, *Empress v. Ramanand*, I.L.R. 3 All. 664 at 667 (1881) ("No court would wish to interfere with those domestic rules and laws which regulate and control the relations between the members of a caste. On the contrary, the tendency would rather be to countenance and protect them."); *Umed Singh v. Emperor*, A.I.R. 1924 All. 299 at 301 ("So long as caste . . . [remains] one of the fundamental characteristics of social life in India, any attempt to minimize, ignore or brush to one side existing regulations, existing sanctions or respect for existing decisions must be regarded as contrary to the public good.").

entertain claims only: (1) that the decision of a caste tribunal had not been arrived at *bona fides*; (2) that the decision was taken under a mistaken belief; (3) that the decision was actually contrary to the rules or usage of the caste; or (4) that it was contrary to natural justice. The last was the most important of these rules. Violations of natural justice included omission of proper notice to the accused and the denial of an opportunity to the accused to be heard and to defend himself.

Here we have a judicial view of caste more congenial to the sectarian or associational models than to the sacral one. Castes are seen as independent bodies with their own internal order, and the rights and duties of individual members follow from this order. This order is not determined by the position of the caste in an overarching order of Hindu society. Although analogies are sometimes drawn from such associations as clubs,[43] corporations, partnerships, or dissenting churches, the courts never subsume the caste group under any of these. It is a group *sui generis*.[44] Although some courts speak of the caste as a voluntary organization in the sense that one can leave it, it was generally conceded that "the caste is a social combination, the members of which are enlisted by birth, not by enrollment."[45]

Is the caste group a "religious body"? We have seen that the courts refused to take cognizance of suits for mere "religious honours" or to enforce obligations they regarded as purely religious. The caste group was recognized as a proper forum for settling these religious questions. The caste was recognized as a corporate body with the right to prescribe and enforce its own religious doctrine, ritual, and leadership.[46] But in many cases it could not be characterized solely by its religious attributes. "The caste is not a religious body, though its usages, like all other Hindu usages, are based upon religious feelings. In religious matters, strictly so called, the members of the caste are governed by their religious preceptors. In social matters they lay down their own laws."[47] Thus the caste unit was not solely religious in its concerns and nature. It was mixed—partly civil and partly religious.[48] Or as a Madras court summed it up, "a caste is a combination of a number of persons governed by a body of usages which differentiate them from others. The usages may refer to social or religious observances, to drink, food, ceremonies, pollution, occupation, or marriage." The caste group, then, is not wholly or solely to be characterized by religion, either in doctrine or in practice.[49]

It is here that we find a departure from the characterization of caste in terms

---

43. See *Appaya v. Padappa*, I.L.R. 23 Bom. 112 (1898).

44. "The Hindu caste is an unique aggregation so wholly unknown to the English law that English decisions, concerning English corporations and partnerships tend rather to confusion than to guidance upon matters relating to caste." *Jethabhai Narsey v. Chapsey Kooverji*, I.L.R. 15 Bom. 599 at 611 (1891).

45. *Raghunath v. Javardhan*, 15 Bom. 599 (1891).

46. See, for example, *Devchand Totarm v. Ghaneshyam*, A.I.R. 1935 Bom. 361. (Jurisdiction of caste includes outcasting of members for adherence to sub-sect said to be outside Vedic religion.)

47. *Raghunath v. Javardhan*, 15 Bom. 599 (1891).

48. *Haroon v. Haji Adam*, 11 Bom. L. Reporter 1267.

49. *Muthuswami v. Masilamani*, I.L.R. 33 Mad. 352 (1909).

of an overarching sacral order of Hinduism. Castes are autonomous units with internal government and characterized partly by religious and partly by non-religious usages. In contradistinction to the personal law[50] and to what was held in the cases involving precedence and disabilities where castes were allocated differential religious honor because of their place in the wider Hindu scheme, here the castes are treated as autonomous and self-sufficient entities whose order proceeds from internal organs.

This detachment from the context of the wider Hindu society comes out clearly in the treatment of non-Hindu groups under the heading of caste autonomy. Here we find that the autonomous caste group is recognized not only among Hindus but also among Muslims, Jews, Sikhs, Jains, and Christians.[51] In this context caste groups are not subsumed under the varnas; they are treated as a special kind of group. Claims of rights and powers which derive from a place in a larger Hindu order are not recognized among non-Hindu groups. But where the rights and powers derive from the internal order, customary and deliberative, of the group as an autonomous entity, they are recognized among all religions, not only among Hindus.

THE NEW DISPENSATION

The Constitution sets forth a general program for the reconstruction of Indian society.[52] In spite of its length, it is undetailed in its treatment of the institution of caste and of the existing group structure of Indian society. But it clearly sets out to secure to individuals equality of status and opportunity,[53] to abolish invidious distinctions among groups,[54] to protect the integrity of a variety of groups—religious, linguistic, and cultural,[55] to give free play to voluntary associations,[56] the widest freedom of association to the individual,[57] and generally the widest personal freedom consonant with the public good.[58] Without pursuing all these in detail, it is clear that the following general principles are consistently in evidence: (1) a commitment to the replacement of ascribed status by voluntary affiliations; (2) an emphasis on the integrity and

50. The personal law inclined away from the sacral view toward a view more like that found in the caste autonomy area in the recognition of castes as units whose customs, where proved, would serve to vary the law of the textbooks.

51. See, for example, *Abdul Kadir v. Dharma*, I.L.R. 20 Bom. 190 (1895), where the court observed that "caste" comprised "any well-defined native community governed for certain internal purposes by its own rules and regulations," and was thus not confined to Hindus. Cf. *Yusef Beg Sahib v. Maliq Md. Syed Sahib*, A.I.R. 1927 Mad. 397, where the court rejected the notion that the word "caste" was confined to Hindus and found that it "refers to any class who keep themselves socially distinct or inherit exclusive privileges."

52. This new dispensation did not arrive on the scene suddenly. It represents the culmination of more than half a century of increasing anti-caste sentiment among reformers, the gradual acceptance by politicians of the need for reform of caste, and a variety of provincial anti-disabilities and temple-entry legislation, and the growing conviction that caste is inimical to democracy and progress and should play a restricted role in the new India.

53. Preamble, Articles 14, 15, 16, 17, 18, 23, 46.

54. Articles 14–17, 25–30.

55. Articles 25–30, 347, 350A, 350B.

56. Articles 19(1)c, 25, 26, 30.

57. *Id.*

58. See generally, Parts III and IV of the Constitution.

autonomy of groups within society; (3) a withdrawal of governmental recognition of rank ordering among groups. In order to see how the new constitutional scheme has affected the judicial view of caste, we shall trace recent developments in the areas previously discussed and in some new problem areas that have emerged since independence.

PERSONAL LAW

The Constitution contains a commitment to replace the system of separate personal laws with a "uniform civil code."[59] In spite of its strictures against discrimination on the ground of religion, the Constitution has been interpreted to permit the continuing application of their respective personal laws to Hindus and Muslims. The continuing validity of disparate rules of personal law and the power of the state to create new rules applicable to particular communities has been upheld.[60] Within the Hindu law itself, the constitutional ban on caste discrimination has not been read as abolishing differences in personal law between Hindus of different castes. Although legal enforcement of disabilities against lower castes was sometimes rationalized in varna terms, the use of varna distinctions in the personal law is not included within the constitutional abolition of untouchability.[61] However, the Hindu Code Acts[62] of 1955–56 have largely abandoned the shastraic basis of Hindu law and established a more or less uniform law for Hindus of all regions and castes. The new law creates the hitherto unknown capacity to marry and adopt across varna lines and, with a few minor exceptions, eliminates all of the distinctions along varna lines embodied in the old law.[63] Varna has virtually been eliminated as an operative legal concept, although for the present the courts are required to apply it to transactions covered by the older law. In addition, the new legislation severely curtails but does not eliminate the opportunities for invoking caste custom in order to vary the generally applicable Hindu law.[64] Where sanctioned by custom, caste tribunals may still dissolve marriages.[65] Where caste is still relevant to the operation of personal law, its significance is as a vessel of custom and

59. Article 44.
60. For example, *State of Bombay v. Narasu Appa Mali,* A.I.R. 1952 Bom. 84.
61. The assignment of a community to a varna has been held not to constitute a deprivation of rights to equality before the law, nor is it religious discrimination. *Sangannagonda v. Kallangonda,* A.I.R. 1960 Mys. 147. The classification of the offspring of a Shudra and his Brahman concubine as a *cāṇḍāla,* the lowest of Untouchables in the traditional scheme, did not strike the court as unconstitutional in *Bachubhai v. Bai Dhanlaxmi,* A.I.R. 1961 Guj. 141.
62. That is, the Hindu Marriage Act of 1955, the Hindu Succession Act of 1956, the Hindu Minority and Guardianship Act of 1956, and the Hindu Adoptions and Maintenance Act of 1956.
63. Derrett (1958) suggests that the only instances in which varna might continue to have effect are succession to sannyasis and determination of the maximum age for adoption. The former is an instance of a varna rule left intact (Shudras cannot become sannyasis); the possibility of variation by caste custom also remains intact. See Derrett (1963, Sec. 592). The latter is an instance where custom may vary the law, and custom here is based at least in part on varna distinctions. See Derrett (1963, Sec. 159 ff.).
64. Derrett (1963, Sec. 13) lists as matters remaining open to customary variation the prohibited degrees for marriage, the maximum age of adoption, the right to dissolution of marriage by a caste tribunal, right to be a sannyasi, right to maintenance out of impartible estates, and other joint family rights.
65. For example, *Premenbhai v. Channoolal,* A.I.R. 1963 M.P. 57.

as a body with its own rules and tribunal rather than as the holder of a position in a larger system. Here, the sacral view of caste has given way entirely to a view of castes as autonomous corporate units.[66]

PRECEDENCE AND DISABILITIES

The Preamble to the Constitution resolves "to secure to all of its citizens . . . Equality of status and opportunity." Accordingly, it confers on all its citizens a fundamental right to be free of discrimination by the state on the ground of caste. The Constitution not only forbids caste discrimination by the government; it goes on to outlaw invidious treatment on the basis of caste by private citizens as well. Article 15(2) prohibits discrimination by private persons in regard to use of facilities and accommodations open to the public, such as wells, tanks, shops, and restaurants.[67] Under these provisions, there is no longer any governmental power to make discriminations among citizens on caste lines.[68] Nor may government enforce any customary right to exclude certain castes from a public facility.[69] Article 17 provides:

"Untouchability" is abolished and its practice in any form is forbidden. The enforcement of any disability arising out of "Untouchability" shall be an offense punishable in accordance with law.

The guarantee of freedom of religion is explicitly qualified to permit temple-entry legislation.[70]

The Untouchability (Offenses) Act (UOA) of 1955[71] outlaws the imposition of disabilities "on grounds of untouchability" in regard to, *inter alia*, entrance and worship at temples, access to shops and restaurants, the practice of occupations and trades, use of water sources, places of public resort and accommodation, public conveyances, hospitals, educational institutions, construction and occu-

---

66. The caste autonomy recognized here is of a limited kind. Castes carry and can administer established customs, possibly they can abrogate an old custom, but they cannot deliberately create new customary law. A caste cannot attract to itself a different body of personal law by changes of name, etc. *Sankaran v. Madhavan*, A.I.R. 1955 Mad. 579. Nor is it possible to form a caste voluntarily which enjoys even this limited prerogative, since it derives from the ancient character of the custom rather than the legislative power of the caste. *Deivani Achi v. Chidambaram Chettiar*, A.I.R. 1954 Mad. 657. Nor can traditional caste powers be transferred to a composite group made up of members of several castes. *Ellappa v. Ellappa*, A.I.R. 1950 Mad. 409.

67. See also Articles 28(3) and 29(2), which forbid discrimination in private educational institutions.

68. See, for example, *State of Madras v. Champakam Dorairjan*, [1951] S.C.J. 313; *Sanghar Umar v. State*, A.I.R. 1952 Saur. 124. Caste cannot be recognized for electoral purposes. The Constitution rules out caste-wise electorates for parliament and state legislatures. Art. 325. Communal electorates in local bodies are unconstitutional. *Nain Sukh Das v. State of U.P.*, A.I.R. 1953, S.C. 384; nor can caste be used as a criterion in delimiting territorial constituencies (by excluding from a ward "houses of Rajputs in the east of the village"). *Bhopal Singh v. State*, A.I.R. 1958 Raj. 41.

69. *Aramugha Konar v. Narayana Asari*, A.I.R. 1958 Mad. 282.

70. Article 25(2)b. When the Constitution was enacted, customary exclusion of lower castes from temples and secular facilities, previously recognized and to some extent enforceable at law, had been transformed into statutory offenses throughout most of India. For a survey of this provincial legislation and its continuing efficacy, see Galanter (1961).

71. Act XXII of 1955.

pation of residential premises, holding of religious ceremonies and processions, and use of jewelry and finery. Enforcement of disabilities is made a crime, punishable by fine or imprisonment, and the power of civil courts to recognize any custom, usage, or right which would result in the enforcement of any disability is withdrawn.

In order to gauge the scope of Article 17 and the UOA, it is necessary to determine the meaning of "untouchability." Although it is yet unclear in detail, judicial construction so far provides some guidelines. The "untouchability" forbidden by the Constitution does not include every instance in which one person is treated as ritually unclean and polluting. It does not include such temporary and expiable states of uncleanliness as that suffered by women in childbirth, mourners, etc.[72] It does not include attribution of impurity to worshippers (vis-à-vis attendants) in sacred places;[73] nor does it include that "untouchability" which follows upon expulsion or excommunication from caste.[74] It is confined to that untouchability ascribed by birth rather than attained in life. Further, it does not include every instance in which one is treated as untouchable in certain respects because of a difference in religion or membership in a different or lower caste. It does not include the use of varna distinctions to demarcate Shudras from the twice-born.[75] It includes, in the words of the first court to pass on the issue explicitly, only those practices directed at "those regarded as 'untouchables' in the course of historic development"; that is, persons relegated "beyond the pale of the caste system on grounds of birth in a particular class."[76] Thus untouchability would not include practices based on avoidance due to a difference of religion or caste, except insofar as the caste was traditionally considered "untouchable" and "outside the pale of the caste system." Thus disabilities imposed, for example, by one group of Brahmans on other Brahmans, by Brahmans on non-Brahmans, by "right-hand" on "left-hand" castes, would all fall outside the prohibition of Article 17.

The meaning of untouchability then is to be determined by reference to those who have traditionally been considered "Untouchables." But it is no easier to define Untouchables than it is to define "untouchability." "Beyond the pale of the caste system" is a misleading and unworkable formulation. Even the lowest castes are within the system of reciprocal rights and duties; their disabilities and prerogatives are articulated to those of other castes. Presumably the Mysore court means by this phrase, outside the four varnas of the classical lawbooks. In reference to their customary rights, Untouchables have sometimes, particularly in southern India, been referred to as a fifth varna, below the Shudras.[77] But in other places they were regarded as Shudras.[78] For purposes of personal law,

---

72. See *Devarajiah v. Padmanna,* A.I.R. 1958 Mys. 84.

73. *Parameswaran Moothathu v. Vasudeva Kurup,* I.L.R. 1960 Ker. 73.

74. *Hadibandhu v. Banamali,* A.I.R. 1960 Or. 33; *Saifuddin Saheb v. State of Bombay.* A.I.R. 1962 S.C. 853.

75. *Sangannagonda v. Kallangonda,* A.I.R. 1960 Mys. 147.

76. *Devarajiah v. Padmanna,* A.I.R. 1958 Mys. 84 at 85. See *Kandra Sethi v. Metra Sahu,* XXIV Cuttack L. T. 364 at 366 (1963).

77. See, for example, *Sankaralinga Nadan v. Raja Rajeshwari Dorai,* 35 I.A.C. 176 (1908).

78. See, for example, *Atmaram v. King-Emperor,* A.I.R. 1924 Nag. 121.

the courts have never attempted to distinguish Untouchables from Shudras.[79] Even where Untouchables are popularly regarded as Shudras, they cannot be equated with them, since there are non-Untouchable groups which belong to this category. Thus, the tests used for distinguishing Shudras from the twice-born cannot be used as a satisfactory measure of untouchability.

Although the abolition of untouchability amounts to a kind of negative recognition of the sacral order of Hinduism, it is not likely that the jurisprudence recognizing that order will find new employment for the purpose of identifying "Untouchables." In attempting to identify Untouchable groups for the purpose of giving them benefits and preferences, the government has not tried to apply general criteria but has adopted the device of compiling lists of castes in each locality. These were drawn up mainly with an eye to low ritual standing, but there is an uneven admixture of other social and economic factors.[80]

Thus the "untouchability" forbidden by law is confined to discrimination against certain not readily defined classes of persons. It includes not every discrimination against them but only those imposed because of their position in the caste system. The provisions making untouchability an offense attempt to distinguish between those disabilities and exclusions imposed on grounds of caste position, and those which derive from religious and sectarian difference. Crucial sections of the Untouchability Offenses Act are qualified to make it an offense to exclude Untouchables only from places "open to other persons professing the same religion or belonging to the same religious denomination or section thereof."[81] Thus the scope of the rights conferred on Untouchables by the UOA depends on the meaning of the phrases "the same religion" and "the same religious denomination or section thereof." To the extent that caste distinctions are conceived of as religious or denominational differences, the rights of Untouchables are limited. Thus exclusion of Untouchables by Jains is not forbidden insofar as it is on the ground that they are non-Jains rather than because of their caste.[82] In spite of some attempt by the lawmakers to minimize such distinctions,[83] courts have (on solid textual grounds) been reluctant to read the act as obviating these distinctions. In *State of Kerala v. Venkiteswara*

---

79. See *Muthusami v. Masilimani*, I.L.R. 33 Mad. 342 (1909); *Maharajah of Kolhapur v. Sundaram Awar*, A.I.R. 1925 Mad. 497 at 521; *Manickam v. Poogavanammal*, A.I.R. 1934 Mad. 323; *Bhola Nath v. Emperor*, A.I.R. 1924 Cal. 616; *Sohan Singh v. Kabla Singh*, A.I.R. 1927 Lah. 706.

80. Such lists derive from earlier attempts (in the 1930's) to find a single set of criteria to measure "untouchability." (These included such tests as whether the caste in question was "polluting" or "debarred" from public facilities—which may admit of no equivocal answer—and whether they were served by "clean" Brahmans—which has only a local and comparative reference.) All attempts to set up tests based on the assumption that "Untouchables" are set off by some uniform and distinctive pattern of practices proved inadequate to isolate the groups which local administrators felt deserving of inclusion. Additional criteria of poverty and illiteracy had to be added. The government lists then give little guide to the meaning of untouchability. There is no adequate inclusive list of all groups considered Untouchable or any single set of criteria for identifying them. For a discussion of the problem of identifying the "Untouchables," see Dushkin (1957, 1961).

81. Sec. 3(1).

82. *Devarajiah v. Padmanna*, A.I.R. 1958 Mys. 84; *State v. Puranchand*, A.I.R. 1958 M.P. 352.

83. See the "Explanation" attached to Sec. 3 of the UOA.

Prabhu,[84] Untouchables were prevented from entering the *nālambalam* of a temple belonging to the Gowda Saraswat Brahman community. Since only members of this community ordinarily entered this part of the temple, the court held that exclusion of Untouchables was not an offense, since they did not belong to the same "denomination or section thereof." The acceptance by the court of denominational lines within Hinduism as limiting the operation of the temple-entry provisions may produce some unanticipated results. For the "religion" and "denomination" qualifiers also appear in other provisions of the Untouchability Offenses Act.[85] Thus judicial solicitude for the sectarian prerogatives of groups within Hinduism may severely limit the rights granted by some of the central provisions of the UOA.[86]

Since untouchability has been interpreted to include only discriminations against Untouchables, the legislation against it has not touched discriminations against other classes of Hindus. Troubled by the anomalous situation in which, while it is an offense to exclude Untouchables from temples, classes of touchable Hindus may be excluded with impunity, several states have responded by enacting supplementary legislation. A Bombay act, for example, makes it an offense to prevent "Hindus of any class or sect from entering or worshipping at a temple to the same extent and in the same manner as any other class or section of Hindus."[87] These laws extend protection to non-Untouchables, and they also overcome the sectarian and denominational limitations which the courts have found in the UOA. Although the states are limited in their power to legislate directly on the subject of untouchability, this legislation will substantially broaden the rights of Untouchables as well, for the rights of the latter under the Untouchability Offenses Act are automatically elevated to a parity with the new rights which the state legislation confers on caste-Hindus.[88] It remains to be seen whether the denominational prerogatives preserved by the Untouchability Offenses Act will be found to have a constitutional foundation.[89]

84. A.I.R. 1961 Ker. 55.

85. The qualification appears in the provisions relating to: use of utensils and other articles kept in restaurants, hotels, etc.; use of wells, water sources, bathing ghats, cremation grounds; the use of "places used for a public or charitable purpose"; the enjoyment of benefits of a charitable trust; and the use of *dharmshalas, sarais,* and *musāfirkhānās.* Sections 4(ii), 4(iv), 4(v), 4(ix). Strangely enough, it does not appear in Section 4(x) regarding "the observance of any . . . religious custom, usage or ceremony or taking part in any religious procession." Thus Untouchables seem to have access to the religious processions of Hindu denominations and sects, but not to their wells, etc.

86. Courts have also read severe private property restrictions into the Act. Thus, a privately owned well which the owner allows to be used by villagers is not covered. *Benudhar Sahu v. State,* I.L.R. 1962 Cuttack 256. Nor are religious performances "in an open space" to which the public is invited. *State of M.P. v. Tikaram,* 1965 M.P.L.J. (Notes of Cases) 7. See *Kandra Sethi v. Metra Sahu,* XXIX Cuttack L.T. 364 (1963).

87. Bombay Hindu Places of Public Worship (Entry Authorization) Act, 1956 (Bombay Act No. XXXI of 1956). United Provinces Temple Entry (Declaration of Rights) Act, 1956 (U.P. Act. No. XXXIII of 1956).

88. *State of Bombay v. Yagna Sastri Purushadasji,* 61 Bom. L. Reporter 700 (1958). (Under the Bombay Act, Satsangis [members of Swaminarayan Sampradaya] could not exclude non-Satsangi Harijans from their temples.)

89. See discussion on pages 328–29 below. Generally, on the relation of denominational prerogatives to temple entry and the abolition of untouchability, see Galanter (1964b).

"Protective Discrimination"

The attack on discrimination is only one side of the attempt to remove the disabilities of the lower castes. For the purpose of securing equality, the government is authorized to depart from indifference to caste in order to favor the Untouchables, tribals, and backward classes. These provisions for "protective discrimination" are the principal exceptions to the constitutional ban on the use of communal criteria by government. The Constitution authorizes government to provide special benefits and preferences to previously disadvantaged sections of the population. Reserved posts in government service, reserved seats in legislatures,[90] reserved places in educational institutions, and an array of preferences and welfare measures have been made available to the Scheduled Castes and, to a lesser extent, to the "backward classes."

As mentioned earlier, the selection of Scheduled Castes has been on the basis of ritual standing, supplemented by social and economic criteria. No uniform tests have been used. Pollution and impurity in the local scale are important tests, but considerations of varna as such played a minor role in the process of selecting these castes.[91]

The provisions for "protective discrimination" extend not only to Untouchables but to "other socially and educationally backward classes." Although the Constitution refers to backward *classes*, caste groups have commonly been the units selected as backward. Low standing in the ritual order was clearly one of the bases upon which caste groups have been deemed backward. But varna as such was never used for this purpose.[92] Increasing criticism within and without the government, and the increasing willingness of the courts to subject preferences for backward classes to close scrutiny, have caused a trend away from caste in favor of noncommunal economic and educational criteria. The Supreme Court in *Balaji v. State of Mysore* struck down a scheme for reservations in colleges for backward classes on the ground that they were selected primarily on the basis of caste; that is, the groups were chosen on the basis of their ritual and social standing.[93] It appeared to be constitutionally permissible for the state to use castes or communities as the units it designated as backward,[94] so long as it selected these units by other criteria; that is, by social, economic, and educational indices. So far, the Supreme Court seemed to reject the sacral model in favor of something along the lines of the organic model. Caste groups might be used, if selected as backward by nonreligious criteria on a relative scale in which they were measured against other caste groups. However, more recently, the Court has indicated that the caste group may be used to select beneficiaries

---

90. As originally enacted, the Constitution provided reserved seats in Parliament and the state legislatures for the Scheduled Castes (that is, Untouchables) and the Scheduled Tribes for a ten year period. This has been extended for another ten year period. Constitution (Eighth Amendment) Act, 1959.

91. See note 80 above.

92. A "varna" test was advocated by Shri S.D.S. Chaurasia, a member of the Backward Classes Commission, but his contention that the backward classes should be equated with Shudras was rejected by the commission (Report 1956: I, 44; III, 22ff.).

93. *Balaji v. State of Mysore*, A.I.R. 1963 S.C. 649.

94. *Id.; Ramakrishna Singh v. State of Mysore*, A.I.R. 1960 Mys. 338.

of preferences on a much narrower scale than the *Balaji* case seemed to imply. In *Chitralekha v. State of Mysore*, the Court suggested that, while it is permissible to use caste (presumably in the sense of standing or rank) "in ascertaining the backwardness of a class of citizens," it is by no means necessary to take caste into account "if [government] can ascertain the backwardness of a group of persons on the basis of other relevant criteria."[95] This confirms the *Balaji* view that caste standing is neither a necessary nor a sufficient criterion of backwardness. The Court then goes on to say that, while caste may be relevant in determining the backwardness of individuals, caste groups are themselves not the classes whose backwardness is to be ascertained. It suggests that if the whole caste is backward it should be included among the Scheduled Castes.

Apparently, caste groups are not to be used as the units or classes which are deemed backward. However, the first High Court to which this case was cited had no difficulty in approving the use of caste units. It upheld the classification of Ezhuvas as a backward class, indicating that this was not based on an assessment of their impurity but rather of the continuance of disabilities to which they were subjected. "Habits of thought die hard and slow, and occupations like toddy-tapping carry their social stigma from one generation to another and through decades of conduct."[96] It is not their location in the varna scheme, but their location in the estimate of others and the impact of this on their opportunities which the state may take into account.

In the designating of the beneficiaries of protective discrimination, the Scheduled Castes are selected by a mixture of ritual and social-economic characteristics. In this respect the government has used the shadow or negative of the sacral view of caste. However, in selecting backward classes, the courts have narrowly confined the use of caste standing: it can be used only as an index of social and economic backwardness and then only in conjunction with other tests. The permissibility of using caste groups as units is open to doubt. Insofar as caste may be used in this area, it is caste conceived in the organic view—as a group with a relative share of social, educational, economic resources, rather than as a group with a given ritual standing.

With membership in caste groups a qualification for preferment of various kinds, it is not surprising that disputes have arisen concerning such membership. In order to qualify for preferences, one must be a member of the listed caste. In *Chatturbhuj Vithaldas Jasani v. Moreshwar Pareshram*, the Supreme Court decided that a Mahar who had joined the Mahanubhava Panth,[97] a Hindu sect which repudiated the multiplicity of gods and the caste system, remained a Mahar (thus eligible to stand for a reserved seat in the legislature). The Court arrived at this conclusion on the ground that he had continued to identify himself as a Mahar and had retained full acceptance by the Mahar community.

95. A.I.R. 1964 S.C. 1823 at 1833. One of the remarkable and confusing aspects of these cases is that the courts manage to use the word caste to mean successively (1) "communal unit" and (2) "caste rank or standing" without feeling any need for clarification or distinction. I have tried here to sort out these meanings.
96. *State of Kerala v. Jacob Mathew*, I.L.R. 1964(2) Ker. 53 at 60.
97. On the role of this sect in Mahar tradition, see Miller (1966).

The Court concluded that "conversion to this sect imports little beyond an intellectual acceptance of certain ideological tenets and does not alter the convert's caste status."[98] Thus the Court saw no distinctive religious content in membership in the caste; its bonds are "social and political ties." "If the individual . . . desires and intends to retain his old social and political ties," and if the old order is tolerant of the new faith and does not expel the convert, the conversion does not affect his caste membership.[99] However, the Court recognizes that there is a religious level to caste affiliation as well. It is not only the convert's own choice that must be taken into account, "but also the views of the body whose religious tenets he has renounced because here the right [to stand for a reserved seat] is a right of the old body, the right conferred upon it as a special privilege to send a member of its own fold to Parliament."[100]

The same question came before the Madras High Court in the case of *Shyamsunder v. Shankar Deo*,[101] where the question was whether the candidate had lost his membership in the Samgar caste by joining the Arya Samaj, a Hindu sect which rejects idolatry and ascription of caste by birth. The Court said there would be no deprivation of caste unless there was either expulsion by the old caste or intentional abandonment or renunciation by the convert. Since there was no evidence of expulsion or ostracism by the old caste, the question was whether there had been a break from the old order "so complete and final that . . . he no longer regarded himself as a member of the Samgar caste."[102] Here the Court felt this was refuted not only by his activities but by his testimony that he believed in idols and in texts repudiated by the Samajists. Again while religious criteria played a secondary role in defining membership in caste, the Court, like the *Jasani* Court, conceived of the caste as having some body of religious tenets. One might be a member while repudiating them, but adhering to them was evidence that one regarded oneself as a member. In these cases, the view of caste fits what we have called the associational model. It is a group characterized by a constellation of social and political ties; it has "religious tenets," though adherence to them is not a requisite for membership so long as the other ties are not severed.

In *V.V. Giri v. D. Suri Dora* the question before the Supreme Court was whether a candidate had lost his membership in the Moka Dora tribe by becoming a Kshatriya. The candidate was born a Moka Dora, and his family had described itself as such in all documents from 1885 to 1923. Since that time they had described themselves as Kshatriyas. There was evidence that the

---

98. [1954] S.C.R. 817 at 840.

99. *Id*. at 839.

100. *Id*. at 839. Perhaps the "religious tenets" language is here only because the Court used as authority the case of *Abraham v. Abraham*, 9 M.I.A. 199 (1863), which involved conversion from one religion to another with retention of personal law.

101. A.I.R. 1960 Mys. 27.

102. *Id*. at 32. The caste referred to as "Samgar" here is evidently the same as that listed as "Samagara" in Census of India, Paper no. 2 (1960): Scheduled Castes and Scheduled Tribes Arranged in Alphabetical Order, p. 84. The Sonar caste, mentioned below, are traditionally goldsmiths and of a higher social standing, usually associated with Vaishya status.

family had adopted Kshatriya customs, celebrated marriages in Kshatriya style, was connected by marriage to Kshatriya families, employed Brahman priests, and wore the sacred thread in the manner of Kshatriyas.[103] The candidate's election was challenged on the ground that he was no longer a Moka Dora and was therefore ineligible to stand for a seat reserved for Scheduled Tribes. The Supreme Court solved the question by deciding that he had not in fact become a Kshatriya because "the caste status of a person in this context would necessarily have to be determined in the light of the recognition received by him from the members of the caste in which he seeks entry." Finding no evidence of such recognition, the court said that "unilateral acts cannot be easily taken to prove that the claim for the higher status . . . is established."[104] This recognition test is essentially a variant on the reputation test for the varna standing of caste groups. It is notable that it completely excludes any religious test of Kshatriyahood. One judge (J. L. Kapur), dissenting, vigorously rejected the majority notion that caste is determined in the first instance by birth and can be varied (at least upward) only by recognition of his claims by members of the group to which he aspires. He put forward a theory that caste rank varies as a consequence of the gunas, karma, and *subhāvanā* and is dependent on actions; he found that the candidate had "by his actions raised himself to the position of a Kshatriya. . . ."[105] The majority did not accept this but did regard the varna order as hierarchic. It was a hierarchy determined by mutual social acceptance, rather than by possession of traits indicative of religious capacity or attainments.

So long as they are dealing with caste within Hinduism, whether it is the precedence or rights of a caste or membership in it, the courts have been unwilling to describe and rationalize these differences in terms of the sacral model of caste. They assign only a minor role to the religious content of caste and avoid invoking the notion of an overarching sacral order in which all castes are hierarchically arranged. The use of their "untouchability" as the criterion for selecting the scheduled castes implies a kind of reverse recognition of the Hindu ritual order. However, it is clear that such recognition cannot be extended to the selection of the "backward classes." The only instance so far in which we have seen implicit reference to a hierarchical ordering is in the case of the tribals. In the Moka Dora case, the Kshatriya status was denied on grounds that implied such a hierarchy, even though it had no specially religious content. However, when we move to questions which concern persons and groups outside "Hinduism" we find that the religious content of caste re-emerges.

103. A.I.R. 1959 S.C. 1318. Apparently the candidate's family was one of a number of families of Mokasadars or large landholders who, according to the Election Tribunal, "would not like to be called Moka Doras but considered themselves Kshatriyas." XV E.L.L. 1 at 38 (1957). The tribunal found that the candidate had "totally given up feeling himself to be a member of the Moka Dora tribe and considers himself a Kshatriya." *Id*. For a comparison of the divergent approaches of the Election Tribunal, the High Court and the Supreme Court in this case, see Galanter (1962, pp. 337ff.).

104. A.I.R. 1959 S.C. at 1327.

105. *Id*. at 1331. "Gunas," etc. means roughly material nature, deeds and temperament.

THE "HINDU" COMPONENT OF CASTE

The Constitution forbids religious discrimination on the part of the state[106] and guarantees freedom of religion.[107] The courts have been vigilant in invalidating governmental measures framed along religious lines.[108] Nevertheless, in some instances religion has been made a qualification for preferential treatment. The president's order specifying Scheduled Castes provided that "no person professing a religion different from Hinduism shall be deemed a member of a Scheduled Caste."[109] Who is a Hindu? What is the role of caste in deciding who is a Hindu? What is the role of Hinduism in determining membership in a caste group?

The legal definition of Hinduism, developed for the purpose of applying appropriate personal law, was not a measure of religious belief, nor was it a description of social behavior so much as a civil status describing everyone subjected to the application of "Hindu law" in the areas reserved for personal law.[110] Heterodox practice, lack of belief, active support of non-Hindu religious groups,[111] expulsion by a group within Hinduism[112]—none of these removed one from the Hindu category, which included all who did not openly renounce it or explicitly accept a hostile religion.[113] The individual could venture as far as he wished over any doctrinal or behavioral borders; the gates would not shut

106. Arts. 15, 16.

107. Arts. 25, 26, 30. On Indian secularism generally, see Smith (1963); Galanter (1965); Seminar 67 (1965).

108. *State of Rajasthan v. Pratap Singh*, A.I.R. 1960 S.C. 1208; *Nain Sukh Das v. State of U.P.*, A.I.R. 1953 S.C. 384; *State of Jammu and Kashmir v. Jagar Nath*, A.I.R. 1958 J and K 14.

109. Constitution (Scheduled Castes) Order, 1950, para. 3. An exception was included for Sikh members of 4 of the 34 Scheduled Castes listed for the Punjab. In 1956, the main provision was expanded to include all Sikhs, so that it now reads "no person who professes a religion different from the Hindu or Sikh religion shall be deemed a member of a Scheduled Caste." The Scheduled Castes and Scheduled Tribes Orders (Amendment) Act, 1956 (Act 63 of 1956), para. 3. Cf. the Government of India (Scheduled Caste) Order, 1936, para. 3, which provided: "No Indian Christian shall be deemed a member of a Scheduled Caste." The Constitution (Scheduled Tribes) Order, 1950, contains no religious qualifications.

110. Or, more accurately, all who would be subject to Hindu law in the absence of proved special custom or of a contingency such as marriage under the Special Marriage Act (III of 1872). On the other hand, it does not include all persons subject to Hindu law. Hindu personal law has sometimes been applied to Christians (see *Abraham v. Abraham, supra*, note 100) and to Muslims (until the passage of the Muslim Personal law (Shariat) Application Act XXXVI of 1937). See also *Chinnaswamy v. Anthonyswamy*, A.I.R. 1961 Ker. 161 (Tamil Vaniya Christian Community of Chittur Taluk governed by Hindu law in matters of inheritance and succession); cf. *Mira Devi v. Aman Kumari*, A.I.R. 1962 M.P. 212 (tribals may be subject to Hindu law although they are not Hindus).

See the broad definition in the Hindu Marriage Act, 1955, Sec. 2, and discussion in Derrett (1963, Sec. 17ff.).

111. *Bhagwan Koer v. Bose*, 30 I.A. 249 (1903). One remains a Hindu even when he joins a sect which has non-Hindu members. *State of Bombay v. Yagna Sastri Purushadasji*, 61 Bom. L. Reporter 700 (1960).

112. *Ratansi D. Morarji v. Admr. General of Madras*, A.I.R. 1928 Mad. 1279 at 1283.

113. The concept of "Muslim" is treated somewhat differently. There are expressions of the same negative (no conversion) test. See *Bhagwan Bakhsh Singh v. Dribijai Singh*, I.L.R. 6 Luck. 487 (1931). Generally it is held that adherence to some minimum of beliefs (the unity of God, the mission of Mohammed, the authority of the Koran) is necessary and sufficient to make one a Muslim. *Narantakath v. Parakkal*, I.L.R. 45 Mad. 986 (1922); *Jiwan Khan v. Habib*, I.L.R. 14 Lah. 518 (1933). Repudiation of these beliefs, even without conversion to another religion, makes one not a Muslim. *Resham Bibi v. Khuda Bakhsh*, I.L.R. 19 Lah. 277 (1938).

behind him if he did not explicitly adhere to another communion.[114] In *Chandrasekhara Mudaliar v. Kulandaivelu Mudaliar*[115] the Supreme Court had to decide on the validity of a consent to adoption by a sapinda who disavowed belief in the religious efficacy of adoption, in Hindu rituals and scriptures, in atman, and salvation. But the Court found that "the fact that he does not believe in such things does not make him any the less a Hindu. . . . He was born a Hindu and continues to be one until he takes to another religion . . . whatever may be his personal predilections or views on Hindu religion and its rituals. . . ."[116]

In the post-constitutional cases involving preferences, the same broad conception of Hinduism has been carried over from the area of personal law. To "profess" Hinduism merely means to be a Hindu by birth or conversion.[117] Unorthodoxy or lack of personal belief in its tenets does not mean lack of profession for this purpose. In effect the test seems to amount to a willingness to refrain from calling oneself something else. Thus, where the election to a reserved seat of an active supporter of Dr. Ambedkar's Buddhist movement was challenged on the ground that he was not a Hindu, the Court found that "it has to be established that the person concerned has publicly entered a religion different from the Hindu . . . religion." Mere declarations falling short of this would not be sufficient.[118] The candidate had supported the movement for mass conversion by serving on the reception committee, editing a newspaper supporting the movement, and attending a rally where an oath, "I abandon the Hindu religion and accept the Buddha religion" was administered by Dr. Ambedkar. When those who wished to convert were asked to stand, the candidate stood. But there was no evidence that he did in fact take the oath; the Court held that in the absence of evidence of such a declaration, he remained a Hindu.[119] The same test of public declaration was recently upheld by the Supreme Court

---

114. No proof of formal abandonment of his new religion is necessary for the convert to effect a successful reconversion to Hinduism. While a mere declaration is not sufficient to restore him to Hinduism, acceptance by a Hindu community with whatever formalities it deems proper—even none at all—is sufficient. *Durgaprasada Rao v. Sundarsanaswami*, A.I.R. 1940 Mad. 513; *Gurusami Nadar v. Irulappa Konar*, A.I.R. 1934 Mad. 630. However, cf. *Marthamma v. Munuswami*, A.I.R. 1951 Mad. 888 at 890, where the primary test is the "intention" of the reconvert; the court says "the religious persuasion of a man now-a-days depends on his 'subjective preference' for any religion."

For purposes of at least certain preferences, re-converts to Hinduism who were born in Scheduled Castes are deemed members of the Scheduled Castes. But those born in another religion (for example, whose fathers were converts) are not treated as members of Scheduled Castes "whatever may be their original family connections." *Report for the Commissioner for Scheduled Castes and Scheduled Tribes* (1953, p. 132). In the personal law cases, acceptance by the community was a measure of one's success in re-entering Hinduism; here, Hindu birth is the condition of gaining membership in the community.

115. A.I.R. 1963 S.C. 185.

116. *Id.* at 200.

117. *Michael v. Venkataswaran*, A.I.R. 1952 Mad. 474.

118. *Karwadi v. Shambharkar*, A.I.R. 1958 Bom. 296 at 297. On the Buddhist movement, see Zelliot (1966).

119. *Karwadi v. Shambharkar*, Id. at 299. The vagaries of the declaration test are illustrated in *Rattan Singh v. Devinder Singh*, VII E.L.R. 234 (1953), XI E.L.R. 67 (1955), where the candidate had at various times described himself as a Mazhabi Sikh, a Harijan Hindu, a Balmiki, and a Balmiki Hindu.

in *Punjabrao v. D. P. Meshram,* where the Court found that a conversion had in fact occurred.[120]

Once it is established that the candidate has "professed" Buddhism, the question arises whether this is a religion "different from the Hindu religion" within the meaning of the Scheduled Castes Order. Converts to Christianity and Islam are, of course, non-Hindus.[121] But Buddhists, Jains, and Sikhs are treated as Hindus for many purposes.[122] Hindu is an equivocal term, sometimes used to refer to adherents of more or less "orthodox" vedic and brahmanical communions and at other times used to embrace the full array of "heterodox" groups, including Sikhs, Jains, and Buddhists. Yet Jains and Buddhists are considered non-Hindus for purposes of preferences; Sikhs were originally excluded and are now mentioned separately.[123] The Supreme Court concluded that "Hindu" in the Scheduled Castes Order "is used in the narrower sense of the orthodox Hindu religion which recognizes castes and contains injunctions based on caste distinctions."[124] This comes close to suggesting a positive definition of Hinduism which goes beyond merely excluding Sikhs, Jains, and Buddhists, to throw doubt on the inclusion of those sects which in one fashion or another repudiate caste distinctions in doctrine or practice. This association of Hinduism with caste distinctions is particularly puzzling in view of the Supreme Court's subsequent indication that invidious caste distinctions are "founded upon superstition, ignorance and complete misunderstanding of the true teachings of Hindu religion . . ."[125]

The *Meshram* Court, while inquiring what it means to "profess" a religion "different from the Hindu" reads the order as requiring that to be treated as a member of a Scheduled Caste "a person . . . must be one who professes either Hindu or Sikh religion."[126] And it notes that "the word 'profess' in the presidential order appears to have been used in the sense of open declaration or practice by a person of the Hindu (or the Sikh) religion."[127] In these dicta the Court comes perilously close to suggesting a positive religious test for membership in Scheduled Castes. In spite of the Court's remarks, it is clear that the Scheduled

120. A.I.R. 1965 S.C. 1179.

121. *Michael v. Venkataswaran,* A.I.R. 1952 Mad. 474.

122. These groups are Hindu for purposes of personal law, but their separateness has been recognized in other contexts, for example, Jains are not "the same religion" as Hindus for purposes of temple-entry legislation. *State v. Puranchand,* A.I.R. 1958 M.P. 352; *Devarajiah v. Padmanna,* A.I.R. 1958 Mys. 84. Yet they are "Hindus" with the definitions contained in most temple-entry acts. Cf. Constitution of India, Art. 25(2)(b) Explanation I. Recently the Supreme Court has indicated that the boundaries of Hinduism for this purpose enfold even sects with historical Hindu connections who currently assert that they constitute a distinct religion. *Sastri Yagnapurushadasji v. Muldas Bhundardas Vaishya,* A.I.R. 1966 S.C. 1119. Differences in regard to the organization of religious trusts may be recognized by having a Hindu religious trusts law which covers Jains and Buddhists but not Sikhs. *Moti Das v. S.P. Sahi,* A.I.R. 1959 S.C. 942.

123. *Gurmukh Singh v. Union of India,* A.I.R. 1952 Pun. 143; *Rattan Singh v. Devinder Singh,* VII E.L.R. 234 (1953), XI E.L.R. 67 (1955). See note 109 above.

124. A.I.R. 1965 S.C. at 1184.

125. *Sastri Yagna Purushadasji v. Muldas Bhundaras Vaishya, supra* note 122, at 1135. In this case the court propounds a normative view of Hinduism which seems to withdraw the mantle of religion from such practices.

126. A.I.R. 1965 S.C. at 1184.

127. *Id.*

Caste Order itself does not establish or sanction such a positive religious test. It does not require anyone to profess Hinduism, much less practice it. It merely requires that he not profess a different religion. In determining this, the profession and practice of Hinduism need be considered, as they are in *Meshram,* only for their evidentiary value.

It is clear, then, that Buddhists are excluded by the presidential order. The Supreme Court merely notes that when a person "has ceased to be a Hindu he cannot derive any benefit from that Order."[128] Persistent efforts by Buddhists to be treated as members of Scheduled Castes have proved unavailing.[129] Their exclusion is usually justified on the ground that conversion to Buddhism operates as loss of caste. "As Buddhism is different from the Hindu religion, any person belonging to a Scheduled Caste ceases to be so if he changes his religion. He is not, therefore, entitled to the facilities provided under the Constitution specifically for the Scheduled Castes."[130] The central government, recognizing that conversion itself is unlikely to improve the condition of the converts, has recommended that the state governments accord the Buddhists the concessions available to backward classes. Such preferences, less in scope and quantity than those for Scheduled Castes, have been granted in some cases.[131]

In *Punjabrao v. Meshram,* the Supreme Court never reaches the question of whether the "Hinduism" test for recipients of preferences infringes the constitutional ban on religious discrimination by the state.[132] The constitutional challenge has been raised in several earlier cases in the High Courts. The judicial response to this challenge presents the problem of characterizing the relation of the caste group to Hinduism.

In *S. Gurmukh Singh v. Union of India,*[133] a Bawaria Sikh protested his exclusion from the Scheduled Castes, in which the President had included Hindu Bawarias. The Court found that Article 341 empowered the President to select those "parts of castes" which he felt should be included and that he could select these parts on the basis of religion. He did not violate Article 15(1), the ban

128. *Id.*
129. A bill to this effect was defeated in the Lok Sabha. *New York Times,* Aug. 30, 1961, p. 2, col. 6. On the problems that the "Hinduism test" presents for the neo-Buddhists, see Isaacs (1965, p. 117 ff.).
130. *Reports of the Commissioner of Scheduled Castes and Scheduled Tribes* (1957–1958, I, 25). This ruling is based squarely on the "Hinduism" requirement of the President's Order. See the statement of Pandit Pant, *Times of India,* Aug. 21, 1957, p. 12, col. 3.
131. *Report of the Commissioner of Scheduled Castes and Scheduled Tribes* (1957–1958, I, 25; II, 60). While some states have included Buddhists within the backward classes, others have continued to treat them like Scheduled Castes for some purposes, and still others have withdrawn all preferential treatment.
In Maharashtra, where over three-quarters of the Buddhists live, they enjoy all concessions and facilities extended to the Scheduled Castes by the state government. They do not enjoy the constitutional provisions for reserved seats or the benefits provided by the central government, especially post-matriculation scholarships and job reservations.
132. The question was never raised. In the Election Tribunal, the candidate contested the fact of the conversion. Apparently, counsel for the challenged candidate were eager to argue that Buddhists were indeed Hindus. The High Court excluded this issue as a factual question which should have been pleaded and proved by evidence, but decided in favor of the candidate, finding no conversion had occurred. The Supreme Court reversed, finding there was a conversion. At no stage was the constitutional issue raised.
133. A.I.R. 1952 Punj. 143.

against religious discrimination, since Article 15(4), which authorizes preferential treatment of the backward classes, operated as an exception to the prohibitions of Article 15(1). The Court conceded that Scheduled Castes were to be designated on the basis of their backwardness. But, finding that the Constitution vested in the President the entire power to make such determinations, the Court refused to review his order by considering whether the Sikh Bawarias were in fact sufficiently backward to be included. In this situation, it is conceded that these non-Hindus either constitute or are members of a caste group; what is decided is that the President's exclusion of that group (or part of the group) is unreviewable.[134]

In *Michael v. Venkataswaran*[135] the religious requirement was upheld against a Paraiyan convert to Christianity who wished to stand for a reserved seat. Even if there are cases in which both the convert and his caste fellows consider him as still being a member of the caste, the Court found, "the general rule, is [that] conversion operates as an expulsion from the caste . . . a convert ceases to have any caste."[136] The presidential order, according to the Court, proceeds on this assumption and takes note of a few exceptions. The Court declined to sit in judgment on the President's determination that similar exceptional conditions do not prevail in other instances. Thus the presidential order was upheld not because of an absence of judicial power to review it but because of its accuracy in the general run of cases.

In *In re Thomas*[137] another bench of the Madras court considered a convert case which did not involve the presidential order. The Madras government had extended school-fee concessions to converts from Scheduled Castes "provided . . . that the conversion was of the . . . student or of his parent. . . ." A Christian student whose grandfather had converted could not, it was held, complain of discrimination, since converts did not belong to the Harijan community. By conversion they had "ceased to belong to any caste because the Christian religion does not recognize a system of castes."[138] The concessions to recent converts were merely an indulgence, and the state could determine the extent of this indulgence.

The theory that acceptance of a non-Hindu religion operates as loss of caste reflects the continued force of the sacral view of caste. The question arises in two kinds of factual situations: first, those involving a caste group or a section

134. The unreviewability of the presidential order would seem open to question in the light of subsequent cases which have firmly established judicial power to review the standards used by government to designate the recipients of preferential treatment. *Balaji v. State of Mysore*, A.I.R. 1963 Mys. 649. There is no indication in the Constitution that executive action, even in pursuance of expressly granted and exclusive constitutional powers, is immune from judicial review for conformity with constitutional guarantees of fundamental rights. See Article 12. The position in the *Gurmukh Singh* case must be seen as one of judicial restraint rather than judicial powerlessness. The restraint there expressed seems out of line with later judicial assertiveness in this area.

135. *Michael v. Venkataswaran*, A.I.R. 1952 Mad. 474.

136. *Id*. at 478.

137. A.I.R. 1953 Mad. 21.

138. *Id*. at 88. The exclusion of neo-Buddhists from the preferences for Scheduled Castes has been similarly justified by the notion that "Buddhism [does] not recognize castes." Statement of Mr. B. N. Datar in Rajya Sabha, Aug. 26, 1957. Reported in *Times of India*, Aug. 27, 1957, p. 10, col. 1.

of a caste made up of members who are non-Hindus; second, those involving an individual convert. In the first type, there is little dispute that such persons as the Sikh Bawarias in the *Gurmukh Singh* case are, in fact, members of a caste in one of the segmental senses of caste encountered in the law. The existence of such caste groups among non-Hindus in India is well known and has long been recognized by the judiciary.[139] To refuse to recognize caste membership among such non-Hindu groups implies that the "caste" of which the court is speaking is not a caste in the sense of a body of persons bound by social ties, but a caste in the sense of a body which occupies a place in the ritual order of Hinduism.[140]

The second type of case is that of the individual convert. In such cases, the question facing the court would seem to be whether the individual convert's acceptance of Christianity, Islam, or Buddhism evidences a loss of membership in the caste group to which he belonged at the time of the conversion. This can be treated as a question of fact, to be answered by evidence about his observable interactions with other members of the group. This was the approach taken in the cases dealing with conversions to sects within Hinduism. It is the approach taken in dealing with converts among the Scheduled Tribes.[141] It is presumably the approach that would be taken with Scheduled Caste converts to Sikhism. But it is not taken with Scheduled Caste converts to other religions. Yet in at least some cases of conversion outside Hinduism, there is evidence that the convert continues to regard himself and to be regarded by others as a member of the old caste.[142] In dealing with these conversions to religions outside Hinduism, the courts have forsaken this empirical approach and have treated the conversion as depriving him of his membership as a matter of law. This conclusion derives not from the facts of the individual case but from a view of castes as the components in the sacral order of Hinduism. When that overarching scheme is abandoned, so is caste membership.

Caste Autonomy

Notwithstanding the common rhetoric about the "casteless" society, the Constitution is quite unclear about the position of the caste group in Indian life. While there are guarantees to preserve the integrity of religious and linguistic

139. Cf. *Report of the Backward Classes Commission* (1956, I, 28ff.).

140. The inclusion of Sikhs along with Hindus in 1956 (see note 109 above) renders this view even less tenable than it might have been earlier. As it stands, caste groups are to be recognized outside of the Hindu fold, but only among Sikhs and not among Christians, Muslims, and Buddhists.

141. *Kartik Oraon v. David Munzni*, A.I.R. 1964 Pat. 201; *Gadipalli Paroyya v. Goyina Rajaryya*, XII E.L.R. 83 (1956).

142. The reports are replete with cases in which converts have lived so indistinguishably with their caste fellows that the courts retrospectively infer a tacit reconversion without either formal abjuration of the new religion or formal expiation and readmittance to Hinduism. *Durgaprasda Rao v. Sundarsauaswaram*, A.I.R. 1940 Mad. 513; *Gurusami Nadar v. Kurulappa Konar*, A.I.R. 1934 Mad. 630; *Venkatramayya v. Seshayya*, A.I.R. 1942 Mad. 193. The "indulgence" extended by the state in the *Thomas* case, *supra* note 137, seems to reflect an awareness that recent converts, if not effective members of their old castes, are at least subject to similar disabilities. And cf. *Muthasami Mudaliar v. Masilami*, I.L.R. 33 Mad. 342 (1909), where lifelong Christians were accepted as members of a Hindu caste.

groups,[143] there are none for the caste group. It would not seem to enjoy any constitutional protection as such. This silence may represent an anticipation that caste will wither away and have no important place in the new India, or it may represent an implicit ratification of the old policy of noninterference.

There is a desire to minimize the impact of caste groupings in public life. The government has discouraged the use of caste as a legal identification.[144] Appeals to caste loyalty in electoral campaigning are forbidden.[145] Promotion of enmity between castes is a serious criminal offense.[146]

Apart from explicit restrictions on caste discrimination, there is a tendency to discourage any arrangements which promote the coherence and integrity of the caste group as such. Thus, for example, the Supreme Court struck down as unreasonable restrictions on property rights laws providing for pre-emption on the basis of vicinage. The Court held that the real purpose of these laws was to promote communal neighborhoods, a purpose which could have no force as public policy, since the desire to promote such exclusiveness could no longer be considered reasonable.[147]

143. Articles 25–30, 350A, 350B.

144. The Registration Act has been amended to exclude the requirement of caste as personal identification. Indian Registration (Amendment) Act, 1956 (Act XVII of 1956) Sec. 2.

145. Representation of the People Act (Act XLIII of 1951), Sec. 123. It is not entirely clear just what sort of appeals are barred by this provision. Appealing to Chambhars to elect a Chambhar brother has been held to be a corrupt election practice. *Lachhiram v. Jamuna Prasad Mukhariya*, 9 E.L.R. 149 (Elec. Tribunal, Gwalior, 1953). So also with appeals to Gadarias to vote for Gadarias and not for Brahmans. *Shiv Dutt v. Bansidas Dhangar [No. 2]*, 9 E.L.R. 325 (Elec. Tribunal, Faizabad, 1954). But an appeal to "all Yadav brethren to do their duty to the country by voting Congress" is not an appeal on grounds of caste. Nor is an appeal to Vishwakarmas and Kalakars to vote for a candidate because of his service to their professions. *Rustom Satin v. Dr. Sampoornanand*, 20 E.L.R. 221 (Allahabad High Court, 1958). Nor is an appeal to voters to support a candidate because their caste organizations support his party (Congress). *Sant Prasad Singh v. Dasu Sinha*, A.I.R. 1964 Pat. 26. Nor is an appeal to a community not to vote for a party on the ground of alleged misdeeds to the community. *Raja Vijai Kumar Tripathi v. Ram Saran Yadav*, 18 E.L.R. 289 (Allahabad High Court, 1958). Nor are appeals to the loyalty of ascriptive groupings smaller than caste (*gotra*). *Pratap Singh v. Nihal Singh*, 3. E.L.R. 31 (Elec. Tribunal, Patiala, 1953). Nor are appeals to classes of persons made up of a number of castes (backward classes). *Raja Vijai Kumar Tripathi v. Ram Saran Yadav, supra*. It appears, then, that the forbidden appeals are only appeals to members of a caste to vote for a member of that caste on grounds of his membership in that caste (or against a member of another caste on grounds of his membership in that other caste). Presumably all but the most unsophisticated politicians can manage to avoid this class of appeals.

146. Section 153-A of the Penal Code (first enacted as Act IV of 1898), which provided up to two years' imprisonment for promoting feelings of enmity between different classes of Indian citizens, was replaced by a new enactment in 1961. (Act XLI of 1961). The new 153-A provides:

Whoever—

(a) by words, either spoken or written, or by signs or by visible representations or otherwise, promotes, or attempts to promote, on grounds of religion, race, language, caste or community or any other ground whatsoever, feelings of enmity or hatred between different religious, racial or language groups or castes or communities, or

(b) commits any act which is prejudicial to the maintenance of harmony between different religious, racial or language groups or castes or communities and which disturbs or is likely to disturb the public tranquility, shall be punished with imprisonment which may extend to three years, or with fine or with both.

For an interesting American analogy, see *Beauharnais v. Illinois*, 343 U.S. 250 (1951).

147. *Bhau Ram v. Baij Nath*, A.I.R. 1962 S.C. 1476. Compare *Ram Swarup v. Munshi*, A.I.R. 1963 S.C. 553, where the Supreme Court took a more lenient view of pre-emption which aimed at preserving the integrity of the village and familial expectations. In this regard the Court's view runs parallel to the government's preference for the village unit over the communal one, for example, in implementation of Panchayati Raj.

What is left of caste autonomy? What remains of the prerogatives previously enjoyed by the caste group? The caste retains the right to own and manage property and to sue in court. Section 9 of the Civil Procedure Code, with its bar on judicial cognizance of "caste questions," is still in force. Courts still refuse to entertain suits involving caste questions (for example, fitness of an officer to manage property),[148] and castes retain their disciplinary powers over their members (for example, a court refused to declare invalid the assessment of a fine for an alleged breach of caste rules).[149] The caste retains its power of excommunication.[150] It is still a good defense to a criminal action for defamation to assert the privilege of communicating news of an excommunication to one's caste fellows.[151] Yet these powers are subject to some restriction. The UOA makes inroads on caste autonomy by making it an offense to expel caste fellows or boycott outsiders for their failure to enforce disabilities.[152] And the Representation of the People Act forbids the use of caste disciplinary machinery for political purposes.[153]

In one sense the autonomy of the caste group is enhanced by the constitutional provisions. One of the basic themes of the Constitution is to eliminate caste as a differentia in the relationship of government to the individual—as subject, voter, or employee. The Constitution enshrines as fundamental law that government must regulate individuals directly and not through the medium of the communal group. The individual is responsible for his own conduct and cannot, by virtue of his membership in a caste, be held accountable for the conduct of others. Thus the imposition of severe police restrictions on specified

148. *Kanji Gagji v. Ghikha Ganda*, A.I.R. 1955 N.U.C. 986.

149. *Bharwad Kama v. Bai Mina*, A.I.R. 1953 Saur. 133.

150. *Varadiah v. Parthasarathy*, 1964 (2) Mad. 417 (in spite of the changing social order "where an individual has done something wrong or prejudicial to the interests of his community, the members of his community which, by virtue of custom or usage, is competent to deal with such matters [can] take a decision by common consent; and so long as such a decision does not offend law, it can be enforced by the will of the community." (*Id.* at 420). But composite groups such as "non-Brahmans" and "caste Hindus" do not enjoy the privilege when they undertake to outcaste for caste offenses. *Ellappa v. Ellappa*, A.I.R. 1950 Mad. 409.
The powers of the caste closely parallel those of the club. Cf. *T. P. Daver v. Victoria Lodge*, A.I.R. 1963 S.C. 1144 (expulsion for "Masonic offenses"). The grounds for judicial intervention in such private groupings are analogous to those employed in judicial review of special governmental tribunals. See *Jugal Kishore v. Sahibganj Municipality*, (reviewable only for lack of jurisdiction, procedural irregularities, or violations of natural justice). See, generally, Chakraverti (1965).

151. *Panduram v. Biswambar*, A.I.R. 1958 Or. 256. For a description of the mechanics of outcasting in the caste here involved (Orissa Telis), see Patnaik (1960). *Manna v. Ram Ghulam*, A.I.R. 1950 All. 619 (a caste member is bound to publish the resolution "for saving himself and the caste from the defilement which would take place by acting against the verdict of excommunication." *Id.* at 620).

152. Untouchability (Offenses) Act, 1955, Sec. 3(2). But cf. *Sarat Chandra Das v. State*, A.I.R. 1952 Or. 351, where it was held that imprecations against a priest for associating with Untouchables and taking food from them was admonition and did not amount to criminal defamation.

153. The Representation of the People Act, 1951 Sec. 123(2), makes it "undue influence" and a corrupt election practice if one:
. . . (i) threatens any candidate, or any elector, or any person in whom a candidate or an elector is interested, with injury of any kind, including social ostracism or excommunication or expulsion from any caste or community; or
(ii) induces or attempts to induce a candidate or an elector to believe that he, or any person in whom he is interested, will become or will be rendered an object of divine displeasure or spiritual censure. . . ."

castes in certain villages on grounds of their proclivity to crime was struck down as unconstitutional, since the regulation depended on caste membership rather than on individual propensity.[154] Similarly, the Supreme Court held unconstitutional a punitive levy on a communal basis, since there were some lawabiding citizens in the penalized communities.[155] Thus it would appear that regulative or penal measures directed at certain castes are beyond the power of government; a caste, then, enjoys a new protection from regulation directed at it as a corporate whole.

The autonomy of the caste group is also affected by the provisions of the Constitution which guaranteed the prerogatives of religious groups. Article 26 guarantees to every "religious denomination or section thereof" the right to establish and maintain religious and charitable institutions, to own and administer property and to "manage its own affairs in matters of religion." It is in the application of these denominational rights that we can see the courts envisaging castes in our sectarian model.

In *Sri Venkataramana Devaru v. State of Mysore* the government sought to apply the Madras Temple Entry Act to a temple which the trustees claimed was exempt as a denominational temple belonging to the Gowda Saraswat Brahman community. The government contended that the temple was "only a communal and not a denominational temple" unless it could be established that there were "religious tenets and beliefs special to the community. . . ."[156] Finding that members of the community brought their own idols to the temple, that they recognized the authority of the head of a particular math, and that others were excluded from certain ceremonies, the Supreme Court concluded that they were indeed a "religious denomination." A denomination's right to manage its own affairs in matters of religion included not only matters of doctrine and belief but also practices regarded by the community as part of its religion, including the restriction of participation in religious services.[157] However, the Court found that the temple-entry rights granted by Article 25 included such denominational temples and overrode the denomination's rights to exclude Untouchables completely. The denomination's rights were not entirely without effect, nevertheless. The Court held that the denomination's rights may be recognized where "what is left to the public is something substantial and not merely the husk of it." Since the other occasions of worship were sufficiently numerous that the public's rights were substantial, the Court was willing to recognize the right of the denomination to exclude all non-Gowda Saraswat Brahmans during special ceremonies and on special occasions.

Thus we find that the caste's assertion of its denominational character enables it to enjoy certain prerogatives. But this view of the caste is of a sect or de-

154. *Sanghar Umar Ranmal v. State*, A.I.R. 1952 Saur. 124.
155. *State of Rajasthan v. Pratap Singh*, A.I.R. 1960 S.C. 1208.
156. A.I.R. 1958 S.C. 255 at 263.
157. More recently, the Supreme Court has indicated that maintenance of caste distinctions in places of worship may not in its view be a genuine tenet of Hinduism entitled to the protection of freedom of religion. See *Sastri Yagnapurushadasji v. Muldas Bhundardas Vaishya*, A.I.R. 1966 S.C. 1119, where the Court indicated that such considerations were superstitious and inconsistent with "the true teachings of Hindu religion."

nomination; its claim rests not on its position in the overarching Hindu order but on its religious distinctiveness.

In *Saifuddin Saheb v. State of Bombay*, the Supreme Court held that the power to excommunicate for infractions of religious discipline is part of the constitutional right of a religious denomination to manage its own affairs in matters of religion.[158] The case, involving excommunication from a Muslim sect, held unconstitutional a Bombay act making excommunication a criminal offense. This does not imply a similar protection for caste groups as such; it would presumably protect only those that can qualify as religious denominations. It probably would not protect excommunication that was merely social and was not "to preserve the essentials of religion." Even if the excommunication were a matter of religious discipline, it would presumably not be constitutionally protected if the breach of discipline involved failure to observe untouchability[159] or if its purpose were political.[160]

Once a caste is recognized as a religious denomination, then as a religious group it is presumably a "minority . . . based on religion" and as such enjoys a constitutional right under Article 30(1) "to establish and administer educational institutions of [its] choice." Article 30(2) provides that, in granting aid to educational institutions, the state shall not "discriminate against any educational institution on the ground that it is under the management of a minority, whether based on religion or language." (On the other hand, once it receives state aid it cannot discriminate on caste lines in admissions.)[161]

To the extent that its religious (or other) distinctiveness can be construed as giving it a "distinct . . . culture of its own," the caste group may merit the protection afforded by Article 29(1), which provides that "Any section of . . . citizens . . . having a distinct language, script, or culture of its own shall have a right to conserve the same." Article 29 has rarely been considered by the courts independently; usually it has been mentioned only in the context of the assertion of rights under Article 30(1). Apparently, every religious denomination or section thereof might qualify as a cultural group. Their right to "conserve" their culture clearly includes the right to transmit this culture. In the *Bombay Education Society* case, the Supreme Court referred to "the right to impart instruction in their own institutions to children of their own community in

158. A.I.R. 1962 S.C. 853.
159. Excommunication on this ground is forbidden by the Untouchability (Offenses) Act, Sec. 7(2). I have seen no post-constitutional case involving this section. (Cf. *Sri Sukratendar Thirtha Swami of Kashi Mutt v. Prabhu*, A.I.R. 1923 Mad. 582, for the old law). The conclusion here is by analogy with the *Devaru* case, *supra* note 156, where the temple-entry rights were held to override the denominational rights. The instant situation might of course be distinguished on the ground that here the excommunicated party is asserting no constitutional right of his own, but is only vicariously asserting the Article 17 rights of the Untouchable. However, Article 17 might be read as conferring directly on every person a right to immunity from caste action against him for the purpose of enforcing untouchability. Cf. *Barrows v. Jackson*, 346 U.S. 249 (1953).
160. Representation of the People Act, Sec. 123 (see note 153 above). Cf. *Ram Dial v. Sant Lal*, A.I.R. 1959 S.C. 855, where Sat Guru's threats of expulsion from the Namdhari sect of Sikhs were found to constitute undue influence, a corrupt practice sufficiently serious to void the election of this candidate.
161. Art. 29(2).

their own language" as the "greater part" of the contents of Article 29.[162] However, more recently the Supreme Court has held that this right extends to political action to preserve the distinctive characteristics of the group, even where this involved resistance to, and disparagement of, the cultural claims of others.[163]

The potential protections of Articles 29 and 30 have been radically enhanced by several recent judgments of the Supreme Court, which refer to these rights as "absolute," in contrast to most fundamental rights, which are subject to "reasonable restrictions" with a view to various public interests. In *Rev. Sidhrajbhai Sabbaji v. State of Gujarat,* the Court invalidated a government order threatening withdrawal of aid and recognition from a teacher-training institution which refused to reserve 80 per cent of its places for government appointees. It held that the right of a Presbyterian Society under Article 30(1) to run its schools was "absolute" and "not to be whittled down by so-called regulative measures conceived in the interest not of the minority educational institution, but of the public or the nation as a whole."[164] Thus governmental regulation of minority educational institutions must be not only reasonable, but "conducive to making the institution an effective vehicle of education for the minority community. . . ." In *Jagdev Singh v. Pratap Singh,* the Supreme Court held that election appeals to vote for a candidate on the ground that he would conserve Hindi (by opposing introduction of Punjabi as a second language in the schools) was not a corrupt election practice, but was instead protected by Article 29(1). "The right conferred upon the section of the citizens . . . to conserve their language script or culture is made by the Constitution absolute. . . ."[165]

Presumably, then, any group which can characterize itself as either "a minority based upon religion" or a "section of citizens with a distinct . . . culture" may qualify for a wide range of protections. The characterization of the caste group by the sectarian model puts it in the constitutionally privileged status of a religious denomination. Once so characterized, the group enjoys, to some extent at least, constitutional protection not only in its right to control its religious premises but also in its rights to excommunicate dissidents, to maintain educational institutions free from government regulation which is not in *its* interest, and to "conserve" its distinctive culture by political means. Of course this applies only to those castes which could qualify as "religious denominations or section[s] thereof." It seems unlikely, however, that any government could allow these privileges to some castes and not to others; and in any event it seems

162. *State of Bombay v. Bombay Education Society,* 17 S.C.J. 678 (1954).

163. *Jagdev Singh v. Pratap Singh,* A.I.R. 1965 S.C. 183.

164. A.I.R. 1963 S.C. 540. Compare the less stringent views in *In re Kerala Education Bill,* A.I.R. 1958 S.C. 956; *Dipendra Nath v. State of Bihar,* A.I.R. 1962 Pat. 101 at 108. (Articles 29 and 30 concern "the sphere of intellect and culture" and do "not involve dispensation from obedience to general regulations made by the state for promoting the common good of the community."); *Arya Pratinidhi Sabha v. State of Bihar,* A.I.R. 1958 Pat. 359.

165. A.I.R. 1965 S.C. 183 at 188. In *Kultur Singh v. Mukhtiar Singh,* A.I.R. 1965 S.C. 141 (decided after *Jagdev Singh*), the Supreme Court, without mentioning Article 29(2) excluded certain religious appeals from the coverage of corrupt practices: "Political issues which form the subject-matter of controversies at election meetings may indirectly and incidentally introduce considerations of language or religion."

probable that all castes could produce enough distinctive ritual or doctrine to qualify as denominations. This view of caste would seem to present difficulties to those proponents of the casteless society who advocate prohibition of communal charities and educational institutions.[166]

NEW MODELS FOR OLD

Before suggesting some of the implications of this new dispensation, let me summarize briefly the recent changes in the legal characterization of caste. Since independence, the sacral view has been drastically impaired. In the personal law, varna distinctions (and with them the necessity of determining the varna standing of caste groups) have been eliminated, at least for the future, although these matters persist for a time. In the area of precedence and disabilities, there has been a withdrawal of all support for precedence based on ritual standing. This withdrawal is embodied in provisions against caste discrimination, in the abolition of untouchability, and in temple-entry laws. The government has reversed its previous policy by now intervening to prevent the imposition of disabilities and to give preferential treatment to those at the bottom of the socioreligious order. In administering these preferences, the courts have avoided giving recognition to the sacral view, at least when dealing with transactions within Hinduism, although the shadow or mirror of it appears in the definition of Untouchables and it appears in an attenuated form in dealing with non-Hindus.

Where the sacral order implicitly remains, its religious content is relatively diffuse and indefinite. But in other post-independence developments we see caste given a more positive religious treatment. Alongside the remnant of the older one, a different image of the caste group is found, seeing the caste group as a religious unit, denomination, or sect distinguished by its own idiosyncratic cult, doctrine, and ritual. This we found in the cases involving temple entry and in the protection of denominational rights.

The associational model which sees the caste as an association characterized by a complex of characteristics (including but not limited to religious ones) has been strengthened since independence. The area of caste autonomy, where it previously prevailed, is largely unimpaired and in some respects enhanced. It retains a minor but important role in the personal law area. It has been accepted in the cases involving group membership, at least within Hinduism.

The organic model, which stresses the relative economic, educational, and occupational attainments of the caste group, is used (along with a mirror image of the sacral view) in the selection of Scheduled Castes for preferential treatment. For a time, this organic view led a rather vigorous life in the area of preferences for the backward classes. Its use for this purpose is now greatly restricted and very possibly fated to extinction.

In short, there has been a decline in the use of the sacral model and increasing reliance on the other models. We may think of the courts during the British

---

166. See, for example, Narayan (1955, pp. 72, 75); Karve (1961, p. 154). ("Contributions to funds intended to benefit castes or communal groups should be stopped by law.").

period as conceiving of castes primarily as graded components in the sacral order of Hinduism and secondarily as autonomous associations. In administering the law, they were sensitive to vertical differences among castes (expressed in varna distinctions and pollution) as well as to horizontal differences (expressed in sectarian distinctiveness and in caste autonomy). The Constitution now forbids the courts to give recognition and support to the vertical, hierarchical distinctions; but other constitutional provisions (guarantees to religious denominations and of the integrity of groups) enjoin the courts to recognize and support the horizontal distinctions. The Constitution can be read as the "disestablishment" of the sacral view of caste—the courts can give no recognition to the integrative hierarchical principle; yet the Constitution recognizes the claims of the component parts of the system. Claims based on the sacral order are foreclosed (in personal law reform, temple entry, abolition of untouchability, non-recognition of exclusionary rights), but claims based on sectarian distinctiveness or group autonomy are not.

While the integrative and hierarchic elements of the caste system may elicit no (or little) legal recognition or protection, the new dispensation does not prevent caste groups from using their resources (including legal protections and powers) to advance their claims in both "old" (socioritual) and "new" (economic, political) hierarchies. Indeed, the new view of caste is one that seems well suited to a situation in which castes have overlapping claims, functions, and positions in each of several hierarchies; in which "horizontal" solidarity and organization within caste groups grows at the expense of "vertical" integration among the castes of a region; in which relations between castes are increasingly independent and competitive and less interdependent and cooperative (Srinivas, 1962, introduction, chaps. 1, 4, 6; Gould, 1963; Rudolph, 1960). In particular, the new legal view of caste furnishes recognition and protection for the new social forms through which caste concerns may be expressed: caste associations, educational societies, political parties, religious societies, unions, etc. It offers scope not only to the endogamous *jāti* but to "the caste-like units which are so active in politics and administration in modern India" (Srinivas, 1962, 6). We may anticipate that the new legal view of caste will not only sanction but stimulate and encourage new forms of organization, new self-images, and new values within caste groups. And the disestablishment of the predominant organizing model of cultural unity may give new vitality to lesser traditions and new scope for innovation.

We can visualize the judiciary as mediating between the Constitution's commitment to a great social transformation and the actualities of Indian society. The courts must combine and rationalize the various components of the constitutional commitment—voluntarism and respect for group integrity on the one hand, and equality and nonrecognition of rank ordering among groups on the other. They must do this in the process of applying these constitutional principles to claims and conflicts which arise within the existing structure of Indian society. In working out the application of these principles, the judiciary have produced a picture of caste which no one proposed and no one anticipated.

We may also visualize the judiciary as mediating between the aspirations of the "non-caste" (or anti-caste) people, those politicians, publicists, and intellectuals who envision a radical transformation to a "casteless" society, and the attitudes and concerns of the "caste people." The courts provide one forum in which conflicting policies, claims, and ambitions are reconciled. In this process, the implementation of strictures against caste does not lead to the results anticipated by the "no-caste" people. And operating through new channels and with new concepts, caste will be transformed in ways not envisioned by the "caste people." It is just because traditional proponents and modern opponents of caste are linked together by the courts (and other mediating institutions, such as political parties) that it can confidently be predicted that what will emerge will be neither the caste society of the imagined past nor the "casteless" society of the imagined future.

BIBLIOGRAPHY

CHAKRAVERTI, SURANJAN.

1965. *Domestic tribunals and administrative juridictions*. Lucknow: Eastern Book Company.

DERRETT, J. DUNCAN M.

1958. Statutory amendments of the personal law of the Hindus since Indian independence. *American Journal of Comparative Law*, 380.

1963. *Introduction to modern Hindu law*. Bombay: Oxford University Press.

DUSHKIN, LELAH.

1957. *The policy of the Indian National Congress toward the depressed classes*. Unpublished master's thesis, University of Pennsylvania.

1961. The backward classes. *Economic Weekly*, 13: 1665–68; 1695–1705; 1729–38.

GALANTER, MARC.

1961. Caste disabilities and Indian federalism. *Journal of the Indian Law Institute*, 3: 205–34.

1962. The problem of group membership: some reflections on the judicial view of Indian society. *Journal of the Indian Law Institute*, 4: 331–58.

1964a. *Hindu law and the development of the modern Indian legal system*. Paper delivered at the 1964 annual meeting of the American Political Science Association, Chicago.

1964b. Temple entry and the Untouchability (Offenses) Act, 1955. *Journal of the Indian Law Institute*, 6: 185–95.

1965. Secularism east and west. *Comparative Studies in Society and History*, 7: 133–59.

GOULD, HAROLD A.

1963. The adaptive functions of caste in contemporary Indian society. *Asian Survey*, 3: 427–38.

HARPER, EDWARD B.

1964. Ritual pollution as an integrator of caste and religion. *Journal of Asian Studies*, 23: 151–97.

INDIA, BACKWARD CLASSES COMMISSION.

1956. Report 1, 3.

INDIA, COMMISSIONER FOR SCHEDULED CASTES AND SCHEDULED TRIBES.

1953. Report.

1957–58. Reports 1, 2.

ISAACS, HAROLD R.

1965. *India's ex-untouchables*. New York: John Day.

JOSHI, RAO BAHADUR P. C.

1913. History of the Pathare Prabhus and their gurus or spiritual guides. *Journal of the Anthropological Society of Bombay*, 10: 100–38.

KARVE, IRAWATI.

1961. Hindu society—an interpretation. Poona: Deccan College.

KIKANI, L. T.

1912. *Caste in courts or rights and powers of castes in social and religious matters as recognized by Indian courts*. Rajkot.

McCORMACK, WILLIAM.

1963. Lingayats as a sect. *Journal of the Royal Anthropological Institute*, 93, Part I: 57–71.

1966. Caste and the British administration of Hindu law. *Journal of Asian and African Studies*, 1: 25–32.

MILLER, ROBERT.

1966. Button, button . . . great tradition, little tradition, whose tradition? *Anthropological Quarterly*, 39: 26–42.

MULLA, DINSHAH FARDUNJI.

1901. *Jurisdiction of courts in matters relating to the rights and powers of castes*. Bombay: Caxton Printing Works.

NARAYAN, SHRIMAN.

1955. Socialist pattern and social revolution. In Myron Weiner (Ed.), *Developing India*. (2 Vols.) Chicago: University of Chicago Press.

ORENSTEIN, HENRY.

1965. The structure of Hindu caste values: A preliminary study of hierarchy and ritual defilement. *Ethnology*, 4: 1–15.

PATNAIK, NITYANANDA.

1960. Outcasting among oilmen for drinking wine. *Man in India*, 40: 1–7.

RAMAKRISHNA AIYAR, C. S.

1918. Caste customs, caste questions and jurisdiction of courts. *Hindu Law Journal*, Madras, 1921; 1 (May, 1918–June, 1919), Sec. IV: 33–68.

RUDOLPH, LLOYD I., and SUSANNE H. RUDOLPH.

1960. The political role of India's caste associations. *Pacific Affairs*, 33: 5–22.

SEMINAR.

1965. No. 67: *Secularism, a symposium on the implication of national policy*.

SINHA, D. P.

1960. Caste dynamics: case from Uttar Pradesh. *Man in India*, 40: 19–29.

SMITH, DONALD E.

1963. *India as a secular state*. Princeton, N.J.: Princeton University Press.

SRINIVAS, M. N.

1962. *Caste in modern India and other essays*. Bombay: Asia Publishing House.

ZELLIOT, ELEANOR.

1966. Buddhism and politics in Maharashtra. In Donald E. Smith (Ed.), *South Asian Religion and Politics*. Princeton, N.J.: Princeton University Press.

LAW REPORTS CITED

A.I.R.   All-India Reporter. Nagpur: D.V. Chitaley, 1914–.

Bom. L. Reporter   The Bombay Law Reporter. Bombay: The Bombay Law Reporter Office, 1899–.

Crim. L. J.   Criminal Law Journal: a monthly legal publication containing full reports of all reportable criminal cases of the High Courts and Supreme Court of India. Nagpur: All India Reporter, Ltd., 1904–.

Cuttack L. T.   Cuttack Law Times. Cuttack: H. P. Bhagat, 1935–.

E.L.R.   Election Law Reports; containing cases on election law decided by the Supreme Court and the High Court of India, opinions of the Election Commission and important decisions of the election tribunals. Delhi: Election Commission of India, 1951–60.

I.A.   The Law Reports . . . Indian appeals: being cases in the Privy council on appeal from the East Indies. London: Council of Law Reporting, 1874–1950.

I.L.R. (All.)   The Indian Law Reports, Allahabad series. Allahabad: Government Press, 1876–.

I.L.R. (Bom.)   The Indian Law Reports, Bombay series, containing cases determined by the High Court at Bombay. . . . Madras: Government Press. 1876–.

I.L.R. (Cal.)   The Indian Law Reports, Calcutta series, containing cases determined by the High Court at Calcutta. . . . Calcutta, 1876–.

I.L.R. (Cuttack)   The Indian Law Reports, Cuttack series, containing cases determined by the High Court of Orissa. . . . Cuttack: Orissa Government Press, 1959–.

I.L.R. (Ker.)   The Indian Law Reports, Kerala series, containing cases determined by the High Court of Kerala. . . . Ernakulam: Government of India, Government Press, 1957–.

I.L.R. (Lah.)   The Indian Law Reports, Lahore series, containing cases determined by the High Court at Lahore. . . . Lahore: Government Book Depot, 1920–47.

I.L.R. (Luck.)   The Indian Law Reports, Lucknow series, containing cases determined by the chief court of Oudh. . . . Allahabad: Government Book Depot, 1926–48.

I.L.R. (Mad.)   The Indian Law Reports, Madras series, containing cases determined by the High Court at Madras. . . . Madras: Government Press, 1876–.

M.I.A.   Reports and cases heard and determined by the Judicial committee of the Privy council. By Edmund F. Moore and J. and H. Clark. London: 1836–72.

M.L.J.   The Madras Law Journal. Madras: R. Narayanaswami Aiyar, 1891–.

M.P.L.J.   The Madhya Pradesh Law Journal. Nagpur: Central Law House, 1956–.

M.W.N.   The Madras Weekly Notes. Madras: N.R.K. Tatachariar, 1910–.

P.R.   Punjab Record. 1866–1919.

S.C.J.   Supreme Court Journal. Mylapore: N. Ramavatnam, 1937–.

S.C.R.   The Supreme Court Reports, containing cases determined by the Supreme Court of India. Delhi: Manager of Publications, 1950–.

Weir   The Law of Offenses and Criminal Procedure (Criminal Rulings) as Expounded by the High Court of Judicature, Madras. Thomas Weir, comp. and annotator. 4th ed. by K. Jagannatha Aiyar. 2 vols. Madras: Srinivasa Varadachari and Co., 1905.

EXPLANATION OF LAW REPORT CITATIONS

Citations of the judgments of courts are given in standard Indian legal form. Thus citations of official reports give the names of the first party on each side, the notation

I.L.R. (indicating Indian Law Reports), the volume number, the title of the series (indicating the court) and the page on which the case begins, and, finally, the date of publication; for example, *Gopal v. Hanmant*, I.L.R. 3 Bom. 273 (1879). Citations to the All-India Reporter, the most popular series of unofficial reports, follow a slightly different pattern; for example, *Sunder Devi v. Jheboo Lal*, A.I.R. 1957 All. 215 (names, A.I.R.-series, year of publication, name of court, page on which case begins). There is a separate A.I.R. volume published each year for each court. The coverage of I.L.R. and A.I.R. is overlapping but not identical. Occasionally cases not found in either of these series are reported in a local or specialized series. The citation of these follows a similar pattern.

PART V:

The Joint Family, Its Structures and Changes

14. REGION, CASTE, AND FAMILY STRUCTURE:
A COMPARATIVE STUDY OF
THE INDIAN "JOINT" FAMILY

PAULINE M. KOLENDA

THIS PAPER is a comparison of 26 sociological and anthropological studies, all carried out in India since 1949, which include quantitative data on the frequency of various types of families.[1] The questions with which the research began were these: Do Indians typically live in joint families? Are there caste differences in the distribution of family types, with the high castes having higher proportions of joint families than the middle and lower castes? Are joint families more characteristic of landowning castes than of landless castes? (A joint family is defined here as a commensal unit composed of two or more related married couples plus their unmarried children. Detailed definitions of family types appear below in the third section of the paper.)

Unexpectedly wide ranges in the proportions of various types of families became evident as the comparisons were made. They suggest that marked regional and subregional differences in family structure exist in India, largely unrecognized heretofore. Considerable attention is given in the paper to these as well as to the questions above. It was necessary, in order to facilitate comparisons, that I go through a preliminary procedure of equating the definitions of family types used by over a score of social scientists, no two of whom used the same definitions, to a standard set of definitions. These definitional translations have been recorded in detail, but because of the bulk of the total set, they are not published here. As with most translations, there is awkwardness and inadequacy in them; most of these are noted in the tables in the fourth section below. I can only hope that on balance the distortions have not been excessive. Two excellent recent studies (Desai, 1964; Nicholas, 1961) have been omitted because reasonably valid translations could not be made.[2]

The process of making comparisons has involved a number of assumptions

1. This research was supported in part by the National Science Foundation, Grant number GS-1261. I owe thanks to Joseph Schwartzberg, Cora Du Bois, and Gerald Berreman for calling my attention to three of the studies included here. Joseph Schwartzberg read and commented on the early version of this paper. Gerald Berreman and Adrian Mayer generously made their field census data available to me. Others, Kathleen Gough, M. G. Kulkarni, and Joan Mencher, answered questions about their village data. I am grateful for so much help and cooperation from them and other authors who responded to my requests for permission to draw on their data.
2. One other recent study (Ghurye, 1960) was omitted because the 20 per cent sample of households reported upon appeared not to be a random sample, representative of the whole village.

about studies with incomplete data on family structure; these assumptions are based upon extrapolation from studies with complete data. Some of the decisions based upon these assumptions, made for purposes of comparison, are probably incorrect. I must hope again, however, that the essential trends of the overall comparisons will be valid, and that the final structure is not entirely a house of cards. The sections below include remarks on the theoretical background of the study, a listing of the studies included, presentation of the definitions, comparisons of the individual studies, and summary comparisons.

THEORETICAL BACKGROUND

The sociologist William Goode has held that most parts of the world are undergoing a family revolution (Goode, 1963). Almost everywhere in the future, he predicts, the predominant type of family will be nuclear in structure, made up of parents and their unmarried children. Larger families that include grandparents, unmarried or widowed uncles and aunts, married children, their spouses and unmarried children, and other more distant kin are likely to disappear as industrialization, urbanization, and Westernization gather momentum. Talcott Parsons, a sociologist who has long inclined toward the same view, has put it this way: "There has been a historic trend to whittle down the size of kinship units in the general direction of isolating the nuclear family" (1961, p. 257).

Versions of the hypothesis that the nuclear family is functionally appropriate for a modern urban industrial economy and that the nuclear-family form will develop wherever a modern urban industrial economy is established are associated variously by different students of family change with the names of Parsons, Weber, Wirth, Linton, Ogburn and Nimkoff, and Burgess and Locke.[3] Whoever may be viewed as its author, this hypothesis has already stimulated much research (Greenfield, 1961; Arensberg, 1955, 1960; Johnson, 1964; Nimkoff and Middleton, 1960; Litwak, 1960a, 1960b; Sussman, 1963; Young and Willmott, 1957); the accumulation of such research should eventuate in a more adequate theory of the relationship between family and economy and between family and other cultural institutions. A number of studies in India have already been guided by this hypothesis (Desai, 1964; Gore, 1961; Kapoor, 1965, p. 54; Morrison, 1959; Ross, 1961; Sarma, 1964; Shahani, 1961).

It is not my purpose here to review the literature relating to this hypothesis, nor to assess the weight of evidence supporting or rejecting it—or, more accurately, refining and developing it into sub-hypotheses. Let me merely say that studies both in India and elsewhere suggest three points. First, a large number of variables placeable under the rubrics of industrialization, urbanization, and Westernization do seem to relate to, or at least to correlate with, a trend toward increasing proportions of nuclear families and decreasing proportions of joint families. In India, factors that appear to be related to this trend are Western

3. Litwak (1960a, 1960b) attributes the hypothesis to Parsons (1953, p. 116). Erwin Johnson (1964) attributes the hypothesis to Max Weber (1950, p. 111). Greenfield (1961) cites the same reference in Weber as well as Ogburn and Nimkoff (1950, pp. 469–73), and Wirth (1938). Aileen Ross (1961) cites Linton (1952, p. 84) and Burgess and Locke (1953, pp. 26–27).

secular education, modern salaried occupations, development of market cash economies displacing agrarian subsistence economies (Bailey, 1957; Epstein, 1962, p. 307) and changes in family law or legal practices relating to joint property (Beals, 1955, pp. 86–87, 91–92; Gough, 1952, pp. 79, 81; Mencher, 1962, pp. 236–37). Partly as a result of population pressure on land, there has been an influx of people, including the more educated, into cities (Gough, 1956, 831–32; Ray, 1956, p. 9; Madan, 1965, pp. 145–51; R. D. Singh, 1962, pp. 44, 77). Where men going to the city leave their wives and children in the village, their departure may actually seem to strengthen the joint family as Basu suggests (1962, p. 90), or it may lead to break-up through various processes, among which are the inequality of earnings of brothers, leading to envy and resentment and the eventual division of households, and a man's taking his wife and children with him to the city and so establishing a nuclear family.

Second, industrialization, modernization, and Westernization in their various manifestations may serve to strengthen the joint family because an economic base has been provided to support a joint family or because more hands are needed in a new family enterprise or because kin can help one another in the striving for upward mobility (Johnson, 1964; Friedl, 1964, p. 574). With respect to India, a number of writers have commented on the development of bridegroom-wealth, or dowry, and its great increase in extent and cost during recent decades, partly as a result of the higher demand for educated husbands (Gough, 1956, p. 834; Mandelbaum, 1957, p. 252; Karve, 1953, pp. 160–61; Sarma, 1963, p. 227). Dowry would appear to function as a stabilizer and to support the joint family and has been a custom related to joint-family living.

Last, Westernization, industrialization, and urbanization may not take place at the same rate or in a neatly meshed, harmonious functional process. Clifford Geertz, referring to post-independence Indonesia, said that that country: "is moving from industrialization without urbanization toward urbanization without industrialization" (1963, p. 145). Referring to modern China, he points out that the joint family may break down without industrialization.

It is clearly possible for development to misfire at any stage, even the initial one. Levy has shown, for example, how many of the social changes prerequisite to industrialization took place in China toward the end of the Ching dynasty—most notably the dissolution of the extended family system—without the promised economic growth following . . . (1963, p. 3, citing Levy, 1955, pp. 496–536).

Perhaps I have said enough to suggest the complexity of the variables, the processes, and the issues involved in the testing of the general hypothesis that the nuclear family is functional for the modern, Western, industrial economy.

More immediately relevant is the fact that the study of family change in India is bedeviled by the lack of baseline data against which to measure change. We have little quantitative evidence on the distribution of family types at early time periods. There is some such evidence. Ghurye (1960), for example, studied a village near Poona for which a census of families had been made by a British resident, Surgeon Thomas Coats, in 1819 (Coats, 1823, p. 182). From genealogies,

Hitchcock was able to make a retrospective estimate of family structure in 1901 for a section of a village *jāti* of Rajputs (Hitchcock, 1956, p. 155). Gould has recently reported two sets of statistics on family structure for the same village, collected in 1954–55 and 1959–60 (Gould, 1966, p. 10). Other anthropologists, some of whom were mentioned above, have reported on change in family structure in particular villages, but there were no existing statistics available for substantiation.

Given the still largely preindustrial condition of India at the present time, and the dearth of baseline statistics on family structure, this paper is meant to provide a baseline that may be useful for students of future change. Furthermore, it may be useful at the present time. Without such a baseline, grounded in reasonably sound statistical data, one may overgeneralize in various ways about the Indian family as it presently exists. The common belief is that Indians generally live in "joint" or extended families. On the other hand, the reader of census reports that show that there are few large families in India may assume that the "joint" family is a romantic myth. The census of India for 1951, for example, showed that less than one-quarter of the population lived in hearth groups with seven or more members (Census, 1951, p. 130). Even social anthropologists agree only in part in their generalizations about the Indian family.

Thus, Irawati Karve suggests that it is the larger or smaller joint family that is typical of India; S. C. Dube, on the other hand, suggests that the nuclear family or small joint family is typical. Karve says that in the north, at least, the joint family divides at the time of its founder's death, and divides, not into nuclear families but into smaller joint families. Dube says that, in villages, children who have grown up and who have "a degree of economic self-sufficiency" break away earlier, presumably before the father's death, and that a complete joint family of any type is rare (Karve, 1953, pp. 10–12; Dube, 1959, p. 213).

Again, while Mandelbaum suggests that the joint family tends to be a rural phenomenon (Mandelbaum, 1957, p. 247), Dube suggests that it is an "urban phenomenon, confined mostly to upper-caste groups in traditional small towns" (Dube, 1963, p. 197). The two writers agree that in rural areas the joint family is characteristic of upper castes rather than of lower castes and that those who accept Western culture are less likely to live in joint families. Dube and Béteille (1964, p. 239) say that the joint family is characteristic of landowning groups rather than of landless groups. Mandelbaum says that it is characteristic of "wealthier strata of society."

In this paper, attention is directed particularly to the hypothesis that the joint family is more characteristic of upper and landowning castes than of lower and landless castes. On the basis of the data available, I also discuss the composition of the "typical" Indian family. Unfortunately, the data available for comparing or contrasting urban and rural families are neither sufficient nor appropriate.

THE STUDIES COMPARED

Twelve different Indian states are represented among the 26 studies compared: West Bengal, Uttar Pradesh, Rajasthan, Maharashtra, Andhra Pradesh,

Madras, Delhi, Kashmir, Madhya Pradesh, Kerala, Orissa, and Mysore. Five types of social units were studied: villages; caste communities; districts, taluks, and census tracts; urban neighborhoods; and classes of high school students. The studies included are listed below.

TWENTY-SIX STUDIES TO BE COMPARED ON FREQUENCY OF FAMILY TYPES

I. VILLAGES

1. Basu; Kanchanpur, Burdwan District, West Bengal (1962).
2. Berreman; Sirkanda in the sub-Himalayas, Dehra Dun District, Uttar Pradesh (1963, unpublished data).
3. Bose, Malhotra, and Bharara; Korna, Jodhpur District, Rajasthan (1963).
4. Dube; Shamirpet, Andhra Pradesh (1955).
5. Gould; Sherupur, Faizabad District, Uttar Pradesh (1959, 1966).
6. Lewis; Rampur, Delhi (1958).
7. Mayer; Ramkheri, Madhya Pradesh (1960, unpublished data).
8. Morrison; Badlapur, Thana District, Maharashtra (1959).
9. Sarma and Sen; four villages in Burdwan District, West Bengal (Sarma, 1964; Sen, 1965).

II. CASTE COMMUNITIES

10. Singh, the Thakurs of Senapur, Jaunpur District, Uttar Pradesh (1962).
11. Cohn, the Untouchable Chamars of Senapur, Jaunpur District, Uttar Pradesh (1961).
12. Gough, the Brahmans of Kumbapettai, Tanjore District, Madras (1956).
13. Madan, the Kashmiri Pandits (Brahmans) of Utrassu-Umanagri, Anantnag District, Kashmir (1965).
14. Ray, Kanaujia Brahmans of Bira-Narasinghapur, Puri District, Orissa (1956).
15. Dumont, enumeration of the household composition of a neighborhood composed of the members of a sub-lineage of Pramalai Kallar of Tengalapatti hamlet, Madurai District, Madras (1957, pp. 54–57).
16. Hitchcock, a *paṭṭī* (ward) of a community of Rajputs of Khalapur, Saharanpur District, Uttar Pradesh (1956).
17. Kolenda, a *basti* (enclave) of Untouchable Chuhras of Khalapur, Saharanpur District, Uttar Pradesh (unpublished field data).
18. Kapoor, two subcastes of Punjabi Khatris living in Chandni Chowk, Old Delhi (1965).
19. Woodruff, a "hutment" of Tamil-speaking Paraiyans living in Bangalore, Mysore (1959).

III. DISTRICTS, TALUKS, CENSUS TRACTS

20. Driver, sample survey of Nagpur District, Maharashtra (1962).
21. Bose and Saxena, sample survey of Jalor District, Rajasthan (1964, 1965a, 1965b).
22. Kulkarni, survey of Gokak Taluk, Belgaum District, Mysore (1960).

23. Malhotra and Sen, sample survey from five Panchayat Samiti areas of Barmer District, Rajasthan (1964).

24. Mencher, census of family types for two census tracts of Angadi, a dispersed village of 12,000 people, in Ernad Taluk, Kozhikode District, Kerala (1962).

IV. URBAN NEIGHBORHOODS MIXED IN CASTE COMPOSITION

25. Sarma, survey of two neighborhoods in Calcutta: Shyambazar area, 45 per cent high caste in composition, and the Lake area, 89 per cent high caste in composition. The high castes were Brahmans, Vaidyas, and Kayasthas (1964).

V. HIGH SCHOOL STUDENTS

26. Shahani, questionnaires on family composition given to students in the two highest classes in high schools in Baroda. Students were from three major castes: Brahmans, Baniyas, and Patidars (1961).

All the studies cited above include frequency tables on the various types of families present in the social unit studied, or they include information sufficient for tabulating frequency tables. In two instances in which the appropriate data or the complete data were not included in published works, the researchers supplied them. Gerald Berreman made available copies of his village household census cards so that they could be analyzed by the categories used in this study; Adrian Mayer re-analyzed his census material, making tabulations for the family types used here.

DEFINITIONS

In order to make comparisons among the studies, it was necessary to translate into a common one the wide variety of typologies used by more than a score of social scientists. It is not an exaggeration to say that no two used the same set of definitions of family types. There are two sides to the definitional problem. First, *what* is shared by the family unit referred to, and, second, *who* shares it, that is, what relatives compose the various types of families?

Turning first to the problem of what the family unit shares we find that most of the studies considered here use *commensality* as a defining criterion. The family is the hearth group, the relatives who eat food from the same kitchen. The hearth group may or may not share a dwelling with other related hearth groups. Five researchers have explicitly stated that more than one hearth group may share a dwelling. Three of these (Hitchcock, 1956, p. 127; Madan, 1965, p. 561; and Kapoor, 1965, p. 56) have presented statistics on the number of dwellings with one, two, or more hearth groups. The other two researchers who indicate that more that one hearth group may reside in a dwelling are Sarma for the multicaste neighborhoods in Calcutta (1964, p. 199) and Mayer (1960, p. 177) for Ramkheri, Madhya Pradesh.

In eight localities, it appears that the hearth group usually also has its own separate dwelling. These are Sirkanda, Dehra Dun District, Uttar Pradesh; the Chuhras of Khalapur, Saharanpur District, Uttar Pradesh; the four villages in

Burdwan District, West Bengal, studied by Sarma and Sen; the Paraiyans of Bangalore; the Nayars of Ernad Taluk, Kerala; the sublineage of Pramalai Kallar of Tengalapatti hamlet, Madurai District, Madras, and the Brahmans of Kumbapettai, Tanjore District, Madras. In three other instances, it is not clear whether the hearth group and residential group coincide, but the researchers define the family as a hearth group. These are the studies of the Thakurs and of the Chamars of Senapur, Jaunpur District, Uttar Pradesh, and the study of Jalor District, Rajasthan.

In four studies, the family seems to be the *residential* family group, spoken of as the "household" in Kanchanpur, Burdwan District, West Bengal (Basu, 1962, p. 89); "residence in the same household" in Nagpur District, Maharashtra (Driver, 1962, p. 113); the "dwelling" in Sherupur, Faizabad District, Uttar Pradesh (Gould, 1959); and the "house site" in Rampur, Delhi (Lewis, 1958, p. 17). In none of these cases is it stated whether these units coincide with the hearth group. In the remaining six studies, the bases for delimiting separate families are not indicated. Of these, two studies were done by researchers of the Central Arid Zone Institute, Jodhpur, Rajasthan. In another of this research institute's studies, of Jalor District, Rajasthan, by Bose and Saxena, the family is defined as the hearth group; perhaps we may assume that the same definition was used in the other two institute studies. In another, Dube's study of Shamirpet, Telengana, the author speaks of married sons' breaking away from their parents soon after marriage (Dube, 1955, p. 133); again perhaps we are justified in assuming that such units are hearth groups, possibly hearth-*cum*-dwelling groups.

We find no definitions or statements useful for inferring the definitions of family or household in the studies of the Brahmans of Bira-Narasinghapur, Orissa; of Gokak Taluk, Belgaum District, Mysore; or of the high-caste high school classes in Baroda. In none of the eleven doubtful studies does any indication appear that the family units enumerated are *not* hearth groups. Since such a criterion for definitions is well known, due to its use by the census of India, and since it has been used in fifteen of the studies, I have somewhat arbitrarily assumed that it is hearth groups which are being compared in these eleven studies. I have most doubts about this regarding the study of Gokak Taluk, Belgaum District; the study of Nagpur District, Maharashtra; the study of the high-caste high school students of Baroda; the study of Rampur, Delhi; and the study of Sherupur, Faizabad District, Uttar Pradesh.

The uniting theme in the definitions used by so many of the researchers, the family as the commensal unit, should not disguise the fact that many definitions in the studies included here list several criteria. Cohn, for example, speaks of the joint family as eating from one chulha (hearth). He says further: "This means sharing property and rights, pocket book, larder, debts, labour and usually one head" (1961, p. 1052). For another example, Mayer describes a household as those who "share a cooking hearth, pool their incomes and have living expenses in common" (1960, p. 177).

Turning now to the other side of the definitional problem: that of the typologies of composition of families (who shares the hearth mentioned above), the multiplicity of definitions used by the various researchers may again be analyzed for similar usage. Particularly useful for my purposes were the nine studies in which the data included full or almost full descriptions of the composition of every family in the population treated. These were the studies of the sub-lineage of Pramalai Kallar of Tengalapatti hamlet, Madurai District, Madras; the section of Rajputs of Khalapur, Saharanpur District, Uttar Pradesh; the Kashmiri Pandits of Anantnag District, Kashmir; the Nayars of Ernad Taluk, Kerala; the sample from Gokak Taluk, Belgaum District, Mysore; the hutment of Paraiyans of Bangalore, Mysore; and the unpublished data referring to Sirkanda, Dehra Dun District, Uttar Pradesh; to Ramkheri, Malwa; and to the Chuhras of Khalapur, Saharanpur District, Uttar Pradesh.

Almost all the studies compared distinguish between joint and nuclear families (the one exception: Kapoor, 1965), although the composition of the units included under these rubrics varies. Fifteen of the studies distinguish types of joint families on the principles of lineal (father-son) links and collateral (brother-brother) links (studies numbered above: 1, 2, 5, 6, 7, 9, 10, 11, 13, 15, 16, 17, 18, 22, 24). Sixteen of these studies specify single-person households (numbers 1, 2, 6, 7, 10, 11, 12, 13, 14, 15, 16, 17, 19, 21, 24, 25). Nine specify subnuclear households (1, 2, 7, 13, 15, 16, 17, 19, 24); twelve specify supplemented nuclear families (2, 7, 12, 13, 14, 15, 16, 17, 19, 20, 22, 24).

The series of compositional categories used in the present study appear below. (Note that I do not include any relatives in the nuclear family category other than parents and unmarried children. I confine this term thus because I think we should use the same definition for the nuclear family in India as in the United States, if we are ever to compare Indian family structure with American family structure. Further, a family is "joint" only if it includes two or more related married couples.)

1. Nuclear family: a couple with or without unmarried children.

2. Supplemented nuclear family: a nuclear family plus one or more unmarried, separated, or widowed relatives of the parents, other than their unmarried children.

3. Subnuclear family: a fragment of a former nuclear family. Typical examples are the widow with unmarried children, or the widower with unmarried children, or siblings—whether unmarried, or widowed, separated, or divorced—living together.

4. Single-person household.

5. Supplemented subnuclear: a group of relatives, members of a formerly complete nuclear family, plus some other unmarried, divorced, or widowed relative who was not a member of the nuclear family. For example, a widow and her unmarried children plus her widowed mother-in-law.

6. Collateral joint family: two or more married couples between whom there is a sibling bond—usually a brother-brother relationship—plus unmarried children.

7. Supplemented collateral joint family: a collateral joint family plus unmarried, divorced, or widowed relatives. Typically, such supplemental relatives are the widowed mother of the married brothers, or the widower father, or an unmarried sibling.

8. Lineal joint family: two couples between whom there is a lineal link, usually between parents and married son, sometimes between parents and married daughter.

9. Supplemented lineal joint family: a lineal joint family plus unmarried, divorced, or widowed relatives who do not belong to either of the lineally linked nuclear families; for example, the father's widower brother or the son's wife's unmarried brother.

10. Lineal-collateral joint family: three or more couples linked lineally and collaterally. Typically, parents and their two or more married sons, plus the unmarried children of the three or more couples.

11. Supplemented lineal-collateral joint family: a lineal-collateral joint family plus unmarried, widowed, separated relatives who belong to none of the nuclear families lineally and collaterally linked; for example, the father's widowed sister or brother, or an unmarried nephew of the father.

12. Other. Some researchers—Woodruff, Kulkarni, Bose and Saxena, and Mencher—included an "other" class of families which they did not define, or about which I could not make reasonable guesses. I have retained their categorization. There were twelve "other" families which I could not classify in the eleven categories above. These were:

1. Among the villagers of Sirkanda, Dehra Dun District, Uttar Pradesh, seven cases as follows:

   3 cases of a Rajput woman living alone with a male servant,
   1 case of a grandmother living with an unmarried grandchild,
   1 case of a grand-uncle living with an unmarried grand-nephew.
   1 case of a woman and unmarried grandchild plus her dead husband's brother,
   1 case of a woman living with her mother's brother's wife.

2. Among the Pramalai Kallar: 1 household composed of a woman and her two unmarried children, her widowed daughter-in-law, and the latter's two unmarried children—two related subnuclear families.

3. Among the Nayars of Ernad Taluk, Kerala: 3 cases of a grandmother living with a single unmarried grandchild; 4 households composed of "miscellaneous matrilineally related kin" (Mencher, 1962, p. 239).

4. Among the Rajputs of Khalapur one household composed of a man and his widowed daughter-in-law.

Except for the last residual category of cases, the set of eleven types above was sufficient for almost every study. The group for which the categories had to be supplemented was the polygynous Khasiya Rajputs of Sirkanda, Dehra Dun, Uttar Pradesh. The group for which the categories had to be redefined was the matrilineal Nayars and some other castes of Angadi Village, Ernad Taluk, Kerala. The modifications made for the data on family structure for those groups are commented upon as they appear in the next section of the paper.

The reader may note that there are four principles upon which the classification rests. First, a joint family *must* include two related married couples. Second, these couples may be related lineally (usually in a father-son relationship, occasionally in a father-daughter relationship), or collaterally (usually in a brother-brother relationship, occasionally in a brother-sister relationship). Third, the unmarried relatives (including widowed or divorced) who are not children of any of the married couples in a family *supplement* the family, whether it is a joint, nuclear, or subnuclear family. Fourth, where there is no married couple and the relatives were formerly part of the same nuclear family, then it is a subnuclear household. If not, it is either an "other" type of household or a single-person household.

Some researchers—Mayer, Cohn, Sarma, Berreman, and Basu—have separately classified joint families in which the married couples are related as parents and married daughter (with her husband and unmarried children), or a married brother with his married sister and their spouses and unmarried children. In some of the tables in the next section, these categories are retained. In the overall analysis, however, I do not distinguish between the ordinary patrilineal or fraternal joint families and these latter types of joint families, deviant in a society practicing patrilineal descent.

There are many additional principles used by researchers that could be added to those above to make categories which might be more accurately descriptive of the families included in each. Some researchers emphasize the number of generations present in a family (Desai, 1964; Madan, 1965, pp. 67–68; Kapoor, 1965, pp. 56–57), whether or not a married couple have children (Basu, 1962, p. 88), whether there is a stepmother present (Basu, 1962, pp. 90–91), whether or not the couple is legally or ceremonially married (Basu, 1962, pp. 88–89; Woodruff, 1959, pp. 28–29); or they differentiate joint families including only two married couples from those including three or more (Morrison, 1959, pp. 51, 53), or indicate the number of supplementary relatives present (Woodruff, 1959, p. 31). If large numbers of researchers had made use of these distinctions, I might have included them in the set of categories for comparative purposes.

The categories I have set up have been based upon the distinctions most commonly used by the researchers themselves. I do not necessarily advocate the future use in research of the dozen categories listed above, but they do represent a set that has operated reasonably well for the comparison of the 26 studies. Needless to say, future comparison would be greatly facilitated if a standard set of family types did come into currency among social scientists studying the family in India.

Some further comments relating to the definition of Indian family types are pertinent here. Some social scientists (Madan, 1962a, pp. 88–89; 1962b; Bailey, 1960, p. 347) have advocated the limitation of the term "joint family" to a group of relatives who form a property-owning group, the co-parcenary family. It is useful to distinguish the co-parcenary family from the residential and commensal family groups, but since the term as used in India seems to refer to the composition of the residential and hearth family as often as it refers to the sharing of joint property—and, of course, they probably usually coincide—it is worth retaining the popular usage along with specifying adjectives: the co-parcenary joint family, the residential joint family, the commensal joint family. One might substitute the term "extended family" to refer to the latter two types, except that it has come to be used in anthropology to refer to a family including three or more generations and thus would not ordinarily refer to what Murdock has called the "fraternal joint family" (1949, p. 33), that is, the collateral joint family. I must admit that my preference for the term "joint" is probably due to the desire to be easily understood by an Indian audience; if social anthropologists prefer the term "extended" or some other I would not seriously object.

What seems far more important is a set of categories that are reasonably descriptive of their contents, so that from a title, it is possible to imagine accurately the compositions of the families included, and that are exhaustive and mutually exclusive. On the whole, past parsimony—too few types—has resulted in lack of clarity and incompleteness. Many studies do not clearly classify single-person households or subnuclear families. Supplemented nuclear families may be mixed with joint families, and so on.

Finally, let me make a comment about the "family cycle." It has become the practice in anthropological studies of families in primitive and peasant societies to emphasize the fact that the various structural types of families are stages in a family cycle (Fortes, 1949; Goody, 1958; Raymond Smith, 1956; Gray and Gulliver, 1964; Campbell, 1964) and to present family types as stages in this cycle. Some studies have referred to Indian family types as stages in a family cycle (Desai, 1964; Gould, 1966; Madan, 1965; Cohn, 1961; Nicholas, 1961; Bose and Saxena, 1965; Shahani, 1961), most of which use statistical evidence.

Let me explain, however, why I do not claim that the eleven types of family used here are stages in a single family cycle. First of all, we oversimplify reality if we speak of a single family cycle. There are a number of different family cycles even in the same Indian village *jāti* community. The most important factors making for variation between them include the time of a man's death in relationship to the ages and marriages of his children, the number of years between the latter in their ages, and variation in obligation of children to parents and to each other, depending upon birth-order and sex. Furthermore, between Indian communities there are important variations in the patterning of cycles, depending upon mores concerning (1) the proper time for married sons to break away from parents, or married brothers to break away from each other, (2) whether widow remarriage is prohibited or allowed, (3) whether women are allowed to live alone, (4) whether women are allowed to head a household, and (5) whether legal divorce initiated by women is allowed. Such factors influence the numbers and proportions of various family types in different regions, as will be shown in latter parts of the paper.

The set of categories is meant to accommodate a variety of cycles; it is not assumed that they form a single set of stages in a single cycle. This is not to deny the importance of recognizing that the form of a particular family changes over time. There probably is rarely a "perpetual nuclear family," as Shahani (1961, p. 1825) has put it; that is, usually the nuclear family is a stage in a cycle with other structural types of families.

COMPARISON

As a strategy for comparing these 26 studies, I have divided them into three types: first, studies of a sample of couples or household heads from a district or taluk (the studies by Driver, Kulkarni, Malhotra and Sen, and Bose and Saxena); second, studies of the households of whole villages (the studies by Bose, Malhotra and Bharara, Gould, Lewis, Dube, Morrison, Mayer, Berreman, Basu, and Sarma); and third, studies of the households of a single-caste community or part-community, or of three high-caste high school classes (the studies by Gough, Ray, Madan, Sarma, Kapoor, Mencher, Hitchcock, Kolenda, Cohn, Singh, Wood-ruff, and Dumont).

Studies at the District and Taluk Level

In 1958, Driver conducted a survey of the head couples of 1 per cent of the households of Nagpur District, Maharashtra; there were 2,314 couples in this sample. Such a sampling procedure automatically excluded single-person households and subnuclear families. Since he defined the joint family in terms of two or more couples and recognized only one type of supplemented nuclear family (that with one parent present), his definitions do not allow for the supplemental presence of unmarried brothers and sisters of the head, or other unmarried or widowed relatives. He also did not separate lineal joint families from collateral joint families.

Some time in the 1950's, Kulkarni took a 5 per cent sample of twelve major Hindu castes, as well as Jains, Muslims, and Christians, from four out of eight geographical zones in Gokak Taluk of Belgaum District, Mysore. Gokak Taluk varies geographically, having hills, highlands, and plains within it. About the four out of the total of eight zones in Gokak Taluk, Kulkarni says:

The first zone, that of the Gokak town, comprises the river-inundated and the central canal irrigated area and also includes a part of the Western hilly tract. Having within it two major towns *viz.*, Gokak and Konnur with 17,694 and 15,232 population respectively, it has also the highest density of 448 persons per square mile. The second zone of Ankalgi includes the Kundarnad valley region in the Southwestern part of the taluka and has a density of 349 persons per square mile. The Dhupdal zone covers the highlands in the northwestern part of the taluka adjacent to the first zone and includes a part of the canal irrigated area. Its density is 376, which is second only to the first zone. The fourth zone, that of the village Mudalgi, refers to the plains of the north covering the last tip of the canal irrigated area in the taluka (Kulkarni, 1960, p. 62).

Although he presented his data in terms of fourteen different family types, and some figures showing the numbers and proportions of single person households for the entire population, Kulkarni did not include either single-person households, subnuclear families, or most types of supplemented joint families.

He also did not distinguish clearly between lineal joint families and one type of supplemented nuclear family (nuclear supplemented by one parent). Kulkarni did recognize the supplemented nuclear types including unmarried brother and/or sister, or widowed sister.

Thus, neither Kulkarni nor Driver included single-person households or sub-nuclear families. Like Kulkarni, Driver failed to distinguish all the various types of supplemented nuclear family. (He does distinguish that in which a single parent is the supplementary relative.) Thus, the categories of the data from Kulkarni's and Driver's studies are quite similar when translated into the set of definitions used for comparison. Below appear tables showing the distribution of family types for Nagpur District, Maharashtra, and for the four zones of Gokak Taluk, Belgaum District, Mysore.

TABLE 1

FAMILY TYPES IN NAGPUR DISTRICT, MAHARASHTRA.

(Studied by Driver)

Family type	Number of Head Couples	% of Head Couples
Nuclear family	1,207	52.2
Supplemented nuclear*	412	17.8
Lineal, collateral, supplemented lineal, supplemented collateral†	606-671	26.3 — 29 ⎞
Lineal-collateral, supplemented lineal-collateral	89-24	3.7 — 1.0 ⎠ 30
Other	—	—
Total	2,314	100%

* Supplemented nuclear family is composed of a nuclear family plus one parent of the head.
† Driver uses a family type of a married couple plus both parents, and either brother(s) or son(s). Depending upon whether such a family includes sons or brothers, it is either lineal or lineal-collateral. There are 65 such families. These families account for the double sets of figures in some categories.

Note the rather large variation in proportion of joint families in Gokak Taluk, a variation of 13 to 17 per cent. In all four zones of Gokak Taluk, however, there is a higher proportion of joint families than in Nagpur, where 30 per cent of families are joint. It is likely too that supplemented nuclear families, those supplemented by unmarried brothers and sisters, are included in the 30 per cent joint families of Nagpur District, so that the proportion of joint families as defined in this study is even less than 30 per cent. Since all of the estimates for Gokak Taluk are higher than the 30 per cent for the Nagpur study, it seems very likely that there is a higher proportion of joint families in Gokak taluk, Mysore, than in Nagpur District, Maharashtra. Consistent with this are the figures indicating a higher proportion of nuclear families in Nagpur District

TABLE 2

PROPORTIONS OF FAMILY TYPES IN 4 ZONES OF GOKAK TALUK, BELGAUM DISTRICT, MYSORE.
(Studied by Kulkarni)

Family Type	Zone 1 Gokak (2 towns included) WEST		Zone 2 Village Ankalgi Heavily Agricultural SOUTHWEST		Zone 3 Village Dhupdal Not so heavily Agricultural NORTHWEST		Zone 4 Village Mudalgi Heavily Agricultural NORTH		TOTAL	
	No.	%	No.	%	No.	%	No.	%	No.	%
Lineal collateral	56	10	18	10	19	16	17	8	110	10
Lineal joint*	86-178	16-33	45-59	24-31	28-41	23-34	62-91	28-42	221-369	22-35
Collateral joint	42	8	15	8	14	12	18	8	89	8
Supplemented nuclear*	43-135	8-25	10-24	6-13	5-18	4-15	11-40	4-18	69-217	7-20
Nuclear	200	37	73	39	38	32	78	36	389	37
Other	18	4	13	6	3	2	4	2	38	3
TOTALS	537	100%	188	100%	120	100%	219	100%	1,064	100%
JOINT:	34%- 51%		42%- 49%		51%- 62%		44%- 58%		37%- 53%	

* Kulkarni uses a family type (man, wife, children) plus "parent or parents." There are 148 such families in all. They could be categorized for the present study as supplemented nuclear or as lineal joint families. These families account for the double sets of figures in some categories of Kulkarni's study.

than in Gokak Taluk, 52.2 per cent in Nagpur versus 32–37 per cent in Gokak Taluk.

It should be remembered, however, that Kulkarni did not sample from 26 small castes in the four zones of Gokak Taluk that he studied; the seeming difference between the two geographical areas could be an artifact of a sampling procedure that excluded small castes, possibly characterized by a high proportion of nuclear families. Inclusion of households from these small castes might have increased somewhat the proportion of nuclear families in Gokak Taluk, Mysore.

Social scientists in the Human Factor Studies Division of the Central Arid Zone Research Institute, Jodhpur, Rajasthan, have reported a number of studies including statistics on family structure (Bose and Saxena, 1964, 1965a, and 1965b; Malhotra and Sen, 1964). In two districts, Jalor and Barmer, Rajasthan, surveys of large numbers of families were carried out. In Jalor a 20 per cent random sample of all families in 41 villages (1 out of every 15 was selected from a list of villages) was selected and surveyed. In Barmer District, one out of every fifteen villages in five Panchayat Samiti areas was selected, and a 20 per cent sample of families selected and surveyed.

In both studies the term "joint" family appears to include supplemented nuclear families, and the nuclear category probably includes single-person and subnuclear households for Barmer District. Note that in both districts the proportions of joint families are close to, but somewhat less than, half. Since it is likely that these figures also include supplemented nuclear families, we may assume that considerably fewer than one-half are joint families as defined for the purposes of the present study. Noteworthy, however, is the closeness of the figures for two districts near each other in western Rajasthan.

TABLE 3*

TYPES OF FAMILIES IN A SAMPLE FROM 41 VILLAGES

IN JALOR DISTRICT, WESTERN RAJASTHAN (Studied by Bose and Saxena)

AND IN A SAMPLE FROM 5 PANCHAYAT SAMITI AREAS, BARMER DISTRICT.

(Studied by Malhotra and Sen)

Family Type	Jalor District		Barmer District	
	No.	%	No.	%
Single-person	23	1.9	—	—
Nuclear†	568	46.5	412	51.76
Other (Subnuclear possibly)‡	62	5.1	—	—
Supplemented nuclear & joint	565	46.5	384	48.24
Totals	1,218	100%	796	100%

* Twenty per cent sample in both studies. Figures for Jalor District from Bose and Saxena (1964, pp. 299–300, and 1965b, p. 196) and for Barmer District from Malhotra and Sen (1964, p. 21).

† The nuclear category probably includes for Barmer District both single-person and possibly some subnuclear types of families.

‡ The authors do not define the "other" type of family, but since it is at first included in a nuclear category, and appears to include children, we may suppose that it is a subnuclear family (Bose and Saxena, 1965, p. 196).

STUDIES AT THE VILLAGE LEVEL

Another study carried out by the researchers of the Central Arid Zone Research Institute was done in the village of Korna, 36 miles from Jodhpur in Rajasthan (Bose, Malhotra, and Bharara, 1963). The investigators were particularly interested in comparing life in dispersed dwellings (*dhanis*) and that in compact settlements. The sample of 200 houses out of a total of 405 houses is made up of 100 from the compact settlements (out of a total of 207 in the settlements) and 100 from *dhanis* (out of a total of 198). As in the studies cited above, the joint category probably included supplemented nuclear families, and the nuclear may include single-person and subnuclear households. In this village, however, over half the families are joint or supplemented nuclear.

The authors, Bose, Malhotra, and Bharara, comment on their data, as shown in Table 4, as follows:

TABLE 4*

FAMILY STRUCTURE IN 100 FAMILIES IN DISPERSED DWELLINGS AND 100 FAMILIES
IN COMPACT SETTLEMENTS FROM VILLAGE KORNA, JODHPUR, RAJASTHAN.
(Studied by Bose, Malhotra, and Bharara)

Family Type	Dispersed No.	%	Compact Settlement No.	%
Nuclear (probably includes subnuclear & single person)	42	42	45	45
Supplemented nuclear & joint	58	58	55	55
	100	100%	100	100%

* Figures from Bose, Malhotra, and Bharara, (1963, p.122).

"The hypothesis that dispersed dwellings have more joint households is not borne out by the data in this study since the difference between the percentages of joint households in the two settlement types is not significant" (Bose, Malhotra, and Bharara, 1963, p. 122). Note that the proportion of joint families is somewhat higher in Korna village, Jodhpur District, than in Barmer and Jalor districts (see Table 3 above).

Four of the village studies use rather few categories for family types. The distributions of families for the villages studied by Gould (1959, 1966), Lewis (1960), Dube (1955), and Morrison (1959) can be presented by the categories nuclear and joint families.

Data from Dube's (1955) study must be treated with caution. I have derived the proportions from the following statement in Dube's book:

[C]ase histories of one hundred and twenty families from the villages were examined. In 34% of the cases sons had separated from their parents within two years of marriage. 36% separated between two and three years after marriage. Separation took place after three, but within five years of marriage in 28% cases. Only 22% of the sons were still found to be living with their parents five years after their marriage. . . . (p. 133).

Those who can hold together for five years generally continue to live under the same roof peacefully for a much longer period. Nevertheless, separation is known to have taken place in some cases even after ten to fifteen years of living together (p. 134).

The percentages given by Dube above add up to 120 per cent. Since there were 120 cases in the sample, I suspect the percentages were actually numbers of cases in each category. If we compute percentages on that basis we find that 34 cases, or 28 per cent, separate from their parents after two years of marriage; 36, or 30 per cent separate between two and three years; 28, or 23.5 per cent, separate after three but within five years; and 22, or 18.5 per cent are still with parents after five'years of marriage.

There are various confusions in this way of presenting data. Dube did not divide families into cohorts representing the varying lengths of time of marriage of the head couple. Some of the marriages must be of less than five years' duration. We do not know how he categorized marriages of one, two, three or four years' duration of couples who have not yet left the parental household. Possibly he limited himself only to couples married five or more years, or possibly he speaks only of marriages of *heads* of households; if so, he overlooks the other married couples in the household. We do not know what the sample of 120 cases represents.

Despite the incompleteness and confusing nature of these data, I have included this study because it suggests an unusually low proportion of joint families. I take the figure 18.5 per cent, those couples still living with parents after five years of marriage, as close to the proportion of lineal joint families in Shamirpet, Telengana.

With the exception of Lewis' category for single-person households shown in Table 5 and a category of supplemented collateral (one parent with married sons) not shown in Table 5, and Morrison's explicit inclusion of one type of supplemented nuclear family (that including a single parent of one of the head couple) with nuclear family, none of these students explains his categorization

TABLE 5

COMPARISON OF FAMILY TYPES IN 4 VILLAGES: SHERUPUR, FAIZABAD DISTRICT, U.P. (Studied by Gould); RAMPUR, DELHI STATE (Studied by Lewis); SHAMIRPET, TELENGANA, ANDHRA PRADESH (Studied by Dube); AND BADLAPUR, THANA DISTRICT, MAHARASHTRA (Studied by Morrison).

Family Type	Uttar Pradesh Sherupur Faizabad Dt.		Delhi Rampur		Andhra Pradesh Shamirpet Telengana		Maharashtra Badlapur Thana Dt.	
	No. of Families	% of Families	No.	%	No.	%	No.	%
Single-person	—	—	2	1	—	—	—	—
Nuclear	19	44	67	45	98	81.5	552*	86
Joint	24	56	81	54	22	18.5	89	14
	43	100%	150	100%	120	100%	641	100%

* Includes an unknown number of supplemented nuclear families, those that consist of a couple and their unmarried children plus one parent of the head couple.

of single person or subnuclear (Dube seems to have omitted such households from his sample) or supplemented nuclear families, nor does any differentiate clearly between lineal and collateral joint types, or the supplemented joint types. It seems likely that for three studies (Lewis', Morrison's, and Gould's), the nuclear category includes some subnuclear households, and for two of the studies (Morrison's and Gould's) it includes single-person households. It seems likely that nuclear families supplemented by husband and wife's unmarried sibling(s) would also be categorized as nuclear by Morrison and by Dube, while for the other two studies (Gould's and Lewis') we may perhaps assume that supplemented nuclear families are included with joint families.

Granted the incompleteness of the data for my purposes, and the tentativeness with which one must treat figures from Dube's study, a comparison of the distribution shows two trends. First, the two places on the Gangetic Plain, one in Uttar Pradesh and one in Delhi State, have very similar distributions, 54 per cent and 56 per cent joint with supplemented nuclear families, as do the two studies from Central India for joint families, 18.5 per cent and 14 per cent. Second, the two geographical areas show very large differences in the proportions of joint and nuclear families. These data suggest that there may be a much higher proportion of joint families on the Gangetic Plain than in Central India.

To compare two other studies, one from Central India and one from the sub-Himalaya region of Uttar Pradesh, let us look at the studies by Mayer (1960) for Ramkheri, Malwa, Madhya Pradesh, and by Berreman (1963) for Sirkanda, Dehra Dun District, Uttar Pradesh. Both anthropologists have provided full data on family types.

In Sirkanda, polygyny is commonly practiced; about 15 per cent of marriages are polygynous (Berreman, 1963, p. 150). It was necessary, therefore, to devise some family types for a community practicing polygyny. In Table 6 a simple polygynous family is composed of a man, his two wives, and their unmarried children. A supplemented polygynous family is composed of the simple polygynous family plus some unmarried, widowed, or divorced relative of the head or of his wives, other than their unmarried children. A sub-polygynous family is usually composed of a woman, one of the wives of a man living elsewhere (perhaps with his other wife), and her unmarried children. A supplemented sub-polygynous is such a household plus an unmarried, divorced, or widowed relative other than one of the children. A polygynous lineal or collateral household includes at least one component family composed of a man and two wives.

In both Ramkheri, M.P., and Sirkanda, U.P., there are about the same proportions of joint families (23 per cent and 21 per cent) and supplemented nuclear families (18 per cent and 16 per cent). In Sirkanda, however, there is a considerably lower proportion of nuclear families (24 per cent in Sirkanda versus 41.5 per cent in Ramkheri), and a much higher proportion of persons in something less than a nuclear family, a household in which no married couple resides (17 per cent in Ramkheri versus 33 per cent in Sirkanda). This difference probably reflects the combination of practices of polygyny and freedom of women, greater for both than on the Gangetic Plain or in Ramkheri, Malwa.

TABLE 6

Comparison of family types in Ramkheri, Madhya Pradesh (Studied by Mayer) and Sirkanda, U.P. (Sub-Himalayas) (Studied by Berreman).

Family Types	RAMKHERI, MALWA				SIRKANDA, SUB-HIMALAYAS, U.P.			
	No. Families	% Families	No. Persons	% Persons	No. Families	% Families	No. Persons	% Persons
Single person	9	4.0	9	1	11	14.0	11	3.0
*Subnuclear	24	13.0	67	7	6	7.0	22	6.0
Supplemented subnuclear & other 2-3 persons less than nuclear households	—	—	—	—	8	10.5	20	5.0
Supplemented sub-polygynous	—	—	—	—	1	1.5	5	1.0
Nuclear	80	41.5	341	37.6	19	24.0	82	21.5
Supplemented nuclear	36	18.0	174	19	13	16.0	69	18.0
Simple polygynous	1	0.5	3	0.4	3	4.0	16	4.0
Supplemented polygynous	—	—	—	—	2	2.0	15	4.0
Polygynous and lineal	—	—	—	—	1	1.5	5	1.0
Polygynous and collateral	—	—	—	—	1	1.5	7	2.0
Lineal	17	8.5	132	14.4	1	1.5	4	1.5
Supplemented lineal	5	2.5	39	4.2	—	—	—	—
Collateral	13	6.5	75	8.2	1	1.5	4	1.5
Supplemented collateral	8	4.0	57	6.2	3	4.0	37	9.5
Lineal-collateral	—	—	—	—	4	5.0	33	9.0
Supplemented lineal-collateral	—	—	—	—	3	4.0	39	10.0
Other joint	3	1.5	15	2.0	2	2.0	12	3.0
Totals	196	100%	912	100%	79	100%	381	100%
Summarized:								
Less than nuclear	33	17.0	76	8.0	26	33.0	58	15.0
Nuclear	80	41.5	341	37.6	19	24.0	82	21.5
Supplemented nuclear	36	18.0	174	19.0	13	16.0	69	18.0
Simple or supplemented polygynous	1	0.5	3	0.4	5	6.0	31	8.0
Joint, polygynous and non-polygynous	46	23.0	318	35.0	16	21.0	141	37.5
	196	100%	912	100%	79	100%	381	100%

* For Ramkheri, the subnuclear category may include some single-person households.

Thus, it is common for a co-wife to live in a fieldhouse or house alone with a servant, or relative, or her unmarried children, while her husband lives with the other co-wife and children.

These two villages appear to rank between Badlapur, Maharashtra, and Shamirpet, Telengana, with their very low proportions of joint families (14 per cent and 18.5 per cent), and the two Gangetic Plain villages with 54 per cent (Rampur, Delhi) and 56 per cent (Sherupur, U.P.) joint with supplemented nuclear families. (Note that, if joint and supplemented nuclear families are combined for Sirkanda and Ramkheri, the proportions are 37 per cent and 41 per cent respectively, less than those of the Gangetic Plain villages, but possibly higher than those for Badlapur and Shamirpet, for which we lack figures on supplemented nuclear families.)

Finally, we compare three studies covering five villages of Burdwan District, West Bengal: the study of four villages reported upon by Sarma (1964) and the study of Kanchanpur Village, made by Basu (1962). The family types used by Sarma and by Basu can be fitted fairly easily. Sarma combines one type of supplemented nuclear family, that in which a single parent lives with a married son and his wife and children with joint families, and one type (unmarried sibling living with married brother and his wife and children) with nuclear families. Basu does not specify supplemented nuclear families. Basu specifies single-person and subnuclear types, while Sarma explicitly combines these types with the nuclear type. Lastly, Basu includes figures for the total population of a village, while Sarma includes figures for around 80 per cent of the families in the villages she studied. Tables presenting family types for these two sets of villages appear below.

TABLE 7

FAMILY TYPES IN KANCHANPUR VILLAGE, BURDWAN DISTRICT, WEST BENGAL
(Studied by Basu)

Family Type	No.	%
Single-person	22	8
Subnuclear*	36	12
Nuclear	116	41
Lineal and lineal-collateral	85	30 ⎫
Collateral joint	23	8 ⎬ 39%
Other joint†	3	1 ⎭
Total	285	100%

* Subnuclear households may include some single-person households, a widow living alone.
† These include a married daughter or married sister's family.

The proportions are strikingly similar for family types for villages of the same district. In Kanchanpur, the proportion of joint (probably including supplemented nuclear families) families is 39 per cent; for the four other villages in Burdwan District the proportions of joint (with one type of supplemented nuclear family included) are 36 per cent, 44 per cent, 45 per cent, and 45 per cent. These proportions cover a narrow range, from 36 per cent to 45 per cent.

These figures appear to be lower than those of the Gangetic Plain villages (54 per cent and 56 per cent for joint with supplemented nuclear). They are about the same as those for Ramkheri, M.P., and Sirkanda, U.P., and perhaps higher in proportions of joint families than Shamirpet, Telengana, or Badlapur, Maharashtra.

STUDIES OF A SINGLE-CASTE OR OF A FEW CASTES

First, let us consider three different studies of the family structure of village *jātis* of Brahmans, one in Madras studied by Gough (1956), one in Orissa studied by Ray (1956), and one in Kashmir studied by Madan (1965). In none of the Brahman *jātis* does there appear to be a high proportion of joint families. Again the range is narrow: 20 per cent to a maximum of 33 per cent. These three studies do not suggest that Brahmans, as a high caste, have high proportions of joint families. The highest proportion of joint families appears among the Kashmiri Pandits; note the very large proportion of single-person and subnuclear families, 22 per cent among the Madras Brahmans. Proportions of nuclear and supplemented nuclear families tend to be similar, differing over a rather narrow range.

The next set of comparisons includes two different neighborhoods in Cal-

TABLE 8

DISTRIBUTION OF FAMILY TYPES IN 4 VILLAGES IN BURDWAN DISTRICT, WEST BENGAL, IN 1953–54.[*]

	Village Bigra		Village Hijalna		Village Mudafar-F†		Village Punyagram		Total	
	No.	%	No.	%	No.	%	No.	%	No.	%
Nuclear (includes single person & supplemented nuclear where unmarried brother or sister of married brother is present)	75	63.56	62	55.86	85	53.8	111	54.14	333	56
Joint with Parents (includes lineal-collateral, supplemented collateral, & supplemented nuclear where only one married son & one parent are present)	28	23.73	34	30.36	42	26.58	62	30.25	166	28
Joint with brothers (collateral joint)	8	6.78	11	9.82	21	13.29	18	8.78	58	10
Joint with others (relatives of wife or mother included)	7	5.93	5	4.46	10	6.33	14	6.83	36	6
Totals	118	100%	112	100%	158	100%	205	100%	593	100%

* Table from Sarma (1964, p. 200).
† The full name of this village is Mudafar-Falahari.

TABLE 9

COMPARISON OF FAMILY STRUCTURE AMONG 3 VILLAGE *Jātis* OF BRAHMANS:
BRAHMANS OF KUMBAPETTAI VILLAGE, TANJORE, MADRAS (Studied by Gough),
BRAHMANS OF BIRA-NARASINGHAPUR, PURI DISTRICT, ORISSA (Studied by Ray),
AND BRAHMANS OF UTRASSU-UMANAGRI, ANANTPUR, KASHMIR (Studied by Madan).

Family Type	Madras Brahmans Families		Orissa Brahmans Families		Persons		Kashmir Brahmans Families	
	No.	%	No.	%	No.	%	No.	%
Single person	8	22	11	7	11	1	3	3
Subnuclear	—	—	—	—	—	—	4	5
Supplemented subnuclear	—	—	—	—	—	—	1	1
Nuclear	13	36	66	40	276	30	27	31
Supplemented nuclear	8	22	44	26	233	25	23	26
Supplemented nuclear or supplemented collateral	—	—	—	—	—	—	104	1-5†
Joint*	7	20	45	27	408	44	25-28	29-33
	36	100%	166	100%	928	100%	87	100%

* Ray's joint families may include some supplemented nuclear families.

† Among the Kashmiri Pandits were four cases (or 5%) composed of a head, his married son or sons, son's or sons' wives, and unmarried children. These are categorized as either supplemented nuclear or supplemented collateral joint families.

cutta studied by Jyotirmoyee Sarma (1964), and two *jātis* of Punjabi Khartris living in Delhi, studied by Saroj Kapoor (1965). The Lake area of Calcutta is largely (89 per cent) high caste, made up of Brahmans, Kayasthas, and Vaidyas; the Shyambazar area is only 45 per cent high caste. The former has a higher proportion of joint families, 58 per cent, than the "less high caste" area, which has only 37 per cent joint families.

It was difficult to fit the definitions of the present study to those used by Kapoor in her study of the Khatris. My calculations indicate that the proportion of joint families (including some supplemented nuclear families) is between 28 per cent and 45 per cent. The high-caste Calcutta neighborhood, the lake area, appears to have the highest proportion of joint families of the three urban neighborhoods, 58 per cent, while the Shyambazar area of Calcutta and the Delhi Khatris show rather similar proportions of joint families.

Both Joan Mencher and John Hitchcock studied traditionally military castes. Mencher studied Nayars in two census tracts of a village, Angadi, in Ernad Taluk, Kozhikode District, Kerala. Tract 18 was largely Nayar, but included some other matrilineal castes; tract 13 contained many Muslims and lower-caste groups, as well as many Nayar households (Mencher, 1962, pp. 238–39).

In order to compare the matrilineal households of these Kerala people with the patrilineal households of the places and castes represented in the other studies, I had to modify the definitions of family types. The lineal-collateral and lineal joint families are equated with "the small *tavari*," defined by Mencher as composed of a woman, her sons and daughters, and the children of one or more daughters. The husbands of the women usually belong to their mothers' or sisters' *tavari*, although occasionally a man lives in his wife's household.

The collateral joint family is Mencher's "two-generational matrilineal household" composed of two sisters and their children, or a woman, her children, and several of her brothers. The subnuclear family is Mencher's "matrilineal segment" composed of a woman with her children, the house belonging to the woman and her husband living with his own matrilineal kin elsewhere. Mencher also includes in this category the households of widowed and divorced women and their children.

Nuclear families are composed of a husband, wife, and children for both Mencher, and for this study. Some "others," as labeled by Mencher, have been equated to my categories: supplemented nuclear families, supplemented lineal families, supplemented collateral joint families, single person households and to a category of "other."

The distribution of the types of families for the two census tracts in Angadi Village, Kerala, is presented in Table 11 below. Note the very high proportions of joint families in the two tracts, 53 per cent and 61 per cent.

Turning to the other traditionally military caste, the Rajputs, John Hitchcock studied a *paṭṭī* (division) of a village *jāti* of Rajputs in Khalapur, Saharanpur District, in northwestern Uttar Pradesh. Note the low proportions of joint households among the Rajputs, 26 per cent.

TABLE 10

COMPARISON OF FAMILY TYPES IN 2 NEIGHBORHOODS OF CALCUTTA (Studied by Sarma) AND 2 *Jātis* OF PUNJABI KHATRIS LIVING IN DELHI (Studied by Kapoor).

	Calcutta				Delhi	
	Lake Area (89% High Caste) Families		Shyambazar (45% High Caste) Families		Two Jātis of Khatri Families	
Family Type	No.	%	No.	%	No.	%
Single person	—	—	6	6	2-12	2-8
Subnuclear*	—	—	—	—		
Nuclear	34	34	36	36	69-105	70-47
Supplemented nuclear	8	8	21	21		
Joint†	59	58	37	37	41-67	28-45
Totals	101	100%	100	100%	148	100%

* For the Khatris, Kapoor includes with single-person and subnuclear families some childless couples. The latter are considered to be nuclear families in the present study; thus, there is a range of cases in both the single-person–subnuclear category and in the nuclear category due to an unknown number, as many as ten, of childless couples. Sarma probably includes subnuclear families in the nuclear category.

† Again for the Khatris, the joint category includes some supplemented nuclear families as well as joint families; hence there is a range in number. There could be as many as 26 supplemented nuclear families in this category. They are also included in the nuclear-supplemented nuclear category.

For contrast, I include in Table 11, as well, the distribution of families in a very small enclave of Untouchable Chuhras or Bhangis of Khalapur. Note that they have a considerably lower proportion of joint families, 12 per cent, than do the Rajputs of the same village (26 per cent). However, the two groups have very similar proportions of nuclear and supplemented nuclear families. The Chuhras have somewhat more families of less than nuclear composition (those with no married couple present).

Thus, it appears that the Nayars have much higher proportions of joint families than do the Rajputs of Khalapur. If, however, we add to the proportion of joint families for the Rajputs, their supplemented nuclear families, 25 per cent, the combined total would be 51 per cent, a proportion comparable to the combined joint and supplemented nuclear families of Sherupur, Uttar Pradesh (56 per cent), and Rampur, Delhi (54 per cent).

Another pair of single-caste studies were made in the same village, the study of the Thakurs of Senapur by R. D. Singh (1962) and the study of the Chamars of Senapur by Bernard S. Cohn (1961). Notice that the really large difference between the Thakurs and the Chamars is in the proportion of collateral joint families, a difference probably reflecting the much slower break-up of the joint

TBALE 11

COMPARISON OF FAMILY TYPES IN 2 LARGELY NAYAR CENSUS TRACTS IN ANGADI VILLAGE, ERNAD TALUK, KERALA (Studied by Mencher) WITH A PATTI OF RAJPUTS OF VILLAGE KHALAPUR, SAHARANPUR DISTRICT, U.P. (Studied by Hitchcock), AND A BASTI OF UNTOUCHABLE CHUHRAS OF KHALAPUR (Studied by Kolenda).

| | Khalapur | | | | Nayars with Some Other Castes* | | | |
| | Rajputs | | Chuhras | | Tract 18 | | Tract 13 | |
Family Types	No.	%	No.	%	No.	%	No.	%
Supplemented lineal collateral	5	5	—	—	—	—	—	—
Lineal-collateral	6	6	1	6				
Lineal	10	9	—	—	37	42	15	29
Supplemented lineal	2	2	—	—	1	1	10	19
Supplemented collateral	3	3	1	6	2	2	?	?
Collateral	1	1	—	—	8	8	7	13
Supplemented nuclear†	26	25	5	32	1	2	?	?
Nuclear‡	37	36	6	38	13	14.5	9	17
Supplemented subnuclear	—	—	1	6	—	—	—	—
Subnuclear	6	6	1	6	15	17	6	12
Single-person	6	6	1	6	5	5.5	?	
Other	1	1	—	—	7	8	5§	10
Totals	103	100%	16	100%	89	100%	52	100%

* Tract 18 is largely Nayar in caste composition. Tract 13 is Nayar plus many Muslim and lower-caste groups.
† There is one polygynous family included in supplemented nuclear category for Rajputs.
‡ There is one polygynous family included in nuclear category for Rajputs.
§ This category may include some of the categories marked above with a question mark.

TABLE 12

COMPARISON OF FAMILY TYPES AMONG THE THAKURS (Studied by Singh) AND
THE CHAMARS (Studied by Cohn) OF SENAPUR, JAUNPUR DISTRICT, U.P.

	Thakurs		Chamars	
Family Type	No.	%	No.	%
Lineal*	19	30.5	24	20
Collateral†	28	44	14	11
Other joint	—	—	4	3
Nuclear‡	12	19	72	59
Single-person	4	6.5	8	7
Totals	63	100%	122	100%

* Singh includes in this category lineal-collateral, supplemented lineal, supplemented lineal collateral, and supplemented nuclear.

† Singh includes here supplemented collateral also.

‡ Singh includes here some supplemented nuclear and subnuclear families. Cohn includes here subnuclear.

family among the Thakurs than among the Chamars. Many Thakur joint families include adult men who are cousins; few Chamar joint families do.

Shahani (1961) studied 258 high school students from three large high castes in Baroda: the Brahmans, Baniyas, and Patidars. It was not possible for me to fit my definitions of family types to Shahani's, so I present her data in terms of joint, supplemented nuclear, and nuclear families. Note the high proportion

TABLE 13

DISTRIBUTION OF FAMILY TYPES AMONG STUDENTS OF THREE HIGH CASTES IN BARODA.
(Studied by Shahani)

	Brahmans		Baniyas		Patidars	
Family Type*	No.	%	No.	%	No.	%
Nuclear	37	54	62	61	28	32
Supplemented subnuclear and subnuclear†	3	4	2	2	5	6
Joint	29	42	38	37	54	62
Totals	69	100%	102	100%	87	100%

* Shahani does not include families joint or supplemented due to the presence of mother's relatives or a widowed sister with her children.

† A family headed by the student's married brother, supplemented at least by the student, probably unmarried.

of joint families among the Patidars (66 per cent) and the low proportion among the Baniyas (37 per cent), with the Brahmans in between (43 per cent) but closest to the Baniyas.

Last, let us compare two Tamil-speaking groups, the Tamil Untouchable Paraiyans of a hutment in Bangalore city, studied by Woodruff, and a sub-lineage of the traditionally criminal, now largely agricultural, Pramalai Kallar of Madurai District, Madras, studied by Louis Dumont. Dumont considers the Pramalai Kallar to be a middle-ranking caste, or Shudra (Dumont, 1957, pp. 5,

TABLE 14

COMPARISON OF FAMILY TYPES AMONG UNTOUCHABLE PARAIYANS OF BANGALORE
(Studied by Woodruff) AND AMONG A SUB-LINEAGE OF EX-CRIMINAL
PRAMALAI KALLAR, A MIDDLE CASTE OF MADURAI DISTRICT, MADRAS.
(Studied by Dumont)

	Bangalore Paraiyans				Pramalai Kallar			
	Families		Persons		Families		Persons	
	No.	%	No.	%	No.	%	No.	%
Single person	14	7.0	7	0.9	1	4	1	1
Subnuclear	16	8.0	35	4.3	2	7	6	5
Nuclear	122	59.0	442	56.0	20	77	85	81
Supplemented nuclear	26	12.4	120	15.3	1	4	5	4
Joint	24	11.6	172	21.5	1	4	5	4
Other*	5	2.0	17	2.0	1	4	6	5
Totals	207	100%	793	100%	26	100%	108	100%

* Other: Woodruff does not describe this set of families. For the Pramalai Kallar sub-lineage the "other" family includes a widow and her two children, her widowed daughter-in-law, and the latter's two children.

16). Among both these Tamil-speaking lower castes the proportion of joint families is very low, 11.6 per cent for the Paraiyans of Bangalore and 4 per cent for the sub-lineage of Pramalai Kallar of Tengalapatti hamlet, western Madurai District, Madras.

CASTE DIFFERENCES IN FAMILY STRUCTURE IN THE VILLAGE AND DISTRICT STUDIES

In this section, we return to the studies discussed earlier to consider the proportions of various types of families in various of the castes. Data on caste in relation to family do not appear in the studies by Driver, Dube, or Sarma. Recently, however, Lalit Kumar Sen has published data on the family structure of categories of castes in the four Burdwan villages surveyed by Sarma (Sen, 1965). In Table 15 appear family types by twelve Hindu castes and three religious communities in Gokak Taluk of Belgaum District, Mysore. Since many of these castes may be unfamiliar to the reader, I list below the occupations and identifications of most of them.

Lingayats	Sectarians who form a dominant land-owning caste in Mysore.
Panchals	Carpenters and goldsmiths (Edgar Thurston says that they include five classes of workers, those who work with gold, silver, brass and copper, iron, and stone) (1909, Vol. 6, p. 43).
Berads	Hunters traditionally.
Hanabars	Husbandmen.

TABLE 15

Relationship between caste and family types in Gokak Taluk, Belgaum District, Mysore (Studied by Kulkarni).

CASTES

Family Type	Brahmans		Lingayats		Marathas		Panchals		Berads		Hamabars		Kurubas		Uppars	
	No.	%	No.	%	No.	%	No.	%	No.	%	No.	%	No.	%	No.	%
All joint	13	37	173	50	44	55.5	28	62	48	48	6	75	54	55	54	64
Lineal-collateral	4	11	27	8	8	10	6	13	9	9	4	50	10	10	17	20
Collateral	1	3	25	7	6	7.5	7	16	6	6	—	—	10	10	5	6
Lineal joint*	8	23	121	35	30	38	15	33	33	33	2	25	34	35	32	38
Supplemented nuclear	1	3	23	7	6	7.5	—	—	12	12	—	—	4	4	4	5
Other	—	—	19	6	2	2	1	2	4	4	—	—	2	2	1	1
Nuclear	21	60	129	37	28	35	16	36	36	36	2	25	38	39	25	30
Cases	35		344		80		45		100		8		98		84	

CASTES

Family Types	Vadars		Holeyas		Madigas		Samagars		Christians		Jains		Muslims	
	No.	%	No.	%	No.	%	No.	%	No.	%	No.	%	No.	%
All joint	15	80	27	52	20	55	6	67	5	34	15	45	62	59
Lineal-collateral	3	16	6	11.5	2	6	2	22	1	7	5	15	7	7
Collateral	6	32	7	13.5	3	8	—	—	1	7	3	9	10	9
Lineal joint*	6	32	14	27	15	41	4	45	3	20	7	21	45	43
Supplemented nuclear			3	6	4	11	1	11	1	7	4	12	1	1
Other	2	10	2	4	1	3	1	11	1	7	1	3	4	4
Nuclear	2	10	20	38	11	31	1	11	8	52	13	40	39	36
Cases	19		52		36		9		15		33		106	

* The lineal joint type probably includes some supplemented nuclear families of the type that includes a single parent of the head of the nuclear family. It does include some supplemented lineal.

Kurubas	Shepherds.
Uppars	Saltmakers.
Vadars	Stone-cutters, mud-carriers, construction workers.
Holeyas	Untouchable agricultural laborers and sweepers.
Madigas	Untouchable rope-makers and agricultural laborers.
Sanagars	Untouchable leatherworkers.

For those cases that are reasonably well represented in Kulkarni's sample, one may note the very high proportion of joint families (including one type of supplemented nuclear family, that supplemented by a single parent of one of the head couple), 62 per cent and 64 per cent, for the Panchals, high-ranking artisans, and for the Uppars, saltmakers, probably agriculturalists today. Only four groups out of the fifteen represented have fewer than 50 per cent joint families. Especially noteworthy is the low proportion of joint families among the Brahmans, only 37 per cent. Only one group, very lightly represented, with fifteen cases, the Christians, have a lower proportion, 34 per cent.

This study is interesting, then, for the overall high proportions of joint families; for the highest proportions being among Shudra artisans and saltmaker-agriculturalists, rather than among dominant land-owners; and for almost the lowest proportion of joint families being among Brahmans.

Malhotra and Sen compare castes divided on the basis of primary occupation for family structure (see Table 16). Although they do not name castes or

TABLE 16

RELATIONSHIP BETWEEN CASTE AND TYPE OF HOUSEHOLD IN A SAMPLE OF FAMILIES FROM 5 PANCHAYAT SAMITI AREAS IN BARMER DISTRICT (Studied by Malhotra and Sen).

	Type of Household			
	Nuclear		Joint†	
Caste Occupation	No.	%	No.	%
Agricultural castes	206	50.0	206	50.0
Castes raising sheep and goats	18	40.0	27	60.0
Occupational castes serving the needs of agriculturists	81	54.4	68	45.6
Castes serving socio-religious needs	12	48.0	13	52.0
Castes serving other needs of the community	84	58.7	59	41.3
	401	51.8	373	48.2

* Table adapted from Malhotra and Sen (1964, p. 25).
† "Joint" families probably includes supplemented nuclear households.

indicate caste rank, so that it is difficult to interpret the import of their findings for the present study, it is worth including here, because it suggests that the castes raising sheep and goats, probably not of the highest rank, have the highest proportion of joint families. Among these shepherd castes are the Raikas (Malhotra and Sen, 1964, p. 27).

THE VILLAGE STUDIES

1. GOULD'S STUDY OF SHERUPUR, FAIZABAD DISTRICT, U.P.

Table 17 shows the numbers of nuclear and joint families in Sherupur by caste. Although there are very few families in each caste, it is noteworthy that there are joint families represented in all castes; that again the highest proportion of joint families is in a Shudra or middle caste (the Kori), and that of the four Brahman families only one is a joint family.

TABLE 17

RELATIONSHIP BETWEEN CASTE AND FAMILY TYPES IN SHERUPUR, FAIZABAD DISTRICT, UTTAR PRADESH (Studied by Gould).*

	Castes							
	Brahman		Kshatriya		Ahir		Marau	
Family Type	No.	%	No.	%	No.	%	No.	%
Joint	1	25	3	60	3	43	2	67
Nuclear	3	75	2	40	4	57	1	33
Totals	44	100%	5	100%	7	100%	3	100%

	Castes							
	Lohar		Kori		Muslim		Chamar	
Family Type	No.	%	No.	%	No.	%	No.	%
Joint	1	50	12	75	1	33	1	33
Nuclear	1	50	4	25	2	67	2	67
Totals	2	100%	16	100%	3	100%	3	100%

* Table adapted from Gould (1959, p. 33).

LEWIS' STUDY OF RAMPUR, DELHI

In Lewis' study of Rampur, Delhi State, all castes specified in the table he includes have some joint families (which probably include supplemented nuclear families); the highest proportion, 70 per cent, is among the dominant land-owning Jats; the lowest proportion, 19 per cent, is among the Untouchable agricultural workers, the Chamars. However, the Brahmans, with 53 per cent and the Untouchable Bhangi sweepers, with 40 per cent, castes at the top and the bottom of the caste hierarchy, are not so remarkably different as are the Jats and Chamars, in the proportions of joint families within each caste group. However, no very strong statement about Bhangis and Brahmans can be made on the basis of such small numbers of cases.

MORRISON'S STUDY OF BADLAPUR, MAHARASHTRA

No caste grouping in Badlapur, Thana District, Bombay, has a high proportion of joint families. The highest proportions, 32.6 per cent and 28.6, occur among the outcastes and the artisans. The Brahmans, well represented with 83 families, have the lowest proportion of joint families, only 6 per cent.

TABLE 18

RELATIONSHIP BETWEEN CASTE AND FAMILY TYPES IN RAMPUR, DELHI

(Studied by Lewis).*

Family Type	Jats No.	%	Brahmans No.	%	Chamars No.	%	Bhangis No.	%	Others† No.	%
Single-person	1	1	0	—	1	5	0	—	0	—
Nuclear	23	29	7	47	16	76	6	60	15	57
Joint	54	70	8	53	4	19	4	40	11	43
	78	100%	15	100%	21	100%	10	100%	26	100%

* Table adapted from Lewis (1958, p. 17).

† Other castes include 7 Kumhars or Potters, 5 Jhinwars or Water-carriers, 4 Dhobis or Washerman, 4 Khatis or Carpenters, 3 Nais or Barbers, 2 Chipis or Calico printers or Tailors, 1 Lohar or Blacksmith, and 1 Baniya or Merchant (Lewis, 1958, p. 16).

TABLE 19

RELATIONSHIP BETWEEN CASTE AND FAMILY TYPES IN BADLAPUR, THANA DISTRICT, MAHARASHTRA (Studied by Morrison).*

Family Type	Castes Brahmans No.	%	Bazaar No.	%	Muslims No.	%	Marathas No.	%
Joint	5	6	11	11.6	12	13.1	7	9.3
Nuclear & Supplemented Nuclear	78	94	84	88.4	80	86.9	68	90.7
Totals	83	100%	95	100%	92	100%	75	100%

Family Type	Castes Traditional Agricul- turalists		Artisans No.	%	Service No.	%	Outcastes No.	%	Scheduled Tribes No.	%
Joint	22	14.9	8	28.6	1	7.7	14	32.6	9	14.1
Nuclear & Supplemented Nuclear	126	85.1	20	71.4	12	92.3	29	67.4	55	85.9
Totals	148	100%	28	100%	13	100%	43	100%	64	100%

* Based on table in Morrison (1959, p. 59).

† Bazaar castes include Shopkeepers, Tailors, Goldsmiths, Oil-sellers, Clerks, and Scribes.

Marathas include Konkani Marathas, Rao Marathas, Maratha Telis, Tilori, and Shinde, who call themselves Maratha Kunbis, Yadavs, and Guravs.

Traditional agriculturists include Agri, Bhoi, Habsani, and Mahadev Koli.

Artisans include Potters, Ironsmiths, Carpenters, Basketmakers, Tinsmiths, Bricklayers, and Weavers.

Service include Barbers and Washermen.

Outcastes include Mahar, Chambhar, and Bhangi.

Scheduled Tribes include tribals, Thakur, and Katkari.

MAYER'S STUDY OF RAMKHERI, MADHYA PRADESH

While Adrian Mayer does not present a table on the distribution of family types by caste, a passage (pp. 172–73) in his book can be analyzed to suggest that 19 out of 26 castes have one or more "extended" (joint) families.

BERREMAN'S STUDY OF SIRKANDA, UTTAR PRADESH (SUB-HIMALAYA ZONE)

In 1957, 87 per cent of the population of Sirkanda were Khasiya Rajputs (Berreman, 1963, p. 29). They belonged to four exogamous patri-sibs (p. 182), and to at least nine different patrilineages (p. 178). Five other castes made up the remainder of the population. Table 20 shows the proportion of various types of families among Rajputs and non-Rajputs, and among the four patri-sibs of the Rajputs. There appear to be no important differences between the more

TABLE 20

COMPARISON OF FAMILY TYPES AMONG 4 KHASIYA RAJPUT SIBS
AND 5 NON-RAJPUT VILLAGE *Jātis* IN THE SUB-HIMALAYA ZONE
OF UTTAR PRADESH (Studied by Berreman).

| | Khasiya Rajputs | | | | | | | | Total Rajputs | | Non-Rajputs | |
| | Sib 1 | | Sib 2 | | Sib 3 | | Sib 4 | | | | | |
Family Types	No.	%	No.	%	No.	%	No.	%				
Single person	3	12	4	12.5	2	22	—	—	9	13.5	2	16.67
Subnuclear, other less than nuclear & supplemented subpolygynous	5	20	7	22	2	22	—	—	14	21	1	8.33
Nuclear	5	20	7	22	3	34	—	—	15	22.5	4	33.33
Supplemented nuclear	5	20	5	15.5	1	11	1	100	12	18	1	8.33
Simple polygynous	1	4	2	6	—	—	—	—	3	4	—	—
Supplemented polygynous	1	4	1	3	—	—	—	—	2	3	—	—
Joint & polygynous	1	4	1	3	—	—	—	—	2	3	—	—
Joint & non-polygynous	4	16	5	16	1	11	—	—	10	15	4	33.34
Totals	25	100%	32	100%	9	100%	1	100%	67	100%	12	100%

sizeable Rajput sibs. The non-Rajput castes show no instances of polygny and show a noticeably higher proportion of joint families: 33.4 per cent as opposed to the Rajput 18 per cent (combining both polygynous and non-polygynous joint families). The Rajputs also show a higher proportion of subnuclear and other small families of less than nuclear structure: 21 per cent for Rajputs as opposed to 8.33 for non-Rajputs. The differences involved in the comparison between castes in Sirkanda cannot be given much weight, however, since the numbers of cases involved, especially for the non-Rajputs, are so small.

TABLE 21

RELATIONSHIP BETWEEN CASTE AND FAMILY TYPES IN KANCHAPUR, BURDWAN DISTRICT, WEST BENGAL (Studied by Basu).*

	CASTES							
	High Castes		Jal-cal		Jal-acal		Exterior	
Family Type	No.	%	No.	%	No.	%	No.	%
Lineal and lineal collateral joint	25	41	20	42	12	27	28	21
Collateral joint	4	7 } 51%	3	6 } 50%	4	9 } 36%	12	9 } 30%
Other joint	2	3	1	2	—	—	—	—
Nuclear	15	24	15	31	19	42	67	51
Subnuclear	9	15	2	4	6	13	19	15
Single person	6	10	7	15	4	9	5	4
	61	100%	48	100%	45	100%	131	100%

* Based on table in Basu (1962, p. 88).

† The high castes include 50 Brahman families, 4 Vaidya families, and 7 Kayastha families. The jal-cal castes are castes from whose hands the Brahmans accept water to drink. Included are 19 families of Sadgops (cultivators), 3 families of Ugra-Kshatriyas (cultivators), 15 families of Gops (milkmen), 5 families of Gandhabaniks (spice dealers), 2 families of Napits (barbers), 1 family each of Kamars (blacksmiths), Tantis (weavers), Moiras (confectioners), and Malakars (unidentified). The jal-acal castes are castes from whose hands the Brahmans do not accept water to drink, but who are not Untouchable. They include 23 families of Subarnabaniks (bankers), 6 families of Chunaris (lime-makers), 1 family of Chutors (carpenters), 9 families of Sunris (liquor-sellers), 5 families of Kaibarttas (fishermen), and 1 family of Vaishnavas (religious mendicants).

The exterior castes and groups include 49 families of Bagdis (field laborers), 22 families of Haris (field laborers), 15 families of Kotals (agriculturalists), 22 families of Bauris (field laborers), 6 families of Muchis (dealers in hides, cobblers), 6 families of Koras (earth cutters), 1 family of Doms (basket makers), 8 families of Santals (tribals), and 2 families of Muslims.

BASU'S STUDY OF KANCHANPUR, BURDWAN DISTRICT, WEST BENGAL

Basu divided the castes in Kanchanpur, West Bengal, into four types. The high castes and the higher middle castes had 51 per cent and 50 per cent joint families, (probably including supplemented nuclear families) respectively; the lower middle-castes had 36 per cent, and the exterior castes 30 per cent.

SEN'S STUDY OF THE FOUR VILLAGES IN BURDWAN DISTRICT, WEST BENGAL

Lalit Kumar Sen recently published an article on the same four villages in West Bengal that Sarma reported upon earlier (Sen, 1965). They both participated in a team study of these villages in 1953–54. Sen actually did the field work in the four villages studied (Sarma, 1959, p. 87).

In his paper, Sen presents a comparison of three groupings of castes, upper, middle, and lower, for proportions of nuclear, extended, and other types of families. He finds the highest proportion of extended families (probably including supplemented nuclear families) in the middle castes, 51 per cent, and identical lower proportions, 37 per cent in both the upper and lower castes. Sen comments: "The common notion that the extended family is characteristic of the upper castes is not confirmed by the data presented in Table 2." Concerning the high proportion of extended families in the middle castes, he says:

"One would suspect the presence of an intervening variable in this relationship. One might hypothesize that the middle classes, as in many societies, show a conservative trend in carefully following the accepted and traditional norms. . . . [In] rural India family norms strongly support the maintenance of an extended family . . ." (Sen., 1965, pp. 7–8).

From these district and village studies a number of hypotheses emerge. First, there appear to be definite regional differences in family structure. Thus, there seem to be higher proportions of joint families in Gokak Taluk, Mysore, than in Nagpur District, Maharashtra, a higher proportion of joint-*cum*-supplemented nuclear families in the Gangetic Plain villages of Rampur, Delhi, and Sherupur, Uttar Pradesh, than in Shamirpet, Andhra Pradesh, or in Badlapur, Maharashtra, or in Ramkheri, Madhya Pradesh, or Sirkanda in the sub-Himalayas.

Second, on the other hand, districts or villages close to each other geographically appear to have quite similar frequency distributions. Among the five villages of Burdwan District, West Bengal, the range of variation in the proportions of joint (with some supplemented nuclear families) was only 9 per cent. (The range was from 36 per cent to 45 per cent.) In other regions, ranges of difference are somewhat greater. Thus, there was a range of difference of 13 per cent to 17 per cent among four geographically diverse zones of Gokak Taluk, Belgaum District, Mysore, and a range of 12 per cent among two samples and one village from three different districts of western Rajasthan. While these latter are fairly sizeable variations, they appear not to be as great as the extreme differences between the Gangetic Plain villages and those of Badlapur and Shamirpet in Central India, differences of over 30 per cent. (Since,

TABLE 22

TYPES OF FAMILY AS RELATED TO CASTE GROUPINGS RANKED UPPER, MIDDLE, AND LOWER
IN 4 VILLAGES IN BURDWAN DISTRICT, WEST BENGAL

(Reported upon by Lalit Kumar Sen.)*

Family Type	Caste†		
	Upper, %	Middle, %	Lower, %
Nuclear	60	46.0	56.0
Extended	37	51.0	37.0
Other	3	3.0	7.0
Total	100%	100%	100%

* Based on table in Sen (1965, p. 7).

† Sarma (1959, p. 91) lists five categories of castes for these four villages. Sen is perhaps using the same set. She included in "A" or high castes the Brahman and Kayastha (for Punyagram and Mudafar-Falahari only); in "B" or middle castes, the Bagdi-Brahman, the Bostom, Chutor, Dom-Brahman, Gandhabanik, Goala, Jugi, Kamakar, Kayastha (for Bigra and Hijalna only), Moira, Napit, Sadgop, Tambuli, Tanti, Ugra-Kshatriya; in "C" or low, she included the Bagdi, the Bauri, Dom, Dule, Garhwal, Ghatwal, Goala (for Bigra only), Hari, Kaivarta, Kalu, Muchi, Namashudra. She also had an "S" category for Santals and an "M" category for Muslims.

The tabulation below, which is taken from Sarma (1959, p. 96), lists the castes and occupations.

Occupations	Castes	Heads of Households
Priests	Brahman	2
	Bagdi-Brahman	5
	Dom-Brahman	3
	Jugi	1
Weaving	Tanti	12
Fishing	Kaivarta	2
	Bagdi (Duley)	1
Carpentry	Chutor	1
Cobbler	Muchi	1
Confectionery	Moira	1
Ironwork	Kamar	2
Grocer	Gandhabanik	1
	Tambuli	2
Boatman	Bagdi (Majhi)	1

however, the figures for Badlapur and Shamirpet probably do not include supplemented nuclear families, and the figures for the Gangetic Plain villages probably do, the differences between the two sets of villages probably are not as great as 30 per cent.)

Third, in some places almost all castes have low proportions of joint families, for example, Badlapur, Thana District, Maharashtra; in some places, almost all castes have high proportions of joint families, for example, Gokak Taluk, Mysore.

Fourth, in some places there appears to be a positive correlation between caste rank and proportions of joint families, for example, Rampur, Delhi, and Kanchanpur, Burdwan District, West Bengal; but in most places proportions of joint families *do not correlate* with caste rank, as in Gokak Taluk, Mysore; Barmer District, Rajasthan; Sherupur, Uttar Pradesh; Badlapur, Thana District, Maharashtra; Sirkanda, Dehra Dun District, Uttar Pradesh; or in the four villages of Burdwan District, West Bengal, studied by Sarma and Sen.

OVERALL COMPARISONS OF REGIONS AND CASTES

In the preceding section, I have tried to compare studies in which family structure is presented for similar social units—district, taluk, high school class, or village or caste—and in terms of similar sets of typologies. In this section, comparability is *imposed* on the studies by an attempt to use the same set of four categories for all of them. These are (1) joint, (2) supplemented nuclear, (3) nuclear, and (4) subnuclear and single-person households. Such a comparison is made difficult by the fact that most of the researchers did not make all these distinctions in definition. Thus, in many studies, supplemented nuclear families have most probably been combined with nuclear families, or with joint families; or subnuclear and single person households have been combined with nuclear households, or omitted altogether. The strategy used here has been to compare studies with full data for these four categories and then to make extrapolations from these to studies which have *not* presented full data. The proportions of the four types of families for the eleven studies presenting separate proportions for each of them are presented in Table 23.

By comparing these eleven studies, it has been possible to find typical ranges for the four types of family. Table 24 shows the actual numbers of studies for each category of family in each decile of percentages. Such a comparison suggests that typically a population has 10 to 19 per cent subnuclear and single-person households; 30 to 39 per cent nuclear families; 20 to 29 per cent supplemented nuclear families; and 20 to 29 per cent joint families.

By taking such an approach we may designate the Brahmans of Madras (22 per cent), the Sirkanda, U.P. villagers (21 per cent), and the Nayars of Tract 18 in Angadi, Kerala (22.5 per cent), as having unusually high proportions of single-person and subnuclear families; the Pramalai Kallar of the Tengalapatti sub-lineage, Madras (77 per cent), the Bangalore Paraiyans (59 per cent), the Brahmans of Orissa (40 per cent), and the villagers of Ramkheri, M.P. (41.5 per cent) as having unusually high proportions of nuclear families; the Chuhras of Khalapur as having an unusually high proportion of supplemented nuclear families (32 per cent); and the Lake area (58 per cent) and Shyambazar area (37 per cent) of Calcutta, the Nayars of Kerala (52 per cent and 61 per cent), and the Kashmiri Pandits (29–33 per cent) as having unusually high proportions of joint families.

By using the standards of these ranges (10–19 per cent subnuclear and single-

TABLE 23

4 FAMILY TYPES FOR 11 STUDIES OF FAMILY STRUCTURE.

Population Studied	Single-Person and Sub-Nuclear	Nuclear	Supplemented Nuclear	Joint	Other	Total
	%	%	%	%	%	%
Pramalai Kallar, Madurai Dt., Madras	11	77	4	4	4	100
Paraiyans, Bangalore, Mysore	15	59	12.4	11.6	2	100
Chuhras, Khalapur, U.P.	12	38	32	12	6	100
Ramkheri, Malwa, M.P.	17	41.5	18	23	0.5	100
Brahmans, Bira-Narasinghapur, Orissa	7	40	26	27	—	100
Sirkanda, Dehra Dun, U.P.	21	24	16	21	18	100
Brahmans, Kumbapettai, Madras	22	36	22	20	—	100
Rajputs, Khalapur, U.P.	12	36	24	26	2	100
Kashmiri Pandits, Utrassu-Umanagri, Anantnag, Kashmir	8	31	26–31	29–34	1	100
Shyambazar, Calcutta (45% high caste)	6	36	21	37	—	100
Lake, Calcutta (89% high caste)	—	34	8	58	—	100
Nayars-Tract 18 Angadi, Kerala	22.5	14.5	3	52	8	100
Nayars-Tract 13, Angadi, Kerala	12	17	—	61	10	100

TABLE 24

PROPORTIONS FOR 4 TYPES OF FAMILIES FOR 11 STUDIES
ARRANGED BY PERCENTAGE DECILES.

For each type of family:	Number of studies in which proportions were:								
	0–9%	10–19%	20–29%	30–39%	40–49%	50–59%	60–69%	70–79%	Total
Single-person and subnuclear	4	6	3	0	0	0	0	0	13
Nuclear	0	2	1	6	2	1	0	1	13
Supplemented nuclear	4	3	5	1	0	0	0	0	13
Joint	1	2	5	2	0	2	1	0	13

person households; 30–39 per cent nuclear households; 20–29 per cent supplemented nuclear households; and 20–29 joint households) we have a crude kind of "typical profile of family structure" in India. With it, we can judge the typicalness or unusualness of the family structures reported upon in the other fifteen studies. In those in which it is likely that supplemented nuclear families have been combined with joint families, we may combine the ranges to say that between 40 and 58 per cent of families would normally be supplemented nuclear *and* joint. Where we think that single-person and subnuclear families may have been combined, we can use the estimate that between 40 and 58 per cent of families should typically be single-person–subnuclear-nuclear households.

Table 25 provides a guide for labeling proportions of families. Medium is

TABLE 25

Ranges	Supplemented nuclear	Joint	Joint combined with supplemented nuclear
High	30% or more	30% or more	59% or more
Medium	20–29%	20–29%	40–58%
Low	up to 19%	up to 19%	up to 39%

Ranges	Single-person and subnuclear	Nuclear	Nuclear, subnuclear and single-person
High	20% or more	40% or over	59% or more
Medium	10–19%	30–39%	40–58%
Low	up to 9%	up to 29%	up to 39%

considered to be at the mode, the proportions appearing in Tables 23 and 24 as the most frequent range for the family type or types in question.

By using such a crude measuring profile, we find that other unusually high proportions are these:

For single-person households: Kanchanpur, West Bengal (20 per cent).

For nuclear with probably some subnuclear families: Chamars of Senapur (59 per cent).

For nuclear: Nagpur, Maharashtra (less than 52.2 per cent, probably between 44 and 52.2 per cent).[4]

4. Driver did not include single-person or subnuclear households. If we try to imagine what his results would have been if he had taken a complete sample of all households that included single-person and subnuclear households, we might guess that up to 19 per cent fell in these categories. In that case, his total of 2,314 households would have represented 81 per cent of the total, and 19 per cent more or 543 more cases would have been single-person or subnuclear. The table would have looked like this.

Single person and subnuclear	543	19%
Nuclear	1207	42.5%
Supplemented nuclear	412	14%
Lineal-collateral, Supplemented lineal	606–671	21%–23%
Supplemented collateral		
Lineal-collateral, Supplemented lineal-collateral	89–24	3.7%–1%
Total	2,857	100%

For nuclear with probably some subnuclear and single-person: Baniyas of
Baroda (61 per cent).

For nuclear with subnuclear and single-person: Shamirpet, Telengana (81.5
per cent), and Badlapur, Maharashtra (86 per cent).

For joint families: the Khatris of Delhi (28–45 per cent).

For joint and some supplemented nuclear families: Thakurs of Senapur, U.P.
(74.5 per cent).

For joint and supplemented nuclear families: Patidars of Baroda (62 per cent).

For joint: Gokak Taluk, Mysore: four zones with ranges of 34–51 per cent; 42–49
per cent; 51–62 per cent; 44–58 per cent. Overall proportions range from
40–53 per cent.

These places, villages, districts, and taluks, and caste communities can be
placed on a continuum with high proportions of nuclear families at one end and
high proportions of joint families at the other. This continuum is presented in
Table 26.

The array of studies placed along such a continuum suggests with respect to
category V, those places and castes with the highest proportions of joint families,
that possibly there is a region with high proportions of joint families in northwestern Mysore, as suggested by the data from Gokak taluk of Belgaum District,
Mysore. The placement of the Nayars of Malabar in a category of high proportions of joint families is probably no surprise, since this caste is famous for its
large matrilineal joint estates. To essay another regional prediction, if we ignore
the urban neighborhoods in Calcutta and Delhi in categories V and IV, in rural
areas there are perhaps higher proportions of joint families on the Gangetic
Plain (Sherupur, U.P., Rampur, Delhi, and Khalapur, U.P.) than in the areas
to the east—Bengal, possibly Orissa (Category II), or to the south—in Central
India, in Madhya Pradesh, and Maharashtra (Category II), and Telengana (Category I), and perhaps about the same or more than to the west in Western
Rajasthan (Categories III and II). (The populations from Madras and from Baroda
are more scattered in the categories of Table 26 than are those of Uttar Pradesh,
Bengal, Maharashtra, and Rajasthan.)

One of the initial questions of the study was: Do high castes have larger
proportions of joint families? Turning to this question, we may consider the
various high castes that are ordinarily considered to be in the various varnas
or divisions of Indian society.[5] They are ranked from high to low; the Brahmans,
the Kshatriyas or warriors, the Vaishya or merchants, the Shudras or servants,
and the Untouchables. The first three are considered to be "twice-born" or
high varnas, and castes that I assume to belong to these varnas in the belief of
the members of other castes in a locality, I shall define as high castes.

First, let us consider various Brahman *jātis* represented among these studies.
We find that Brahmans have high proportions of joint families among the
Kashmiri Pandits (34 per cent), and in the Lake area of Calcutta, which is 89

5. The concept of varna cannot be discussed here. For my present purposes I use it as a
system of caste ranking which is almost universally known in India and to which rankings of
castes in a local system are usually equated.

TABLE 26

PLACES AND CASTE COMMUNITIES ARRANGED ALONG A CONTINUUM OF HIGH NUCLEAR–HIGH JOINT FAMILY PROPORTIONS.

PLACES

| HIGH NUCLEAR | | | | HIGH JOINT |
I	II	III	IV	V
Shamirpet, Telengana	Ramkheri, Malwa, M.P. Barmer, Dt., Rajasthan	Korna, Jodhpur, Rajasthan Sirkanda, Dehra Dun,* U.P.	Shyambazar, Calcutta	Lake, Calcutta
Badalapur, Maharashtra	Jalor Dt., Rajasthan	Sherupur, U.P. Rampur, Delhi		Gokak Taluk, Mysore
	Kanchanpur, W. Bengal* 4 villages in Burdwan Dt. West Bengal Nagpur, Maharashtra			

CASTES

| | | | | |
I	II	III	IV	V
Pramalai Kallar, Madras Paraiyans, Bangalore (originally from Madras)	Brahmans, Orissa Brahmans, Baroda	Madras Brahmans* Chuhras, Khalapur,† U.P. Rajputs, Khalapur, U.P.	Kashmiri Brahmans Khatris, Delhi	Nayars, Kerala Thakurs, Senapur, U.P.
Chamars of Senapur, U.P. Baniyas of Baroda				Patidars, Baroda

* These castes or communities have unusually high proportions of single-person and subnuclear households, 20% or more.
† The Chuhras of Khalapur have an unusually high proportion of supplemented nuclear families, 32%.

per cent high caste (made up of Brahmans, Kayasthas, and Vaidyas), 58 per cent. Brahmans have medium proportions among the Brahmans of Tanjore District, Madras (20 per cent joint), in Bira-Narasingapura village, Puri District, Orissa (27 per cent), and in Gokak Taluk, Mysore (37 per cent joint, with some supplemented nuclear families), and Kanchanpur, West Bengal, where 50 out of 61 high-caste families are Brahmans (51 per cent high-caste families are joint and supplemented nuclear families), in Rampur, Delhi (54 per cent for both joint and supplemented nuclear families), and in Baroda (42 per cent for both joint and supplemented nuclear families). Brahmans have low proportions of joint families in the four Burdwan villages studied by Sarma and Sen (where high castes, which include 33 Brahman and 19 Kayastha families, have 37 per cent joint and supplemented nuclear families), in Sherupur, U.P. (out of four Brahman families, only one is joint or supplemented nuclear), and in Badlapur, Maharashtra (6 per cent joint for a population of 83 Brahman families).

These comparisons suggest that Brahmans may have high, medium, or low proportions of joint families in various places. As pointed out earlier, Brahmans may have much lower proportions of joint families than do castes of lower rank in a particular locality. This is particularly striking in Gokak Taluk and in Badlapur, Maharashtra (see tables 15 and 19 above).

There are three village *jātis* who are considered by themselves and others to be members of the Kshatriya or warrior varna. These are the Thakurs of Senapur, with 74.5 per cent joint and supplemented nuclear families, a high proportion, and the Kshatriya of Sherupur, U.P., where three of the five families live in joint or supplemented nuclear families, and the Rajputs of Khalapur, U.P., who have a medium proportion of joint families, 26 per cent. Marathas, who are sometimes considered to be Kshatriyas, are represented with 80 families in Gokak Taluk, Mysore, with a high proportion of joint families, 55.5 per cent; and with 75 families in Badlapur, Maharasthra, with a very low proportion of 9.3 per cent joint families.

There is only one group of Baniyas represented, the Baniya high school boys of Baroda, with a low proportion of 37 per cent joint and supplemented nuclear families. Other castes sometimes considered to be "twice-born," in the three highest varnas, include the Kayasthas, Vaidyas, Khatris, and Lingayats. Kayasthas and Vaidyas who live in the Lake area of Calcutta would appear to have a high proportion of joint families: 58 per cent. Those seven Kayastha and four Vaidya families out of 61 high-caste families in Kanchanpur, West Bengal, may have a medium proportion of joint and supplemented nuclear families. (The entire 61 families of Brahmans, Kayasthas, and Vaidyas have a 51 per cent proportion of joint and supplemented nuclear families.) The Khatris of Delhi appear to have a high proportion of joint families, 28–45 per cent. The 344 Lingayat families represented in the sample of Gokak Taluk, Mysore, have 50 per cent joint, with some supplemented nuclear families, a high proportion.

Turning from "twice-born" varnas to Shudra castes, we find that proportions of joint families among those *jātis* represented vary from high to low. Some, probably all landed and dominant castes in the localities represented, have high proportions of joint families: the Nayars of Kerala (52 per cent, 61 per cent), the Patidars of Baroda (62 per cent joint and supplemented nuclear), the Jats of Rampur, Delhi (70 per cent joint and supplemented nuclear). Castes less well known as landowners but of Shudra varna also have high proportions of joint families: castes raising sheep and goats including Raikas caste in Barmer District, Rajasthan (60 per cent joint and supplemented nuclear out of 45 families); in Gokak Taluk, the Panchals (62 per cent joint out of 45 families), the Berads (48 per cent joint out of 100 families), the Hanabars (75 per cent joint, with some supplemented nuclear out of only 8 families), the Kurubas (55 per cent joint, with some supplemented nuclear out of 98 families), the Uppars (64 per cent joint, with some supplemented nuclear out of 84 families), the Vadars (80 per cent joint, with some supplemented nuclear out of 19 families), the Christians (34 per cent joint, with some supplemented nuclear out of 15 families), the Jains (45 per cent, with some supplemented nuclear out of 33 families), and the Muslims (59 per cent joint, with some supplemented nuclear out of 106 families); in Sherupur, Faizabad District, Uttar Pradesh, the Murau (2 out of 3 families are joint and supplemented nuclear) and Koris (75 per cent joint and supplemented nuclear of 16 families), and the non-Rajputs of Sirkanda, U.P. (4 of 12 are joint families). Other middle castes, Shudra castes, have medium or low proportions of joint families. These are:

Medium proportions (20–29 per cent joint or 40–58 per cent joint and supplemented nuclear)

All middle occupational castes in Barmer, Rajasthan, except those raising sheep and goats (see Table 16).

Ahirs and Lohars of Sherupur, U.P. (3 of 7 families of Ahirs are joint or supplemented nuclear, and 1 of 2 families of Lohars).

Artisan castes of Badlapur, Maharashtra (28.6 per cent joint of 28 families) (see Table 19 above for names of castes).

Jal-cal castes of Kanchanpur, West Bengal (50 per cent joint and supplemented nuclear of 48 families) (see Table 21 for names of castes).

Middle castes of Rampur, Delhi (57 per cent joint and supplemented nuclear out of 26 families) (see Table 18 for names of castes).

Middle castes of 4 villages in Burdwan District, West Bengal (51 per cent of 193 families).

Low Proportions (up to 19 per cent joint, or up to 39 per cent joint and supplemented nuclear)

Jal-acal castes of Kanchanpur, West Bengal (36 per cent joint or supplemented nuclear of 45 families) (see Table 21 for names of castes).

Muslims of Sherupur, U.P. (1 out of 3 families is joint or supplemented nuclear).

Bazaar castes (11.6 per cent joint of 95 families), Muslims (13.1 per cent of 92 families), traditional agriculturalists (14.9 per cent joint of 148 families), service castes (7.7 per cent of 13 families)—all of Badlapur, Maharashtra (see Table 19 for names of castes).

Pramalai Kallar, a sub-lineage of Tengalapatti hamlet, Madurai District, Madras (4 per cent joint).

Turning lastly to Untouchables, we find again that some have high, some have medium, and some have low proportions of joint families. These are listed below.

High joint (30 per cent or more joint or 59 per cent or more joint and supplemented nuclear)

Holeyas (52 per cent joint, with some supplemented nuclear out of 36 families), and Sanagars (6 out of 9 families) of Gokak Taluk.

Outcastes (Mahar, Chambhar, and Bhangi) of Badlapur, Maharashtra (32.6 per cent of 43 families).

Medium joint (20–29 per cent joint or 40–58 per cent joint and supplemented nuclear)

Bhangis of Rampur, Delhi (40 per cent joint and supplemented nuclear).

Low joint (up to 19 per cent joint or up to 39 per cent joint and supplemented nuclear)

Chamars of Sherupur, U.P. (33 per cent joint and supplemented nuclear).
Chamars of Rampur, Delhi (19 per cent joint and supplemented nuclear).
Chamars of Senapur, U.P. (34 per cent joint and supplemented nuclear).
Chuhras of Khalapur, U.P. (12 per cent joint).
Scheduled Tribes (Tribals, Thakur, and Katkari) of Badlapur, Maharashtra, 14.1 per cent joint).
Exterior castes of Kanchanpur, Burdwan (30 per cent joint and supplemented nuclear of 131 families) (see Table 21 for names of castes).
Lower castes of 4 villages in Burdwan District, West Bengal (37 per cent joint and supplemented nuclear for 400 families) (see Table 22 for names of castes).
Paraiyans of Bangalore (11.6 per cent joint).

These comparisons suggest that there is no simple correlation between caste rank and proportion of joint families. Within each varna, there are some *jāti* groups somewhere with high, with medium, and with low proportions of joint families reported. Clearly, there does appear to be a tendency for Untouchable *jātis* to have lower proportions of joint families. Table 27 gives a kind of "straw

TABLE 27

STRAW COUNT OF *Jāti* GROUPS RANKED BY VARNA AND PROPORTIONS
OF JOINT FAMILIES REPRESENTED IN THE 26 STUDIES.

	Varnas					
Proportions of	*Twice-Born*		*Shudras*		*Untouchables*	
Joint Families	*No.*	*%*	*No.*	*%*	*No.*	*%*
High	9	39	16	25.5	6	16
Medium	9	39	26 or more	41.5	1	2
Low	5	22	21	33	31	82
	23	100%	63 or more	100%	38	100%

count" of the *jāti* groups represented here. Such a count cannot be anything but suggestive of the relationship between caste rank and proportions of joint families. It suggests that twice-born castes are somewhat more likely to have high proportions of joint families than are Shudra *jātis*; both twice-born and Shudras are much more likely to have middle proportions of joint families than are Untouchables. Untouchables are much more likely to have low proportions of joint families than are Shudras and twice-born. The hypothesis this table suggests is that the sharpest division is between the Untouchables and the other castes in proportions of joint families.

A second question we asked initially was: Are joint families more prevalent among landed castes than among landless castes? Unfortunately, we lack data on land ownership for many localities or caste communities included here; or again, in some instances we know about land ownership but lack statistics on family structure for the various castes within a locality. However, some facts seem clear.

First of all, in every category along the continuum of nuclearity-jointness, there are castes that are landed, castes that represent in their respective localities dominant castes owning most of the land. These are for each family type, from high nuclear to high joint, from Table 26:

I   Pramalai Kallar-landed (Dumont, 1957, p. 122), although almost 20 per cent are landless in the whole hamlet of Tengalapatti.

II   Brahmans of Bira-Narasinghapur, Puri District, Orissa, own almost all the land in the village (Ray, 1956, pp. 14, 8), originally land granted by a king.

III Brahmans of Kumbapettai, Tanjore District, Madras, own two-thirds of the land in the village (Gough, 1960, p. 18).
Rajputs of Khalapur, Saharanpur District, U.P., own over 90 per cent of the land in the village.

IV   Kashmiri Pandits of Utrassu-Umanagri, Anantnag District, Kashmir, control almost all the land in the village (Madan, 1965, pp. 159–50).

V   Thakurs of Senapur, Jaunpur District, U.P., own almost all the land in the village (Cohn, 1961, p. 1052).
Nayars of Angadi village Ernad Taluka, Kozhikode District, Kerala, are landed (Mencher, 1962, pp. 231, 236).

The fact that there are landed castes in every category indicates that having land and being the dominant caste in a locality is not a cause for high proportions or even medium proportions of joint families.

The following facts emerge if we look within villages and ask if the landed castes or families within a village are more likely to have joint family structures (villages and localities arranged by the categories in Table 26).

CATEGORY II

1. Kanchanpur, Burdwan District, West Bengal (see Table 28 for relationship between caste rank and amount of land owned). The difference in land ownership is most marked between the exterior castes (plus Santals and Muslims) versus all

TABLE 28
Relationship between caste rank and land-holding
in Kanchanpur, Burdwan District, West Bengal.*

Amount of	Castes							
Land Owned	High		Jal-cal		Jal-Acal		Exterior	
	No.	%	No.	%	No.	%	No.	%
None	6	10	5	10	9	20	111	85
Up to 5 bighas	14	22	14	30	7	15	12	9
5–20 bighas	25	40	24	50	21	47	7	5
21–50 bighas	14	22	4	8	8	18	1	1
50 or more bighas	4	6	1	2	—	—	—	—
	63	100%	48	100%	45	100%	131	100%

* Table adapted from Basu (1962, p. 53).

† The high castes include 50 Brahman families, 4 Vaidya families, and 7 Kayastha families. The *jal-cal* castes are castes from whose hands the Brahmans accept water to drink. Included are 19 families of Sadgops (cultivators), 3 families of Ugra-Kshatriyas (cultivators), 15 families of Gops (milkmen), 5 families of Tantis (weavers), Moiras (confectioners), and Malakars (unidentified). The *jal-acal* castes are castes from whose hands the Brahmans do not accept water to drink, but who are not Untouchable. They include 23 families of Subarnabaniks (bankers), 6 families of Chunaris (lime-makers), 1 family of Chutors (carpenters), 9 families of Sunris (liquor-sellers), 5 families of Kaibarttas (fishermen), and 1 family of Vaishnavas (religious mendicants).

The exterior castes and groups include 49 families of Bagdis (field laborers), 22 families of Haris (field laborers), 15 families of Kotals (agriculturalists), 22 families of Bauris (earth cutters), 1 family of Doms (basketmakers), 8 families of Santals (tribals), and 2 families of Muslims.

other castes (85 per cent landless versus 13 per cent landless among other castes). While the *jal-acal* castes have a somewhat higher proportion of landless families, 20 per cent as compared to 10 per cent each among the *jal-cal* and high castes, the differences in amount of land held between the high, the *jal-cal*, and the *jal-acal* castes are not as great as the differences in their family structure. If the reader will refer back to Table 21, he will note that joint (probably with supplemented nuclear) families are 51 per cent for high castes, 50 per cent for *jal-cal* castes, 36 per cent for *jal-acal* castes, and 30 per cent for exterior, Santals, and Muslims. The comparison of the two sets of proportions suggests that, while there is some correlation between land ownership and higher proportions of joint families, it is not a closely coordinated or strong relationship in Kanchanpur.

2. Four villages in Burdwan District studied by Sarma and Sen. Table 22 indicates that the middle castes in these four villages have a higher proportion of joint (probably with supplemented nuclear) families. Table 29 shows that owner-cultivators do have higher proportions of joint families (with supplemented nuclear families) than do other occupational groups: sharecropper, non-cultivating owner, agricultural laborer, and others. Thus, while the data suggest that high castes do not have especially high proportions of joint families in these villages, the owner-cultivators of land do have higher proportions (64.86 per cent).

3. Barmer District, Rajasthan. Table 16 showed that it was the castes raising sheep and goats which had the highest proportion of joint (with supplemented

TABLE 29

FAMILY TYPES AND OCCUPATIONAL GROUPS IN 4 VILLAGES OF BURDWAN DISTRICT, WEST BENGAL.*

Family Type	Owner-Cultivator		Share-cropper		Non-Cultivating Owner		Agricultural Laborer		Others		Total
	No.	%	No.	%	No.	%	No.	%	No.	%	
Nuclear	39	35.14	63	42.57	32	58.49	95	75.40	104	67.74	333
Collateral joint	17	15.31	19	12.85	5	9.43	4	3.17	13	8.39	58
Lineal, lineal-collateral, supplemented collateral, supplemented nuclear where one married son & one parent are present	43	38.74	53	35.81	16	30.19	22	17.46	32	20.75	166
Joint with relatives of wife or mother included	12	10.81	13	8.78	1	1.89	5	3.97	5	3.22	36
Total	111	100%	148	100.01%	54	100%	126	100%	154	100%	593

* Table adapted from Sarma (1964, p. 201).

383

nuclear families) in the sample from Barmer District. The range of proportions among the other castes is very narrow—a little over 10 per cent (41.3–52 per cent). Such data do not suggest that the landed castes have a higher proportion of joint families.

CATEGORY III

1. Rampur, Delhi. The caste owning all the land, the Jats, have the highest proportion of joint and supplemented nuclear families (see Table 18). However, other castes, the Brahmans with 53 per cent joint and supplemented nuclear families and the Bhangis with 43 per cent joint and supplemented nuclear families, have medium proportions despite the dependence on Jats for land (in the case of five agriculturalist out of fifteen Brahman families), and the landlessness of ten Brahman families and all of the Bhangis (Lewis, 1958, p. 88). Thus, despite land-lessness, these castes have medium proportions of joint families.

2. Sirkanda, Dehra Dun District, Uttar Pradesh. Table 20 suggests that the very small numbers of non-Rajputs in Sirkanda have a higher proportion of joint families than do the Rajputs. All castes appear to own some land (Berreman, 1963, p. 16), although the low castes, 10 per cent of the population, own only 2 per cent of the land (p. 40). In any case, since there does not seem to be a positive correlation between rank of caste and proportion of joint families, disproportionate landowning cannot be an explanation in Sirkanda.

Although we lack data for other places represented in the various studies, a review of five places does not suggest a *close* relationship between landowning and high proportions of joint families for caste units. There appears to be a relation-ship between landowning, provided one is also a cultivator, and a higher propor-tion of joint families in the four villages of Burdwan. In Rampur, Delhi, and in Kanchanpur, West Bengal, castes owning a greater proportion of land have higher proportions of joint families, but the contrast in rank is sharper than that of land ownership with respect to proportion of joint families.

Thus far, I have tended to reject two hypotheses and have concluded that:

1. Except for the tendency of the Untouchable castes represented to have low proportions of joint families, castes in the other four varnas vary in having high, medium, or low proportions of joint families. Hence, there does not appear to be a close relationship between caste rank and proportion of joint families.

2. There does *not* appear to be a *strong* closely coordinated relationship between landowning castes and castes with high proportions of joint families.

In the course of this research, I did note differences in customary time of break-up of joint families. Thus in some places, as among the Thakurs of Khalapur, joint families tend *not* to break up until the heads are first cousins. In other places, they tend to break up after married brothers have lived together for a time after the father's death, as among the Kashmiri Pandits of Utrassu-Umanagri. In other places they break up shortly after marriage, as in Shamirpet, Telengana, and among the Pramalai Kallar. Thus, if we consider the categories of castes and localities in Table 26 we find:

CATEGORY I

Except for Badlapur, Maharashtra, for which I lack information, all the castes and communities in Category I are characterized by break-up of the joint family shortly after a son's marriage, within a few years at most, certainly. This would normally be before the father's death (Dube, 1955, p. 133; Dumont, 1957, p. 174; Woodruff, 1959, p. 17; Cohn, 1961, p. 1052; Shahani, 1961, p. 1827).

CATEGORY II

We lack information for Barmer District, Rajasthan, and for the Brahmans of Orissa, and for Nagpur, Maharashtra. In Ramkheri, "there are frequent partitions of joint households" (Mayer, 1960, p. 241); one gathers that married brothers seldom stay together (pp. 241, 181). Partition, it appears, takes place either before or after the father's death. For Jalor District, Rajasthan, Bose and Saxena say that "most brothers separate after a few years of marriage, or on the death of their parents." (1965, pp. 31, 33). In the four villages of Burdwan and in Kanchanpur, it seems to be customary for brothers, at least in the higher castes, to divide property at or shortly after the father's death (Basu, 1962, p. 90; Sarma, 1964, p. 194). We lack information for the Brahmans of Orissa, but for the Brahmans of Baroda, Shahani says, "Even before his children are old enough to marry, he [the Brahman father] separates to form a nuclear family" (Shahani, 1961, pp. 1825–26).

Thus the castes and communities in Category II appear to be characterized by partition of the joint household before, at, or shortly after the father's death.

CATEGORY III

We lack information for Korna, Jodhpur, Rajasthan, and for Sherupur, U.P. In Sirkanda, division takes place casually and frequently as parts of a coparcenary joint family move to a field house or a second house to live (Berreman, 1963, pp. 34–37).

In Rampur, Delhi, and among Madras Brahmans, division takes place at the father's death or shortly thereafter (Lewis, 1958, p. 105; Gough, 1956, pp. 837, 839). Among Khalapur Chuhras and Khalapur Rajputs, division takes place before the father's death (Kolenda, unpublished field notes; Hitchcock, 1956, p. 141).

CATEGORY IV

We lack information on Shyambazar.

Among the Kashmiri Pandits for whom Madan gives statistical evidence, 80 per cent of the divisions take place between married brothers (Madan, 1965, p. 56).

Among Khatris of Delhi, division takes place after the birth of two or three children; Kapoor does not relate this to the death of the father or the marriage of the brother, but she does refer to the early separation of households (Kapoor, 1965, pp. 59, 60).

CATEGORY V

I lack information for the Lake area, Calcutta, and Gokak Taluk, Mysore.

Both Singh for the Thakurs of Senapur and Shahani for the Patidars of Baroda (Shahani, 1961, p. 1825) say that there are among these groups some families headed by married first cousins, the married sons of married brothers. Singh says that the time of break-up of Senapur joint families is typically in the third generation, between first cousins (Singh, 1962, pp. 70–71).

Among Nayars it is only recently that the law has changed to favor break-up into smaller estates (Mencher, 1962, pp. 236–37).

While these data are scanty, they do suggest that the five categories along the continuum of jointness and nuclearity do differ among themselves in the patterned time of break-up of the commensal joint family; at the extreme in Category I, joint family break-up takes place for a man within a few years of his marriage; this is normally likely to be well before his father's death. In Categories II and III, break-up may take place before, at, or after the father's death. In Category IV, break-up takes place between married brothers presumably after the father's death, and in Category V, either between married brothers or between married first cousins. (An amplification of this concern with differences in time of breakup appears in Kolenda, 1967.)

Our last initial question was: Do Indians typically live in joint families? Unfortunately, most studies do not include statistics on the number of people included in the various types of families. Nine studies do include such statistics. A perusal of these statistics, presented in Table 30, suggest that when about 30 per cent of families are joint in a community, the majority of persons, more than half of the population, live in joint families. Referring back to Table 26, the nine localities or castes listed under IV and V would probably have the majority of their members in joint families. Those in III may or may not; those in II and I probably do *not* have a majority of persons living in joint families.

If we consider the ten studies giving statistics on persons included for the proportion of persons in both joint and supplemented nuclear families, we may estimate that when 35 per cent of the families are either joint or supplemented nuclear, most of the population is in these two types of families. Such a standard would cover Categories V, IV, III, and II in Table 26. Only in the populations listed under I would most persons not live in either joint or supplemented nuclear families.

The nine studies on which I base these estimates can hardly be considered representative of India as a whole; they do not represent a systematic random sample of Indian villages, districts, or castes. Therefore, I hesitate to go on to the next obvious generalization: that Indians typically live in either joint or supplemented nuclear families. If we refer back to statements by Karve and Dube cited at the beginning of the paper—Karve's statement that it is the larger or smaller joint family that is typical in India, and Dube's that it is the small joint family or nuclear family that is typical—we may say that both are right in saying that the small joint family is the typical Indian family, provided that by

TABLE 30

PROPORTION OF POPULATION INCLUDED IN JOINT AND SUPPLEMENTED NUCLEAR FAMILIES IN TEN STUDIES.

Studies Compared	Proportion of Joint Families %	Proportion Population in Joint Families %	Proportion of Supplemented Nuclear Families %	Proportion Population in Supp. Nuclear %	Proportion of Both Joint and Supp. Nuclear Families %	Proportion Population in Both Joint and Supp. Nuclear Families %
Thakurs of Senapur	—	—	—	—	74.5	94
Jalor District, Rajasthan	—	—	—	—	46.5	56
Barmer District, Rajasthan	—	—	—	—	48.2	58
Brahmans of Bira-Narasinghapur, Puri District, Orissa	27	44	26	25	53	69
Ramkheri, Malwa, Madhya Pradesh	23	35	18	19	41	54
Sirkanda, Dehra Dun District, U.P.	21	37.5	16	18	37	55.5
Badlapur, Thana, Maharashtra	14	21.9	Combined with Nuclear	—	—	—
Paraiyans of Bangalore	11.6	16.5	12.4	15	24	31.5
Pramalai Kallar Sub-lineage, Madras	4	4	4	4	8	8

387

this term the joint family and the supplemented nuclear family, as defined in this study, are included. As for Karve's "large joint family," it is my impression from having classified so many Indian families, that the family including more than two married couples is rare (see column in Table 31 for proportions of families including three or more couples: lineal-collateral). If by a large joint family, a family with more than two married couples is meant, then these data suggest that it is unusual. As for Dube's statement that it is the nuclear family that is also typical, we may agree that often the most numerous type of family represented is the nuclear family. If we compare the four main types of family— single person, subnuclear, nuclear, supplemented nuclear, and joint—referring to Table 26, among the castes and communities listed under I and II, the most numerous type of family is the nuclear family; it is not the most numerous type of family in IV and V. Those in III divide, with the nuclear being most numerous in Sirkanda, and among the Madras Brahmans, the Chuhras of Khalapur, and the Rajputs of Khalapur, but not the most numerous type in Sherupur, U.P., Rampur, Delhi, or Korna, Jodhpur. Thus, among the 29 localities or caste groups represented here, in 18 the nuclear family is the most numerous family type. But, as suggested above, although it is the most numerous type of family, it is probably not the type including the majority of persons, except in communities and castes such as those listed under I in Table 26.

A last question is this: Are there more lineal joint families than collateral joint families in India? For only twelve caste groups or communities is it possible to compare the proportions of lineal versus collateral families, or more precisely the proportion of lineal and supplemented lineal joint families *versus* the proportion of collateral, supplemented collateral, lineal-collateral, and supplemented lineal-collateral families? In Table 31, these ten studies are listed with the proportions of these two categories of families presented. In three studies, there clearly appears to be a higher proportion of the lineal type than of the collateral type. These are Gokak Taluk, Mysore; Ramkheri, M.P.; and the Chamars of Senapur. In five studies, the collateral types are in higher proportion than the lineal types: Sirkanda, U.P., among the Kashmiri Pandits, among the Khalapur Rajputs, among the Khalapur Chuhras, and among the Thakurs of Senapur. In three cases, it is unclear, although it would seem likely that there are more of the lineal type than the collateral: Kanchanpur, West Bengal, the four Burdwan villages studied by Sarma and Sen, and among the Nayars of Angadi, Kerala.

Among the Madras Brahmans, there appear to be no collateral joint families; among the Pramalai Kallar, the one joint family is "deviant," made up of a widower, his son and his wife, and his married daughter and her husband (Dumont, 1957, p. 57).

For other studies we do not know the breakdown of types of joint families— for Barmer District, Jalor District, or Korna Village in Rajasthan, or for Rampur, Delhi; Sherupur, U.P.; or Nagpur, Maharashtra, or for Badlapur, Maharashtra, for the Orissa Brahmans, for the Khatris of Delhi, Bangalore Paraiyans, or the two mixed-caste communities of Calcutta, or the three Baroda caste groups.

TABLE 31

Proportions of "Lineal" and "Collateral" joint families in eleven studies.

Studies	Lineal and Supplemented Lineal	Supplemented Lineal-Collateral, Supplemented Collateral, Lineal-Collateral, Collateral COLLATERAL	Three or More Couples: Supplemented Collateral Lineal-Collateral ONLY	Other Joint
Gokak Taluk, Mysore	20.7–34.7%	18.8%	10.4%	—
Ramkheri, Madhya Pradesh	11%	10.5%	0	1.5%
Sirkanda, Dehra Dun, U.P.	3%	16%	9%	2%
Kanchanpur, Burdwan, W. Bengal	Less than 30%	8% plus less than 30% additional	Less than 30%	1%
4 Villages in Burdwan, W. Bengal	Less than 28%	More than 10%	Unclear	6%
Kashmiri Pandits, Utrassu-Umanagri	12%	17–22%	Less than 5%	—
Rajputs of Khalapur, U.P.	11%	15%	11%	—
Nayars of Angadi-Tract 18	44% or less	8% or more	—	—
Nayars of Angadi-Tract 13	48% or less	13% or more	Less than 29%	—
Chuhras of Khalapur, U.P.	0	12%	6%	—
Thakurs of Senapur, U.P.	Less than 30.5%	More than 44%	Unclear	—
Chamars of Senapur, U.P.	20%	11%	Unclear	3%

389

While the evidence on this question is thin, it does not overwhelmingly support the assumption that lineal joint families greatly outweigh collateral joint families. However, it should be remembered that lineal-collateral families were included with collateral joint families above. It may be that there are, overall, few families composed of married brothers whose parents are both dead. This suggests that married brothers with or without parents present may sometimes be more numerous than simple lineal (that is, stem families) or supplemented lineal families.

SUMMARY STATEMENT

By comparing twenty-six studies which included frequencies of family types for villages, caste communities, and other populations, I have tried to answer, tentatively, some questions about family structure.

The first question was: Is the joint family more characteristic of higher castes than of lower castes? Comparisons suggest that it is least characteristic of local *jātis* of Untouchables. It may be somewhat more characteristic of higher "twice-born" castes, but Brahmans, attributed high-caste rank widely over India, more characteristically have average or medium proportions of joint families rather than high proportions. Among the studies considered here, there were instances of *jātis* of all five of the varnas having high, medium, and low proportions of joint families. At best, there is only a partial correlation between caste rank and proportions of joint families.

The second question was: Is the joint family more characteristic of landed castes than of landless castes? The evidence on this was slight. The evidence we did have suggested that landed castes may vary in proportions of joint families from high to low, and that caste *rank* seems, in seven villages and one district compared, to be more closely related to the size of the proportions of joint families than does land ownership.

The third question was: What is the typical Indian family? An estimate based on ten studies suggested that not until a community has 30 per cent joint families does the majority of the population live in joint families.

While these studies suggest that most Indians do *not* live in joint families, as defined here, they do suggest that most (rural people at least) live in either a joint or a supplemented nuclear family. While the majority of people may live in such joint and supplemented nuclear families, the majority of families, defined here as commensal units, are probably nuclear in structure.

Emerging during the research were other hypotheses. First, there appear to be regional differences in proportions of joint families. It may be that there are higher proportions of joint families on the Gangetic Plain than in Central India (represented by studies in Maharashtra, Madhya Pradesh, and western Rajasthan), or in West Bengal. There may be high proportions of joint families among most castes in northwestern Mysore State. There also appear to be places such as Gokak Taluk, Belgaum District, Mysore, in which all castes appear to have high proportions of joint families, and places such as Badlapur, Thana District,

Maharashtra, where almost all local caste groups have low proportions of joint families.

Second, there appear to be definite differences in the customary time of break-up of the joint family in various places in India, and the differences in the mores of break-up correlate with the proportions of joint families. Those with earlier break-up—when a married son establishes his own household separate from his father's within a few months or years after his marriage—correlate with low proportions of joint families; those with medium break-up when married sons break up at or shortly after the death of the father—with medium proportions of joint family; and with slow break-up—where married sons continue to live together for long periods after their father's death, even until their own sons are grown and married, so that families headed by first cousins occur—with high proportions of joint families.

Third, in three places more than one-fifth of the households were occupied by a single person or by a subnuclear family. These places are characterized either by prohibition of widow remarriage as in Bengal (Karve, 1953, p. 97) and among Madras Brahmans, or by polygyny as among the Rajputs of Sirkanda, U.P., in the sub-Himalayas. In all three places, women are allowed to live alone and to head a household. Among the Khasiya Rajputs in Sirkanda, U.P., who practice polygyny extensively, it is common for a co-wife to live alone with a servant, relative, or her unmarried children, while her husband lives with another wife and children, or with others of his relatives. This pattern ties in with a pattern of co-parcenary joint families' owning two or more houses, often one in the village and at least one in the fields.

Although the findings above are based upon comparisons of 26 studies, they must be considered at best tentative findings and, at worst, merely suggestive of new hypotheses and new avenues of research on the Indian family. Comparison has been hobbled throughout by the fact that researchers did not categorize their data on family structure in the same way. In this study I have tried to make the various sets of data comparable, but the process has often involved assumptions on my part, assumptions which are not arbitrary but which undoubtedly have involved guesswork.

Perhaps the main contribution this study can make is to stimulate social scientists in India to be more questioning about the phenomena of family structure, more doubtful about the standard hypotheses explaining the presence or absence of the joint family, more open to new possibilities in formulating hypotheses about the latter, more careful in precise definition, and more thorough in reporting their field data on family structure.

Throughout this study I have been treating commensal families, hearth groups. I may have treated some studies mistakenly because other units were actually counted. In any case, this is only one way to define the functioning family group. One could focus upon the residential family or upon the co-parcenary family, or upon the kinship neighborhood (Sarma's term, 1964). Needed especially are studies considering all of these family units and the interrelationships between them. It may be that almost all rural Indians live in kinship neighborhoods—their relatives live next door. As yet, little data on the relationships between neighbors have been published, except for data on caste composition and lineage. A notable example of the kind of mapping of kinship neighborhoods needed is that by Dumont for the Pramalai Kallar sub-lineage of Tengalapatti hamlet, Madurai District, Madras (1957, pp. 52–53).

It may be that the division in the interests of sociologists and social anthropologists, with the former more interested in the residential family and the latter more interested in the lineage or local kin group, has acted as a kind of barrier to the study of the family in all the social units in which it can be considered to be manifested—units that fit one within another as part of a single congery, the Indian family. Undoubtedly the appropriate data have already been collected for many localities and could be prepared for publication.

BIBLIOGRAPHY

ARENSBERG, CONRAD M.

1955. American communities. *American Anthropologist*, 66: 1143–62.

1960. The American family in the perspective of other cultures. In Eli Ginsberg (Ed.), *The nation's children, 1: Family and social change*. Washington, D.C.: White House Conference.

BAILEY, F. G.

1957. *Caste and the economic frontier*. Manchester: Manchester University Press.

1960. The joint-family in India: A framework for discussion. *Economic Weekly*, 12: 345–52.

BASU, TARA KRISHNA.

1962. *The Bengal peasant from time to time*. New York and Calcutta: Asia Publishing House.

BEALS, ALAN R.

1955. Interplay among factors of change in a Mysore village. In McKim Marriott (Ed.), *Village India*. Chicago: University of Chicago Press.

BERREMAN, GERALD D.

1963. *Hindus of the Himalayas*. Berkeley and Los Angeles: University of California Press.

n.d. Unpublished village census.

BÉTEILLE, ANDRÉ.

1964. Family and social change in India and other South Asian countries. *Economic Weekly*, 16: 237–44.

BOSE, A. B., S. P. MALHOTRA, and LAL PAUL BHARARA.

1963. Socio-economic difference in dispersed dwelling and compact settlement types in arid regions. *Man in India*, 43: 119–30.

BOSE, A. B., and P. C. SAXENA.

1964. Composition of rural households in Rajasthan (studies in households III). *Indian Journal of Social Research*, 1964: 299–308.

1965a. Composition and size of rural joint households (studies in households IV). *Indian Journal of Social Research*, 1965: 30–40.

1965b. Some characteristics of nuclear households. *Man in India*, 45: 195–200.

BURGESS, E. W., and H. J. LOCKE.

1953. *The Family*. New York: American Book.

CAMPBELL, J. K.

1964. *Honour, family and patronage*. Oxford: Oxford University Press.

CENSUS OF INDIA, 1951.

1957. Selections from census of India, 1951. In *Introduction to the civilization of India; changing dimensions of Indian culture*. Chicago: University of Chicago Press.

COATS, THOMAS.

1823. Account of the present state of the township of Lony. *Transactions of the Literary Society of Bombay*, 3: 172–264.

COHN, BERNARD S.

1961. Chamar family in a North Indian village; a structural conttingent. *Economic Weekly*, 13: 1051–55.

DESAI, I. P.

1964. *Some aspects of family in Mahuva*. New York: Asia Publishing House.

DRIVER, EDWIN D.

1962. Family structure and socio-economic status in Central India. *Sociological Bulletin*, 11: 112–20.

DUBE, S. C.

1955. *Indian village*. London: Routledge and Kegan Paul.

1959. Social structure and change in Indian peasant communities. In A. R. Desai (Ed.), *Rural sociology in India*. Bombay: Indian Society of Agricultural Economics, Vora and Company.

1963. Men's and women's roles in India: a sociological review. In Barbara Ward (Ed.), *Women in the new Asia*. United Nations Educational, Scientific and Cultural Organization.

DUMONT, LOUIS.

1957. *Une sous-caste de l'Inde du Sud*. Paris: Mouton.

EPSTEIN, T. SCARLETT.

1962. *Economic development and social change in South India*. Manchester: Manchester University Press.

FRIEDL, ERNESTINE.

1964. Lagging emulation in post-peasant society. *American Anthropologist*, 66: 569–86.

FORTES, MEYER.

1949. *The web of kinship among the Tallensi*. London: International African Institute Oxford University Press.

GEERTZ, CLIFFORD.

1963a. *Agricultural involution*. Berkeley and Los Angeles: University of California Press.

1963b. *Peddlers and princes*. Chicago: University of Chicago Press.

GHURYE, G. S.

1960. *After a century and a quarter*. Bombay: Popular Book Company.

GOODE, WILLIAM J.

1963. *World revolution and family patterns*. London: The Free Press of Glencoe, Collier-Macmillan.

GOODY, JACK (Ed.)

1958. *The developmental cycle in domestic groups*. Cambridge: Cambridge University Press, for the Department of Archaeology and Anthropology.

GORE, MADHAV SADASHIV.

1961. *The impact of industrialization and urbanization on the Aggarwal family in Delhi area*. Unpublished Ph.D. dissertation, Columbia University.

GOUGH, E. KATHLEEN.

1952. Changing kinship usages in the setting of political and economic change among the Nayars of Malabar. *Journal of the Royal Anthropological Institute*, 82: 71–88.

1956. Brahman kinship in a Tamil village. *American Anthropologist*, 58: 826–53.

1960. Caste in a Tanjore village. In E. R. Leach (Ed.), *Aspects of caste in South India, Ceylon and North-West Pakistan*. Cambridge: Cambridge University Press.

GOULD, HAROLD A.

1959. *Family and kinship in a North Indian village*. Unpublished Ph.D. dissertation, Washington University, St. Louis.

1966. *Time-dimension and structural change in an Indian kinship system: a problem of conceptual refinement*. Unpublished paper read at the meetings of the Association for Asian Studies, New York, April 5, 1966.

GRAY, ROBERT F., and P. H. GULLIVER (Eds.).

1964. *The family estate in Africa*. Boston: Boston University Press.

GREENFIELD, SIDNEY M.

1961. Industrialization and the family in sociological theory. *American Journal of Sociology*, 47: 312–22.

HITCHCOCK, JOHN T.

1956. *The Rājpūts of Khālāpur: A study of kinship, social stratification and politics*. Unpublished Ph.D. dissertation, Cornell University.

JOHNSON, ERWIN.

1964. The stem family and its extension in present day Japan. *American Anthropologist*, 66: 839–51.

KAPOOR, SAROJ.

1965. Family and kinship groups among the Khatris in Delhi. *Sociological Bulletin*, 14: 54–63.

KARVE, IRAWATI.

1953. *Kinship organization in India*. Poona: Deccan College Post-Graduate and Research Institute.

KOLENDA, PAULINE M.

1967. *Regional differences in Indian family structure*. In Robert Crane (Ed.), *Region and regionalism in South Asian studies*. Durham, N.C.: Duke University Press.

KULKARNI, M. G.

1960. Family pattern in Gokak Taluka. *Sociological Bulletin*, 9: 60–81.

LEWIS, OSCAR.

1958. *Village life in Northern India*. Urbana: University of Illinois Press.

LEVY, M. J.

1955. Contrasting factors in the modernization of China and Japan. In Simon Kuznets, Wilbert E. Moore, and Joseph J. Spengler (Eds.), *Economic growth: Brazil, India, Japan*. Durham, N.C.: Duke University Press.

LINTON, RALPH.

1952. Cultural and personality factors affecting economic growth. In Bert F. Hoselitz (Ed.), *The progress of underdeveloped areas*. Chicago: University of Chicago Press.

LITWAK, EUGENE.

1960a. Occupational mobility and extended family cohesion. *American Sociological Review*, 25: 9–20.

1960b. Geographical mobility and family cohesion. *American Sociological Review*, 25: 385–94.

MADAN, T. N.

1962a. The Hindu joint family. *Man*, 62: 88–89.

1962b. The joint family: a terminological clarification. *International Journal of Comparative Sociology*, 3: 1–16.

1965. *Family and kinship: A study of the Pandits of rural Kashmir*. New York: Asia Publishing House.

MALHOTRA, S. P., and MOHAN LAL A. SEN.

1964. A comparative study of the socio-economic characteristics of nuclear and joint households (II). *Journal of Family Welfare*, 1964: 21–32.

MANDELBAUM, DAVID.

1957. The family in India. In *Introduction to civilization of India: changing dimensions of Indian society and culture*. Chicago: University of Chicago Press.

MAYER, ADRIAN C.

1960. *Caste and kinship in central India*. Berkeley and Los Angeles: University of California Press.

n. d. Unpublished village census.

MENCHER, JOAN P.

1962. Changing familial roles among South Malabar Nayars. *Southwestern Journal of Anthropology*, 18: 230–45.

MORRISON, WILLIAM A.

1959. Family types in Badlapur: an analysis of a changing institution in a Maharashtrian village. *Sociological Bulletin*, 8: 45–67.

MURDOCK, G. P.

1949. *Social Structure*. New York: Macmillan.

NICHOLAS, RALPH W.

1961. Economics of family types in two West Bengal villages. *Economic Weekly*, 13: 1057–60.

NIMKOFF, M. F., and RUSSELL MIDDLETON.

1960. Types of families and types of economy. *American Journal of Sociology*, 66: 215–225.

OGBURN, WILLIAM F., and MEYER F. NIMKOFF.

1950. *Sociology*. Boston: Houghton Mifflin.

PARSONS, TALCOTT.

1953. Revised analytical approach to the theory of social stratification. In Reinhard Bendix and Seymour Martin Lipset (Eds.), *Class, status and power*. Glencoe, Ill.: The Free Press.

1961. Introduction to part two: Differentiation and variation in social structures. In Talcott Parsons, Edward Shils, Kaspar D. Naegele, and Jesse R. Pitts (Eds.), *Theories of society*. New York: The Free Press of Glencoe.

RAY, AJIT.

1956. A Brahmin village of the Sasana type in the district of Puri, Orissa. *Man in India*, 36: 7–16.

ROSS, AILEEN D.

1961. *The Hindu family in its urban setting*. Toronto: University of Toronto Press.

SARMA, JYOTIRMOYEE.

1959. The secular status of castes. *Eastern Anthropologist*, 12: 87–106.

1964. The nuclearization of joint family households in West Bengal. *Man in India*, 44: 193–206.

SEN, LALIT KUMAR.

1965. Family in four Indian villages. *Man in India*, 45: 1–16.

SHAHANI, SAVITRI.

1961. The joint family: a case study. *Economic Weekly*, 13: 1823–28.

SINGH, RUDRA DATT.

1962. *Family organization in a North India village: a study in culture change.* Unpublished Ph.D. dissertation, Cornell University.

SMITH, RAYMOND.

1956. *Negro family in British Guiana.* London: Routledge and Kegan Paul.

SUSSMAN, MARVIN B.

1963. The isolated nuclear family: fact or fiction? In Marvin B. Sussman (Ed.), *Sourcebook in marriage and the family.* Boston: Houghton Mifflin.

THURSTON, EDGAR.

1901. *Castes and tribes of southern India.* Madras: Government Press.

WEBER, MAX.

1950. *General economic history.* Glencoe, Ill.: The Free Press.

WIRTH, LOUIS.

1938. Urbanism as a way of life. *American Journal of Sociology*, 40: 1–24.

WOODRUFF, GERTRUDE MARVIN.

1959. *An Adidravida settlement in Bangalore, India.* Unpublished Ph.D. dissertation, Radcliffe College.

YOUNG, MICHAEL, and PETER WILLMOTT.

1957. *Family and kinship in East London.* London: Routledge and Kegan Paul.

15. CHITPAVAN BRAHMAN FAMILY HISTORIES: SOURCES FOR A STUDY OF SOCIAL STRUCTURE AND SOCIAL CHANGE IN MAHARASHTRA

MAUREEN L. P. PATTERSON

INTRODUCTION

SIXTY-FOUR FAMILY HISTORIES (Marathi: *kula-vṛttānta, kula-vṛtta, gharāṇyācā itihāsa*) were published between 1914 and 1963 in Maharashtra. Over thirty more are reported to be in preparation at the present time. All the volumes are, and are to be, in Marathi. The books range in length from 64 to 1,150 pages and deal with family groups ranging in size from 159 to 2,946 males living at the date of compilation.

Forty-nine of the 64 volumes deal with Chitpavan Brahman families and are written by Chitpavans. (The others are divided among Deshastha Rigvedi, Karhade Brahman, Shuklayajurvedi, Madhyandin, and Maratha families.) It is generally agreed that Chitpavan Brahman family-history writing may be divided into two time periods, 1914 to 1933 and 1934 to the present (Pendse, 1949, p. 8). During the first period only five Chitpavan volumes were compiled and published, while the second period witnessed the publication of 45, of which 21 came out during the 1940's alone.

As of 1961, it was claimed that about 41,000 (27 per cent) of the 150,000 living Chitpavan Brahman males had been covered in the histories published; or in other terms, over 72 of the approximately 330 surnames had been covered (Ketkar, 1961, p. 526).

These volumes draw heavily upon historical sources, which include: family records; documents and papers collected by famous Maharashtrian historians such as Rajwade, Parasnis, and Sardesai; records and registries kept at pilgrimage centers by priests traditionally patronized by specific client families. Further, the compilers use school enrollment lists (reaching back into the nineteenth century) and the annual public announcements of high school and college graduation, as well as membership rolls of district local boards, municipalities, and the legislatures, to obtain data on family members.

In May, 1938, while Krishnaji Vinayak Pendse was working on his *Pendse kula-vṛttānta,* he applied to the government of Bombay for permission to go through the Peshwa Daftar[1] to look for references to members of his family in

---

1. This collection comprises over 27,000 bundles of records in Marathi and about 8,000 files in English owned by the state government and located in Poona. These are the records kept by the Chitpavan Brahman Peshwas' ("Prime Ministers'") administration, 1714–1818.

the eighteenth- and early nineteenth-century administrative records. His request was turned down. So he and several other family historians formed an organization, the *Kula-vṛttānta Saṅgha* (family history association), with the express and immediate purpose of putting pressure on the government to permit access to the Daftar. A Chitpavan member of the Bombay legislature brought the matter to the attention of the government; eminent historians discussed the matter at the annual meeting of the Indian Historical Records Commission; and the then Prime Minister of Bombay (B. G. Kher, a Karhade Brahman) received a personal appeal from Pendse, who had become secretary of the *Kula-vṛttānta Saṅgha*. Finally, on December 7, 1938, the government acceded to this pressure and henceforth permitted writers of family histories access to the primary sources.

Having achieved its objective, however, the *Kula-vṛttānta Saṅgha* did not disband. Instead, its members decided to constitute it as the central clearinghouse of information on family history research, financing, writing, and publication. Pendse remained the secretary and still was in May, 1962, when I interviewed him in Poona. The establishment of the *Kula-vṛttānta Saṅgha* in 1938 and the publication of Pendse's booklet *Kula-vṛttānta-mārga-darśana* in 1949 represent high points in the gradual institutionalization of Chitpavan family history writing.

REGIONAL SETTING

The cultural-linguistic region of Maharashtra has two major subdivisions: the Desh and the Konkan. The *Desh* is more or less synonymous with the Marathi-speaking section of the Deccan plateau. This, centered on the upper Godavari valley, is the old heartland of Maharashtra, the area in which Marathi emerged as a language and cultural vehicle around the eleventh or twelfth century. This is the homeland of the fighting Maratha and Kunbi castes, as well as of the Deshastha Brahmans, who produced most of the region's great literary and religious figures between the thirteenth and nineteenth centuries.

The *Konkan* is the second major subdivision of Maharashtra. This is the coastal lowland between the Western Ghats and the Arabian Sea, and comprises the three districts of Thana, Kolaba, and Ratnagiri. The Konkan lowland stretches some 330 miles from well north of Bombay City to Goa on the south. This area is between thirty and fifty miles wide. While Marathi is the language of these three districts, it gives way to Konkani (a separate language rather than a dialect) as the spoken language in Goa, though standard Marathi remains the literary language of most Hindus in Goa. Kannada takes over as the predominant language in adjacent North Kanara District of Mysore State.

While the Konkan is tied to the Desh by half a dozen tortuous routes up and over the Western Ghats (the Sahyadri Mountains, in Marathi), it differs in basic climatic and agricultural respects from the plateau. For example, its rainfall of eighty to a hundred inches is four times that of the Desh around Poona; rice is the dominant crop in the Konkan in contrast to millet on the plateau; mangoes, coconuts, and lately some jute contrast with the cotton, tobacco, groundnuts, and sugar cane on the Desh.

But possibly the most significant difference between the Desh and the Konkan is one of attitude. To put it briefly, the Konkan has always been a zone of contact between India and countries to the west of her, and the coastal Konkan districts, together with Konkani-speaking Goa and the coastal towns of North Kanara, have been exposed for centuries to influences and persons from across the Arabian Sea. The string of ports from Bombay south to Karwar has had in turn Roman, Greek, Arab, Abyssinian, Portuguese, Dutch, and English traders, invaders, visitors, or settlers. It is this stretch of coast, too, which has received at one time or another such immigrant groups as the Bene Israel, Parsis, Kudaldeshkar Brahmans, Gaud Saraswat Brahmans, and Chitpavan Brahmans. It is not pertinent to the present discussion to go into the place of origin or reason for immigration of any of these groups. What is pertinent is that each of these groups has been an intrusive group, physically and culturally differentiated from the others as well as from the population into which they all came.

One further point is that each of these groups appears to have settled in different sections of the coastal territory, adjoining rather than intermingling with the settlements of the others. In this way, the Bene Israel came to be associated with the northern part of Kolaba District; Chitpavans, with the southern section of Ratnagiri (including what was formerly the small Sawantwadi princely state); Gaud Saraswat Brahmans, with Goa and the adjacent coastal section of North Kanara District.

Of all these groups, the Chitpavan Brahmans were apparently the last to arrive, and so they ended up with that section of the coast which is by and large the least fertile and which has the fewest good ports. It would seem that Ratnagiri District, being thus the least desirable, was easily available, in a frontier-like way, and that little competition and few obstacles faced the Chitpavans as they went about settling down.

Traditionally, Chitpavans explain their origin according to the story in the *Sahyādrī Khaṇḍa*:

Parashurama slew all the Kshatriyas on earth and was so defiled by this slaughter that ordinary Brahmans refused to perform any ceremonies for him. At that time the bodies of fourteen shipwrecked foreigners were cast up on the shore of the sea which then washed the foot of the Sahyadris. Parashurama purified these corpses by burning them on a funeral pyre, or *cita*, restored them to life, and taught them Brahman rites. These Brahmans, *cita + pāvana* ["pure from the pyre"], performed rites for Parashurama and he wished to reward them with a grant of land. He prayed the sea to give him some of its domain; it agreed to retire as far west as Parashurama could shoot an arrow from the crest of the Sahyadris. The arrow was shot and reclaimed a belt of land about thirty miles broad. The banks of the Vashishthi River, about forty miles north of Ratnagiri town, were set apart for the new Brahmans, and in memory of the process by which they were produced they were called "Chitpavans" and their chief settlement was called Chitpolan, or later Chiplun [my adaptation from the account given by Enthoven (1920, p. 242)].

Most of the *kula-vṛttāntas* give the Parashurama story in quite considerable detail, with much elaboration and interpretation.

From consideration of the several immigrant groups, one more point emerges that serves to distinguish the Chitpavan Brahmans from the others: all but the Chitpavans show a basically north-south (that is, coastal) pattern in eighteenth- and nineteenth-century migration and mobility. The Chitpavan pattern is characteristically east-west (that is, up over the Sahyadris onto the Desh, to Poona and beyond). This may perhaps be tied, on the one hand, to the Chitpavan association with administration and government at all levels, and, on the other hand, to the preoccupation of Parsis, Bene Israel, and Saraswats, for example, with trade and commerce in general and in particular with activities centered on the eighteenth- and nineteenth-century British establishment at Bombay.

EMERGENCE OF THE CHITPAVAN BRAHMANS

Parashurama notwithstanding, very little is known about or heard of Chitpavans until about 1707 A.D., when one individual, Balaji Vishvanath Bhat, appeared on the scene in the Poona-Satara area. He was brought from Ratnagiri District by an official of the Maratha government and, on account of his administrative ability and general efficiency, he quickly gained the attention of the King, Shahu, grandson of the great Shivaji Chhatrapati. Shahu was so pleased with Balaji's work that in 1713 he appointed the Ratnagiri man as his Peshwa, or prime minister. Balaji Vishvanath succeeded in stemming Mughal military advances, ran a well-organized administration, and by the year of his untimely death in 1720 had laid the groundwork for the subsequent Maharashtrian occupation of a very large part of India. Balaji Vishvanath Bhat was succeeded in the Peshwaship by his son, Bajirao, and thus began a century of power based in Poona, with the top position held by members of this Chitpavan Brahman family.

Balaji Vishvanath's appointment as Peshwa started a steady flow of Chitpavan migrants from Ratnagiri District to the *de facto* seat of power in Poona. The Peshwa entrusted all manner of important offices to his kinsmen and caste fellows. From Poona, Chitpavans were dispatched as diplomats, administrators, and military men all over the country. Not all remained loyal to the Peshwa in Poona; we find them later settling down as advisers or generals at rival seats of power in Nagpur or other centers of Maratha (that is, non-Brahman) princes, for example, at Baroda, Indore, Dewas, and Gwalior.

By the latter part of the eighteenth century, Chitpavans had gained very great political power in Poona and the territory under its control, and, as a concomitant of political power, they had obtained very considerable economic power as well. The virtual usurpation by Chitpavan Brahmans of the Maratha king's power (despite the Peshwa's ceremonial trip to Satara to be invested by the Chhatrapati) led inevitably to feelings of mutual distrust on the part of Marathas and Chitpavans. This particular aspect of Brahman–non-Brahman conflict has been manifested in many ways over the years and down to the present day—we may recall the anti-Brahmanism of 1948 following Gandhi's assassination by a Chitpavan as the most violent recent outburst (see Patterson, 1952).

The last Peshwa was defeated by the British in 1818, but as a result of Elphinstone's policies in the 1820's the Chitpavans gained as much as they lost in military defeat. They were encouraged to continue in their traditional roles of *śāstri* and pundit and also were encouraged to go in for Western learning. They did so and very successfully, and soon came to hold the same types of subordinate administrative jobs in the British regime that they had held during the Peshwai. By the end of the nineteenth century, Chitpavans had obtained far more than their proportionate share of leading positions in politics, education, social reform, journalism, literature, and so forth; this was overwhelmingly the case in Poona, but was unmistakably so also in Bombay, Nagpur, and other urban centers. While some Chitpavans have attained great wealth, this is unusual; most caste members, and there are now close to 300,000, are modest of means and in aspirations. Wherever they may be, Chitpavans seem to retain a lively consciousness of a great common bond and, often nostalgically, of a common place of origin in India, that is, Ratnagiri District.

BACKGROUND FOR FAMILY HISTORY WRITING

Historical writing is not new to Maharashtra. It is not quite accurate to say, as the historian Sardesai (1949, p. 26) does, that it is a "creation of the nineteenth century" or of the days of the British raj, "started in imitation of the great prose writers of the West." In fact, in this respect I tend to agree with V. G. Dighe (1961, p. 473) that "The impetus to history-writing came with the rise of the Maratha state in the seventeenth century. . . . The need was felt by the Marathas to record their military exploits and political experience in writing, and this took the form of chronologies, ballads, annals, family accounts, and chronicles." Actually, Sardesai (1949, p. 24) turns around somewhat and seems to agree with Dighe in the following passage:

The Marathas can rightly boast of possessing in a printed form, Bakhars or chronicles, personal and public letters, news-reports, accounts, government documents, sanads and decisions, treaties, genealogies, diaries and chronological entries, and various other forms of historical material, which probably no other people of India has, in the same proportion or of the same variety.

All through the Peshwai, for instance, letters, orders, financial transactions, grants of land, etc., were carefully recorded and thousands of documents accumulated; these are now stored in Poona. Some 45 large volumes of selections from what is called the Peshwa's Daftar have been published to date and comprise a storehouse of historical material unmatched in other regions.

In addition to official government documents such as the Peshwa's Daftar, the Maharashtrian historical genius expressed itself in stirring ballads and songs glorifying the adventures and achievements of Shivaji and his followers. This was historical expression at the popular level, and these captivating songs aided in prompting people to be conscious of historical events and in setting the stage for the writing of history.

The expansion of British administration in the nineteenth century spurred his-

torical writing, in large part as a result of the individual interests of such administrators as Elphinstone and Grant Duff. Various papers were written, for example,
for the English court of arbitration, justifying the accession of one prince rather
than another to Shivaji's throne at Satara. Furthermore, at the district and local
levels, British administrators, first haphazardly and later systematically, went about
collecting information on the territories they were to govern, consciously or unconsciously stimulating local residents to commit to writing salient features of
their family's or locality's past.

Again, in the nineteenth century, Maharashtrians who began to learn of English literature appear to have been particularly attracted to the historical novels
of Sir Walter Scott. Before the turn of the century, writers such as Hari Narayan
Apte and Nath Madhav had adopted Scott as their model and were turning out
dozens of historical novels based largely on Maratha and early Rajput history.
This literary fascination with history has as its twentieth-century counterpart the
immense popularity of historical movies, especially those so admirably made by
Shantaram and Pendharkar.

Another factor which should be included in any consideration of the sources
and stimuli for family-history writing is the age-old and well-known Brahman
tendency toward classification and quantification. In fact, it seems to me that it
is this very emphasis on categorization and statistical detail that distinguishes the
Brahman from the much more discursive non-Brahman family histories.

These then are some of the factors which, in my opinion, have gone into the
creation of an atmosphere conducive to the time-consuming and arduous job of
writing family histories. In a word, family-history writing emerged out of the
background of historical documentation of the Peshwai, out of the absorption
and adaptation in the nineteenth century of Western models, and from a traditional propensity for classification.

Many of the *kula-vṛttāntas* mention the fact that a great amount of genealogical
and family-history writing has been done in the West. And several writers use
this fact to urge more and more families to get their histories written. One (Khare,
1940, p. 1) specifies an article in the *Scientific American* which is purported to
state that so far 1,200 family histories have been published in the United States.
Unfortunately, I have not been able to trace the article; apparently the citation
is incorrect—this is not to say that references in these books cannot be trusted,
for, so far, this is the first I have found that does not work! In any case, it seems
clear that the Chitpavan authors are using American and British examples in order
to spur their caste fellows to greater effort in family-history writing so that they
may "keep up with" the West.

THE CHITPAVAN FAMILY HISTORIES, 1914–1964

The year 1914 is generally considered to be the starting point for modern family-history writing. It was in 1914 that Govindrao Vinayak Apte published his
Āpte gharānyācā itihāsa. This book was compiled on the basis of research in historical documents, interviews with individuals, and a five-point questionnaire

which Apte had published in a number of Marathi newspapers. The five questions were prefaced by a short statement of the reasons for and the context of the inquiry. My translation of the whole follows:

Public invitation

Among a man's duties a very important one is to publish in book form research done in many different ways into early authentic history. Since the work of historical research is very difficult and laborious, there must be a number of devoted researchers in this work. One's *kulasvāmī* [male family deity] is powerful in contributing to success in this.

My aim is to publish in due course complete information regarding Deshastha, Konkanastha and other Brahmans. Therefore I am now making efforts to collect whatever information I can on Gokhale, Patwardhan, Paranjpe, Bapat, Lele, Ranadye, Sathe and Sathaye. This is an invitation to persons of these surnames to send answers to the following questions to the address below:

1. What is your original village in the Konkan?
2. Who are your *kulasvāmī* and *kuladevī* [female family deity], and what is their village?
3. Who lives in which place in the Konkan, on the Desh, or any other place?
4. What land, *ināin* [inalienable land grant], jagir or hereditary position is held in the Desh or Konkan?
5. Give the names of the three principal wage-earners in your house and if you have any more information put it on the line after the name; give briefly information on any particularly wealthy person in your family, and if possible please send a photo. What is the full name and address of the wage-earners in the households?

   Please send in copies of deeds, land grants, etc.

Dharmapuri Shri Datta Mandir   Yours etc.
Post. Wai   Govind Vinayak Apte
Dist. Satara   Author of Apte Family History

The response to the plea was reportedly remarkably good, and the book was written and published. Possibly it would not have attracted much notice if Lokamanya Bal Gangadhar Tilak had not written an enthusiastic review of it in his paper, *Kesarī* in which he praised Apte for leading the way in publicizing the valorous deeds and sterling character of his forefathers. And Tilak emphasized that everyone should learn about his own forefathers and should follow the examples they set in service to Maharashtra. Tilak's favorable reception of the book was interpreted by Apte as a command to do further writing, and he set about to write the histories of three more families, besides encouraging and organizing the writing of several more histories by members of their respective families. Apte died suddenly in 1925, but he had started something that was to become even more developed and well organized than he could have imagined. For example, by 1944 when the *Lele kula-vṛttānta* was started, the list of questions in the initial inquiry had grown to eleven and now included requests for information on education, marriage relationships, occupation, etc. By the time Pendse wrote his guide to family-history writing in 1949, the questionnaire comprised fifteen rather detailed questions, including three on family deities, rituals, and special observances, and others covering several additional topics not previously asked about. In 1962, when the Thosar volume was being prepared, the questionnaire had 56 points to be filled in and covered four legal-size sheets. These materials are made available to the compilers by the *Kula-vṛttānta Saṅgha* in Poona, which, under Pendse's direction, urges a standardized format through which it is hoped that the books will become uniform and comparable documents of social and cultural history. Since 1939, there has clearly been a conscious attempt to tie the findings in one volume in with those in another; some of the tabular materials show, for instance, how family A has produced more college graduates than families B and C.

TABLE OF CONTENTS OF A REPRESENTATIVE *KULA-VṚTTĀNTA*

The *Marāṭhe kula-vṛttānta* (Marathe, 1946, pp. xvi, 780) covers a total of 2,862 living males as of the date of compilation. Of this number, 2,204 have the surname Marathe and the remaining individuals, 658, are divided among six sub-surnames as follows: Vidhvans, 240; Chakradev, 144; Khambete, 175; Joshi, 55; Jail, 29; Ratate, 15. All are considered to be branches (*gharāṇā*) of the Marathe *kula*, and it seems probable that before long the sub-surname will disappear and will be transformed into simply the name of the branch. This type of process appears to be frequent. All branches belong to the same *gotra* (Kapi), *veda* (Rigveda), *śākhā* (Shakala), and *sūtra* (Ashvalayana). The xvi + 780 pages of the book are divided as follows:

(1) The initial section contains a list of photographs of sculptures of eleven deities, at various sites, and the photographs themselves.

(2) The foreword discusses the difficulties encountered in writing the book, including the first attempt, unsuccessful because of lack of money, in the 1930's. It describes the sources of information and the methods used in gathering it: taking notes at Nasik and other pilgrim centers; checking through lists of members of all sorts of local bodies, examination results, lists of marriages given in other *kula-vṛttāntas*; advertising in a dozen or so newspapers (space usually donated by publishers who were themselves Chitpavans); mailing of questionnaires; if possible visiting each village in Konkan where members are reported to be; acknowledgments and thanks to various persons.

(3) This is a list of the 115 branches of the *kula*, most of them with geographical labels.

(4) Pages 1–7 of the body of the text are devoted to general information about the Marathe *kula*: description of the *poṭ-ādnāṃv* or "sub-surnames" attached to the Marathe *kula*; notes on the *gotra, śākhā, sūtra, pravaras* (kinship categories based on the legendary ancestors of the family and on the Vedic texts and commentaries accepted as authoritative by the family); comment on origin of surname; and notes on original place of residence, Ratnagiri-Goa. As of 1946, thirteen generations can be traced for some of the branches, fewer generations for others. The author gives details about *kuladevatā* and *kulācāra* (deities and rituals) which differ according to branches of *kula*.

(5) Genealogical tables and biographies (pages 7–628) form the main part of

the volume, wherein the details gathered during research are organized and presented according to *gharāṇā* or "branch of the family."

The biographies vary in length, from one line to a page or so for well-known persons; the entries are all by male members of the family, with names of wife and daughters given within the entry (wife's father's name is usually given in full and his place of residence if known; also name of daughter's husband and place he comes from).

Whatever information has been collected on education, occupation, travels, etc., is given briefly; birth date and death date also, where known. Much more information is given for contemporary or early twentieth-century persons.

A short paragraph at the beginning of the table and biographies for each *gharāṇā* tells who started that particular branch and where; if the branch was started by someone who had migrated, details are given; for example, branch number 63 is called "Ajgaon-Ichalkaranji," indicating that originally it was in Ajgaon, but one member moved to Ichalkaranji when granted land there in the early nineteenth century.

(6) This section lists names about whom information has not been found. Its purpose is to alert *kula* members to these lacunae, so that the second edition of the book may be more complete.

(7) This is a list of individuals mentioned prominently in historical documents. Names and page references to the relevant biographies are given.

(8) This section of the volume, the analytical summary (pp. 632–94), is typical of the majority of Chitpavan family histories. It is this section, in all these histories, which is crucial to the use of these books for sociological analysis.

The purpose is to draw a profile of the whole Marathe *kula*, thus forming a basis for comparison with other *kulas*. All the details given in the preceding biographies which could be reduced to statistical tables are so handled in this part. These topics are as follows:

(a) List of *gharāṇās* in the *kula*, with number of living males and total number of males ever recorded given for each branch; also number of generations recorded for each branch—these statistics make it possible to see which branch is expanding and which is about to vanish.

(b) Age structure: number of living males by five-year age groups. This is followed by a table showing number of grandfathers and great-grandfathers living at time of compilation, together with frequency of five-or-more brothers of Marathe *kula* and of sub-surname (*gharāṇā* 104 has eight brothers).

(c) Education: tables show number of living males at primary, secondary, and college level; then number of degree-holders (B.A., M.A., LL.B., Ph.D., etc.). A separate table shows number of females at various educational levels and in certain professions (nurse-midwife, writer, etc.).

(d) Occupation: twelve categories of occupations are listed, with the number in each: government service (two categories); teaching (English, and Marathi); railway service; nongovernment employment; trade and commerce; medicine (Western and indigenous); law; agriculture; religious mendicancy; retirement.

(e) Residential distribution: the 2,862 living males are listed by name according to city, town, or village of current residence. The total number of Marathes in a given place is indicated after the name of the town, for example, Poona (302), Calcutta (14), New York (1). A page reference to the biography section is given after the individual's name.

Since the origin of all Marathes is Ratnagiri District, we can see how members of the *kula* have spread within thirteen generations; of 2,862 males, 312 are shown in Ratnagiri District at the time of writing. Preliminary analysis shows that persons tend to live in villages in the Konkan homeland and in towns and cities after leaving Ratnagiri. There is evidence in this and other volumes to show an association between living in Ratnagiri and agricultural occupation; agricultural pursuits are not followed after migration to the Desh.

(f) Marriage relationships: the total of 5,362 marriages recorded in the biographies is analyzed by family into which marriage took place; in twenty pages, families are listed in alphabetical order, with total number of marriages, for example, Apte (152), Gokhale (265); page numbers refer back to biographies so that one can obtain details on each.

A paragraph after the statistics rather pointedly tells of 27 cases of prohibited *sagotra* and *sapravara marriages,* and of 29 cases of marriage with non-Chitpavan Brahmans or non-Brahmans (also with page references to biographies for details).

(g) List of individual males given or taken in adoption, with *kula* to or from which each came, with page references.

(h) List of *kula-vṛttāntas* published to date, organized by *gotra* and accompanied by a number of living males covered in each volume.

(i) List of contributors: 265 persons gave a total of Rs. 5,610 over the period 1940 to 1946; the total expense was Rs. 6,384. (We are not told where the balance came from. It might have been from the sale of some of the 480 copies printed, which were priced at Rs. 10 each; names are given with the amount each gave, from Rs. 1,000 from one, to Rs. 25 and Rs. 10 from very many, down to Rs. 2 from one person.)

(9) Index of individuals: this takes up 71 pages and is an alphabetical list of all males mentioned in the text. An asterisk before the name denotes that the person is living at the time of compilation. A page number after the name indicates where detail on him is to be found. An analysis of the 259 personal names given to Marathe males shows the frequency with which names are given: the most popular is Ramachandra, occurring 401 times for 7,339 males recorded; Mahadeva is next, with 241; Vishnu occurs 235 times; Hari occurs 181 times, etc.

The volume is completed by three pages of information received just prior to printing; and four blank pages designed for the reader to use for adding information as he gains it.

Differences do occur in different books. In some books, for example, there is a tendency to include more data about women in the *kula,* and some books go so far as to have a separate index of women members. Most of the books have a large number of photographs, usually representing the contemporary family group, but sometimes showing older men and women in traditional dress. Since the nineteenth-century Chitpavan society put the value of a widow at more or less nil, it is amazing how many photographs of widows are included.

THE STRUCTURE OF THE CHITPAVAN BRAHMAN CASTE

If the Maharashtrian Brahman "caste cluster," to use Irawati Karve's phrase (1958b, p. 883), comprises 24 castes with a combined population of about 1,500,000, then the Chitpavan caste, with approximately 300,000 persons, comprises only one-fifth of all Brahmans in the region, or in other terms, much less than 1 per cent of all Maharashtrians.

The internal structure and working of the Chitpavan caste is one of the things we seem to be able to reconstruct from details given in the *kula-vṛttānta* volumes. Following is a diagram, based on these books, of some of the basic units within the caste, that is, the number of exogamous divisions and subdivisions within the endogamous *jāti* or *dñyāti*.

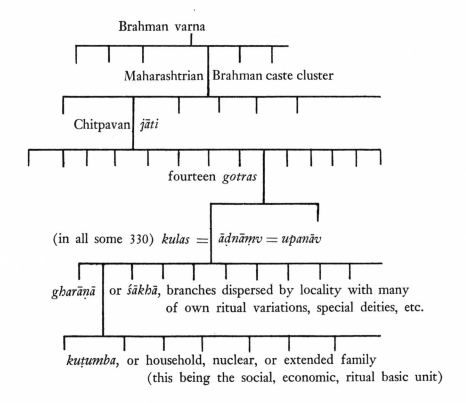

Gotra: a *gotra* is generally defined as an exogamous patrilineal sibship whose members trace their descent back to a common ancestral rishi, or a rishi held in common by more than one *gotra*. The fourteen Chitpavan *gotras*[2] are grouped

2. We may recall the legend that the fourteen bodies washed up on the shores of the Konkan became the fourteen Brahmans purified by Parashurama.

into six *gaṭas* or *gaṇas*, five of two *gotras* each and one with three *gotras*. The fourteenth *gotra* remains outside this structure and has a special characteristic.

Bharadvaja Rishi   Kashyapa Rishi   Vasishtha Rishi

Kapi, Gargya, Bharadvaja	Kashyapa, Shandilya	Kaundinya, Vasishtha	
Kaushika, Babhravya	Jamadagnya, Vatsa	Nityundan, Vishnuvriddha	Atri

Vishvamitra Rishi   Bhrigu Rishi   Angiras Rishi   Atri Rishi

Families belonging to *gotras* within the same box are not permitted to intermarry because the *gotra* founders are supposed to be related through descent from the same rishi. However, those *kulas* which belong to the fourteenth *gotra*, Atri, are not restricted as to marriages with persons of any other *gotra*. The Atri *gotra* thus appears to perform the function of knitting together the entire *jāti*. The Marathi phrase, *Atri āṇī sarvāṃśī maitrī*, meaning "Atri and friendship with all," seems to describe this function; this statement appears in many of the *kula-vṛttāntas* in a discussion of relationships among *kulas* and *gotras*. The Atri *gotra* may in fact be the crucial link that makes for Irawati Karve's statement that the Chitpavan caste "shows an evenly spun web of kinship" (1958a, p. 135). Perhaps it is the *gotra* system which is the organizing and regulating mechanism between the *kula* structure and the overall *jāti*.

Kula: The word *kula* means "family," in the sense of an agnatic kin group, and it refers to groups which range in size from less than 100 living males to more than 2,000.[3] *Kula* is usually synonymous with *ādnāṃv* or *upanāv*, meaning "surname" in these books. A tradition committed to writing (in metrical sloka form) in about 1850 states that the fourteen *gotras* comprised "originally" (though what period is meant is not clear) sixty *kulas* or *ādnāṃvs*, that is, surnames. These varied in distribution from one per *gotra* to twelve. Fission, as a result of migration, etc., has increased the number of surnames to somewhere between 300 and 360. The number of *kulas* per *gotra* ranges from five to about ninety.

Gharāṇā: Each *kula* is divided into *gharāṇās* (or *śākhās* [both terms occur]). A *gharāṇā* is a branch of the family set up in a locality removed from the original location of the *kula* (which was usually, if not always, Ratnagiri District). Some *kulas* have well over 100 *gharāṇās*, while others have only a dozen or so. The branches are always designated by town or village names, and some have two

3. These are the figures given for *kulas* for which books have been written; they are probably low, if anything, because of difficulties of contacting all family members. Figures given in the books are of course for the year just prior to the publication of the book so that the statistics are not synchronic. There are, however, no other sources available for estimating the size of a *kula*.

or three names (hyphenated) which indicate the sequence of settlement and further migration in the first two or three generations after leaving the original place.

Āḍnāṃv: Chitpavan surnames, and particularly the "original" ones, are quite distinctive. They fall into several categories. Most of the books dwell at length on their meaning and derivation. A rough classification of the surnames is as follows: (1) Some are short, just two characters in the Marathi syllabary and more or less monosyllabic in English, for example, Jog, Ok, Bal, Bam, Vad; (2) some are without any clear meaning: Gadgil, Bapat, Achwal, etc.; (3) some are descriptive: Gore (fair), Kale (dark); (4) some refer to territorial divisions: Konkane, Marathe, Kanade; (5) others indicate locality, probably the residence of an ancestor, through the use of the suffix "kar," thus: Agarkar, "from Agar"; Karandikar, "from Karandi," Ketkar, etc.; (6) Quite a few nowadays are occupational terms, such as Vaidya, Pandit, Bhat, Joshi, Mahajan, Muzumdar, etc. These names are recently acquired, and usually families with such names can show that they were originally Gokhales, or Bapats, etc.

SOME TENTATIVE CONCLUSIONS

My study, which deals only with the Chitpavan *kula-vṛttāntas,* brings up several questions. We may ask, for instance, why were these books compiled? How can the books be interpreted? What problems of objectivity are involved? How can these books be used? What do they really represent?

A theme that runs through the books with increasing frequency as we get closer and closer to the present is that the family organization is felt to be good in itself and to be an end in itself. Within the context of a hostile world, some of the authors seem to be saying that it is comforting to know who one's family members, *kula-bandhu,* are, and to watch how they are adjusting to changing circumstances. And for Chitpavans to think in terms of a hostile world is perhaps not totally unrealistic, because of the frankly anti-Chitpavan Brahman atmosphere abroad in large areas of Maharashtra—the anti-Brahmanism that came to a head in the violent attacks on Chitpavan property in 1948 when it became known that a Chitpavan had assassinated Gandhi. Perhaps it is not coincidental that the increase in family-history writing begins at the same time (in the 1930's) as the somewhat frantic organization of "Brahman protection societies" (*Brāhmaṇa Hitasaṃrakṣaka Saṅgha,* in Satara and Pandharpur), the Chitpavan-dominated *Rāṣṭrīya Svayaṃsevaka Saṅgha* (R.S.S.), and so forth—all of which organization seems to have reached a peak in the 1940's along with a peak in anti-Brahmanism, that is to say, anti-Chitpavanism.

It has been suggested that the vogue of *kula-vṛttānta* writing is essentially escapist; that it reflects a general wistful backward-looking attitude, remembering the glories of the days of the Peshwai, or even more recently of the days of B. G. Tilak. Perhaps the Chitpavans' looking back at the Peshwai should be considered more as a genuine fascination with all aspects of history, and as a genuine desire to contribute toward a more favorable discussion of Maharashtra's part in eighteenth-century Indian history.

Some of the uses of these books for social science research may be as sources for the study of social change. For instance, the books show changing occupational patterns as a family branch has been established somewhere outside of the Konkan; government service has replaced agriculture or revenue farming, or work as a mendicant priest; or, in latter days, government service has become less desirable than entrepreneurial activities or employment in nongovernment service, because of anti-Brahmanism. Further, the books indicate that there is a tendency for attainment of higher educational levels to be associated with migration out of the Konkan. Also, the books show what Chitpavans aspire to nowadays: ownership of a house; job security (but no more is government service considered so safe as it used to be; private industry or the military services are now seen as relatively safe from anti-Chitpavan discrimination); etc.

These family histories can be used as sources for a study of the structure and dynamics of the Chitpavan caste. R. P. Paranjpe's (1940, p. 5) comment on the books indicates his belief that they are useful sociological tools which reflect a cross-section of the caste based on a random sample. It seems to me that if these books were documents meant to create the most favorable image possible of the caste, much in them that actually is not favorable, would of course not be included. These books are essentially books by and for Chitpavans; they are not available in the general book market, but mainly from the publisher-compiler himself; and they are printed in very small editions. They attempt to describe reality, and they succeed to the extent that the dedicated compilers are able to gather sufficient information from their *kula-bandhus*. This realism, and the fact that the movement is steadily going on, that new volumes or second editions are coming out year by year, indicate to me their significance for serious study of Maharashtrian Brahman caste society.

BIBLIOGRAPHY

APTE, GOVIND VINAYAK.
    1914. *Āpte gharānyācā itihāsa* ("Apte family history"). The author.
DIGHE, V. G.
    1961. Modern historical writing in Marathi. In C. H. Philips (Ed.), *Historians of India, Pakistan and Ceylon*. London: Oxford University Press.
ENTHOVEN, R. E.
    1920. *The tribes and castes of Bombay*. Vol. 1. Bombay: Government Central Press.
KARVE, IRAWATI.
    1958a. What is caste? (1) Caste as extended kin. *Economic Weekly*, 10: 125–38.
    1958b. What is caste? (2) Caste as a status group. *Economic Weekly*, 10: 881–88.
KETKAR, RAMACHANDRA VASUDEV.
    1961. *Ketkar kula-vṛttānta* ("Ketkar family histtory"). Bombay: The author.
KHARE, MORO HARI.
    1940. *Khare kula-vṛttānta* ("Khare family history"). Poona: The author.
MARATHE, KRISHNARAO GOVIND.
    1946. *Marāṭhe kula-vṛttānta* ("Marathe family history"). Poona: D.G. Joshi.

PARANJPE, RAGHUNATH PURUSHOTTAM.

1940. *Svāgat* ("Welcoming preface"). In Govind Vasudev Bhave (Ed.), *Bhāve-kula-vṛttānta* ("Bhave family history"). Poona: The author.

PATTERSON, MAUREEN L. P.

1952. *Brahman versus non-Brahman conflict in Maharashtra.* Unpublished master's thesis, University of Pennsylvania.

PENDSE, KRISHNAJI VINAYAK.

1949. *Kula-vṛttānta-mārga-darśana* ("Guide to family histories"). Poona: The author.

SARDESAI, GOVIND SAKHARAM.

1949. *Main currents of Maratha history.* (Rev. ed.) Bombay: Phoenix Publications.

16. TIME-DIMENSION AND STRUCTURAL CHANGE IN AN INDIAN KINSHIP SYSTEM: A PROBLEM OF CONCEPTUAL REFINEMENT

HAROLD A. GOULD

NOT MANY YEARS AGO, it became evident to thoughtful students of Indian social structure that studies of the Indian family were failing to provide an adequate basis for determining the relationship between variations in family structure and the changing structure of Indian society. Empirical data on the family were not lacking; by the end of the 1950's there existed a considerable body of empirical data on the Indian family, particularly in its rural manifestations, which encompassed at least 80 per cent of the country's population. What was lacking were conceptual tools suitable for meaningful organization and analysis of the data that existed. It is to this problem that the present paper primarily addresses itself.

Perhaps the greatest deficiency in most early attempts to understand developmental trends in the Indian family was the tendency to view the family as a series or variety of static entities and then to apply to these entities criteria of change that had been devised in the context of the West's experience during the early stages of the industrial revolution; that is, Indian families were generally characterized as either "nuclear" or "joint," and then some statement was made about change based on the proportion of nuclear to joint families. The latter judgment arose from a generalization propounded by both the Marxist and the American schools of sociological thought to the effect that urbanization and industrialization break down the extended family and make the neolocal nuclear family a necessary and inevitable substitute for it.

As good an illustration as any of such ill-advised reification and naive conceptualization is contained in the book *Social Profiles of a Metropolis*, written by Radhakamal Mukerjee and Baljit Singh (1961). In this "social survey of Lucknow," the authors assert:

The urban family at present is in transition towards the natural family [sic] comprising the couple and their unmarried children. But the transition is in no way complete, and many families still exhibit the features of a joint family—with several generations and a large number of relations living together (p. 37).

It is clear that Mukerjee and Singh do not for a moment question the assumption that urbanization must lead to the neolocal nuclear family, or what they revealingly call the *natural* family. They do not even *suggest* alternative possibilities, let alone explore some of these possibilities scientifically before drawing their evolutionary conclusions.

One of the first social scientists to oppose the notion that the Indian family was meeting the challenges of modernization by becoming nuclear was I. P. Desai (see Kapadia, 1958, pp. 261–66). Because his survey data revealed from several different standpoints that in the mid-1950's the ratio of people living jointly to those living in nuclear families was about three to one, Desai asked pointedly, "How far are we correct in assuming the growth of the spirit of individualism?" Reinforcing this view, Kapadia (1958, pp. 264–65) says, "The traditional family comprising a man, his father, his grandfather and his collaterals within three generations, has not yet considerably decreased."

Bernard S. Cohn (1961, pp. 1051–55) and Ralph Nicholas (1961, pp. 1057–60) were among the first to attempt an anthropological interpretation of structural trends in the Indian family. Each of these writers from his respective empirical vantage point (Cohn in Uttar Pradesh, Nicholas in West Bengal), came to realize that static categorizations of the Indian family are a misleading basis for talking about its structure, and what appears to be change in structure on superficial examination may not be seen as such when less static categorizations are employed.

A key phrase in Nicholas's study of the economics of family types is: "What creates the appearance that the joint family system is breaking down is that in each generation a number of joint families are partitioned" (p. 1060). And from Cohn's study of Chamar families in Senapur, we hear: "Most field workers who talk about family structure in India freeze processes which take place over time" (p. 1051). Cohn continues: "We freeze process to talk about it, but we should not lose sight of the fact that for Chamars the joint family is a structural contingent not a fixed form" (p. 1055).

What Nicholas and Cohn are suggesting is that we cannot speak meaningfully of structural change in the Indian family until we first establish some basis for differentiating such processes from the merely normal rearrangements through time which the Indian family, like the human family everywhere, undergoes as a result of the vicissitudes of demography, economy, mobility, etc. One consequence of these *normal rearrangements* will be the inevitable emergence of a certain quantum of nuclear families whose existence will in no sense demonstrate that the presence of nuclear families is automatic evidence of disintegrating extended families.

Fortes and other British social anthropologists have provided us with an admirable conceptual tool for dealing systematically with the necessary distinction that is being made here. This, of course, is the so-called developmental cycle thesis, which accords specific recognition to patterned rearrangements of family structure through time. Fortes writes:

What are the institutional mechanisms and customary activities of social reproduction in a particular society and how do they operate? . . . In all human societies, the workshop, so to speak, of social reproduction is the domestic group. . . . The domestic group goes through a cycle analogous to the growth cycle of a living organism. The group as a unit retains the same form, but its members, and the activities which unite them, go through a regular sequence of changes during the cycle which culminates in the dissolution of the original unit and its replacement by one or more units of the same kind (1958, p. 2).

The question that comes immediately to mind, then, is whether it is possible to identify the "institutional mechanisms and customary activities of social reproduction" in Indian society, or at least in some region of it. For, if we can make this identification, we can go a long way toward facilitating studies of change in the Indian family by being able scientifically to determine the fact that some observed activities are not legitimately characterizable as change. It is my contention that a "developmental cycle" can be posited for India and that empirical investigations do substantiate its reality. In what follows, however, I shall be speaking exclusively about North India, both because it is the area I know best and because the entire subcontinent is too vast a mosaic to be dealt with in a single, brief essay. The logic of my argument, I would nevertheless contend, is amenable to eventual application to the whole of India.

A developmental cycle is a kind of net outcome of the convergence within the domestic group of numerous forces generated by human social life; that is, it arises as a consequence not only of the formal structure and logical contradictions of the kinship system but also of such demographic realities as birth, death, and sex ratios, and of the economic environment in which society as a whole and the domestic group in particular exist. Under the constant impact of such powerful and complex forces, it is not surprising that the domestic group does not simply manifest a single structure which it maintains for all time. Naturally, each culture has an ideal family structure, either implicitly or explicitly expressed, toward which actual domestic organization is oriented so long as no radical process of change is introduced into the society. In India, this is the so-called joint family, which has been recognized as the cultural ideal of domestic organization by anthropology and traditional Hindu law alike. In Mitakshara succession, for example, the traditional legal system for adjudicating kinship matters over much of India, the "joint and undivided family" is spoken of as "the normal condition of Hindu society," according to Mulla (1952, p. 238). It is joint "not only in estate but also in food and worship." And it is this cultural ideal which many Indian and non-Indian social scientists have reified in such a fashion that where *in practice* nuclear families have been found they have been taken as evidence of the decay of the joint family. But, as Cohn (1961, p. 1052) so rightly observes: "There are several important factors which make the achievement of the ideal joint family difficult among the Chamars"—and, I might add, among Indians in general. Clearly, one of the main reasons for trying to approximate this ideal as fully and as frequently as possible is that it facilitates corporate activity in pursuit of economic, social, and religious ends.

Mitakshara succession essentially provides a jural basis for maintaining a household consisting of male agnates, their wives, and their daughters until the latter are wed. Male agnates comprise the unit of property ownership and control; they form, in other words, what Mitakshara law calls a co-parcenary; they are a sort of corporation of patrilineally related male kinsmen who share equally the property, the productivity, and the liabilities of the domestic group. Wives, unwed daughters, and occasionally certain other individuals, enjoy rights of maintenance but not rights of inheritance in virtue of their membership in the household.[1]

At the same time, Mitakshara succession makes provision for partition of the joint property whenever that is the desire of any legal co-parcener who is of age. In practice, however, it is rare for a partition to be called for in the lifetime of the patriarch. Patriarchal authority is so absolute as to discourage sons from making such a demand while their father still lives. The ancient sages, notes Kapadia (1958, p. 208), were opposed to father-son partitions. They decreed that "sons who enforce partitions against the wish of the father should not be invited to the sraddha dinner."

Evidently, the clause legitimizing partitions was primarily designed to protect brothers from each other after the patriarch died. Without such a provision, an eldest brother, in particular, could appropriate to himself the family property, thereby denying sustenance to the remaining co-parceners. This appears to be implied in Manu (IX: 104–111), where it is said (as quoted by Kapadia, 1958, pp. 207–208):

After the death of the father and of the mother, the brothers, having assembled, may divide among themselves in equal shares, the estate for they have no power (over it) while the parents live. Or, the eldest alone may take the whole paternal estate and the others shall live under him just as (they lived) under their father. . . . Either let them thus live together or (get) apart if each desires. . . .

There is, in other words, less potentiality for solidarity among siblings than there is between parents and children in the North Indian kinship system. Brothers' rights in the co-parcenary were protected after the patriarch's death by giving each a veto power in the form of the right to call for partition in case he did not believe the joint property was being used to his personal advantage.

A further source of potential disruption is the competition offered to lineal solidarity by conjugal ties as they develop. The rule enjoining village exogamy means that brides are invariably outsiders to their husbands' community and household. Since she has no jural rights in either her natal or her affinal household, the wife's security rests almost entirely with her capacity to manipulate the conjugal relationship to her advantage. To put the matter in another way, we can say that a wife's power in her affinal household grows in proportion as she can divert her husband's loyalties away from his lineal and toward his conjugal ties. As the domestic group matures, the wife's power grows with the birth of children and the simple fact of her increasing familiarity with the manipulative potentialities inherent in her relations to her affines. When the patriarch dies, the strongest link in the chain of lineal authority is broken, and thereafter the balance of power usually swings over to the side of the conjugal relationship. Most partitions of joint families occur at this juncture.

1. The new Succession Law of 1956 actually gives wives and daughters inheritance rights equal to those of male agnates, but the effects of this legislation remain to be felt in the peasant society.

The change from an earlier paramountcy of lineal over conjugal ties to a later paramountcy of conjugal over lineal ties has been widely documented in the anthropological literature. Dube (1955, pp. 142–43) gives a compelling account of how the wife manipulates the conjugal relationship. In my own work, I found villagers repeatedly saying that rivalries between the brothers' wives is a major source of friction and of the ultimate partition of the joint family. Cohn (1961, p. 1053) says: "After disputes over food sharing, the most common cause for separations among Chamars is disputes between wives of brothers or between wives and their husbands' mothers."

Obviously, the foregoing suggests that some kind of limits on the size and composition of Indian domestic groups are imposed by the logic of the groups' structure. This is not to say, to be sure, that changing environmental conditions have not affected the working of this "logic." It seems highly probable that the rapid growth of population, the increasing monetization and individuation of economic life, the wider opportunities for physical and social mobility and many other related factors have had the effect of further emphasizing conjugal ties at the expense of lineal ties and thus of accelerating the trend toward partition after the patriarch's demise. But I suspect this to be more a matter of degree than of kind. At any rate, the sum total of the forces currently at work in the North Indian family results, in my opinion, in its passing through three phases, during each of which a characteristic set of events occurs. These may be stated as follows: Phase 1: Replacement of daughters by daughters-in-law. Phase 2: Demise of the senior male agnate. Phase 3: Severance of male siblings' co-parcenary ties. Each time these three sets of events occurred in sequence, a North Indian domestic group has moved through an entire developmental cycle and in doing so has replaced itself with one or more units of the same kin. Now let us examine these phases more closely.

Phase 1: Replacement of daughters with daughters-in-law. This is the period when a North Indian joint family is moving toward what Nicholas (1961) calls a father-son joint family. As daughters approach reproductive age, tradition requires that they be sent as brides to another household outside the natal village. The village exogamy rule means that daughters-in-law are imported from alien communities, while daughters are exported to alien communities. In the end, therefore, daughters, who are not legitimate candidates for carrying on the family, are entirely replaced in the household by daughters-in-law, who are. For analytical convenience, this phase can be divided into two subphases:

Subphase A: From the first *gaunā* to occur in the family to the point where 50 per cent of all *gaunās* have occurred.

Gaunā is the ceremonialized departure of a daughter for her affinal household and simultaneously the receipt of a daughter-in-law into her affinal household, depending on one's vantage point. During Subphase A, the daughters predominate over daughters-in-law in the household, so that the latter are not only subordinate to mothers-in-law but are outranked by a host of their husband's lineal kinsmen, both male and female.

Subphase B: From the point at which 50 per cent of all *gaunās* have occurred to the point at which all daughters have been replaced by daughters-in-law.

In this subphase, the balance begins to swing in favor of conjugal over lineal ties. Husband-wife relationships predominate within the domestic group and grow deeper and more complex with the birth of children. Unimpeded lineal loyalties become progressively less easy to sustain as men are confronted with choices between the welfare of their own wives and children and that of the corporate unilineal group writ large. However, patriarchal authority remains decisively powerful and usually holds the group together despite mounting internal stresses. *Subphase B* represents the maximal development of the father-son joint family, and in its size and complexity corresponds to the ideal of the Hindu joint family.

Phase 2: Demise of the senior male agnate. With the death of the patriarch, the structure of the joint family alters dramatically. It ceases to be a father-son joint family, held together by revered patriarchal authority, and becomes what we may call a fraternal joint family. This is inherently the most unstable type, and consequently is normally the least enduring phase of the developmental cycle. An eldest brother enjoys neither the moral stature nor the jural authority which would be required for him genuinely to replace the father and serve as a focus, to the same degree, of lineal loyalties. Fraternal joint families, therefore, lead rapidly to partitions of the co-parcenary, except in rare and highly specialized circumstances. At this stage, conjugal ties almost entirely override lineal ties.

Phase 3: Severence of male siblings' co-parcenary ties. As already noted, Mitakshara law says that the demand for partition must be respected. The division of the joint property among the legal co-parceners is accompanied by the establishment of separate living quarters for each conjugal pair. This may be done by erecting new walls in the ancestral household, by constructing new domiciles, or both. Partition leads, then, to the establishment of *nuclear families*, which then set about repeating the developmental cycle. Such nuclear families are, in other words, what Cohn has called structural contingents, mere milestones on the circular pathway of temporal changes in the domestic group. Their occurrence has nothing to do with the disintegration of the joint family system; on the contrary, they are a part of that system.

This phase may also be differentiated into two subphases:

Subphase A: From the point of partition of a co-parcenary to the first marital ceremony conducted for a child of the newly formed unit.

It must be remembered that marriages normally occur long before cohabitation commences, that is, long before *gaunās* occur. But the first marriage ceremony in the unit signifies that movement toward the multinucleated domestic group is proceeding, that the calculations and maneuvers by which the head of a household endeavors to assure the eventual replacement of his daughters by daughters-in-law are activated. Until this event occurs, however, the domestic group is a relatively simple social structure.

Subphase B: From the first marital ceremony conducted for a child of the newly formed unit until the first *gaunā*.

Although still "nuclear" in structure, the family is at this point, as suggested above, experiencing a rapid increase in the complexity of its social activities. Marriages are being contracted and offspring are being prepared for the assumption of adult economic roles and cohabitation with their spouses. And when the first *gaunā* occurs, the developmental cycle has been completed; phase 1 has once more been reached.

It should be obvious after what has been said that a mere counting of nuclear families in a community or region can in itself yield very little information about changes in family structure unless the developmental cycle has been worked out. For at two different points in time, the ratio of joint to nuclear families will almost never be the same, simply because the families comprising the population being studied will be so differentially affected by the developmental cycle. At times an earlier sampling will show a higher proportion of nuclear families than a later sampling, and vice versa. In the one instance the naive observer would assert that the extended family is becoming more prevalent as time passes, while in the other instance he would form precisely the opposite opinion. And in either case he would be wrong.

A brief illustration of this point can be provided through the use of some data from Sherupur, the eastern Uttar Pradesh village I have known since 1954. There are 43 households on which I have data for the periods 1954–55 and 1955–60. Comparing the two sets of data on these same households with respect to phases of the developmental cycle reveals considerable variation in the brief span of five years.

PHASES OF THE DEVELOPMENTAL CYCLE DISPLAYED BY 43 DOMESTIC GROUPS
OF SHERUPUR IN 1954–55 AND 1959–60.

Phase of Developmental Cycle	1954–55		1959–60	
	No. Domestic Groups	% Domestic Groups	No. Domestic Groups	% Domestic Groups
1	14	33	21	49
A	6	14	9	21
B	8	19	12	28
2	10	24	8	19
3	18	44	14	34
A	13	31	9	21
B	5	13	5	13

Since phase 3 consists entirely of nuclear families, and phases 1 and 2 of joint families, the unwary observer would no doubt conclude that in Sherupur the trend is toward an increase in the prevalence of the joint-family system. Actually, of course, no such trend is provable on the basis of the data, for they reflect merely the random vicissitudes of the developmental cycle. True structural change would be indicated only if, say, sons were separating from fathers on a large scale and departing from the village to live neolocally and were, in turn, compelling their own children to do likewise. But such a thing is not happening.

Time does not permit us to venture into the domain of urban family structure. It must suffice to say that data I possess suggest that, among menials who migrate to the city, there is a marked tendency to adhere to traditional kinship principles, especially as these promote corporate arrangements. Life in the city does lead to some interesting modifications in kinship structure, but mostly these modifications represent efforts to preserve as high a degree of corporation as possible under the conditions. Among modern business and professional elites, on the other hand, there is evidence of some radical changes in the structure of domestic organization and in the developmental cycle. These appear to be in response to the demands in the high-status modern occupational order for virtually unlimited spatial mobility.

Along with the obvious utility of developmental cycle theory as a means of distinguishing true structural change in kinship systems from mere temporal rearrangements in their structure, this approach enables us to avoid the tendency to establish a "type" of family to fit every minor variation in the personnel of domestic groups. Obviously, some variations in personnel reflect genuinely important transitions from one phase of domestic organization to the next, while some are merely incidental and deserve no special recognition. I cannot go into all such variations, but the status of the widowed mother is a good illustration of the point I wish to make.

Women have rights to maintenance in their husband's joint family under the provisions of Mitakshara succession, but not rights of inheritance. Therefore, when the patriarch dies, the widowed mother is simply retained as a member of what is now a fraternal joint family. If and when the fraternal joint family is partitioned, the widowed mother will be absorbed as a person with rights to maintenance into one of her sons' nuclear households. Her presence in one of these households does not make it structurally any different from the other units which have formed through the partition. For the mother, once she is widowed, plays no role in the processes which are crucial to the movement of the domestic group into its subsequent phases of development.

CONCLUSION

This paper merely scratches the surface of a problem that requires exhaustive research if we are to ever make meaningful statements about changes in the family structure of societies like India. So little attention has been paid to the difference between normal rearrangements of domestic organization through time and genuinely new structural innovations that one wonders whether any studies of the subject now extant provide us with reliable information. Certainly, the primary failings in studies of the Indian family have been the regrettable tendency to define structure in static terms and the unfortunate use of outmoded theoretical formulations to deal with the matter of changes in its structure.

BIBLIOGRAPHY

Cohn, Bernard S.
1961. Chamar family in a North Indian village. *Economic Weekly*, 13: 1051–55.

Dube, S. C.
1955. *Indian village*. Ithaca, N.C.: Cornell University Press.

Fortes, Meyer.
1958. Introduction to J. Goody (Ed.), *The development cycle in domestic groups*. Cambridge: Cambridge University Press.

Kapadia, K. M.
1958. *Marriage and family in India*. (2d ed.) Bombay: Oxford University Press.

Mukerjee, Radhakamal, and Baljit Singh.
1961. *Social profiles of a metropolis*. London: Asia Publishing House.

Mulla, D. S.
1952. *Principles of Hindu law*. (11th ed.) Calcutta: The Eastern Law House.

17. THE INDIAN JOINT FAMILY
IN MODERN INDUSTRY

MILTON SINGER

INTRODUCTION

THE RELATIONSHIP of industrialization to family organization in Europe and the United States has long been a subject for discussion and theorizing. The earlier views of the economic historians and social critics, which blamed "the industrial revolution" or "private property" for destroying "the family" by putting men, women, and children into factories for long hours, have been replaced by the less apocalyptic views of the sociologists, who have restated the relationship as a transformation in family type. According to this theory, the extended pre-industrial family system has been transformed under the influence of industrialization into a nuclear or elementary family system. Support for this theory has been marshaled in statistics that purport to show an increasing trend toward nuclear families in industrial countries, as well as in the argument that the structure of the extended family system is functionally adapted to an agricultural society but dysfunctional in an industrial society, while the nuclear family is functionally adaptive in an industrial society but dysfunctional in an agricultural society.

Although treated as axiomatic in many sociology textbooks, this theory has been challenged during the last fifteen years from three different directions: the documentation by social anthropologists of the variety of family systems in different parts of the world; the discovery by social historians that the nuclear family may have been prevalent and a cultural norm in Europe and the United States even before industrialization; and the finding by sociologists and social anthropologists that many families in American and European cities maintain widespread kin ties.[1]

These findings have reopened many of the questions previously considered to be settled about the relations of family organization to industrialization. Some sociologists have tried to take account of the comparative study of family systems in reformulating the general theory. Goode (1963); Nimkoff (1965); Levy (1966); and Moore and Feldman (1960); among others, show familiarity with cross-cultural studies and a strong interest in them. Levy's recent formulation is perhaps characteristic of this group of sociological writers:

---

1. For example, Levy and Fallers (1959); Furstenberg (1966); Greenfield (1961); Firth (1964, 1956); Schneider and Homans (1955); Cumming and Schneider (1961); Sussman and Burchinal (1962); Bruner (1963).

One of the special characteristics of relatively modernized societies is their quite unusual type of family unit. Whatever the previous ideal family structure was, during the transition toward relative modernization, the ideals always change toward what anthropologists and sociologists call a multilineal conjugal family, unless they already took that form (1966, p. 74).

Social and cultural anthropologists would be more likely to stress the variety of adaptations to industrialization, as well as the initial variety of kinship structures. There are some anthropologists, however, whose interest in universal generalizations is almost as strong as that of the sociologists and who are tentatively reformulating the relationship of industry to family organization in terms as general as those of the sociologists. Among the products of these approaches, Raymond Firth's recent paper (1964), "Family and Kinship in Industrial Society," illustrates a characteristic familiarity with recent sociological and historical studies and a lucid trial reformulation of a general theory. This reformulation, based on recent studies of kinship in London, is more circumspect and differentiated than the sociologists'.

What the development towards an industrial society probably does is to break down the formal structure of kin groups, except perhaps that of the elementary family, which is most resistant. The lineage, the extended family, the large co-operative cognatic kin unit is likely not to survive as its members disperse into industrial employment and their traditional resources and authority structures lose meaning. But personal kin ties tend to be retained on a selective basis. Indeed, they may be even strengthened if the physical isolation of the elementary family is promoted by industrial, urban, conditions. There is no reason then to think that extra-familial kin ties are likely to decrease in our modern Western society. They fulfill a function which, though not strikingly obvious, is almost certainly important for the social life of individuals and family units (p. 83).

The present paper will attempt to trace the implications of some recent studies of the relationship of the Indian joint family to urbanization and industrialization, including a preliminary study of my own in Madras City. I shall be interested not only in the extent to which the Indian case fits the kind of generalization formulated by Levy and Firth but even more in the new approaches which the Indian case suggests for a study of the problem within the framework of social anthropology.

IS THE JOINT FAMILY BREAKING DOWN?

Recent discussions of what is happening to the Indian joint family under the influence of urbanization, industrialization, and modernization parallel in many respects the general trends just summarized. The tendency of these discussions is to question earlier conclusions that the joint family is breaking down and is being replaced by the nuclear family. Census data previously used to support such conclusions are now being reinterpreted or disqualified on the grounds that such data gave only information about household size, an unreliable index of family type. The entire question of rural-urban distributions of joint and nuclear families is being reconsidered in the census, other statistical surveys, and in case studies.

These reconsiderations and the new studies based on them offer a considerable challenge to the thesis of a linear transformation of the joint family into a nuclear family under the influence of urbanization and industrialization. They show, for example, that large joint families are more prevalent in urban than in rural areas and vary in prevalence with region and caste, that nuclear households are as prevalent in villages as in cities, and that such rural-urban distributions may have been common in the past. They also show that nuclear households, in both villages and cities, may, with the changing domestic cycle of marriages and births, grow into joint households, and decline with separations and deaths into nuclear households again. "Jointness" in these studies has become a complex, multidimensional thing including common residence and meals, common worship, common property, and the maintenance of kin ties even among separated households which may no longer have any joint property.

With this growing sophistication, it is no longer possible to support conclusions about the breakdown of the joint family by citing statistics on the frequency of nuclear households. The burden of proof has shifted: one must distinguish the cultural ideal of the joint family from its actual occurrence, and attitudes and sentiments from behavior. Different types of joint families (lineal, collateral, and others) must be distinguished, as must different types of nuclear families. One writer has, in fact, proposed a classification of joint family types based on different aspects of jointness as well as on the number of generations within a household (Desai, 1964).

In view of this increasing complexity, questions of how we are to define "joint family" or "nuclear family" are now frequently raised. Is a household composed of parents and their married sons and daughters-in-law who have not yet had children to be classified as nuclear or as joint? Some writers would classify such a household as nuclear because it does not consist of at least three generations. Others classify it as joint because it represents a phase in a domestic cycle which will soon grow into a proper joint household as grandchildren are born. Others carry the domestic cycle analysis one step further and see a joint family growing out of every nuclear family.

The authors of these studies and discussions have reacted so strongly against the "breakdown" and linear transformation theories that they sometimes give the impression that the joint family never changes except by eternal recurrence of the nuclear-to-joint-to-nuclear domestic cycle of growth and decline.[2]

Yet despite all this new evidence and argument, one continues to suspect that the joint family has been changing. Even if one accepts the validity of the domestic cycle analysis, the question remains unanswered whether the rate of reformation

2. Among the contributors to the discussion have been I. P. Desai (1955, 1956), K. M. Kapadia (1959), Orenstein (1961), Cohn (1961), Bailey (1961), T. N. Madan (1962), Shah (1964), Kolenda (1968), and H. Gould (1968).
Studies reflecting the new trend include I. P. Desai (1964), M. S. Gore (1961), K. M. Kapadia (1958), I. Karve (n.d.; 1965), T. N. Madan (1965), A. C. Mayer (1960), Orans (1965), A. Ross (1961), and W. Rowe (1964).

of joint families out of their nuclear "seeds" is greater or less than it was in the past, and similarly for the rate of fission of joint families into nuclear. And what about the argument of functional incompatibility of the joint family with urban life and industrial organization? How can that have any cogency if the joint family never changes but only recurs? The "no-change" critics have, I believe, introduced greater sophistication into the discussion but have yet to come to grips with the problem of change.

By arguing that a joint family is more than a matter of household size or composition, of common residence or common property, or of the ratio of nuclear to joint households, etc., these critics have introduced, albeit implicitly, the more abstract concept of the joint family as a social structure embedded within the framework of a specific kind of social system. As a social structure, a joint family is a network of social relations among persons related in specified ways. These social relations are crystallized in a set of mutual obligations within a framework of law or customary usages which defines appropriate norms of behavior for each category of relative. Whether a particular group of persons constitutes a joint family depends on whether this group of persons is held together by the kind of social network in question, that is, whether the individuals within it are disposed to discharge toward one another the set of rights and duties specified in their religious scriptures, legal code, and customary usages. The presence or absence of joint residence, joint property, a particular set of kin, etc., is relevant only insofar as it is a part of the total structure of obligations. The presence of any particular feature does not necessarily make a group of people a joint family, nor does its absence deprive the group of that status.

This concept of social structure, as is well known, derives from Radcliffe-Brown. Its application to the Indian joint family may be carried one step further by noting that, as a social system, the joint family may be analyzed into several distinct components: the kinship terminology; the categories of relatives designated by the terminology; and the rules of marriage, residence, descent, inheritance, and authority, etc. The Indian joint family is usually characterized in terms of these components as follows: it is patrilineal in descent, patrilocal in residence, patriarchical in authority, and has an inheritance rule that divides family property equally among adult males lineally related within at least four generations. Since there are significant variations in each of these components in different regions, castes and tribes, and religious groups, such a characterization cannot be taken for *the* Indian joint family. It may, however, be taken as a characterization of a dominant structural type of Indian joint family. And I shall so take it in this paper, setting aside for the time being the matrilineal systems and the other "deviations" from this dominant type.

We can now approach the problem of change of this structural type in two ways: *synchronically*, by investigating the conditions of equilibrium of the social system in terms of the mutual adjustments of the component parts so as to maintain or restore the structural type, or *diachronically*, by investigating adjustments which may lead to changes in the type. Radcliffe-Brown called the first type of change *social physiology* and the second *structural change*. We may characterize the recent trend of discussion among social anthropologists and sociologists of the Indian joint family as moving from morphology to social physiology but not quite yet arrived at structural change.[3]

THE GENEALOGICAL METHOD FOR
THE STUDY OF SOCIAL CHANGE

In their collection of data from which they construct the social structure and the social system of a particular community, one of the field methods social anthropologists generally use is "the genealogical method." This was first developed by W. H. R. Rivers on the Torres Straits Expedition, when he started collecting genealogies to see whether psychological traits he was studying were correlated with any genetic differences. He soon found that the genealogies, when collected to include basic demographic and social characteristics such as age, sex, kinship terminologies and behavior, personal names, clan names, local residence, migrations, and social groups, also provided systematic information about social organization which could be later analyzed and internally checked. As it was later refined by Radcliffe-Brown and his students, the genealogical method became a standard technique for collecting the data from which was constructed the kinship system and the wider social structure, including the rules of marriage, residence, descent, inheritance, etc.

Curiously, this method has not been much used by social anthropologists for the study of social change. I say "curiously" because some of the components of a social system constructed with the use of the genealogical method include rules of descent, succession, and inheritance. All such rules stipulate intergenerational patterns of behavior, and, in constructing a social system which includes such rules, the social anthropologists are interested not only in the norms stipulating the patterns but also in the extent to which actual behavior conforms to these norms over several generations. They circumvent the problem of intergenerational change by treating the constructed social system within a synchronic perspective of at most three overlapping generations, by postulating the stability and recurrence of the system through longer periods of time, and by treating the "native" genealogies as mythological charters for the present social structure rather than as records of history (for example, Fortes, 1953).

Not all social anthropologists, however, have bypassed the problem of historical change in social systems. Among those who have given serious attention to this problem are Eggan, Murdock, Lévi-Strauss, Leach, Firth, and Redfield. Most of these social anthropologists have not, however, made use of the genealogical method for this purpose. Eggan, one of the first social anthropologists to combine structural and functional analysis with historical and archeological data, has shown the operation of such basic processes of change in North American Indian social structures as acculturation to white and Indian models, ecological adaptation, and cyclical alternation between "lineage" and "generational" systems (1966).

3. F. G. Bailey (1960) is exceptional in trying to deal at least hypothetically with structural change in the joint family.

Murdock has surveyed statistically a world ethnographic sample to arrive at generalizations about the sequence and interrelations of changes. In his work *Social Structure* his tentative conclusion was that "rules of descent and the kin groups resulting from them rank highest in relative efficacy among the major groups of kinship determinants, followed by forms of marriage and the consequent family types" (1949, p. 182). But he also adds that "the rule of residence is normally the first aspect of a social system to undergo modification in the process of change from one relatively stable equilibrium to another, the last aspect to change being kinship terminology" (1949, p. 183).

Lévi-Strauss shares Murdock's interest in a universal formulation of the processes of social change, but he does not find any linear sequence of changes among the components of a social system. His theory, on the contrary, is "dialectical." It assumes that the structures of kinship terminologies are to some extent independent of the systems of attitude and behavior expressed by them. When contradictions occur in these structures, changes will occur in the systems of behavior and attitude which tend to resolve the contradictions. Such changes will, in turn, lead to changes in the terminologies, and so on (1963). Leach has challenged the assumption of stability by analyzing a case where native models of the society fluctuate between two poles (1954).

Despite the intention of each to formulate a general theory of social change, neither Murdock nor Lévi-Strauss deals with the kinds of changes in a social system brought about by industrialization, or even by urbanization. Murdock omits these kinds of changes because his world ethnographic sample does not include a sufficient number of such cases to be dealt with statistically, and Lévi-Strauss omits them because he is personally more interested in studying primitive cultures before they disappear.

Among social anthropologists, Robert Redfield was most interested in the question of what happens to preindustrial social and cultural systems as they undergo urbanization and industrialization. In his Yucatan studies he examined the special case of one such preindustrial system in contact with one special variant of urban, industrial civilization. In his later writings he also became interested in the same question in China and in India, where living traditions of indigenous urbanism provide a different setting and content for the process of industrialization. Redfield saw in the broad transformation of Yucatan folk culture and society into a modern, urban culture and society the operation of such processes as acculturation to the new models diffusing outward from urban centers, but he did not believe that this was the fundamental process at work in the situation. That process, for him, consisted in an intricate series of interrelated changes in social and cultural organization set in motion by the increasing contacts of a folk culture and society with a modern, urban culture and society.

Redfield's generalized formulation of the sequence and results of these changes, which he proposed as a hypothesis, is well known: primitive and peasant societies tend, when they come into contact with urban societies, to change from a "folk"-type culture and society into an "urban" type through a series of interdependent changes, in the direction of increasing individualism, secularism, and cultural disorganization (Redfield, 1941). It is also well known that Redfield's theoretical framework was shaped by the writings of Maine, Durkheim, Tönnies, and Weber, among others. His distinctive contribution, however, does not rest on these ideas and ideal types but rather on the empirical research he designed to test and refine the theoretical framework.

It is easy enough to say, for instance, that societies have been changing from a kin-based system of "status" to a non-kin-based system of "contract." But what Redfield set out to document in detail was the nature of the transformation in the case of a specific society; and he tried to do this by comparing four contemporary communities, arranged along a folk-urban continuum in Yucatan.

Valuable as these methods and results have been, they have not depended in any essential way on a diachronic use of the genealogical method. Nor are they in any way in conflict with such a use of the genealogical method (see Bruner, 1955, 1956).

Rivers himself did not restrict the use of the genealogical method to synchronic analysis. Although he may have overemphasized a deterministic interpretation of the correlations between kinship terms, behavior, and social institutions, he also made quite explicit his belief that the method can be used for the study of historical change. In his 1910 paper on the genealogical method, he says that it is possible "to write a full and fairly accurate account of the recent history of a savage community by taking a complete genealogical record of the community as a concrete background." "Genealogical details," he adds, "give definiteness to the narrative and serve the same purpose as dates in the history of civilized communities" (1910, pp. 81–82). Rivers believed that the application of such an approach to the inheritance of property, for example, was not limited to establishing a normative rule but included also a detailed history. By the use of the method, "it is possible to take a given piece of land and inquire into its history, perhaps from the time when it was first cultivated. The history of its divisions and subdivisions on various occasions may be minutely traced" (1910, p. 7).

Sharing Haddon's interest in recovering disappearing primitive cultures, Rivers also suggested that his genealogical method could provide a history of these cultures both before and after European influence.

The greatest merit of the genealogical method is that it often takes us back to a time before European influence. It may give us records of marriage and descent and other features of social organization one hundred years ago, while events a century old may be obtained in abundance in all the communities with whom I have myself worked, and I believe that with proper care they could be obtained from nearly every people. . . .
Further, the course of the pedigrees is itself sometimes sufficient to demonstrate the gradual effect of the new influences which have affected the people (p. 11).

I should like to suggest a return to Rivers' naive faith, as it may now seem to some, in the genealogical method as a method for studying historical change in social systems. With the benefit of its now well-understood use for constructing synchronic social systems, and with our knowledge of the pitfalls of "conjectural history," we are ready to explore its possibilities for the study of historical change in such systems. These possibilities seem especially promising for the study of those societies, such as some in India, China, Japan, or Europe, where there is an abundance of historical and archeological documentation to check the inferences drawn from oral genealogies. How much can be learned about social change from genealogical records of remote periods has been demonstrated by some recent studies of social mobility in China (Ping-ti-Ho, 1962; Hsu, 1965; Marsh, 1961; Kracke, 1953). The problem of the historical accuracy of genealogies, moreover, is less acute for the recent periods in which significant changes have occurred within a span of two or three generations. Many studies of social mobility and related changes rarely go beyond three generations from the present. One recent sociological study of intergenerational transmission of social traits is based on data obtained from a sample of three-generation families (Aldous and Hill, 1965; see also Chow, 1966; Fei, 1953; M. Freedman, 1958; F. Hsu, 1948; E. Wolf, 1966).

It is not, however, necessary to restrict the genealogical method to a three-generation depth, since historical, archeological, and other forms of indirect evidence may be available on which to base inferences about longer time periods. Students of human genetics are frequently able to trace distributive patterns of genetic traits in family pedigrees of four or more generations. Why should the student of social change restrict himself to three generations in tracing the pedigree patterns of culturally transmitted traits?

Conducting his research in the Torres Straits, India, and Melanesia during the heyday of European colonialism, Rivers was, of course, aware of the colonial distrust of "native testimony." But he satisfied himself that the accuracy of oral genealogies could be verified by cross checking and by careful observation of the context in which they were collected (1910, p. 10).

Rivers did not get to make any intensive application of his genealogical method to the study of *recent* historical changes. His work on the history of Melanesian society tended to concentrate on conjectural, long-run historical reconstructions. The application of his method for the study of recent history is long overdue (Cunnison, 1951; Barnes, 1954).

THE GENEALOGY OF INDIAN INDUSTRIALIZATION

An application of the genealogical method to a study of the relations of the Indian joint family to developing industrialization would be easily understood in India. This intelligibility derives primarily not from familiarity with the sociologists' thesis of breakdown, although the impact of rapid change has aroused some concern, but from the idiom of family and kin, which is, so to speak, endemic and pervasive in the language of the people. Examples of this idiom are easily found. The accepted view of the Vedas is that their different branches were revealed to different seers and transmitted in the different family lines to the present. Brahmans and members of other orthodox upper castes are still likely to identify themselves in terms of the particular Veda which belongs to their family line, as well as in terms of *gotra* and lineage. The great epic, the *Mahābhā-rata*, tells the story of a quarrel between relatives which was so bloody and intense that Arjuna shrank from killing his kinsmen until persuaded by his divine charioteer Krishna that his duty as a warrior left him no choice. The Puranas, in principle at least, are supposed to chronicle the histories of royal dynasties, their migrations, and their descent from the pantheon of deities. There is in fact an "origin story" for practically every caste, tribe, sect, village, town, and temple, which traces its history from particular "founders" through the genealogies of their descendants. These stories are more often "origin myths" than true histories, although they may frequently embody genuine events which have been recorded by professional genealogists.

For Indians these "origin stories" are perhaps more significant as "charters," in Malinowski's sense, justifying present status and status aspirations, than as historical records. This may be one reason why sociologists, social anthropologists, and historians tend to avoid use of the genealogical approach to social change: they are afraid they may end up writing another "origin myth" for some social group in search of illustrious "founders." Besides, the history of industrialization in India is so recent, hardly a hundred years old, that it would not be very plausible for any group to claim a long family tradition in industrial employment. For these reasons, perhaps, recent students of change in Indian family structure have preferred other methods, such as contrasting the acculturating trends of Westernization and Sanskritization among upper and lower caste families, respectively (Srinivas, 1942; Cohn, 1955), the adaptations of village families to different ecological and economic conditions (Bailey, 1957; Epstein, 1962; Nicholas, 1961; Leach, 1961), or comparisons along a rural-urban continuum (Orans, 1965; Gore, 1961). Genealogies are collected, to be sure, but usually for the purpose of constructing synchronic kinship systems, not for the purpose of studying changes in such systems in relation to changes in the social components. Where genealogies have been used diachronically, as in personal memoirs or in selected family histories, they have been used incidentally, or to illustrate their functions as "social charters," not in the context of a systematic approach to the study of social change. A few exceptions are beginning to appear, but in general the method is still not recognized or accepted. (Shah and Shroff, 1958; Karve, 1963; Cohn, 1961; Rowe, 1968; Patterson, 1968; Tandon, 1961; Sinha, 1962; Freed, 1963).

The risks in the genealogical method are worth taking, however. It is a method which offers a good prospect of avoiding several sterile assumptions which have beset the study of modernization in India and elsewhere. One of these is the assumption that modernization is an abstract force, in the form of industry or urbanism, confronting the force of traditionalism in the form of traditional societies and traditional cultures. Another is that such confrontation must lead to the breakdown of the traditional social and cultural forms, or, if in a particular case this breakdown does not occur, then the forces of traditionalism must have been too strong and we should expect a failure of modernization and a persistence of the traditional forms. In reference to Indian modernization these assumptions have usually led to sweeping generalizations about the incompatibility between the joint family, the caste system, and Hinduism, on the one hand, and the forces of modern industry, urbanization, science, technology, and education, on the other. The research problem is then posed as one of either demonstrating the breakdown of these "traditional" institutions under the influence of the forces of modernization or, if this is not possible, demonstrating that the persistence of the "traditional" institutions is a major obstacle to modernization. Since the "modern" and the "traditional" so often coexist in India, we are led by the application of such reasoning to the conclusion that either India is an anomaly or it is in a state of "transition" from a traditional to a modern society.

The genealogical approach, by contrast, need not assume that the joint family, and other traditional institutions, either are passive recipients of the "impact" of modernizing forces or are inert survivals, and obstacles to modernization; nor need it treat the varying mixtures of the modern and the traditional as anomalies. By looking at the development of industry through family histories, a perspective is opened on how particular groups of people adapt their traditional institutions to changing conditions and how, under such circumstances, they may evolve new institutions. The problem of what happens with the growth of industry to the joint family, as a characteristic traditional institution, can then be investigated in a concrete way without prejudging the incompatibility of joint family structure with industrialization.

Conclusions about the functional incompatibility of industry and the structure of the joint family, insofar as they are empirically based, usually cite three kinds of supporting evidence: (1) the prevalence of the nuclear family in countries that have become industrialized, such as England and the United States; (2) examples of how well adapted the joint family was in an agricultural condition of society; and (3) examples of industrial backwardness in countries where an extended or joint family is prevalent. I have already referred to the second thoughts which historians and sociologists are having about the first kind of evidence, suggesting that a nuclear-type family may have preceded industrialization in these countries, and that industrialization may actually broaden the network of some kinds of kin ties. There is also a special kind of fallacy to be noted in the use of the second and third kind of evidence. This involves a comparison of cases of successful adaptation of the joint family to agricultural conditions with cases of unsuccessful adaptation under industrial conditions. And since the duration and geographical scope of agricultural conditions are so much more extensive than those of industrial ones, the selection is doubly biased: the end product of a prolonged and widespread process of trial-and-error adjustments is compared with the early, sporadic efforts at adapting to industrialization.

This kind of biased selection of the evidence can be avoided and a more adequate understanding achieved of the functional relations between industrialization and the joint family by studying successful industrial families in the context of a society with a strong tradition of joint family organization. Such a study would select a group of successful industrial leaders and would try to trace their family histories in terms of basic social components: residence, household size and composition, maintenance of kin ties, occupational succession, subcaste affiliation, education, control and inheritance of joint property, authority structure and household management, religious beliefs and practices, etc. The patterns of intergenerational persistence or change in these components can then be interpreted in relation to the associated processes of urbanization, industrialization, and modernization in which the families are involved. These interpretations would not be linear, causal statements about the effects of urbanism or industry on the joint family, but would rather analyze the variety of forms which the joint family structure assumes in specific urban and industrial conditions in terms of their adaptive, functional significance under these conditions, and would identify the major variables which might account for the observed variety of adaptations. Generalizations drawn from this kind of study would of course be quite restricted in scope, being limited by the nature of the sample and the stage of industrialization of the society from which it is drawn. They would nevertheless suggest hypotheses about basic processes of adaptive change which could be tested with other family histories in more advanced stages of industrialization.

INDUSTRIAL LEADERSHIP AND
THE JOINT FAMILY IN MADRAS CITY

INTRODUCTION

I have started such a study by collecting the family histories of nineteen outstanding industrial leaders in Madras City. These were selected on the basis of their local reputations as successful industrial leaders and by the capitalization of their companies. A detailed report of this study will be published elsewhere. In the present context those preliminary results which throw new light on the question of functional compatibility between the joint family and industry will be summarized. The organization of the summary will emphasize those factors generally regarded as destructive to the joint family, namely, residential mobility, occupational mobility, scientific and technical education, monetization, industrial organization, and so on.

The study is preliminary and incomplete in several respects. It deals primarily with the families of industrial leaders (owners and managers) and not with those of workers and other industrial employees. The analysis and conclusions are not, therefore, intended to apply to all industrial occupations. A more serious limitation arises from the fact that I had no opportunity to collect the "traditional" kinship systems of the families studied. The absence of such data makes it very difficult to generalize about trends of change in their kinship systems brought about by industrialization. To some extent this defect can be mitigated by reference to some of the excellent kinship studies now available on some of the South Indian groups (for example, Dumont, 1957, and references; Gough, 1956, 1961; Leach, 1961; Mencher, 1965, Srinivas, 1942; Yalman, 1962, 1967), and I have used these where relevant. But in view of the numerous variations among different families, castes, communities, and regions, the use of such studies does not solve the problem. In a complete study, the "traditional" kinship systems of just those families who have moved into industry and urban living would have to be reconstructed as they existed in their native villages and towns. Such a reconstruction would take its point of departure from the genealogies provided by living members, and one would need to supplement these with local historical studies of these families.

Most of the data were collected from January through March of 1964, when I was in India; some of the background information was collected on two earlier trips in 1954–55 and in 1960–61. The industrialists were selected by asking knowledgeable people, including industrialists themselves around Madras City and in other places, to name the leading industrialists of the city, and by identifying the owners or managing directors of companies in the city with a capitalization that would fall into the census definition of "large" or "very large" industry. In the end, the two lists coincided fairly closely. A general manager of a successful public sector industry was also included for comparative purposes, as well as the State Minister of Industries. Three industrialists on the original list had to be dropped because they were not in the city during the period of the study.

Statistical and historical information about industrial development and particular industries in Madras City and Madras State was obtained from the State Ministry of Industries, from the Superintendent of the Census in Madras City, from the Madras Record Office, from the records of the Commercial Office of the American Consulate in Madras, as well as from literature published by some of the companies.

There are nineteen industrial leaders in the study, representing eighteen different families. Seventeen are heads of industries in the private sector, one is a general manager of a public sector industry, and one is State Minister of Industries. Nine of them are Brahmans, four are Chettiyars, one a Gujarati Hindu, one an Andhra Kamma, one a Mudaliyar, two are Muslims, and one is a Syrian Christian.

The products manufactured by the companies owned or managed by the eighteen industrial leaders include textiles, automobiles, trucks, buses, tires, batteries, bicycles and bicycle parts, railway wagons and coaches, diesel engines, railway wheels and rims, cement and cement-manufacturing machinery, carborundum, chemicals, plastics, chemical fertilizers, insulators and electronic equipment, farm equipment, leather, sugar, liquor, and candy. The total number of employees of these companies in 1964 was 45,470, and the total paid-up capital was Rs. 272, 247,380.

The nineteen industrial leaders, and their eighteen different families, are not necessarily a "representative sample" of industrial leaders in Madras State or in India. They are a group of identified individuals and families known to be playing a significant role in industrial development. The Minister of Industries has referred to them as "the cream of the industrial class." For purposes of an inquiry into the social elements and motivations of a newly emerging class of successful industrial entrepreneurs, it is precisely "the cream," the pace-setters and creators of new standards, that needs at this point, I believe, to be studied.

INTERGENERATIONAL CHANGE

The dominant intergenerational pattern among the families of the industrial leaders seems to be change and mobility. Even if we restrict the perspective to the three-generation span that is usually taken to mark a synchronic cycle, the changes are numerous and striking. While all of the industrial leaders were born in a village or small town, all of them now live in a metropolitan center. The majority of them, about twelve out of nineteen, live in small nuclear households with their unmarried children. When their daughters marry, they go to live with or near their husband's family. When the sons marry, they are "kicked out" of the parent's home, as one leader who likes American slang described it. The trend to a smaller number of children is unmistakable: in only one case out of eighteen has a leader had significantly more children than his father. He was an only child but has eight children himself. In the other cases the reverse trend is dominant, usually going from a range of five to eight children for the father to a range of one to three for the son. Belief in and practice of birth control are widespread among the leaders. One of them had himself sterilized about 24 years ago and persuaded all the male members of his family and about 3,000 of his male employees to do the same.

The changes in occupational patterns are equally striking. Most of the industrial leaders have entered industry recently: ten between 1931 and 1940, five between 1941 and 1950, three between 1951 and 1960, and one in 1962. Their previous occupations were in commerce chiefly (nine), and to a lesser extent in government service (four) and salaried employment (four). Their fathers' occupations also tended to concentrate in commerce (eleven) and in government service (four), and so did their paternal grandfathers' occupations; seven in commerce, two in government service, two in law. Other than these concentrations the residual occupations of the other fathers, grandfathers, and great-grandfathers is generally given as landlord.

The high frequency of previous occupations in commerce, that is, trade and banking, is not primarily explained by traditional caste occupations, since nine of the industrial leaders were Brahmans and only four belonged to the traditional South Indian merchant community, the Chettiyars.

Seven of the nineteen industrial leaders were the founders of their own companies and were also the first in their families to enter industry. In six other cases, the father was the founder and family pioneer, in one case a father-in-law, in one a mother's brother, and in one a grandfather. In only one case had the company been founded outside of the family, by British merchants in 1785.

A college education is not a prerequisite for industrial leadership, to judge from the educational background of the Madras industrialists. Five of the nineteen have never been to any kind of college, and three of these were founders of the companies they now head. Of the fourteen who had "some college" education, eight had specialized training (two were chartered accountants, three obtained Bachelor of Science degrees, two obtained Master of Arts degrees in economics, and one specialized in automotive engineering). Of the four "founders" in the college-educated group, three had some specialized education and one did not. But there seems to be no specific kind of specialized education that qualifies for industrial leadership in this group. One chartered accountant (F) is a founder and another (J) is not. Of the three who had Bachelor of Science degrees (L, N, M), one of whom was a founder, none seemed to think that their specialized science education prepared them for their industrial roles, and two of these, in fact, shifted to advanced work in economics and politics. The third said that, if he were reborn, about the only change he would make would be to take a degree in economics instead of in geology. Those who did take advanced degrees in economics (H, E) seem to make good use of their training in the analysis of industrial problems for specific industries as well as the problems of industrial development in India generally. Three of the leaders taught themselves engineering (A, K, and M), one on the basis of no previous college training, one on the basis of an arts degree, and one on the basis of a B.Sc. in geology and an M.A. in arts. Some experience in related occupations and in the technical training programs in India during World War II, sponsored by the British, gave them the opportunity for this specialized learning. Only the automotive engineer (I) passed directly from his specialized training into a line of work in his father's enterprises which made full use of his training.

Over a four-generation perspective there is a definite upgrading of educational qualifications, as well as a tendency for the families to specialize in engineering and scientific fields. None of the fathers or grandfathers of those industrial leaders without college education had any college education themselves. On the other hand, all the sons of these leaders are college trained or are now in college, and in at least three of these families (A, R, S), the sons have received technical engineering training in England.

Of the fourteen fathers of industrial leaders with some college education, five fathers had some college training, four had none, and in five cases the information was not definite. Of fourteen paternal grandfathers, seven had not been to college, four had received legal training, and the information was not available in three cases. Two of the grandfathers without college training were identified as a "Sanskrit pundit" and a "Tamil poet," designations which imply a high level of learning within the traditional culture.

The sons of the college-trained leaders have for the most part exceeded their fathers in level of education completed, in degree of specialization in science and engineering, and in going abroad for their specialized training. Nine of the fourteen leaders, for example, have sons who have been trained in engineering or in industrial chemistry; and in six of these cases, the specialized education was received in England or the United States. In several cases where the sons are now in school, the fathers are planning to send them abroad for scientific or technical training. One 13-year-old, the son of a leader who himself had about two years in a commercial college, is already being prepared to enter Harvard.

STRUCTURAL CHANGE OR STRUCTURAL PERSISTENCE?

Were we to concentrate on these evidences of intergenerational change in residence, household size and composition, occupation, and education, we should be compelled to conclude that the trend to the nuclear family is unmistakable and that this trend is functionally associated with the move to the city and industrial entrepreneurship. Such a conclusion would, however, be incomplete and misleading, since the evidence presented was deliberately selected to answer the question:

are there any intergenerational changes that indicate a structural change in the joint family system associated with urbanization and industrialization? Suppose we now raise the question of whether there is any evidence for the intergenerational *persistence* of the joint family system. Such evidence is not hard to come by. In fact, for every item of evidence indicating structural change, there is a complementary item of evidence indicating structural continuity and persistence. So, for example, the move to the city has not destroyed large family households. At least four of the leaders maintain very large joint households and another three have moderately large ones. When the married sons are "kicked out" they may not be kicked very far. They may be given a bungalow in a family compound or a house nearby. Contact is also maintained with relatives in village and town through visits to them on the occasion of weddings, births, deaths, etc., and through philanthropies in the form of a school, a college, a clinic or hospital, or renovation of a local temple. Relatives also come to the city for life cycle rites or to ask for help, and they send children to be raised and educated in the city.

The occupational mobility into industry appears less discontinuous in the light of the background of experience in closely related occupations of trade and banking which most of the leaders and their families possessed. The growth patterns of most of the family industries show that those who were in trade or banking had opportunities to learn about manufacturing processes, costs, market conditions, new ventures, possible sources of capital, etc. And those leaders who came from government service also shared access to such opportunities through special assignments, wartime experience and training, unusual contacts, etc. Even the new trend toward highly specialized training in science, engineering, and business administration among the sons, nephews, and grandsons of the industrial leaders represents but a new version of the old principle of families specializing in one or several closely related occupational lines. The character of the occupation may be changing but not necessarily the principle of family specialization.

How this transition from the "older modern" to the "newer modern" occupation has been made is illustrated by the example of L's family. Law and government figure in the older generation. L's father and grandfather and his father's five brothers were all in government service and were chiefly employed in railway offices. Five brothers-in-law were also in government service; one brother was a teacher, another brother was a lawyer. The brothers' and sisters' sons and the leaders' own children reflect the newer trend toward a specialized technical profession. His own son has a Ph.D. in chemistry, as has his elder brother's son; a younger brother's son is an electrical engineer. Among his four sisters' sons, four are engineers, one has a Ph.D. in chemistry and is employed by the Indian atomic energy commission, one is a medical officer in the air force, and there are among them as well a university professor, a government administrator, and an army officer. This also illustrates the diversification of government services, which have come to include many different kinds of highly trained technical professions.

The evidences for structural persistence and continuity could be greatly expanded, and so could the evidences for structural change. Rather than continue to match the two kinds of evidence item for item, I want now to discuss what to make of such apparently conflicting evidence. The usual rule of evidence, which says to consider the preponderance of evidence and draw the conclusion accordingly, does not seem to apply in this case. Qualitatively, the evidence for structural persistence and continuity seems to me just as strong as the evidence for structural change. Quantitatively, the evidence seems to favor the hypothesis of structural change, at least in the sense that there are more nuclear households than joint households among the industrial leaders in the city. But this quantitative preponderance of nuclear households does not necessarily indicate a breakdown in the joint family system for reasons already given: families living in nuclear households continue to maintain numerous joint family obligations and, for the most part, continue to subscribe to the norms of that system. Even those one or two exceptional families who self-consciously subscribe to the norms of a Western-style nuclear family have not abandoned their joint family obligations and many features of that system, such as arranged marriages, separation of the sexes in eating and visiting, and joint domestic worship. From the perspective of the domestic cycle, there are indications as well that as children grow up and are married the pattern of modified joint households will reappear.

If the available evidence does not favor the hypothesis of structural change over the hypothesis of structural persistence and continuity, or conversely, what conclusion can be drawn? I should like to suggest, since there is strong and unequivocal evidence for both hypotheses, that we conclude, contrary to the usual view, that structural change and structural persistence are not mutually exclusive phenomena, that both are occurring simultaneously. Once we accept this conclusion we can then put such questions to the evidence as: "In spite of the many changes taking place in the joint family system, what evidence is there for the persistence of that system?" and "In spite of the evidence of persistence of the joint family system, what changes are occurring that are new and tending to modify the system?"

On the previous assumption of the mutual exclusiveness of structural change and structural persistence, to put both of these questions to the same set of data created a sense of paradox, if not contradiction. With this assumption dropped, the paradox is gone too. Moreover, we are now free to concentrate on the dynamics of the processes of functional adaptation involved in the changes and persistences rather than on typological analysis of family structures.

ADAPTIVE PROCESSES

Among the families of the Madras industrial leaders the following processes of functional adaptation operate to maintain or modify joint family structures in an urban and industrial setting:

COMPARTMENTALIZATION

The separation of work and residence that comes with modern industry and urban life is more than a physical separation. It also symbolizes separate spheres of conduct and norms: the home becomes the sphere of religion and traditional values; office and factory become the sphere of business and modern values. The home is culturally defined as the domain of one's family, one's caste, one's religious community; and the norms appropriate to these groups are in operation there. The office and factory, on the other hand, are defined as a domain which includes non-relatives, other castes and religious communities, and foreigners. The norms of behavior in this context are quite different from the home context: English is used, Western dress is worn, intercaste contact is frequent, food and drink may be taken which are not served at home, and the techniques and concepts of modern science and technology engage the attention. When the industrialist goes home he symbolizes the change in context by changing into traditional dress and by speaking Tamil or his regional language.

Compartmentalization is an adaptive process which permits the incorporation of innovative patterns of thought and behavior associated with modern industry without too direct a collision with traditional modes of thought and behavior. So long as the rest of the family is maintaining the traditional observances, the industrial leader, and his employees as well, feel free to depart from the traditional patterns in the office, in the factory, on trips abroad, and elsewhere outside of the home.

Vicarious Ritualization

Compartmentalization may reduce the conflicts between the traditional and the modern spheres, but it does not eliminate them altogether. Other processes of adaptation are necessary to cope with the remaining conflicts and instabilities engendered by modernization. If an industrial leader spends twelve to fourteen hours a day in his office or preoccupied with business affairs, he cannot give as many hours as his father or grandfather gave to ritual and ceremonial observances or to scriptural study. Although most of the Hindu industrialists are convinced they are good Hindus, this belief is based not on a personal conformity to ritual observances but on a "vicarious ritualization." They contract their daily ablutions and prayers from four hours to fifteen minutes, done while shaving or washing, but maintain that symbolically "the worship is no less." Similarly, weddings, birth ceremonies, sacred thread ceremonies, and the other life cycle rites have all been contracted, and some have been consolidated. Weddings which took at least a week in the village are now done in a single day with a religious ceremony in the morning and a reception in the evening in a public hall hired for the purpose.

On all these occasions the industrial leader does not assume personal responsibility for carrying out the ritual observances. He delegates that responsibility to professional domestic priests whom he employs for the purpose and to his wife and children, who have the time. He also increases his personal religious merit by making gifts to the priests, to temples and maths, and by supporting charitable endowments of all kinds.

Vicarious ritualization is one of the major ways in which the family of an industrial leader has been able to "Sanskritize" its domestic and social life at the same time that the leader has been "modernizing" life at the factory and office.

Separation of Ownership and Control

The separation of work and residence and the process of compartmentalization have not prevented the carryover of certain principles and practices of joint family organization into the sphere of industrial organization. Except for the public sector industry and one private sector company, all the other companies are family firms. This is true even of the very largest public limited companies in which the controlling family owns only a small fraction of the stock. Effective family control has been maintained through a number of different organizational devices, the most important of which is to have the company's affairs managed by a "managing agency" which is owned and controlled by the family, to organize the company as a subsidiary of a "parent" company which is family controlled, and to appoint members of the family to the managing directorship and to the board of directors of the company. These devices of indirect control of industrial firms are also familiar in the United States and Europe, where they have also developed with the separation of ownership from control in the modern corporation. And it is probable that they were introduced into Indian business under British and Western auspices. I should like to suggest, however, that the separation of ownership from control has parallels in the structure of the joint family, and these parallels make it relatively easy for Indian joint families to adapt the principles and practices of household management to industrial organization.

Controlling authority in the Indian joint family resides in the family head or manager, usually the father or eldest male. He makes the major decisions on all important questions, including the disposition of joint family property. Generally he is expected to consult other members of the family, but his decisions are supposed to be binding on all once made. If the manager of the family is the father, he "owns" a portion of the joint family property. This portion may be but a fraction of the whole, since, in the South Indian patrilineal system, he shares the joint family property with his sons, grandsons, and great-grandsons. Each of them has a right to a portion of the joint property when it is divided, a right to ask for a division, if of age, or through his guardian, if not, and a right to be consulted on important decisions concerning the management of joint family affairs. Members of the joint family who are not co-parceners are entitled to maintenance but do not have a say in the management or in the questions of partition.

The relationship of the manager of a joint family to the co-parceners and other family members is thus analogous to the relationship of the managing director of a company to its board of directors and stockholders. In each case there is a separation of ownership from control. The controlling authority does not necessarily own a major portion of the shares but has the major responsibility for making major policy decisions on the affairs of the group with due consultation. And in each case the maintenance of an undivided, expanding organization depends on the decision-making abilities of the manager and the acceptance of his authority by the "owners."

HOUSEHOLD MANAGEMENT IN INDUSTRY

The structural and organizational parallelism between joint family management and business management is not merely formal. It is appreciated by the industrial leaders and sometimes made the basis of a direct extension of the same principles from the rural joint family household into modern industry. In fact, the tables of organization of some of the industrial firms resemble a genealogical chart of the coparceners of joint family property.

The process of extension usually begins with the way in which the father trains his sons. There are seven families among our group who have clearly extended the traditional pattern of joint-family organization in their industries. In three of these (C, I, R), the father, who was the founder of the family industries, was quite aware of the advantages of joint-family organization in industry and deliberately set about to train his sons from an early age to this pattern. The description of one of these three families (I) is quite characteristic of all of them.

The father, who died in 1955 and was described by one of his sons as a very severe "disciplinarian," had inculcated mutual respect and tolerance in his five sons from an early age. Each of the sons was encouraged to pursue an educational career suited to his interests and abilities in engineering, finance, arts, or business administration. Except for the eldest son, who lives in the family village and manages the family lands, each of the other four sons has a specialized industrial responsibility, managing a separate operation in the family business. In addition, two grandsons have also been trained and brought into the business, and several others are being trained to come in.

The "founding father" laid down the following rules for the conduct of all family enterprises:

(1) No member of the family should have property of his own or outside investments.

(2) No member should maintain a separate bank account outside the joint-family account; all of a member's financial transactions should be known to the others.

(3) All profits should be reinvested in the family business.

(4) Shares in the business should be held only by the descendants in the male line.

(5) All the houses and automobiles used by the family should be owned by the company and be made available to family members when they work for the company. In addition, each son's wife could draw a fixed allowance for the expenses of her separate household and for entertainment and travel.

These rules, which are simply an adaptation of traditional joint-family practices to industrial life, were in practice modified in some respects. When the father retired, he sold his holdings in the business, which were equal with those of each son, to his five sons at par value, in equal shares, for about fifteen lakhs of rupees. He then gave the cash to his three daughters. Each son is supposed to provide for a similar division in his will. This procedure is intended to keep the holdings in the family and also to avoid "son-in-law problems." Recently, however, some of the granddaughters as well as grandsons have been given shares in the business. And, after the father died, the brothers agreed to leave their estate to a family trust, which will then run the business. Such a trust is required under present laws to spend 75 per cent of its holdings for the purposes for which it was created but may retain 25 per cent subject to municipal and business taxes. At the present time the family makes a variety of charitable contributions, religious and secular, of about two lakhs of rupees per year.

All major company decisions are discussed at informal meetings of the brothers, which take place at least once a month. These decisions require complete consensus, on the assumption that if anyone has a reasonable proposal he should be able to persuade the others. Two members of the third generation, sons of the oldest brother, are already on the board of directors of the company, and several others are being groomed for such posts.

CYCLES OF AUTHORITY

There are indications that some younger sons, and grandsons, of the present generation of founders are not generally content to follow in their father's or grandfather's footsteps and need to be given scope and opportunity for making their own decisions, if the family industrial enterprises are to be kept within the family. In several families, fathers and grandfathers are aware of this restlessness in the younger generation and have given the young men special "projects" to manage and develop. One hears more cases of such restlessness among the third generation than among the second generation: grandsons of founders are more likely to break away from their father and the family business than are sons of founders. There is probably an alternating generational cycle at work here which is a function of the structure of authority and affection in the joint family, as modified by the personality of the father, and by the changing structure of opportunities.

A strong father, who has himself broken with *his* father, may succeed in raising his sons as a loyal "band of brothers" who will not break away from him or insist on a division of the family property, even after he is dead. But the more successful he is in this, the more submissive his sons will have become, and the less authoritarian they will be as fathers. Other things equal, this is probably the "psychodynamic" explanation of the relatively greater rebelliousness of the third generation over the second.

Other things are rarely equal, however. A man may not have enough sons, or opportunities for industrial leadership may change from generation to generation and in relation to opportunities for political and other kinds of leadership. The recent emergence of industry as a field for leadership in Madras State is underlined by the fact that, of the nineteen leaders interviewed, eight were the first generation of their family in industry, ten were second generation, and only one was third generation.

In starting industrial enterprises, the present generation of seven founders departed from traditional family occupations and started on new paths. It is therefore relevant to ask whether the founders also "broke" psychologically with their fathers. The information on this point is quite interesting. In one case the father strongly disapproved the son's occupational choice (F), in three cases the sons quarreled with the fathers and left home between the ages of 17 and 21 (A, H, Q) to make their own way in Madras City. Two of these quarrels concerned the father's alienation of the mother's affections by taking a concubine or a second wife. In one of these quarrels, the son set up a new household at the age of 18 with his mother and his mother's brother just one year after arriving in Madras City. The mother's brother was also his partner in the firm he eventually founded.

In two other cases (D, K), the fathers died when the sons were still young, aged 6 months and 13 years, respectively. One of these fatherless boys was raised in Colombo, Ceylon, by his mother's brother, who also became his father-in-law and who initiated him into the business of trade and moneylending. When he started his own industrial enterprise, he took as a partner his mother's sister's husband. The second fatherless boy was raised by an elder brother whom he eventually took as a partner in his first industrial venture.

Six of the seven leaders who were founders, then, did experience some kind of psychological break with their fathers. Of the twelve "non-founders" there are two who mentioned losing their fathers while still young (N, P), and none mentioned quarrels with the fathers. One leader who lost his father was raised and adopted by one of his father's brothers, was taken into the family business, and is now a managing director of one of the family's industrial subsidiaries. In the second case, the father died when the son was 7; the boy was sent to Madras City to be raised and educated by his mother's brother, who had already founded a successful family business in trade. He has since succeeded his uncle as leader of the family business. None of the other ten non-founding leaders seemed to have experienced a psychological break with his father, or at least none revealed any special feeling about this problem. All but one are continuing in the family business.

The role of substitute father in cases were a leader lost or quarreled with his father and left home was taken by a mother's brother in three cases (A, D, P), by an elder brother in one case (K), by a father's brother in one case (N), by employers in two cases (F, Q), and by an unspecified person in the last case (H). The substitute father generally also initiated the boy into business and became closely associated with him in an industrial career. What kind of person became the substitute father depended in part on the reasons for the break with the father and in part on the availability of brothers, uncles, sympathetic employers, etc.

Before we conclude, however, as some American studies have done, that a psychological break with the father is a necessary or sufficient condition for industrial leadership, we should remember that most of the ten non-founders who presumably suffered no psychological break with the father have already demonstrated effective and successful industrial leadership. We should also need more information than we have about whether the fathers of the non-founders who were themselves founders experienced a break with *their* fathers, as well as information about the relations of the present founders to their sons, and about those sons who broke with their fathers and did not become industrial leaders.

CONCLUSION

Until quite recently, a prevailing sociological theory asserted that the joint and extended family structure was everywhere and inevitably transformed into nuclear family structures under the influence of urbanization and industrialization. This theory based itself on the alleged history of such transformations in Europe and the United States and on the alleged functional incompatibilities of joint and extended family structures with such requirements of urban and industrial life as residential and occupational mobility, a highly complex and specialized division of labor, a monetized economy, advanced scientific and technical training, large capital requirements, and corporate organization. The comparative studies by social anthropologists of diverse family systems did not at first seriously challenge this theory because they dealt chiefly with the simpler societies and because they tended to concentrate on synchronic analysis of presumably stable social systems. This situation generated a series of false dilemmas between generalization and comparison, between world-wide uniformities and regional and cultural diversities, and between structural transformation and structural stability, etc. Only as sociologists have become interested in the comparative studies of social systems, and social anthropologists in structural change within complex societies, have these false dilemmas ceased to dominate discussion and has a more productive convergence of sociological and anthropological approaches begun to develop.

One of these newer approaches is the use of family histories to study social and cultural change, including change in family systems. This method has been used by sociologists and social historians to study social and occupational mobility. It has also been used in genetics and medicine to trace pedigree patterns in the inheritance of selected traits. In social anthropology, however, the approach, known after W. H. R. Rivers as the "genealogical method," has been somewhat arbitrarily restricted to oral genealogies and the synchronic study of social systems. Rivers himself did not so restrict the method but looked upon it as a promising way to get data for recent social history. I should like to suggest that Rivers' genealogical method, if freed from the synchronic restriction, does indeed offer a powerful means of collecting social data for the study of both structural change and structural continuity of family systems and of other kinds of social structure. It seems to be an especially appropriate method for the study of what happens to the Indian joint family in an urban and industrial setting.

In a preliminary application of the method to study a group of outstandingly successful industrial leaders in Madras City, I found that, while there have been striking changes within three generations in residential, occupational, educational and social mobility, as well as in patterns of ritual observances, these changes have not transformed the traditional joint family structure into isolated nuclear families. On the contrary, the urban and industrial members of a family maintain numerous ties and obligations with the members of the family who have remained in the ancestral village or town or have moved elsewhere. And within the urban and industrial setting a modified joint family organization is emerging. The metropolitan industrial center has simply become a new arena for the working of the joint family system.

The natural history of the process is similar to the changing relations of the "stem" and "branch" families in Japan, although primogeniture is not a regular feature of the Indian joint family. When a member of the Indian joint family first moves to the city and goes into industry, he may become a "deviant" and peripheral outpost in relation to his family's ancestral seat and traditional occupation. As he succeeds and prospers, however, when he marries, begets children, and builds an urban house and an industrial empire, he soon establishes a "branch" center in relation to the ancestral estate. Eventually, as ties with the natal village or town become attenuated, as more relatives move into the city and into industrial occupations, the urban "branch" may become a new "stem" sending out new shoots into other cities and towns with every new branch office or plant of the family company.

This natural history is characterized by the operation of adaptive processes, some of which change the structure of the traditional joint family system and some of which minimize the conflicts with the new conditions. Among such adaptive processes identified in Madras are *compartmentalization* of the domestic and social sphere as "traditional and religious" and of the industrial sphere as "modern and secular"; *vicarious ritualization*; the separation of ownership and control both in the organization of the family and in the organization of the industrial corporation; and the extension of the practices and principles of household management of the rural joint family to business management.

The possibility and effectiveness of these adaptations depend on the existence of structural congruities between the joint family system and the requirements of modern industry and urban life; upon the intelligence, motivation, and ability of the actors; and upon a favorable legal structure and climate of opinion.

It is perfectly true that modern industry in India is characterized generally by such features as urban location, the separation of place of work from the place of residence, a widely extended market for its products and services, a monetized economy with an institutionalized credit system, a complex division of labor and an occupational structure based on highly specialized technology requiring scientific research and technical training, a separation of legal ownership from management, and a hierarchical structure of management interested in the intergenerational continuity of the enterprise. But it is not at all true that the joint family system is structurally and functionally incompatible with these features of modern industry and therefore either is a major obstacle to the development of industry or is inevitably destroyed by the progress of industry. On the contrary, the foregoing evidence drawn from the family histories of successful Madras industrial leaders suggests that the traditional joint family system and many of the practices associated with it offer some distinct advantages for organizing an industrial enterprise.

The joint family provides a nucleus of capital which can be used for the technical and specialized education of its members, for starting new ventures, and for operating or expanding existing industries. In the living four generations of a common ancestor, his sons, grandsons, and great-grandsons who constitute the co-parceners of joint-family property at a given time, the family provides a well-structured pattern of authority, succession, and inheritance based on the relationships of father and sons, brother and brother, uncle and nephew. This structure, as it turns out, also meets many of the requirements of industrial organization for direction, management, diversification, and continuity. Decisions can be taken by mutual consultation and consensus. The varied talents of family members can be trained and utilized for a variety of industrial operations—fiscal, administrative, engineering, etc.—as these develop, within the parent company and in the establishment of subsidiaries. And, as older members retire and withdraw from active life, the continuity of capital and management is replenished from the pool of joint-family friends and personnel. With a living horizon of three or four generations visible at any given time, its extensibility into the future limited only by the family's fertility, the scope for industrial foresight and planning seems practically unlimited.

This structural congruence between joint-family organization and the organization of industrial firms seems at first sight to be so great that one wonders how the opinion of their inherent incompatibility ever got started. The harmonies we have sketched are to be found in the hypothetical "ideal" circumstances only. In practice there may be many disturbing factors: an insufficiency of mutual trust and cooperation among the co-parceners, or an insufficiency of sons and grandsons, or inadequacies of ability and motivation. And, in addition to these internal failures, there are the external disturbances emanating from discouraging laws and taxes, public criticism, unfavorable economic conditions, industrial problems including the growing capital requirements, and the threats of nationalization. In view of these many sources of possible disturbances of the "ideal" pattern of adjustment, it is surprising to find, among the cases of our industrial leaders, several approximations to the "ideal."

The relative frequency of occurrence of joint families versus nuclear families in industry, however, has not been a major interest of this study. This has not been a statistical survey but an analysis of a small number of identified families who have produced successful industrial leaders. The major interest of the analysis has been in the ways in which these families have functionally adapted their pre-industrial social structures to industry, in the varied range of these adaptations, and in the major variable factors which account for this range. Among these factors we have identified the following as perhaps the most important: the demographic patterns of births and deaths in particular family lines; the patterns of child rearing, especially of sons by fathers; the occurrence of "pioneer" types of personalities; the availability of economic opportunities; the tax structure and the legal framework generally; national industrial policy; and the attitudes of public opinion toward family dynasties in industry. Secular and religious ideologies play their part, too, but chiefly through their influence on the other factors. Hinduism, as such, is not a major factor, although the way in which specific Hindu rites and doctrines have been adapted by these industrial families shows analogies with Max Weber's analysis of the relation of the Protestant ethic to the rise of European capitalism. That, however, is a subject for another paper!

The internal and external limitations on the joint-family in industry are not absolute or decisive. They must be taken into account in assessing the future of the family firm, but they may also be modified by counter efforts. The Hindu Code's admission of daughters to equal inheritance with sons, for example, would seem to undermine the patrilineal, patrilocal kind of joint-family organization of industry, by bringing in daughters and their husbands and children. Yet there is no intrinsic reason why the patrilineal, patrilocal family pattern should not eventually adapt itself to the broader pattern if that proves functional for industrial organization. In fact, we have noted several cases where sons-in-law have been brought into the business because there were not enough sons available. It is likely that urban residence patterns will minimize the distance married daughters move away from the parental household. The psychological tension between father-in-law and son-in-law is not in any case any greater than that between father and sons, and the tension among brothers-in-law is probably no greater than that among brothers.

The reluctance of sons to follow their father's occupational careers can also be neutralized, as some of the industrialists have found, by giving the sons responsibilities that will satisfy their desires for challenge, initiative, and independence.

In any case, the future of the Indian joint family in industry does not depend on the conversion of Hindus to a Protestant ethic or on the increasing spread of nuclear-type families. Such changes may only change the specific forms of family organization without destroying the family principle. What is more likely to destroy the family basis of industrial organization is a tax policy which makes it impossible for families to accumulate sufficient capital for starting or expanding a business, or a policy of nationalizing the private-sector industries. Although many of the industrial leaders said that they would be willing to continue as managers of public sector industries in the event of nationalization, one wonders whether their motivations would not undergo profound changes if their industrial activity were completely divorced from family organization.

BIBLIOGRAPHY

ALDOUS, J., and R. HILL.
   1965. Social cohesion, lineage type, and intergenerational transmission. *Social Forces*, 43: 471–82.

BAILEY, F. G.
   1957. *Caste and the economic frontier.* Manchester: Manchester University Press.
   1960. A framework for discussion. *Economic Weekly*, 12: 345–52.

BARNES, J. A.
   1954. *Politics in a changing society.* London: Oxford University Press.

BENNETT, J. W., and E. ISHINO.
   1966. *Paternalism in the Japanese economy.* Minneapolis: University of Minnesota Press.

BERNA, J. J.
   1960. *Industrial entrepreneurship in Madras State.* New York: Asia Publishing House.

BÉTEILLE, A.
   1964. Family and social change in India and other South Asian countries. *Economic Weekly*, 16: 237–44.

BRUNER, EDWARD M.
   1963. Medan: the role of kinship in an Indonesian city. In Alexander Spoehr (Ed.), *Pacific Port Towns and Cities.* Honolulu: Bishop Museum.

1956. Primary group experience and the processes of acculturation. *American Anthropologist*, 58: 605–623.

CHOW, YUNG-TEH.
1966. *Social mobility in China*. New York: Atherton Press.

CHOWDHRY, K. K.
1965. Social and cultural factors in management development in India. Geneva: Unesco.

COHN, BERNARD S.
1955. The changing status of a depressed caste. In McK. Marriott (Ed.), *Village India*. Chicago: University of Chicago Press.

1961. Chamar family in a North Indian village. *Economic Weekly*, 13: 1051–55.

CROZIER, DOROTHY.
1965. Kinship and occupational succession. *Sociological Review*, 13: 15–43.

CUMMING, E., and D. M. SCHNEIDER.
1961. Sibling solidarity: a property of American kinship. *American Anthropologist*, 63: 498–507.

CUNNISON, I.
1951. *History of the Luapula*. London: Oxford University Press.

DERRETT, J. D. M.
1962. The history of the juridical framework of the joint Hindu family. *Contributions to Indian Sociology*, 6: 17–47.

1963. *Introduction to modern Hindu law*. Bombay: Oxford University Press.

DESAI, I. P.
1955. (Ed.) Symposium: caste and joint family. *Sociological Bulletin*, 4: 85–146.

1964. *Some aspects of family in Mahuva*. New York: Asia Publishing House.

DUMONT, L.
1957. *Hierarchy and marriage alliance in South Indian kinship*. Occasional Paper No. 12, The Royal Anthropological Institute of Great Britain and Ireland.

1966. Book review of *Une sous-caste Inde du Sud* and *Hierarchy* and *Marriage alliance in South Indian kinship*. *Current Anthropology*, 7: 327–46.

EGGAN, FRED.
1966. *The American Indian*. Chicago: Aldine Publishing Company.

1968. Kinship systems. In *International Encyclopedia of the Social Sciences*.

ELDER, J.
1964. Brahmans in an industrial setting, a case study. In W. B. Hamilton (Ed.), *The transfer of institutions*. Durham, N.C.: Duke University Press.

EPSTEIN, S.
1962. *Economic development and social change in South India*. Manchester: Manchester University Press.

FEI, HSIAO TUNG.
1939. *Peasant life in China*. London: G. Routledge and Sons.

1953. *China's gentry*. (Ed. by M. P. Redfield.) Chicago: University of Chicago Press.

FIRTH, R.
1956. *Two studies of kinship in London*. London: Athlone Press.

1964. Family and kinship in industrial society. Sociological Review Monograph No. 8. Keele.

FORTES, MEYER.
1953. The structure of unilineal descent groups. *American Anthropologist*, 55: 17–41.

FREED, S. A.

1963. Fictive kinship in a North Indian village. *Ethnology*, 2: 86–103.

FRIEDMAN, M.

1958. *Lineage organization in southeastern China.* London: Athlone Press.

FURSTENBERG, F. F.

1966. Industrialization and the American family: a look backward. *American Socio-logical Review*, 31:326–37.

GADGIL, D. R.

1959. *Origins of the modern Indian business class.* New York: Institute of Public Relations.

GEERTZ, C.

1966. *Person, time, and conduct in Bali: an essay in cultural analysis.* New Haven: South East Asia Studies, Yale University Press.

GOODE, WILLIAM J.

1963. *World revolution and family patterns.* New York: Free Press of Glencoe.

GOODY, J. (Ed.).

1958. *The development cycle in domestic groups.* Cambridge: Cambridge University Press.

GORE, M. S.

1961. *The impact of industrialization and urbanization on the Aggarwal family in Delhi area.* Unpublished Ph.D. dissertation, Columbia University.

GOUGH, E. KATHLEEN.

1956. Brahman kinship in a Tamil village. *American Anthropologist*, 58: 826–63.

1961. The modern disintegration of matrilineal descent groups. In D. Schneider and K. Gough (Eds.), *Matrilineal kinship.* Berkeley: University of California Press.

GOULD, H. A.

1965. Lucknow rickshawallas: the social organization of an occupational category. In K. Ishwaran and R. Piddington (Eds.), *Kinship and geographical mobility.* Leiden: E. J. Brill.

1968. Time-dimension and structural change in an Indian kinship system. In M. Singer and B. S. Cohn (Eds.), *Structure and change in Indian society.* Chicago: Aldine Pub-lishing Company.

GREENFIELD, S. M.

1961. Industrialization and the family in sociological theory. *American Journal of Sociology*, 67: 312–22.

GULATI, I. S., and K. S. GULATI.

1962. *The undivided Hindu family, its tax privileges.* New York: Asia Publishing House.

HO, PING-TI.

1962. *The ladder of success in Imperial China, aspects of social mobility, 1368–1911.* New York: Columbia University Press.

HSU, C.

1965. *Ancient China in transition: An analysis of social mobility, 722–227 B.C.* Stan-ford: Stanford University Press.

HSU, F. L. K.

1948. *Under the ancestors' shadow.* New York: Columbia University Press.

1952. *Religion, science and human crisis.* London: Routledge and Kegan Paul.

1963. *Clan, caste, and club.* Princeton, N.J.: D. Van Nostrand.

JOHNSON, ERWIN.

1964. The stem family and its extension in present day Japan. *American Anthro-pologist*, 66: 839–51.

KAPADIA, K. M.

1958. *Marriage and family in India.* Madras: Oxford University Press.

1959. The family in transition. *Sociological Bulletin,* 8(2): 68–99.

KARVE, IRAWATI.

1963. A family through six generations. In L. K. Bala Ratnam (Ed.), *Anthropology on the march.* Madras: Book Centre.

1965. *Kinship organization in India.* (2d ed.) Bombay: Asia Publishing House.

KOLENDA, PAULINE M.

1968. Region, caste, and family structure: A comparative study of the Indian "joint" family. In M. Singer and B. S. Cohn (Eds.), *Structure and change in Indian society.* Chicago: Aldine Publishing Company.

KRACKE, E. A., JR.

1953. *Civil service in early Sung China, 960–1067.* Cambridge: Harvard University Press.

KURIAN, GEORGE.

1961. *The Indian family in transition.* The Hague: Mouton and Company.

LAMB, H. B.

1959. Business organization and leadership in India today. In R. L. Park and I. Tinker (Eds.), *Leadership and political institutions in India.* Princeton: Princeton University Press.

LAMBERT, R.

1965. *Workers, factories, and social change in India.* Princeton: Princeton University Press.

LEACH, E. R.

1954. *The political systems of highland Burma.* London: London School of Economics and Political Science.

1961. *Pul Eliya, a village in Ceylon.* Cambridge: Cambridge University Press.

LEWIS, O.

1959. *Five families.* New York: Basic Books.

LÉVI-STRAUSS, C.

1963. *Structural anthropology.* New York: Basic Books.

LEVY, MARION J., JR.

1949. *The family revolution in modern China.* Cambridge: Harvard University Press.

1966. *Modernization and the structure of societies.* (2 vols.) Princeton: Princeton University Press.

LEVY, MARION J., JR., and LLOYD FALLERS.

1959. The family: some comparative considerations. *American Anthropologist,* 61: 647–51.

LIPSET, SEYMOUR M., and REINHARD BENDIX.

1964. *Social mobility in industrial society.* Berkeley: University of California Press.

LITWAK, EUGENE.

1960. Occupational mobility and extended family cohesion. *American Sociological Review,* 25: 9–20.

McCRORY, J. T.

1956. *Small industry in a North Indian town.* New Delhi: Gov. of India.

MADAN, T. M.

1962. The Hindu joint family. *Man,* 62: 88–89.

1965. *Family and kinship: a study of the Pandits of rural Kashmir.* New York: Asia Publishing House.

MANDELBAUM, DAVID G.
1949. The family in India. In Ruth Anshen (Ed.), *The family and its functions and destiny*. New York: Harper.

MARSH, R. M.
1961. *The Mandarins: the circulation of elites in China, 1600–1900*. Glencoe, Ill.: The Free Press.

MAYER, A. L.
1960. *Caste and kinship in central India*. Berkeley: University of California Press.

MENCHER, J.
1965. The Nayars of South Malabor. In M. F. Nimkoff (Ed.), *Comparative family systems*. Boston: Houghton Mifflin.

MOORE, W., and A. S. FELDMAN (Eds.).
1960. *Labor commitment and social change in developing areas*. New York: Social Science Research Council.

MURDOCK, G. P.
1949. *Social structure*. New York: Macmillan.

NICHOLAS, R.
1961. Economy of family types in two West Bengal villages. *Economic Weekly*, 13: 1057–60.

NIMKOFF, M. F. (Ed.).
1965. *Comparative family systems*. Boston: Houghton Mifflin.

NIMKOFF, M. F.
1960. Is the joint family an obstacle to industrialization? *International Journal of Comparative Sociology*, 1: 109–118.

ORANS, M.
1965. *A tribe in search of a great tradition*. Detroit: Wayne State University Press.

ORENSTEIN, HENRY.
1961. The recent history of the extended family in India. *Social Problems*, 8: 341–50.

PATTERSON, MAUREEN L. P.
1967. Chitpavan Brahman family histories. In M. Singer and B. S. Cohn (Eds.), *Structure and change in Indian society*. Chicago: Aldine Publishing Company.

REDFIELD, R.
1941. *The folk culture of Yucatan*. Chicago: University of Chicago Press.

RIVERS, W. H. R.
1910. The genealogical method of anthropological inquiry. *Sociological Review*, 3: 1–12.

ROSS, AILEEN D.
1961. *The Hindu family in its urban setting*. Toronto: University of Toronto Press.

ROWE, WILLIAM L.
1960. The marriage network and structural change in a North Indian community. *Southwestern Journal of Anthropology*, 16: 299–311.

N.d. Caste, kinship and association in urban India. In E. Bruner and A. Southall, (Eds), *Urban Anthropology*. In press.

1967. Mobility in the nineteenth-century caste system. In M. Singer and B. S. Cohn (Eds.), *Structure and change in Indian society*. Chicago: Aldine Publishing Company.

SCHNEIDER, D. M., and K. GOUGH (Eds.).
1961. *Matrilineal kinship*. Berkeley: University of California Press.

SCHNEIDER, D. M. and G. C. HOMANS.
1955. Kinship terminology and the American kinship system. *American Anthropologist*, 57: 1194–1208.

SHAH, A. M.

1964. Basic terms and concepts in the study of family in India. *Indian Economic and Social History Review*, 1: 1–36.

SHAH, A. M., and R. G. SHROFF.

1959. The Vahīvancā Barots of Gujerat: A caste of genealogists and mythographers. In M. Singer (Ed.), *Traditional India*. Philadelphia: American Folklore Society.

SINHA, S.

1962. State formation and Rajput myth in tribal central India. *Man in India*, 42: 35–80.

SRINIVAS, M. N.

1942. *Marriage and family in Mysore*. Bombay: New Book Co.

1966. *Social change in modern India*. Berkeley: University of California Press.

SURYA, N. C.

1966. Development of ego-structure in the Hindu joint family. Conference on Mental Health in Asia and the Pacific, held at the East-West Center, Honolulu, March 28–April 1, 1966. (Unpublished.)

SUSSMAN, M. B.

1959. The isolated nuclear family: fact or fiction? *Social Problems*, 6: 333–40.

SUSSMAN, M. B., and L. B. BURCHINAL.

1962. Kin family network. *Marriage and Family Living*, 24: 231–40.

TANDON, P.

1961. *Punjabi century (1857–1947)*. London: Chatto and Windus.

WOLF, E. R.

1966. Kinship, friendship, and patron-client relations in complex societies. In M. Banton (Ed.), *The social anthropology of complex societies*. New York: Praeger.

YALMAN, N. O.

1962. The structure of the Sinhalese kindred. *American Anthropologist*, 64: 548–75.

1967. *Under the bo tree: studies in caste, kinship and marriage in the interior of Ceylon*. Berkeley and Los Angeles: University of California Press.

YOUNG, M., and P. WILLMOTT.

1957. *Family and kinship in East London*. Baltimore: Penguin Books.

PART VI:
Language and Social Structure

18. SOCIAL DIALECT AND SEMANTIC STRUCTURE
IN SOUTH ASIA

WILLIAM BRIGHT

T HE RECENTLY GROWING FIELD of sociolinguistics may be defined as the study
of the relationships between language and society; this is correct, but
vague. Modern sociolinguistic study differs from earlier interests in these
relationships in that it views both language and society as structures, rather than
as mere collections of items. It represents a departure, at the same time, from previous trends in linguistics which attempted to ignore social influences and to
treat language as homogeneous or monolithic; it focuses, rather, on linguistic
diversity within the social unit, and on the correlations between such diversity
on one hand and social functions on the other hand.

It is possible to distinguish several dimensions of linguistic study, each involving two or more alternative features. Thus, studies of sociolinguistic diversity
may be classified along a dimension of *extent*, with three possible features: *multidialectal*, where socially conditioned varieties of a single language are used
within a single society, such as "U" versus "non-U" speech in Great Britain
(Ross, 1954); *multilingual*, where different languages are used within a single
society, as English and French are in Canada; and *multisocietal*, where contrastive
studies are made of the functions of diverse languages within separate societies.

A second dimension of sociolinguistic study concerns the conditioning factors
of linguistic diversity—the socially defined elements which determine the choice,
within a particular society, of alternative linguistic forms. This dimension commonly involves three features. One is the social identity of the *sender*[1]: this may
be defined in terms of social strata, as in the case of "U" versus "non-U" British
usage mentioned above, or in terms of other socially recognized classes of speakers, as where differences are found between men's and women's speech. A second
conditioning factor is the social identity of the *receiver*, or, in some cases, the
person spoken about; this factor is involved in the use of special honorific speech
styles widely reported from the Orient and from Oceania. The third conditioning
factor is that of the social *setting*, including all relevant elements other than the
identities of the persons involved in the communication. This factor conditions
such usage as, for instance, the reported special language used by the Apaches
when on the warpath (Opler and Hoijer, 1940); more commonly, it conditions
widespread differences between formal and informal language, differences which
have been variously labelled as literary versus colloquial, written versus spoken,

1. Terms here are from Hymes (1962, p. 25).

non-casual versus casual, and "high" versus "low" (where these last terms refer not to social strata but to differences of prestige between, for example, literature and informal conversation). In societies with formal and informal styles which are sharply divergent yet genetically related, such as the standard French and the Creole language used side by side in Haiti, we characterize the situation as one of *diglossia* (Ferguson, 1959).

In South Asia, we have of course to deal with sociolinguistic diversity both of the multilingual type—as in the competition between English, Hindi, and regional languages—and of the multidialectal type. It is the latter which concerns us here. If we consider the variant forms of Kannada, for instance, first eliminating the element of geographical dialect differences, we find at least two kinds of socially conditioned diversity. The identity of the receiver is, to be sure, not as important in India as elsewhere; specifically honorific styles are not prominent there. The factor of situation, however, carries great weight. Specifically, some situations are socially defined as formal and require the use of formal Kannada; these situations include the acts of writing (in most cases), of public address, and of performance on the stage. Other situations are socially defined as informal and condition the use of informal Kannada; these include most situations of communication with family, friends, and casual acquaintances. The differences between formal and informal Kannada are great, and a situation of diglossia clearly exists. The same is apparently true of the other major South Indian languages, and (in a less clear-cut way) of Bengali. In Hindi, on the other hand, though there are certainly differences between formal and informal usage, the division is less sharp and more comparable to what we are familiar with in most European languages.

However, the factor of formality in linguistic diversity is not our primary interest in the present context. We are concerned rather with the identity of the sender as a conditioning factor and specifically with his caste affiliation, as it is correlated with differences of caste dialect. Such differences have been widely reported; the general picture is of a dichotomy between Touchable and Untouchable usage in North India, as against a three-way division in South India between Brahman, non-Brahman, and Untouchable dialects. It should be made clear that caste dialects are independent of the dichotomy between formal and informal styles. It may be true that the higher castes more often have the opportunity to receive an education and thereby to become proficient in the formal style. But formal usage is quite a separate system from high-caste informal usage; it is used in a substantially uniform way by all educated people, whatever their caste background may be.

Descriptions of Indian caste dialects, like other sociolinguistic studies, have usually been organized along another dimension, corresponding to the divisions of language structure recognized by descriptive linguists. The features usually noted under this heading are phonological, grammatical, and lexical. Under the phonological rubric, we may be told, for example, that Brahman Kannada initial /h/ corresponds to non-Brahman zero, in examples like Br. *haalu*, NBr. *aalu*, "milk". Under grammar, it is explained that Brahman Kannada has the locative morpheme *-alli* corresponding to NBr. *-aagi*. Under lexicon, such differences as Br. *sinima*, NBr. *bayskoopu*, "movies," are noted (Bright, 1960).

Most of the data of this kind which have been published essentially involve differences of phonological shape between semantically equivalent utterances. That is, both Brahman and non-Brahman dialects have morphemes meaning "milk, locative, movies"; these morphemes have the differing phonemic shapes *haalu* vs. *aalu*, *-alli* vs. *-aagi*, and *sinima* vs. *bayskoopu*, respectively. These differences may be accounted for historically in a variety of ways, involving considerations such as regular sound change, borrowing, or analogical change. But the fact remains that such comparisons do not point to any differences in structure between the two caste dialects compared. The dialects have the same grammatical units, but in different phonological shapes. If we use the term "morphophonemics" to refer to the part of linguistic description which accounts for the phonological shapes of grammatical elements, then we may say that the type of description of caste dialects which has been illustrated above is altogether a matter of morphophonemic comparison.

In some publications, to be sure, comparisons of caste dialects have also pointed out that one dialect has a different inventory of basic elements than another. Under phonology, for instance, it can be stated that the difference between Kannada Br. *haalu*, NBr. *aalu*, "milk," reflects the fact that the Brahman dialect has an /h/ phoneme while the non-Brahman dialect does not; furthermore, the Brahman phonemes /f z š/ are also lacking in the non-Brahman dialect. Under the heading of grammar, however, it becomes harder to find reports of structural differences. It is clear that sometimes one variety of a language will use inflectional machinery where another variety will use syntactic constructions, as in formal Urdu *savaalo javaab* ("question-and-answer") versus informal *savaal aur javaab* (Gumperz and Naim, 1960, p. 116). But such comparisons reflect differences in means of expression, not differences in underlying grammatical categories. And under the lexical heading, we again find very scant report of differences deeper than those of the morphophonemic level.

The suggestion I would like to make is that caste dialects may differ not only in various ways that are phonologically definable but also in important ways which are reflected in differences of grammar and vocabulary, but which derive basically from different semantic structures; that is, caste dialects, like separate languages (but probably to a lesser degree) may reflect different ways of classifying nonlinguistic phenomena, whether subjective or objective.

The scarcity of data on these differences probably reflects several factors. For one thing, semantic differences are less obvious to the investigator than the other types which have been mentioned. In addition, semantic structure has only recently become a favored area of research for descriptive linguists. Even so, the published data on Indian social dialects provide evidence which is quite adequate to establish that difference in semantic structures is in fact present. The following are illustrative of the data to be found:

(1) In the Tamil of Kumbakonam and Chidambaram, according to Bloch (1910, pp. 18–19), the Brahman dialect distinguishes terms for "elder sister's husband," and "younger sister's husband," and "wife's brother"; certain non-Brahman groups use a single term.

(2) In the Tamil of Kumbakonam and Tirumangalam, Brahmans use a single term for "wife's sister," but non-Brahmans distinguish "wife's older sister" from "wife's younger sister" (Bloch, 1910, pp. 18–19).

(3) In the Kannada of Dharwar, Brahmans address mother and elder sister with the same forms, while non-Brahmans (Lingayats) make a distinction. There is a similar pattern in addressing father and elder brother (McCormack, 1960, pp. 86–87).[2]

(4) Also in Dharwar, Brahmans use a single morpheme -*u* of general purpose address; Lingayats distinguish -*apa*, used to men, from -*be*, used to women; and Untouchables add special elements for addressing a son-in-law and for addressing affinal kin (McCormack, 1960, pp. 86, 90).

(5) Again in Dharwar, Brahmans and Lingayats distinguish two cases of the noun which can be called Accusative and Dative, but the Untouchable dialect shows merger of the two cases into one (McCormack, 1960, pp. 89–90).

(6) According to Ramaswami Aiyar (1936, p. 903), the Brahman dialect of Tulu has a single third-person honorific pronoun *aaru*, where the non-Brahman dialect retains a distinction (made elsewhere in both dialects) between *aaru*, "he (honorific) there," and *meeru*, "he (honorific) here."

In addition to the above cases, it may be of interest to point to some data on semantic differences between formal and informal styles in Indian languages:

(1) In Hindi, formal usage tends to distinguish *yah*, "this," from *ye*, "these," and *vah*, "that," from *ve*, "those." Informal usage tends to obliterate the singular-plural distinction, employing *ye*, "this, these," and *vo*, "that, those" (Gumperz and Naim, 1960, p. 115).

(2) Formal Hindi distinguishes *yadi* or *agar*, "if," from *yadyapi*, "although," and formal Urdu distinguishes *agar*, "if," from *agarci* or *haalaaki*, "although"; but informal Hindi-Urdu merges the two meanings as *agar*, "if, although" (Gumperz and Naim, 1960, p. 115).

(3) Formal Kannada distinguishes present and future tenses; informal Kannada has a single "non-past," with forms corresponding to the formal present tense (Bright, 1958, p. 21).

(4) Formal Kannada and Tamil distinguish neuter singular from neuter plural in demonstratives and (as subject markers) in verb forms; but many informal dialects use just one form (corresponding to the formal singular) for both singular and plural meanings.

(5) In the Tamil reported by Shanmugam Pillai (1960, p. 38), the formal style has a single third person plural pronoun, indifferent as to gender; but the informal style adds pronouns with specific masculine and feminine reference.

---

2. It was McCormack's data that elicited the comment by Friedrich (1961, p. 167), that "the comparative componental analysis of the kinship terms in two contiguous caste dialects is perhaps of greater theoretical significance than the relatively banal issue of language as 'an index of social status.'" However, such comparative componental kinship analyses from caste dialects are still not available. In a recent paper, Shanmugam Pillai (1965) compares kin terms from thirteen castes in a Tamil community, but his interest is in the terms peculiar to single castes, and he does not give the complete data which would permit a semantic analysis.

Differences in semantic structure, like those illustrated above both for caste dialects and for formal-informal styles, have, it may well be supposed, counterparts in other sections of the total social structures with which they are associated. It would be unduly venturous at this point, given the scarcity of data, to launch into wider speculations and to suggest that semantic differences between caste dialects may reflect differences in value systems from one caste to another.[3] But if field workers will turn their attention to semantic structures, and if more data on the subject are made available, then it may indeed be possible to fit semantic diversity into a larger understanding of how caste functions.

BIBLIOGRAPHY

BLOCH, JULES.

1910. Castes et dialectes en Tamoul. *Mémoires de la Société de Linguistique*, 16: 1–30.

BRIGHT, WILLIAM.

1958. *An outline of colloquial Kannada*. Poona: Deccan College.

1960. Linguistic Change in some Indian caste dialects. In Charles A. Ferguson and John J. Gumperz (Eds.), *Linguistic diversity in South Asia*. Indiana University Research Center in Anthropology, Folklore, and Linguistics, Publication no. 13 (*International Journal of American Linguistics*, 26(3), pt. III).

FERGUSON, CHARLES A.

1959. Diglossia. *Word*, 15: 325–40.

FERGUSON, CHARLES A., and JOHN J. GUMPERZ (Eds.).

1960. *Linguistic diversity in South Asia*. Indiana University Research Center in Anthropology, Folklore, and Linguistics, Publication no. 13 (*International Journal of American Linguistics*, 26(3), pt. III).

FRIEDRICH, PAUL.

1961. Review of Ferguson and Gumperz, *Linguistic diversity in South Asia. Language*, 37: 163–68.

GUMPERZ, JOHN J., and C. M. NAIM.

1960. Formal and informal standards in the Hindi regional language area. In Charles A. Ferguson and John J. Gumperz (Eds.), *Linguistic diversity in South Asia*. Indiana University Research Center in Anthropology, Folklore, and Linguistics, Publication no. 13 (*International Journal of American Linguistics*, 26(3), pt. III).

HYMES, DELL.

1962. The ethnography of speaking. In Thomas Gladwin and William Sturtevant (Eds.), *Anthropology and human behavior*. Washington, D.C.: Anthropological Society of Washington.

McCORMACK, WILLIAM.

1960. Social dialects in Dharwar Kannada. In Charles A. Ferguson and John J. Gumperz, *Linguistic diversity in South Asia*. Indiana University Research Center in Anthropology, Folklore, and Linguistics, Publication no. 13 (*International Journal of American Linguistics*, 26(3), pt. III).

OPLER, MORRIS, and HARRY HOIJER.

1940. The raid and war-path language of the Chiricahua Apache. *American Anthropologist*, 42: 617–34.

3. See Friedrich's suggestion that "conservatism in phonemics and grammar . . . might be the linguistic aspect of the deeply internalized values of caste status among the Brahmins" (1961, p. 164).

PILLAI, M. SHANMUGAM.

1960. Tamil—literary and colloquial. In Charles A. Ferguson and John J. Gumperz (Eds.), *Linguistic diversity in South Asia.* Indiana University Research Center in Anthropology, Folklore, and Linguistics, Publication no. 13 (*International Journal of American Linguistics,* 26(3), pt. III).

1965. Caste isoglosses in kinship terms. *Anthropological Linguistics,* 7(3): 59–66.

RAMASWAMI AIYAR, L. V.

1936. Materials for a sketch of Tulu phonology. *Indian Linguistics,* 6: 385–438.

Ross, ALAN S. C.

1954. Linguistic class indicators in present-day English. *Neuphilologische Mitteilungen,* 55: 20–56.

19. THE STRUCTURE OF VARIATION:
A STUDY IN CASTE DIALECTS

A. K. RAMANUJAN

THIS IS A STUDY in the structure of variation in Brahman and non-Brahman caste-dialects.[1] Though this paper inventories in reasonable detail the iso-glosses for two caste dialects, the chief purpose is to show that these caste-isoglosses are not isolated, piecemeal differences but are patterned in certain ways. It is part of a larger search for configurations that pattern isogloss formation in social dialects. Morphological isoglosses, especially paradigms, are found to be specially useful for this purpose (see section on free variants below).

Two colloquial varieties of Indian Tamil, the I(yengar) and the M(udaliyar) dialects, are chosen as examples. The Tengalai Iyengar dialect is a well-marked B(rahman) dialect, distinctly recognized as such by the Tengalai Iyengars them-selves and by other castes in the speech community. The Mudaliyar dialect is considered an upper-caste N(on-) B(rahman) dialect. Both are easily available everywhere in the Tamil area, so that regional variants can be separated from caste variants. Only those isoglosses shared by the members of a community in different regions are considered the "markers."

It has been pointed out in the literature again and again (for example, Bloch, 1910, Bright, 1960, Bright and Ramanujan, 1964, Pillai, 1960, Zvelebil, 1960, 1964) that variation in Tamil is regional as well as social.[2] The social parameters are educated/uneducated, urban/rural, formal/informal, $caste_1$/$caste_2$ and so on. There are differences in the speech of different subcastes, for example, Mudaliyar/

1. The data are mostly drawn from my own recordings and field notes, checked against and supplemented by printed sources cited below. The field work (1963–64) on Tamil, Kannada, and Tulu social dialects was made possible by a grant from the American Institute of Indian Studies. I wish to acknowledge here my indebtedness to the Institute.

While most of the conventions of transcription for Tamil are well known to fellow workers (such as that underlined $\underline{n}$, $\underline{r}$, are alveolar, $ṇ$, $ṭ$, etc., are retroflex), we may mention two devia-tions: long vowels are shown by double letters, for example, /aa/, /ii/, and unrounded [ɯ] is written /u/.

2. *Social* and *caste* dialects should be distinguished. A *caste* dialect is only one kind of *social* dialect. Formal and informal varieties of speech could also be considered social dialects, as their linguistic features co-vary with social contexts. On the other hand, formal and informal varieties are like styles in that they may, and usually do, coexist in the repertory of the same speaker. Anyone who controls the formal dialects will also have an informal dialect, except in self-conscious "pathological" cases of purism. Caste dialects, like regional dialects, tend to be mutually exclusive, that is, a person who speaks a Brahman dialect may or may not speak any other. In intercaste or interregional communication, imperfect stereotypes of other dialects may be used, as suggested below in the discussion of free variants. Some of these distinctions are roughly shown in the diagram below. The interaction and mixture of formal/informal, and of the various caste and regional dialects is a fascinating study, but we will refer to it here only in passing where relevant.

461

Chettiyar, both non-Brahman, or Iyer/Iyengar, both Brahman. Without going into details, the main dialect divisions may be diagrammed as follows:

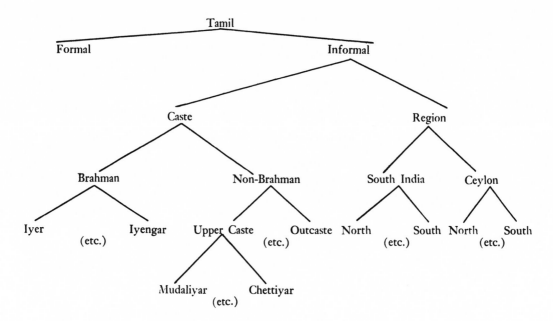

In this rather simplified diagram of the dialect picture, the urban/rural, educated/ uneducated, Hindu/Muslim contrasts are omitted, as no exact information is available on such matters yet. The regional divisions are impressionistic (see Zvelebil, 1964, for suggestions). There are no branchings under the formal variety, for caste and regional differences are mostly neutralized in the formal style.

We could have placed all the regional branchings under both the Brahman and non-Brahman nodes, or vice versa. There is good reason to believe that region and caste are independent variables; every Tamil speaker must be identified for both. Some isoglosses are clearly geographical. (For a qualification of this view see section on the function of a social dialect below.) For instance, roughly south of Tirunelveli and Ramanathapuram we hear *nuppadu* for "thirty"; north of Tirunelveli it is *muppadu*. In the written dialect and educated Tirunelveli speech it is *muppadu*. Uneducated B and uneducated NB speakers (say, children just beginning school) were found to say *nuppadu*. So the form may be unambiguously assigned to uneducated Tirunelveli or Ramanathapuram Tamil rather than to any caste.

The variety of competing subcaste forms within the B and NB dialects was reduced by the choice of just two subcastes for intensive analysis. Any comparison with other B or NB subcastes will show that all B subcastes are distinguishable in speech from any NB subcaste, that is, B subcastes like Iyer and Iyengar share overall speech features, despite differences; NB subcastes (like Mudaliyar, Chettiyar, Vellala) also have recognizable overall features.

All our informants were urban and educated. The dimension of "horizontal" dialect variety was eliminated by choosing our data from three cities, Madras, Mayuram, and Madurai, and considering only the a-geographic variants for each dialect.

THE VERB SYSTEM

Let us begin with what is obviously the most conservative subpart of the language, the verb-system. The forms in the first Tamil column represent the W(ritten) or Formal dialect. It will be assumed here that in most cases W furnishes us with the underlying, even historically prior, base-forms (for evidence and argument, see Ramanujan, 1963). W forms are given in transliteration; I and M forms are written in a phonemic transcription.

The relevant morphological variations are most marked in (a) the present tense and (b) in the III person neuter singular past. The endings are *italicized*.[3]

Verbs: Present Tense, Neuter Singular

Gloss	W	I	M
It is	1. iru*kkiṟatu*	iru*kku*	iru*kkudu*
It kills	2. kol*kiṟatu*	kol*radu*	kol*ludu*
It walks	3. naṭa*kkiṟatu*	naḍa*kradu*	naḍa*kkudu*
It comes	4. varu*kiṟatu*	var*adu*	var*udu*
It goes	5. poo*kiṟatu*	poo*radu*	poo*vudu*

Note that W has only two forms for the neuter present tense. 1 and 3 are strong verbs, they take -*kkiṟatu*; 2, 4, 5, are weak verbs, they take -*kiṟatu*. The I forms have four different shapes for the same endings: -*kku*, -*radu*, -*kradu*, -*adu*. The M forms have only two, corresponding to the W forms; -*udu* (the -v- in poo-v-*udu* is inserted automatically by general rule) and -*kkudu*.

Verbs: Present Tense, Masculine Singular

	W	I	M
He is	1. iru*kkiṟaaṉ*	iru*kkāā*	iru*krāā*
He kills	2. kol*kiṟaaṉ*	kol*rāā*	kol*rāā*
He walks	3. naṭa*kkiṟaaṉ*	naḍa*krāā*	naḍa*krāā*
He comes	4. varu*kiṟaaṉ*	var*āā*	var*rāā*

Note that W has again only two kinds of endings, and M likewise has two, whereas I has four.

---

3. As the concern of this paper is to illustrate a grammatical "drift" or configuration, and not morphological identification of segments, the technicalities of morphology are kept to a minimum. For instance, in the next paradigm, we could identify -*kku* of I iru + *kku* as a "portmanteau" morph representing two morphemes, that is, present tense and III person neuter. We could point out the vowel harmony in the M endings, for example, *udu*. Or we could set up rules deriving from a single base both B and NB forms. Such a presentation would show formally what we describe informally here: given W as the base, the B dialect would require (a) more rules, (b) rules with more restricted conditions, i.e., more provisions for exceptions, than the NB dialect.

Verbs: Past Tense, Neuter Singular

		W	I	M
It was	1.	irunt*atu*	irund*udu*	irund*uccu*
It killed	2.	koṇr*atu*	konn*udu*	konn*uccu*
It walked	3.	naṭant*atu*	naḍand*udu*	naḍand*uccu*
It came	4.	vant*atu*	vand*udu*	vand*uccu*
It went	5.	pooyi*ṟṟu*	poo*ccu*	poo*ccu*
It brought	6.	vaaṅki*ṟṟu*	vaaṅgi*ttu*	vaaṅgi*ccu*

Here *W* has only two forms for the neuter personal endings: *-atu* and *-ṟṟu*. I has three: *-udu*, *-ccu*, *-ttu*. The M forms have only one basic *-(u)ccu*, obviously generalizing the *pooccu*-paradigm (5), shared by both dialects.

Verbs: New Classes

   When we examine the morphophonemic classes of verbs in W, I, and M, we find again that I has a few more than M, i.e. *uṭkaar* "sit."

		W	I	M
He sat	1.	uṭkaarndaaṇ	okkaaṇḍãã[4]	okkaandãã

The I form is unique in the language in having retroflexes only in the past tense suffix. A retroflex consonant in the past would ordinarily entail a retroflex in the stem-final. But in *uṭkaar*, the stem-final is *r*. The M forms fit the paradigm of other verbs such as *seer*, "join":

Present	okkaarrãã	seerrãã
Past	okkaandãã	seendãã
Future	okkaaruvãã	seeruvãã

The reflexive post-verb *-koḷ* is another example. While *-koḷ* has many regional variants, the overall I and M markers may be fairly represented by the following:

		W	I	M
He is doing	(reflexive)	paṇṇi*kkoḷ*kiṟaaṇ	paṇṇi*kki*rãã	paṇṇi*kid*rãã
He did	(reflexive)	paṇṇi*kkoṇ*ṭaaṇ	paṇṇi*ndãã*	paṇṇi*kiṭṭ*ãã
He will do	(reflexive)	paṇṇi*kkoḷ*vaaṇ	paṇṇi*ppãã*[5]	paṇṇi*kid*uvãã

The W forms of -koḷ are morphophonemically regular:

Present	-koḷkiṟaaṇ
Past	-koṇṭaaṇ
Future	-koḷvaaṇ

The I forms are unusual. But for the retroflex *-ṇḍ-* (as in the *uṭkaar* paradigm above), the whole conjugation of *-koḷ-* is assimilated to the tense endings of a strong verb like *naḍa*:

4. Most I dialects I have recorded seem to have this form; some have okkaandãã. Since writing this paper I have found *naharu* "move"—*nahaṇḍãã* "he moved" in a Ramanathapuram Nadar (NB) dialect.
5. Often a free variant, *paṇṇikkuvãã*, which makes the paradigm wholly "irregular."

	I and M	I Reflexive -koḷ
He walks	naḍakkarāā	-kkirāā
He walked	naḍandāā	-ṇḍāā
He will walk	naḍappāā	-ppāā

On the other hand, the reflexive -koḷ in M has been re-worked on the model of viḍu, "leave, let go," the only other important and frequent aspect-marker in the language. Adverbial participle + viḍu gives us the completive aspect of the verb, adverbial participle + koḷ gives us the reflexive. Unlike the -viḍu and -koḷ forms of I, in M both aspect markers belong to the same general class, the viḍu-class:

	M Adv PP. + koḷ	I and M viḍu	I and M Adv PP. + viḍu
Present	paṇṇikidrāā	vidrāā	paṇṇidrāā
Past	paṇṇikiṭṭāā	viṭṭāā	paṇṇiṭṭāā[6]
Future	paṇṇikiḍuvāā	viḍuvāā	paṇṇiḍuvāā

	I Adv PP. + koḷ
Present	paṇṇikkirāā
Past	paṇṇiṇḍāā
Future	paṇṇippāā

In every one of the above four examples (one may easily cite other verbs as evidence), we find that the Brahman I is the overdifferentiated dialect compared to the other two. M has invariably regularized its paradigm, even where W has "irregularities" as in the past neuter singular or has two different classes of verbs like -koḷ and viḍu. Neither I nor M is close to W. Both have innovated in their different ways.

Such analogical leveling or regularizing of forms in M (filling out and symmetrizing paradigms) is not confined to the verbs. We see the same tendency in other subsystems also; we will cite here only a few examples from pronouns. The examples will also point up the special differentiating developments in I.

PRONOUNS

Pronouns: I and II Person Singular

		W	I	M
I	1.	naaṉ	nāā	nāā
My	2.	eṉ	en, ē	en, ē
To me	3.	eṉakku	neekku	enakku
You	4.	ṉii	nii	nii
Your (sg.)	5.	uṉ	on, õ	on, õ
To you	6.	uṉakku	nookku	onakku

6. There are further special features in I for Adv. PP. + viḍu, not found in W or M. In the neuter past, I has *paṇṇiḍuttu* when one would expect *paṇṇiṭṭudu*, found both in W (*paṇṇivittatu*) and M. In fast M speech, there are further assimilations: both *paṇṇikiṭṭāā* and *paṇṇi(vi)ṭṭāā* are pronounced *paṇṇiṭṭāā*.

M corresponds to W exactly, by regular rules like vowel + final nasal in W = nasalized vowel in M, I (2); *u* becomes *o* if the next syllable has an *a* (6) etc. *on* in (5) is probably a back-formation from *onakku.*

But I has two unpredictable forms: *neekku* (3) and *nookku* (6).[7] To my knowledge, these are the only two examples in the language of this kind of metathesis and vowel change (quite common in Telugu under different conditions):

enakku $\longrightarrow$ ne-akku $\longrightarrow$ neekku

unakku $\longrightarrow$ onakku $\longrightarrow$ no-akku $\longrightarrow$ nookku

Pronouns: III Person

	W	*I*	*M*
He	avaṇ	avã	avã (or avẽ)
She	avaḷ	avo	ava

	W	*I*	*M*
He/She (polite)	avar	avar	avaru
They (he/she)	avarkaḷ	avaa	avanga
They (masculine)	—	—	avanuha
They (feminine)	—	—	avaḷuha

Here the M forms are the overdifferentiated ones, but they are perfect examples of the M tendency to generalize and fill out paradigms. Both W and I have gender distinctions in the singular, but are defective in having none in the plural. M fills it out with *avanuha* "they—masculine" and *avaḷuha* "they—feminine."

	W		*I*		*M*	
	Sg.	Pl.	Sg.	Pl.	Sg.	Pl.
masc.	avar	avarkaḷ	avã	avaa	avã	avanuha
fem.	avaḷ	avarkaḷ	avo	avaa	ava	avaḷuha

The componential diagrams below point up the fuller symmetry of M as compared with W and I:

W and I

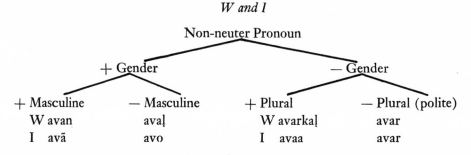

Non-neuter Pronoun

+ Gender   − Gender

+ Masculine   − Masculine   + Plural   − Plural (polite)
W avan   avaḷ   W avarkaḷ   avar
I   avã   avo   I   avaa   avar

7. Zvelebil (1964, p. 254) says that "an Aiyangar (Vaishnavite) Brahman would not tend to use the form /ne:kku/ . . . but /enakku/." But my data attest /neekku/ for both Iyer and Iyengar speakers.

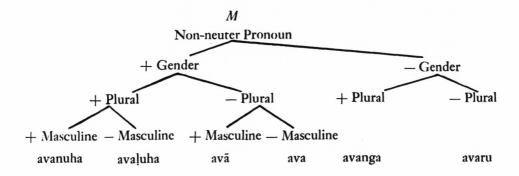

DERIVATIONAL EXAMPLES

Words in the feminine gender can often be derived from the masculine forms by the addition of *-cci,* in W, M, or I.

	W		M and I	
	Masculine	Feminine	Masculine	Feminine
outcaste	paraiyan	paraicci	parayā	paracci
cowherd	itaiyan	itaicci	edeyā	edecci

M generalizes this suffix and adds it to many feminine kinship terms:

	W	I	M
younger sister	1. tankai	tange	tangacci
sister-in-law	2. maittuni	maccini	maccinicci
(sister of spouse)			
sister-in-law	3. No cognate	No cognate	attaacci
(elder brother's wife)			

Similarly, one finds that where I has two separate unrelated words for relationships like "brother" and "brother's wife," M has two derivationally related words (1, 2 below); often one is derived from the other by the addition of a general feminine suffix (3, 4).

	W	I	M
son-in-law	1. marumakan, maappillai	maaple	marumahā
daughter-in-law	2. marumakal, naattuppen	maattuponnu	marumaha (l)
elder brother	3. annaa, annan	annaa	annaa, annā
elder brother's	4. anni (?)	manni	anni
wife			

anni has the same feminine suffix (*-i*) as the following:

	W	M and I	
grandfather	1. paattan	paattā	
grandmother	2. paatti	paatti	
blind man	3. kurutan	kurudā	
blind woman	4. kuruti	kurudi	etc.

These grammatical configurations, of generalization (M) and specialization (I) in paradigms, appear in other parts of the grammar also. Many phonological and lexico-semantic examples can be given. Here we will content ourselves with a couple from each domain. There are syntactic examples also but they are too complex for brief presentation.

PHONOLOGY

Generally, I tends to have more contrasts than M in every position. For instance, medially in M the retroflex *ṇ* and *ḷ* do not contrast with alveolar *ṉ* and *ḻ*; nor does *ṛ* (retroflex continuant) contrast with *ḷ* (retroflex lateral). The retroflex/alveolar contrast in nasals and liquids is characteristic of I.

	W	I	M
calf	1. kaṉru	kannu	kaṇṇu~kannu (free variants)
eye	2. kaṇṇu	kaṇṇu	kaṇṇu~kannu
stone	3. kallu	kallu	kaḷḷu~kallu
toddy	4. kaḷḷu	kaḷḷu	kaḷḷu~kallu
road	5. vaṛi	vaṛi	vaḷi~vali
outdoors	6. veḷi	veḷi	veḷi~veli

LOAN-PHONOLOGY

This is probably the right place to talk about the phonology of loan-words like *buumi*, "earth," *bayō*, "fear," *bassu*, "bus." Urban dialects, Brahman as well as non-Brahman, keep the initial voiced consonants and other such "non-Tamil" features of such loan-words. Furthermore, "non-Tamil" features like initial voiced stops (for example, *bassu*, "bus"), postnasal voiceless stops (for example, *pampu*, "pump"), seem to decrease in frequency as we go from Madras toward the south (see Pillai, 1963). But it is probably true that Brahman speakers everywhere tend to pronounce English and Sanskrit loan-words with a semblance of English and Sanskrit pronunciations, and resist their assimilation to the Tamil system (for example, by de-voicing initial voiced stops in *buumi*, *bassu*, etc.). This resistance seems to fit in, not so much with the prevalence of literacy (which, certainly, is *one* contributing factor), but with the general conservation in Brahman speech of differences, of contrasts in the system. We will return to this shortly.

VOWELS

Confining ourselves to the native vocabulary, we find many more contrasts preserved in I than in M; for instance, in final position, *e* and *a*, *ā* and *ō* do not contrast in M.

	W	I	M
me (accus.)	1. eṉṉai	enne	enna [ᵞennaˤ]
what	2. ṉṉa	enna [ᵞennaˤ]	enna [ᵞennaˤ]

Most final *a*'s are somewhat fronted in both M and I. But in M, final *e*'s are backed toward *a*, so the two vowels are indistinguishable.

Similarly, the final ã and õ of I tend to run together in M.

	W	I	M
he	1. avaṉ	avã	avã
tree	2. maram	marõ	marã

Thus, there seems to be not only a smaller inventory of phonemic contrasts, there is also a neutralization of contrasts in many positions in M.

LEXIS

KINSHIP TERMS

In the sphere of lexis and semantics there are many examples again of the same phenomenon. There are many more names for kin in I than there are in M.[8] (This, of course, correlates with different marriage practices, but the results fit the general I and M patterns.)

	M	I
son-in-law	1. marumahã	maaple
younger sister's husband	2. maccãã	maaple
wife's brother	3. maccãã	maccina
elder sister's husband	4. maccãã	attimbeer

(see Bloch, 1910)

FOOD-WORDS

In the domain of food-words, Brahman speech in general and I in particular are notoriously overspecialized (see Bloch, 1910); the intimate relationships of food and ritual are relevant here. It may also be noted in passing that the B-words, especially I-words, make little distinction between temple food-offerings and the food served at home. For instance, the I-word for cooked rice (*saadõ*) is obviously derived from a Sanskrit loan-word, *prasaadõ*, "food-offering in a temple." During ceremonial feasts, the word *prasaadõ* itself is regularly used instead of *saadõ* "cooked rice." NB (here M) speech uses the B-words exclusively for ceremonial cooking (*taḷihe*) and temple food (*prasaadõ*). We need not go into the details and wider implications of these distinctions. Neither do we need to point out the purely lexical differences between I and M. The B proliferation of lexical items (and the resulting extra divisions in the "semantic space") is well illustrated in the literature. One example will suffice:

	I	M
drinking water	1. tiirtõ	taṇṇi
water in general	2. jalõ	taṇṇi
non-drinkable water	3. taṇṇi	taṇṇi

8. See Pillai, 1965, where he shows that the Brahmans and the Muslims have the highest "caste-marked" isoglosses in kinship terms. See especially pages 64–65, which support the thesis of this paper. Pillai does not list the M kin terms listed by me (for example, *maccãã*) because he defines "caste-markers" as lexical items characteristic of each caste. A word like *maccãã* would be found in Mudaliyar as well as in other NB castes.

In the light of the remarks made above, we must add that M uses *tiirtō* for the holy water they receive from the priest in the temple. I qualifies it usually by an adjective: *perumaaḷ tiirtō* "god's holy water."

FREE VARIANTS

Most of the above statements regarding I and M could be made with minor modifications with regard to other Brahman and non-Brahman caste dialects. We have ignored here the fact that Brahmans generally use some non-Brahman forms (like *kaḷuvu* for *alambu*, "wash," *paṇṇikiṭṭu* for *paṇṇiṇḍu*, "having done" [reflexive]) when speaking to non-Brahman addressees. Similarly we have ignored the fact that, in phonology and lexis, many non-Brahmans (certainly M) have several I forms as free variants: "bird," I *paṭsi*, M *parave~paṭsi*; "cooked rice," I *saadō*, M *sooru~saadō* (see above for free variants in phonology).[9] But the grammatical items we have cited throughout do not usually have such free variants. This is one reason why morphology, rather than phonology or lexis, seems crucial and decisive in this contrastive study.

GENERAL REMARKS

At first glance, it appears that I innovates more than M. But a closer look shows that both I and M innovate (compared to W), but in different directions: I toward differentiation, M toward generalization, of paradigmatic patterns. In no simple sense is one dialect more "conservative" or "archaic" or resistant to innovation than the other. It must be noted also that bilingualism on the part of the Brahman speakers does not really account for the innovations, as either both dialects have many of the same loan forms with different distributions and in differently adapted shapes ("worship," I *puuje*, M *puuse*), or in both cases the innovations are intra-linguistic (as in the verb morphology, see section on verbs above). What seems relevant is the fact that M assimilates many of the loan-words (*puuje* ⟶ *puuse*) but I does not; I keeps the non-native characteristics intact and unassimilated, just as it keeps the irregularities of its morphology unassimilated. Of course, both literacy (in the community, not necessarily in the individual informant) and precise knowledge of other languages help in the general process of this fastidious upkeep of differences.

EVIDENCE FROM TULU

That literacy is not crucial is suggested by examples from Tulu. Tulu was first suggested as a test case by Bright (1960). Phenomena similar to those in

---

9. Pillai (1965, p. 65) observes: "The Mudaliyārs tried to imitate the speech of the brahmins to elevate themselves in the social hierarchy. Even now it is a common scene in some of the Mudaliyār families for the older people to reprimand the younger generation for speaking like sudras when they don't speak like brahmins. This is perhaps the reason for the greater percentage of common core [in kinship terms] between the brahmins and the mudaliyar. But if the castes in group IV [fishermen] and V [paḍayachi] tried to imitate the brahmins, they would be subject to ridicule." The wide and systematic differences in the grammatical systems of I and M dialects demonstrated in this paper appear all the more striking in the light of the above remarks.

Tamil characterize Shivalli (Brahman) and Banta (non-Brahman) dialects. Among the many examples, only one will be presented here.

	B	NB
of the tree	1. maroto	marota
of the water	2. niirudo	niiruda
of the boy	3. aaṇuno	aaṇuda
of the trouble	4. kaṣṭanta	kaṣṭada
	5. arita of the rice	kurita of the sheep
	(a variant)	

(See Aiyar, 1932. The forms are given here in phonemic writing. Aiyar gives them in broad phonetic transcription.)

Note here again the four forms (five, including the variant 5) in B and the two in NB genitives. Locatives and datives also exhibit such overdifferentiations in B. "The negative ending (i)ri is sometimes fully conjugated for gender, number and person in a few negative tenses in the Brahmins' dialect" (Aiyar, 1932, p. 905).

THE FUNCTION OF A SOCIAL DIALECT

Some suggestions may be hazarded as possible explanations for these structured differences in dialect change. First of all, the I or even the whole Brahman community is a minority. It is isolated by ritual status. The dialect differences appear to be used as expressions of social identity. This is confirmed by the fact that most of the grammatical *characteristics* of I are unaffected by regional variation; they are insulated and preserved by the sense of social identity. There is also a greater range of variation among NB dialects both regionally and sect-wise, than among the B dialects. Anyone attempting Tamil dialect-geography necessarily must concentrate on the NB dialects.

The self-identifying function of a dialect for a given community is evidenced dramatically in Tulu, which had no script or written literature till recently. The Shivalli Brahmans are characterized by their phonology, which has simply one-to-one correspondences for certain consonants of the non-Brahman dialects.

	B	NB
coconut tree	1. taaɭe	taare
see	2. ʃuup-	tuup-
which?	3. jaane	daane

But significantly, in one of the most common words, where NB has j, B reverses its usual correspondence $(j = d)$:

	B	NB
not	id*d*i	iʄʄi

Evidence is indirectly supplied also by the number of lexical items that the Smarta Iyer Brahman shares with non-Brahman castes:

	I (Iyengar)	*Iyer and M*
a soup-like dish	saattumadu	rasõ
a sweet porridge	tirukkaṇṇamadu	paayasõ
basil	tiruttoḷaa	toḷasi etc.

The fact that I Brahmans are a more recently formed sect than the Iyers may have something to do with further discriminations in this vocabulary of self-identity.

LINGUISTIC SELF-CONSCIOUSNESS

The self-consciousness regarding linguistic markers (which we offer as one of the forces conserving morphological differences etc.) is attested again by the amount of linguistic correction vis à vis NB forms in a B home. In fact, many of the NB forms are constantly used in B homes only with emotional charges: when one is angry with a child or when one is ironic or pejorative.

	I	*M*
worship	1. puuje	puuse
punishment for children	2. puuse	
food	3. saadõ	sooru (saadõ as free variant)
food (pejorative term)	4. sooru	
eat	5. saapḍu	tinnu (saapḍu as free variant)
guzzle, etc. (pejorative)	6. tinnu	

VERBAL CULTURE

The general B conservation of traditions, the attention paid to exactitude in the oral learning of texts, may also be mentioned as possibly relevant to the daily maintenance of linguistic differences, "irregularities," and non-native pronunciations. (For some insightful remarks on the relation of phonology to internalized value systems in caste dialects, see Friedrich, 1961.)

CONCLUSION

One may, in closing, say that the function of B dialects seems to be self-identification, intracaste communication; their structure is a product of this functioning process. The characteristics of NB dialects seem to be (as seen in its general simplification of paradigms, etc.) the result of their functioning as intercaste media of communication (compare Bombay Hindi and its simplifications of Hindi grammar). It is not surprising, therefore, that the colloquial standard that appears to be developing all over Tamilnad is based on non-Brahman colloquials.

BIBLIOGRAPHY

BLOCH, JULES.
1910. Castes et dialectes en Tamoul. *Mémoires de la Société de Linguistique*, 16: 1–20.

BRIGEL, J.
1872. *A grammar of the Tulu language*. Mangalore.

BRIGHT, WILLIAM.
1960a. Linguistic change in some South Indian dialects. In Charles A. Ferguson and John J. Gumperz (Eds.), *Linguistic diversity in South Asia*. Indiana University Research Center in Anthropology, Folklore, and Linguistics, Publication no. 13 (*International Journal of American Linguistics*, 26(3), pt. III).

1960b. Social dialect and language history. *Current Anthropology*, 1: 324–25.

BRIGHT, WILLIAM, and A. K. RAMANUJAN.
1962. *A study of Tamil dialects*. Chicago: University of Chicago. (Mimeographed.)

1964. Sociolinguistic variation and language change. In *Proceedings of the Ninth International Congress of Linguistics*, The Hague.

FERGUSON, CHARLES A., and JOHN J. GUMPERZ.
1960. Linguistic diversity in South Asia. Indiana University Research Center in Anthropology, Folklore, and Linguistics, Publication no. 13 (*International Journal of American Linguistics*, 26(3), pt. III).

FISCHER, JOHN L.
1958. Social influences in the choice of a linguistic variant. *Word*, 14: 47–56.

FRIEDRICH, PAUL.
1961. Review of Ferguson and Gumperz, *Linguistic diversity in South Asia*. *Language*, 37: 163–68.

MATTHEWS, GORDON.
1942. The vulgar pronunciation of Tamil. *Bulletin of the School of Oriental Studies* (London), 10: 992–97.

PILLAI, M. SHANMUGAM.
1960. Tamil—literary and colloquial. In Charles A. Ferguson and John J. Gumperz (Eds.), *Linguistic diversity in South Asia*. Indiana University Research Center in Anthropology, Folklore, and Linguistics, Publication no. 13 (*International Journal of American Linguistics*, 26(3), pt. III).

1962. A Tamil dialect of Ceylon. *Indian Linguistics*, 23: 90–98.

1965a. Caste isoglosses in kinship terms. *Anthropological Linguistics*, 7(3): 59–66.

1965b. Merger of literary and colloquial Tamil. *Anthropological Linguistics*, 7(4): 98–103.

RAMANUJAN, A. K.
1963. *Spoken and written Tamil: the verb*. Chicago: University of Chicago. (Mimeographed.)

RAMASWAMY AIYAR, L. V.
1932. Tulu prose texts in two dialects. *Bulletin of the School of Oriental Studies* (London), 6: 897–931.

SJOBERG, ANDRE F.
1962. Co-existent phonemic systems in Telugu. *Word*, 18: 115–26.

VINSON, JULIEN.
1895. Les variants phonetiques de la prononciation populaire tamoule. *Centenaire de l'Ecole des Langues Orientales Vivantes* (Paris): 115–26.

ZENGEL, MARJORIE S.

1962. Literacy as a factor in language change. *American Anthropologist*, 64: 132–39.

ZVELEBIL, KAMIL.

1959. Dialects of Tamil, I–II. *Archiv Orientálni*, 27: 272–317, 572–603.

1960. Dialects of Tamil, III. *Archiv Orientálni*, 28: 414–56.

1961. Some features of Dindigul Tamil. *Te. Po. Mī Maṇiviṟā Malar* (T. P. Meenak-shisundaram Commemoration Volume), Coimbatore, 424–46.

1963. On finite verb terminations in colloquial Tamil. *Archiv Orientálni*, 31: 109–118.

1964. Spoken language of Tamilnad. *Archiv Orientálni*, 32: 237–64.

20. OCCUPATION AND RESIDENCE
IN RELATION TO DHARWAR DIALECTS

WILLIAM McCORMACK

INTRODUCTION

Previous studies of Kannada social dialects have shown that linguistic differences in spoken Kannada correlate with the major sociocultural division between Brahman (hereafter B) and non-Brahman (hereafter NB) castes. For example, Bright and Ramanujan have demonstrated that these "class dialects innovate independently of one another, and in two ways . . . conscious [upper class or B] and unconscious [lower class or NB]" (1964, p. 1112). The present study moves to build on the earlier work, though it is also understood that only a beginning has been made in exploring social class differences in Kannada language variability; that there are sundry complicating regional distinctions as well, as in self-selection of the linguistic elements which differentiate B from NB; and that the features which mark social identity of Kannada speakers are relatively trivial from the standpoint of an overall core or deep structure for the language. Thus to characterize B semantic structure as "elaborated code" and NB semantic structure as "restricted code," as is done below for Dharwar dialects of Kannada, would seem to reinforce Bright's and Ramanujan's point about the conscious/unconscious qualitative polarity for B and NB linguistic change, respectively (Bernstein, 1964a, 1964b, 1964c; Lawton, 1963). The thrust of studies of socially distinctive features of speech, both in India and elsewhere, has been to indicate that a social structural component exists for language. The studies from India seem the more significant because many of the linguistic markers of social identity in the caste social interaction situation are consciously recognized by a sizable percentage of speakers (McCormack, 1960; Gumperz, 1965, p. 86).

The present study adopts a correlational model for connecting selected variables of the sociocultural context, namely, the residential situation of speakers and the occupational role of speakers' family head, with morphological and semantic variables of the spoken language as derived from elicited texts. In a general sense, the study represents a correlation of language signs to the life styles of their users. Alternatively, one might view the approach as involving a contrastive study of "speech-cultures" as between B and NB. In this regard, Gumperz' concept of "verbal repertoire" as the linguistic corollary of status and role interactions ("speech varieties [in a community] each associated with particular kinds of social relationships"), and Bernstein's hypotheses on the relationships between speech coding and social structure, seem most relevant (Gumperz, 1965, p. 85;

Bernstein, 1964c). Also relevant to speech cultures in Dharwar are the data, included below, on family use of second languages, that is, spoken Marathi, spoken and written English, and written literary Kannada.

Since this study proceeds from analysis of texts that were tape-recorded in speakers' homes by two Indian interviewers, and of a supplementary questionnaire administered after the texts were elicited, there is no direct indication of the appearance of the tabulated linguistic variables in "natural" speech settings. This is indeed a limitation, for although I have observed a considerable amount of speech interaction in Dharwar in connection with other linguistic and cultural studies, much of this observation has pertained to males, whereas the respondents for this study were females. Of course, and however regrettable, observation has traditionally played a small role in dialectology, linguists as a rule having drawn their linguistic boundaries on the basis of printed lists and texts. There were experimental controls in this study: a specified procedure was followed in drawing a sample of interviewees, though this procedure was not successful in achieving a random selection of Dharwar families; a standard pictorial stimulus was used to elicit texts, rather than a verbal stimulus, which might have skewed results in the direction of more verbally oriented respondents; instrumentation was used, in the form of a tape recorder; and the elicited texts were subjected to quantification, tabulation, and simple statistical analysis.

So far as the comparative value of this study is concerned, it appears that occupational role is a key variable in understanding the generation of class dialects in India, England, and America alike. In view of this, Gumperz' characterization of Indian linguistic variability in terms of "argot," which has connotations of trade jargon and cant, is particularly appropriate. At the same time, the present study establishes a correlation between the occupational role of family-household head and the speech of the female respondent, and the implication of this, and of Bernstein's work as well, is that "argot" and "mother tongue" (or vernacular) are to a degree overlapping categories. It would follow that Gumperz' very appropriate term, "argot," is not to be construed too narrowly as "any speech variety distinct from that used around the home and by the local peer group," at least not in Dharwar.

The texts on which this study is based were elicited from 62 women, 18 B and 44 NB, who were residents of Dharwar City, Dharwar District, northern Mysore State, in the summer of 1963.[1] The 1961 Indian census of Dharwar described it as Mysore State's tenth city in size, with a total population of 77,163 persons. The Department of Social Anthropology and Social Welfare of the Karnatak University, Dharwar, had completed a first sampling for its own census of Dharwar by April of 1963. From this, I drew at random a sample of every hundredth household until a hundred households were drawn (at an estimated average of five persons per Indian household, the universe for this sample was approximately 50,000 persons).

1. The research reported here was performed pursuant to a contract with the United States Office of Education, Department of Health, Education, and Welfare. I also wish to acknowledge supplementary grants from the American Council of Learned Societies and the Research Committee of Duke University.

It was assumed that the incompleteness of the university's census at that time might not affect the language study, but this assumption proved wrong. Our questionnaires revealed marked selection against agriculturalists and, in an areal sampling sense, against those suburbs which are more outlying and difficult to reach and which are populated mainly by farmers. Of the 100 households, less than 10 per cent were in agriculture, as compared to the 1961 census figure of 12 per cent for Dharwar. More particularly, only two of the nineteen Lingayat households in our sample were agriculturalist, as against our guess-estimate of 50 per cent of Dharwar's Lingayat households. On the whole, the sample was biased against blue-collar occupations generally and thus against castes whose members are primarily blue collar. While the 1961 census of Dharwar reports about 37.7 per cent employment in government service and teaching—the main components of our "white-collar" category—we found that at least 60 per cent of our B households, and 45 per cent of our NB households, fell in that category.

The 18 B women of the sample belonged to four subcastes, and the 44 NB women belonged to eighteen subcastes, nine of which are affiliated with the Lingayat caste-sect. Most heavily represented in the B group was the Vaishnava Brahman subcaste, with thirteen respondents, and in the NB group, the Lingayat Panchamsali, with nine respondents. The Panchamsali, according to the 1881 census for Dharwar District, are the most numerous of the twenty-odd Lingayat subcastes in the district. They are traditionally agriculturalist, and comprised then, and probably now, about half the Lingayat population of the district, being about three and one-half times as numerous as the next most populous Lingayat sub-caste, the priestly Jangamas.

Two of the B women had migrated from Karwar and Belgaum districts, re-spectively, while ten of the NB women had come from districts other than Dharwar, chiefly from Belgaum District. Non-native speakers of Kannada were excluded from the final sample.

As for residential distribution within Dharwar, eight NB women and nine B women lived in two of three residential areas where B's were in the majority. The remaining women in the sample were distributed among seventeen out of 27 residential areas, wards, or suburbs, where NB's were in the majority.

The interview procedures started with a request to a woman in each of the 100 households of our original sample to respond verbally to the stimulus of eleven line drawings depicting people in Indian sociocultural situations, plus one calendar photo of a temple. The respondent, usually a wife but in two cases a daughter, then described the pictured material in her "normal" spoken style of Kannada. Ultimately, the 100 households were reduced to 62, by nearly 40 per cent, through circumstances beyond the control of the interviewers. Some house-holds contained no women, some families had removed from the city, still other families were not Kannada-speaking, and six respondents were of families that were unwilling to cooperate. Of these six, all were NB, four were blue-collar in occupation, and two were of "ex-Untouchable" castes—all perhaps explanatory of their not understanding the purpose of a study of their speech. At the conclu-sion of the taping session, the interviewers, a local NB male college student and a female anthropologist from northern India, elicited replies to a questionnaire. This included items on the caste and sect of the respondent, her age, the occupation of the male household head, the places of origin of both husband and wife, the date of their in-migration to Dharwar, and the languages known and the publications read in the household.[2]

SOCIAL VARIABILITY INDEXED BY GRAMMATICAL MARKERS

The 62 texts were scored first for frequency of substitutions for selected grammatical traits that represent public norms for the respondent's B or NB caste. Sixteen substitutions were scored in all (Table 1), but the texts were divided into

TABLE 1
REGIONAL AND SOCIAL DISPERSION OF MARKER TRAITS.

Grammatical Meaning	Brahman*		Non-Brahman	
	Dharwar	Bangalore	Dharwar	Bangalore
It is	ədə	ide	ayti	ayti
Inside	-olage	-alli	-aaga	-aaga
Infinitive	-likke	-ook	-aak	-aak
Participle	-oo	-oo	-aa	-aa
Sit	kuut-	kuut-	kunt-	kunt-
Reflexive	koo-	koo-	kont-	kont-
Go	hoog-	hoog-	hoṇt- (and hok-)	(h)ok-
Even though	-aadru	-aadru	-aara	-aara
Verbal compound	-ir-	-ir-	(absent)	(absent)
Indefinite	-o	-o	-a	-a

* All the forms characteristic of Brahmans, save —ook, can be described as "literary," that is, occurring normally in the written language. None of the non-Brahman forms are in the same sense literary.

B and NB sets from the beginning, so that only eight substitutions were scored per group. Of the total sixteen, twelve were "paired" in the sense that the NB's use of a B form such as ədə was scored, and a B's use of the NB equivalent, ayti, likewise was scored. The six "pairs," so defined, were as follows: ədə/ayti, -olage/ -aaga, -likke/-aak, -oo/-aa, kuut-/kunt-, koo-/kont-. The remaining four were not paired: hoṇt- and -aara were scored as substitutions in B texts, and -ir- (in verbal compounds) and -o were scored as substitutions in NB texts. Although we have preferred to discuss these traits as "morphological," since all, or nearly all, are structurally equivalent in their use in sentences, they might more strictly be classed as differences in "lexicon," that is, differences in selection of forms. A possible exception would be the last two, -ir- and -o (indefinite), which might be viewed as NB adoption of a B (and a more literary) syntactic pattern. The rea-

2. I wish to express thanks to Marion Diengdoh Pugh, who collected and transcribed the Kannada texts, and to Shri R.S. Hiremath and Shrimati Suneela Ramaswamy, who assisted Miss Pugh in collection and transcription respectively.

sons for selecting these particular sixteen traits for scoring were discussed in an earlier paper on Dharwar dialects (McCormack, 1960), and will not be repeated here except to note that the traits were originally chosen with the help of a panel of Dharwar college students who, on the basis of them, successfully identified social dialects of speakers from taped interviews with those speakers.

It was asserted in the earlier paper on Dharwar dialects that grammatical markers of social identity are self-consciously perceived by Dharwar speakers. Confirmation comes from the present study, as there is a significant positive intratextual association $(P < .02)$[3] between NB adoption of B traits and NB adoption of features borrowed from written literary Kannada—an association that would be expected in view of the Dharwar stereotype of B's: that they speak "like books" (Bennur, 1959). Viewed more widely, the Kannada situation of course represents a variety of "diglossia," according to which the literacy of the B elite group reinforces their using written forms as an integral part of their distinctive speech patterns (Ferguson, 1959). An interesting and additional aspect of Dharwar diglossia, however, is the identification of use of Marathi with the B elite group—this because the historic Maratha Empire dominated the Karnatak region in which Dharwar is situated, and B's, Peshwas, and other local B's formed that empire's administrative cadre. Thus fourteen of the eighteen B respondents of our sample reported use of Marathi by some family member, and a significant association $(P = .0167)$ was established between NB speakers' adoption of B morphological elements and their reporting some family knowledge of Marathi. A similar situation appeared with regard to English, for fifteen of eighteen B respondents reported that English was spoken by a family member. This is consistent with recruitment policy and administrative practice in higher education and government in the region today. The association between NB use of English and NB adoption of B morphology was significant at the probability level of $P = .07$.

Labov has reported, for phonological markers of social identity in New York City speech, that a speaker's awareness of a norm may be correlated with his frequency of violating the norm in casual speech (Labov, 1965, p. 109). A similar situation may exist in Dharwar, if the paradigm could be expressed as follows: greater awareness of (phonological) norm / higher frequency of own violation of it : high frequency of NB adoption of (morphological) trait associated with B speech / high frequency of B adoption of the equivalent trait associated with NB speech. The adage "set a thief to catch a thief" would cover the phenomenon in terms of folk psychology, "projection" being the pertinent psychoanalytical term, and "hypercorrection" being another related concept that is familiar to both students of language change and language teachers. However, a statistical demonstration of intercorrelation of B and NB groups on the paired morphological traits runs into the difficulty of the rank-frequency constant in language (Zipf, 1935), so that similar possibilities of occurrence of substitutions in both B and NB texts might be due to this and/or to equivalence in "grammati-

3. This figure for probability, and all which follow unless otherwise specified, was reached by applying the chi square test to a fourfold contingency table.

cal" meaning of the pairs. Labov's data did not suffer from any such shortcoming, since his correlations were figured between subjective statements by respondents about norms and the same respondents' violations of these norms in speech behavior. If it is hypothesized that Dharwar B's and NB's share a perception that B speakers are "wordy," very verbal, or "learned" (Bennur, 1959), this stereotype of B's would afford a possible measure of the B group's position as norm-setters in the significant association (P < .01 by the median test of association in a fourfold table situation; [McNemar, 1962, p. 376]) between the length of an NB speaker's text, by word count, and the frequency of B morphological traits appearing in that text. Again, however, the association between length of text and frequency of NB substitutions of B elements may reflect only that a greater opportunity for deviance to be expressed in frequency terms exists in the longer texts.

B deviance, that is, substitution by B's of NB morphological elements, did not reveal a significant association with either of the primary sociocultural variables tabulated in this study. It is possible that our outside-view classification of eleven B families and seven B families into W (white collar) and BL (blue collar) categories, respectively, was simply not meaningful from the inside view, since the roles traditionally ascribed to B's, those of priest and government administrator, are W. That is, all B's may be perceived by self and by others as W rather than BL, irrespective of their real employment situations and job roles. Neither did any statistically meaningful relationships emerge between B residence in NB residential areas and the frequency of B adoption of NB traits. Idiosyncratic and rural background might be relevant in explaining B adoption of NB morphology, since 25 per cent of the total B sample's usage of NB traits was contributed by one speaker of rural origin who resided in an NB ward. It was perhaps true of her that in spirit she had never left the village—a context where B phonological norms, at least, closely approximate NB speech.

Of the two sociocultural variables, residence and occupation, only W occupation by NB's reached a statistically significant level of association with frequency of NB speaker's adoption of B traits. Thus, by the median test employed in conjunction with the chi square technique for a fourfold table of frequencies comparison, there was obtained a probability level for association of W occupation and NB adoption of B traits which indicates a chance association of this magnitude would be reached but once in fourteen times (P = .07).[4] While these results do not of themselves lend strong import to the relationship between NB occupational role and selection of B morphological traits, they do form part of an overall picture in which occupational role is a predictor of NB approximation of B-style "elaborated code" semantic features, of NB adoption of B-style literary borrowings in speech, and so on. A further argument for a significant relationship between the variable of occupational role and B features in NB speech is an apparently distinctive W, as compared to BL, pattern of selectivity from among

4. Yates's correction for continuity was embodied in the formula for frequency comparison for a fourfold table by the chi square technique as suggested by McNemar (1962, p. 226):

$$\chi^2 = \frac{N(|BC-AD|-N/2)^2}{(A+B)(C+D)(A+C)(B+D)}$$

the B morphological traits. Thus in a sample of 38 NB's, 20 W (52.6 per cent) and 18 BL (47.4 per cent), the W contribution to the total frequency of occurrences of each of the B traits was as follows: ǝḍǝ 89.8 per cent; *koo-*, 81.8 per cent; *kuut-*, 71.6 per cent; *oḷage*, 70.5 per cent; *-ir-*, 69.4 per cent; *-oo*, 65.2 per cent; *-likke*, 64.28 per cent; *-o* 46.3 per cent. The finding that ǝḍǝ is the form most favored in the dialect of W, NB families accords with the general impression, based on observations in "natural" speech settings, as well as on speakers' subjective statements about norms, that the ǝḍǝ/*ayti* pair is most salient for marking B versus NB social identity of a speaker. Still greater weight accrues to the variable of occupation in that regular reading habits failed to relate significantly (P = .219) to NB adoption of B morphological traits. No other direct information on the amount of formal education of respondents was solicited, but if years of schooling can be assumed to correlate negatively with age of respondents—since female schooling is recent even for B's in Dharwar—then the absence from both NB and B groups of significant associations between age and frequency of substitutions of grammatical traits would seem to strengthen the argument for the importance of the association obtained between features of speech and occupational status of household head.

SEMANTIC FEATURES OF THE TEXTS: ELABORATED AND RESTRICTED CODES

First comparative inspection of B and NB texts immediately yielded the impression of a difference between the two sets which has hitherto been described for English and American speech as "elaborated" versus "restricted" code and/or as "middle" versus "lower" class dialect (Bernstein, 1964b, 1964c; Lawton, 1963; Schatzman and Strauss, 1955). The more precise recent thinking on this subject has been by Bernstein (1964a, pp. 259–60; see also Lawton, 1963), who describes an ideal-type restricted code as follows:

The pure form of a *restricted* code would be one where the lexicon is wholly predictable; therefore also the organizing structure. . . . If the code is restricted, by definition so is verbal planning. . . . The bond relating the thinker to the concrete and descriptive will become progressively tighter with the cumulative effect of the use of the restricted code.

In point of fact, B's proved to be more dramatic in description, to take an interest in the actions of people in the pictured situations, and to use lexicon that was less predictable from the pictures themselves, while NB's revealed a more exclusive concern with descriptive details such as how the pictured figures actually looked with respect to dress, physical appearance, and so on. So striking is this difference between B's and NB's that the single B respondent who confined herself to concrete detail, and who was also second among B's in frequency of substitutions of NB morphological elements, perhaps deserves pause as to her family's claim to B status. This speaker was a member of a family practicing the goldsmith trade, and goldsmiths, as a caste in South India, have long claimed B status, but with small success. At the same time, it should be cautioned that by far the major content of all texts, both B and NB, was "restricted" in that it was overwhelmingly concrete and descriptive. On the other hand, this may represent, at least in part, the fact that pictorial stimuli alone were used in the eliciting situation.[5]

To compare the 62 texts for the presence or absence of elaborated code features, selected indicators were resorted to. Elaborated code was redefined in terms of two components; P, or the attribution of purposive behavior to the pictured figures (indicating a degree of verbal planning), and E, or the attribution of emotion to the figures (indicating a degree of orientation to other persons). E without P appeared in the text of one B respondent, but in none of the NB texts. Combined EP appeared in the texts of six B respondents and six NB respondents. P alone was far the most common, appearing in the texts of 10 B respondents and 24 NB respondents. The total numbers of respondents who attributed E, EP, or P to the pictured figures were seventeen B's (94 per cent of Bs) and thirty NB's (68 per cent of NBs). Of course, if the goldsmith interviewee is re-ranked from B to NB, the percentage figure for B respondents rises to 100 per cent and for NB respondents decreases slightly. In scoring for elaborated code, one attribution of E, EP, or P to a pictured figure was reckoned sufficient to have indicated the presence of elaborated code in the text—this because the nondirection employed by the interviewers, in order to elicit as much text as possible, yielded responses to individual pictures which were differential in length and occasionally absent. In this situation, a comparative frequency count for E, EP, or P could not be sufficiently controlled. It is to be noted, however, that multiple appearances of EP and P were not limited to B texts.

Since the strongest association obtained in this study was between elaborated-code semantic features in NB texts and W occupation of the NB families concerned, the discussion of the inevitable complexities and ambiguities of defining occupations as W has been reserved for this time. By an original and "minimal" categorization, eighteen NB households were included in the W category, and all eighteen respondents from these households appeared among the thirty NB respondents displaying elaborated-code features. However, the finding presented in the section above, on the association of NB adoption of B morphology with W occupation, was based on a "maximal" categorization of 25 NB households as W, the respondents from which also all displayed elaborated-code features. According to the maximal W category, 25 of 30 NB elaborated-code scores are explained by W occupation, and this makes a stronger case for the pivotal role of occupation than does eighteen out of thirty. Either way, there is the association for NB texts of W occupation and presence of elaborated-code features.

Since all, or nearly all, B respondents displayed elaborated-code scores, there was no differential response to be examined in terms of W versus BL occupation, or, indeed, in terms of residential differences.

Unlike the situation for NB adoption of B morphology, it is quite probable that formal education plays a direct role in the appearance of elaborated-code

5. It is not known, for example, how much the interviewers' directive to respondents to "describe the pictures" may have had a consequence of eliciting concrete, descriptive responses.

features among NB's. The evidence for NB's stems from a significant association (P = .037) between respondent-reported regular family reading habits and elaborated-code score. However, it would be more in keeping with the total direction of our findings, including that on the relationships between B morphology and W occupation, to regard this association as merely incidental, and derived from a common and high correlation of both reported reading habits and elaborated-code scores with W occupation. It is an additional fact that only three of seventeen "reading" families occur in the BL category.

DISCUSSION

The present study has explored a series of relationships involving, on the linguistic side, morphological sets that mark a speaker's social identity in a more or less self-conscious way, and features of elaborated versus restricted semantic complexity that seem less likely to rise to the social consciousness of speakers, *qua* language. Nevertheless, both sets of features, morphological and semantic, have been shown to be associated with (1) B status as ascribed by the caste system, and (2) NB status as achieved via W occupational role. If a social-functional idiom were to be adopted here,[6] Merton's distinction between manifest or direct, and latent or indirect, functions of social roles, institutional patterns, social norms, and so on (Merton, 1957, p. 51), would seem to be applicable to our data on B/NB speech cultures. Thus morphology can be seen as directly marking a speaker's social identity (manifest function), and elaborated code semantic features can be seen as indirectly adaptive, through verbal planning and person-orientation, to W occupational role (latent function). In these terms, the appearance of BL occupations for B speakers is either functionally anomalous or dysfunctional. It is probable that most Dharwar speakers do not perceive it so; for example the assumption is still made (in a still but partially secularized—de-Brahmanized—culture) that W occupation is a constant ascriptive aspect of B caste status. On the other hand, the present data at least pose the possibility that, once an association of B status and BL occupational role is perceived, this situation would be upsetting for related linguistic norms, expectations, and speech-cultural values, unless there is also a redefinition of values concerning BL occupational role.

6. Various other models for a mediational structure which might meaningfully link the sociocultural and speech variables isolated by this study have been considered. The most promising came from communication engineering (information theory), from which the hypothesis was derived that a linkage might exist between social decision-making power, that is, "information" (Cherry, 1957, pp. 242–43) and B speech-culture. However, no empirical test was discovered to support this hypothesis, and one test contributed negative evidence. The latter attempted to measure information content of the texts by a specificity index. For this, a sample of 14 B's and 29 NB's who responded to the calendar-picture stimulus were scored as S±, according to whether they somehow specified the name, location, or builder of the pictured temple (S+), or not (S−). The S scoring, however, did not correlate (in the conventional chi square frequency comparison employed for a series of fourfold tables) with any of the sociocultural or speech variables of this study. The test for association of S score with B status, W occupation, length of text, residential situation of speaker, and semantic complexity (as indexed by E, EP, and P components) produced figures which were remarkably close to those one would expect on the basis of chance association alone.

BIBLIOGRAPHY

BENNUR, C. S.
1959. Communal stereotypes of high school children. In G. S. Halappa (Ed.), *Studies in education and culture, in honour of Shri D. C. Pavate*. Dharwar: Karnatak University.

BERNSTEIN, BASIL.
1964a. Aspects of language and learning in the genesis of the social process. In Dell Hymes (Ed.), *Language in culture and society*. New York: Harper and Row.

1964b. Elaborated and restricted codes: Their social origins and some consequences. In J. J. Gumperz and Dell Hymes (Eds.), *The ethnography of communication. American Anthropologist* 66 (6), Pt. 2.

1964c. Social class, speech systems, and psycho-therapy. In Frank Riessman, Jerome Cohen, and Arthur Pearl (Eds.), *Mental health of the poor*. New York: Free Press of Glencoe.

BRIGHT, WILLIAM.
1960. Linguistic change in some Indian caste dialects. In C. A. Ferguson and J. J. Gumperz (Eds.), *Linguistic diversity in South Asia. (International Journal of American Linguistics*, 26(3), pt. III.)

BRIGHT, WILLIAM, and A. K. RAMANUJAN.
1964. Sociolinguistic variation and language change. In *Proceedings of the Ninth International Congress of Linguists, Cambridge, Massachusetts, 1962*. The Hague: Mouton.

CHERRY, E. COLIN.
1957. *On human communication*. Cambridge, Mass.: The MIT Press; New York: John Wiley and Sons.

FERGUSON, CHARLES A.
1959. Diglossia. *Word*, 15: 325–40.

GUMPERZ, JOHN J.
1961. Speech variation and the study of Indian civilization. *American Anthropologist*, 63: 976–88.

1965. Linguistic repertoires, grammars and second language instruction. In Charles W. Kreidler (Ed.), *Report of the 16th Annual Round Table Meeting on Linguistics and Language Studies* (Monograph Series on Languages and Linguistics 18). Washington, D.C.: Georgetown University Press.

LABOV, WILLIAM.
1964. Phonological correlates of social stratification. In J. J. Gumperz and Dell Hymes (Eds.), *The ethnography of communication. American Anthropologist*, vol. 66, no. 6, pt. 2.)

1965. On the mechanism of linguistic change. In Charles W. Kreidler (Ed.), *Annual Round Table Meeting on Linguistics and Language Studies* (Monograph Series on Languages and Linguistics 18). Washington, D.C.: Georgetown University Press.

LAWTON, DENIS.
1963. Social class differences in language development: A study of some samples of written work. *Language and Speech*, 6: 120–43.

McCORMACK, WILLIAM.
1960. Social dialects in Dharwar Kannada. In C. A. Ferguson and J. J. Gumperz (Eds.), *Linguistic diversity in South Asia. (International Journal of American Linguistics*, 26(3), pt. III.)

McNemar, Quinn.
  1962. *Psychological statistics.* New York: John Wiley and Sons.

Merton, Robert K.
  1957. *Social theory and social structure.* (Rev. ed.) Glencoe, Ill.: The Free Press.

Schatzman, Leonard, and Anselm Strauss.
  1955. Social class and modes of communication. *American Journal of Sociology,* 60: 329–38.

Zipf, George K.
  1935. *The psycho-biology of language.* Boston: Houghton Mifflin.

PARTICIPANTS IN THE CONFERENCE
(EXTERNAL)

Kathleen Aberle
Department of Anthropology
Simon Fraser University
Vancouver, B.C.

Conrad M. Arensberg
Department of Anthropology
Columbia University
New York

Alan Beals
Department of Anthropology
Stanford University
Palo Alto, California

Gerald Berreman
Department of Anthropology
University of California
Berkeley

William Bright
Department of Anthropology
University of California
Los Angeles

Cora DuBois
Peabody Museum
Harvard University
Cambridge, Massachusetts

Joseph W. Elder
Department of Sociology
University of Wisconsin
Madison

Stanley Freed
American Museum of Natural History
New York

Harold A. Gould
Department of Anthropology
University of Illinois

Allen Grimshaw
Department of Sociology
Indiana University
Bloomington

John Gumperz
Department of Near Eastern Languages
University of California
Berkeley

Edward B. Harper
Department of Anthropology
University of Washington
Seattle

Henry Hart
Department of Political Science
University of Wisconsin
Madison

Harold Isaacs
Massachusetts Institute of Technology
Cambridge

Iravati Karve
Deccan College
Poona, India

Pauline M. Kolenda
Department of Sociology and
  Anthropology
University of Houston

Owen M. Lynch
Department of Anthropology
Harpur College
Binghamton, New York

David G. Mandelbaum
Department of Anthropology
University of California
Berkeley

William McCormack
Department of Anthropology
Duke University
Durham, North Carolina

Joan Mencher
Department of Anthropology
Columbia University
New York

Beatrice Miller
Robert Miller
Department of Anthropology
University of Wisconsin
Madison

Morris D. Morris
Department of Economics
University of Washington
Seattle

Ralph W. Nicholas
Department of Anthropology
Michigan State University
East Lansing

Morris E. Opler
Department of Anthropology
Cornell University
Ithaca, New York

Mrs. Lita Binns Osmundsen
Wenner-Gren Foundation
New York

Henry Orenstein
Department of Anthropology
Brooklyn College
New York

William L. Rowe
Department of Sociology and
    Anthropology
Duke University
Durham, North Carolina

Joseph E. Schwartzberg
Department of Geography
University of Minnesota
Minneapolis

James Silverberg
Department of Anthropology
University of Wisconsin
Milwaukee

Robert Smith
Department of Anthropology
Cornell University
Ithaca, New York

M. N. Srinivas
Department of Sociology
School of Economics
Delhi University
Delhi, India

Stephen Tyler
Department of Anthropology
University of California
Davis

(INTERNAL)

Leonard Binder
Department of Political Science
University of Chicago

Bernard S. Cohn
Departments of Anthropology
    and History
University of Chicago

Edward Dimock
Department of South Asian
    Languages and Civilizations
University of Chicago

Fred Eggan
Department of Anthropology
University of Chicago

Lloyd A. Fallers
Department of Anthropology
University of Chicago

Marc Galanter
Social Sciences Collegiate Division
University of Chicago

Eric Hamp
Department of Linguistics
University of Chicago

Leighton Hazlehurst, Postdoctoral Fellow
Department of Anthropology
University of Chicago

McKim Marriott
Department of Anthropology
University of Chicago

Manning Nash
Professor of Anthropology in
    Graduate School of Business
University of Chicago

Maureen L. P. Patterson
Bibliographic Specialist
South Asia Library
University of Chicago

A. K. Ramanujan
Department of South Asian
    Languages and Civilizations
University of Chicago

Susanne Rudolph
Social Sciences Collegiate Division
University of Chicago

Lloyd I. Rudolph
Department of Political Science
University of Chicago

David Schneider
Department of Anthropology
University of Chicago

Edward Shils
Committee on Social Thought
University of Chicago

Milton Singer
Department of Anthropology
University of Chicago

Melford Spiro
Department of Anthropology
University of Chicago

Sol Tax
Department of Anthropology
University of Chicago

J. A. B. van Buitenen
Department of South Asian
    Languages and Civilizations
University of Chicago

Nur Yalman
Department of Anthropology
University of Chicago

Norman H. Zide
Department of South Asian
    Languages and Civilizations
University of Chicago

INDEX

INDEX *

A

Abu'l Fazl 'Allami, 5
Abvāb, 249, 257, 268
Achhut Anand, 218
Adams, William, 9
Ādi Hindū Āndolan (Original Hindu Movement), 218, 221, 227
Ādnāṃv, 404–409
Agamas, 305
Agni, 122
Agra City, 209–211, 213–35
Agra University, 213
Ā'in-i-Akbari, 5, 191
Aiyappan, A. A., 23
Akbar, 5
Al-Biruni, 4
Aldous, J., 430
Aligarh City, 231
Aligarh District, 133
Allahabad City, 105, 204
Allahabad District, 102
Almond, Gabriel A., 220, 223
Amar Ujālā, 230
Ambala District, 287
Ambedkar, B. R., 221, 223–25, 227, 231, 235, 321
American Council of Learned Societies, 476
American Institute of Indian Studies, 173, 461
Amritsar District, 100
Anantnag District, 343, 346, 360, 374, 381
Andhra Pradesh, 45–46, 277, 343 ff.
Andrews, Charles Freer, 10
Angiras, 122–23, 127
Apastamba, 115, 119, 122–27
Apte, Govindrao Vinayak, 402–403
Apte, Hari Narayan, 402
Arensberg, Conrad M., 209, 340
Arya Samaj, 194, 215–16, 218–19, 223, 288, 318
Atkins, John, 66
Atma Ram, Swami, 215
Atri, 118–22, 124–27
Attitudes, toward autocracy, 184–85
toward caste-avoidance taboos, 182–84
toward fate, 181–82
traditional and non-traditional, 175
Aurangzeb, 6
Authority, patriarchal, in joint family, 33, 37, 416–18, 426, 440 ff.
personal, as aim of village politicians, 255, 260
of village headman, 252–53, 263–65, 268–69
See also Patron-client relationship
Azamgarh District, 106

B

Backward Classes Movement, 193–96, 274 *See also Ādi Hindū Āndolan*; Dravida Munnetra Kazhagam; Political participation; Republican Party; Scheduled Castes Federation
Baden-Powell, B. H., 19–20, 25, 267, 269–72
Baghelkhand, 99
Bailey, F. G., x, 34, 39, 54, 59, 192–93, 199, 202, 211, 225, 228, 243–47, 262, 272–74, 277–78, 295, 341, 348, 425, 427, 431
Baines, Athelstane, 190
Bajirao, 400
Balaji Visvanath Bhat, 400
Balambhatta, 122
Ballia District, 106
Banaras, 12, 41
Bangalore, 343, 345–46, 363–64, 373–74, 377, 387–88, 478
Bankura District, 111
Barber, Bernard, 209
Barbosa, Duarte, 5
Barmer District, 344, 353–54, 366, 373, 377, 379, 382, 385, 387–88
Barnes, J. A., 430
Baroda, 344–45, 363, 376–79, 385–86, 388, 400
Baroda University, 31
Barrier, Norman G., 21
Barth, Ernest A. T., x, 59–60, 71
Barth, Fredrik, 170, 211, 271, 295
Basu, Saran Chandra, 202
Basu, Tara Krishna, 341, 343, 345, 348, 350, 358, 370–71, 385
Baudhayana, 116, 118, 120–25
Beals, Alan R., 36, 43–44, 46–47, 270, 276, 341
Belgaum District, 343, 345–46, 350–52, 364–65, 376, 390, 477
Bengal, Buchanan's accounts of, 14
caste structure of, 95, 108–111
Colebrooke's accounts of, 12–13
land revenue settlements in, 11–12
land tenure systems in, 270
studies of family structure in, 343 ff.
village politics in, 247–64 ff.
Bengali, 9
Bennur, C. S., 479–80
Berko, J., 129
Bernstein, Basil, 475–76, 481
Berreman, Gerald D., 59, 277, 339, 343–44, 348, 350, 356–57, 369, 384–85

---

* References to particular castes, sub-castes, and tribes will be found under the entry "Castes, sub-castes, and tribes," and references to particular villages will be found under the entry "Villages."